Windows 98

Paul McFedries

SAMS

201 West 103rd Street
Indianapolis, IN 46290

To Karen for proving that, yes, dogs and cats can get along.

Copyright © 1998 by Sams Publishing

International Standard Book Number: 0-672-31235-2

Library of Congress Catalog Card Number: 97-69860

Printed in the United States of America

First Printing: May 1998

00 99 98   4   3   2   1

Trademarks

Executive Editor
Jeff Koch

Acquisitions Editor
Kim Spilker

Development Editor
Sandy Doell

Managing Editor
Sarah Kearns

Project Editors
Rebecca M. Mounts
Maureen A. McDaniel
Tom Dinse

Copy Editor
Nancy Albright

Indexer
Craig Small

Technical Editor
Greg Guntle

Production
Carol Bowers
Mona Brown
Ayanna Lacey
Gene Redding

Overview

Contents

About the Author

Paul McFedries is a computer consultant, programmer, and freelance writer. He has worked with computers in one form or another since 1975, he has a degree in mathematics, and he can swap out a hard drive in seconds flat; yet still, inexplicably, he has a life. He is the author or coauthor of more than two dozen computer books that have sold over one million copies worldwide. His titles include the Sams Publishing books *Paul McFedries' Microsoft Office 97 Unleashed* and *Visual Basic for Applications Unleashed* and the Que book *The Complete Idiot's Guide to Windows 98.*

Acknowledgments, Kudos, Plaudits, and Assorted Pats on the Back

Being an author is the most wonderful vocation (I don't think of it as a job) I can imagine. I get to play with words, I get to talk about things I'm intensely interested in, and I get some big-time warm, fuzzy feelings when people write to me to tell me that, in some small way, something I've written has helped them.

However, just because my name is the only one that appears on the cover, don't think that this book is solely my creation. Any book, but especially a project as massive as this one, is the result of the efforts of many hard-working people. The Sams editorial staff, in particular, never fails to impress me with their dedication, work ethic, and commitment to quality. You'll find a list of all the people who worked on this book near the front, but there are a few I'd like to thank personally:

Jeff Koch: Jeff is the Executive Editor, which makes him the unofficial "CEO" of the book. With his laid-back style and ever-present sense of humor, Jeff was always a pleasure to work with. Jeff, I look forward to collaborating on many more projects in the future.

Kim Spilker: Kim was the Acquisitions Editor for this book, which means that she "acquired" me to write it. I'm honored that she would choose me for such an important project, and I thank her for the confidence she has shown in my abilities.

Brian-Kent Proffitt: As the original Development Editor for this book, it was Brian's job to work with me in determining the overall structure of the book and to make sure that all the relevant topics were covered in an order that made sense. If we succeeded in this (and I think we did), it's due in no small part to Brian's experience, knowledge, and unmatched judgment. Thanks, Brian, for your hard work and dedication. I wish you all the best in your new career.

Sandy Doell: Sandy had the unenviable task of taking over as Development Editor in midstream. That's no easy feat on a huge project such as this, but Sandy's experience and keen eye for detail enabled her to pull it off with style, grace, and good humor. Sandy, it was both an honor and a joy to work with you.

Tom Dinse, Maureen McDaniel, and Rebecca Mounts: As the book's Project Editors, this trio's daunting task was to gather everything together and make it presentable for the production process. Some last minute outline changes forced Tom to work even harder than usual, but he handled the extra workload without a hitch or a complaint. Maureen and Rebecca had the unenviable task of taking over as Project Editors late in the cycle, but thanks to their unparalleled competence and good humor, they managed to get the book dressed for the production prom without a hitch. Thanks to all of you for an outstanding effort.

Nancy Albright: As Copy Editor, Nancy has the often thankless task of turning an author's ugly prose into a thing of grammatical beauty. Well, her job is thankless no more because I truly appreciate the efforts to which she went to beautify this book.

Peter Kuo: Peter is a NetWare guru who wrote all the NetWare material in Part VI, "Unleashing Windows 98 Communications and Networking." Once again, Peter, thank you for a job well done.

Greg Guntle: Greg was the book's Technical Editor. This means that he verified all my facts and tried out all my techniques to make sure I didn't steer you in the wrong direction. That's a tough and tedious job, but Greg was more than up to the challenge.

Introduction

We shall not cease from exploration
And the end of all our exploring
Will be to arrive where we started
And know the place for the first time.
—*T. S. Eliot*

Here we go again. It seems like only yesterday that we were desperately trying to escape the onslaught of hype and puffery that accompanied the launch of Windows 95. Now here we are with Microsoft's latest bouncing baby operating system: Windows 98. Is this just "Windows 95 plus 3"? On the surface, it would seem so. If all you want from Windows is the ability to launch your word processor and spreadsheet programs, you probably won't notice much difference between the old Windows and the new one.

However, if your operating system needs aren't so superficial (and your purchase of this book would indicate just that), Windows 98 has no shortage of new trinkets and baubles for you to discover. Whether it's Web integration, a boatload of new and improved Internet utilities, support for the latest three-letter hardware gadgets—MMX, AGP, USB, and DVD, to name just a few—or the massive collection of system tools, Windows 98 is no mere name change. (I run through the complete list of new Windows 98 features in Chapter 4, "What's New and Noteworthy in Windows 98.")

On the other hand, Windows 98 still carries some Windows 95 baggage. It still takes forever to load (although not quite as long as Windows 95), it's still hobbled by some 16-bit code, and general protection faults still rear their annoying heads from time to time. Not only that, but some useful Windows 95 tools—such as Microsoft Fax—have been dropped inexplicably from the lineup.

My goal in writing *Windows 98 Unleashed* is to cover the good, the bad, and the ugly of Windows 98. In particular, I give you complete coverage of the intermediate-to-advanced features of Windows 98. This means that I bypass basic topics, such as wielding the mouse, in favor of more complex operations, such as working with the Registry, setting up hardware profiles, networking, and getting connected to the Internet.

I've tried to keep the chapters focused on the topic at hand and unburdened with long-winded theoretical discussions. However, there are plenty of situations in which you won't be able to unleash the full power of Windows 98 and truly understand what's going on unless you have a solid base on which to stand. In these cases, I give you whatever theory and background you need to get up to speed. From there, I get right down to brass tacks without any further fuss and bother. To keep the chapters uncluttered, I've made a few assumptions about what you know and what you don't know:

- I assume that you have knowledge of rudimentary computer concepts, such as files and folders.
- I assume that you're familiar with the basic Windows skills: mouse maneuvering, dialog box negotiation, pull-down menu jockeying, and so on.
- I assume that you can operate peripherals attached to your computer, such as the keyboard and printer.
- I assume that you've used Windows for a while and are comfortable with concepts such as toolbars, scroll bars, and, of course, windows.
- I assume that you have a brain that you're willing to use and a good supply of innate curiosity.

How This Book Is Organized

To help you find the information you need, this book is divided into nine parts that group related tasks. The next few sections offer a summary of each part.

Part I: Unleashing Windows 98 Installation and Startup

The chapters in Part I get your advanced Windows 98 education off to a flying start by covering the ins and outs of the installation process. From there, you learn a myriad of ways to get Windows 98 off the ground and, once you do, I give you a tour of the landscape, including an in-depth look at what's new in the Windows 98 package.

Part II: Unleashing Windows 98 Customization and Optimization

With this introduction out of the way, in Part II you dive into the deep end of advanced Windows work: customizing, performance tuning, optimization, and hardware considerations. I've also included a couple of chapters that show you how to work with that most important of Windows 98 features: the Registry.

Part III: Unleashing Files, Folders, and Disks

Part III takes a hard look at how to use Windows 98 to work with files, folders, and disks. You also learn how to back up your data, as well as some invaluable techniques for protecting that data.

Part IV: Unleashing Day-to-Day Windows 98

Part IV takes your basic, workaday Windows chores and reveals their inner mysteries, allowing you to become more productive. Topics include installing and uninstalling applications, sharing data, fonts, printing, notebook computers, and the Windows 98 DOS prompt.

Part V: Unleashing Multimedia: The Sights and Sounds of Windows 98

Windows 98 is rich in multimedia goodies, and Part V shows you how to work with them to your best advantage. You get a frame-by-frame look at Windows 98 video, including the new Broadcast Architecture and the nitty-gritty of audio in Windows 98.

Part VI: Unleashing Windows 98 Communications and Networking

Compared to Windows 3.*x,* the communications tools that come with Windows 98 are first-rate. I show you how to take full advantage of all they have to offer in Part VI. You get the full scoop on modem communications and how to configure your modem in Windows 98. Once that's done, I show you how to work with two communications applets: Phone Dialer and HyperTerminal.

The rest of the chapters in Part VI give you all the background and know-how you need to get your Windows 98 machine on the network and to work with network resources once you're there.

Part VII: Unleashing Windows 98 for the Internet and Intranet

To close out this book, Part VII shows you how to set up and work with Windows 98's Internet and intranet features. You get the details behind TCP/IP and the specifics of how to get an Internet connection up and running in Windows 98. Finally, the last few chapters show you how to wield a number of Internet programs, including Internet Explorer, Outlook Express, NetMeeting, and FrontPage Express.

This Book's Special Features

To make your life easier, this book includes various features and conventions that help you get the most out of this book and Windows 98 itself.

Steps: Throughout the book, I've broken many Windows 98 tasks into easy-to-follow step-by-step procedures.

Things you type: Whenever I suggest that you type something, what you type appears in a monospace font.

Filenames: These also appear in monospace.

DOS commands: DOS commands and their syntax use the monospace font as well. Command placeholders (which stand for what you actually type) appear in an *italic monospace* font.

Pull-down menu commands: I use the following style for all application menu commands: *Menu*|*Command,* where *Menu* is the name of the menu that you pull down and *Command* is the name of the command you select. Here's an example: File| Open. This means that you pull down the File menu and select the Open command.

New to 98

New Windows 98 features icon: Programs and files that are new in Windows 98 are marked with the New to 98 icon.

Code continuation character: When a line of code is too long to fit on only one line of this book, it is broken at a convenient place and continued to the next line. The continuation of the line is preceded by a code continuation character (➥). You should type a line of code that has this character as one long line without breaking it.

This book also uses the following boxes to draw your attention to important (or merely interesting) information:

NOTE

The Note box presents asides that give you more information about the current topic. These tidbits provide extra insights that give you a better understanding of the task at hand. In many cases, they refer you to other sections of the book for more information.

TROUBLESHOOTING

Troubleshooting boxes point out common Windows 98 problems and tell you how to solve them.

TIP

The Tip box tells you about Windows 98 methods that are easier, faster, or more efficient than the standard methods.

CAUTION

The all-important Caution box tells you about potential accidents waiting to happen. There are always ways to mess things up when you're working with computers. These boxes help you avoid at least some of the pitfalls.

How to Contact Me

If you have any comments about this book, or if you wish to register a complaint or a compliment (I prefer the latter), please don't hesitate to send a missive my way. If you're still into the snail mail thing, just address your note to Sams Publishing, and I'll be sure to get it. If you're online, however, please drop me a line at the following email address:

paul@mcfedries.com

Better yet, feel free to drop by my Web site, have a look around, and sign the Guest Book:

http://www.mcfedries.com/

PART

I

Unleashing Windows 98 Installation and Startup

Preparing for the Windows 98 Installation

CHAPTER 1

> *In preparing for battle I have always found that plans are useless, but planning is*
> *indispensable.*
>
> *—Dwight D. Eisenhower*

Before you can unleash the power of Windows 98, you need to unleash Windows 98 on your system (or on your users' systems). Still, that's no big deal, right? Don't you just slip the CD-ROM into the drive, run some kind of setup program, and then kick back while Windows handles all the dirty work for you? Well, that might be true if you were installing just another run-of-the-mill application, but you're dealing with your computer's operating system (OS) here. This isn't some dinky little utility you can toss willy-nilly onto your hard drive to check out. Windows 98 is a demanding program that will take over your whole system, so you need to be prepared for the ordeal to come.

Before diving into the deep end of the Windows 98 installation, you should dip a toe or two into the waters to make sure that you know what's in store. That's just what you do in this chapter as you explore the setup process in depth, and as you get yourself and your computer ready for the installation. Then, in Chapter 2, "From Disc to Disk: Installing Windows 98," I'll take you through the entire setup procedure, whether you're installing Windows 98 "clean" or upgrading from another operating system.

Windows 98 System Requirements

Personal computing is governed by two inexorable, and not unrelated, "laws":

> **Moore's Law:** Processing power doubles every 18 months (from Gordon Moore, cofounder of Intel).

> **Parkinson's Law of Data:** Data expands to fill the space available for storage (from the original Parkinson's Law: Work expands to fill the time available).

These two observations help explain why, when the computers we use are becoming increasingly powerful, our day-to-day tasks never really seem all that much faster. The leaps in processing power and memory are being matched by the increasing complexity and resource requirements of the latest programs. So the computer you're using today might be twice as muscular as the one you were using a year and a half ago, but the applications you're using are twice the size and require twice as many resources.

Windows fits neatly into this scenario. With each new release of Microsoft's flagship operating system, the hardware requirements become more stringent, and our computers' processing power is taxed a little more. Windows 98 is no exception. Even though Microsoft spent an enormous amount of time and effort trying to shoehorn Windows 98 into a minimal system configuration, you need a reasonably powerful computer if you don't want to spend most of your day cursing the dreaded hourglass icon. (Windows changes your mouse pointer into an hourglass when it's performing a lengthy task that prevents you from using your computer.) Table 1.1 presents a rundown of the minimal and reasonable system requirements you need to install and work with Windows 98.

Table 1.1. System requirements for Windows 98.

System Component	What You Need
DOS version	**Minimum:** DOS 3.31. **Reasonable:** DOS 5.0 or higher. DOS 4.0 was so buggy that you're really taking a chance installing Windows 98 over it.
Processor	**Minimum:** 66 MHz 486DX2 **Reasonable:** Pentium, Pentium MMX, or Pentium II. Note, however, that Pentium Pro systems do not run Windows 98 noticeably faster than other Pentiums running at the same clock speed. The Pentium Pros are optimized for pure 32-bit code (such as you find in Windows NT), and Windows 98 contains enough 16-bit code to prevent any significant speed increases.
Memory	**Minimum:** 16MB. **Reasonable:** Windows 98 runs much better with 24MB of RAM. For best results, I recommend at least 32MB, with 64MB being the bottom line for the truly impatient.
Hard disk free space	**Minimum:** The minimum amount of space required by Windows 98 Setup is 225MB. **Reasonable:** A full install of Windows 98 could use up as much as 400MB of hard disk space. (See the following Note box.) Setup may also require another 45–50MB for the backup copies of your system files, and Windows 98 will need 20MB or 30MB for its dynamic swap file.
Video	**Minimum:** VGA, 14-inch monitor. **Reasonable:** Super VGA, 17-inch monitor. Windows 98 enables you to open and work with many more applications at once than did Windows 3.*x*. So to maximize screen space, your video card and monitor should be capable of displaying 256 colors at 1024×768 resolution. If you plan on using Windows 98's multimedia features (such as video), a video card that can handle true color (16 million colors) and DirectX is a must. You need to install a second adapter to take advantage of Windows 98's multiple monitor support.

continues

Table 1.1. continued

System Component	What You Need
Peripherals	**Minimum:** 3 1/2-inch high-density floppy drive, CD-ROM drive, and a mouse (Microsoft or compatible). **Reasonable:** If you plan on using The Microsoft Network, Microsoft Fax, HyperTerminal, or any other communications packages, you need a modem or a fax/modem. To take advantage of Windows 98's built-in sound support, you need a sound card and speakers. If you plan on using Windows 98's networking features, your system must have a network interface card installed.

HARD DISK SPACE REQUIREMENTS

Here are a few things to keep in mind when thinking about Windows 98's hard disk requirements:

- These recommendations for hard disk free space are higher than what Windows 98 actually usurps. They include about 45–50 extra megabytes that are used by Setup for temporary files that it creates during the installation process (and deletes when it's done).

- The actual number of megabytes required by Windows 98 depends on the installation options you select. For more information on these options, see the section in Chapter 2 titled "Setup Options."

- Windows 98's disk space requirements are also a function of the cluster size used on the target partition (see Chapter 9, "Peformance Tuning: Optimization Memory and Disk Access").

- You don't have to install Windows 98 on your system's boot drive (usually drive C). If you have a hard disk partitioned into multiple drives, or if you have multiple physical disk drives, you can install Windows 98 on any drive. Note, however, that Setup will install about 3MB of files on the boot drive. (Don't assume, however, that you can therefore partition your boot drive down to 3MB. Setup normally uses the boot drive to install its temporary files, so you really need your boot drive to be at least 15MB. On the other hand, it is possible to specify a location for Setup's temporary files. See "Setup's Command-Line Options" in Chapter 2.)

- Most Windows applications like to add optional components (such as DLL files, fonts, and Help files) to either the main Windows directory or Windows's SYSTEM subdirectory. So even if you install these programs on a different drive, this extra clutter will still add to the disk space needs of whatever drive you use to install Windows.

In addition to these requirements, your system must also meet the following guidelines:

■ Your system's BIOS shouldn't be any older than January 1994. Windows 98 often seems to have trouble with any BIOS older than that.

■ Your hard disk must have a DOS FAT (File Allocation Table) partition. Windows 98 doesn't recognize, and therefore can't be installed onto, drives partitioned as NTFS (Windows NT File System) or HPFS (OS/2's High Performance File System).

■ If your computer's boot drive is compressed, it must have at least 3MB of uncompressed space available. Windows 98 works with disks that have been compressed with DoubleSpace, DriveSpace, Stacker 3.0 and 4.*x*, and SuperStor compression schemes.

■ If you have the Windows 98 upgrade package, you must either have Windows 3.*x* installed on your system or have the original installation disks. If you have the full Windows 98 package, your system doesn't need to have an existing operating system.

Preparing Your System: A Checklist

Installing a new operating system—especially one that makes relatively radical changes to your system, as Windows 98 does—is definitely a "look before you leap" operation. Your computer's operating system is just too important; you shouldn't dive blindly into the installation process. To make sure that things go well, and to prevent any permanent damage in case disaster strikes, you need to practice "safe" installing. This means taking some time beforehand to run through a few precautionary measures and to make sure that your system is ready to welcome Windows 98. To that end, the next few sections run through a checklist of items you should take care of before firing up the Setup program.

Check Your System Requirements

Before getting too involved in the Setup process, you need to make sure that your computer is capable of supporting Windows 98. Go back over the system requirements I outlined earlier to make sure that your machine is Windows 98–ready.

Back Up Your Files

Although the vast majority of Windows 98 installations make it through without a hitch, there's another law that software (particularly complex operating system software) always seems to follow: Murphy's Law (that is, if anything can go wrong, it will). Windows 98 Setup has a Smart Recovery option that should get you out of most jams, but you should still make backup copies of important files, in case Smart Recovery is, for once, just not smart enough. Here are some suggestions for files to archive:

■ All your data files. If you're reinstalling Windows 98, be sure to back up your Exchange personal folder file (usually named Exchange.pst) and your personal address book (usually named Exchange.pab).

■ Important configuration files, such as AUTOEXEC.BAT and CONFIG.SYS (in your hard drive's root directory), WIN.INI, SYSTEM.INI, all your password list files (*.PWL), and all your GRP files (in your main Windows directory).

■ Windows 95 users should back up their Registry files. Be sure to make copies of both SYSTEM.DAT and USER.DAT (both are hidden files in your main Windows 95 folder).

■ Configuration files used by your applications. Windows applications usually store their configuration data in INI files in your main Windows directory. If you're running Windows 95, however, most of your application configuration settings will be stored in the Registry.

If you use backup software to archive your files, make sure that when you move to Windows 98 you keep not only the backup program, but also any "catalog" files that the program needs in order to restore the files. These catalogs spell out which files you backed up, their original locations, and where the files were backed up.

Clean Up Your Hard Disk

To maximize the amount of free space on your hard disk (and just for the sake of doing some spring cleaning), you should go through your hard disk with a fine-toothed comb, looking for unnecessary files you can delete. Here are some candidates:

Old DOS uninstall files: As I mentioned earlier, if you installed DOS 6 on your system, the program backs up your existing DOS files in a directory called OLD_DOS.1. (If you've upgraded more than once, you might also have an OLD_DOS.2 directory.) Setup will detect and offer to delete these files for you, but it's perfectly safe to delete them by hand in advance. In fact, it's better to do it in advance if you plan on defragmenting your hard drive (as I'll suggest shortly).

Stray TMP files that Windows 3.*x* hasn't deleted: Windows 3.*x* stores temporary files in a directory named TEMP. (This is usually C:\WINDOWS\TEMP. To find out for sure, examine the SET TEMP= line in your AUTOEXEC.BAT file.) These files have a .TMP extension, and Windows normally deletes them when you exit the program. (Other programs might also store temporary files in this directory.) If, however, your system crashes, or if a power failure shuts down your system before you get a chance to exit Windows, you might end up with a few TMP stragglers clinging to the TEMP directory. Exit Windows and then clean out the TEMP directory.

EXIT WINDOWS BEFORE DELETING TMP FILES

It's very important that you exit Windows completely before deleting anything from the TEMP directory. If you do this while Windows is running—even if you do it from a Windows DOS session—you run the risk of losing data or having Windows lock up on you.

Unneeded backup files created by applications: Many programs create backup files as you work. It's likely you don't need these backups, so you can delete them. Most backups have the extension .BAK, although you also see some with the extensions .TMP and .$$$. To make this chore easier, use File Manager's Search feature to scope out the BAK files on your hard drive. In File Manager, select the root directory, and then select File | Search. Type *.bak in the Search dialog box and click OK. A new window appears, showing all the BAK files on your system. You can delete the files from there. If you don't have Windows 3.*x*, run the following DOS command from the root directory: dir *.bak /s.

Unused programs and data files: Most people have hard disks that are littered with the rusting hulks of programs they tried a few times and then gave up on. Now is as good a time as any to remove this detritus from your system once and for all.

Turn Off Internet Explorer 4's Web Integration

If you're upgrading from Windows 95 with Internet Explorer 4 installed, Microsoft recommends that you turn off Web integration and return to the default Windows 95 shell. To do this, open My Computer and select View | Options to display the Options dialog box. In the General tab, activate the Classic style option and then click OK.

Reset "Numeric Tails"

One common Windows 95 tip that made the rounds (including earlier editions of this book) was a Registry tweak that prevented Windows 95 from adding "numeric tails" (such as ~1 and ~2) to the end of the DOS filenames. (See Chapter 4, "What's New and Noteworthy in Windows 98," to learn more about numeric tails and the relationship between DOS filenames and Windows 98's long filenames.)

Microsoft warns that this setting is incompatible with the Windows 98 upgrade process. This is probably because some DOS folder names have been hard-wired into the Setup code. If numeric tails have been disabled, this code will fail because the folders will be created with DOS names different than the ones Setup expects.

To turn off this feature, open the Registry Editor and head for the following key (see Chapter 12, "Getting to Know the Windows 98 Registry," to learn how to work with the Registry Editor):

HKEY_LOCAL_MACHINE\System\CurrentControlSet\control\FileSystem

Delete the NameNumericTail setting.

If You're Upgrading, Prepare Windows

If you're upgrading to Windows 98 from an existing version of Windows 3.*x*, here are a few chores to run through to make sure that the upgrade is a smooth one:

■ You can free up a large chunk of disk territory by getting rid of your Windows 3.*x* permanent swap file (assuming that you have one). In Windows 3.*x*, open the Control

Panel, open the 386 Enhanced icon, and click the Virtual Memory button. If you see Permanent in the Type field, click the Change>> button. If you don't plan on dual-booting between Windows 98 and Windows 3.*x*, select None from the Type drop-down list (the one in the New Settings box); otherwise, select Temporary (in this case, the swap file will exist only while Windows 3.*x* is active).

■ If you are starting Windows 98 Setup from within Windows 3.*x*, shut down all programs except Program Manager. If you have any other files open, Setup might not be able to install some of the new Windows 98 files properly. (Besides, having other programs open slows the whole installation process.)

■ If you have programs in your Startup group, Setup will add them automatically to the new Startup folder in Windows 98. However, some of your existing programs might not work with Windows 98, so you should clean out your existing Startup folder to prevent problems when Windows 98 starts.

■ If you're using a replacement shell (such as the Norton Desktop), disable it before starting Setup. You do this by opening SYSTEM.INI (it's in your main Windows folder), finding the [Boot] section, and editing the shell= line so that it reads as follows:

```
shell=progman.exe
```

■ Setup deletes Write, the little word processor that came with Windows 3.*x*. If you've grown accustomed to Write and want to preserve it, you need to store WRITE.EXE (and, if necessary, Write's Help file, WRITE.HLP) in a separate directory. After installation is complete, you can restore these files to their Write-ful place. (Note that you'll find a file named WRITE.EXE already in your Windows folder. That's just a stub that loads WordPad, the new Windows 98 word processor. Don't worry, though: Overwriting or renaming this file has no effect on WordPad.)

■ Similarly, Setup also deletes Paintbrush and replaces it with the new Paint program. Although Paint is generally an improvement over Paintbrush, it's disappointing that Paint can't save files in the PCX graphics format. (It can read PCX files, but it can save files only in Windows' native BMP format.) If you'd like to preserve the ability to write PCX files, you need to save the following Paintbrush files in a separate directory: PBRUSH.EXE, PBRUSH.DLL, and PBRUSH.HLP. When the installation is complete, copy these files to your main Windows 98 folder. (Again, note that Windows 98 already has a PBRUSH.EXE file, which is a stub that loads Paint. You need to overwrite or rename this file.)

Check and Defragment Your Hard Disk

As you learned earlier, Setup uses ScanDisk to give your hard disk a quick once-over before settling down to the serious business of installation. Sure, a "quick once-over" is better than nothing, but you should be more thorough. Specifically, use either the Windows 95 ScanDisk program or the DOS 6.2x ScanDisk utility (or some other disk-checking utility, such as Norton Disk Doctor) to give your hard disk a "surface" scan. The surface scan (it's called a *Thorough* scan in ScanDisk) checks your hard disk for physical imperfections that could lead to trouble down the road. (I discuss the Windows 98 version of ScanDisk in Chapter 15, "Disk Driving: The Windows 98 Disk Utilities.")

Don't forget to do a virus check if you have anti-virus software. Viruses have been known to wreak havoc on the Windows 98 Setup program (in addition to their other less-endearing qualities, such as locking up your system and trashing your hard drive).

When that's done, you should next defragment the files on your hard drive. This action ensures that Setup will store the Windows 98 files with optimal efficiency, which will improve performance and lessen the risk of corrupted data. (I explain file fragmentation in all its glorious detail, as well as how to use the Windows 98 Disk Defragmenter utility, in Chapter 9.)

Create a Bootable Floppy Disk

If you don't have one already, you should make a bootable floppy disk. That way, if Setup makes a complete mess of your boot drive (which is entirely possible, because Setup does tamper with the master boot record), you can still boot your system and make repairs.

If you have Windows 95, your best bet is to create a startup disk. See Chapter 17, "Wielding the Windows 98 System Tools," for the details. Otherwise, insert a disk in drive A, and then use either of the following methods to make the disk bootable:

- In File Manager, select Disk | Make System Disk. Insert a disk in drive A and click OK in the Make System Disk dialog box.
- At the DOS prompt, enter the following command:

  FORMAT A: /S

(Although DOS has a SYS command that will make a formatted disk bootable, you're better off using FORMAT. By formatting the disk, you can be sure that you're starting with a "fresh" disk that isn't cluttered with other files or, more important, doesn't have any viruses lurking in the weeds.)

After you've created a system disk, you need to copy a few more files in order to create a true "emergency disk" you can use to investigate and troubleshoot problems. The number of files you copy depends on the capacity of the disk and what you have in the way of recovery software. Here are some suggestions:

A text editor: This enables you to make changes to your configuration files. If you have at least DOS 5, use the Edit program (copy both EDIT.COM and QBASIC.EXE from your DOS directory).

Your computer's setup program: Some computers come with a setup program on a separate disk (it might be called something like SETUP.EXE). In many cases, you just need to rerun this program to get your hard disk back up and running.

Recovery utilities: If you've accidentally deleted one or more of the system files or if you've accidentally formatted your hard disk, you can recover with special software. If you have DOS 5 or 6, copy UNDELETE.EXE and UNFORMAT.COM from your DOS directory. You should also include FDISK.EXE, the DOS partitioning utility, in case you end up with a corrupted partition table. ATTRIB.EXE is useful if you have to adjust the attributes of a file. I'd also recommend SYS.COM, the DOS utility that makes a drive bootable by copying the system files. If you have any other utility programs you like to use, copy the appropriate files.

Startup files: Copy your current AUTOEXEC.BAT and CONFIG.SYS files from your root directory. To make sure that DOS doesn't try to execute these files at startup, however, you should rename them (because I boot from drive C, I call mine AUTOEXEC.C and CONFIG.C).

Disk diagnostics: If you have DOS 6 or Windows 3.1, copy MSD.EXE, the Microsoft diagnostics program.

Virus checker: In case your hard disk goes down for the count because of a virus, you should include an anti-virus program on your emergency disk. Make sure that the program can "disinfect" (and not just detect) viruses.

Hardware drivers: Include any drivers you need for devices such as a CD-ROM drive, removable hard disk, SCSI controller, disk compression (such as DBLSPACE.BIN), and so on.

Ideally, you should create new AUTOEXEC.BAT and CONFIG.SYS files for the bootable disk. One easy way to do this is to use your existing AUTOEXEC.BAT and CONFIG.SYS files as starting points. Edit them to change hard drive references to drive A. For example, if you have the line C:\SCSI\ASPI2DOS.SYS in your regular CONFIG.SYS, change it to read just A:\ASPI2DOS.SYS in the bootable disk version (assuming, of course, that you've copied the file ASPI2DOS.SYS to the bootable disk). You might need to try a few reboots with the bootable disk in drive A to get things working right.

Shut Down Any Unnecessary TSRs

As I mentioned earlier, TSRs and device drivers can cause Setup to choke, so you should remove all unnecessary memory-resident programs before starting Setup. This is particularly true of virus detection software. Because Setup alters your system's master boot record, any virus scanner in memory will assume that a virus attack is under way. The battle between Setup and the anti-virus program will most likely cause your system to hang, and you might not be able to reboot.

Here are the only TSRs and device drivers you need: drivers for disk partitions, hard disks, networking, video, CD-ROMs, SCSI controllers, and whatever other devices are crucial to the operation of your system.

To remove TSRs, you can either run a command at the DOS prompt (some TSR commands have switches that remove them from memory) or disable the appropriate lines in CONFIG.SYS and AUTOEXEC.BAT. You do this by appending REM and a space to the beginning of the line so that DOS will ignore the line at startup. You need to reboot your machine to put these changes into effect.

Use MSD to Print a System Report

It's a good idea to take a "snapshot" of your current system configuration before running Setup. If you have Windows 3.1 or higher on your system, you have a handy utility in your main Windows directory called MSD (Microsoft Diagnostics). You can use MSD to print a report showing all your major system parameters, including important hardware configuration values such as IRQ settings and memory addresses. Here are the steps to follow to print this report:

1. Exit Windows. You can run MSD from within Windows, but you need to run it outside Windows to get the most accurate picture of your system.

2. Type msd and press Enter. You see the MSD window, shown in Figure 1.1.

FIGURE 1.1.

You can use MSD to print a system configuration report.

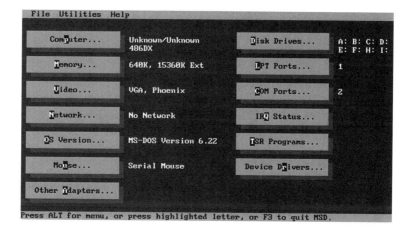

3. Select File | Print Report. MSD displays a dialog box filled with printing options.

4. In the Report Information section, activate the Report All check box.

5. In the Print to section, select the port to which your printer is attached.

6. Make sure that your printer is turned on and then click OK.

7. Fill out the Customer Information dialog box, if desired, and click OK. MSD prints the report.

8. Select File | Exit or press F3 to exit MSD.

Some Notes About Dual- (and Multi-) Booting

The last thing you need to mull over before getting down to the nitty-gritty of the Setup program is whether you want to run Windows 98 exclusively or "dual-boot" with another operating system. Dual-booting means that when you start your computer, you have the option of running Windows 98 or some other operating system, such as Windows 3.*x*. It's even possible to multi-boot, which means having the choice of three or more operating systems at startup. The next few sections show you how to dual-boot Windows 98 with various other systems.

YOU CAN'T DUAL-BOOT WITH WINDOWS 95

Windows 98 replaces the Windows 95 system files, so you can't dual-boot between Windows 98 and Windows 95.

Dual-Booting and FAT32

Windows 98 supports the new FAT32 file system that was originally introduced in the OSR2 release of Windows 95. FAT32 brings a number of advantages to the file allocation table, the most notable of which are 32-bit speed and vastly improved storage efficiency. Windows 98 goes OSR2 one better by providing a utility for converting 16-bit FAT partitions to FAT32, *without* losing data. (I show you how this utility works in Chapter 9.) In other words, you almost certainly want to upgrade your hard disk to FAT32.

However, you want to think twice about FAT32 if you really need to dual-boot between Windows 98 and another operating system. That's because Windows 98 disables its dual-boot functionality on a drive that uses FAT32.

You can get around this limitation by strategically partitioning your hard drive as follows:

- Create a boot partition (drive C). Leave this partition as FAT16, which will leave Windows 98's dual-boot feature enabled.
- Create a partition for Windows 98 and convert it to FAT32.
- Create one or two FAT32 partitions for your programs and data files.
- Create another partition for the operating system you want to dual-boot with Windows 98. You can use either FAT16 or the operating system's native file system (such as NTFS for Windows NT or HPFS for OS/2). Don't use FAT32, however, because no other operating system can recognize FAT32 partitions.

Dual-Booting with Windows 3.*x*

If you've been using Windows 3.*x*, setting up your system to dual-boot with Windows 98 has its advantages. For one thing, you get to start Windows 98 with a clean slate and without any of the DLL and INI file baggage that your Windows 3.*x* installation might have accumulated over the years. For another, it's handy to be able to return to Windows 3.*x* at any time in case you have a program that Windows 98 doesn't like.

On the downside, dual-booting with Windows 98 means your program and configuration settings won't migrate to Windows 98. You have to reinstall most of your applications, reconfigure your network, and so on.

RUN WINDOWS 3.*X* PROGRAMS WITHOUT REINSTALLING

Actually, you might be able to get away with not having to reinstall some of your applications in Windows 98. Some enlightened programs store all the files they need (including DLLs and INI files) in their own directory. These all-too-rare applications should run fine under Windows 98. Most other applications store files in the Windows 3.*x* main directories: \WINDOWS and \WINDOWS\SYSTEM. If you try to run these programs from Windows 98, they'll fail because they can't find these files. The solution? Add the Windows 3.*x* directories to your Windows 98 path. In AUTOEXEC.BAT, look for the PATH statement. If you installed Windows 98 in a directory named WIN95, it should look like this:

PATH C:\WIN95;C:\WIN95\COMMAND;C:\DOS

If Windows 3.*x* is in C:\WINDOWS, edit this statement so that it reads as follows:

PATH C:\WIN95;C:\WIN95\COMMAND;C:\DOS;C:\WINDOWS;C:\WINDOWS\SYSTEM

CONVERTING PROGRAM GROUPS IN WINDOWS 98

If you have some carefully constructed program groups in Windows 3.*x*, you might not like the idea of losing them when you install Windows 98 in a separate directory. Well, you don't have to, because Windows 98 has a utility called Program Group Converter (GRPCONV.EXE) that can convert existing Program Manager groups into Windows 98 Start menu folders. First, for each program group you want to convert, copy the appropriate GRP file from your main Windows 3.*x* directory to your main Windows 98 directory. Open the Windows 98 Start menu, select Run, type grpconv /m, and click OK. In the Select a Group to Convert dialog box, highlight one of the program group files and click Open. When you're asked whether you're sure you want to convert the group, click Yes. The group is converted into a Start menu folder, and the Select a Group to Convert dialog box is redisplayed. Repeat the process for any other groups you want to convert.

Installing Windows 98 if Windows 3.*x* Is Already Installed

As long as your system is running DOS 5.*x* or 6.*x*, dual-booting with an existing version of Windows 3.*x* is a no-brainer. When Setup asks you to specify the directory to use for Windows 98, be sure to choose a different directory than the one you're currently using for Windows 3.*x*. Setup leaves your existing version of Windows (and DOS) intact, and you can run them normally any time you like.

You do this by first rebooting your computer. While the machine is rebooting, hold down the Ctrl key. You eventually see the following menu:

```
Microsoft Windows 98 Startup Menu
=====================================

    1. Normal
    2. Logged (\BOOTLOG.TXT)
    3. Safe mode
    4. Step-by-step confirmation
    5. Command prompt only
    6. Safe mode command prompt only
    7. Previous version of MS-DOS

Enter a choice: 1
```

(If you're running Windows 98 on a network, you see a total of eight choices.) Highlight the Previous version of MS-DOS item and press Enter to load your old DOS version. Windows 98 uses your old system and configuration files (IO.DOS, MSDOS.DOS, COMMAND.DOS, CONFIG.DOS, and AUTOEXEC.DOS) to load your previous DOS version.

BYPASSING THE STARTUP MENU

For faster service, you can load the previous version of DOS without using the Windows 98 Startup menu. When your computer beeps to indicate that it has completed its Power-On Self Test (POST), press F4.

Installing Windows 3.*x* if Windows 98 Is Already Installed

In Chapter 2 I'll show you how to install Windows 98 on a clean system (that is, a system with a freshly formatted boot drive). But what happens if, after you've installed Windows 98, you find you need to reinstall Windows 3.*x* (for example, to run a program that Windows 98 doesn't get along with)? It's still possible to dual-boot between the two systems, but it takes a bit more work. Here are the steps to follow:

1. Using the bootable disk you created before installing Windows 98, copy IO.SYS to IO.DOS in the root directory of your boot drive. You can use one of two methods:

   ■ In Windows 98, open Explorer, select View | Folder Options, and then display the View tab. Activate the Show all files option, deactivate the Hide file extensions for known file types check box, and click OK. Select drive A and copy IO.SYS to a separate directory (not your root directory). Rename IO.SYS to IO.DOS, and then move it into the root directory. (If Windows 98 asks whether you're sure you want to rename the file, click Yes.)

   ■ At the DOS prompt, run the following two commands to remove any attributes from IO.SYS and copy it to IO.DOS in the root directory:

   ```
   attrib -h -r -s a:\io.sys
   copy a:\io.sys c:\io.dos
   ```

2. Repeat step 2 for MSDOS.SYS (in other words, copy it to MSDOS.DOS in the root directory).

3. Copy COMMAND.COM to COMMAND.DOS, AUTOEXEC.BAT to AUTOEXEC.DOS, and CONFIG.SYS to CONFIG.DOS (again, your destination in each case is the root directory).

4. Copy any device drivers your system needs to the hard drive. You might want to create a separate directory to hold these files and avoid cluttering the root directory.

5. Adjust CONFIG.DOS and AUTOEXEC.DOS so that the device driver lines point to the appropriate files on the hard drive.

6. Open the file MSDOS.SYS (it's in the root directory) in your favorite text editor, find the [Options] section, and add the line BootMulti=1. The file should now look something like this:

```
[Options]
BootGUI=1
BootMulti=1
```

7. Save the file.

At this point, you should be able to load the version of DOS you used for your bootable disk. Make sure that the disk is removed from the drive, restart Windows 98, and follow the instructions given earlier for booting to the previous version of MS-DOS.

You can now reinstall Windows 3.*x*. Make sure, of course, that you install into a different directory than the one you used for Windows 98. When Windows 3.*x* asks about modifying your CONFIG.SYS and AUTOEXEC.BAT files, go ahead and let it do so. This might seem counterintuitive because the files used by your previous version of DOS are CONFIG.DOS and AUTOEXEC.DOS. But when Windows 98 loads the previous DOS version, it does two things:

■ It temporarily renames CONFIG.SYS to CONFIG.W40 and AUTOEXEC.BAT to AUTOEXEC.W40 (it also renames COMMAND.COM to COMMAND.W40).

■ It restores CONFIG.DOS to CONFIG.SYS and AUTOEXEC.DOS to AUTOEXEC.BAT (and COMMAND.DOS to COMMAND.COM).

The upshot of all this is that you can let Windows 3.*x* modify CONFIG.SYS and AUTOEXEC.BAT without fear of crippling your Windows 98 setup.

Dual-Booting with Windows NT

Windows 98 and Windows NT are happy to share the same machine, so dual-booting between the two is no problem. You do, however, need to watch out for a few things:

■ Your hard disk must have a FAT16 boot partition and a FAT16 or FAT32 partition into which you can install Windows 98. If your hard disk uses only an NTFS (NT File System) partition, you won't be able to install Windows 98.

■ Windows 98 doesn't understand NTFS, so even if you install Windows 98 into a separate FAT partition, you won't be able to read NTFS partitions from within Windows 98.

■ The Windows 98 compression scheme (DriveSpace) is different from the one used by Windows NT 3.51, and more important, the two are incompatible. So even if both Windows 98 and Windows NT are installed on a FAT partition, they won't be able to read each other's compressed files.

HOW TO AVOID REINSTALLING APPS IN NT

To avoid reinstalling all your Windows 98 applications in Windows NT, there's a way to make NT recognize and run some (but not all) of your existing applications. In NT's Control Panel, open the System icon. In the System dialog box that appears, highlight the Path line in the System Environment Variables section. Move down to the Value text box, and then add the following string to the end of the existing value:

`;C:\WINDOWS;C:\WINDOWS\SYSTEM`

Yes, that's a semicolon at the beginning. If you installed Windows 98 in a directory other than `C:\WINDOWS`, make the appropriate change to the string. Click the Set button and then click OK to put the change into effect.

Installing Windows NT After Installing Windows 98

There's no problem loading Windows NT on your system after Windows 98 is installed. In fact, if you can manage it, it's always best to install Windows 98 first and then install Windows NT. (If NT is already on your system, though, I'll show you how to install Windows 98 alongside it in the next section.) To ensure a hassle-free setup, you need to do only two things:

■ In Windows 98, open the DOS command prompt, change to the directory where the Windows NT source files are stored, and enter the command winnt /w. The /w switch enables the Windows NT Setup program to operate under Windows 98.

■ When Setup asks which directory you want to use to install Windows NT, be sure to specify a different directory than the one you used for Windows 98.

After Windows NT is ensconced on your system, rebooting will display NT's OS Loader menu:

```
OS Loader V4.00
Please select the operating system to start:
    Windows NT Workstation Version 4.00
    Windows NT Workstation Version 4.00 (VGA mode)
    Microsoft Windows
Use á and â to move the highlight to your choice.
Press Enter to Choose.
```

Highlight the operating system you want to work with and then press Enter.

Installing Windows 98 After Installing Windows NT

If Windows NT is already installed on your system, setting up a dual-boot system with Windows 98 requires a few extra steps. How you run the Windows 98 Setup program depends on how Windows NT is configured:

- If you installed NT over DOS or alongside Windows 3.*x*, you should see the OS Loader menu at startup (as described in the preceding section). In this case, select either DOS or Windows from the menu and then run Windows 98 Setup.

- If you have no other operating system to work with, boot from a floppy disk that has a previous version of MS-DOS. When you run Windows 98 Setup, it will trash NT's master boot record. To fix this, insert your NT boot floppy, reboot, and follow the onscreen instructions. When you get to the Welcome to Setup screen, select the Repair option by pressing R. This will restore the boot sector and give you a choice of operating systems in the OS Loader menu.

Dual-Booting with OS/2 Warp

These days, many people are wondering which of the three major operating systems—Windows 98, Windows NT, or OS/2 Warp—is best suited to their needs. Each system boasts certain advantages over the other, and to be sure, each has its pitfalls. The best way to compare one OS against another is to load a couple of them onto your system and dual-boot between them. If you're comparing Windows 98 and OS/2, here are some notes to think about beforehand:

- Your hard disk must have a FAT16 boot partition and a FAT16 or FAT32 partition into which you can install Windows 98. You can't install Windows 98 into an OS/2 HPFS partition.

- Windows 98 won't work with HPFS, so even if you install Windows 98 into a separate FAT partition, you won't be able to read HPFS partitions from within Windows 98.

- Windows 98 won't migrate any existing OS/2 settings.

- If you were running Windows 3.*x* applications under OS/2, you might have to reinstall them under Windows 98.

Ideally, you should install OS/2 first and then install Windows 98. When installing OS/2, be sure to create a "startable" Boot Manager partition and a separate "bootable" FAT partition for Windows 98 (you do all this inside OS/2's FDISK utility). If OS/2 is already installed, run the FDISK utility from within OS/2 to create the Boot Manager and FAT partitions.

Use a bootable floppy to boot your computer to DOS, and then run the Windows 98 Setup program. Boot Manager will display a message warning you that continuing with Setup will disable Boot Manager. Why does Setup disable Boot Manager? Because Setup needs to reboot your system a couple of times during the installation process. If Boot Manager is active, Setup has no way of knowing which operating system will be used to boot the computer. To make sure that Windows 98 is booted during Setup's restarts, Boot Manager's partition information is removed. That's OK, though, because you restore Boot Manager later.

After Windows 98 is safely installed, insert your OS/2 boot disk and restart the system. Now run OS/2's FDISK utility to restore the Boot Manager partition. With Boot Manager back up and running, the Boot Manager menu will give you a choice of either OS/2 or Windows 98 each time you restart your computer.

Multi-Booting with Three or More Operating Systems

For maximum OS flexibility, you want to have three or more systems available on your machine so that you can multi-boot among them. Depending on the operating systems you want to use, this isn't all that much more work than setting up a dual-boot system.

If you want to use Windows 3.*x*, Windows 98, and Windows NT, go ahead and install all three operating systems, in separate directories, using the dual-boot guidelines outlined earlier. The best installation sequence is to install Windows 3.*x* first, then Windows 98, then Windows NT. As explained earlier, each time you start your machine, you see the Windows NT Boot Loader menu. Here's how to boot each operating system:

■ To boot Windows NT, select the Windows NT Workstation option.

■ To boot to Windows 98, select the Windows option.

■ To boot to Windows 3.*x*, select the Windows option. Then, when you see the Starting Windows 98... message, press F4 to load the previous version of DOS.

If you want to multi-boot with OS/2, Windows 98, and some other operating system, install OS/2 first and use Boot Manager to set up bootable partitions for the other operating systems. Install the other operating systems into these partitions, use OS/2's FDISK utility to repair the Boot Manager partition (if necessary), and use the Boot Manager menu to select the operating system you want to use.

If you don't have OS/2, you can use one of the other multi-boot programs that are around. You might want to check out any of the following:

■ System Commander
   $99.95 from V Communications
   408-296-4224
   http://www.v-com.com/

■ Partition Magic
   $69.95 from PowerQuest Corporation
   800-379-2566
   http://www.powerquest.com/

- Wizard of OS
  $99 from Modular Software Systems
  360-886-8882
  `http://www.netusa.com/pcsoft/library/p_960.htm`

Summary

This chapter explained the Windows 98 installation process in depth. As you saw, even though Windows 98 Setup is the friendliest and most intelligent of the Windows install programs, the installation process is far from trivial. You have upgrade issues to consider and preparatory chores to perform. Still, thanks to innovations such as the CD-ROM–based installation and the Hardware Detection Manager, Windows 98 Setup is a relatively painless affair.

Here's a list of chapters where you find related information:

- For more information about the Windows 98 Startup menu and `MSDOS.SYS`, check out Chapter 3, "Start Me Up: Controlling Windows 98 Startup."

- To get your feet wet with the new Windows 98 interface and tools, read Chapter 4, "What's New and Noteworthy in Windows 98."

- Plug and Play and other hardware-related issues are covered in Chapter 10, "Getting the Most Out of Device Manager and Hardware Profiles."

- I offer extended coverage of ScanDisk in Chapter 17, "Wielding the Windows 98 System Tools."

- Printer installation is covered in Chapter 21, "Prescriptions for Perfect Printing."

- For network installations, try Chapter 28, "Setting Up Windows 98 for Networking."

From Disc to Disk: Installing Windows 98

CHAPTER 2

IN THIS CHAPTER

Would not this be that best beginning which would naturally and proverbially lead to the best end?

—*Plato*

This chapter takes you through the entire setup procedure, whether you're installing Windows 98 "clean" or upgrading from another operating system. For good measure, I'll also take you through the installation of individual Windows 98 components, and I'll even show you how to uninstall Windows 98.

Getting Setup Started

At long last, we get down to brass tacks and run the Windows 98 Setup program. This section takes you through the specifics of the procedure, including the various prompts and dialog boxes you can expect.

How you start Setup depends on how you want to install Windows 98, which version you're using, and which operating system (if any) is currently installed on your machine. The next couple of sections run through the various possibilities.

Performing a Clean Installation

In many ways, the best Windows 98 installation method starts with a clean slate. In other words, you wipe everything off your hard drive (after first backing up your data, of course) and install Windows 98 on the freshly formatted disk. This is called a clean installation. Its chief advantage is that you can be sure you're not saddling Windows 98 with any excess (and potentially troublesome) baggage from an earlier operating system. It also serves to rid your system of excess files that might be hanging around, it freshens the hard disk sectors, and it puts the boot to any viruses that might be hiding out on your hard disk. The disadvantage, of course, is that you need to reinstall all your programs.

Here's how to get started with a clean Windows 98 installation:

1. Back up all your important data, including the configuration files used by your programs.

2. If you haven't done so already, create a bootable disk as described in Chapter 1, "Preparing for the Windows 98 Installation." Make sure that the disk has the FORMAT.COM and FDISK.EXE programs on it.

3. Insert the bootable disk and restart your computer. Watch the startup routine carefully, looking for any error messages that might crop up. When you get to the DOS prompt, check to make sure that all the devices you need (CD-ROM, SCSI controller, and so on) are functioning properly.

4. At this point, you might want to consider using FDISK to repartition your hard drive. At the very least, you should have one partition for your operating system files and another for your program and data files. This way, if you ever have to attempt a clean installation again, you need only reformat the drive that contains the operating system; you can leave the data drive intact. If you want to load multiple operating systems on the computer, consider creating a partition for each operating system.

FDISK IS DESTRUCTIVE!

Note that when you partition a disk, FDISK destroys all the disk's data. So after you've changed your partitions, there's no going back! If you don't feel like trashing your data, consider a nondestructive partitioning program such as Partition Magic.

5. Enter the command `format c: /s` to format drive C and install the DOS system files. DOS displays the following message:
   ```
   WARNING: ALL DATA ON NON_REMOVABLE DISK
   DRIVE C: WILL BE LOST!
   Proceed with Format (Y/N)?
   ```

6. Press Y and then press Enter to start the format. When DOS is done, it will prompt you for a volume label. If you like, you can type a label of 11 or fewer characters and then press Enter (don't use a space or any of the following characters in your label: + = \ ¦ [ ] ; : , . < > ? /). If you don't want to include a label now, just press Enter; you can use Windows 98 to label your disk, as described in Chapter 14, "File and Folder Tricks and Techniques."

7. If you used FDISK to create any other drives, format them as well (but don't add the /s switch).

Now that your hard disk is scrubbed clean, it's time to install Windows 98. Before doing so, follow these steps:

1. Copy the hard disk versions of AUTOEXEC.BAT and CONFIG.SYS from the boot disk to the hard drive's root directory. In Chapter 1, "Preparing for the Windows 98 Installation," I suggested that you name these files AUTOEXEC.C and CONFIG.C, so you also need to rename the copied versions.

2. Copy your system's device drivers from the boot disk to the hard disk.

3. Remove the boot disk and restart your computer.

If all went well, your system should boot to the c:\ prompt, and your CD-ROM drive will be available. (If it's not, make sure that the DEVICE= line in CONFIG.SYS points to the location of your CD-ROM driver. Also, make sure that the MSCDEX.EXE line in AUTOEXEC.BAT points to the correct location of MSCDEX.EXE.) Switch to the CD-ROM drive, type setup, and press Enter to start Windows 98 Setup.

Options for Starting Setup

Here's a list of the options you have for starting Setup, depending on which operating system you have installed:

Upgrading from Windows 95: Insert the Windows 98 CD-ROM. Assuming you have AutoRun enabled, a dialog box will ask whether you want to upgrade Windows. Click Yes to launch the Setup program. (If AutoRun is disabled, double-click Setup.exe in the CD-ROM's root folder.)

Installing from Windows 3.*x* (Windows 3.1 or Windows for Workgroups): First, insert the Windows 98 CD-ROM or Disk 1 in the appropriate drive. In Program Manager, select File | Run, enter *drive*:\setup.exe (where *drive* is the letter of the drive containing the Setup disk) in the Run dialog box, and click OK. (Alternatively, you can run Setup from the DOS prompt, as described next.)

Installing from DOS or Windows 3.0: In either case, you must run Setup from the DOS prompt. First, insert the Windows 98 CD-ROM. Type *drive*: (where *drive* is the letter of your CD-ROM drive) and press Enter. Type setup and press Enter.

Installing Windows 98 on a computer that doesn't have DOS: In this case, follow the instructions in the preceding section for performing a clean install.

Moving to Windows 98 from other operating systems: For all other operating systems—including Windows NT and OS/2—you need to get to a DOS prompt—either by dual-booting or by restarting your system with a bootable DOS floppy in drive A. Insert the CD-ROM, change to the appropriate drive, type setup, and press Enter.

Running Setup from Your Hard Disk

Compared to floppy disks, it's a true pleasure installing Windows 98 from CD-ROM. However, Setup can still take quite a while if you have a slow CD-ROM drive. If you have enough room on your system, you can speed up the Windows 98 installation considerably by copying all the source files to your hard drive. Use Windows Explorer (Windows 95), File Manager (Windows 3.*x*), or the XCOPY command (DOS) to copy the CD-ROM's \WIN98 directory to your hard drive. (Don't copy any of the other directories on the CD-ROM!) Note that these files will consume a little over 112MB of hard disk acreage.

To start the installation, run the SETUP.EXE program in the WIN98 directory on your hard disk.

Setup's Command-Line Options

Setup boasts quite a number of command-line switches you can use to control the way Setup operates. A *switch* is an extra parameter you tack on to the end of the setup command. Each switch consists of a slash (/) followed by one or more characters. For example, the /? switch doesn't start Setup at all. Rather, it displays a list of all the available switches. Note that you must include a space between the setup command and the switch, like so:

setup /?

Here's the general syntax for the setup command:

setup [*batch*] *switches*

Here, *batch* is an optional file that specifies various settings for a custom batch setup. Table 2.1 details some of the more important Setup switches. (Note that you must use the switches with the exact uppercase and lowercase letters shown in the table.)

Table 2.1. Setup's command-line switches.

Switch	*Description*
/?	Provides a brief summary of the available Setup switches.
/C	Tells Setup not to run SMARTDrive.
/d	Tells Setup not to use your existing copy of Windows.
/id	Tells Setup not to check for the minimum disk space required to install Windows 98.
/iL	Tells Setup to load the Logitech mouse driver rather than the Microsoft mouse driver.
/in	Tells Setup not to run the Network Setup module.
/it	Tells Setup not to check for the presence of dirty or deadly TSRs.
/ih	Tells Setup to run ScanDisk in the foreground (if you start Setup from within Windows 3.*x*).
/iq	Tells Setup not to check your drive for cross-linked files. This switch is valid only if you use the /is switch to bypass ScanDisk or if ScanDisk fails.
/is	Tells Setup not to run ScanDisk.
/IW	Tells Setup not to display the License Agreement.
/T:dir	Specifies an alternative directory in which Setup should store its temporary files. (Note that Setup will delete *all* the files in this directory when it's done!)

After Setup Is Under Way

With Setup off the launch pad, you receive several prompts before the installation process begins in earnest. If you started Setup from DOS, you see the following prompt:

```
Setup is now going to perform a routine check on your system.

To continue, Press Enter. To quit Setup, press ESC.
```

Press Enter and Setup performs the ScanDisk check you learned about earlier. If ScanDisk finds any problems, it tells you and gives you various options on how to proceed. (I discuss ScanDisk in detail in Chapter 17, "Wielding the Windows 98 System Tools.") When ScanDisk has completed its labors, press X to select the Exit button (which appears only if you started Setup from DOS) to continue with Setup. At this point, the DOS version of Setup switches to Windows mode for the rest of the installation.

New to 98

Regardless of the method you use to launch Setup, you eventually see the Windows 98 Setup screen shown in Figure 2.1. The margin on the left outlines the broad steps that Setup will take, provides an estimate for the time remaining in the installation procedure, and provides other "informational details" as the install proceeds.

FIGURE 2.1.

The revamped Windows 98 Setup screen.

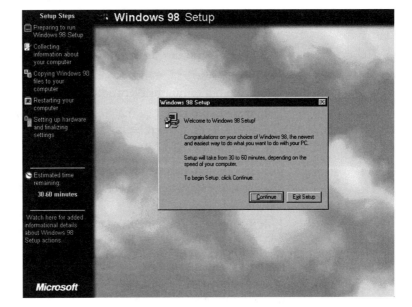

Click Continue to proceed with the installation. Here's a summary of the steps you may take while Setup readies the Setup Wizard:

1. If Setup finds an OLD_DOS.X directory (which contains uninstall data for a previous version of DOS), it asks whether you want to remove these files (see Figure 2.2). Because you don't need them any more, you should probably select Yes to free up the disk space. Otherwise, just click No to leave them alone.

FIGURE 2.2.

You see this dialog box if you have old DOS uninstall files cluttering your hard disk.

2. Setup might display a warning about low disk space or some other condition that could prevent Windows 98 from installing. You might have no choice but to quit Setup, but in some cases you can click OK to proceed.

3. If you have any other programs running, Setup displays a dialog box recommending that you shut them down (see Figure 2.3). To close any running programs, press Alt+Tab to switch to each program, and close them. When you're finished, click OK to continue with the installation.

FIGURE 2.3.

You should shut down any running Windows programs before continuing.

4. The program initializes the Setup Wizard. This Wizard is a series of dialog boxes that takes you through the entire installation procedure.

5. If you have the upgrade version of Windows 98, Setup searches your hard drive for an existing version of Windows. However, if you're performing a clean install, your old version of Windows will have been deleted when you formatted your hard drive, and so the search will fail. That's not a problem because Setup can verify the upgrade using your original Windows CD-ROM or floppy disks. To do this, insert your original Windows CD-ROM or, if you have floppy disks, insert Disk 1. In the Windows 98 Upgrade Verification dialog box, enter the path to the disk (or click Browse to select the path), and then click OK. Note that if you're using floppy disks, Setup will prompt you to enter several of the disks.

6. When the Wizard is ready, Setup displays the Windows 98 software license agreement. Read the license agreement (if you dare!), click the I accept the agreement option, and then click Next >.

Supplying the Setup Wizard with Information

As I mentioned earlier, the Setup Wizard's job is to display a series of dialog boxes that asks you for various tidbits of information Setup needs in order to install Windows 98 to your liking. Windows 95 upgraders don't have to worry about this too much because Setup Wizard uses the existing configuration. For those installing over a different operating system or onto a clean hard disk, this section explains the various dialog boxes you'll see and outlines what Setup expects from you.

Before we get started, let's review how wizards work. Each Setup Wizard dialog box contains various buttons at the bottom. You can use these buttons to move forward and backward through the installation process. Table 2.2 outlines the function of each button.

Table 2.2. The Setup Wizard's command buttons.

Button	Description
< Back	Takes you back to the previous Setup Wizard dialog box.
Next >	Accepts the data in the current dialog box and moves ahead to the next dialog box.
Cancel	Quits the installation process.

The next few sections give you a rundown of the Setup Wizard dialog boxes.

Select Directory

The Select Directory dialog box gives you two options: You can install Windows 98 in your current Windows 3.*x* or Windows 95 directory (usually C:\WINDOWS), or you can use a different directory. For the former choice, just click the Next > button. For the latter, activate the Other directory option and click Next >.

Change Directory

The Change Directory dialog box appears if you selected the Other directory option in the Choose Directory dialog box. Enter the new directory in the dialog box and click Next >. Setup then warns you that installing Windows 98 in a new directory means you will have to reinstall your programs, and it asks whether you want to continue. Click Yes.

Save System Files

If you're installing Windows 98 over Windows 3.*x* or Windows 95, the Save System Files dialog box asks whether you want to save your system files. Saving them lets you uninstall Windows 98, so it's a good idea. Here's how you do it:

1. Make sure that the Yes option is activated.

2. Click Next >. Windows gathers the system files and then prompts you for the disk drive to use to store them.

3. Use the Hard disk drop-down list to select the drive you want to use.

DISK SPACE REQUIREMENTS FOR SAVED SYSTEM FILES

Saving your system files uses up another 45–50MB of hard disk space.

4. Click OK. Setup stows the system files on the drive you selected.

Setup Options

You use the Setup Options dialog box, shown in Figure 2.4, to specify the Windows 98 components you want installed. Select the option you want and click Next >.

FIGURE 2.4.

Use the Setup Options dialog box to choose the type of installation you want.

Which Setup option should you choose? That depends on two factors: the amount of hard disk space you have available and the optional Windows 98 components you need. Here's a summary of what you get with each option (I'll discuss each option in more detail a little later):

Typical: Installs the Windows 98 components that will be needed (in Microsoft's estimation, anyway) by most Windows 98 users.

Portable: Uses less disk space than the Typical option, but focuses on components suited to portable computers.

Compact: Bypasses all the optional Windows 98 components to save disk space.

Custom: Enables you to pick and choose specific Windows 98 components (although, as you'll see, you can "customize" any of the Setup options).

To help you make this decision, I've put together a couple of tables that spell out not only how much disk space each option uses, but also which components are included in each option.

YOU CAN INSTALL AND REMOVE COMPONENTS LATER

Don't worry if you're not sure which components you need. You can always add and remove components from within Windows 98. See the section titled "Adding and Removing Windows 98 Components," later in this chapter.

For starters, Table 2.3 presents approximate hard disk space requirements for each Setup option (including the extra disk space that Setup needs for its temporary files). These are only approximate because the actual number depends on the hardware you have in your system (Setup installs different device drivers depending on the hardware it detects) and whether you're installing Windows 98 on a network (Setup installs extra networking software). Also, the figure shown for the Custom option assumes that you're selecting all the Windows 98 components.

Table 2.3. Disk space used by each Setup option.

Install Option	Disk Space
Compact	177.4MB
Portable	192.9MB
Typical	202.2MB
Custom (All)	347.1MB

Table 2.4 details which Windows 98 components Setup installs for each option. Here are some notes about this table:

- There is no column for Custom because you use the Custom option to hand-pick the components you want.

- The Component column groups the Windows 98 components according to how they appear in the Select Components Setup Wizard dialog box (which you get to later in the installation process). For example, the Select Components dialog box has an Accessories component, which has several "subcomponents," such as Briefcase and Calculator.

Table 2.4. Windows 98 components associated with each Setup option.

Component	Typical	Portable	Compact
Accessibility:			
Accessibility Options	Yes	Yes	Yes
Accessibility Tools			

Component	Typical	Portable	Compact
Accessories:			
Briefcase			
Calculator	Yes		
Desktop Wallpaper			
Document Templates	Yes		
Games			
Imaging	Yes		
Mouse Pointers			
Paint	Yes		
Quick View			
Screen Savers:			
Additional Screen Savers			
Flying Windows	Yes		
OpenGL Screen Savers	Yes		
Windows Scripting Host	Yes	Yes	
WordPad	Yes	Yes	
Communications:			
Dial-Up Networking	Yes	Yes	Yes
Dial-Up Server			
Direct Cable Connection		Yes	
HyperTerminal		Yes	
Infrared			
Microsoft Chat 2.1			
Microsoft NetMeeting	Yes		
Phone Dialer	Yes	Yes	
Virtual Private Networking		Yes	
Desktop Themes			
Internet Tools:			
Microsoft FrontPage Express	Yes	Yes	
Microsoft VRML 2.0 Viewer			
Microsoft Wallet			

2

FROM DISC TO
DISK: INSTALLING
WINDOWS 98

continues

Table 2.4. continued

Component	Typical	Portable	Compact
Personal Web Server	Yes	Yes	
Real Audio Player 4.0			
Web Publishing Wizard			
Web-Based Enterprise Mgmt			
Microsoft Outlook Express	Yes	Yes	
Multilanguage Support			
Multimedia:			
Audio Compression[1]	Yes	Yes	Yes
CD Player[2]	Yes	Yes	Yes
DVD Player[3]			
Macromedia Shockwave Director	Yes		
Macromedia Shockwave Flash	Yes		
Media Player	Yes	Yes	
Microsoft NetShow Player 2.0			
Multimedia Sound Schemes			
Sample Sounds			
Sound Recorder[1]	Yes	Yes	
Video Compression	Yes	Yes	
Volume Control[1]	Yes	Yes	
Online Services	Yes	Yes	Yes
System Tools:			
Backup			
Character Map			
Clipboard Viewer[4]			
Disk compression tools[5]		Yes	
Drive Converter (FAT32)	Yes	Yes	
Group policies			
Net Watcher			
System Monitor			

Component	Typical	Portable	Compact

System Resource Meter

Web TV for Windows

[1]Setup installs these components automatically if you specified that you have a sound card in your system.

[2]Setup installs this component automatically if it detects a CD-ROM drive.

[3]Setup only displays this option if it detects a DVD decoder card that is supported by Windows 98.

[4]Setup installs this component automatically if you upgrade over Windows 3.x (not Windows for Workgroups).

[5]Setup installs this component automatically if it detects DoubleSpace or DriveSpace.

User Information

The User Information dialog box, shown in Figure 2.5, asks you for your name and, optionally, your company name. Fill in the appropriate values and click Next >.

FIGURE 2.5.
Use this dialog box to enter your name and, optionally, your company name.

Windows Components

If you chose the Typical, Portable, or Compact Setup option, you next see the Windows Components dialog box. This dialog box presents you with two options:

Install the most common components (recommended): If you activate this option, Setup installs the default components for the Setup option you selected earlier (as listed in Table 2.4).

Show me the list of components so I can choose: If you activate this option, Setup displays the Select Components dialog box (discussed in the next section) so that you can customize the component selection.

Make your choice and click Next >.

Select Components

The Select Components dialog box, shown in Figure 2.6, appears either if you chose the Custom Setup option or if you activated the Show me the list of components so I can choose option in the Windows Components dialog box.

FIGURE 2.6.

Use the Select Components dialog box to pick and choose the specific Windows 98 components you want to install.

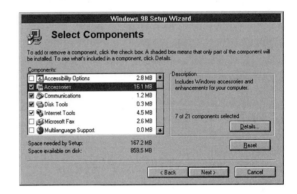

Here's how you use this dialog box to select components:

■ To install a component, activate its check box.

■ To bypass a component, deactivate its check box.

■ Some options (such as Accessories and Communications) consist of multiple components. To choose specific components for any of these options, highlight the option and click the Details button. In the dialog box that appears (Figure 2.7 shows the dialog box for the Accessories components), choose the components you want to install and click OK.

FIGURE 2.7.

For options with multiple components, clicking the Details button brings up a dialog box that lists the available components.

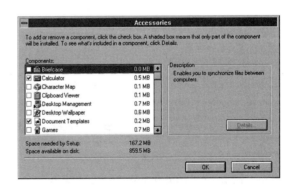

When you've completed your choices, click Next >.

NETWORK INSTALLATION INSTRUCTIONS

At this point in the installation, Setup might ask you to enter network information. I put off a discussion of network installation issues until later in this book. See Chapter 28, "Setting Up Windows 98 for Networking."

Identification

If you're upgrading from Windows for Workgroups, Setup asks you to supply three pieces of networking information:

Computer name: This is the name by which your computer will be identified on the network.

Workgroup: This is the name of the network workgroup or domain to which your computer belongs.

Computer Description: Use this text box to enter a brief description of your computer. This description will be visible to other network users.

Computer Settings

If you selected the Custom Setup option, Setup displays the Computer Settings dialog box. Use this dialog box to select the keyboard layout and the Windows 98 language support you want to use.

After reviewing the settings, you might find you need to make some changes. If so, here are the steps to follow:

1. Highlight the item you want to adjust.
2. Click the Change button. Setup displays a dialog box with a list of available choices.
3. Use the list to highlight the option you want.
4. Click OK to return to the Change Settings dialog box.
5. Repeat steps 1 through 4 to adjust other settings.
6. When you're done, click Next >.

Establishing Your Location

Windows 98's support for Active Channels includes a number of channel sets, each of which is designed with a specific country in mind. In the Establishing Your Location dialog box, Setup asks you to select the country you want to work with.

Startup Disk

The Setup Wizard now asks whether you want to create a startup disk, as described earlier. Whether or not you want to create a startup disk, click Next >. Setup gathers the files it needs and then prompts you to insert a disk in your floppy drive. You have two choices at this point:

- If you want a startup disk, insert the floppy and then click OK to begin the copying. When Setup has completed its startup disk labors, remove the disk and click OK to return to the wizard.
- If you don't want a startup disk, click Cancel. (If you already have a disk in the drive, click OK if Setup prompts you to remove the disk.

Start Copying Files

Setup is now ready to start installing the Windows 98 files on your computer. When you see the Start Copying Files dialog box, click Next > to crank up the copying process.

When Setup is done, one of two things will happen:

- If you started Setup from DOS, a dialog box will appear. Remove your boot floppy (if necessary) and then click OK.
- If you're upgrading from Windows 95, Setup will automatically reboot your machine. (A warning dialog box with a 15-second countdown will appear.)

Setup now reboots your computer and attempts to start Windows 98 for the first time.

Finishing the Installation

For the final phase of the installation, Setup configures your hardware and takes you through a few tasks designed to configure Windows 98 the way you want. The next few sections run through each of these tasks.

Hardware Detection

After rebooting, Setup runs through its hardware detection phase in which it attempts to locate and configure both Plug and Play and legacy devices. (Setup runs the full hardware detection routine only if you're not upgrading from Windows 95.)

As Setup comes across particular devices, a wizard may show up to help you configure the hardware. For example, if your computer has one or more PC Card (PCMCIA) slots, the PC Card Wizard will make an appearance, as shown in Figure 2.9. (I discuss this wizard in Chapter 11, "Device Advice: Dealing with Devices in Windows 98.")

FIGURE 2.9.

During the hardware detection phase, Setup may ask a wizard or two to help you configure devices.

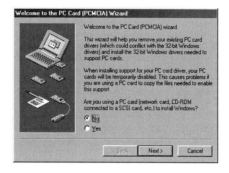

Depending on what happens during this phase, Setup may reboot your computer when the hardware detection is complete.

Setting the Time Zone

Setup next displays the Date/Time Properties dialog box, shown in Figure 2.10. You use this dialog box to specify your time zone. This is important for networked computers that need to keep file time stamps synchronized. Also, Windows 98 understands daylight savings time and adjusts for it automatically if you specify your correct time zone. This dialog box defaults to the Pacific time zone. If you live in a different time zone, you can either select it from the drop-down list or use the left- and right-arrow keys to select it visually on the map. Click Close when you're done.

FIGURE 2.10.

Use this dialog box to tell Windows 98 which time zone you live in.

Entering a Windows Password

When Setup finishes its configuration chores, it will likely reboot your computer once again. During this final Setup phase, you are asked to enter a username and password. You have several ways to proceed, depending on whether your computer is (or will be) connected to a network.

For a standalone machine (you see the Enter Windows Password dialog box), you can leave the user name and password fields blank and click OK. A password is optional on a standalone computer, so Windows 98 won't bother you with this dialog box again in future startups.

For a networked machine (you see the Enter Network Password dialog box), you can't bypass the password dialog box, but you do have two ways to handle it:

- Enter a user name and password. You are required to enter these values each time you log on to Windows.

- Enter a user name and leave the password field blank. This way, each time Windows prompts you for a password, you can just press Enter to dismiss the dialog box.

If you do enter a password, Setup asks you to confirm it by displaying the Set Windows Password dialog box. Reenter your password and click OK.

The Home Stretch

Setup is just about done at this point. It may perform one last hardware check and configure whatever new devices it finds. You eventually see the Welcome to Windows 98 dialog box, shown in Figure 2.11.

FIGURE 2.11.
The sign of a successful setup: the Welcome to Windows 98 dialog box.

Do You Need AUTOEXEC.BAT and CONFIG.SYS?

As I mentioned earlier in this chapter, Setup creates its own AUTOEXEC.BAT and CONFIG.SYS files, based on your existing files, and renames the existing files with .DOS extensions. The only reason you need these files in Windows 98 is to load real-mode drivers for devices such as sound cards and CD-ROM drives. However, Windows 98 comes with protected-mode drivers for just about any kind of hardware you can throw at it. This means you might not need your real-mode drivers, so you might not need AUTOEXEC.BAT and CONFIG.SYS.

To test whether you need them, rename your AUTOEXEC.BAT and CONFIG.SYS files (to, for example, AUTOEXEC.98 and CONFIG.98). Restart your system and see whether Windows 98 loads properly. If it does, you're in luck: You don't have to bother with AUTOEXEC.BAT and CONFIG.SYS at all! The advantages of this are quicker load times and increased conventional memory.

On the other hand, you might not be using your startup files to load any device drivers. Many people keep AUTOEXEC.BAT on hand only to set a few DOS environment variables (for, say, a Sound Blaster card). In this case, you can still eliminate your AUTOEXEC.BAT file by using a Windows 98 utility called WINSET. This utility works like the DOS SET command, except that it modifies environment variables for Windows 98's global DOS environment. (In contrast, if you run the SET command within a DOS session, the change applies only to that session.) By including the appropriate WINSET commands in a batch file and then including that batch file in your Windows 98 Startup folder, you eliminate the need for an AUTOEXEC.BAT file.

WINSET is available on the Windows 98 CD-ROM in the \tools\apptools\envvars folder. Copy the WINSET.EXE file to your main Windows 98 folder and then use the following syntax:

```
WINSET variable=string
```

variable   The name of the environment variable.

string   The value you want to assign to the variable.

For example, suppose you use the following command in AUTOEXEC.BAT to set the default parameters for the DIR command:

```
SET DIRCMD=/OGN /P
```

To do the same thing with WINSET, you'd use the following command:

```
WINSET DIRCMD=/OGN /P
```

Adding and Removing Windows 98 Components

The Windows 98 components you installed during Setup are by no means set in stone. You're free at any time to add new components and to remove components you don't need. The good news is that, thanks to its Add/Remove Programs feature, Windows 98 makes it a breeze to install and uninstall chunks of the system. (If you want to delete Windows entirely, head for the section titled "Uninstalling Windows 98," later in this chapter.)

For starters, you need to get to the Windows Setup tab of the Add/Remove Programs Properties dialog box:

1. Select Start | Settings | Control Panel.

2. In the Control Panel window, open the Add/Remove Programs icon to display the Add/Remove Programs Properties dialog box.

3. Select the Windows Setup tab, shown in Figure 2.12.

FIGURE 2.12.

Use the Windows Setup tab to add or remove pieces of Windows 98.

As you can see, this dialog box is reminiscent of the Setup Wizard's Select Components dialog box. In this case, though, you interpret the component check boxes as explained here:

- If a component's check box is activated, the component is already installed.

- If a component's check box is deactivated, the component isn't currently installed.

- If a component's check box has a gray background, the item contains multiple components, and only some of them are installed. (To find out how many of the item's components are installed, highlight the item and look inside the Description box. You see something like `3 of 4 components selected`.)

Adding Windows 98 Components

Adding components is a simple matter of activating the appropriate check boxes. If an item contains multiple components, highlight it and click the Details button to see the list of components. Activate the check boxes for the components you want to install and then click OK to get back to the Windows Setup tab.

When you're done, click OK. Windows Setup will likely ask you to insert your Windows 98 CD-ROM. Insert the disk and click OK to continue. Depending on the components you're adding, Windows 98 might ask you to restart your computer. If it does, click Yes to let Windows 98 handle this job for you. When the restart is complete, the new programs are ready for action.

Adding Components from the Windows 98 CD-ROM

The Windows 98 CD-ROM contains not only the basic Windows 98 files, but also a truckload of other programs and files, including extra device drivers, handy utilities, multimedia files, and more. I'll be talking about many of these files as you trudge through this book, but here's the general procedure for installing files from the CD-ROM:

1. In the Windows Setup tab, click the Have Disk button. The Install From Disk dialog box appears.

2. Use the Copy manufacturer's files from box to enter the drive letter containing the Windows 98 CD-ROM and the full path of the folder containing the files you want to install. If you're not sure of the path, click the Browse button, use the Open dialog box to highlight the drive and path, and click OK to return to the Install From Disk dialog box.

3. Click OK. Windows 98 displays the Have Disk dialog box with a list of components to install.

4. Activate the check boxes for the components you want to install.

5. Click Install. Windows 98 installs the components and returns you to the Windows Setup tab. (In some cases, Windows 98 might need to restart your computer.)

Extracting Files from the Windows 98 Cabinet Archives

Rather than installing CD-ROM components and programs, you may need to extract a file or two from one of the Windows 98 cabinet (CAB) files. (Cabinet files are special compressed archives that contain most of the Windows 98 system files.) To do this, you must first discover which cabinet contains the file you need, and then extract the file from that cabinet. Here are the steps to follow:

1. Insert the Windows 98 CD-ROM and then use Windows Explorer to select the Win98 folder.

2. Select Explorer's Tools | Find | Files or Folders command.

3. In the Named text box, enter `*.cab`.

4. In the Containing text box, type the name of the file you want to extract.

5. Click Find Now.

6. If Find locates the cabinet that contains your file, double-click the cabinet to open it. (The capability of viewing the contents of a cabinet archive is a new feature in Windows 98.)

   New to
   98

7. Either highlight the file and select File | Extract, or right-click the file and click Extract.

8. Use the Browse for Folder dialog box to select the folder for the extracted file, and then click OK.

Using the Web to Update Your Windows 98 Configuration

Windows 95 proved that Microsoft was no longer content to rest on its laurels between operating system releases. In addition to a retail add-on (Microsoft Plus!), a service pack, and two

OEM service releases, Microsoft also made available on its Web site numerous driver upgrades, bug fixes, and utilities. This was a real boon to administrators and power users who wanted the latest technology because it usually meant a faster and more stable system.

The problem, however, was that these upgrades were often difficult to implement. Because most of the enhancements went through only limited beta testing, Microsoft was leery of making them available to the general public. As a result, even if you somehow found out about an upgraded component, you still had to track it down and install it yourself.

New to **98**
There is little doubt that Windows 98 will continue this idea of the operating system as a work in progress. However, the Microsoft engineers have come up with a way to make the upgrade process as automatic as possible. A new feature called Windows Update uses a World Wide Web site as the starting point for all upgrades. From this site, an installed ActiveX control examines your system and displays a list of the drivers, components, and programs for which newer versions are available. You can then select the items you need, and a couple of mouse clicks later the upgrades are downloaded and installed.

Assuming you have an Internet connection set up (if not, see Chapter 32, "Windows 98 and the Internet"), you can get to the Windows Update site by selecting the Start | Windows Update command. You can also dial the following Web address into your browser:

```
http://www.microsoft.com/windowsupdate/
```

Either way, you end up at the Web page shown in Figure 2.13. (Note that like many Web sites, the Windows Update site changes frequently, so what you see when you get there may not look like the page shown in Figure 2.13.)

FIGURE 2.13.

The Windows Update home page.

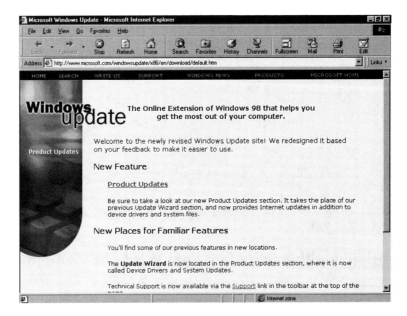

From here, click the Product Updates link. Here are some notes:

■ You need to be a registered Windows user to access this site, so you may have to run through the Registration Wizard before going any further.

■ The Windows Update site requires that several ActiveX controls be installed on your computer. This means you may also see a few dialog boxes that ask you whether you want these controls installed. For best results, make sure you install each control when prompted.

When all that's done, the Update Wizard proceeds to examine your system (which may take several minutes). When the system scan is complete, Windows Update displays a list of Internet Explorer components and tells you the status of each component: Already Installed, Upgrade Available, or Not Installed. Activate the check boxes for the components you want to add, and then click Download.

Note that there is also a Device Drivers and System Files section that contains a link to the Update Wizard page. Click that link and, on the page that appears, click Update. The Update Wizard checks your device drivers and system files and then displays a page similar to the one shown in Figure 2.14. The Available Updates box lists the drivers and components that you can install. Click an update to display a description in the Description box.

FIGURE 2.14.
When the scan of your system is done, this page shows you a list of the available updates.

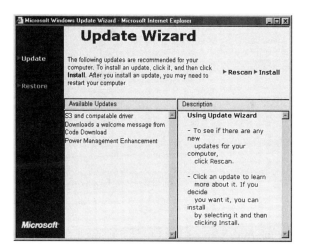

To install an update, click it and then click Install. Windows Update downloads the component and then installs it automatically. Note that in some cases you may have to restart your computer after the upgrade is complete.

Removing Windows 98 Components

If you've installed a Windows 98 component that you know you won't need in the future, you should delete it. This frees up disk space and reduces the clutter in the Start menu's folders.

In the Windows Setup tab, deactivate the check boxes for the components you want to expunge. Again, if an item has multiple components, highlight it, click Details, deactivate the appropriate check boxes, and click OK.

When you've finished deactivating check boxes, click OK. Windows 98 removes the components and might ask you to restart your computer.

Removing Your Old Windows Files

When you're sure you want to stick with Windows 98 for the duration, you'll likely want to get rid of your old Windows 3.*x* or Windows 95 files (assuming you saved them during the Windows 98 install). Windows 98 can handle this for you automatically. Just follow these steps:

1. Select Start | Settings | Control Panel.

2. In the Control Panel window, open the Add/Remove Programs icon to display the Add/Remove Programs Properties dialog box.

3. In the list box in the Install/Uninstall tab, highlight the appropriate option (such as Remove Windows 95 system files [Uninstall info]). See Figure 2.15.

FIGURE 2.15.

Use the Install/
Uninstall tab to remove
your old Windows 95
files.

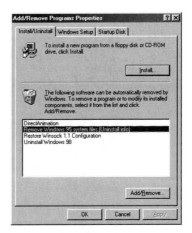

4. Click the Add/Remove button. If you saved your old system files during Setup, Windows 98 uses the dialog box shown in Figure 2.16 to warn you that this uninstall information will be deleted.

FIGURE 2.16.

Windows 98 warns you
that your uninstall
information will be
deleted.

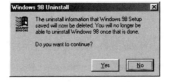

5. Click Yes. Windows 98 deletes the Windows 95 uninstall files and tells you that you can no longer uninstall Windows 98.

6. Click OK.

Uninstalling Windows 98

If for some reason you and Windows 98 just aren't getting along, you can always get a divorce. In other words, you can always uninstall Windows 98 and put that part of your life behind you. Uninstalling Windows 98 can be easy or hard, depending on how you installed it in the first place:

The easy method: If you upgraded over Windows 95, told Setup to save backup copies of your system files, and haven't compressed your hard drive with DriveSpace, you can use Windows 98's Uninstall feature to remove Windows 98.

The hard method: If you installed Windows 98 in a separate directory, or if you've already deleted your old Windows 95 files, you need to uninstall Windows 98 by hand.

Using the Windows 98 Uninstall Feature

If Setup saved your Windows 3.*x* or Windows 95 system files during an upgrade (and if you haven't deleted your old Windows 3.*x* files), kicking Windows 98 off your system is easy. In this case, Windows 98 has all the information it needs to remove itself, and the job is all automated by the new Uninstall feature. Table 2.5 lists the various files that Uninstall uses.

Table 2.5. Files used by the Windows 98 Uninstall feature.

Filename	Purpose
SETUPLOG.TXT	Contains an entry pointing to the location of the WINUNDO.DAT and WINUNDO.INI files.
SUHDLOG.DAT	Contains a copy of all master boot records and partition boot records on the system both before and after the upgrade to Windows 98. Is used to restore the original boot sectors.
WINUNDO.DAT	Contains a compressed backup of the Windows 95 system files.
WINUNDO.INI	Contains a listing of files backed up in the WINUNDO.DAT file, as well as the new Windows 98 files installed by Setup.

Uninstall also restores the saved system files (IO.DOS, MSDOS.DOS, COMMAND.DOS, CONFIG.DOS, and AUTOEXEC.DOS) to their original names (IO.SYS, MSDOS.SYS, COMMAND.COM, CONFIG.SYS, and AUTOEXEC.BAT).

Here are the steps to follow to uninstall Windows 98:

1. Select Start | Settings | Control Panel.

2. In the Control Panel window, open the Add/Remove Programs icon to display the Add/Remove Programs Properties dialog box.

3. In the list box, highlight Uninstall Windows 98.

4. Click the Add/Remove button. Windows 98 displays a dialog box with several warnings, as shown in Figure 2.17.

FIGURE 2.17.

Windows 98 displays this dialog box when you begin the uninstall procedure.

5. Click Yes. Windows 98 displays another dialog box to tell you that Uninstall is about to check for disk errors and remove all the long filename information created by Windows 98.

6. Click Yes. Uninstall runs ScanDisk to check your hard disk for problems. When ScanDisk is done, another dialog box appears to tell you that Uninstall is ready to do its thing.

7. Click Yes. Uninstall shuts down your computer, removes the Windows 98 files, and restores your previous configuration (this process takes several minutes).

8. When Uninstall is finished, remove any floppy disks you might have in your computer and then press Enter to restart your machine and load Windows 95.

ALTERNATIVE UNINSTALL STARTUPS

If you can't load Windows 98 (which would be a good reason for uninstalling it!), you can still run the Uninstall program. You have two choices:

- If you have a Windows 98 startup disk, reboot your system with the disk in drive A, and when you get to the A:\ prompt, type uninstall, press Enter, and follow the onscreen instructions.

- If you have a disk that boots to your previous operating system, reboot your system with the disk in drive A, and when you get to the A:\ prompt, type c:\windows\command\uninstall (assuming that you installed Windows 98 in the C:\WINDOWS directory), press Enter, and follow the onscreen instructions.

Uninstalling Windows 98 by Hand

If you installed Windows 98 alongside Windows 3.*x* in a separate directory, or if you've already removed your old Windows 95 files, it takes quite a bit more work to uninstall Windows 98. Note that you must have a bootable disk that boots your system to the previous version of Windows or DOS, and that this disk must have the SYS.COM utility on it.

If you're uninstalling to Windows 3.*x*, you need to make a slight adjustment to the ScanDisk initialization file. Using Notepad or some other text editor, open SCANDISK.INI (look in Windows 98's COMMAND subfolder) and find the [ENVIRONMENT] section. You need to make two adjustments:

> LabelCheck=On: This tells ScanDisk to check disk volume labels for invalid characters.
>
> SpaceCheck=On: This tells ScanDisk to check for invalid spaces in filenames.

When you're done, save the file and exit the text editor. Now follow these steps:

1. Restart your system, and when you hear the beep that signifies the Power-On Self Test is complete, press F8 to display the Windows 98 Startup menu. Then select the Command prompt only option. When you get to DOS, make sure that you're in the root directory (if you're not sure, type cd\ and press Enter).

2. Use the following two commands to copy the files DELTREE.EXE, SCANDISK.EXE, and SCANDISK.INI from \WINDOWS\COMMAND to the root directory (if you installed Windows 98 in a directory other than C:\WINDOWS, substitute the appropriate directory in the following commands):

```
copy c:\windows\command\deltree.exe
copy c:\windows\command\scandisk.*
```

3. If you're uninstalling to Windows 3.*x*, Run ScanDisk to remove all volume labels and filenames that your previous version of DOS will consider invalid. Type scandisk *drive*: (where *drive* is the drive on which Windows is installed) and press Enter. If you have other drives, run ScanDisk on them as well.

4. Use the DELTREE utility to delete all the Windows 98 files on your system. Here are the commands to run (note that the /y switch suppresses the DELTREE confirmation prompt; if you want to be prompted, remove /y from each command; also, in the first command, replace windows with the name of your main Windows 98 directory, if it's different):

```
deltree /y windows
deltree /y recycled
deltree /y winboot.*
deltree /y io.sys
deltree /y msdos.sys
deltree /y commmand.com
deltree /y config.sys
deltree /y autoexec.bat
deltree /y detlog.txt
deltree /y netlog.txt
```

```
deltree /y setuplog.txt
deltree /y suhdlog.dat
deltree /y system.1st
deltree /y d??space.bin
```

5. Rename CONFIG.DOS to CONFIG.SYS and AUTOEXEC.DOS to AUTOEXEC.BAT using the following commands:

```
ren config.dos config.sys
ren autoexec.dos autoexec.bat
```

6. Insert the bootable disk containing your previous version of DOS in drive A and restart your computer.

7. Type sys c: (assuming that drive C is your boot drive; if drive C is compressed, substitute the letter of the host drive—such as H—for drive C) and press Enter. This command transfers the system files for the previous DOS version and overwrites the Windows 98 master boot record.

8. Remove the disk and restart your computer to boot to the previous version of Windows or DOS. Note that if you didn't save the old Windows 95 system files, you have to reinstall Windows 95.

Summary

This chapter showed you how to use Setup to install Windows 98 on your system. You also learned how to add and remove Windows 98 components, as well as how to uninstall Windows 98.

Here's a list of chapters where you will find related information:

- I gave you some preparatory background for the Setup process in Chapter 1, "Preparing for the Windows 98 Installation."

- For more information about the Windows 98 Startup menu and MSDOS.SYS, check out Chapter 3, "Start Me Up: Controlling Windows 98 Startup."

- To get your feet wet with the new Windows 98 interface and tools, read Chapter 4, "What's New and Noteworthy in Windows 98."

- Plug and Play and other hardware-related issues are covered in Chapter 10, "Getting the Most Out of Device Manager and Hardware Profiles."

- I give extended coverage of ScanDisk in Chapter 17, "Wielding the Windows 98 System Tools."

- Printer installation is covered in Chapter 21, "Prescriptions for Perfect Printing."

- For network installations, try Chapter 28, "Setting Up Windows 98 for Networking."

Start Me Up: Controlling Windows 98 Startup

IN THIS CHAPTER

CHAPTER 3

The White Rabbit put on his spectacles. "Where shall I begin, your Majesty?" he asked.

"Begin at the beginning," the King said, very gravely, "and go on till you come to the end: then stop."

—*Lewis Carroll,* Alice's Adventures in Wonderland

Assuming Windows 98 is now safely installed, you can begin your journey, appropriately enough, at the beginning: the startup process. At first blush, this might seem like a surprising topic for an entire chapter. After all, the Windows 98 startup procedure gives new meaning to the term no-brainer: You turn on your system, and a few seconds later, Windows 98 reports for duty. What's to write about?

You'd be surprised. The progress of a typical boot appears uneventful only because Windows 98 uses a whole host of default options for startup. By changing these defaults, you can take control of the startup process and make Windows 98 start your way. This chapter takes you through the entire startup process, from go to whoa, and shows you the options you can use to customize it.

The Boot Process, from Powerup to Startup

To better help you understand your Windows 98 startup options, let's take a closer look at what happens each time you fire up your machine. Although a computer performs dozens of actions during the boot process, most of them appeal only to wireheads and other hardware hackers. (A *wirehead* is, broadly speaking, an expert in the hardware aspects of PCs.) For our purposes, we can reduce the entire journey to the following 12-step program:

1. When you flip the switch on your computer (or press the Restart button, if the machine is already running), the system performs various hardware checks. The system's microprocessor executes the ROM BIOS code, which, among other things, performs the Power-On Self Test (POST). The POST detects and tests memory, ports, and basic devices, such as the video adapter, keyboard, and disk drives. (You hear your floppy disk motors kick in briefly and the drive lights come on.) If the system has a Plug and Play BIOS, the BIOS also enumerates and tests the PnP-compliant devices in the system. If the POST goes well, you hear a single beep.

2. Now the BIOS code looks for a boot sector on drive A (the drive light illuminates once more). If no disk is in the drive, the BIOS turns its attention to the hard disk and looks for the active (that is, bootable) partition and its boot sector.

THE STARTUP DISK SECRET

This explains why the Windows 98 Emergency Startup Disk lets you regain control of your system in the event of a hard-drive crash. The BIOS first looks for a bootable disk in drive A. If it finds one, it bypasses the hard drive altogether. This is also why your startup disk must be readable by drive A: The BIOS normally doesn't attempt to boot from drive B (although some systems have CMOS settings that let you reverse drives A and B).

3. With the boot sector located, the BIOS program runs the boot sector as a program. The Windows 98 boot sector runs IO.SYS, which is basically just DOS. IO.SYS (which combines the functionality of both IO.SYS and MSDOS.SYS from previous DOS versions) initializes some device drivers and performs a few real-mode chores.

4. IO.SYS reads MSDOS.SYS. Note that MSDOS.SYS does not have the same functionality as MSDOS.SYS in previous DOS versions. The Windows 98 MSDOS.SYS is a text file that controls various startup options. (See "Custom Startups with MSDOS.SYS," later in this chapter.)

5. IO.SYS reads CONFIG.SYS, if it exists, and processes its statements (real-mode device drivers and so forth).

6. IO.SYS reads AUTOEXEC.BAT, if it exists, and processes its commands.

7. IO.SYS reads the Registry and loads a number of drivers and settings. Here's a partial list:

DBLSPACE.BIN or DRVSPACE.BIN: The disk compression driver.

HIMEM.SYS: The real-mode extended memory manager. Note that IO.SYS doesn't load this driver if a HIMEM.SYS line already exists in CONFIG.SYS.

IFSHLP.SYS: The Installable File System Helper, which helps load VFAT and other Windows 98 installable file systems.

SETVER.EXE: A program that handles operating system version number requests from legacy applications. If an application requires a particular version of DOS, SETVER can "lie" to the application and thus fool the program into running properly.

DOS=HIGH: Loads DOS into the high memory area (HMA). If you load EMM386.EXE in CONFIG.SYS, IO.SYS also includes the UMB parameter, which enables memory management using upper memory blocks. Note, however, that IO.SYS doesn't load EMM386; if you need to use it, include the appropriate DEVICE line in CONFIG.SYS.

FILES=30: Determines the number of file handles to create. Windows 98 doesn't use this setting, and it's included only for backward compatibility with legacy programs. If you have DOS programs that require a higher value, include a FILES setting in CONFIG.SYS.

LASTDRIVE=Z: Determines the last drive letter that can be assigned to a disk drive. This is another setting that's needed only for backward compatibility; Windows 98 doesn't use this setting.

BUFFERS=30: Determines the number of file buffers to create for applications using file I/O calls to IO.SYS; it's not required by Windows 98. To specify a different value, include a BUFFERS line in CONFIG.SYS.

STACKS=9,256: Determines the number of stack frames and the size of each frame. For backward compatibility only. To specify different values, add a STACKS line to CONFIG.SYS.

SHELL=COMMAND.COM /P: Determines the name of the command-line interpreter.

FCBS=4: Determines the number of file control blocks that can be open at any one time. For backward compatibility only.

DON'T USE VALUES LOWER THAN THE DEFAULTS

If you plan to add (or modify) FILES, BUFFERS, or STACKS in CONFIG.SYS, make sure that the values you use are greater than or equal to those used in IO.SYS.

8. IO.SYS switches the processor into protected mode and then calls on VMM32.VXD to load the Windows 98 protected-mode drivers.

9. Plug and Play information—new devices detected during the initial boot phase, removed devices, hardware conflicts, and so on—is processed. Windows 98 might ask you to insert a source disk to load new drivers.

10. Windows 98 is started, and the Windows 98 GUI and other core subsystems are loaded.

11. Windows 98 prompts you for a password if you're logging onto a network or if you specified a password for the Windows logon.

12. The contents of the Startup folder are processed.

The three most obvious ways to customize this startup procedure are to insert a bootable disk (such as the Windows 98 Emergency Startup Disk) before the POST is done, modify CONFIG.SYS, and modify AUTOEXEC.BAT. However, Windows 98 also provides some less obvious routes for personalizing your startup:

■ Invoke the Windows 98 Startup menu after the POST is complete.

■ Edit the MSDOS.SYS file to change the default startup options.

■ Use one of the first two methods to boot to the DOS prompt, and then run Windows from there with command-line switches.

■ Add programs or documents to the Windows 98 Startup folder.

The next three sections cover the first three of these techniques. To learn how to add applications and documents to the Startup folder, see Chapter 14, "File and Folder Tricks and Techniques."

Custom Startups with the Windows 98 Startup Menu

In the 3.*x* versions of Windows, you had to run the win command (the WIN.COM file) to start Windows. This was handy because if you were having trouble with Windows (a garbled display, for example), you could always boot to the DOS prompt, fix the problem (by editing an INI file, for example), and then restart. Even if you had the win command in AUTOEXEC.BAT, you could always bypass it by commenting it out.

Although Windows 98 still has WIN.COM, you never really use it because, as you've seen, Windows 98 loads automatically. So what do you do if you need to bypass Windows 98? You could put a bootable disk in drive A, but that's not always convenient. Instead, Windows 98 comes with a Startup menu that gives you various options for loading Windows 98, booting to the DOS prompt, or even loading your old DOS version.

Unfortunately, it's a bit harder to get the Windows 98 startup menu than it was to get to the Windows 95 menu. In Windows 95, you used to look for the Starting Windows 95... message immediately after the completion of the POST. You then had two seconds to press F8. Although Windows 98 displays the Starting Windows 98... message, the system designers decided to shorten startup times by eliminating the two-second buffer. This makes it much more difficult to get to the startup menu, but not impossible. To get to the Windows 98 startup menu, you have two choices:

New to **98**

- ■ Press and hold down the Ctrl key sometime before the end of the POST. Because Ctrl doesn't add anything to the keyboard buffer, you can keep the key pressed until the startup menu appears. This works on most systems, although it may cause a SCSI card to interrupt its initialization chores, so you need to be careful.

- ■ Press F8 immediately after you hear the beep that signals the end of the POST. This method does not work on all systems, so I don't recommend using it.

Here's an example of the Startup menu:

```
Microsoft Windows 98 Startup Menu
=====================================

   1. Normal
   2. Logged (\BOOTLOG.TXT)
   3. Safe mode
   4. Step-by-step confirmation
   5. Command prompt only
   6. Safe mode command prompt only
   7. Previous version of MS-DOS

Enter a choice: 1        Time remaining: 30
```

The layout of the Startup menu depends on your Windows 98 configuration, as explained here:

■ You see only the Safe mode with network support option if you installed network support with Windows 98.

■ You see only the Safe mode without compression option if you have a drive that has been compressed.

■ You see only the Previous version of MS-DOS option if you installed Windows 98 on a machine that had an existing version of DOS.

The Normal option loads Windows 98 in the usual fashion. You can use the other options to control the rest of the startup procedure.

Logged (\BOOTLOG.TXT)

This option is the same as the Normal option, except that Windows 98 logs the boot process in a text file named BOOTLOG.TXT, which you find in the boot drive's root folder. BOOTLOG.TXT is useful as a troubleshooting tool, especially if Windows 98 is hanging during startup. (See "Troubleshooting Windows 98 Startup" later in this chapter.)

Safe Mode

If you're having trouble with Windows 98—for example, if a corrupt or incorrect video driver is mangling your display, or if Windows 98 won't start—you can use the Safe mode option to run a stripped-down version of Windows 98. Note that if Windows 98 failed to start properly, rebooting will display the Windows 98 Startup menu automatically, with the Safe mode option highlighted. You also see the following message:

```
Warning: Windows did not finish loading on the previous attempt.
Choose Safe mode, to start Windows with a minimal set of drivers.
```

Here's what happens when Windows 98 boots in Safe mode:

1. Windows 98 bypasses CONFIG.SYS, AUTOEXEC.BAT, and the Registry.

2. HIMEM.SYS is loaded. Note that Safe mode does not process any command-line switches for HIMEM.SYS. If your system requires switches (such as /M, the machine switch), you won't be able to run Safe mode. For an alternative, see "Troubleshooting Windows 98 Startup," later in this chapter.

3. IFSHLP.SYS, a real-mode file that helps install the Windows 98 Installable File System (IFS), is loaded. The IFS adds support for VFAT, CDFS (CD-ROM file system), and other Windows 98 file systems.

4. The MSDOS.SYS file is checked for the location of the Windows 98 files. (I'll talk more about MSDOS.SYS later.)

5. If the Windows 98 files are found, the command win /d:m (which enables a Safe-mode boot) is executed, and COMMAND.COM is skipped. If the Windows 98 files aren't found, COMMAND.COM is executed instead. (For more info on command-line switches for starting Windows 98, see "Command-Line Switches for Starting Windows 98," later in this chapter.)

6. Windows 98 loads only the virtual device drivers (VxDs) for the keyboard, mouse, and standard VGA display.

7. Windows 98 processes SYSTEM.INI and WIN.INI as detailed here:

   ■ The [Boot] and [386Enh] sections of the SYSTEM.INI file are bypassed.

   ■ However, Windows 98 does run the shell= and drivers= lines from SYSTEM.INI's [Boot] section.

   ■ The Load= and Run= lines in the [Windows] section of WIN.INI are bypassed.

8. Windows 98 resizes the desktop to a resolution of 640×480 using the Standard VGA display driver.

9. The dialog box shown in Figure 3.1 appears to remind you that Windows 98 is running in Safe mode. Click OK to finish loading Windows 98.

FIGURE 3.1.

This dialog box appears each time you start Windows 98 in Safe mode.

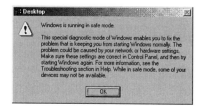

When Windows 98 finally loads, the desktop reminds you that you're in Safe mode by displaying Safe mode in each corner.

Step-by-Step Confirmation

This option enables you to step through each command in IO.SYS, CONFIG.SYS, and AUTOEXEC.BAT and confirm whether you want Windows 98 to run the command. This technique is invaluable for isolating problems. By stepping though the commands, you can watch your screen for error messages and try to narrow the problem to a specific command or driver. (For more details, see the section "A Step-by-Step Strategy," later in this chapter.)

When you select this option, Windows 98 prompts you like this:

```
Process the system registry [Enter=Y,Esc=N]?
```

To load the driver or run the command, press Enter or Y; to bypass the command or driver, press Esc or N.

Command Prompt Only

This option boots you to DOS; it doesn't load the Windows 98 GUI, and it doesn't process Windows 98's protected-mode drivers. This option does, however, process CONFIG.SYS and AUTOEXEC.BAT, if you have them.

This option boots quickly to the DOS prompt, so it's useful for running DOS programs or performing quick file maintenance chores. When you're at the prompt, you can start Windows 98 by typing WIN and pressing Enter. You'll want to use this option each time you need to start Windows 98 with command-line switches.

Safe Mode Command Prompt Only

This option runs Safe mode, but it boots you to DOS without loading the Windows 98 GUI or any protected-mode drivers. CONFIG.SYS and AUTOEXEC.BAT are also bypassed.

Previous Version of MS-DOS

If your system had an existing version of DOS when you installed Windows 98, Setup renames your old startup files and saves them in the root directory as IO.DOS, MSDOS.DOS, COMMAND.DOS, CONFIG.DOS, and AUTOEXEC.DOS. When you select the Previous version of MS-DOS option, Windows 98 takes the following actions:

- Renames IO.SYS to JO.SYS, MSDOS.SYS to MSDOS.W40, COMMAND.COM to COMMAND.W40, CONFIG.SYS to CONFIG.W40, and AUTOEXEC.BAT to AUTOEXEC.W40
- Renames IO.DOS to IO.SYS, MSDOS.DOS to MSDOS.SYS, COMMAND.DOS to COMMAND.COM, CONFIG.DOS to CONFIG.SYS, and AUTOEXEC.DOS to AUTOEXEC.BAT

Windows 98 then boots your system, and your previous version of DOS loads.

Shortcut Keys for Startup Menu Options

To save a bit of time, Windows 98 recognizes several shortcut keys for some of the Startup menu options. These are called BootKeys. I've spelled out the available keys and key combinations in Table 3.1. As before, you must press the key or key combination immediately after the POST ends.

Table 3.1. BootKeys for Windows 98 Startup options.

BootKey	Startup Menu Equivalent
F4	Previous version of MS-DOS
F5	Safe mode
Shift-F5	Safe mode command prompt only
Shift-F8	Step-by-step confirmation

Custom Startups with MSDOS.SYS

In days of yore, before "Windows" and "hype" were synonyms, DOS used two system files to pull itself up by its own bootstraps. Those system files were IO.SYS, which provided the system initialization code, and MSDOS.SYS, which was called by IO.SYS and which served to load the basic system drivers, determine equipment status, and perform a few other first-thing-in-the-morning routines.

In the Windows 98 scheme of things, however, these MSDOS.SYS functions have been rolled into IO.SYS, and the new MSDOS.SYS is a text file that controls certain Windows 98 startup parameters. This section shows you how to edit MSDOS.SYS and explains all the options you can use to customize your startup.

Opening MSDOS.SYS

MSDOS.SYS is a read-only, hidden system file that resides in the root folder of your boot drive (usually drive C). To view and edit this file, you need to make a few adjustments, as described in the following steps:

1. In Explorer, select View | Options to display the Options dialog box.
2. Activate the Show all files option and click OK.
3. In the Folders pane, highlight the root folder of your boot drive.
4. Find Msdos.sys in the contents pane, right-click it, and select Properties from the context menu. The Msdos.sys Properties dialog box, shown in Figure 3.2, appears.
5. Deactivate the Read-only check box and click OK.

FIGURE 3.2.

Use this dialog box to adjust the read-only attribute of MSDOS.SYS.

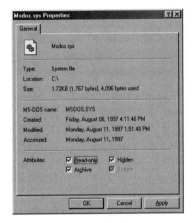

EDITING MSDOS.SYS FROM THE COMMAND LINE

If you need to edit MSDOS.SYS from the command line (by using EDIT.COM), enter the following command to change the file's attributes:

```
attrib -r -h -s c:\msdos.sys
```

(Note that this command assumes drive C is your boot drive. If that isn't the case, you need to edit the command accordingly.) After you've finished editing the file, run the following command to reset the attributes:

```
attrib +r +h +s c:\msdos.sys
```

You can now use Notepad or some other text editor to open the file. When you do, you see a file similar to the one shown in Figure 3.3. Note that MSDOS.SYS is divided into two sections—[Paths] and [Options]—which I'll discuss next. When you've finished editing the file, save it and then return to Explorer to reset the file's read-only attribute.

WHAT'S WITH ALL THE X'S?

MSDOS.SYS, you no doubt have noticed, contains 19 lines that consist mostly of the letter x. The note above these lines says that they "are required for compatibility with other programs." What does this mean? It seems that some older programs—especially virus protection utilities—expect MSDOS.SYS to be larger than 1,024 bytes. If a virus checker sees that MSDOS.SYS is less than 1024 bytes, it might assume that your system has been infected with a virus. These extra lines push the MSDOS.SYS file size beyond 1024 bytes.

FIGURE 3.3.

A typical MSDOS.SYS *file.*

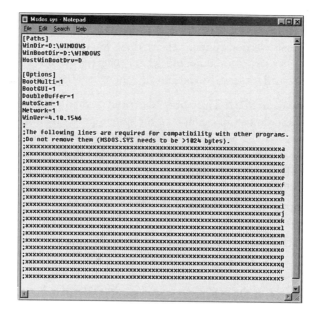

MSDOS.SYS **MIGHT BE TOO SMALL**

The Windows 98 Startup disk has a SYS utility that transfers the system files (including MSDOS.SYS) to your boot drive. Note, however, that the MSDOS.SYS file that gets transferred is less than 1024 bytes. To be safe, you should add the dummy lines shown in Figure 3.3 to make sure that MSDOS.SYS meets the minimum size requirements.

The [Paths] Section

The first section in MSDOS.SYS is called [Paths]. It includes information that enables IO.SYS to locate the Windows 98 files, including the Registry. This section includes three settings:

WinDir: This is the path you specified for the Windows installation during Setup. This is your main Windows 98 folder.

WinBootDir: This path specifies the location of the files needed to boot Windows 98. By default, WinBootDir is the same as WinDir.

HostWinBootDrv: This is the drive letter from which Windows boots.

The [Options] Section

The [Options] section contains the settings you can use to customize various aspects of the Windows 98 startup. Although the default [Options] section contains only four or five entries, there are actually at least 16 you can add and edit. Here's the rundown:

AutoScan=0|1|2: This option determines whether Windows 98 runs ScanDisk after a bad shutdown (for example, if the system power is switched off before you exit Windows 98). When AutoScan is set to 1 (the default), Windows 98 warns you that your system was shut down improperly and then runs the real-mode version of ScanDisk. If you set AutoScan to 2, Windows 98 bypasses the prompt and runs ScanDisk automatically. If AutoScan is 0, Windows 98 doesn't run ScanDisk. (See Chapter 17, "Wielding the Windows 98 System Tools," for a more detailed explanation of this feature.)

BootFailSafe=0|1: Determines whether Windows 98 boots in Safe mode automatically. If BootFailSafe is 0 (the default), Windows 98 boots in Safe mode only if you select one of the Startup menu's Safe mode options or if the system failed to start properly on the preceding boot. If BootFailSafe is 1, your computer boots in Safe mode automatically.

BootGUI=1|0: Determines whether IO.SYS loads the Windows 98 GUI. If BootGUI is 1 (the default), the GUI is loaded; if BootGUI is 0, your system boots to the command line (this is the same as selecting Command prompt only from the Windows 98 Startup menu).

BootKeys=1|0: Determines whether the BootKeys are enabled. If BootKeys is 1 (the default), you can use the BootKeys to invoke, or choose an item from, the Windows 98 Startup menu; if BootKeys is 0, the BootKeys are disabled.

BootMenu=0|1: Determines whether the Windows 98 Startup menu appears automatically. If BootMenu is 0 (the default), you have to press F8 before the Starting Windows 98... message disappears to get the Startup menu; if BootMenu is 1, the Startup menu appears without user intervention. Note that when this setting is 1, the Startup menu runs a countdown, after which it selects the default option automatically. (See BootMenuDefault to set the default option; see BootMenuDelay to set the length of the countdown.)

BootMenuDefault=*value*: Determines which of the Startup menu options is highlighted automatically when you invoke the menu. Here, *value* is the number of the option you want to highlight. The default value is 1 (the Normal option) if the system started normally on the previous boot; the default value is 4 (Safe mode) if the system encountered problems on the previous boot.

BootMenuDelay=*seconds*: Determines the length of the countdown that appears with the Startup menu if `BootMenu` is 1.

BootMulti=1|0: Determines whether the system supports a dual-boot with your previous version of DOS. If `BootMulti` is 1, the Previous version of MS-DOS command appears on the Startup menu; if `BootMulti` is 0, this command doesn't appear.

BootWarn=1|0: Determines whether `IO.SYS` runs Safe mode automatically if it encountered problems on the previous boot. If `BootWarn` is 1 (the default) and the previous boot was incomplete, `IO.SYS` invokes the Startup menu, sets the Safe mode option as the default, and displays a warning message; if `BootWarn` is 0 and the previous boot was incomplete, `IO.SYS` loads Windows 98 normally.

BootWin=1|0: Determines whether `IO.SYS` runs Windows 98 or your previous version of DOS. If `BootWin` is 1 (the default), `IO.SYS` loads Windows 98; if `BootWin` is 0, `IO.SYS` loads your previous version of DOS (equivalent to selecting the Previous version of MS-DOS command on the Startup menu).

DoubleBuffer=0|1|2: Determines whether `IO.SYS` loads double buffering for SCSI drive memory caching. If `DoubleBuffer` is 0, double buffering is disabled; if `DoubleBuffer` is 1 (the default), `IO.SYS` enables double buffering only for controllers that require it; if `DoubleBuffer` is 2, `IO.SYS` enables double buffering whether the controller needs it or not.

DBLSpace=1|0: Determines whether `IO.SYS` loads `DBLSPACE.BIN` (the DOS 6.*x* disk compression driver) automatically. If `DBLSpace` is 1 (the default), `DBLSPACE.BIN` is loaded automatically; if `DBLSpace` is 0, `DBLSPACE.BIN` isn't loaded.

DRVSpace=1|0: Determines whether `IO.SYS` loads `DRVSPACE.BIN` (the Windows 98 disk compression driver) automatically. If `DRVSpace` is 1 (the default), `DRVSPACE.BIN` is loaded automatically; if `DRVSpace` is 0, `DRVSPACE.BIN` isn't loaded.

LoadTop=1|0: Determines whether `COMMAND.COM` and `DRVSPACE.BIN` are loaded into the Upper Memory Area (UMA). If `LoadTop` is 1 (the default), `IO.SYS` loads `COMMAND.COM` and `DRVSPACE.BIN` into the UMA and increases the amount of free conventional memory; if `LoadTop` is 0, `IO.SYS` loads `COMMAND.COM` and `DRVSPACE.BIN` into conventional memory. This might eliminate conflicts with NetWare or any other programs or drivers that load into specific addresses of the UMA and might therefore butt heads with `COMMAND.COM` or `DRVSPACE.BIN`.

Logo=1|0: Determines whether `IO.SYS` displays the animated Windows 98 logo at startup. If `Logo` is 1 (the default), the logo is displayed; if `Logo` is 0, the logo isn't displayed. The latter setting might also help to avoid conflicts with some third-party memory management utilities. (If you want to try your hand at creating a custom startup logo, check out the next section.)

3

Controlling Windows 98 Startup

> **BYPASSING THE WINDOWS 98 LOGO AD HOC**
>
> You can also bypass the animated Windows 98 startup logo by pressing Esc when the logo appears. Note that this also enables you to see the progress of the commands in your CONFIG.SYS and AUTOEXEC.BAT files. Bear in mind, however, that some video cards can't handle the mode switch that occurs when you press Esc. You know this is the case on your system if you see a garbled display after you press Esc.

Creating Your Own Startup Logo

The Windows 98 startup logo is nice enough, but you might prefer to see your own custom screen. For example, you might want to display your company logo or a message to other users of the computer. Impossible? Not at all, as you'll see in this section.

The secret is to create or modify a bitmap and store it in the root folder of your boot drive under the name LOGO.SYS. You can use Paint to do this, so begin by selecting Start | Programs | Accessories | Paint. LOGO.SYS uses a 320×400 bitmap, and the image you use must be the same size. (This is despite the fact that IO.SYS displays LOGO.SYS at 640×480. Go figure.) How you proceed from here depends on whether you want to create a new image or use an existing image.

If you're creating a new image, follow these steps:

1. Select Image | Attributes (or press Ctrl+E) to display the Attributes dialog box.
2. Enter 320 in the Width text box and 400 in the Height text box.
3. Click OK to return to the image.
4. Create your image.
5. Select File | Save (or press Ctrl+S) and save the bitmap as LOGO.SYS in the boot drive's root folder.

If you want to use an existing image, follow these steps:

1. Select File | Open (or press Ctrl+O) to display the Open dialog box.
2. Highlight the file you want to use and click Open.
3. Select Image | Attributes (or press Ctrl+E). In the Attributes dialog box, check the Width and Height text boxes to get the current dimensions of the image.

4. If the file is 320×400, skip to step 5. Otherwise, you need to resize the bitmap. First, resize the horizontal dimension to 320 pixels by selecting Image | Stretch/Skew (or pressing Ctrl+W), entering an appropriate percentage in the Horizontal text box (the one in the Stretch group), and clicking OK. For example, if your bitmap is 640 pixels wide, you enter 50, as shown in Figure 3.4.

FIGURE 3.4.

Use the Stretch and Skew dialog box to size your image to 320×400.

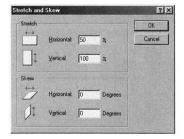

5. Resize the vertical dimension to 400 pixels by selecting Image | Stretch/Skew again, entering an appropriate percentage in the Vertical text box (again, the one in the Stretch group), and clicking OK. For example, if your bitmap is 500 pixels wide, you enter 80. Your image should now be 320×400.

ADJUSTING THE STRETCH

These stretch percentages might not give you an image that's exactly 320×400. For example, if your image is 480 pixels vertically, an 83 percent stretch would bring the image down to 399 pixels. In this case, use the Image Attributes dialog box to enter the exact dimension.

6. Modify the image, if necessary. (For example, stretching the image might mess up some of the colors, so you might need to make some adjustments.)
7. Select File | Save As and save the bitmap as LOGO.SYS in the boot drive's root folder.

The next time you start Windows 98, your image will appear as the startup logo.

Command-Line Switches for Starting Windows 98

If you boot to the command line, you can load the Windows 98 GUI and the protected-mode drivers by typing win and pressing Enter to run WIN.COM. You can also modify the startup by specifying switches with WIN.COM according to the following syntax:

```
WIN [/?] [/B] [/W] /WX [/D:[F] [M] [N] [S] [T] [V] [X]]
```

Table 3.2 describes these switches and how they modify the startup.

Table 3.2. `WIN.COM` switches.

Switch	Description
`/?`	Displays a partial list of the available `WIN.COM` switches.
`/B`	Logs the startup progress to a `BOOTLOG.TXT` in the boot drive's root directory. This is the same as selecting the `Logged` (`\BOOTLOG.TXT`) option in the Windows 98 Startup menu.
`/W`	Restores `CONFIG.SYS` from `CONFIG.WOS` and `AUTOEXEC.BAT` from `AUTOEXEC.WOS`, and then prompts you to press any key to start Windows 98.
`/WX`	Restores `CONFIG.SYS` from `CONFIG.WOS` and `AUTOEXEC.BAT` from `AUTOEXEC.WOS`, and then starts Windows 98.
`/D:`	Used for troubleshooting the Windows 98 startup. It's used in conjunction with other switches, as described in the following entries.
`/D:F`	Disables 32-bit disk access and forces all drive access to go through the real-mode mapper (RMM). Normally, the RMM provides compatibility with real-mode device drivers that have no protected-mode counterparts. This switch is equivalent to setting `32BitDiskAccess=FALSE` in `SYSTEM.INI`.
`/D:M`	Starts Windows 98 in Safe mode. This is equivalent to selecting the Safe mode option on the Windows 98 Startup menu.
`/D:N`	Starts Windows 98 in Safe mode, but also enables networking support. This is equivalent to selecting the Safe mode with networking option on the Windows 98 Startup menu.
`/D:S`	Tells Windows 98 not to use the ROM address space between F000:0000 and 1MB for a break point. This switch is equivalent to setting `SystemROMBreakPoint=FALSE` in `SYSTEM.INI`.
`/D:T`	Starts Windows 98 in a mode similar to that used by Setup. Internal and external VxDs aren't loaded, no EMS page frame is set up, and FastDisk isn't enabled.
`/D:V`	Tells Windows 98 that the ROM routine will handle interrupts from the hard disk controller. This is equivalent to setting `VirtualHDIRQ=FALSE` in `SYSTEM.INI`.
`/D:X`	Excludes the entire adapter range of the UMA from memory addresses that Windows 98 scans to find unused upper memory blocks. This is equivalent to setting `EMMExclude=A000-FFFF` in `SYSTEM.INI`.

> **WHAT ARE WOS FILES?**
>
> As you'll learn in Chapter 23, "DOS Isn't Dead: Unleashing the DOS Shell," you can set up a program to run in MS-DOS mode and specify custom `CONFIG.SYS` and `AUTOEXEC.BAT` files for the program. When you then run the program, Windows 98 renames the existing `CONFIG.SYS` file to `CONFIG.WOS` and renames `AUTOEXEC.BAT` to `AUTOEXEC.WOS`.

Troubleshooting Windows 98 Startup

Computers are often frustrating beasts, but few things in computerdom are as hair-pullingly, teeth-gnashingly frustrating as an operating system that won't operate. To help save some wear and tear on your hair and teeth, this section outlines a few common startup difficulties and their solutions.

> **WINDOWS 98'S SYSTEM TROUBLESHOOTER**
>
> For fine-tuned control over the Windows 98 startup, you should check out the new System Troubleshooter utility. It provides a graphical front-end for all the various startup components, and you can use simple check boxes to toggle startup items on and off. I discuss this utility in Chapter 17, "Wielding the Windows 98 System Tools."
>
> Chapter 17 also discusses the new Automatic Skip Driver utility, which you can use to troubleshoot hung startups caused by a defective device or device driver.

New to **98**

3

CONTROLLING
WINDOWS 98
STARTUP

When to Use the Various Startup Menu Options

You saw earlier that Windows 98 has some useful options on its Startup menu. But under what circumstances should you use each option? Well, because there is some overlap in what each option brings to the table, there are no hard and fast rules. It is possible, however, to lay down some general guidelines.

You should use the Safe mode option if one of the following conditions occurs:

- Windows 98 doesn't start after the POST ends.
- Windows 98 seems to stall for an extended period.
- Windows 98 doesn't work correctly or produces unexpected results.
- You can't print to a local printer (although you can try some other troubleshooting steps for printing problems; see Chapter 21, "Prescriptions for Perfect Printing").
- Your video display is distorted and, possibly, unreadable.
- Your computer stalls repeatedly.

■ Your computer suddenly slows down.

■ You need to test an intermittent error condition.

You should use the Logged (\BOOTLOG.TXT) option in the following situations:

■ The Windows 98 startup hangs after switching to protected mode.

■ You need a detailed record of the startup process.

■ You suspect (after using one of the other Startup menu options) that a protected-mode driver is causing Windows 98 startup to fail.

After starting (or attempting to start) Windows 98 with this option, you end up with a file named BOOTLOG.TXT in your boot drive's root folder. This is a text file, so you can examine it with any text editor. For example, you could boot to the DOS prompt (using the Command prompt only or Safe mode command prompt only option) and then use EDIT.COM to examine the file.

Scour the file for a couple of lines that look like this:

```
[0016586B] Loading Vxd = vmouse
[0016586B] LoadFailed  = vmouse
```

These lines tell you which driver Windows 98 choked on during the startup. You probably need to reinstall the driver, as described in Chapter 11, "Device Advice: Dealing with Devices in Windows 98." Note, however, that there are a few cases in which a LoadFailed message doesn't necessarily indicate a problem. Here's a summary of these exceptions:

```
LoadFailed = dsound.vxd
```

DSOUND.VXD is the library of DirectSound routines. (See Chapter 24, "DirectX and Windows 98 Video," for explanations of the various DirectX components.) The failure of this driver to load properly might mean only that you have no DirectSound-enabled games on your system.

```
LoadFailed = ebios
```

You see this message if the extended BIOS driver didn't find an extended BIOS on your system.

```
LoadFailed = ndis2sup.vxd
```

This message might mean only that the NDIS 2 support driver didn't locate any NDIS 2 drivers to support.

```
LoadFailed = vpowerd
```

VPOWERD is the Advanced Power Management (APM) driver. If your system doesn't support APM, this driver will fail to load.

```
LoadFailed = vserver.vxd
```

VSERVER.VXD attempts to saves memory by loading later in the boot process only if it's needed.

```
LoadFailed = vshare
```

It's likely that VSHARE loaded successfully earlier in the boot process. This second copy of VSHARE realizes that VSHARE is already loaded, so it fails.

```
InitCompleteFailed=SDVXD
```

This line indicates that a temporary disk cache used by Windows 98 to speed the boot process has been unloaded from memory.

You should use the Safe mode command prompt only option if you're facing one of the following situations:

- Windows 98 won't start, even with the Safe mode option.
- You want to use WIN.COM's command-line switches (see Table 3.2).
- You want to run a program from the command line (such as EDIT.COM to edit a startup file).
- You want to avoid loading HIMEM.SYS or IFSHLP.SYS.

You should use the Safe mode without compression option in the following situations:

- Your computer hangs each time it tries to access a compressed drive.
- A Corrupt CVF error occurs during the startup process.
- Windows 98 fails to start, and it won't start if you use either the Safe mode or the Safe mode command prompt only option.
- You want to prevent IO.SYS from loading the compression driver (DBLSPACE.BIN or DRVSPACE.BIN).

You should use the Safe mode with network support option if one of the following situations occurs:

- Windows 98 fails to start using any of the other Safe mode options.
- The drivers or programs you need in order to repair a problem exist on a shared network resource.
- You need access to email or other network-based communications for technical support.
- Your computer is running a shared Windows 98 installation.

You should use the Step-by-step confirmation option if one of the following conditions is true:

- The Windows 98 startup fails while processing any of the startup files.
- You need to check for failure messages related to real-mode drivers while processing CONFIG.SYS and AUTOEXEC.BAT.

3

CONTROLLING
WINDOWS 98
STARTUP

- You need to check for failure messages related to the IO.SYS commands.
- You need to check for failure messages related to the Registry.
- You need to verify that the expected drivers are being loaded.
- You need to bypass a specific driver or a set of drivers.

A Step-by-Step Strategy

If Windows 98 starts in Safe mode, your next move should be to try the Step-by-step confirmation option in the Startup menu. Rather than just guessing at which options you should load and which you should avoid, let's put together a strategy. Table 3.3 lists the various prompts you see during a step-by-step boot. Columns A, B, C, and D list various response combinations you should try.

Table 3.3. Response combinations for a step-by-step boot.

Step-by-Step Prompt	*A*	*B*	*C*	*D*
Load DoubleSpace driver?	Yes	No	Yes	Yes
Process the system registry?	Yes	Yes	Yes	No
Create a startup log file (BOOTLOG.TXT)?	Yes	Yes	Yes	Yes
Process your startup device drivers (CONFIG.SYS)?	No	No	Yes	Yes
Process your startup command file (AUTOEXEC.BAT)?	No	No	Yes	Yes
Load the Windows graphical user interface?	Yes	Yes	Yes	Yes
Load all Windows drivers?	No	Yes	No	Yes
filename.vxd?	N/A	Yes	N/A	Yes

Option A: If Windows 98 starts properly when you use the responses in option A, you know you have a problem with a device driver or TSR. Use options B and C (see the following paragraphs) to narrow down the problem. If Windows fails to start when you use the responses in option A, try option D.

Option B: If Windows 98 starts properly when you use the responses in option B, you know you have a problem with a real-mode device driver or TSR in CONFIG.SYS or AUTOEXEC.BAT. You can pinpoint the problem by stepping through these files. If Windows 98 fails to start when you use the responses in option B, try option C.

Option C: If Windows 98 starts properly when you use the responses in option C, you know you have a problem with a protected-mode device driver. You have three choices:

- Run the Startup menu's Logged (`\BOOTLOG.TXT`) option to see which driver is causing the problem.

- Do another step-by-step startup, select Yes to the `Load all Windows drivers?` Prompt, and then select Yes for each of the individual protected-mode drivers (VXDs). If Windows 98 hangs after loading one of these drivers, you've found the culprit.

- Turn to Chapter 11 and read the section titled "Troubleshooting Protected-Mode Driver Problems."

  If Windows fails to start when you use the responses in option C, try option D.

Option D: If Windows 98 starts properly when you use the responses in option D, you know you have a problem with the Registry. See Chapter 13, "A Few Good Hacks: Some Useful Registry Tweaks." If Windows fails to start when you use the responses in option D, `SYSTEM.INI` or `WIN.INI` likely has a problem. Rename these two files (to, for example, `SYSTEM.SAV` and `WIN.SAV`), rename `SYSTEM.CB` to `SYSTEM.INI`, and reboot normally. If Windows 98 loads successfully, you need to examine the original `SYSTEM.INI` and `WIN.INI` files for problems (such as attempting to load a device driver that no longer exists on your system).

RECOVERING YOUR MOUSE

When you reboot with `SYSTEM.CB` saved as `SYSTEM.INI`, your mouse probably won't work. To fix this problem, first add the following line to the `[boot]` section of the new `SYSTEM.INI` file:

```
mouse.drv=mouse.drv
```

Then add the following line to the `[386Enh]` section:

```
mouse=*vmouse, msmouse.vxd
```

THE SYSTEM CONFIGURATION UTILITY

Windows 98 has made troubleshooting startup woes a bit easier thanks to its new System Configuration Utility. This utility acts as a kind of front-end for controlling how Windows 98 starts. The utility presents a collection of check boxes that enable you to pick and choose which elements of the startup procedure are executed and which are bypassed. You can skip large chunks—such as `CONFIG.SYS` and `AUTOEXEC.BAT`—as well as individual lines in the

New to
98

continues

continued

startup files. The System Configuration Utility also enables you to make backup copies of your system files.

To run the System Configuration Utility, select Start | Run, type msconfig in the Run dialog box, and then click OK.

Windows 98 Won't Start in Safe Mode

If Windows 98 is so intractable that it won't even start in Safe mode, your system is likely afflicted with one of the following problems:

- Your system is infected with a virus. See Chapter 17 for more information on viruses and how to get rid of them.

- Your system has incorrect CMOS settings. Run the machine's CMOS setup program to see whether any of these settings needs to be changed or whether the CMOS battery needs to be replaced.

- Your system has a hardware conflict. See Chapter 11 for hardware troubleshooting procedures.

- There is a problem with a SCSI device. In this case, your system may hang during the SCSI BIOS initialization process. Try removing devices from the SCSI chain until your system starts normally.

- You need to make an adjustment to MSDOS.SYS. For example, I mentioned earlier that some third-party memory managers don't like LOGO.SYS, so you might need to change the Logo setting to 0.

- If your system uses an Intel Triton PCI controller or a PCI-based display adapter, you might need to use the special VGA.DRV or VGA.VXD video drivers from the Windows 98 CD-ROM.

Another possibility is that your system needs to run HIMEM.SYS with a machine switch, such as the following:

```
DEVICE=c:\windows\himem.sys /machine:1
```

Windows 98 normally runs HIMEM.SYS from IO.SYS. If, however, you need a machine switch, you must add it to the HIMEM.SYS line in CONFIG.SYS because you can't edit IO.SYS. The problem is that a Safe-mode boot doesn't process CONFIG.SYS; therefore, the machine switch doesn't get processed and your system might hang. Here's how to get a Safe-mode boot and process HIMEM.SYS with the machine switch:

1. Reboot, display the Windows 98 Startup menu, and select the Step-by-step confirmation option.

2. Respond to the prompts as follows:

Process the system registry?	No
Create a startup log file (BOOTLOG.TXT)?	Yes
Process your startup device drivers (CONFIG.SYS)?	Yes
Individual CONFIG.SYS device prompts	Yes
Process your startup command file (AUTOEXEC.BAT)?	No
Load the Windows graphical user interface?	No
Load all Windows drivers?	No

3. At the DOS prompt, type win /d:m and press Enter to start Windows 98 in Safe mode.

Miscellaneous Startup Snags

This section runs through a few more common startup complaints.

When you start your computer, the Windows 98 Startup menu is displayed automatically, and the following message appears:

```
Warning: Windows has detected a registry/configuration error.
Choose Safe mode, to start Windows with a minimal set of drivers.
```

This error indicates that the Registry files (they're hidden files named SYSTEM.DAT and USER.DAT in your main Windows directory) are either missing or corrupted. You need to boot Windows 98 in Safe mode.

Windows 98 first tries to restore the Registry from its backup copies. (Each time the Registry is modified, Windows 98 saves a backup of the current Registry files in SYSTEM.DA0 and USER.DA0.) You see the Registry Problem dialog box with an explanation of the problem. Click the Restore From Backup and Restart button.

If it restores the backups, Windows 98 will prompt you to restart your computer. Click Yes to reboot.

If it can't restore the backups, Windows 98 suggests that you shut down your system and reinstall Windows 98. Although you might have to reinstall Windows 98 as a last resort, you can still try two other things:

- If you have your own backup copies of the Registry files on floppy disk (this is always a good idea), you can restore those files from there.
- Reboot to the command prompt and check MSDOS.SYS. Make sure that the WinDir and WinBootDir settings point to the correct folder (that is, your main Windows 98 folder, which is where the Registry files are stored).

When you start your computer, you hear the beep that signals the end of the POST, followed by the It is now safe to turn off your computer message.

This behavior can occur if the VMM32.VXD file is missing or damaged. The Windows 98 disks and CD-ROM do include a version of VMM32.VXD. Extracting this version of the file won't solve the problem, however, because it's an incomplete version of the file. You have to run Setup again to re-create a system-specific VMM32.VXD file. Here are the steps to follow:

1. Restart your computer and hold down the Ctrl key. Then choose Command prompt only from the Startup menu.

2. Enter the following command to change to the System folder (assuming that Windows 98 is installed in \WINDOWS):

   ```
   cd \windows\system
   ```

3. Enter the following command:

   ```
   ren vmm32.vxd vmm32.old
   ```

4. Repeat step 1.

5. Reinstall Windows 98.

A DOS program you were running in MS-DOS mode starts every time you restart your computer.

As you'll learn in Chapter 23, it's possible to create custom CONFIG.SYS and AUTOEXEC.BAT files for each of your DOS applications. In this case, Windows 98 uses these new startup files to replace the current CONFIG.SYS and AUTOEXEC.BAT files (which are renamed to CONFIG.WOS and AUTOEXEC.WOS).

If you restart or turn off your computer while running the DOS program, Windows 98 doesn't get a chance to restore the correct CONFIG.SYS and AUTOEXEC.BAT files. Instead, the program-specific startup files are executed, and you end up back in the DOS program. The solution is to exit the program normally to allow Windows 98 to restore the correct startup files.

When you start Windows 98, you receive one of the following error messages and are then dumped at the DOS prompt:

```
The following file is missing or corrupted: WIN.COM
```

```
Program too big to fit in memory
```

```
Cannot find WIN.COM, unable to continue loading Windows
```

These errors imply that WIN.COM either is missing or has been damaged. Windows 98 expects WIN.COM to be 24,971 bytes. If WIN.COM weighs in less than that, you see the first error message; if WIN.COM is larger, you see the second error message; if WIN.COM is missing in action, you see the third error. The solution in all cases is to re-create WIN.COM from your Windows 98 CD-ROM or installation disks.

Here are the steps to follow:

1. If your CD-ROM drive uses protected-mode drivers, insert your Windows 98 Startup disk in drive A and reboot. (I'm assuming here that you have access to real-mode drivers for your CD-ROM on the Startup disk.) If your CD-ROM uses real-mode drivers, reboot your computer, display the Windows 98 Startup menu, and select the Command prompt only option.

2. Insert the Windows 98 CD-ROM.

3. Enter the following command (where *drive* is the letter of your CD-ROM drive; this command assumes that your main Windows folder is C:\WINDOWS):

```
extract drive:\win98\win98_29.cab win.cnf /L c:\windows\win.cnf
```

WIN.CNF is actually WIN.COM, so you need to rename it. The following commands change to the main Windows folder (you must change the first command if your Windows folder is different from C:\WINDOWS), delete the existing (and presumably corrupted) WIN.COM file, and rename WIN.CNF to WIN.COM:

```
c:
cd\windows
del win.com
ren win.cnf win.com
```

When you're done, restart your computer, and Windows 98 should load properly.

When you start Windows 98, you receive the following error message:

```
VFAT Device Initialization Failed
A device or resource required by VFAT is not present
or is unavailable. VFAT cannot continue loading.
System halted.
```

This error message suggests one of the following problems:

- CONFIG.SYS contains a line pointing to a previous version of IFSHLP.SYS. Windows 98 has a protected-mode version of the IFSHLP.SYS driver, so CONFIG.SYS shouldn't be loading it. In this case, reboot, invoke the Windows 98 Startup menu, and select the Safe mode command prompt only option. When you get to the DOS prompt, open CONFIG.SYS in a text editor and remove the DEVICE line that loads IFSHLP.SYS.

- IFSHLP.SYS is missing from the Windows folder. In this case, you need to extract IFSHLP.SYS from the Windows 98 CD-ROM or from Disk 12 of the source floppy disks. Follow the steps outlined in the preceding solution. Use the following EXTRACT command:

  ```
  extract drive:\win98\win98_47.cab ifshlp.sys /L c:\windows\ifshlp.sys
  ```

- The [Paths] section in MSDOS.SYS is incorrect. Reboot to the command prompt and check MSDOS.SYS. Make sure that the WinDir and WinBootDir settings point to your main Windows folder.

■ A file named WINBOOT.INI still exists in the root folder of the boot drive. Windows 98 creates WINBOOT.INI in the root folder if it detects that the previous startup was incomplete. It normally deletes this file after you run a successful boot. If Windows 98 doesn't do this for some reason, reboot, display the Windows 98 Startup menu, and select the Safe mode command prompt only option. At the DOS prompt, delete WINBOOT.INI and restart your computer.

You want the ability to toggle the Num Lock and Caps Lock keys at startup.

Unfortunately, Windows 98 doesn't have a built-in mechanism for toggling Num Lock and Caps Lock. You can do this if you have Microsoft's IntelliType software installed on your system (I'll show you how it's done in Chapter 8, "Customizing the Mouse, Keyboard, and Other Input Devices"). Otherwise, you need to use the DOS DEBUG program to create your own utilities for toggling these keys.

Let's begin with Num Lock. If you want to create a program that turns Num Lock off, create a new text file, name it NUMOFF.SCR, and enter the code shown in Listing 3.1. (The blank line after the int 21 line means that you press Enter. This returns you to the DEBUG prompt.)

Listing 3.1. A DEBUG script that turns Num Lock off.

```
a 100
mov ax,0040
mov ds,ax
and byte ptr [0017],df
mov ax,4c00
int 21

r cx
000f
n NUMOFF.COM
w
q
```

At the DOS prompt, enter the following command:

```
DEBUG < NUMOFF.SCR
```

This creates a program named NUMOFF.COM, which will turn Num Lock off.

If you want to turn Num Lock back on, create a text file named NUMON.SCR and enter the code shown in Listing 3.2.

Listing 3.2. A DEBUG script that turns Num Lock on.

```
a 100
mov ax,0040
mov ds,ax
or byte ptr [0017],20
mov ax,4c00
int 21
```

```
r cx
000f
n NUMON.COM
w
q
```

At the DOS prompt, enter the following command:

```
DEBUG < NUMON.SCR
```

This creates a program named NUMON.COM, which turns Num Lock on.

You can create similar DEBUG scripts for toggling Caps Lock. To turn Caps Lock off, create a text file named CAPSOFF.SCR and enter the code shown in Listing 3.3.

Listing 3.3. A DEBUG script that turns Caps Lock off.

```
a 100
mov ax,0040
mov ds,ax
and byte ptr [0017],bf
mov ax,4c00
int 21

r cx
000f
n CAPSOFF.COM
w
q
```

At the DOS prompt, enter the following command:

```
DEBUG < CAPSOFF.SCR
```

This creates a program named CAPSOFF.COM, which turns Caps Lock off.

Finally, to turn Caps Lock on, create a text file named CAPSON.SCR and enter the code shown in Listing 3.4.

Listing 3.4. A DEBUG script that turns Caps Lock on.

```
a 100
mov ax,0040
mov ds,ax
or byte ptr [0017],40
mov ax,4c00
int 21

r cx
000f
n CAPSON.COM
w
q
```

3

CONTROLLING
WINDOWS 98
STARTUP

At the DOS prompt, enter the following command:

```
DEBUG < CAPSON.SCR
```

You now have a program named CAPSON.COM, which turns Caps Lock on.

Understanding the Windows 98 Shutdown Process

We began at the beginning by looking at how Windows 98 starts up. Now we'll end at the ending by examining the Windows 98 shutdown process.

The Shut Down Command

One of the cardinal rules when working with Windows 3.*x* was that you should always exit Windows and wait until you got to the DOS prompt before turning off your computer. This gave the Windows cache a chance to flush, and it prevented damage to Program Manager's groups and icons.

This rule still applies to Windows 98 and is, in fact, even more important, for the following reasons:

- Windows 98's write-behind cache waits for idle CPU time before it writes data from the cache to the hard disk. If you turn off your machine willy-nilly, you could lose valuable data that Windows 98 hasn't yet saved to disk. (I discuss write-behind caching in more detail in Chapter 9, "Performance Tuning: Optimizing Memory and Disk Access.")

- Windows 98 waits until shutdown to update any Registry settings that have changed. Turning off your system prematurely causes you to lose unsaved configuration data, and your system might not work properly.

- At shutdown, Windows 98 warns you if any network users are connected to any of your shared resources. Turning off your machine without going through the proper channels disconnects those users and interrupts their current operation (such as a file download or a print job).

To avoid all these problems (and the ulcers that go with them), always run through the Windows 98 shutdown procedure before shutting off your machine for the night. You begin by selecting Start | Shut Down. Windows 98 displays the Shut Down Windows dialog box, shown in Figure 3.5.

FIGURE 3.5.

*The Shut Down
Windows dialog box:
a requisite part of any
system shutdown.*

Use the Shut Down Windows dialog box to select one of the following options and click OK:

Stand by: Select this option to place your computer in standby mode, which powers down only certain components (such as your monitor and hard drive). You can then power up these components by pressing a key or jiggling the mouse. Note that you see this option only if your system supports Advanced Power Management (see Chapter 11).

Shut down: Select this option if you'll be turning off your machine. After you hear a flourish of trumpets (the Windows 98 closing WAV file), you see the Windows is shutting down bitmap. After Windows 98 has completed its shutdown duties, you see a screen that says It's now safe to turn off your computer. This is your go-ahead to turn off the computer. If you change your mind and decide to restart Windows 98, just press Ctrl+Alt+Delete.

Restart: Select this option to give Windows 98 a fresh start. In this case, Windows 98 performs the equivalent of a cold reboot: The POST is run again, and you have a chance to invoke the Windows 98 Startup menu.

3

CONTROLLING
WINDOWS 98
STARTUP

A FASTER RESTART

If you need just a quick restart to update a Registry setting or some other small change, the Restart option is overkill (not to mention time-consuming). Luckily, there is a quicker way. After selecting the Restart option, hold down Shift and click OK. This tells Windows 98 to bypass the cold reboot. Instead, you see a Windows is now restarting message (at which point it's OK to release the Shift key), and Windows 98 restarts almost immediately.

A FASTER REBOOT

If you do want to perform a cold reboot, you can do so without having to display the Shut Down Windows dialog box. First, create a new batch file (named, say, REBOOT.BAT) and include only the following command in it:

```
@EXIT
```

continues

> *continued*
>
> Right-click the batch file and select Properties from the context menu. In the Program tab, activate the Close on exit check box and then click the Advanced button. In the Advanced Program Settings dialog box, activate the MS-DOS mode check box and deactivate the Warn before entering MS-DOS mode check box. Click OK and then click OK again to create a DOS-mode shortcut for the batch file. Copy this shortcut to the desktop and then double-click the shortcut whenever you want to reboot your system. (See Chapter 23 to learn more about MS-DOS mode.)

Restart in MS-DOS mode: Select this option to exit the Windows 98 GUI and get to the DOS prompt. Note that this option has nothing whatsoever to do with restarting your computer. Nothing is rebooted and no initialization files are run; you're simply exiting to DOS the way you used to with Windows 3.*x*. To get back to Windows 98, type win or exit and press Enter.

The Log Off Command

If Windows 98 networking is enabled, or if you've set up different user profiles (which I'll show you how to do in Chapter 7, "Setting Accessibility Options, User Profiles, and More"), you see a Log Off *User* command on the Start menu, where *User* is the name of the user who is currently logged on.

Selecting this command shuts down all your programs and then redisplays the Enter Network Password dialog box so that you can enter a different user name and password. Note that this option is not the same as Restart the computer, because Windows 98 doesn't perform its shutdown chores.

ANOTHER WAY TO RESET WINDOWS 98

The Log Off command is a useful way to reset Windows 98 and get a fresh batch of system resources. You just log on with the same user name.

What do you do, though, if you want to reset Windows 98 but your system doesn't have the Log Off command? No sweat. Press Ctrl+Alt+Delete to display the Close Program dialog box, highlight Explorer, and click End Task. Because Explorer is the Windows 98 shell, the Shut Down Windows dialog box appears. Click Cancel. The Explorer dialog box appears a few seconds later, complaining that the "program is not responding." Don't worry about that; just click End Task. This shuts down the shell, but Windows 98 restarts it right away.

Customizing the Windows 98 Shutdown Screens

You saw earlier how the Windows 98 startup logo was a bitmap file named LOGO.SYS (see the section "Creating Your Own Startup Logo"). Well, as you might imagine, the two Windows 98 shutdown screens are also bitmaps, and they also have the unintuitive SYS extension.

The Windows is shutting down screen is actually a bitmap file named LOGOW.SYS (LOGO Wait), shown in Figure 3.6. The It's now safe to turn off your computer screen is the bitmap file LOGOS.SYS (LOGO Shutdown), shown in Figure 3.7. Both files are in your main Windows 98 folder.

FIGURE 3.6.

The LOGOW.SYS *bitmap.*

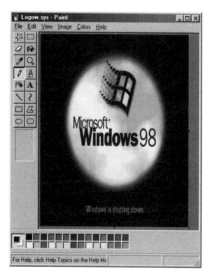

FIGURE 3.7.

The LOGOS.SYS *bitmap.*

As before, you can rename these files, create your own, and name them LOGOW.SYS and LOGOS.SYS. (Make sure that each bitmap is 320×400.) For the LOGOS.SYS file, you could create a message saying that you've gone to lunch or that you're at a meeting. Paint's Text tool is perfect for these applications.

Summary

This chapter got your Windows 98 education off to a rousing start with a close look at the Windows 98 startup process. You worked through the full startup procedure; learned how to customize the startup by using the Startup menu, MSDOS.SYS, and WIN.COM's command-line switches; solved some common startup problems; and examined the shutdown process. You even learned how to create your own startup and shutdown logos.

Here's a list of chapters where you'll find related information:

- For other Windows 98 customization techniques, see Chapters 5 through 8.

- The various memory-related concepts that I glossed over in this chapter—upper memory, high memory, conventional memory, caching, and resources—are explained in detail in Chapter 9, "Performance Tuning: Optimizing Memory and Disk Access."

- To learn more about device drivers—especially the difference between real-mode drivers and protected-mode drivers—head for Chapter 10, "Getting the Most Out of Device Manager and Hardware Profiles."

- You will find lots of background information about the Registry in Chapter 12, "Getting to Know the Windows 98 Registry."

- To learn how to add applications and documents to the Startup folder, see Chapter 14, "File and Folder Tricks and Techniques."

- To learn about MS-DOS mode, see Chapter 23, "DOS Isn't Dead: Unleashing the DOS Shell."

What's New and Noteworthy in Windows 98

CHAPTER 4

The world can doubtless never be well known by theory: practice is absolutely necessary; but surely it is of great use to a young man, before he sets out for that country, full of mazes, windings, and turnings, to have at least a general map of it, made by some experienced traveler.

—*Lord Chesterfield*

The whole point of this book is to traverse the seldom-seen nooks and crannies of Windows 98. My goal is to shepherd you through the thickets and thatches of the Windows 98 landscape in an effort to discover new and useful information and uncover hidden techniques. These newfound treasures will let you squeeze the most out of your Windows 98 investment, whether you're a single-copy user or a thousand-copy administrator.

Before setting out on your travels, however, you need to take a moment to get your bearings and scope out the lay of the new Windows 98 land. In other words, before lighting out for the hinterland, it helps if you first get to know the heartland. That's the job of this chapter. Here, you check out all the new Windows 98 features added or changed since Windows 95 first shipped. And if you're upgrading to Windows 98 from Windows 3.x, I'll run through a few concepts you need to know to get up to speed with your new operating system.

The Web Comes to the Desktop

One of the key design features of Windows 98 is the widespread implementation of the World Wide Web browser interface. So, yes, you still use a browser to navigate Web sites, but you also use browser-like actions to navigate your local disks and to launch applications. This integrated Internet shell brings the following features to the Windows 98 table (all of these features are covered in Chapter 5, "Web Integration and the Active Desktop"):

One-click icon and program launching: With Web integration activated, Windows 98 underlines the names of icons and files so that they resemble Web page links. Launching an icon or file requires only a single click.

No-click icon and file selection: Along similar lines, Web integration also enables you to select an icon or file just by hovering the mouse over the object. You can use the Shift and Ctrl keys to select multiple items (again, without clicking).

View folders as Web pages: Each folder on your system can be viewed as though it was a Web page. In fact, each folder can contain a hidden HTML file that displays the contents of the folder in an ActiveX control and leaves you free to tweak the rest of the folder/page using standard HTML tags as well as the new Dynamic HTML techniques implemented in Internet Explorer 4. Figure 4.1 shows the Control Panel folder displayed as a Web page.

The Active Desktop: The Windows 98 desktop doesn't have to be the static, blank expanse that it was in Windows 95. Instead, with Windows 98's new Active Desktop concept, the desktop is really a container object that can hold HTML content, Java applets, and ActiveX controls, as well as the new push media supported by Internet Explorer 4. In fact, Windows 98 comes with a special *channel bar* that plays host to numerous push media that utilize the Channel Definition Format (CDF).

FIGURE 4.1.

The Control Panel folder viewed as a Web page.

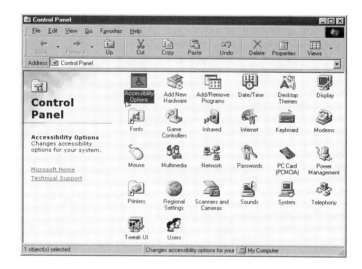

Windows 98 Knows the Internet

Microsoft's new "hard core" approach to the Internet materialized a few months after Windows 95 hit the shelves. So although Windows 95 had drastically better Internet support than Windows 3.*x*, it was obvious that the Internet was still only a minor part of the overall Windows picture. Since then, it seems that just about everything Microsoft has done has been in some way related to the Internet. So it's no surprise that the Windows 98 tool chest is overflowing with Internet features and utilities. Here are the highlights:

Internet Explorer 4 built in: The big news on the Windows 98 Internet front is the incorporation of Internet Explorer 4 as an integral part of the operating system. This means that you not only get a standalone browser, but Internet Explorer features can also be found throughout the Windows 98 interface. For example, the taskbar and folder windows all have an Address toolbar into which you can type Web addresses, and there are Back and Forward buttons that enable you to "surf" your folders. Also, Windows Explorer has the browser technology built in, so you can navigate the Web alongside your local drives and network resources (see Figure 4.2). For the full story on Internet Explorer and the browser features incorporated into the Windows 98 interface, see Chapter 33, "Exploring the Web with Internet Explorer."

FIGURE 4.2.

In Windows 98,
exploring Web sites isn't
all that different than
exploring your
computer's local
resources.

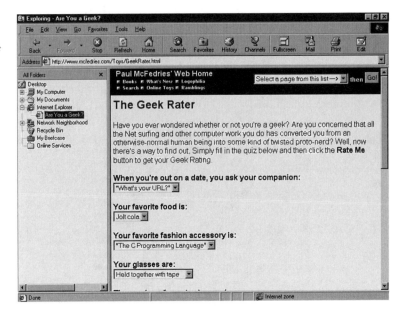

Internet Explorer 4 features: The fact that Internet Explorer is built into Windows 98 isn't the whole story, of course. Version 4 of Internet Explorer is chock-full of new features, including support for push technology and Dynamic HTML, enhanced security, improved history and search features, and numerous user interface improvements. Again, you'll find all of this covered in depth in Chapter 33.

Internet Connection Wizard: Getting connected to the Internet has never been easier, thanks to Windows 98's new Internet Connection Wizard. This wizard takes you through the entire process in the usual step-by-step wizard fashion, and it will even poll your Internet service provider for details about your connection. See Chapter 32, "Windows 98 and the Internet," to find out more.

The Online Services folder: For even easier Internet connections, Windows 98 comes with a special Online Services folder. This folder contains icons for a few service providers, including America Online, CompuServe, and The Microsoft Network. See Chapter 32 to learn more.

Web-based upgrades with Windows Update: As you saw in Chapter 2, "From Disc to Disk: Installing Windows 98," Microsoft has a new Web site devoted to analyzing your system and telling you whether updated Windows 98 device drivers and programs are available.

Outlook Express for Internet mail and news: Although Windows Messaging (formerly Microsoft Exchange) is still around in Windows 98, Internet email users will almost certainly prefer to use the new Outlook Express client. A subset of the Outlook desktop information manager, Outlook Express is optimized for the Internet and includes several new features, including the ability to specify multiple email accounts.

This aspect of Outlook Express is covered in Chapter 34, "Outlook Express and Internet Email." You can also use Outlook Express to read and post to Usenet newsgroups. I'll show you how it's done in Chapter 35, "Outlook Express and Usenet News."

Support for Lightweight Directory Access Protocol (LDAP): Outlook Express also comes with support for the LDAP standard for searching public and private address directories. As well, the Windows 98 Start menu comes with a new Find | People command that also supports LDAP.

Web publishing tools: If you're more interested in creating Web content than reading it, Windows 98 has a few tools that can help. FrontPage Express is a WYSIWYG HTML editor that takes much of the drudgery out of coding and designing Web pages; the Web Publishing Wizard takes you through the process of getting all your files from your computer to your server. Both of these tools are covered in Chapter 37, "Web Page Publishing with Windows 98."

Remote conferencing with NetMeeting: Internet-based phone calls and intranet-based video conferencing are two of the hottest areas in communications right now. To take advantage of this, Windows 98 includes the NetMeeting conferencing software. You get the full scoop on this fascinating bit of technology in Chapter 36, "Remote Collaboration with Microsoft NetMeeting."

Microsoft Wallet: This is a secure storage area you can add to Internet Explorer 4.0. You use it to store payment data, such as credit card numbers, ATM card data, digital certificates, and so on. With this information safely stowed away, you can conduct transactions on the Internet conveniently and without worrying about security. See Chapter 33 for the details.

Support for New Hardware Gadgets

Although Web integration and the built-in Internet tools will be the stars of the Windows 98 show, there's quite a sizable supporting cast to consider. Besides new universal drivers and mini-drivers that work with hundreds of new devices and models, the most significant changes are the new features that support many of the latest hardware standards. Here's a summary:

FAT32: First introduced in the OSR2 release of Windows 98, FAT32 is a 32-bit file system that provides faster disk access and greater storage efficiency. The latter comes via smaller cluster sizes for large hard disks (4KB clusters for disks up to 8GB).

Drive Converter (FAT32): To help you make the move to FAT32, Windows 98 comes with a utility that will convert FAT16 partitions to the new FAT32 structure *without* trashing your data (see Figure 4.3). I show you how to use this utility in Chapter 9, "Performance Tuning: Optimizing Memory and Disk Access."

FIGURE 4.3.

The FAT32 Converter can update any FAT16 partition without harming the existing data.

Win32 Driver Model (WDM): This is a new specification for writing device drivers so that a single driver works on both Windows 98 and Windows NT. See Chapter 10, "Getting the Most Out of Device Manager and Hardware Profiles," for details.

Multiple Display Support: This is one of Windows 98's more intriguing features. It enables you to add two or more PCI display adapters to your system and attach a monitor to each. The result is a desktop that spans all the attached monitors. You learn how to implement this handy feature in Chapter 11, "Device Advice: Dealing with Devices in Windows 98."

Other display adapter enhancements: Windows 98 includes several other new features for display adapters, including refresh rate support, the ability to set graphics acceleration from the Display Properties dialog box, and support for hardware panning at lower resolutions. This is all covered in Chapter 11.

MMX support: Windows 98 implements support for third-party programs that take advantage of Intel's Pentium Multimedia Extensions (MMX). See Chapter 11.

Power management enhancements: Windows 98 supports Advanced Power Management (APM) 1.2, including modem wake-on-ring, a Control Panel Power icon, support for multiple batteries, and drive spin down (which allows machines to place the hard disk in low-power mode when not in use). Windows 98 also implements the Advanced Configuration and Power Interface (ACPI) 1.0, which is a cross-platform power management specification implemented at the OS level instead of the BIOS level. ACPI is the basis for the OnNow initiative, the goal of which is to have PCs turn on as quickly as most consumer electronic devices do. See Chapter 11 to learn more.

Universal Serial Bus (USB) support: Windows 98 can work with USB controllers as well as USB input devices (keyboards, mice, joysticks, and so on) that support the Human Interface Device (HID) standard.

IEEE 1394 (FireWire): Windows 98 has built-in support for the IEEE 1394 bus (aka FireWire), as well as mini-drivers for some controllers (such as the Adaptec AHA-8940).

Digital Versatile Disc (DVD) support: Windows 98 ships with drivers that support DVD-ROM drives as storage devices (see Chapter 11), as well as movie playback from DVD drives and consumer devices (see Chapter 24, "DirectX and Windows 98 Video").

Image and video capture: Windows 98 supports a number of devices that capture still images (scanners and digital cameras) and video streams (conferencing cameras and IEEE 1394 desktop video camcorders). Again, Chapter 24 is the place to go to learn about this technology.

PC Card support: Windows 98 comes with drivers that enable the OS to work with Cardbus (PC Card 32) devices, 3.3 volt PC Card devices, and Global Positioning Satellite devices (see Chapter 11).

IRQ steering: Windows 98 supports the new PCI IRQ steering (sometimes called IRQ routing) feature, which enables the system to "steer" an interrupt request to the next available IRQ (see Chapter 10).

Infrared device support: Windows 98 continues to support standard Serial Infrared (SIR) devices, including IrDA 1.0- and IrDA 2.0-compliant devices and infrared LAN connectivity. Windows 98 also supports the new Fast Infrared (FIR) standard for data transfers up to 4MBps (compared to just 115.2KBps for SIR devices). I tell you how to set up and use infrared devices in Chapter 11.

Storage devices: Windows 98 has increased support for storage devices, including support for IDE Bus Mastering, 120MB Floptical drives, CD changers, Zip drives, and Jaz drives. I discuss the various drive types supported by Windows 98 in Chapter 11.

Accelerated Graphics Port (AGP) support: Windows 98 has built-in support for AGP, which is a bus specification that brings high-performance graphics operations to mainstream PCs. See Chapter 11 for more information.

Hardware profile tweaks: The hardware profile feature boasts a few user interface enhancements in Windows 98 (see Chapter 10 for details).

New Windows 98 System Tools

Windows 98 comes loaded for bear with many new and improved tools for keeping your system running smoothly and efficiently. (This is on top of the performance improvements Microsoft claims have been implemented in Windows 98. See Chapter 9 to learn more about Windows 98 performance.) Here's a quick look at these tools:

Updated FAT32 utilities: All the Windows 98 disk utilities have been redesigned to work with FAT32, including Format, Disk Defragmenter, and ScanDisk (and their DOS counterparts), as well as FDISK. The latter is covered in Chapter 8, "Customizing the Mouse, Keyboard, and Other Input Devices," and the other utilities are covered throughout Part III, "Unleashing Files, Folders, and Disks."

Backup: Windows 98's Backup utility is a version of the backup software that comes with Seagate drives. It sports an improved interface, wizards for backing up and restoring, a plethora of new options, and support for SCSI tape drives and many other tape backup devices. And unlike the Windows 95 Backup, this version will also back up Registry files. Using this utility to back up and restore your data is the subject of Chapter 16, "Working with a Net: The Windows 98 Backup Utility."

System Recovery: In the event of an unrecoverable crash, you can format your hard disk and then use System Recovery to restore your system to its previous state automatically. (You must run a complete backup for this to work, however. See Chapter 17, "Wielding the Windows 98 System Tools," for the details.)

ScanDisk check on boot: ScanDisk now runs automatically at boot time if the system was shut down improperly (see Chapter 17).

Application Tuning: This feature enhances Disk Defragmenter by optimizing your hard disk in such a way as to place the program files you use most often contiguously on the disk. This, in turn, should reduce application load times.

Disk Cleanup: You use this utility to reduce the wasted hard disk space taken up by the Recycle Bin, stray temporary files, downloaded Internet objects, and so on. See Chapter 9.

Task Scheduler: This feature replaces the System Agent that came with Microsoft Plus!. It enables you to schedule programs and utilities to run at regular intervals. Because this utility will mostly be used to schedule system maintenance tasks, I've included it in Chapter 17 along with the other system tools.

Maintenance Wizard: This wizard takes you through the process of setting up and scheduling automatic system maintenance (ScanDisk, Disk Defragmenter, the deletion of unnecessary files, and more).

System File Checker: This new utility monitors your system files and can be used to restore a previous configuration should any of these files become corrupted, missing, or overwritten. I show you how it works in Chapter 17.

System Troubleshooter: If you're having trouble starting Windows 98, the new System Troubleshooter can help. It enables you to toggle items on and off in startup files such as CONFIG.SYS, AUTOEXEC.BAT, and WIN.INI. It also provides access to numerous WIN.COM switches and other startup options. See Chapter 17 for the details.

Microsoft System Information utility: This utility acts as a central storage area for all the pertinent information about your system. It gives you access to hardware data, device drivers in use, network resources, running tasks, and much more (see Figure 4.4). You can also use it to invoke utilities such as ScanDisk, System File Checker, and Automatic Skip Driver Agent. Chapter 17 shows you how to wield this tool.

Automatic Skip Driver Agent: If Windows 98 hangs because of a defective device driver or a device failure, you can use the Automatic Skip Driver Agent utility to tell Windows 98 to bypass the driver or device on subsequent boots. Once again, head for Chapter 17 to get the skinny.

FIGURE 4.4.

The Windows 98 System Information utility.

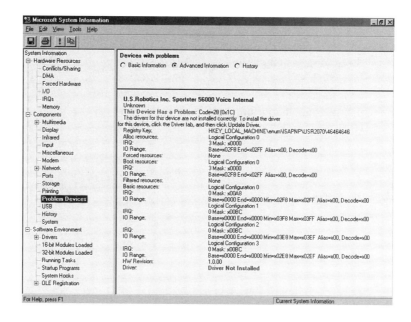

DriveSpace3: Windows 98's version of DriveSpace supports compressed volume files up to 2GB in size. It also includes the Compression Agent for background compression. You find complete coverage of DriveSpace3 in Chapter 15, "Disk Driving: The Windows 98 Disk Utilities."

Registry Scan: This utility (it comes in both a real-mode flavor and a protected-mode flavor) scans the Registry to look for corruption in the files. If a problem is found, Registry Scan can attempt to fix the problem. The real-mode version of Registry Scan is invoked automatically at startup and creates a backup copy of the Registry files automatically. See Chapter 17 for details.

Improved Dr. Watson: The Dr. Watson utility intercepts software faults and takes a snapshot of your system's state at the time of the fault. The Windows 98 version of the utility has been improved to include more system detail in its reports.

New Multimedia Bells and Whistles

The new features you've seen so far will certainly appeal to your left brain. However, Windows 98 has no shortage of right brain treats, as well. Here's a quick look at these new and improved multimedia marvels:

Broadcast Architecture and Web TV for Windows: Windows 98 supports the new Broadcast Architecture, which essentially turns your computer into a receiver for television signals. The Broadcast Architecture also supports signals that are enhanced with data, such as Web pages and other information. Windows 98 comes with Web

4

WHAT'S NEW IN
WINDOWS 98

TV for Windows, which enables you to select and view these television signals. I cover Broadcast Architecture and the Web TV for Windows in Chapter 24.

Streaming content support via NetShow: Windows 98 comes with the NetShow player, which enables you to view multimedia content streamed over the Internet or an intranet using the Active Streaming Format (ASF), as shown in Figure 4.5. I discuss content streaming and show you how to use the NetShow player in Chapter 24.

FIGURE 4.5.

No more long downloads. Windows 98 lets you view rich multimedia content streamed to the NetShow player.

DirectX 5: This is the latest set of graphics API functions and is fully supported by Windows 98. New features implemented in DirectX 5 include AGP support, MMX support in both Direct3D and DirectDraw, DirectX applications spread over multiple monitors, and an overall improvement in speed and robustness. See Chapter 24 for the DirectX details.

OpenGL support: Windows 98 understands the OpenGL graphics libraries and even comes with a few OpenGL 3D screen savers.

Kodak Imaging: This is an image viewer that supports a number of graphics formats. It also integrates with Microsoft Fax and supports image scanners via TWAIN32. See Chapter 11 and CD Chapter 3, "Using Microsoft Fax to Send and Receive Faxes."

Communications and Networking

The Internet may be all the rage, but most corporate administrators are more interested in keeping their local area networks (LANs) running smoothly, improving remote access to their LANs, extending those LANs to their customers, and implementing higher-speed technologies. The communications gurus at Microsoft are aware of this, of course, so they included in Windows 98 many new communications and networking features:

Dial-Up Networking enhancements: Windows 98 incorporates several new Dial-Up Networking features, including an improved properties sheet, hands-free dial-up, support for scripting, and the ability to set up a Windows 98 machine as a dial-up server. I cover all of this in Chapter 30, "Remote Computing with Dial-Up Networking."

ISDN 1.1 Accelerator pack: Windows 98 bundles the ISDN Accelerator pack, which enables Dial-Up Networking to work with an ISDN adapter card.

Virtual Private Networking and PPTP: Windows 98 supports the Point-to-Point Tunneling Protocol (PPTP), which enables you to establish an extended private network (called a Virtual Private Network) over a public network such as the Internet. See Chapter 30 to get the full details.

Multilink Bandwidth Aggregation: This is a communications feature that enables Windows 98 to combine the bandwidth from multiple lines into a single, larger pipe.

TCP/IP improvements: The Windows 98 TCP/IP stack boasts a number of enhancements, including support for Autonet Addressing, TCP large windows, Selective Acknowledgements, Fast Retransmission, and Fast Recovery. I give you an overview of TCP/IP concepts and implementation in Chapter 31, "Implementing TCP/IP for Internet and Intranet Connections."

Windows Sockets (WinSock) 2: This is an update to the WinSock 1.1 support found in Windows 95. WinSock 2 implements a protocol-independent interface, which means it can work with protocols other than TCP/IP. It also utilizes protocol-independent name resolution, so it works not only with DNS, but also with domains such as SAP and X.500.

Resource ReSerVation Protocol (RSVP): This is a new networking protocol that Microsoft has proposed as an Internet standard. It's used to guarantee a particular level of transmission service by reserving in advance the network resources required by the transmission.

New modem support: The Windows 98 Unimodem driver implements support for VoiceView modems, controllerless modems, and Sierra modems. See Chapter 26, "Getting Started with Modem Communications."

Updated telephony support: Windows 98 supports the new TAPI 2.1 telephony standard.

Distributed Common Object Model (DCOM): DCOM extends the Common Object Model (see Chapter 19, "Sharing Data in Windows 98: The Clipboard and OLE") so that component-based applications can communicate across a network.

Novell NetWare 4.*x* client: Windows 98 includes the full client for NetWare 4.*x*, including client support NetWare Directory Services. See Chapter 28, "Setting Up Windows 98 for Networking."

NDIS 5 and ATM support: Windows 98 supports the NDIS 5 network interface, which means Windows 98 can work with Asynchronous Transfer Mode (ATM) network adapters, as well as LAN Emulation (LANE) over ATM.

32-bit Data Link Control (DLC): Windows 98 includes the 32-bit DLC protocol for accessing IBM mainframe and AS/400 computers. Although I don't discuss the DLC protocol in this book, I show you how to install network protocols in Chapter 28.

Other New Shell and Customization Features

The Windows 95 shell was a big hit with most people, but that didn't stop the Microsoft engineers from making changes. The Windows 98 shell boasts quite a collection of improvements, as well as many new tools for customizing Windows 98 to suit the way you work. Here's the rundown:

A better Setup program: The improvements in Windows 98 really begin at the beginning: in the Setup program. This is particularly true if you're upgrading from Windows 95 because the Windows 98 Setup program makes use of the Registry to carry over all your settings (including hardware configurations). This means that the installation process requires very little user input (Setup even reboots the computer automatically as needed). Even for full installs, Setup streamlines the process and is a bit smarter when it comes to hardware detection. (The latter now occurs after the first reboot so that Setup can take full advantage of any Plug and Play data it receives.) The Setup nitty-gritty can be found in Chapter 1, "Preparing for the Windows 98 Installation," and Chapter 2.

Global Windows Address Book: Windows 98 implements a common address book—called the Windows Address Book—that can be used among multiple applications (including Outlook Express and Internet Explorer).

My Documents folder: Setup creates a folder named My Documents on the same drive on which you installed Windows 98. This folder is intended to be used as a storage area for the documents you create while working in Windows 98. The common Open and Save As dialog boxes have been tweaked so that they default to this folder. See Chapter 14, "File and Folder Tricks and Techniques."

Easier user profiles: As in Windows 95, Windows 98 enables you to establish user profiles to create custom configurations for multiple users of a single machine. A new Users Control Panel icon makes it easier to set up and maintain these profiles.

Wheel mouse support: Windows 98 has built-in support for the Microsoft Intellimouse with the extra wheel "button." In most Windows 98 windows, you can scroll up or down by rotating the wheel. See Chapter 8.

Microsoft Plus! display enhancements: All of the display customization features found in the Microsoft Plus! add-on for Windows 95 have been incorporated into Windows 98. These include full-window drag, font smoothing, wallpaper stretching, and customizable desktop icons. I show you how to work with all of these enhancements in Chapter 6, "Customizing the Taskbar, Start Menu, and Display."

QuickRes—on-the-fly color depth changes: Windows 98 bundles the QuickRes utility (formerly part of the Windows 95 Power Toys collection), which enables you to make on-the-fly changes to the color depth used by your graphics adapter (Windows 95 required a reboot to put this change into effect). Windows 98 also places a display settings icon in the taskbar for quick adjustments to both color depth and display resolution. All this is covered in Chapter 6.

Easier Start menu customization: Windows 98 enables you to reposition Start menu items by dragging them up or down within a menu. I explain this technique in more detail in Chapter 6.

Improved Accessibility options: Windows 98 continues the excellent support for the needs of disabled users that was pioneered in Windows 95. To make these Accessibility options even easier to use, Windows 98 comes with a new Accessibility Wizard that provides an intuitive, easy-to-use front-end for most of the settings (see Figure 4.6). Windows 98 also includes a new utility called the Microsoft Magnifier that enables you to "zoom in" on the screen and thus view the contents at increased magnification. I offer complete coverage of Windows 98's accessibility features in Chapter 7, "Setting Accessibility Options, User Profiles, and More."

FIGURE 4.6.

The Accessibility Wizard makes it easier than ever to customize Windows for users with special needs.

New interface animation effects: The Windows 98 interface has been tweaked to include effects such as sliding menus, color highlighting of toolbar icons, and ToolTips for things such as the window Maximize and Minimize buttons. The Windows 98 CD-ROM comes with a utility called TweakUI that enables you to control some of these settings, and I show you how it works in Chapter 6.

Revamped Help system: Windows 98 implements a new Help system front-end called HelpDesk. This is a Web page that resides on your computer and gives you access to Local Help (the Windows 98 Help system) or to Internet-based Help resources. The Help system itself has been retooled as HTML and now runs inside a custom browser window.

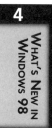

Making the Move from Windows 3.x

As you've seen so far, Windows 98 is brimful to bursting with tools and features that are either brand new or updates of those found in Windows 95. So even though Windows 98 is by no means a radical makeover of Windows 95, upgraders still have a bit of a learning curve ahead of them.

That curve is all the more steep for those making the big leap from Windows 3.*x* to Windows 98. And judging by Windows 95's only so-so reception in corporate offices, it's likely that a lot of people will be making that leap. If you're one of those people, or if you have users who are in that boat, the rest of this chapter provides a few crucial pointers that should help ease the transition.

The Desktop: Your New Windows Home

Assuming that Windows 98 is safely ensconced on your system, each time you boot your machine, you'll be whisked (or walked, depending on how powerful your computer is) right into Windows 98. Along the way, you might have to pass through a checkpoint or two—such as a network login—but you eventually end up at the desktop, shown in Figure 4.7.

FIGURE 4.7.

The Windows 98 desktop.

If you're a former Windows 3.*x* user, the first thing you notice is that Program Manager is nowhere in sight. In its stead, you're presented with a vast, black expanse studded with a few icons. This rather Spartan expanse is the desktop, and it's where most of the Windows 98 action occurs. The Windows 98 designers have consigned Program Manager—with its untidy collection of program groups and program items—to the dustbin of operating system history.

PROGRAM MANAGER RIDES THE PINE

Actually, Program Manager is only in semiretirement, occupying a spot on the bench while the Windows 98 upstarts hog the spotlight. If you find that you miss Program Manager, or if you want to fire it up for old time's sake, select Start | Run, type progman in the Run dialog box, and click OK. Believe me, though, spending only an hour or two with the new Windows 98 interface will be enough to make you forget that Program Manager ever existed.

Although Windows 3.*x* had a "desktop," the Windows 98 desktop is a more accurate representation of the metaphor because it behaves more like the top of a desk. So, yes, your application windows still appear on the desktop as they did in Windows 3.*x*, but the Windows 98 desktop can handle many more items:

- **Icons that take you to specific Windows 98 features.** For example, the Mail icon opens Outlook Express, Windows 98's Internet email and newsgroup client.

- **Pointers to applications.** These pointers, called *shortcuts*, let you launch an application simply by either clicking the shortcut's icon (if Web integration is enabled; see Chapter 5) or double-clicking the icon (if Web integration is disabled).

- **Shortcuts to files, folders, and drives.** As you'll see a bit later, shortcuts can point to much more than just programs.

- **Channels, Web pages, and other "live" content.** The default Windows 98 desktop is called the Active Desktop, and it can contain content that can be updated, such as channels that are "pushed" to the desktop from remote sites.

- **Data snippets.** You can store text, graphics, and other data on the desktop for handy reuse.

Overall, the Windows 98 desktop is a much more versatile and powerful way to work than anything you saw in Windows 3.*x*.

Some New Windows 98 Concepts You Should Know

Before we start poking and prodding Windows 98's new interface and tools, we need to take a second to nail down a few concepts and ideas that Microsoft has introduced since the days when Windows 3.*x* ruled the earth. Of course, Windows 98 is such a radical departure from those older versions of Windows that I could spend a hundred pages going over its many theoretical and architectural innovations. Instead, the next few sections target just those concepts that form a ubiquitous part of the Windows 98 topography.

Understanding Windows 98 Objects

One of the major differences between Windows 98 and Windows 3.*x*—and one of the keys to using Windows 98 powerfully and efficiently—is the idea of the object-oriented user interface. This means that Windows 98 views most of what you see—such as the desktop, the icons, and the taskbar—as objects: separate entities with their own properties and actions.

What does this mean in the real world? Well, let's consider a real-world analogy: a car. A car is an object, to be sure, but what does it mean to say that it has its own "properties and actions"?

The car's properties are simply its physical characteristics: its model, color, engine size, and so on. The car's actions, on the other hand, define what you can do with the car: accelerate, brake, and so on.

The Windows 98 interface is populated with all kinds of objects, each of which has its own properties and actions. This means that you have unprecedented control over the appearance and operation of most of the basic building blocks of the interface.

Object Context Menus

To show you the power of Windows 98 objects, let's examine one of the interface's most useful features: context menus. Move the mouse pointer so that it rests anywhere on an empty part of the desktop and then right-click. You immediately see a small menu, as shown in Figure 4.8. This is called a *context menu* (or sometimes a *shortcut menu*). As you'll see, these context menus are a pervasive feature of the Windows 98 terrain.

FIGURE 4.8.

Right-click the desktop to display this example of a context menu.

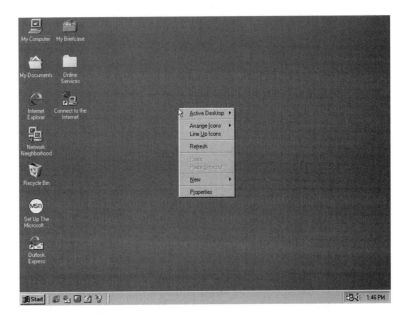

Why are they called *context* menus? Well, the purpose of the menu is to give you easy access to some of the object's properties and actions. But each type of object has a unique collection of properties and actions, so each object type needs a different menu. Which menu appears depends on which object you right-click. In other words, it depends on the *context* of the right-click.

After you have the context menu displayed, you can click one of its commands to either modify the object's properties or run one of the object's actions. If you decide you don't want to do anything with the context menu, you can close it by pressing Esc or by left-clicking elsewhere.

Object Properties

An object's properties govern, for the most part, the look and feel of the object. For example, right-click the desktop to display the context menu shown earlier in Figure 4.8 (if it isn't displayed already) and then click the Properties command. Many of the Windows 98 context menus you'll deal with will have a Properties command, and it almost always displays a Properties dialog box (also called a *properties sheet*) specific to the underlying object. In this case, the Display Properties dialog box, shown in Figure 4.9, appears.

FIGURE 4.9.

The properties sheet for the desktop object.

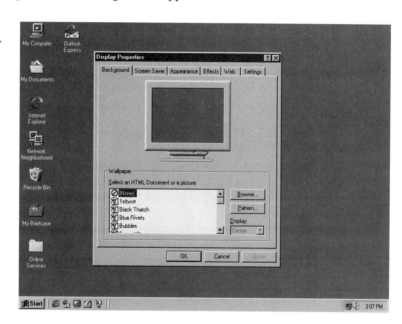

WINDOWS 98'S DIALOG BOXES

Windows 98 makes extensive use of so-called *tabbed* dialog boxes such as the one shown in Figure 4.9. The "tabs" are the headings that run across the top of the dialog box, just below the title bar. (In Figure 4.9, they're Background, Screen Saver, and so on.) When you activate a tab, a new set of controls appears. You navigate the tabs either by clicking them or by using the Ctrl+Tab and Ctrl+Shift+Tab key combinations.

Notice that the dialog boxes in Windows 98 have a couple of buttons in the upper-right corner. The button with the ✕ is the Close button; it's equivalent to clicking the Cancel command button. The button with the question mark (?) is part of the Windows 98 Help system. If you click this button and then click a control, a message appears that gives you a brief description of the control. (This button doesn't appear on all dialog boxes.)

I won't cover the options in this dialog box in depth here (see Chapter 6), but you might want to poke around the tabs to get an idea of the kinds of properties you can work with. Remember, this is the properties sheet for the *desktop*, so the options control the look of the desktop and the look of any objects displayed on the desktop. For example, the Background tab lets you specify a pattern or a wallpaper to cover the desktop. Similarly, the Appearance tab lets you set the color of the desktop (as well as other objects that appear on the desktop, such as menus and window title bars).

When you're finished with the dialog box, you can close it by clicking Cancel, clicking the Close button, or pressing Esc.

Object Actions

An object's actions (they're sometimes called *methods*) define the kinds of actions you can take with the object. For example, try this little experiment:

1. Move the mouse pointer over one of the desktop icons.
2. Hold down the left mouse button and move the mouse pointer slightly to the left. This causes the icon to move to the left as well.
3. Release the mouse button.
4. Right-click the desktop to display its context menu (shown in Figure 4.8).
5. Click the Line up Icons command. Windows 98 moves the icon back to its original position.

In this simple example, you see that one of the desktop object's "actions" is to line up the icons in apple-pie order. Similarly, you can use the Arrange Icons command to display a cascade menu of commands that sort the icons in various ways, and you can use the New command to create new desktop objects, such as folders and documents. (Again, I cover all this ground in later chapters.)

Folders: Directories and Then Some

I mentioned in Chapter 1 that Windows 98 has tossed out the word *directory* and replaced it with *folder*. This is in keeping with the revamped desktop metaphor in Windows 98. After all, the real world's filing cabinets don't use "directories" to store their memos, forms, contracts, and other paperish bric-a-brac; they use file folders. So it makes sense that our electronic filing cabinets (hard disks, floppy disks, and CD-ROMs) should store their documents in folders as well.

However, if Microsoft had introduced the term "folder" merely as a replacement and an update for "directory," we could all yawn a couple of times and go back to what we were doing. But Windows 98's folders go beyond just disk directories, to the point where they are truly universal storage areas. So, yes, your hard disk is filled with folders that contain programs and data, but plenty of other folders also contain other, less obvious, objects:

■ The desktop itself is a folder. This is the Big Kahuna, the Top Dog, the Numero Uno of folderdom; it serves as a container for all the other folders associated with your system. (This concept will become clearer later in the book when you work with Windows Explorer.)

■ Disks (hard, floppy, CD-ROM, Zip, Jaz, and so on) are folders containing not only the files in their root, but also other garden-variety folders used to store programs and data.

■ The Start menu's submenus are all folders containing shortcuts to programs and documents.

■ Control Panel is a folder containing icons that let you customize various aspects of Windows 98.

■ The Printers folder contains icons for all the printers you've installed in Windows 98.

■ The Recycle Bin is a folder that contains files you've deleted.

■ The Network Neighborhood is a folder that contains computers, workgroups, and domains associated with your network.

This folder-happy nature might sound like a lot of foolishness (folderol, if you will), but it has important ramifications for people looking to unleash Windows 98's full potential. In other words, because you can view the contents of any folder by using Windows Explorer, you have full access to all of Windows 98's folders. This makes it blindingly simple to customize these folders: You can add new objects, rename or delete existing objects, and work with the properties and actions of objects. As you work through this book, you'll see that I return to this basic concept again and again.

Long Filenames (Finally!)

Ask DOS or Windows 3.*x* users to catalog their operating system pet peeves, and it will be a rare list that doesn't include "8.3 filename format." They're referring, of course, to the Procrustean filename restrictions foisted on us by DOS: a primary name with an eight-character maximum, followed by a period (.), followed by an extension with a three-character maximum. This constraint has led to hard disks all over the world being littered with filenames like 1STQTR96.XLS and LTR2MOM.DOC. While trying in vain to decipher these filename hieroglyphics, DOS and Windows users would look on in envy at Macintosh, UNIX, and Windows NT mavens with their longer filenames and wonder, "Why not us?"

The problem was that the entire DOS (and Windows 3.*x*) world was built on the creaky foundations of the file allocation table (FAT) file system. The FAT file structure carved the 8.3 filename format in stone, and any attempt to change this would result in that hobgoblin of DOS functionality: complete incompatibility with all existing applications!

Not to be dissuaded by the impossible, the wizards at Microsoft were determined to build long filename support into Windows 98 and maintain compatibility with existing files. So, using an obscure loophole in the FAT file structure, they set up a new file system called the virtual file allocation table (VFAT), which broke through the 8.3 barrier. VFAT now lets you use long, sentence-like filenames (and folder names). As a bonus, for an extra level of readability, you can even use spaces, multiple periods, and the following characters:

~ ' ! @ # $ % ^ & ( ) _ - + = [ ] ; ' ,

Not only that, but, yes, Microsoft was able to maintain compatibility with existing 8.3 filenames and the 16-bit applications that require them.

So just how long can your filenames be? Well, according to Microsoft, the limit is 255 characters, but that's not right. Here's the correct rule: The total number of characters in the pathname—that's the filename plus the file's path information (drive and folder)—cannot exceed 253.

For example, if you create a file in the root folder of drive C, your path is three characters long (`c:\`), so the maximum length of the filename is 250 characters. If you create a verbosely named file and then try to copy it into, say, the `c:\WINDOWS` folder, you get an error message because the new pathname is actually 260 characters (250 for the filename plus 10 for the path).

Understanding Long Filenames

One of the keys to understanding how Windows 98 works is understanding how it converts long filenames into 8.3 filenames, so let's take a closer look. When converting a long filename to an 8.3 filename, VFAT goes through no fewer than seven steps:

1. All spaces are removed from the long filename.
2. All characters that are illegal under DOS (such as ; and =) are replaced by the underscore character (_).
3. The resulting primary name is truncated at six characters.
4. The first three characters in the extension are kept.
5. A tilde (˜) and a 1 are appended to the six-character primary name.
6. All letters in the filename are converted to uppercase.
7. VFAT checks to see whether the resulting 8.3 filename is unique in the folder. If it's not, the 1 at the end of the primary name is changed to 2. If it's still not unique, the number is incremented until a unique filename is found.

For example, consider the following 10 long filenames:

```
Testing, testing, one.txt
Testing, testing, two.txt
Testing, testing, three.txt
Testing, testing, four.txt
Testing, testing, five.txt
Testing, testing, six.txt
Testing, testing, seven.txt
Testing, testing, eight.txt
Testing, testing, nine.txt
Testing, testing, ten.txt
```

The VFAT system converts these files to the following in 8.3 format:

```
TESTIN~1.TXT
TESTIN~2.TXT
TESTIN~3.TXT
TESTIN~4.TXT
```

```
TESTIN~5.TXT
TESTIN~6.TXT
TESTIN~7.TXT
TESTIN~8.TXT
TESTIN~9.TXT
TESTI~10.TXT
```

Notice that in the last filename, VFAT truncates the primary name to five characters because the trailing number is now in double digits.

Although this conversion is an admirable attempt to maintain compatibility with older systems, the addition of two (and sometimes three) superfluous characters (the tilde and the number) at the end of the primary name isn't a great solution. The problem is that you're now down to just six (or even five) characters in the primary name, which gives you even less flexibility with respect to naming files. This is of little importance if you'll be using your files only on a Windows 98 (or Windows NT) system, but it can make a big difference if you'll be distributing your files to people still using DOS or Windows 3.*x*.

How Did They Do It?

So just how did Microsoft perform the seemingly impossible task of giving us long filenames and backward compatibility? Well, they did it by keeping track of two names for every file and directory: a regular 8.3 name and a long name. When you create a file with a long name, VFAT creates a regular FAT-compatible directory entry as well as a secondary directory entry. This new entry stores the first 26 bytes of the long filename. If the name is longer than that, VFAT just keeps adding secondary directory entries until the entire name is concatenated. The 8.3 name is stored in the initial directory entry, so complete compatibility is maintained.

Why don't older programs get confused by all these extra directory entries? Cleverly, Microsoft took advantage of an obscure property of the FAT system. In the FAT file structure, each file has a 32-byte directory entry that specifies, among other things, the file's name, its extension, the date and time it was created, and the file's attributes: read-only, hidden, and so on.

The obscurity is that, under DOS, it isn't logical for a file to have the following four attributes set: read-only, hidden, system, and volume label. In fact, DOS will just ignore any directory entry that has these four attributes set. So that's what VFAT does: It sets these four attributes on all the secondary directory entries so that they'll be ignored by all older programs.

This works for older programs because they use the built-in DOS enumeration functions to work with filenames. However, many older disk utilities (such as Norton Disk Doctor) bypass DOS and work with directory entries directly. Such utilities see VFAT's secondary directory entries as corrupted entries that aren't associated with any file. When they "fix" them, you lose your long filenames.

To avoid this problem, use only disk utilities that were made to run under VFAT. (If you don't have any VFAT-compatible utilities, you can use Microsoft's LFNBK utility to avoid problems with older disk utilities. See Chapter 17 for details.)

4

WHAT'S NEW IN
WINDOWS 98

Shortcuts (Or, Can I Get There from Here?)

When I introduced you to your new desktop abode earlier, I mentioned that one thing you can place on the desktop is the *shortcut.* In a way, a shortcut is similar to a program item in the old Windows 3.*x* Program Manager. For example, you can set up a shortcut or a program item for an application, and clicking the new object then launches the application. In both cases, the object is *not* the application itself; instead, it merely points to the file that runs the application, and if you delete the pointer, it has no effect on the application.

But shortcuts go far beyond the capabilities of program items. For one thing, you can create them anywhere you please. Unlike a program item, a shortcut is a separate file (it uses the .LNK extension), so you can store a shortcut inside any folder, including the desktop. Not only that, but shortcuts can point to many kinds of Windows 98 objects: programs, documents, disk drives, folders, Web sites—even printers. As you'll see throughout this book, this functionality gives you tremendous flexibility when you're customizing your system to suit the way you work.

RECOGNIZING A SHORTCUT

You can tell a particular icon is a shortcut by looking for a small arrow attached to the icon. For an example, check out the Connect to the Internet icon on the desktop.

A Tour of the Taskbar

One of the reasons a world in love with the DOS command line was dragged (kicking and screaming, in some cases) into the Windows way of doing things a few years back was that Windows made it so much easier to do two things: launch applications and navigate among multiple open applications. After all, what could be easier than double-clicking an icon to fire up a program or pressing Alt+Tab to cycle through several running apps?

However, after we got used to doing things this way and started pushing its limits, cracks started to form:

- The more applications we installed, the more crowded and cumbersome Program Manager became. It seemed that every install program liked to create its own program group and populate it with not only the icon that started the installed application, but also readme files, Help files, and so on. So, yes, double-clicking an icon was an easy way to start a program, but *finding* the icon became a real needle-in-a-haystack exercise.

■ Windows 3.*x*, although by no means the best multitasking operating system around, still enabled us to open lots of small- to medium-sized applications. Pressing Alt+Tab is a reasonable way to navigate two or three open programs, but it gets tiresome cycling through six or seven.

■ Windows offered no easy way to know which programs were running, which was a real problem considering that it was possible to open multiple copies of accessories such as Write and Notepad. You could minimize all your windows and adjust the active window so that it didn't cover the bottom of the screen, but that was a pain. You could use the Task List, but that was an awkward tool at best.

The Windows 98 solution to all these problems (although it's an imperfect solution, as you'll see) is the *taskbar*: the gray strip that runs across the bottom of the screen, as shown in Figure 4.10. The next few sections describe the taskbar and show you how it improves on the Windows 3.*x* tools.

FIGURE 4.10.

The Windows 98 taskbar.

Start button

Quick Launch

Taskbar

System tray

The Start Button: The Windows 98 Launch Pad

Perhaps the most recognized feature of Windows 98 is the Start button in the lower-left corner. (This isn't even remotely surprising, considering that most of Microsoft's Windows 95 marketing—both pre- and post-launch—featured the Start button in some way, and there was, of course, the famous multimillion-dollar license to use the Rolling Stones song "Start Me Up.") This is as it should be because the Start button is the doorway into most of Windows 98's features.

Several methods are available for accessing the Start button:

■ Click it with the mouse.

■ Press Ctrl+Esc.

■ If you have the Microsoft Natural Keyboard or some other Windows 98-ready keyboard, press the Windows logo key (⊞).

In each case, the Start menu appears, as shown in Figure 4.11.

FIGURE 4.11.

Clicking the Start button opens the Start menu.

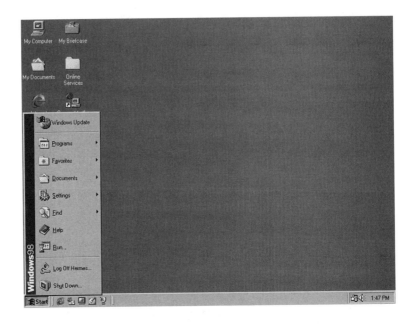

DON'T FORGET THE QUICK LAUNCH TOOLBAR

New to
98

One of the new innovations in Windows 98 is the Quick Launch toolbar beside the Start button. Each of these icons represents a feature of Windows 98, and you can load that feature simply by clicking the appropriate Quick Launch icon. Here's a summary:

Click	To
	Load Internet Explorer (see Chapter 33)
	Load Outlook Express (see Chapters 34 and 35)
	Launch Web TV for Windows (see Chapter 24)
	Minimize all windows and see the desktop (see Chapter 6)
	Load the Active Channel Viewer (see Chapter 5)

Here's a summary of the commands that appear on the Start menu:

Shut Down: You select this command when you want to either restart Windows 98 or shut down your computer. It displays the Shut Down Windows dialog box, which gives you various options (I discussed them in Chapter 3, "Start Me Up: Controlling Windows 98 Startup").

Eject PC: This command appears only on some notebook docking stations. You use this command to separate the notebook from the docking station.

Log Off *User***:** This command logs the current user off the network and redisplays the Windows login dialog box. (This command can also be used to switch users if you've set up Windows 98 with multiple user profiles.)

Run: This command is the Windows 98 equivalent of the Run command on Program Manager's File menu. It displays the Run dialog box, which lets you run programs by entering the name of the file that starts the application (you'll often need to include the appropriate drive and folder as well). It's handy if the program you want to run doesn't appear on any of the Start menu's other folders, or if you need to specify command-line parameters.

USING LONG FILENAMES IN THE RUN DIALOG BOX

In the Run dialog box, if you enter a filename that includes a space, Windows 98 generates an error. To avoid this problem, enclose the filename in quotation marks. For example, suppose you want to run WordPad with the following command:

```
c:\program files\accessories\wordpad.exe
```

In the Run dialog box, you must enter this command like so:

```
"c:\program files\accessories\wordpad.exe"
```

Alternatively, you can use the DOS 8.3 filename without quotes:

```
c:\progra~1\access~1\wordpad.exe
```

Help: This command loads the Windows Help window, which is your entry into the Windows 98 Help system.

Find: This command displays a menu that contains several tools for finding files (see Chapter 14), folders, network computers, information on the Internet, or people in LDAP databases.

Settings: Selecting this command displays a menu with three items: Control Panel (which opens the Control Panel folder, discussed later in this chapter), Printers (which opens the Printers folder, discussed in Chapter 21, "Prescriptions for Perfect Printing"), and Taskbar (which displays the Taskbar Properties dialog box, discussed in Chapter 6).

4

WHAT'S NEW IN
WINDOWS 98

Documents: This command displays the Documents folder, which contains a list of the last 15 documents you worked with in any of your applications. (In this sense, a document is any file you work with in a program. It could be a spreadsheet, a drawing, a letter, or whatever.) When you select a document from this folder, Windows launches the appropriate program and loads the document automatically.

Favorites: This command also displays a submenu. In this case, you get access to the various channels supported by the Active Desktop, as well as a list of the Web sites you've designated as your favorites (see Chapter 33).

Programs: This command opens the Programs menu, which contains shortcuts to various applications, Windows 98 components, and other folders. If you upgraded over Windows 3.*x*, you'll find your old program groups in the Programs folder. To launch a program, just click its Start menu shortcut. (I'll show you how to add more folders and shortcuts to the Start menu in Chapter 6.)

Windows Update: This command takes you to the Windows Update Web site, where you can download and install updates to device drivers, systems files, and more. See Chapter 2.

CLICKLESS FOLDER OPENING

Normally, you open a Start menu folder by clicking an item. (You can also highlight an item and press either Enter or the left-arrow key.) If you're feeling lazy, or if your clicking finger is out of commission, you can still open the folder by hovering the mouse pointer over the item for a second or two.

The Start menu's folder-within-a-folder concept is, to my mind, one of the least attractive facets of the Windows 98 interface. The problem is that you often have to drill down several folders to get to the shortcut you need. For example, if I want to run ScanDisk, I have to click Start, then Programs, then Accessories, then System Tools, and then finally ScanDisk, as shown in Figure 4.12. It's still better than opening and closing program groups, but it's far from ideal. I'll show you a few pointers for streamlining program startups in Chapters 6 and 14.

Navigating Applications with the Taskbar

After you've opened some programs or windows from the Start menu (or the desktop icons), the taskbar really comes into its own. To see why, look at Figure 4.13. Here I have three application windows open: FreeCell, WordPad, and Calculator.

Notice how the taskbar sports an icon for each running program. The taskbar tells you two things: which programs are running and which of those programs has the focus (is the active program). On the taskbar, the program with the focus is shown with a "pressed" button (Calculator in Figure 4.13). That's a nice improvement over Windows 3.*x*, because now you can tell at a glance exactly which programs and folders are open.

FIGURE 4.12.
Windows 98 often makes you jump through quite a few Start menu hoops to find the shortcut you need.

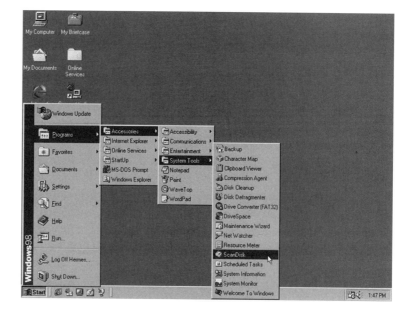

FIGURE 4.13.
Each running program has its own taskbar icon.

Running programs

Active program

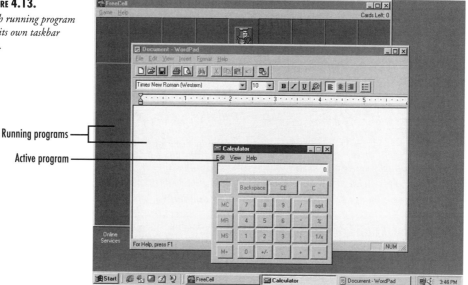

But there's more to the taskbar than that. You can also use it to navigate among running programs. To activate a window, simply click its taskbar icon, and Windows 98 immediately brings the window to the foreground and gives it the focus. This feature is particularly handy when you're working with maximized windows where you can't see any piece of the other open windows. Even when you maximize a window, *the taskbar stays visible onscreen,* so other windows remain only a mouse-click away.

GETTING THE PROGRAM NAME

One of the problems you run into is that after you've opened a few programs, Windows 98 shrinks the buttons so that they can all fit on the taskbar. As a result, some buttons are bound to show only part of the program name. To see the entire name, point the mouse at the button and leave it there for a couple of seconds. Windows 98 then displays a small banner above the button that spells out the entire program name. See Chapter 6 to learn how to give yourself more taskbar room.

A WORD ABOUT WINDOWS 98'S WINDOWS

As you can see in Figure 4.13, the windows in Windows 98 look slightly different from the ones you might be used to in Windows 3.x. For starters, the old Control menu box in the upper-left corner has been replaced by an icon. (The icon you see depends on the window.) Also, the arrangement of the buttons in the upper-right corner is different:

Click	To
[_]	Minimize the window
[□]	Maximize the window
[X]	Close the window

Yes, having the Maximize and Close buttons side by side is a bit uncomfortable at first. You'll probably shut down a few windows that you were trying to maximize—as I did— before you get used to the new layout. If you forget what a particular button does, hover the mouse pointer over the button and a ToolTip will appear with the button's name.

The taskbar isn't the only program navigation game in town. Windows 98 also lets you navigate open programs by using old-fashioned Windows 3.1 methods:

- You can cycle through the icons of the programs by pressing Alt+Tab (or Alt+Shift+Tab to cycle backward).

- If you'd prefer to see the entire application window as you cycle, try Alt+Esc (or Alt+Shift+Esc).

- If you liked the Task Manager in Windows 3.1, you can still use it in Windows 98. Unfortunately, you can't display it by double-clicking the desktop, as before. Instead, select Start|Run, type taskman.exe in the Run dialog box, and click OK.

The System Tray

The right side of the taskbar is devoted to the *system tray* (sometimes called the *notification area*). Here, Windows 98 displays icons that provide you with information and let you know when certain background processes are active. At the very least you see the current time. (Hold the mouse pointer over this icon for a second or two to see the current date. Double-click this icon to display the Date/Time Properties dialog box.) Table 4.1 lists a few of the icons you're likely to see.

Table 4.1. Some icons that Windows 98 displays in the system tray.

Icon	Chapter(s) where it's covered	Description
	25	Volume Control icon (appears only if you have a sound card in your system). Double-click this icon to display the Volume Control applet.
	17	Task Scheduler icon. Double-click this icon to display the Task Scheduler window.
	9	Resource Meter icon. Displays a graphical view of the available system resources. If you hover the mouse pointer over this icon for a second or two, Windows 98 displays the exact state of the system resources. Alternatively, you can double-click the icon to see the resources displayed in a dialog box.
	26	Modem Status icon. This icon appears when you've established a modem connection with another site. Double-click this icon to see the number of bytes sent and received during the session and the total connect time.
	35	New Mail icon. This icon appears when you receive new mail in Outlook Express.
	21	Printing icon. This icon appears while Windows 98 is processing a print job. Double-click this icon to open the printer.

continues

Table 4.1. continued

Icon	Chapter(s) where it's covered	Description
	11	AC Power icon. This icon appears on a portable computer that is connected to its AC power supply.
	11	Battery Meter icon. This icon appears on a portable computer that is running on its battery.
	7	MouseKeys icon. This icon appears if you activate the MouseKeys feature in the Accessibility Options.
	7	StickyKeys icon. This icon appears if you activate the StickyKeys feature in the Accessibility Options.
	7	FilterKeys icon. This icon appears if you activate the FilterKeys feature in the Accessibility Options.
	6	Display Settings icon. You can use this icon to view the current screen resolution and color depth, as well as to change these values.
	7	Keyboard Language icon. The current keyboard language.

Besides the icons listed in Table 4.1, some applications display their own icons in this area.

Control Panel: The Windows 98 Customization Center

If you were a Windows 3.x user, you're no doubt intimately familiar with the Control Panel, that motley collection of icons that allowed you to customize your system to suit your tastes. You'll be happy to know that the Control Panel still exists in Windows 98 and that it has been beefed up to give you even greater customization options.

To display the Control Panel folder, select Start | Settings | Control Panel. You can also get to the Control Panel folder by highlighting Control Panel in Explorer's Folders pane or by launching the Control Panel icon in My Computer. Figure 4.14 shows the Control Panel folder that appears.

I'll be taking you through each of these icons in later chapters, but Table 4.2 summarizes the available icons and describes each one's role in the Windows 98 world.

FIGURE 4.14.

As it did in Windows 3.x, Control Panel still gives you lots of customization options.

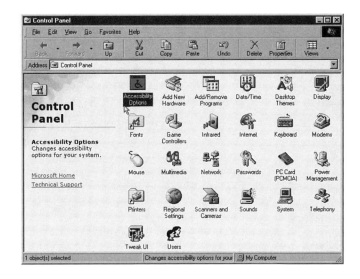

Table 4.2. Control Panel icons.

Icon	Chapter(s) where it's covered	Description
	7	Enables you to customize Windows 98 to give the disabled easier access.
	11	Runs the Add New Hardware Wizard to enable Windows 98 to detect new hardware devices on your system. You can also specify new devices manually.
	2, 15, 18	Used for installing and uninstalling applications and Windows 98 components. Also has an option for creating a Windows 98 Startup disk.
	N/A	Enables you to set the current date and time as well as specify your time zone.
	6	Enables you to specify a desktop theme (wallpaper, icons, mouse pointers, and so on).
	6	Opens the Display Properties dialog box.
	20	Enables you to view and install fonts on your system.

4

WHAT'S NEW IN WINDOWS 98

continues

Table 4.2. continued

Icon	Chapter(s) where it's covered	Description
	8	Displays the Game Controllers dialog box, which lets you modify various attributes for joysticks and other game devices.
	11	Enables you to set options for infrared devices on your system.
	33	Enables you to modify your system's Internet configuration.
	8	Displays the Keyboard Properties dialog box, which enables you to modify various keyboard attributes.
	26	Used for installing and configuring modems.
	8	Displays the Mouse Properties dialog box, which enables you to modify various attributes for the mouse and the mouse pointer.
	24, 25	Contains options for configuring multimedia properties for sound, video, MIDI, and more.
	28	Enables you to install network devices and protocols and adjust their properties.
	7, 28	Enables you to change your Windows password and set up user profiles.
	11	Used to enable PC Card sockets and modify PC Card settings.
	11	Sets various Advanced Power Management properties for portable computers.
	21	Used for installing and configuring printers.
	7	Specifies various default international settings, such as the currency symbol and date format.

Icon	Chapter(s) where it's covered	Description
	24	Setup and configuration for scanners and digital cameras.
	25	Enables you to map sounds to various Windows 98 events.
	10, 11	Gives you access to the Device Manager and enables you to establish hardware profiles.
	26	Enables you to configure dialing locations and telephony device drivers.
	6	Gives you many options for customizing the Windows 98 user interface.
	7	Provides an easier methods for setting up user profiles.

Summary

This chapter took you on a tour of Windows 98. You saw many new sights along the way, and some of what you saw went by rather quickly. Not to worry, though. I'll return to many of these topics and discuss them in greater detail later in this book.

That completes your initial look at Windows 98. From here, you get right down to some handy techniques as you run through Windows 98's extensive customization and optimization features in Part II, "Unleashing Windows 98 Customization and Optimization." First up: an in-depth look at the new Web integration and Active Desktop features.

II

PART

Unleashing Windows 98 Customization and Optimization

Web Integration and the Active Desktop

*Form and function are a unity, two sides of one coin. In order to enhance function,
appropriate form must exist or be created.*

—*Ida P. Rolf*

I don't think it's much of a stretch to say that Web integration is the most significant new
feature found in the Windows 98 package. Sure, the built-in support for USB, DVD, and other
cutting-edge hardware is welcome, and few power users will sniff at the large collection of system
tools bundled with Windows 98, and most new users will be happy that so many wizards
are on the Windows 98 team. But Web integration is more important than all these innovations
for the simple reason that it will affect almost everything you do in Windows 98:

■ As a user, Web integration fundamentally changes how you interact with the operating system.

■ As an administrator or solutions provider, Web integration offers you previously
unheard-of levels of customization and control of user's desktops.

This chapter gets you up to speed with this important new technology. I'll begin by showing
you how Web integration affects the Windows 98 interface (including how to turn Web integration
off if you don't like those interface changes). From there, I'll show you how to take
control of Web integration and use its power to customize your system like never before. I'll
then turn your attention to the Active Desktop aspect of Web integration. You'll even learn
how to create your own channels.

Why Integrate the Web?

Windows has always used the desktop as its metaphor of choice. Although the metaphor was
never perfectly realized, Microsoft continued to improve upon it with each new Windows release,
and the desktop became a true work area with the radical interface innovations introduced
with Windows 95. So why are we now moving away from the desktop and towards the
"Webtop"?

Well, there are a number of reasons. For one, the desktop metaphor just wasn't intuitive enough
for many new users. In particular, Microsoft's research consistently showed that new and inexperienced
users just didn't get double-clicking. This is particularly true when the interface
implements clicks and double-clicks inconsistently. For example, to launch a desktop icon in
Windows 95, you had to double-click the icon, but to launch an application from the Start
menu, you only had to click the item.

The inconsistencies began to pile up when the Web became the rage. Not only were there interface
inconsistencies (*everything* on a Web page requires only a single click), but also inconsistencies
in how data is managed. On the Web, you click special hypertext links to jump to
other documents and sites and then use the browser's Forward and Back buttons to retrace
your steps. The Windows interface, conversely, was purely hierarchical. That is, you'd open
one folder, open a subfolder, open another subfolder, and so on.

This wasn't a terrible thing at first, but then two important concepts came to light:

- Intranets became popular. An *intranet* is a local area network that uses Internet technologies (such as TCP/IP and HTTP). This meant that users could access network information using browsers instead of file managers.

- The Internet Explorer 3.0 browser pioneered the idea of the *active document container*. This meant that the browser could display not only Web pages, but also non-HTML documents (such as an Excel workbook) and folder contents.

In other words, the differences between what was local and what was remote started to blur. However, users still had two completely different ways to access remote and local data.

Perhaps the final nail in the desktop's coffin was the realization by many system administrators that the Internet's technologies could be used to solve some pressing problems locally. An intranet with a browser-based front-end was a great way to disseminate information to employees and to keep that information up-to-date. New technologies such as Java, scripting, and streamed audio and video feeds were easily implemented in this new TCP/IP-based environment. The problem, though, is that much of the support for these technologies was being built into the browser. At some point, it became obvious that this support could and should be built into the operating system itself.

In sum, there are four reasons why we need to move away from the desktop metaphor:

- Interface inconsistencies: clicking versus double-clicking
- The blurring of local and remote resources
- Resource access inconsistencies: a hyperlink structure versus a hierarchical structure
- The need to embed support for Internet technologies with the operating system

Web integration is Microsoft's answer to all of these issues:

- The interface becomes consistent (double-clicking is almost eliminated).
- Remote and local resources can be accessed from the same application.
- You can access all resources using a consistent, browser-like interface (the underlying structure is still hierarchical, but you don't have to approach it that way).
- The operating system supports Internet technologies right out of the box.

And as you'll see later in this chapter, Web integration not only solves existing problems, but adds powerful new functionality to the system. For example, you can view the desktop and any folder as though they were Web pages. This means you can use simple HTML techniques to customize these items at will.

Working with Web Integration

Now that you understand why Microsoft implemented Web integration in Windows 98, let's see how it works and how you can control it.

How Web Integration Affects the Windows 98 Interface

When Web integration is turned on, it produces the following changes in the Windows 98 interface:

Clickable items resemble hyperlinks: When you hover your mouse pointer over certain items, Windows 98 turns the item's text blue and underlines it. This makes the item resemble a hypertext link in a Web page, and it gives you a visual indication that the item is "clickable." (That is, something will happen if you click the item.)

One-click launching: Whether it's an icon on the desktop, a file in Explorer, or a list box item in a dialog box, you can launch everything in Windows 98 with a single click. There are now very few areas where you still need to double-click anything.

ONE-CLICK LAUNCHING CAN BE DANGEROUS

After you get used to it, launching programs and documents with a single click is definitely an easier way to work, and it certainly saves wear and tear on your clicking finger. However, you need to be cautious until it becomes second nature. Early in my Web integration career I tried to select a REG file that included all the Registry information from another computer (see Chapter 12, "Getting to Know the Windows 98 Registry," to learn about REG files). Unfortunately, I clicked the file and thus "launched" it, which meant that it imported all the other computer's Registry settings into my computer's Registry, a nightmare from which it took me days to recover.

No-click selecting: To select an item, just hover your mouse pointer over the item. After a second or two, Windows 98 will highlight the item to indicate that it's selected. You can also select multiple items without having to click a thing:

■ To select multiple, contiguous items, move the mouse pointer over the first item until it's selected. Then hold down Shift and move the mouse pointer over the last item. Windows 98 will then select all the items between and including the first and last items.

■ To select multiple, noncontiguous items, hold down Ctrl and move the mouse pointer over each item in turn. Remember to pause briefly over each item to give Windows 98 time to select it.

Folders become Web pages: Web integration means that you can view any folder as though it was a Web page. As you can see in Figure 5.1, this gives the folder a nicer look and it also provides built-in functionality for displaying descriptions of the folder's contents.

The Active Desktop becomes available: The Active Desktop is really an HTML-based layer that sits underneath the normal icon layer that you're used to seeing. The Active Desktop can therefore host anything that you could put inside a Web page, including images, Java applets, Web page scripts, ActiveX controls, and lots more.

FIGURE 5.1.

Web integration enables you to view your folders as though they were Web pages.

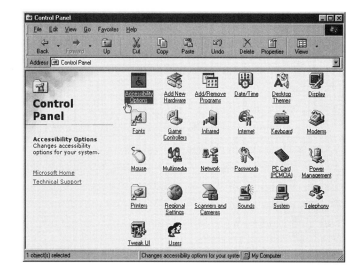

Turning Web Integration On and Off

Microsoft made it easy to turn Web integration off and on at will. To do so, select the Start | Settings | Folders Options. You see the Folder Options dialog box, shown in Figure 5.2. Two of the options in the Folder tab toggle Windows 98 between Web integration and the old Windows 95 interface:

Web style: This is the Web integration option. When you activate this option, Windows 98 asks if you want to use the single-click method for opening an icon. Activate Yes or No, as appropriate, and then click OK.

Classic style: This is the interface used in Windows 95. Selecting this option means you return to double-clicking to launch icons and files and single-clicking to select objects.

FIGURE 5.2.

Use the Folder Options dialog box to toggle Web integration on and off.

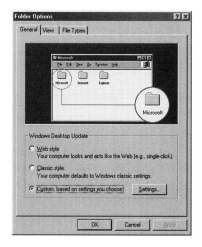

The Folder tab also sports a third option: Custom, based on settings you choose. This option enables you to create a custom configuration somewhere between Web integration and the "classic" interface. If you activate this option and then click the Settings button that becomes enabled, you see the Custom Settings dialog box shown in Figure 5.3. Here's a rundown of the controls in this dialog box:

Active Desktop: These options enable you to turn the Active Desktop on and off. See "Customizing the Active Desktop," later in this chapter.

Open each folder in the same window: Activate this option if you prefer to navigate folders by using a single window that changes with each opened folder.

Open each folder in its own window: If you prefer to leave the windows open for the previous folders you display, activate this option.

For all folders with HTML content: If you activate this option, Windows 98 displays every folder window as a Web page. (Folders are not shown as Web pages in Windows Explorer.)

Only for folders where I select "as Web Page" (View menu): Activating this settings means that you have to display each folder as a Web page by hand.

Single-click to open an item (point to select): Activating this option enables the one-click launching and no-click selecting feature. Windows 98 also enables the following option buttons:

> **Underline icon titles consistent with my browser settings:** If you turn on this option, Windows 98 formats all clickable objects with the current browser settings for displaying links (the default is underlined with blue text).

> **Underline icon titles only when I point at them:** In this case, Windows 98 applies the link formatting to a clickable object only when you point at that object.

Double-click to open an item (single-click to select): Activate this option to use the "classic" mouse techniques for launching and selecting.

Toggling Web Page View On and Off

With Web integration on, the default settings for folders are as follows:

■ All folder windows are shown in Web page view.

■ Folders displayed within Explorer show only the folder contents.

Either way, you can easily toggle the Web page view on or off for any folder by toggling the View | as Web Page command on or off. Figure 5.4 shows a folder displayed as a Web page in Explorer. This view is particularly handy if you're running Explorer without showing the file details and with file extensions turned off. If you want to find out more about a file, select it. Explorer displays the file data on the left side of the contents pane: the filename with extension, the document type, the date and time the file was last modified, and the size of the file.

FIGURE 5.3.
Use this dialog box to set up a custom folder configuration.

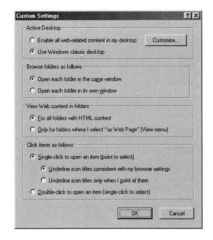

FIGURE 5.4.
Use the View | as Web Page command to toggle the Web page view on and off.

Select a file to see the file details

Creating Custom Web Views for Your Folders

The Web view is an interesting innovation with features that should appeal to both novices and power users. But the Web view becomes truly useful when you realize that the view is fully customizable, from simple tweaks, such as changing the folder background, to full-blown renovations using HTML and other Web technologies. There is no end to the uses to which this level of customization can be put:

■ Display your corporate logo in each folder.

■ Add custom links for technical support, key corporate sites, or email addresses.

5

WEB INTEGRATION
AND THE ACTIVE
DESKTOP

- Rearrange the folder layout. For example, you could create a margin on the left side of the folder window and use that margin to display messages, graphics, links, and so on.

- Trap folder events (such as hovering the mouse over an object) and set up custom responses to those events (such as displaying help information).

The next two sections show you how to customize the Web view for a folder.

Changing the Folder Background

The simplest way to give a folder a new look is to specify a custom background image. Here are the steps to follow:

1. Open the folder you want to customize.

2. Select View | Customize this Folder. Windows 98 loads the Customize this Folder wizard.

3. Activate Choose a background picture and click Next >.

4. In the next wizard dialog box, use the list box to choose a background image (see Figure 5.5). If the image you want resides outside the mail Windows 98 folder, click Browse and select the image you want from the Open dialog box that appears.

FIGURE 5.5.

Use this dialog to choose the background picture and text colors.

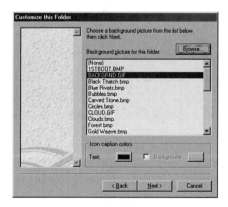

5. Use the controls in the Icon caption colors group to set the text color of the folder's icon titles.

6. Click Next >.

7. Click Finish. Windows 98 applies the custom background to the folder (see Figure 5.6).

FIGURE 5.6.
A folder with a background image.

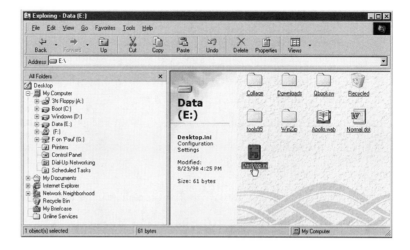

CUSTOM BACKGROUND SETTINGS

When you apply a custom background to a folder, Windows 98 creates a hidden initialization file called `Desktop.ini` within the folder. This file stores the data for the custom background and text colors.

For the background, you see a line similar to the following:

`IconArea_Image=C:\WINDOWS\BACKGRND.GIF`

If you modified the text colors, you see the following lines:

`IconArea_Text=0x00rrggbb`
`IconArea_TextBackground=0x00rrggbb`

Here, *rrggbb* is an RGB color code where *rr* is the red value, *gg* is the green value, and *bb* is the blue value. These are hexadecimal values between 0 and FF.

Creating an HTML Document to Customize a Folder

Modifying the folder background certainly adds a bit of pizzazz to a folder, but there is a lot more you can do, as you'll see in this section and the next.

Before continuing, you need to understand just what you're dealing with when you display a folder in Web view. At first it might seem that Windows 98 is only displaying the folder *as though* it was a Web page, but that's not the case. No, you really are looking at an honest-to-goodness HTML document. The folder contents are displayed courtesy of a special ActiveX object, but the rest of the "page" is standard (albeit advanced) HTML. This means that you can customize any folder to your heart's content just by modifying the underlying HTML document. You have two ways to proceed:

■ Use Notepad to modify the folder's HTML document.

■ Use Windows 98's HTML folder template to modify the layout of all the folders on your system.

Note that I don't recommend modifying a folder template using FrontPage Express because it doesn't understand some of the more advanced features of the template. This means FrontPage Express doesn't show the template properly, which makes it difficult to modify the template safely.

The next two sections take you through both the techniques mentioned above.

Modifying a Folder's HTML Document in Notepad

If you're comfortable with HTML, the easiest way to modify a folder's HTML document is to edit the HTML tags directly using Notepad. There are three ways to go about this:

■ In the Customize This Folder dialog box, activate Create or edit an HTML document and click Next >. When Windows 98 tells you that you're about to start the template editor, click Next > again to open the template within Notepad.

■ Head for the Web folder, which is under your main Windows 98 folder. Copy the Folder.htt file and paste it inside the folder you want to customize.

■ Start a new text file in the folder and name it Folder.htt.

> **WHERE TO GET HTML KNOW-HOW**
>
> This section assumes that you're familiar with HTML tags. If you're not, Chapter 37, "Web Page Publishing with Windows 98," tells you just about everything you need to know. I don't cover scripting, however, and the default HTML folder template uses JavaScript to interact with the Dynamic HTML objects with the page. I'd suggest picking up a copy of the book *Dynamic Web Publishing Unleashed* (Sams.net, 1997).

For the latter two techniques, you need to open Folder.htt in Notepad by following these steps:

1. Right-click the file and click Open With in the context menu.

2. In the program list that appears, highlight NOTEPAD.

3. If you always want to edit HTT files in Notepad, leave the Always use this program to open this file check box activated.

4. Click OK.

All HTML documents have a header section (between the `<head>` and `</head>` tags) and a body section (between the `<body>` and `</body>` tags), and the folder template is no exception. Let's begin by examining the first half of the body, shown in Figure 5.7.

FIGURE 5.7.

The body section of the HTML folder template.

The banner across the top of a My Computer folder

The information panel on the left side of the folder

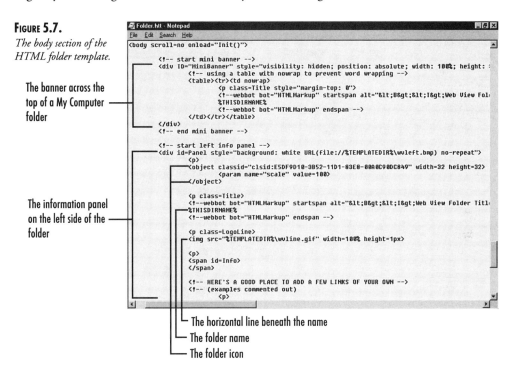

The horizontal line beneath the name
The folder name
The folder icon

As pointed out in Figure 5.7, we can discern two distinct sections in this part of the body.

The first section comprises the first set of `<div>` and `</div>` tags (`ID="MiniBanner"`), and it represents the banner that runs across the top of the folder window in Web page view. Note that this banner appears only when you open the folder within a My Computer window (instead of within Windows Explorer). The name of the folder is given by the `%THISDIRNAME%` environment variable.

The second section is the second set of `<div>` and `</div>` tags (`ID=Panel`), and it represents the information panel on the left side of the Web page folder view. This section contains the following elements:

- An `<object>` tag displays the folder icon.
- The `%THISDIRNAME%` environment variable displays the name of the folder.
- A `<span>` tag sets up the spot where Windows 98 displays prompts and the information for each highlighted file, as you'll see a bit later.

■ The file then suggests that that the next area is "a good place to add a few links of your own" (see Figure 5.8) To do this, edit the sample links accordingly and then remove the two comment lines:

```
<!-- (examples commented out)
-->
```

FIGURE 5.8.

The second half of the body.

Add your own links here ————

Thumbnail viewer ————

Status message ————

Folder-based media ————

The FileList control ————

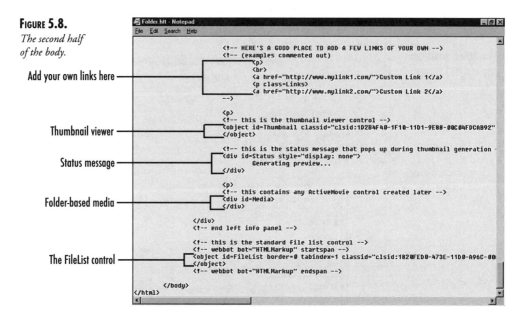

■ Another `<object>` tag adds the Thumbnail Viewer control. This is an ActiveX control that displays the contents of some files, particularly images, HTML documents, movies, and sound files.

■ Another `<div>` tag (`ID=Status`) sets up an area for displaying status messages while generating the thumbnails.

■ The last `<div>` tag (`ID=Media`) sets up an area that displays an ActiveMovie control. You get either a movie player (if the highlighted file is a movie or animation file) or a sound player (if the highlighted file is a sound file).

The rest of the body uses an `<object>` tag to add another ActiveX control, called `FileList`. This control displays the contents of the folder.

The bulk of the header consists of several sets of `<script>` and `</script>` tags, each with a number of JavaScript procedures. The first `<script>` set sets up a number of variables. For example, the `L_Prompt_Text` variable holds the prompt text displayed within the information panel (the default is "Select an item to view its description"). The procedures in this section perform various initialization and housekeeping chores.

The main programming work is performed by the JavaScript statements contained with the following <script> tag:

```
<script language="JavaScript" for="FileList"
➥event="SelectionChanged">
```

The purpose of this script is to handle the SelectionChanged event for the FileList object. That is, each time you select a different object in the folder, Windows 98 executes this procedure. Here's a summary of what happens:

1. The variable fldr is assigned to the Folder property of FileList.

2. The information panel is cleared of any pending status messages, thumbnails, and media players.

3. The variable items is assigned to the SelectedItems().Item(0) property of FileList. This is the selected object.

4. The object's file type, last modified date, and file size are all gathered by slightly different calls to the GetDetailsOf function. Each new piece of data is appended to the text variable.

5. In Dynamic HTML, the innerHTML property represents all the HTML tags and text within an object. The procedure now sets the innerHTML property of the Info object (explained earlier) to the value of the text variable.

6. The script finishes by creating the thumbnail for the file, if necessary.

Again, feel free to play with this code. You could, for example, examine the filename returned by GetDetailsOf and display a special message for a given file (such as instructions for a Setup file).

SPECIFYING A DIFFERENT NAME OR PATH

By default, Windows 98 looks for a file named Folder.htt in the current folder. However, this behavior can be controlled via the following lines in the folder's Desktop.ini file:

```
PersistFile=Folder.htt
PersistMoniker=file://Folder.htt
```

You can use the PersistFile entry to change the default name for the folder's HTML document. You can use the PersistMoniker entry to change the default location for the file.

Working with Web Page Folder Templates

You've seen so far that Windows 98's HTML folder documents offer powerful customization choices. This is downright revolutionary because these customizations are based for the most part on existing HTML standards. (Microsoft has submitted Dynamic HTML as a potential HTML standard and, as of this writing, it looks as if the World Wide Web Consortium will agree.)

5

WEB INTEGRATION AND THE ACTIVE DESKTOP

The problem, though, is that it's a pain to have to customize folders individually. If you set up your HTML document correctly, you could get away with copying `Folder.htt` into your other folders, but that's still a lot of work.

Fortunately, Windows 98 also supports Web page folder *templates*. A template is a sort of global HTML document that Windows 98 uses as the default if it doesn't find a `Folder.htt` file within a folder. You find the template in the Web subfolder of your main Windows 98 folder. This file is identical to the `Folder.htt` you looked at in the last section, so you can customize it in the same way.

The Web folder actually has several HTT files, eight of which you may find useful:

> **Controlp.htt:** This is the HTML document that Windows 98 uses to display the Control Panel folder as a Web page.
>
> **Dialup.htt:** This is the HTML document that Windows 98 uses to display the Dial-Up Networking folder as a Web page.
>
> **Mycomp.htt:** This is the HTML document that Windows 98 uses to display the My Computer folder as a Web page.
>
> **Nethood.htt:** This is the HTML document that Windows 98 uses to display the Network Neighborhood folder as a Web page.
>
> **Printers.htt:** This is the HTML document that Windows 98 uses to display the Printers folder as a Web page.
>
> **Recycle.htt:** This is the HTML document that Windows 98 uses to display the Recycle Bin folder as a Web page.
>
> **Safemode.htt:** This is the HTML document that Windows 98 uses to display the Active Desktop as a Web page during safe mode.
>
> **Schedule.htt:** This is the HTML document that Windows 98 uses to display the Scheduled Tasks folder as a Web page.

WEB VIEW STYLE SHEET

Windows 98 uses a global style sheet within all of its HTML folder templates. If you're familiar with style sheets, you can modify this file to further customize the Web view. Look for the file named `Webview.css` in the Web subfolder.

Customizing the Active Desktop

A big part of this Web integration technology is, of course, the Active Desktop. As with the Web view for folders, Microsoft has again incorporated standard Internet technologies to come up with a completely new desktop paradigm. The Active Desktop actually consists of three layers:

Icon layer: This is the "top" layer and it displays the standard desktop icons (My Computer, My Documents, and so on) and whatever shortcuts you've added to the desktop. This is, in other words, the desktop you came to know and (possibly) love in Windows 95.

HTML desktop background layer: This layer sits underneath the icon layer, so in that sense it's a lot like desktop wallpaper. This is wallpaper on steroids, however, because this layer is really an HTML document. That's right: your desktop is now a Web page and can display all Web page content, including images, links, applets, and more. As you'll learn a bit later (see "Changing the HTML Desktop Wallpaper"), you can specify any local or intranet-based HTML document as your HTML desktop background.

Desktop items layer: This layer sits between the icon layer and the desktop background layer. Its purpose is to act as a container for the various *desktop items* you can plop onto the desktop. These items include other Web pages, Java applets, ActiveX controls, and images. Because these items aren't embedded within a Web page, they can be sized and moved on the desktop to achieve the look you want. See "Adding Desktop Items," later in this section.

Toggling the Active Desktop On and Off

As with the other interface changes wrought by Web integration, you can turn the Active Desktop on or off at will. Note, however, that the HTML desktop background layer and the desktop items layer are two pieces of the same puzzle and can be turned on and off only in tandem.

To toggle the Active Desktop on or off, first right-click an empty part of the desktop and then click Active Desktop in the context menu that appears. Toggling the View As Web Page command on and off will turn the Active Desktop on and off (see Figure 5.9).

Changing the HTML Desktop Wallpaper

With the Active Desktop enabled, you can now customize the HTML desktop wallpaper layer. You have two ways to approach this:

- Customize the default desktop Web page.
- Specify a Web page that already exists locally or on your intranet, or that you create yourself.

Customizing the Default Desktop Web Page

Windows 98's default HTML document for the desktop is `Windows98.htm`, which you find in the Web\Wallpaper subfolder of your main Windows 98 folder. This is a regular HTML document (see Figure 5.10) that sets a background color and displays the Windows 98 logo, which is also set up as a link to the Windows 98 Web site.

5

WEB INTEGRATION AND THE ACTIVE DESKTOP

Figure 5.9.

You need to activate the View As Web Page command to enable the Activate Desktop.

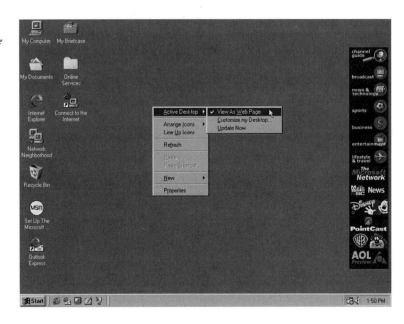

So modifying the HTML desktop wallpaper layer is a simple matter of editing this file with your own tags. To update the desktop after you've saved your changes, right-click the desktop and then click Refresh in the shortcut menu.

Figure 5.10.

`Windows98.htm` *is Windows 98's default desktop Web page.*

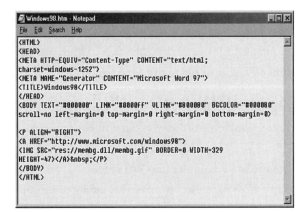

Specifying a Custom Desktop Web Page

It should be obvious by now that you can also customize the HTML desktop wallpaper layer by creating a custom Web page. Here are a few things to think about as you create the page:

■ You can specify only a local page or a page on your network (intranet). You can't use pages that reside on the Internet.

■ Along similar lines, use either local paths or UNC network paths for things like images and videos. If you use URLs, Windows 98 won't display the resources.

■ Keep the layout and dimensions of the desktop in mind as you construct the page. Set up your content so that it isn't obscured by the desktop icons. Also, there's no way to scroll down or to the right, so make sure your content fits inside the desktop area.

■ The Web page doesn't get interpreted by a Web server, so don't include server-specific tags (such as INCLUDE tags).

TURNING OFF DESKTOP ICONS

If you like, you can tell Windows 98 not to display the desktop icons when you view the desktop as a Web page. To do this, select Start | Settings | Folder Options, and then select the View tab in the properties sheet that appears. Activate the Hide icons when desktop is viewed as a Web page check box and then click OK.

When your page is ready to roll, follow these steps to set it up as your desktop Web page:

1. Open the Display Properties dialog box and select the Background tab, as described earlier.

2. Click Browse.

3. Use the Browse dialog box to highlight the Web page you want to use, and then click Open.

4. Click OK.

EASIER PAGE SELECTION

You can avoid having to browse for your desktop Web page by copying or moving the HTML file to the Web\Wallpaper folder. This way, the file will appear in the Wallpaper list in the Background tab.

Adding Desktop Items

As I mentioned in the last section, you have to be a bit careful when it comes to setting up a custom desktop Web page, because you don't want all those icons getting in the way. One way around this is to work with the desktop items layer. You can still add the same type of content—Web pages, ActiveX controls, Java applets, images, and so on—but each item sits inside its own window (which is actually an instance of the Web browser or, more specifically, the WebBrowser ActiveX control). This enables you to resize the items and move them anywhere on the desktop you like. (Note, however, that the regular desktop icons will always display on top of these HTML items.)

5

WEB INTEGRATION
AND THE ACTIVE
DESKTOP

To add items to the desktop, first open the Display Properties dialog box and select the Web tab, shown in Figure 5.11.

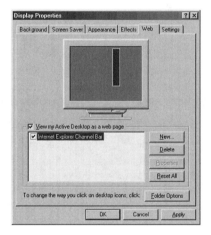

Now click the New button. Windows 98 asks whether you want to connect to Microsoft's Active Desktop Gallery Web site. This page contains various items you can place on your desktop, including a stock ticker, a weather map, and more. If you want to see what's on the Active Desktop Gallery site, click Yes and you are whisked to a page similar to the one shown in Figure 5.12.

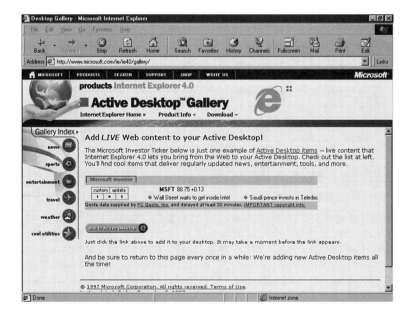

Click a category in the Gallery Index and then click one of the links to see an example of the desktop item. You'll likely also see some kind of "Add to Active Desktop" button. Click that button and you see the Add item to Active Desktop dialog box, shown in Figure 5.13. What's happening here is that you're "subscribing" to the item, which means it will update on a regular schedule. (I'll describe subscriptions in detail when I discuss Internet Explorer in Chapter 33, "Exploring the Web with Internet Explorer.") Click OK to download the item.

FIGURE 5.13.

You see this dialog box when you add an item to your desktop.

Alternatively, you can bypass the Active Desktop Gallery and add new desktop items by hand. When Windows 98 prompts you to go to the Gallery, click No. In this case, you see the New Active Desktop Item dialog box, shown in Figure 5.14. Enter the URL of the resource you want to add and then click OK.

FIGURE 5.14.

Use this dialog box to specify the URL of the desktop item you want to add.

So how do you add images, applets, ActiveX controls, and the like? Well, you can't add them directly. Instead, you must wrap the object inside an HTML document and then add that document to the desktop. If you want to display just a Java applet, for example, you'd include only the appropriate <APPLET> tag inside the page. Note, however, that you get more control over how the item is displayed on the desktop if you also create a Channel Definition Format (CDF) file. This enables you to specify that you're dealing with a desktop item (by setting the USAGE value to "DesktopComponent") and also to specify the correct height and width for the item.

Working with Desktop Items

Figure 5.15 shows a desktop with a couple of items added from the Active Desktop Gallery. Notice that when you pass the mouse over an item, the item sprouts a border. You can use the following techniques to work with the item:

- Drag a border to resize the item.
- Drag the top border to move the item.
- Click the arrow in the upper-left corner to display the Control menu.
- Click the Close button in the upper-right corner to remove the item from the desktop.

FIGURE 5.15.

A desktop with a couple of items.

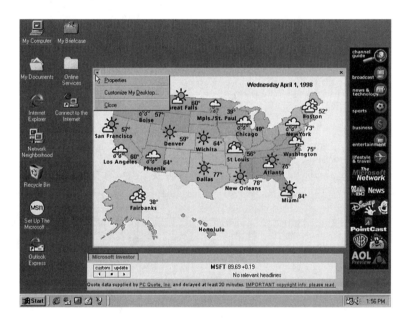

You can also work with your items from the Web tab in the Display Properties dialog box. As you can see in Figure 5.16, Windows 98 displays each installed item in the Items on the Active Desktop list. Here's a list of the techniques you can use to work with the items from this tab:

- To modify an item's properties (such as the subscription schedule), highlight the item and then click Properties.
- To disable an item, deactivate its check box.
- To remove an item from the list, highlight it and click Delete. When Windows 98 asks whether you're sure, click Yes.

■ To disable all the desktop items (as well as the underlying desktop Web page),
deactivate the View my Active Desktop as a web page check box. When you click OK,
Windows 98 may warn you that the current wallpaper can be shown only if the Active
Desktop is enabled. Click No to disable the wallpaper.

Figure 5.16.

*The Web tab lists all
the installed desktop
items.*

Summary

This chapter introduced you to the key new feature in Windows 98: Web integration. I began
by explaining the rationale behind integrating Windows and the Web. From there, I showed
you how to work with Web integration, including how to turn it on and off, how to view a
folder as a Web page, and how to create custom Web page views for your folders. I then turned
to the Active Desktop and showed you how to work with the desktop Web page and how to
add desktop items.

Here's a list of chapters in which you'll find related information:

■ Some of the settings you saw in this chapter are controlled by certain Registry values.
I'll tell you about them in Chapter 13, "A Few Good Hacks: Some Useful Registry
Tweaks."

■ For more ways to customize folders in Windows 98, see Chapter 14, "File and Folder
Tricks and Techniques."

■ I show you how to get on the Internet in Chapter 32, "Windows 98 and the
Internet."

■ To learn how to use Internet Explorer, see Chapter 33, "Exploring the Web with
Internet Explorer."

■ Most of the information you need to properly customize Web integration and the
Active Desktop can be found in Chapter 37, "Web Page Publishing with Windows
98." Here, you'll learn about HTML, FrontPage Express, and the Channel Definition
Format.

5

**Web Integration
and the Active
Desktop**

Customizing the Taskbar, Start Menu, and Display

Whoso would be a man, must be a nonconformist.

—Ralph Waldo Emerson

Microsoft spent countless hours and untold millions of dollars testing and retesting the Windows 98 interface in its usability labs. It's important, however, to remember that Windows 98 is Microsoft's operating system for the masses. With an expected installed base running in the tens of millions, it's only natural that the Windows UI would incorporate lots of "lowest-common-denominator" thinking. So, in the end, you have an interface that most people find easy to use most of the time; an interface that's skewed toward accommodating neophytes and the newly digital; an interface designed for a "typical" computer user, whoever the heck he or she is.

In other words, unless you consider yourself a typical user (and your purchase of this book proves otherwise), Windows 98 in its right-out-of-the-box getup won't be right for you. Fortunately, you'll find no shortage of options and programs that will help you remake Windows 98 in your own image, and that's just what this chapter shows you how to do. After all, you weren't produced by a cookie cutter, so why should your operating system look like it was?

Tweaking the Taskbar

The taskbar is so convenient and such an elegantly simple idea that it might be worth the price of Windows 98 admission all by itself. Sure, if I'm switching constantly back and forth between a couple of applications, nothing's faster than a quick slam of the Alt+Tab "cool switch." But when it comes to navigating several open programs, or just knowing what's up and running, the taskbar can't be beat.

That's not to say it's perfect, however. For example, if you have too many windows open, the taskbar buttons become too small, and you can't make out the window titles; and folks with small screens or video cards that have limited resolution might resent giving up a strip of screen real estate.

Fortunately, these quibbles are easily dealt with because the taskbar is quite flexible. Let's look at some of the features that make the taskbar such a tractable tool.

Sizing the Taskbar

If you don't mind giving up even more screen acreage, there's a sure cure for taskbar button crunch: Make the taskbar bigger. For example, take a look at the taskbar shown in Figure 6.1. With 10 windows open (not an outrageous number), the taskbar buttons become too small to read, so the taskbar itself loses much of its convenience.

FIGURE 6.1.

Taskbar overpopulation: too many windows and too little space.

Surprisingly, however, the taskbar's height isn't fixed at a single row of icons. You can, if you like, expand the taskbar to take up approximately half the screen. On a 640×480 screen, for example, this gives you a maximum of 9 rows; a 1280×1024 display handles a whopping 20 rows.

To try this, follow these steps:

1. Move the mouse pointer to the top edge of the taskbar; the pointer turns into a two-headed arrow.
2. Drag the edge of the taskbar up until the second row appears. This will give you the Quick Launch toolbar on the top row and the taskbar on the bottom row.
3. Drag the left edge of the taskbar and drop it just to the right of the Quick Launch toolbar. This positions the two toolbars side-by-side.

Figure 6.2 shows the same taskbar displayed with two rows. As you can see, the individual buttons are much easier to read.

FIGURE 6.2.
The taskbar displayed with two rows of icons.

HIDE QUICK LAUNCH

Another way to squeeze out a bit more room for the taskbar is to hide the Quick Launch toolbar. To do so, right-click an empty spot on the taskbar. In the context menu that appears, click Toolbars and then click Quick Launch to deactivate it.

VIEWING TASKBAR BUTTON TEXT

Not interested in making the desktop any smaller than it actually is? You can still figure out the full window title that appears on any taskbar button. Just let the mouse pointer linger over a button. After a second or two, a small banner appears that spells out the entire window title.

Moving the Taskbar

As you saw in the last section, the position of the taskbar isn't set in stone either. Although its default position is the bottom edge of the screen, you can move it to the top edge, the left edge, or the right edge. For example, when I'm writing, I like to maximize the vertical area of my word processor's window so that I can see as much text as possible at a glance. One easy way to gain more vertical space is to move the taskbar to one of the side edges.

To move the taskbar, position the mouse pointer over an empty part of the taskbar. Now drag the pointer to the edge of the screen where you want to position the taskbar. As you approach the edge, the taskbar leaps into place. Also note that you can size the taskbar from any edge.

Figure 6.3 shows the taskbar on the left edge of the screen. Notice how the desktop icons are shifted to the right to remain visible.

FIGURE 6.3.

You can move the taskbar to any edge of the screen.

Displaying and Creating Taskbar Toolbars

In Windows 98, the taskbar acts somewhat like a mini-application. The purpose of this "application" is to display a button for each running program and to enable you to switch from one program to another. And like most applications these days, the taskbar also has its own toolbars which, in this case, enable you to launch programs and documents. The Windows 98 taskbar comes with four default toolbars:

Address: This toolbar contains a text box into which you can type Internet addresses. When you press Enter, Windows 98 loads the address into Internet Explorer. (In other words, this toolbar works just like the Address Bar used by Internet Explorer.)

Links: This toolbar contains several buttons that link you to predefined Internet sites. This is the same as the Links toolbar in Internet Explorer.

Quick Launch: This is a collection of one-click icons that launch Internet Explorer, Outlook Express, TV Viewer, and the Internet Explorer channels. There's also an icon to clear the desktop (see the sidebar, below).

Desktop: This toolbar contains all the desktop icons.

To toggle these toolbars on and off, first right-click an empty spot on the taskbar. In the context menu that appears, click Toolbars and then click the toolbar you want to work with.

EASY ACCESS TO THE DESKTOP

The desktop is a handy place to put shortcuts to folders, documents, and applications, and as you'll see a bit later, a quick right-click on the desktop can quickly get you to the Display Properties dialog box. The problem, though, is that you might not always have access to the desktop, because one or more maximized windows might stand in your way.

One solution would be to right-click an empty area of the taskbar and select Minimize All Windows to clear the desktop; this works, but it's a bit of a pain. A better solution is to click the Show Desktop button in the Quick Launch toolbar.

 The Show Desktop icon

New to
98

Taskbar Toolbar Options

After you've displayed a toolbar, there are a number of options you can work with to customize the look of the toolbar. Right-click an empty section of the toolbar and then click one of the following commands:

View: This command displays a submenu with two options: Large and Small. These commands determine the size of the toolbar's icons.

Show Text: This command toggles the icon titles on and off.

Refresh: This command refreshes the toolbar's contents.

Show Title: This command toggles the toolbar title (displayed to the left of the icons) on and off.

Creating New Taskbar Toolbars

Besides the predefined taskbar toolbars, you can also create new toolbars that display the contents of any folder on your system. Here are the steps to follow:

1. Right-click an empty spot on the toolbar to display the content menu.
2. Click Toolbars | New Toolbar. Windows 98 displays the New Toolbar dialog box, shown in Figure 6.4.
3. Use the folder list provided to highlight the folder you want to display as a toolbar.
4. Click OK. Windows 98 creates the new toolbar.

Figure 6.5 shows the Control Panel folder as a toolbar. Notice that I've turned off the icon titles (that is, I deactivated the Show Text command).

FIGURE 6.4.

Use the New Toolbar dialog box to choose the folder you want to display as a taskbar toolbar.

FIGURE 6.5.

The Control Panel folder as a taskbar toolbar.

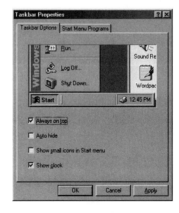

Taskbar Properties

The taskbar is a Windows 98 object, so it has various properties you can set for some extra customization fun. To check out these properties, try either of the following methods:

■ Select Start | Settings | Taskbar & Start Menu.

■ Right-click an empty part of the taskbar and select Properties from the context menu.

Windows 98 displays the Taskbar Properties dialog box, shown in Figure 6.6.

FIGURE 6.6.

Use the Taskbar Properties dialog box to set a few taskbar options.

Customizing the Taskbar, Start Menu, and Display

CHAPTER 6

147

6

THE TASKBAR,
START MENU, AND
DISPLAY

The Taskbar Options tab presents several check boxes that control the behavior of the taskbar. After you've made your selections, you can put them into effect either by clicking the Apply button (to see the effect of the selected options without dismissing the dialog box) or by clicking OK. Here are the options that affect the taskbar:

Always on top: In Windows 3.*x*, a maximized window took up the entire screen, lock, stock, and barrel. In Windows 98, however, a maximized window consumes only the entire desktop; the taskbar remains visible. If you'd prefer to hand over all the screen to your applications, deactivate the Always on top check box.

DISPLAYING THE TASKBAR

With Always on top deactivated, a maximized window will cover the taskbar. To display the taskbar again, press Ctrl+Esc (or the Windows logo key) to display both the taskbar and the Start menu and press Esc by itself to close the Start menu.

Auto hide: This option provides an alternative method for giving your windows extra room on the desktop. When you activate the Auto hide check box, the taskbar sinks below the bottom edge of the screen (assuming, of course, that the taskbar is still situated on the bottom edge). All that remains is a thin gray line. Move the mouse pointer over this line, however, and the taskbar slides back into view; move the pointer off the taskbar, and the taskbar resumes its position below the screen's horizon. In other words, the taskbar appears onscreen only when you need it.

ADJUSTING THE WIDTH OF THE TASKBAR'S GRAY LINE

The width of the gray line that the taskbar leaves behind when Auto hide is activated is the same as the width of the window borders. I'll show you how to adjust this width later (see the section "Display Settings: A Desktop to Call Your Own").

Show small icons in Start menu: If you activate this check box, Windows 98 displays the Start menu and its folders with smaller icons. This reduces the overall size of each menu and makes the menus marginally easier to navigate. The trade-off is that the icons are a bit harder to see, and the individual items are closer together, making them a slightly harder target to hit with the mouse.

Show Clock: This check box toggles the Clock in the lower-right corner on and off.

THE TASKBAR'S ACTIONS

If the taskbar is an object, what are its actions? Well, you saw a few of them already when I showed you how to work with the toolbars. To see the others, right-click an empty part of the taskbar to display the context menu. Here's a review of the other options in this menu:

Cascade Windows: This command arranges all the nonminimized windows in an overlapping, diagonal pattern. When you select this command, the taskbar's context menu gains an Undo Cascade command that you can use to undo the arrangement.

Tile Windows Horizontally: This command arranges the nonminimized windows into evenly sized horizontal strips that cover the desktop. To reverse this procedure, select Undo Tile from the taskbar's context menu.

Tile Windows Vertically: This command arranges the nonminimized windows into evenly sized vertical strips that cover the desktop. To reverse this procedure, select Undo Tile from the taskbar's context menu.

Minimize All Windows: Clears the desktop by minimizing each open window to its taskbar icon. To restore the windows, select Undo Minimize All from the taskbar's context menu.

Customizing the Start Menu

I mentioned in Chapter 4, "What's New and Noteworthy in Windows 98," that even though the Start menu is leaps and bounds ahead of Program Manager, it's still not a particularly satisfying application launcher. It's not so bad if the item you need is on the Start menu itself, or on one of its immediate submenus (such as Programs or Settings). But if you find yourself constantly opening three or even four menus, the whole thing loses its appeal very quickly. When you think about it, though, the problem isn't so much that the Start menu itself is a bad idea; it's just that, in its default incarnation, the Start menu is organized poorly.

For example, Windows 98 comes with a Drive Converter utility that converts a FAT16 partition into a FAT32 partition. To run it, you select Start | Programs | Accessories | System Tools | Drive Converter (FAT 32). That's five clicks in all, which isn't outrageous considering that this is an obscure program that you'll use only once or twice (if at all).

On the other hand, the CD Player applet is an essential tool for those who enjoy listening to music while they slave away. Unfortunately, you have to expend the same amount of energy to run CD Player (Start | Programs | Accessories | Entertainment | CD Player) as you do to run Drive Converter.

6

THE TASKBAR, START MENU, AND DISPLAY

In other words, although the Start menu has a hierarchical structure, its layout is only semi-hierarchical: Some popular programs are easily accessible (such as Windows Explorer on the Programs menu), whereas others are tucked away in obscure nooks (such as CD Player on the Entertainment menu).

INSTALL PROGRAMS JUST MAKE THINGS WORSE

Just to add to the confusion, the install programs for most Windows applications add a folder and a few shortcuts to the Programs menu. Some (such as Microsoft Office) are even rude enough to toss a few shortcuts onto the Start menu itself.

The solution? Scrap Microsoft's inefficient Start menu layout and customize the menus to create a hierarchy of programs that suits the way you work, like this:

- Move the programs, accessories, and documents you use most often into higher layers of the Start menu tree.
- Move the items you use less often into lower layers of the Start menu.

Windows 98 gives you two ways to customize your Start menu in this manner: Use the Taskbar Properties dialog box to add and remove Start menu shortcuts, or work with the Start Menu folder directly.

QUICK START MENU RENOVATIONS

If all you want to do is move an item up or down within one of the Start submenus, Windows 98 offers a quicker method. Open the Start submenu you want to work with and then use your mouse to drag the item up or down within the menu. (Note that this doesn't work with folder items.)

New to **98**

Adding and Removing Start Menu Shortcuts

For simple Start menu customization needs, the Taskbar Properties dialog box offers a couple of tools that enable you to add and remove Start menu shortcuts. First, display the Taskbar Properties dialog box by right-clicking an empty part of the Taskbar and selecting Properties from the context menu, or by selecting Start | Settings | Taskbar & Start Menu. Now select the Start Menu Programs tab, shown in Figure 6.7.

FIGURE 6.7.

Use the Start Menu Programs tab to customize your Start menu.

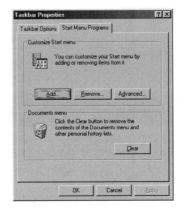

Adding a Shortcut

If the Start menu doesn't contain an item for a program or document you use regularly, you can easily add a shortcut to whichever menu you like. Even if a Start menu already has an item for a program or document, you might want to create a second shortcut in a different folder. (I'll show you how to delete the old shortcut in the next section.) To add a new shortcut to one of the Start menus, follow these steps:

1. Click the Add button. Windows 98 displays the Create Shortcut dialog box.

2. If you know the full path (drive, folder, and filename) of the program, accessory, or document you want to add to the Start menu, enter it in the Command line text box (see Figure 6.8).

   If you're not sure of the correct path, click Browse, use the Browse dialog box to highlight the appropriate file, and click Open.

FIGURE 6.8.

Use the Create Shortcut dialog box to specify the shortcut you want to add.

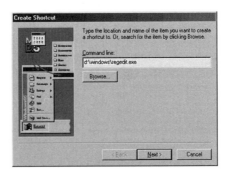

3. Click Next >. The Select Program Folder dialog box, shown in Figure 6.9, appears.

Customizing the Taskbar, Start Menu, and Display

CHAPTER 6

151

6

THE TASKBAR,
START MENU, AND
DISPLAY

FIGURE 6.9.

*Your next step is to use
this dialog box to choose
a Start menu home for
the new shortcut.*

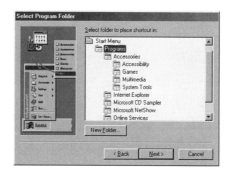

4. If you want to create a new folder for the shortcut, first highlight the folder you want to use as the parent. (For example, if you want to create a new folder off the Start menu, highlight Start Menu.) Now click the New Folder button, type the folder name, and press Enter.

    If you'd prefer to use an existing folder, highlight the folder name.

5. Click Next >. The Select a Title for the Program dialog box appears. This is the text that will appear on the menu.

6. Enter a title and then click Next >. The Select an Icon dialog box appears.

7. Highlight the icon you want to use for the shortcut, and then click Finish. Windows 98 adds the new shortcut (and the new folder, if you created one) to the Start menu tree.

Removing a Shortcut

If there is a Start menu shortcut you never use, or if you've added an existing shortcut to a different folder, you can delete the unneeded shortcut to make the menus easier to navigate. (Note that deleting a shortcut has absolutely no effect on the underlying program or document; all you're removing is a shortcut file that points to the real McCoy.) Here's the procedure:

1. In the Start Menu Programs tab, click the Remove button. Windows 98 displays the Remove Shortcuts/Folders dialog box.

2. Highlight the shortcut or folder you want to delete (see Figure 6.10).

3. Click the Remove button. If you delete a folder, Windows 98 asks whether you're sure you want to go through with the deletion.

4. Click Yes.

5. Repeat steps 2 through 4 to delete any other shortcuts or folders.

6. When you're done, click Close.

A FASTER WAY TO DELETE A START MENU SHORTCUT

An easier way to delete a shortcut is to click Start and open the menu that contains the shortcut. Right-click the shortcut and then click Delete.

FIGURE 6.10.

Use this dialog box to select the shortcut or folder you want to delete.

Dealing with the Documents Menu

Notice in Figure 6.7 that the Start Menu Programs tab has a Documents menu group. Clicking the Clear button in this group removes all the items from the Start menu's Documents menu (which, you'll recall, stores shortcuts to the last 15 documents you worked on).

Windows 98 stores the shortcuts for the Documents menu in the Recent folder (which is a subfolder of your main Windows 98 folder). So instead of clearing the Documents menu via the Start Menu Programs tab, you can simply delete the shortcuts that appear in the Recent folder.

For faster service, you can also use the following DOS command to clear the Documents menu (I'm assuming here that your main Windows 98 folder is C:\Windows):

```
DEL c:\windows\recent\*.lnk
```

You can run this command from a DOS session or the Run dialog box, place this command within your AUTOEXEC.BAT file (before the WIN command), or create a separate batch file that runs only this command. For the latter, you could create a shortcut for the batch file and place this shortcut either on your desktop or inside the Startup folder.

USE A BATCH FILE TO ADD DOCUMENTS TO THE RECENT FOLDER

Besides clearing the Recent folder, you can also use batch file commands to add shortcuts for oft-used documents to the Recent folder. First, create shortcuts for your documents in a separate folder (this folder should contain no other shortcut files). Then create a batch file command that copies these shortcuts into the Recent folder. For example, if the shortcuts are stored in the C:\Windows\MyDocs folder, the following command will copy them to the Recent folder:

```
COPY c:\windows\mydocs\*.lnk c:\windows\recent
```

Customizing the Taskbar, Start Menu, and Display

CHAPTER 6

153

6

THE TASKBAR,
START MENU, AND
DISPLAY

THE RECENT FOLDER AND USER PROFILES

If you've implemented user profiles on your system (as described in Chapter 7, "Setting Accessibility Options, User Profiles, and More"), note that each user will have his or her own Recent folder that will appear in the following Windows 98 subfolder (where *User* is the name of the user):

`\Profiles\User\Recent`

Working with the Start Menu Folder Directly

All this adding and removing of shortcuts works fine, but if you truly want to unleash the program-launching prowess of the Start menu, you need a less cumbersome approach. The key to this new approach is that the Start menu is really just a folder that branches off from your main Windows folder. If Windows 98 is installed in C:\Windows, for example, the Start Menu folder is C:\Windows\Start Menu. This allows you to work with the contents of the Start menu within Explorer (or even My Computer, if you like).

To display the Start Menu folder, use either of the following techniques:

- In Explorer, open your main Windows 98 folder and then highlight the Start Menu folder.

- Right-click the Start button and select Explore from the context menu.

Figure 6.11 shows the Explorer window with the Start Menu folder highlighted.

FIGURE 6.11.

You can use Explorer to customize the Start Menu folder directly.

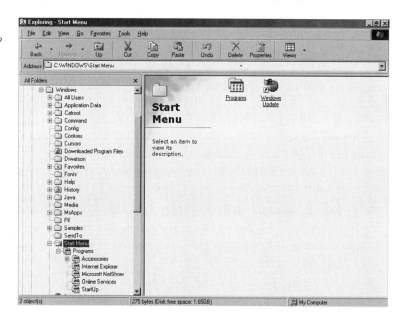

THE START MENU FOLDER AND USER PROFILES

As with the Recent folder, if you're working with user profiles, each user will have his or her own Start Menu folder, which will appear in the following Windows 98 subfolder (where *User* is the name of the user):

`\Profiles\`*User*`\Start Menu`

AVOID THE ADVANCED BUTTON

Another way to open an Explorer window on the Start Menu folder is to click the Advanced button in the Start Menu Programs tab of the Taskbar Properties dialog box. Unfortunately, the window that appears gives you access to only the Start Menu folder; the rest of your folders and drives are off limits. That makes this technique less attractive, so I'd suggest avoiding it.

The first thing you notice is that the Start Menu folder doesn't display all the items in the Start menu. In fact, it shows only two: Programs and Windows Update. Unfortunately, the items that appear below the Programs command in the Start menu are part of the Windows 98 interface, so you can't change them. That's not a big deal, though, because you still have lots of customization possibilities.

As you can see in Figure 6.11, the Start Menu folder contains subfolders that correspond to each submenu. For example, the Programs folder has a subfolder named Accessories; the Accessories folder has subfolders named Entertainment, System Tools; and so on.

Taken together, the Start Menu folder and all its subfolders constitute what I'll call the Start Menu hierarchy. How you work with the Start menu's contents—the folders and shortcuts—depends on whether you're working inside this hierarchy or outside it.

Working Within the Start Menu Hierarchy

Working within the Start Menu hierarchy means you're moving or copying existing shortcuts or Start Menu subfolders, or creating new subfolders below Start Menu. This is all straightforward, and you can use any of the techniques for copying, moving, renaming, and deleting objects that you'd normally use in Windows Explorer. Here are a few notes to bear in mind:

- Feel free to move any of the Start Menu subfolders to a different parent. For example, if you find that you constantly use the programs in the System Tools folder, you can put it within closer reach by moving it to, say, the Programs folder or even the Start Menu folder itself.

- You can create new folders, and they'll appear as new menus off the Start menu (depending on which folder you use for the parent).

■ If you move or copy an object to the Start Menu folder, it appears above the Programs command at the top of the Start menu. In Figure 6.12, for example, I've moved three objects into the Start Menu folder: the Games folder and the shortcuts for Backup and CD Player.

FIGURE 6.12.

Objects copied to the Start Menu folder appear at the top of the Start menu.

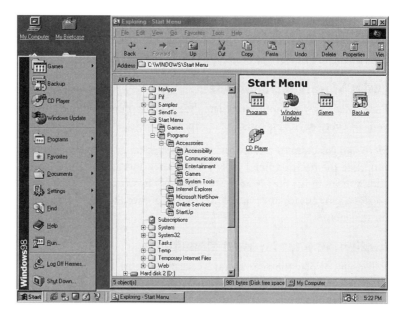

Working Outside the Start Menu Hierarchy

If you want to work with objects that exist outside the Start Menu hierarchy, you need to be a little more careful. That's because when you perform a copy or move operation in Explorer, you're copying or moving the object itself. And moving, for example, an executable file into a Start Menu folder can cause all kinds of problems because the program (and Windows 98) probably expects the file to reside in a certain location.

To avoid these kinds of snafus, always paste a copied or cut file or folder as a shortcut. Here's how:

■ Copy or cut the object normally, highlight the Start Menu folder you want to use as the destination, and select Edit | Paste Shortcut. (You can also right-click inside the destination folder's Contents pane and select Paste Shortcut from the context menu.)

■ If you're dragging an executable file, Explorer assumes that you want to create a shortcut, so you can just drop the file on the destination folder.

■ If you want to drag any other type of object (that is, a document or a folder), you can't use the traditional drag-and-drop technique. Instead, you need to right-drag the object (hold down the right mouse button and drag the object) and then drop it on the destination folder. In the context menu that appears, select Create Shortcut(s) Here.

Start Menu Tricks

Let's finish our look at customizing the Start menu with a few interesting tricks and techniques.

Easier Start Menu Shortcuts

For easy access, you should populate the main Start menu with those programs and documents you use every day. This puts these important objects just a couple of mouse clicks away.

Here's an easy way to create shortcuts that appear at the top of the Start menu: Drag the appropriate file from Explorer or My Computer and drop it on the Start button. Windows 98 adds a shortcut for the file at the top of the Start menu. Note that Windows 98 automatically creates a shortcut for any type of file; there's no need to right-drag documents (or even folders, for that matter).

Accelerator Keys for Start Menu Items

When you display the Start menu, you can select an item quickly by pressing the first letter of the item's name. If you add several shortcuts to the top of the Start menu, however, you might end up with more than one item that begins with the same letter. To avoid conflicts, rename each of these items so that they begin with a number. For example, renaming "Backup" to "1 Backup" means you can select this item by pressing 1. Figure 6.13 shows a sample Start menu that uses this technique.

Adding Control Panel Icons to the Start Menu

The eagle-eyed in the crowd will have noticed that the Start menu shown in Figure 6.13 has two Control Panel icons: Display Properties and Network Properties. How did I get them there? Easy: I just highlighted the Control Panel folder in Explorer and then dragged the icons onto the Start button. You can do the same thing with items in the Printers folder and the Dial-Up Networking folder.

You might think that you could just drag the Control Panel folder and drop it on the Start button to create a new menu that displays each Control Panel icon. Unfortunately, the shortcut created just opens the Control Panel window. Alternatively, you could create a new folder off the Start Menu folder—called, say, Control Panel—and then drag all the Control Panel icons into this new folder.

Customizing the Taskbar, Start Menu, and Display

CHAPTER 6

157

6

THE TASKBAR,
START MENU, AND
DISPLAY

FIGURE 6.13.

Prefacing Start menu names with a number prevents accelerator key conflicts.

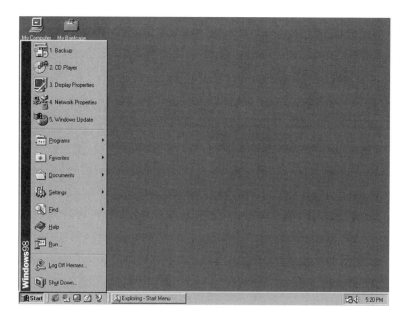

This technique works, but it means that every time an application adds an icon to the Control Panel (and there's no shortage of programs that do this) you have to remember to update your Start Menu folder. To avoid this chore, create a new folder off the Start Menu folder, and give it the following name:

```
Control Panel.{21EC2020-3AEA-1069-A2DD-08002B30309D}
```

Actually, the text to the left of the period can be any string you like; it's just the name that appears on the Start menu. The long value to the right of the period is Control Panel's resource identifier. As you can see in Figure 6.14, the menu it creates contains all the Control Panel icons. The advantage of this technique is that Windows 98 updates the menu automatically whenever Control Panel icons are added or removed.

You can also achieve the same effect with the Printers, Dial-Up Networking, and Scheduled Tasks folders. For the Printers folder, create a new folder with the following name:

```
Printers.{2227A280-3AEA-1069-A2DE-08002B30309D}
```

For the Dial-Up Networking folder, create a new folder with this name:

```
Dial-Up Networking.{992CFFA0-F557-101A-88EC-00DD010CCC48}
```

For the Scheduled Tasks folder, create a new folder with the following name:

```
Scheduled Tasks.{D6277990-4C6A-11CF-8D87-00AA0060F5BF}
```

In all cases, the string to the left of the period is what appears on the menu, so it can be whatever you like.

FIGURE 6.14.

A menu of Control Panel icons.

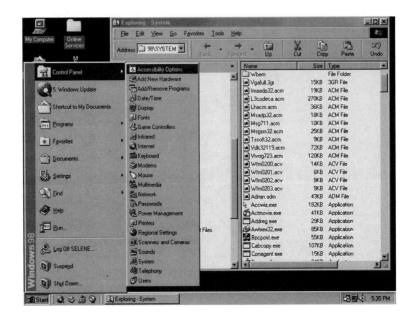

There's even another method you can use to create shortcuts for Control Panel icons. It's not nearly as efficient as the methods we've examined so far, but it demonstrates some interesting facts about how Control Panel works.

The idea is that, for each Control Panel icon you want to use, you create a new shortcut in the appropriate folder. When the Create Shortcut dialog box appears, use the Command line text box to enter a command with the following syntax:

```
C:\WINDOWS\CONTROL.EXE CPL_NAME.CPL [MODULE]
```

If you installed Windows 98 in a folder other than C:\WINDOWS, make the appropriate substitution. Here, CPL_NAME.CPL is the name of the CPL (Control Panel) file that corresponds to the icon, and MODULE is an optional parameter used with MAIN.CPL. Table 6.1 lists the command lines to use with various Control Panel icons. (The Control Panel icons that are missing—such as Add New Hardware and Sounds—can't be accessed with this technique.)

Table 6.1. Shortcut parameters for Control Panel icons.

Control Panel Icon	Command Line
Accessibility Options	C:\WINDOWS\CONTROL.EXE ACCESS.CPL
Add/Remove Programs	C:\WINDOWS\CONTROL.EXE APPWIZ.CPL
Date/Time	C:\WINDOWS\CONTROL.EXE TIMEDATE.CPL
Desktop Themes	C:\WINDOWS\CONTROL.EXE THEMES.CPL
Display	C:\WINDOWS\CONTROL.EXE DESK.CPL

6

Control Panel Icon	*Command Line*
Fonts	C:\WINDOWS\CONTROL.EXE MAIN.CPL FONTS
Infrared	C:\WINDOWS\CONTROL.EXE INFRARED.CPL
Internet	C:\WINDOWS\CONTROL.EXE INETCPL.CPL
Game Controllers	C:\WINDOWS\CONTROL.EXE JOY.CPL
Keyboard	C:\WINDOWS\CONTROL.EXE MAIN.CPL KEYBOARD
Mail	C:\WINDOWS\CONTROL.EXE MLCFG32.CPL
Microsoft Mail Postoffice	C:\WINDOWS\CONTROL.EXE WGPOCPL.CPL
Modems	C:\WINDOWS\CONTROL.EXE MODEM.CPL
Mouse	C:\WINDOWS\CONTROL.EXE MAIN.CPL MOUSE
Multimedia	C:\WINDOWS\CONTROL.EXE MMSYS.CPL
Network	C:\WINDOWS\CONTROL.EXE NETCPL.CPL
Passwords	C:\WINDOWS\CONTROL.EXE PASSWORD.CPL
Power Management	C:\WINDOWS\CONTROL.EXE POWERCFG.CPL
Printers	C:\WINDOWS\CONTROL.EXE MAIN.CPL PRINTERS
Regional Settings	C:\WINDOWS\CONTROL.EXE INTL.CPL
Telephony	C:\WINDOWS\CONTROL.EXE TELEPHON.CPL
Scanners and Cameras	C:\WINDOWS\CONTROL.EXE STICPL.CPL
System	C:\WINDOWS\CONTROL.EXE SYSDM.CPL

HIDING CONTROL PANEL ICONS

Depending on your system's configuration, you might have two dozen or more Control Panel icons to deal with. If there are any icons you never use, it's possible to hide them and thus reduce Control Panel clutter. This is also handy for system administrators who want to keep certain icons out of reach of their users.

To see how this works, first open CONTROL.INI (which you find in your main Windows 98 folder). In the section labeled [don't load], enter the name of the CPL file that corresponds to the Control Panel icon you want to hide, followed by =yes. For example, to hide the Passwords (PASSWORD.CPL) icon, you would set up CONTROL.INI as follows:

```
[don't load]
password.cpl=yes
```

Exit and save your work to put the new settings into effect.

Display Settings: A Desktop to Call Your Own

You saw in the last chapter that you can use the Active Desktop to turn a ho-hum desktop into a veritable entertainment center. The Windows 98 desktop also boasts a number of other display settings that enable you to further customize the look of the Windows interface. To get to these settings, use either of the following techniques:

- Right-click an empty area of the desktop and click Properties in the context menu.
- Select Start | Settings | Control Panel and open the Display icon in the Control Panel folder.

Whichever method you choose, the Display Properties dialog box, shown in Figure 6.15, is displayed. The next few sections take you through each of the tabs in this dialog box. (Note that while you're working in this dialog box, you can click the Apply button at any time to see what effect the choices you've made will have on your desktop. When you're done, click OK— or possibly Close, depending on the options you chose—to put your changes into effect.)

FIGURE 6.15.

Use this dialog box to alter your desktop's properties.

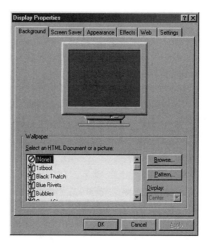

Wallpapering the Desktop

Windows 98's desktop metaphor is implemented in a fairly consistent manner through the interface, but it hits a bit of a snag when it comes to wallpaper. The problem is that wallpaper is a bitmap image that covers some or all of the desktop. Of course, in the real world, wallpaper covers walls, not the tops of desks, so someone on the Windows design team is guilty of mixing his metaphors.

Choosing a Wallpaper

This semantic quibble aside, wallpaper is an easy way to spruce up an otherwise drab desktop. As you learned in the last chapter, Windows 98 supports two kinds of wallpaper: Web pages

(HTM files) and bitmaps (BMP and DIB files). You learned about the former in the last chapter, so I'll discuss only the latter here.

To try out a bitmap wallpaper, select a bitmap file from the Wallpaper list in the Background tab. In the Display list, activating the Center option places the image in the center of the screen; if the image is smaller than the desktop, activating the Tile option displays multiple copies of the image so that it covers the entire desktop. (Most of the bitmaps in the Wallpaper list are tiny, so you have to select Tile to get the full effect.)

Note that the listed bitmaps all reside in the main Windows folder. If you have a bitmap (either a BMP file or a DIB—Device-Independent Bitmap—file) in another folder, click the Browse button, highlight the file in the Browse dialog box, and click OK.

Creating a Custom Wallpaper

Because the wallpapers are just bitmaps, you don't need to do anything special to create your own images to use as wallpaper. By using Paint or any other graphics program that can work with files in BMP or DIB format, create your image (or convert it to BMP or DIB), and save it in your main Windows 98 folder. Alternatively, you can scan an image and save the scan in the Windows folder as a BMP or DIB file.

If you have an image you'd like to use as a wallpaper but you can't move it into the Windows folder, Paint has a couple of commands that can help. Open the image in Paint and then select one of the following File menu commands:

>**Set As Wallpaper (Tiled):** This command sets the current image as the desktop wallpaper and displays the image tiled.

>**Set As Wallpaper (Centered):** This command sets the current image as the desktop wallpaper and displays the image centered.

Working with Desktop Patterns

If you select (None) in the Wallpaper list, the Windows 98 desktop returns to a large, unbroken expanse of unremitting teal. However, the Pattern button also becomes active, so you can define a pattern to break up the desktop monotony.

Choosing a Predefined Pattern

To choose one of these patterns, follow these steps:

1. In the Background tab, make sure that (None) is selected in the Wallpaper list.
2. Click the Pattern button to display the Pattern dialog box shown in Figure 6.16.
3. Use the Pattern list to highlight a pattern. (The Preview box gives you some idea of what the pattern will look like.)
4. When you find a pattern you like, click OK.

FIGURE 6.16.

Use the Pattern dialog box to select one of Windows 98's predefined desktop patterns.

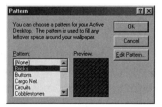

Creating Your Own Pattern

Some of the predefined patterns are just plain hard on the eyes, but a few are quite creative. If you want to try your hand at creating a pattern, follow these steps:

1. Display the Pattern dialog box, as described in the last section.

2. In the Pattern list, select a pattern to work with.

3. Click the Edit Pattern button. The Pattern Editor dialog box appears, as shown in Figure 6.17.

FIGURE 6.17.

Use the Pattern Editor to create your own desktop pattern.

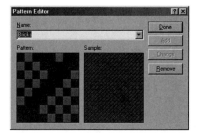

4. Create a pattern by clicking inside the Pattern box. Each click toggles a pixel between the desktop color and black. As you click, the Sample box shows you what the pattern will look like.

5. When you're done, use the Name text box to enter a name for the pattern.

6. Click the Add button to add the pattern to the list.

7. Click Done to return to the Display Properties dialog box.

Setting the Screen Saver

Back when most people worked in character-mode applications, monitors weren't as advanced as those used today. One of the problems people faced was leaving their monitors turned on and idle for extended periods and ending up with characters burned permanently into the screen. Screen savers were invented to help prevent this from happening. The screen saver resided in memory and kicked in only after the computer had been idle for some predetermined length of time. The screen saver would display some kind of moving pattern, so burn-in could never occur.

Nowadays, though, it's pretty tough to burn an image into your screen. Improvements in monitor quality and the graphical nature of Windows 98 have made such a fate virtually impossible. Curiously, though, screen savers are still around and are, in fact, flourishing. The reason: Modern screen savers, with their flying toasters and psychedelic patterns, are a lot of fun!

Windows 98 comes with a few of its own screen savers for good measure. To try them, select the Screen Saver tab in the Display Properties dialog box, as shown in Figure 6.18.

FIGURE 6.18.

Use this dialog box to set up a screen saver.

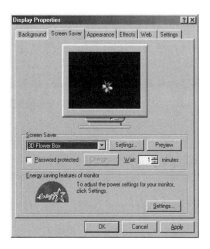

Selecting a Screen Saver

The various screen savers that ship with Windows 98 are shown in the Screen Saver drop-down list. After you've chosen a screen saver, you can use the following controls to set it up:

Wait: This spinner controls the amount of time your computer must be inactive before the screen saver goes to work. You can enter a number between 1 and 60 minutes.

Preview: Click this button to give the screen saver a trial run. To return to the dialog box, move the mouse or press any key.

Password protected: If you activate this check box, Windows 98 requires you to enter a password before it shuts down the screen saver and returns the normal screen. To set the password, click the Change button, enter the password in the Change Password dialog box (note that you must enter it twice), and click OK. When Windows 98 tells you that the password has been changed, click OK.

PASSWORD PROTECTION? NOT!

If you think entering a password for the screen saver will protect your system from snoops, think again. All someone has to do is turn off and restart your computer, open the Display Properties dialog box, and clear the Password protected check box! Windows 98 doesn't bat an eye. (If you do use a password, though, this is a handy technique to know in case you forget your password.)

Settings: Click this button to set various options for the screen saver. The Options dialog box that appears depends on which screen saver you chose.

MONITOR POWER SETTINGS

If you're wondering about the Energy saving features of monitor group, turn to Chapter 11, "Device Advice: Dealing with Devices in Windows 98," to learn about this and other Windows 98 power management features.

Creating an Instant Screen Saver

If you deal with sensitive data (or if you like to sneak in a quick game of Duke Nukem now and then), you probably want to guard against visitors accidentally seeing what's on your screen. Short of always locking your door, an easy way to do this is to create an "instant" screen saver that can be activated using a quick key combination. To try this out, follow these steps:

1. Find your favorite screen saver file (it will have the .SCR extension) in the Windows 98 System folder.
2. Right-drag the file from Explorer, drop it on the desktop, and click Create Shortcut(s) Here. Windows 98 creates a desktop shortcut for the file.
3. Right-click the shortcut, and then choose Properties from the context menu.
4. In the properties sheet that appears, activate the Shortcut tab, click inside the Shortcut key box, and press the key you want to use as part of the Ctrl+Alt key combination. (For example, if you press Z, Windows 98 sets the key combination to Ctrl+Alt+Z.)
5. Click OK.

Now, no matter which application you're working in, you can activate your screen saver immediately simply by pressing the key combination you defined in step 4.

Renovating the Desktop: Colors, Fonts, and Sizes

If you're truly determined to put your personal stamp on the Windows 98 interface, the Appearance tab in the Display Properties dialog box is a great place to start. This tab, shown in Figure 6.19, is brimful to bursting with controls and options that enable you to specify the colors, fonts, and sizes that Windows 98 uses to display objects on the desktop.

FIGURE 6.19.

Use the Appearance tab to give the desktop and its objects a makeover.

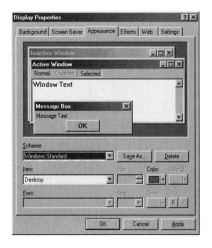

The Appearance tab is divided into two sections. The top half shows a fake desktop displaying a few objects; the bottom half contains the various controls you use to alter the appearance. The idea is that as you work with the controls, the fake objects reflect how your new desktop will look.

Selecting a Scheme

The easiest way to alter the appearance of the Windows 98 desktop is to select one of the 33 predefined schemes. A scheme is a collection of desktop attributes that includes the color of the desktop and window title bars, the fonts used in dialog boxes and pull-down menus, the size of window borders and desktop icons, and much more.

Use the Scheme list to choose a scheme name that sounds interesting, and then check out the fake desktop to see how things look. Note that, if your eyesight isn't what it used to be (and some of these schemes—such as the Pumpkin and Wheat eyesores—might make your eyesight worse!), several of the schemes use larger fonts. Look for the scheme names that end with either (large) or (extra large).

Creating a Custom Scheme

Some of the schemes look as though they were created in the Phyllis Diller House of Design. If you think you can do better, it's easy enough to create your own scheme. The basic procedure is to select an object from the Item drop-down list and then use the other controls—such as Size, Color, and Font—to customize the item. Note that not all the controls are available for each option. (For example, it doesn't make sense to specify a font for the scrollbars.)

A QUICK WAY TO SELECT ITEMS

Another way to select some of objects in the Item list is to click the appropriate part of the fake desktop. For example, clicking the title bar of the active window selects the Active Title Bar item.

Here's a rundown of the various objects available in the Item list:

3D Objects: Dialog box command buttons and tabs, caption buttons (see the "Caption Buttons" entry), scrollbars, status bars, taskbar, and window borders. You can set the background color and font color for these objects.

Active Title Bar: The title bar of the window that has the focus. Windows 98 displays title bar backgrounds as a gradient. To control this gradient, use both the Color 1 and Color 2 palettes. You can also set the size (height) of the title bar, as well as the font, font size, font color, and font style of the title bar text.

Active Window Border: The border surrounding the window that has the focus. You can set the border's width and color. Note that the width setting also controls the width of the taskbar when the Auto hide option is activated (as described earlier).

Application Background: The background on which windows are displayed in applications that support the Multiple Document Interface (MDI). You can set the color of the background.

Application Background: Sets the default color for the background of each application window.

Caption Buttons: The buttons that appear in the upper-right corner of windows and dialog boxes. You can set the size of these buttons.

Desktop: The desktop color. Note that this setting also controls the color of the backgrounds used with the desktop icons. You see this background color only if your desktop is covered with either a pattern or wallpaper.

Icon: The icons that appear on the desktop. You can set the icon size as well as the font attributes of the icon titles. Note that this font setting also controls the fonts displayed in Explorer and all open folders (such as Control Panel and My Computer).

Icon Spacing (Horizontal): The distance allotted (in pixels) between desktop and folder icons on the left and right.

Icon Spacing (Vertical): The distance allotted (in pixels) between desktop and folder icons on the top and bottom.

Inactive Title Bar: The title bars of the open windows that don't have the focus. You can set the size (height) and gradient colors of the bar, as well as the font, font size, and font color of the title bar text.

Customizing the Taskbar, Start Menu, and Display

CHAPTER **6**

167

6

THE TASKBAR,
START MENU, AND
DISPLAY

Inactive Window Border: The borders surrounding the open windows that don't have the focus. You can set the border's width and color.

Menu: The window menu bar. You can set the size (height) and background color of the menu bar, as well as the font attributes of the menu bar text.

Message Box: Message boxes, such as error messages and information prompts. (Note that this setting doesn't apply to regular dialog boxes.) You can set the font attributes of the message text.

Mouse Highlight: With Web integration turned on, this item controls the color that items turn when they're highlighted by hovering the mouse over them.

Palette Title: The application of this item is unknown.

Scrollbar: The scroll bars that appear in windows and list boxes. You can set the width (or height, depending on the orientation) of the scrollbars.

Selected Items: The currently selected menu in a menu bar and the currently selected command in a menu. You can set the height and background color of the selection bar, as well as the font attributes of the item text.

ToolTip: The small banners that appear if you hover the mouse pointer over a toolbar for a couple of seconds. You can set the background color and the font attributes of the ToolTip text. Note that the ToolTip font size also controls the size of a window's status bar text.

Window: The window background and text. You can set the color of these items.

When you're done, click the Save As button. In the Save Scheme dialog box that appears, enter a name for the scheme in the text box provided and click OK. Your newly created color scheme appears in the Scheme list.

If you've created some schemes you no longer need, you should delete them to make the Scheme list easier to navigate. To delete a scheme, highlight it in the Scheme list and click the Delete button.

Creating Your Own Colors

You might have noticed that the Appearance tab's Color lists have an Other button. You can use this option to pick a different color from Windows 98's color palette, or you can create your own color. When you click the Other button, you see the Color dialog box, shown in Figure 6.20.

If you want to use one of the colors displayed in the Basic colors area, click it and then click OK.

To create your own color, you can use one of two methods. The first method uses the fact that you can create any color in the spectrum by mixing the three primary colors: red, green, and blue. The Color dialog box lets you enter specific numbers between 0 and 255 for each of these colors, by using the Red, Green, and Blue text boxes. A lower number means the color is less intense, and a higher number means the color is more intense.

FIGURE 6.20.

Use this dialog box to choose or create a different color.

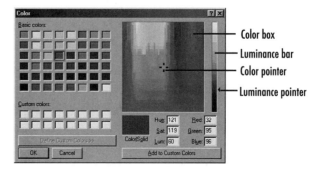

— Color box
— Luminance bar
— Color pointer
— Luminance pointer

To give you some idea of how this works, see Table 6.2, which lists eight common colors and their respective red, green, and blue numbers.

Table 6.2. The red, green, and blue numbers for eight common colors.

Color	Red	Green	Blue
Black	0	0	0
White	255	255	255
Red	255	0	0
Green	0	255	0
Blue	0	0	255
Yellow	255	255	0
Magenta	255	0	255
Cyan	0	255	255

GRAYSCALE COLORS

Whenever the Red, Green, and Blue values are equal, you get a grayscale color. Lower numbers produce darker grays, and higher numbers produce lighter grays.

The second method for selecting colors involves setting three attributes: hue, saturation, and luminance.

Hue: This number (which is more or less equivalent to the term *color*) measures the position on the color spectrum. Lower numbers indicate a position near the red end, and higher numbers move through the yellow, green, blue, and violet parts of the spectrum. As you increase the hue, the color pointer moves from left to right.

Sat: This number is a measure of the purity of a given hue. A saturation setting of 240 means that the hue is a pure color. Lower numbers indicate that more gray is mixed with the hue until, at 0, the color becomes part of the gray-scale. As you increase the saturation, the color pointer moves toward the top of the color box.

Lum: This number is a measure of the brightness of a color. Lower numbers are darker, and higher numbers are brighter. The luminance bar to the right of the color box shows the luminance scale for the selected color. As you increase the luminance, the slider moves toward the top of the bar.

To create a custom color, you can either enter values in the text boxes, as just described, or use the mouse to click inside the color box and luminance bar. The Color | Solid box shows the selected color on the left and the nearest solid color on the right (if you're using a 16-color video driver). If you think you'll want to reuse the color down the road, click the Add to Custom Colors button to place the color in one of the boxes in the Custom colors area. When you're done, click OK.

CUSTOMIZING WITH DESKTOP THEMES

You saw earlier how Windows 98 lets you select desktop schemes that govern the look of various objects, including menu bars, window borders and title bars, icons, and more. You can take this idea a step further with *desktop themes*. A theme is also a collection of object properties, but it covers more ground than a simple scheme. Each theme specifies various settings for not only windows and message boxes, but also a screen saver, a wallpaper, mouse pointers, sounds, desktop icons, and more.

To try out some of these desktop themes, select Start | Settings | Control Panel and then open the Desktop Themes icon in the Control Panel folder.

Note that many of the desktop themes require a color depth of 16 bits (high color) or more. Each theme shows the color requirements beside its name (for example, 256 color, high color) in the Theme drop-down list.

Changing the Effects Properties

The controls in the Effects tab (see Figure 6.21) deal with various visual effects. Here's a rundown of the goodies you get on this tab:

Desktop icons: This group lets you modify the icon for the three basic desktop folders: My Computer, Network Neighborhood, and Recycle Bin (both the full and the empty icons). Highlight the icon you want to change, click the Change Icon button, choose the new icon from the Change Icon dialog box, and click OK. To change an icon back to its original, highlight it and click the Default Icon button.

Hide icons when the desktop is viewed as a Web page: If you activate this check box, Windows 98 removes the desktop icons whenever you display the desktop as a Web page.

Use large icons: Activating this check box increases the size of the desktop icons (and any other folder) from the default value of 32 pixels on each side, to 48 pixels.

Show icons using all possible colors: When activated, this check box tells Windows 98 to use all the available colors to display the desktop icons. If you have a slower computer or video card and you find that Windows 98 takes a long time to refresh your desktop, deactivate this option.

Animate windows, menus, and lists: When this option is activated, Windows 98 displays menus by using an animation that makes it appear as though the menus "scroll" onto the screen. If you deactivate this feature, menus appear instantly.

Smooth edges of screen fonts: If you activate this check box, Windows 98 smoothes the jagged edges of large fonts, which makes them more readable. You need to have your display set up with a color depth of at least high color (16 bits) to use this feature.

Show window contents while dragging: This check box toggles full-window drag on and off. When it's deactivated, Windows 98 shows only the outline of any window you drag with the mouse (by dragging the title bar); if you activate full-window drag, however, Windows 98 displays the window's contents while you're dragging. You need a fast video card to make the full-window drag feature worthwhile.

FIGURE 6.21.

The Effects tab contains various settings for visual effects.

Changing the Display Settings

The Settings tab of the Display Properties dialog box, shown in Figure 6.22, controls various properties of your video display. These properties include the color depth, the resolution, and the default font size. The options available for each property depend on the type of video card and monitor you have and are limited by the capabilities of this hardware. Because of that, you can also use this tab to change your video driver or monitor type (although I don't cover how you do this until Chapter 11).

FIGURE 6.22.

Use the Settings tab to customize your video display.

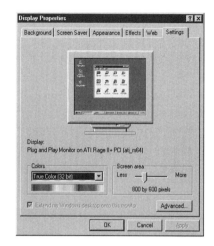

WORKING WITH MULTIPLE MONITORS

If you have multiple video cards and monitors attached to your system, you see a different Settings tab than the one shown in Figure 6.22. I'll show you how to enable and work with Windows 98's multiple-monitor support in Chapter 11.

Changing the Screen Resolution

The Screen area slider controls the screen resolution. Move the slider to the left to get a lower resolution; move the slider to the right to get a higher resolution. The maximum available resolution depends on your video hardware and on the current color depth (see the next section). If you select a higher screen resolution, Windows 98 might have to reduce the color depth.

Changing screen resolution in Windows 3.*x* meant having to restart Windows to put the new setting into effect. However, Windows 98 enables you to change the resolution without restarting.

If you change the resolution and then click OK (or Apply), Windows 98 displays a dialog box that tells you your desktop will be resized. Click OK, and your display resolution is changed automatically. A new dialog box appears to ask whether you want to keep the new setting. Click Yes if you want to keep the new resolution. To return to the original resolution, either click No or wait 15 seconds and Windows 98 will restore the resolution automatically.

Changing the Color Depth

The Colors drop-down list contains the four basic color palettes: 16 color, 256 color, High Color (16 bit), and True Color (32 bit). The latter two depths give you 65,536 colors and 16,777,216 colors, respectively.

In general, fewer colors speed up your display, but you need higher color depths to display complex graphics. Note, too, that the number of colors available at a given resolution is limited by your video adapter. Also, if you select a higher color depth, Windows 98 might have to reduce the resolution.

Windows 95 required a restart after a color depth change, but Windows 98 allows you to make color depth adjustments on-the-fly. When you change the color depth and click OK or Apply, you see the dialog box shown in Figure 6.23. You can either apply the change without rebooting, or you can reboot to ensure compatibility. (The latter should be an issue only if you're dropping to a lower color depth. In other words, if you're using an application that expects, for example, 32-bit color, you could have problems if you drop down to 16-bit color or lower.)

Figure 6.23.

Windows 98 displays this warning when you change color depths.

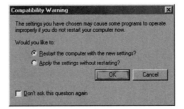

SETTING THE DEFAULT FOR COLOR DEPTH CHANGES

Windows 98 gives you two ways to set the default response for color depth changes:

- In the Compatibility Warning dialog box, choose the option you want to set as the default and activate the Don't ask this question again check box.

- In the Settings tab, click Advanced Properties and then display the General tab in the properties sheet that appears. Use the options in the Compatibility group to set the default behavior.

Changing the Size of the System Font

In the Settings tab, click Advanced Properties and then display the General tab in the properties sheet that appears. The Font Size drop-down list contains options that control the size of the Windows 98 system font (the font Windows 98 uses for objects such as desktop icons, taskbar text, dialog boxes, menus, and windows). If this option isn't available, your video hardware doesn't support custom font sizes.

Actually, the name "Font size" is a bit of a misnomer because it might lead you to expect that it lets you specify a particular point size. That's not the case, however. Instead, Font size serves to scale the existing fonts so that they consume a larger or smaller amount of screen real estate. For example, suppose that a standard 10-point font uses up 100 pixels per inch; increasing this value to, say, 125 pixels per inch makes the font appear 25 percent larger. For this reason, a name such as "Font scale" would probably have made more sense.

The default value is Small Fonts, which displays the standard 10-point Arial font at 96 pixels per inch; alternatively, you can select Large Fonts, which displays the standard 10-point Arial font at 120 pixels per inch (a 25 percent increase).

If you'd prefer to customize the font size, select Other in the Font size list to display the Custom Font Size dialog box, shown in Figure 6.24. Either select one of the five percentages in the drop-down list (75%, 100%, 125%, 150%, or 200%) or drag the mouse pointer along the ruler to set a specific percentage. The available values are between 20% and 500%. When you're done, click OK to return to the Settings tab. When you apply the new font scale, Windows 98 prompts you to restart your computer.

FIGURE 6.24.

Use this dialog box to set the font size manually.

CHANGING DISPLAY SETTINGS FROM THE TASKBAR

Notice that the General tab has a Show settings icon on task bar check box. When this check box is activated, Windows 98 adds a display settings icon to the system tray. Clicking this icon produces a list of all the resolutions and color depths that your video card supports. Click one of these values to change your display settings.

TweakUI: The Interface Power Toy

Soon after Windows 95 was released, a few Microsoft programmers put together some small programs that extended the functionality of Windows. These utilities were called Power Toys, and some of them were quite handy. In fact, one of them—called QuickRes—is now part of Windows 98. (It's the on-the-fly color depth changer you saw earlier.) Another Power Toy is also available on the Windows 98 CD-ROM. It's called TweakUI, and it's crammed with options for changing and working with the Windows 98 user interface.

New to **98**

To install TweakUI, follow these steps:

1. Insert the Windows 98 CD-ROM. Hold down Shift while inserting the disc. This will bypass the AutoRun program on the CD.

2. Using Windows Explorer, display the /tools/ResKit/Powertoy folder.

3. Right-click the tweakui.inf file and then click Install in the context menu.

To run TweakUI, open the Control Panel and launch the TweakUI icon. I'll tell you about the various settings available in TweakUI throughout the book. For now, here's a summary of the tabs that contain settings related to the customization options discussed in this chapter:

> **Control Panel:** This tab presents a list of all the installed Control Panel icons. You can use the check boxes to toggle the display of any icon on and off.

> **Desktop:** This tab displays a list of special desktop icons you can toggle on or off. You can also save some icons as files for display in other folders. (This is similar to the trick I showed you earlier for displaying the Control Panel folder off the Start menu.)

> **Paranoia:** This tab has a Clear Document history at logon check box which you can activate to remove all shortcuts from the Recent folder at startup.

> **Repair:** The Windows shell will occasionally display the wrong icon for a particular desktop item. When that happens, select Rebuild Icons in this tab and then click Repair Now.

Summary

This chapter showed you how to remake Windows 98 in your own image. I showed you how to customize the taskbar and Start menu, how to modify the desktop appearance and display settings, and how to work with the TweakUI utility. Here's a list of chapters where you'll find related information:

- I showed you how to customize your Windows 98 startup in Chapter 3, "Start Me Up: Controlling Windows 98 Startup."

- To learn about Web integration and its effect on the Windows 98 interface, see Chapter 5, "Web Integration and the Active Desktop."

- Customization options related to accessibility, user profiles, and region settings are the focus of Chapter 7, "Setting Accessibility Options, User Profiles, and More."

- To learn how to customize your mouse, keyboard, and game controllers, see Chapter 8, "Customizing the Mouse, Keyboard, and Other Input Devices."

- I cover adding and changing device drivers in Chapter 11, "Device Advice: Dealing with Devices in Windows 98."

- Chapter 11 is also the place to go for information on changing the settings for your display adapter and monitor.

- The Registry gives you tremendous power to customize Windows 98. I take you through lots of examples in Chapter 13, "A Few Good Hacks: Some Useful Registry Tweaks."

- To learn how to customize the Startup folder, see Chapter 14, "File and Folder Tricks and Techniques."

- I show you how to associate sounds with various Windows 98 events in Chapter 25, "Windows 98 Audio Features."

Setting Accessibility Options, User Profiles, and More

CHAPTER 7

The great challenge which faces us is to assure that, in our society of bigness, we do not strangle the voice of creativity, that the rules of the game do not come to overshadow its purpose, that the grand orchestration of society leaves ample room for the man who marches to the music of another drummer.

—Hubert H. Humphrey

This chapter continues your look at the Windows 98 customization options. In particular, I'll take you through three separate customization scenarios. First, I'll discuss the various accessibility settings that Windows 98 provides for handicapped and disabled users. This section will include coverage of the new Accessibility Wizard and Microsoft Magnifier tools. Next, I'll show you how to set up your computer for multiple users so that each person has access to his or her own custom version of Windows 98. Finally, I'll close the chapter with a look at the regional settings, which are options that determine how Windows 98 deals with various international issues (such as how numbers and currency values are displayed).

Accessible Windows: Working with the Accessibility Settings

Although the rest of the world has, over the past few years, striven to increase access for the disabled (in the form of Braille elevator buttons, wheelchair ramps, and handicapped parking spaces, to name a few changes), the computer industry has until recently lagged sadly behind. Most disabled people either had to somehow adapt to the existing systems or use expensive add-ons and software to meet their particular needs.

Windows 95 changed all that by offering a wide selection of accessibility options that let disabled persons customize their systems themselves. Windows 98 continues to offer these tools and adds a couple of new tools to the mix: the Accessibility Wizard and Microsoft Magnifier (which I'll discuss later in this section).

You find the accessibility options in the Accessibility Properties dialog box, shown in Figure 7.1. To display this properties sheet, open the Control Panel and launch the Accessibility Options icon. You can activate your selected options by clicking Apply or OK.

Easier Access to the Keyboard

The Keyboard tab offers several options that make it easier for you to work with your keyboard. The next few sections give you a rundown.

StickyKeys: Easier Key Combinations

If you have trouble with certain key combinations (such as combining Ctrl and Alt with the function keys—a tough stretch even for people with full mobility in their hands) activate the Use StickyKeys check box to enable the StickyKeys feature.

FIGURE 7.1.

Use this dialog box to customize Windows 98's accessibility options for disabled persons.

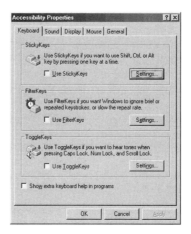

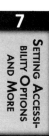

When StickyKeys is on, you can press a modifier key (such as Ctrl, Alt, Shift, or any combination of these), and the key remains active until you press another key. For example, to use the Ctrl+S key combination, you press Ctrl and then S. Note, as well, that Windows 98 beeps the speaker each time you press a modifier key.

Click the Settings button to display the Settings for StickyKeys dialog box (see Figure 7.2) and work with the following StickyKeys options:

Use shortcut: If you activate this check box, you can toggle StickyKeys on and off by pressing the Shift key five times. When you turn StickyKeys on in this manner, Windows 98 displays a dialog box asking you to confirm that you want StickyKeys turned on.

Press modifier key twice to lock: When this check box is activated, you can lock any modifier key by pressing it twice. To unlock the key, press it once.

Turn StickyKeys off if two keys are pressed at once: When this check box is activated, Windows 98 deactivates the StickyKeys feature whenever you press a combination in the normal manner (that is, hold down a modifier key and press another key). If you're sharing your computer with another user who doesn't require StickyKeys, deactivate this check box. That way, you still can take advantage of StickyKeys and the other person will be able to use key combinations in the usual fashion.

Make sounds when modifier key is pressed: This check box toggles the StickyKeys sounds on and off.

Show StickyKeys status on screen: When this check box is activated, Windows 98 displays the StickyKeys icon in the system tray. Double-clicking this icon opens the Accessibility Properties dialog box. You can also display the Accessibility Settings icons in a separate status window for easier access. To do so, right-click any accessibility icon in the system tray and then click the Show Status Window command.

Figure 7.2.
Use this dialog box to customize the StickyKeys feature.

FilterKeys: Ignoring Unwanted Keystrokes

If you tend to hold keys down too long or press keys multiple times, the FilterKeys feature lets you filter out the extra characters that appear in these situations. In the Keyboard tab, activate the Use FilterKeys check box to enable this feature. Windows 98 tells you that the FilterKeys feature is active by displaying a stopwatch icon in the taskbar's system tray.

Click the Settings button to display the Settings for FilterKeys dialog box (see Figure 7.3) and customize FilterKeys:

> **Use shortcut:** Activating this check box means you can toggle StickyKeys on and off by holding down the right Shift key for eight seconds. When you turn StickyKeys on in this manner, Windows 98 displays a dialog box asking you to confirm that you want StickyKeys turned on.

> **Ignore repeated keystrokes:** When this option is activated, Windows 98 ignores repeated keystrokes that occur within a specific threshold (the default is half a second). To change this threshold, click Settings and use the Advanced Settings for FilterKeys dialog box to set a longer or shorter time interval.

> **Ignore quick keystrokes and slow down the repeat rate:** If you activate this option instead, Windows 98 does two things:

> ■ It ignores keystrokes in which the key is held down for less than a specified threshold (the default is 1 second). This feature is called *SlowKeys*.

> ■ For the keyboard repeat rate, it sets up slower values than those specified in the Keyboard Control Panel (discussed in the next chapter). This feature is called *RepeatKeys*.

> Click the Settings button to set the values for both SlowKeys and RepeatKeys.

> **Beep when keys pressed or accepted:** This check box toggles the FilterKeys sounds on and off.

> **Show FilterKey status on screen:** When this check box is activated, Windows 98 displays the FilterKeys icon in the system tray. Double-clicking this icon opens the Accessibility Properties dialog box.

FIGURE 7.3.

The settings in this dialog box enable you to customize the FilterKeys feature.

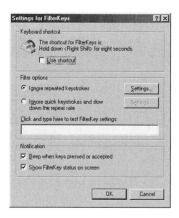

ToggleKeys: "Lock" Key Notification

Enabling the ToggleKeys feature (by activating the Use ToggleKeys check box) tells Windows 98 to beep the speaker when you press Caps Lock, Num Lock, and Scroll Lock. Windows 98 plays a higher pitched sound when these keys are turned on, and it plays a lower pitched sound when they're turned off.

Click the Settings button to display the Settings for ToggleKeys dialog box. The Use shortcut check box toggles the ToggleKeys shortcut (holding down Num Lock for five seconds) on and off.

For the Hearing Impaired: SoundSentry and ShowSounds

The Sound tab, shown in Figure 7.4, contains a couple of options to assist those who are hearing impaired:

SoundSentry: The SoundSentry feature displays a visual indicator each time your system makes a sound. By default, SoundSentry flashes the caption bar of the active window. (You can change this default by clicking the Settings button.) To enable SoundSentry, activate the Use SoundSentry check box.

ShowSounds: The ShowSounds feature displays a visual equivalent for sounds generated by your programs. To enable ShowSounds, activate the Use ShowSounds check box.

A USEFUL TOOL FOR THOSE WHO ARE HEARING IMPAIRED

Another useful tool for those who are hearing impaired is the WinPopup utility. This program enables users to converse via short messages over the network. To run WinPopup, select Start | Run, type `winpopup` in the Run dialog box, and then click OK.

FIGURE 7.4.

Use the Sound tab to generate visual cues for audible Windows 98 events.

For the Visually Impaired: High Contrast

Windows 98 has no shortage of options for those who are visually impaired. Here's a summary of some of the customization options that can improve the visibility of Windows 98 objects:

- In the Appearance tab of the Display Properties dialog box, you can select any of the "large" or "extra large" schemes (as described in Chapter 6, "Customizing the Taskbar, Start Menu, and Display"). You can also increase the size of fonts and objects by using the other controls on this tab.

- In the Settings tab of the Display Properties dialog box, you can use the Font size feature to scale fonts to a larger size (again, see Chapter 6).

- In the Pointer tab of the Mouse Properties dialog box, you can select one of the schemes that produces larger pointer sizes (see Chapter 8, "Customizing the Mouse, Keyboard, and Other Input Devices").

- In the Motion tab of the Mouse Properties dialog box, you can activate the Pointer trail feature to display trails as you move the mouse (this is also described in Chapter 8).

- Use the new Microsoft Magnifier (see "A Zoom with a View: Microsoft Magnifier," later in this chapter).

The Display tab of the Accessibility Properties dialog box offers yet another feature for increasing the visibility of screen components: High Contrast. If you activate the Use High Contrast check box and apply this setting, Windows 98 changes the desktop's colors and fonts to make the screen easier to read. Figure 7.5 shows an example (read the next sidebar to see how I got my screen to look like this).

FIGURE 7.5.
The High Contrast feature makes it easier to view the desktop's components.

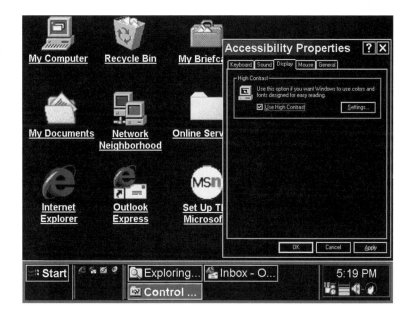

INCREASE THE ICON SIZE IN HIGH CONTRAST MODE

One of the problems with High Contrast mode is that the desktop icon text doesn't fit inside the standard icon size. To fix this problem, open the Display Properties dialog box, select the Appearance tab, select Icon in the Item drop-down list, crank up the Size spinner to 72, and click OK. Now right-click the desktop, click Arrange Icons in the context menu, and then click by Name. These are the steps I used to get the desktop shown in Figure 7.5.

There are also a few High Contrast options you can work with by clicking the Settings button. The Settings for High Contrast dialog box that appears gives you the following options:

Use shortcut: If you activate this check box, you can toggle High Contrast on and off by pressing the following key combination: Left Alt+Left Shift+Print Screen.

High Contrast color scheme: Use these controls to set the color scheme that Windows 98 uses for the High Contrast display. The default is White on black, but you can also choose Black on white or Custom. The latter enables you to choose one of the predefined desktop color schemes.

Moving the Mouse Pointer via the Keyboard: MouseKeys

The Mouse tab of the Accessibility Options dialog box controls the MouseKeys feature. If you activate the Use MouseKeys check box, Windows 98 enables you to move the mouse pointer by using the arrow keys on the keyboard's numeric keypad. (Make sure that you have Num Lock turned on, however. Note, too, that MouseKeys doesn't work with the separate arrow-key keypads found on most modern keyboards.)

Besides the basic arrow movements, you can also use the numeric keypad keys outlined in Table 7.1.

Table 7.1. Numeric keypad keys to use with the MouseKeys feature.

Key	Equivalent Mouse Action
5	Click
+	Double-click
/	Select the left mouse button
*	Select both mouse buttons
–	Select the right mouse button
Insert	Lock the selected button
Delete	Release the selected button

Here's how you use these keys:

■ To click an object, use the arrow keys to move the pointer over the object, press the slash key (/) to select the left mouse button (if it isn't selected already), and press 5 to click.

DETERMINING THE SELECTED MOUSE BUTTON

How do you know which mouse button is currently selected? When you activate MouseKeys, Windows 98 adds a mouse icon to the information area. It indicates the currently selected button by shading the equivalent button on the mouse icon.

■ To double-click an object, use the arrow keys to move the pointer over the object, press the slash key (/) to select the left mouse button, and press the plus sign (+) to double-click.

■ To right-click an object, use the arrow keys to move the pointer over the object, press the minus sign (–) to select the right mouse button, and press 5.

■ To drag-and-drop an object, use the arrow keys to move the pointer over the object, press the slash key (/) to select the left mouse button, press Insert to lock the button, use the arrow keys to move the object to its destination, and press Delete to release the button and drop the object.

■ To right-drag-and-drop an object, use the arrow keys to move the pointer over the object; press the minus sign (–) to select the right mouse button; press Insert to lock the button; use the arrow keys to move the object to its destination; and then press Delete to release the button, drop the object, and display the context menu.

Clicking the Settings button brings up the Settings for MouseKeys dialog box, shown in Figure 7.6. Here's a summary of the options available in this dialog box:

Use shortcut: Activating this check box enables you to turn MouseKeys on and off by pressing the following key combination: Left Alt+Left Shift+Num Lock.

Top speed: Use this slider to set the maximum speed the mouse pointer moves when you hold down an arrow key.

Acceleration: Use this slider to specify how quickly the mouse pointer achieves its top speed after you hold down an arrow key.

Hold down Ctrl to speed up and Shift to slow down: When this check box is turned on, you can hold down the Ctrl key to make the mouse pointer travel faster when you're holding down an arrow key. To slow down the pointer, hold down Shift.

Use MouseKeys when Num Lock is: These options determine the relationship between MouseKeys and the Num Lock key. When On is activated (this is the default), for example, Windows 98 will use MouseKeys whenever you have Num Lock turned on. If you then turn off Num Lock, you can use the regular arrow keys.

Show MouseKey status on screen: When this check box is activated, Windows 98 displays the MouseKeys icon in the system tray. Double-clicking this icon opens the Accessibility Properties dialog box.

FIGURE 7.6.

Use this dialog box to customize the MouseKeys feature.

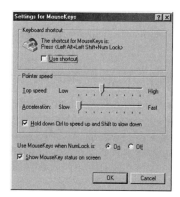

General Options for All Accessibility Settings

The General tab of the Accessibility Properties dialog box, shown in Figure 7.7, contains the following options that apply to all the accessibility features:

Turn off accessibility features after idle for *x* minutes: If you want to leave the accessibility options turned on all the time, deactivate this check box. Otherwise, activate the check box to put a time limit on the accessibility options. Also, enter the number of minutes after which all the options are turned off.

Notification: Activate the Give warning message when turning a feature on check box to tell Windows 98 to display a message whenever a feature is activated. Activate the Make a sound when turning a feature on or off check box to tell Windows 98 to beep the speaker each time a feature is turned on or off.

SerialKey devices: A SerialKey device is an alternative input device (also known as an augmentative communications device) attached to the system's serial port. These devices let the user send equivalent mouse or keyboard commands via the serial port. To enable support for SerialKey devices, activate the Support SerialKey devices check box. Click the Settings button to specify a serial port and baud rate.

FIGURE 7.7.

Use the General tab to set various options that apply to all the accessibility features.

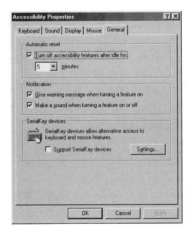

Easier Accessibility Access: The Accessibility Wizard

As you've seen so far, Windows 98 has a large and complex set of accessibility options. Newer users may find all those check boxes and sliders intimidating, so Microsoft added a new Accessibility Wizard to give users a step-by-step approach to accessibility. To launch the Wizard, select Start | Programs | Accessories | Accessibility | Accessibility Settings Wizard. Windows 98 displays the first of the Wizard's dialog boxes, as shown in Figure 7.8.

The Accessibility Wizard leads you through a series of dialog boxes that cover three different areas of accessibility: vision, hearing, and mobility.

Most of the dialog boxes presented by the Wizard provide similar options to those you saw earlier in the Accessibility Properties dialog box. In some cases, however, the Wizard provides extra tools for choosing your options. In particular, the Wizard will often supply you with a number of samples from which to choose. For example, in Figure 7.8 you can see that the Wizard provides several text samples and you choose the smallest one that you can read.

FIGURE 7.8.
*The Accessibility
Wizard: an easier
way to customize
accessibility.*

A Zoom with a View: Microsoft Magnifier

Some visually impaired users have trouble reading only very small items or making out *New to* **98** the detail in an icon or image. In this case, it's probably overkill to revamp the entire display. A better solution would be the ability to magnify just the problematic areas. Happily, Windows 98 introduces just such a solution: Microsoft Magnifier. This utility sets aside the top part of the screen as a "magnification area." Microsoft Magnifier uses this area to display a magnified version of the active part of the screen (that is, the part of the screen where the mouse or keyboard is active).

To give Microsoft Magnifier a test drive, select Start | Programs | Accessories | Accessibility | Magnifier. As you can see in Figure 7.9, a new window appears in the top part of the screen (this is called the Stationary Window), and the Microsoft Magnifier window appears. As you move the mouse, use the arrow keys to navigate, or type text, a magnified version appears in the stationary window.

You can also use the controls in the Microsoft Magnifier window to customize the application:

Magnification level: Use this spinner to set the magnification used in the stationary window (enter a value between 2 and 12).

Track mouse cursor: When this check box is activated, Microsoft Magnifier follows the mouse cursor and displays the area surrounding the mouse pointer in the stationary window.

Track keyboard focus: When this check box is activated, Microsoft Magnifier tracks the navigation keys and displays whatever object has the focus in the stationary window.

Track text editing: When this check box is activated, Microsoft Magnifier watches for text being entered and displays the text in the stationary window.

Invert colors: When this check box is activated, the stationary window displays the current area with opposite colors.

FIGURE 7.9.
Microsoft Magnifier displays a magnified view of the active screen area.

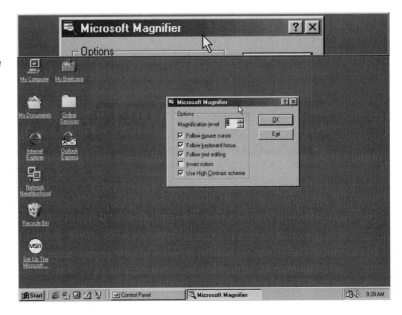

Use High Contrast scheme: When this check box is activated, Windows switches the display to the High Contrast color scheme I discussed earlier.

Personalized Windows: Working with User Profiles

Do you share your computer with other people either at work or at home? Then you're no doubt all too aware of one undeniable fact of human psychology: People are individuals with minds of their own! One person prefers Windows in a black-and-purple color scheme; another person just loves that annoying "Pinstripe" wallpaper; yet another person prefers to have a zillion shortcuts on the Windows 98 desktop; and, of course, everybody uses a different mix of applications. How can you possibly satisfy all these diverse tastes and prevent people from coming to blows?

It's a lot easier than you might think. Windows 98 lets you set up a different user profile for each person who uses the computer. Each profile includes all the customization options we've covered in the last three chapters, such as colors, patterns, wallpapers, shortcut icons, the screen saver, and programs that appear on the Start menu. You can also set up personal versions of the Favorites folder, the My Documents folder, and Internet Explorer features such as cookie files and the History list. This means that each person can customize Windows 98 to his heart's content without foisting his tastes on anyone else.

> ## THE PASSWORDS METHOD IS OBSOLETE
>
> In Windows 95, you established user profiles via the Passwords Control Panel. Although you can still use that method, the Users Control Panel gives you much more flexibility in setting up and managing users.

Creating a User Profile

To begin, you should set up your own "supervisor" profile. To do so, follow these steps:

1. Select Start | Settings | Control Panel and open the Users icon. Windows 98 displays the Enable Multi-user Settings dialog box.

2. Click Next >. The Add User dialog box appears.

3. Enter your username and then click Next >. The Enter New Password dialog box appears.

4. Enter a password for your profile (twice) and then click Next >. (Note that although the password is optional, it's a good idea to enter one for your supervisor profile.) Windows 98 displays the Personalized Items Settings dialog box, as shown in Figure 7.10.

FIGURE 7.10.

Use the Personalized Items Settings dialog box to select the folders to be included in the new user profile.

5. Activate the check boxes for the folders you want to personalize. Note, too, that you can either create the folders as duplicates of the existing folders or start them out empty. When you're done, click Next >.

6. Click Finish. Windows 98 creates the new folders for your user profile and then asks if you want to restart Windows.

7. Click Yes.

When Windows 98 reloads (and each subsequent time you restart Windows 98), you see the Welcome to Windows dialog box. The idea here is that all people who use the computer will have their own usernames, which Windows will use to save their settings. So when you log on, you type your username in the User name field, type the optional password in the Password field, and click OK.

Note that, for each user, Windows 98 creates a new subfolder in the Profiles folder. For example, if you create a profile for a user named Biff, you end up with the following new folder (assuming that your main Windows 98 folder is C:\Windows):

C:\Windows\Profiles\Biff

This new folder contains several subfolders that you can use to store various shortcuts for the user. These subfolders include Desktop, Recent, SendTo, and Start Menu.

FASTER LOGONS

Don't forget that if someone else is logged on to Windows 98 and you prefer to use your settings, you don't have to restart Windows 98. Instead, select Start | Log Off *User* (where *User* is the name of the currently logged on user). When Windows 98 asks whether you're sure you want to log off, click Yes.

NOTE: ACCESSING THE ORIGINAL DESKTOP

The settings for each new user are based on the original desktop configuration that existed when you enabled user profiles. If you want to change this configuration, restart Windows and, when you get to the logon dialog box, click Cancel. This will force Windows 98 to load the original desktop.

Working with User Settings

After you create your supervisor user profile, each time you launch the Users Control Panel you see the User Settings dialog box, shown in Figure 7.11. This dialog box offers the following buttons:

New User: Runs through the previous procedure for creating another user profile.

Delete: Deletes the currently highlighted user.

Make a Copy: This button also runs through the previous procedure for creating another user profile. However, when you get to the Choose Personalized Folders dialog box, the selected folders will be the same as those of whatever user was highlighted when you clicked Make a Copy.

Set Password: Enables you to alter a user's password.

Change Settings: Displays the Choose Personalized Folders dialog box.

FIGURE 7.11.

The User Settings dialog box enables you to work with the user profiles established on your machine.

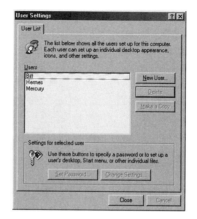

Worldwide Windows: Customizing the Regional Settings

If you'll be writing documents to send to foreign countries, you need to tailor certain aspects of your writing for your readership. For example, if you'll be using foreign currency amounts, not only will you need to use the appropriate currency symbol, but you also will want to place the symbol in the correct position relative to the amount. In Germany, for example, the deutsche mark symbol (DM) is placed after the amount (for example, 5,000 DM). Similarly, date formats are different around the world. In the United States, for example, 12/11/98 means December 11, 1998; in Great Britain, however, 12/11/98 is interpreted as the 12th of November, 1998.

To make your documents easier for foreign readers (and to avoid being embarrassingly late for some appointments!), Windows 98 supports different regional settings for various countries. These settings apply to all Windows applications, and they set the defaults for such things as number formats, currency symbols, and date and time formats.

To view these settings, select Start | Settings | Control Panel and then open the Regional Settings icon from the Control Panel folder. Windows 98 displays the Regional Settings Properties dialog box, shown in Figure 7.12. Use the drop-down list to select the country whose settings you want to work with and click OK. Windows 98 then prompts you to restart the computer.

If you need to change only a few settings, use the following tabs:

Number: The controls on this tab determine the default format for numeric values, including the number of decimal places, the negative number format, and the measurement system (Metric or U.S.).

Currency: The controls on this tab determine the default format for currency values, including the currency symbol and its position.

FIGURE 7.12.

Use this dialog box to set the default values for various regional settings used by your Windows applications.

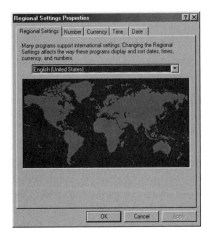

Time: The controls on this tab determine the default format for time values, including the time style and the time separator.

Date: The controls on this tab determine the default format for date values, including the short date style and separator and the long date style.

When you've made your selections, click OK.

Summary

This chapter continued your Windows 98 customization tour by showing you how to work with accessibility options, user profiles, and regional settings. Here's a list of chapters where you'll find related information:

- To learn about Web integration and its effect on the Windows 98 interface, see Chapter 5, "Web Integration and the Active Desktop."

- I cover a host of visual customization options in Chapter 6, "Customizing the Taskbar, Start Menu, and Display."

- To learn how to customize your mouse, keyboard, and game controllers, see Chapter 8, "Customizing the Mouse, Keyboard, and Other Input Devices."

- I show you how to associate sounds with various Windows 98 events in Chapter 25, "Windows 98 Audio Features."

Customizing the Mouse, Keyboard, and Other Input Devices

CHAPTER 8

IN THIS CHAPTER

The mark of our time is its revulsion against imposed patterns.

—*Marshall McLuhan*

Windows 98's new interface is not only slick, but it's also more efficient than the one in Windows 95, and it's infinitely more attractive than the ugly mug we had to look at every day with Windows 3.*x*. But Windows 98 would be just another pretty interface if it didn't afford us some flexibility in terms of how we interact with that interface. In other words, under different circumstances we demand different input devices—whether a mouse, keyboard, or joystick—and we demand a certain level of customization so that these input devices operate the way we want them to. To that end, this chapter looks at the various customization options Windows 98 makes available to mouse, keyboard, and joystick users.

Manipulating Mouse Properties

Much of Windows 98 was made with the mouse in mind, so it's important that you're comfortable handling the little rodent. To help out, Windows 98 offers the Mouse Properties dialog box, shown in Figure 8.1. (If you have IntelliPoint software installed, your dialog box will have a different layout. See "Extra IntelliPoint Goodies," later in this chapter.) To display this dialog box, select Start | Settings | Control Panel and then activate the Mouse icon from the Control Panel folder. As usual, you can put your new settings into effect at any time by clicking the Apply button. When you're done, click OK to vacate the dialog box.

FIGURE 8.1.

*Use the Mouse
Properties dialog box to
customize your mouse.*

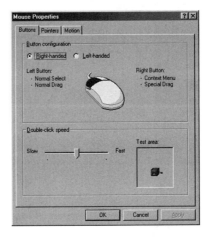

Setting Up the Mouse for Southpaws

With Windows 98's Web integration, you click the left mouse button to launch an object, and you drag with the left mouse button held down to copy or move an object. Similarly, you click the right mouse button to display the context menu for the current object, and you drag with the right mouse button held down to display the "special drag" context menu when you drop the object.

If you're a left-hander and this "rightist" orientation bothers you, it's easy enough to reverse things: Just activate the Left-handed option in the Buttons tab of the Mouse Properties dialog box. After you've applied this new setting, here's how it affects your mouse movements:

- You now click and double-click with the right mouse button.
- To drag something, you now press and hold down the right button.
- To display a context menu, you now left-click an object.
- To perform the "special drag" in Explorer, you now hold down the left mouse button.

Setting the Double-Click Speed

One of the things a mouse-aware program must do is distinguish between two consecutive single-clicks and a double-click. For example, if you click once, wait five seconds, and then click again, that would qualify as two single-clicks in most people's books. But what if there's only a second between clicks? Or half a second? This threshold is called the *double-click speed*: Anything faster is handled as a double-click; anything slower is handled as two single clicks.

You can adjust this threshold by using the Double-click speed slider in the Buttons tab of the Mouse Properties dialog box. You have two options:

- If you find that Windows 98 doesn't always recognize your double-clicks, set up a slower double-click speed by moving the slider bar to the left.
- If you find that Windows 98 is sometimes interpreting two consecutive single clicks as a double-click, set up a faster double-click speed by moving the slider bar to the right.

To test the new speed, double-click the Test area. If Windows 98 recognizes your double-click, a Jack-in-the-box pops up.

Trying Different Pointers on for Size

As you trudge through Windows 98, you'll notice that the mouse pointer busies itself by changing into different icons depending on what you're doing. There's the standard arrow for selecting everything from check boxes to files and folders, there's the two-headed arrow for sizing window borders, and, of course, there's the dreaded hourglass icon that appears whenever a program or Windows 98 is too busy to bother with you right now. (However, as you'll see in Chapter 9, "Performance Tuning: Optimizing Memory and Disk Access," the preemptive multitasking used with 32-bit applications means that seeing an hourglass icon in one program usually doesn't prevent you from working in a different program.)

Surprisingly, the pointers used by Windows 98 in these and other situations aren't fixed. You can specify pointers of different shapes and sizes, and Windows 98 even supports animated pointers (such as an hourglass with falling sand). To see how you can specify different pointers, in the Mouse Properties dialog box select the Pointers tab, shown in Figure 8.2.

8

CUSTOMIZING THE MOUSE AND OTHER DEVICES

FIGURE 8.2.

Use the Pointers tab to select a different set of mouse pointers.

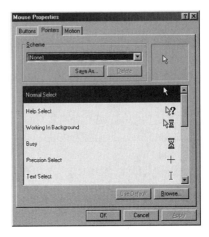

The easiest way to try out different pointers is to choose one of the pointer schemes that comes with Windows 98. To select a scheme, use the Scheme drop-down list and then take a look at the sample pointers in the box below the list to see what they look like.

TRY THE LARGER POINTERS FOR EASIER VISIBILITY

The Scheme list has several items that produce much bigger pointers—look for the scheme names ending with (large) and (extra large). These mutant pointers are handy if you're having trouble picking up the regular pointers in a sea of windows (especially on some cramped notebook screens).

If you feel like creating a scheme of your own, here are the steps to follow:

1. Highlight the type of pointer you want to change.
2. Click the Browse button. Windows 98 displays the Browse dialog box and opens the Cursors folder (this is a subfolder of your main Windows 98 folder).
3. Choose the pointer you want to use and click Open.
4. Repeat steps 1 through 3 to customize any other pointers.
5. To save your scheme, click the Save As button, enter a name in the Save Scheme dialog box, and click OK.

RESETTING THE POINTERS

If you'd prefer to return your mouse pointers to their natural state, click the Use Default button.

Controlling the Tracking Speed

When you move the mouse, Windows 98 translates this movement and tracks the mouse pointer onscreen accordingly. How quickly the mouse moves across the screen is called the *tracking speed*. If this speed is out of whack (for example, if you move the mouse furiously but the pointer just creeps along, or, conversely, if the slightest hand tremor causes the pointer to race across the screen), your mouse is likely to end up in the nearest garbage can.

The good news is that adjusting the tracking speed is a snap. In the Mouse Properties dialog box, select the Motion tab, shown in Figure 8.3. Then take a look at the Pointer speed slider. You can do two things with this control:

■ If the mouse pointer is flying around the screen, slow it down by dragging the slider bar to the left.

■ If the pointer is too slow, drag the slider bar to the right.

If you'd like to test the new setting, click the Apply button and then try moving the mouse around.

FIGURE 8.3.
The Motion tab controls the mouse tracking speed and mouse trails (see the next section).

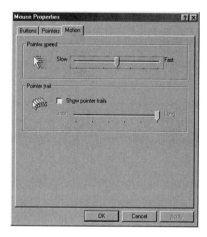

Activating Pointer Trails

Many people with notebook computers or eyesight that isn't quite what it used to be complained they had trouble finding the little mouse pointer on their screen. So Microsoft, ever sensitive, included a Pointer trail feature in Windows 98. (Not all video displays support this feature, however.) When you activate the Show pointer trails check box and move the mouse, you see a trail of pointers following behind the main pointer. You can also use the slider bar to make the trail longer or shorter.

CHANGING THE MOUSE DRIVER

The General tab on the Mouse Properties dialog box enables you to change your mouse driver. I cover the general steps for changing hardware drivers in Chapter 11, "Device Advice: Dealing with Devices in Windows 98."

Extra IntelliPoint Goodies

When Microsoft introduced version 2.0 of its mouse back in 1993, it also updated the mouse utilities with a few extra options. The latest iteration of this software is IntelliPoint 2.0, and it comes with a fistful of controls for tailoring your mouse to suit your style. This section reviews the new tidbits that come with IntelliPoint 2.0.

INTELLIPOINT 2.0 AND WINDOWS 98

IntelliPoint 2.0 was designed to work with Windows 95. If you install Windows 98 over your old IntelliPoint settings, some of the functionality may become disabled. You need to either upgrade to a version of IntelliPoint designed for Windows 98 (not available as this book went to press) or reinstall IntelliPoint 2.0.

Note, as well, that some of the IntelliPoint 2.0 options aren't compatible with Windows 98's Web integration.

When you activate the Control Panel's Mouse icon (or if you select Start | Programs | Microsoft Input Devices | Mouse | IntelliPoint 2.0), you see the dialog box shown in Figure 8.4. This dialog box incorporates all the options found in the standard Mouse properties sheet and adds quite a few more. The Pointers tab is identical, and the Basics tab provides alternative controls for the pointer speed, double-click speed, and button selection. The rest of the tabs have extra tools that are explained in the next few sections.

FIGURE 8.4.

The revised Mouse Properties dialog box that comes with IntelliPoint 2.0.

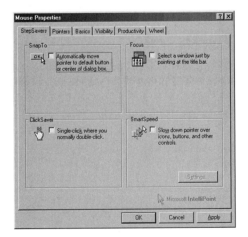

The StepSavers Tab

The StepSavers tab, shown in Figure 8.4, contains four options related to mouse movements:

SnapTo: This is a handy feature that can make it easier to navigate dialog boxes. Most dialog boxes have a default command button (usually the OK button, but not always) that you can select by pressing Enter. When you activate the SnapTo check box, Windows 98 automatically places the mouse pointer over the default button. So, to select this button, you just click.

Focus: When you enable this check box, you can activate any open window by hovering the mouse pointer over the window's title bar.

ClickSaver: If you activate this option, you can use a single click in place of a double-click if you've turned Windows 98's Web integration off.

SmartSpeed: Most mouse movements involve tracking across the screen to a specific element, such as a title bar, scroll bar, window border, dialog box button, toolbar icon, and so on. When you activate this check box, Windows 98 slows down the mouse pointer when it tracks over one of these elements. Click the Settings button to control how much the pointer slows down.

The Visibility Tab

The Visibility tab, shown in Figure 8.5, contains various options that control the visibility of the mouse pointer in different circumstances:

Sonar: This is a handy option if you find yourself losing the mouse pointer in a sea of windows, text, and toolbars. When you activate this check box, pressing Ctrl displays a series of concentric circles that zero in on the mouse pointer.

Vanish: Activate this check box to make the mouse pointer disappear whenever you begin typing. The pointer will reappear as soon as you move the mouse.

Trails: This is the same mouse trails option that I discussed earlier.

PointerWrap: This is one of my favorite features of the new mouse. If you activate this button and then, for example, move the mouse pointer off the left edge of the screen, it reappears on the right side. It's not for everyone, and it does take some getting used to, but it can make mousing around remarkably easier.

FIGURE 8.5.

The Visibility tab controls the appearance of the pointer.

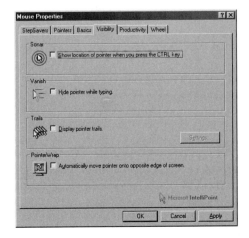

The Productivity Tab

The Productivity tab, shown in Figure 8.6 is really just a mixed bag of options. Here's a summary:

Odometer: If you activate the Turn on the Odometer check box, Windows 98 tracks all your mouse movements and translates them into feet and (eventually) miles. No, I'm not sure why anyone would want to know this.

Orientation: If you have a unique way of holding the mouse, or if the ergonomics of your workspace dictate that you can't use the standard mouse movements, the controls in the Orientation group may be able to help. The idea here is that you tell IntelliPoint which mouse direction is "up" for you. Normally, "up" means moving the mouse forward (that is, toward the cable). To define a different direction, click Set Orientation and then follow the instructions. (To return the mouse to its standard behavior, click Use Defaults.)

ClickLock: If you activate this check box, IntelliPoint enables you to drag an object without holding down the mouse button. That is, you click the object, hold down the mouse button for a second or two, and then release the button. IntelliPoint acts as if the mouse button is still held down. You can then move the mouse to drag the object. When you're done, click the object again. To control the amount of time you have to hold down the mouse button to lock it, click Settings.

FIGURE 8.6.

Use the Productivity tab to tell Windows 98 which way is "up" for you.

The Wheel Tab: Customizing the Wheel "Button"

The latest Microsoft mouse—the IntelliMouse—ships with an extra wheel "button" between the two regular buttons. Windows 98 includes built-in support for this wheel, which means you can use it to scroll up and down within windows, text boxes, list boxes, and within any application that uses the standard Windows 98 controls. Here's how the wheel works:

■ Rotating the wheel forward or backward scrolls up or down within the current object. The default scroll is 3 lines at a time. (The wheel is ratcheted, so you can rotate in discrete movements.)

■ Clicking the wheel within a scrollable object locks the scroll function. You can then scroll up or down by moving the mouse itself forward or back.

You can use the Wheel tab, shown in Figure 8.7, to turn wheel support on or off or for customizing the wheel's behavior.

FIGURE 8.7.

You can use the Wheel tab to control Windows 98's wheel support.

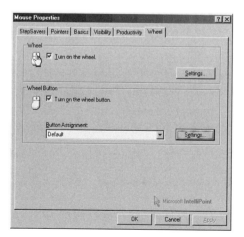

New to **98**

8

CUSTOMIZING THE MOUSE AND OTHER DEVICES

For starters, use the Turn on the wheel check box to toggle Windows 98's wheel support on and off. When wheel support is activated, click Settings to work with the following options:

Reverse the response your programs have when you rotate the wheel: Activate this check box to reverse the wheel's rotation behavior. (For example, rotating the wheel forward scrolls *down*.)

Scroll *x* lines at a time: Activate this option to scroll the specified number of lines with each discrete wheel rotation.

Scroll one "screen" a time: Activate this option to scroll by one screenful of information with each discrete wheel rotation (equivalent to pressing Page Up or Page Down).

Use the Turn on the wheel button check box to toggle the button aspect of the wheel on and off. When this option is activated, use the Button Assignment list to specify how Windows 98 should interpret a wheel click. You can also click Settings to set how fast the pointer moves when you drag the mouse after pressing the wheel button.

Customizing the Mouse with TweakUI

The TweakUI utility that I told you about in Chapter 7, "Setting Accessibility Options, User Profiles, and More," offers a few wheel-related settings, as shown in Figure 8.8. Here's a summary:

Menu speed: This setting controls how quickly Windows 98 displays a submenu when you hover the mouse over an item in a context menu. To test it out, right-click the Test Icon.

Double-click: This spinner controls how close (in pixels) two clicks must be before Windows 98 will recognize them as a double-click. If you find that the mouse moves when you double-click, try a higher pixel value.

Drag: This spinner controls how far (in pixels) an object must be moved before Windows 98 assumes you are dragging the object. If you find that Windows 98 often moves an object slightly when you click it, increase the pixel setting.

Use mouse wheel for scrolling: This check box toggles the scrolling feature of the wheel on and off.

Scroll a page at a time: If scrolling is enabled, activate this option to scroll one "page" with each discrete wheel rotation (equivalent to pressing Page Up or Page Down).

Scroll by *x* lines at a time: If scrolling is enabled, activate this option to scroll the specified number of lines with each discrete wheel rotation.

FIGURE 8.8.
You can use TweakUI to tweak the wheel settings for the IntelliMouse.

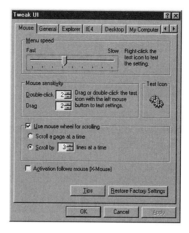

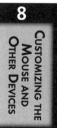

Customizing the Keyboard

Although a mouse makes many everyday Windows 98 tasks easier, we're still a long way from having to ditch our trusty keyboards. In fact, after you get used to a few Windows 98 keyboard shortcuts, you'll find yourself reaching for the mouse less and less. This section shows you a few techniques for customizing your keyboard.

Setting the Delay and Repeat Rate

When you press and hold down a key on the keyboard, you notice two things: First, when you press the key, there is a slight *delay* before the second letter appears; second, the subsequent characters appear at a constant rate (called the *repeat rate*). Beginning keyboardists are usually better off with a longer delay and a slower repeat rate. More experienced typists, on the other hand, would probably prefer a short delay combined with a fast repeat rate.

Happily, Windows 98 lets you change both these values. To see how, select Start | Settings | Control Panel and then open the Control Panel's Keyboard icon. Windows 98 displays the Keyboard Properties dialog box, shown in Figure 8.9.

You control the delay by using the Repeat delay slider. Move the slider bar (by dragging it with the mouse or by using the left- and right-arrow keys) to the left for a longer delay or to the right for a shorter delay.

As you've no doubt guessed by now, the Repeat rate slider controls the repeat rate. Move the slider bar to the left for a slower rate or to the right for a faster one.

To try out the new settings, head for the Click here and hold down a key to test repeat rate text box. Press and hold down any key and check out the delay and the repeat rate.

FIGURE 8.9.

Use the Keyboard Properties dialog box to adjust your keyboard's delay and repeat rate.

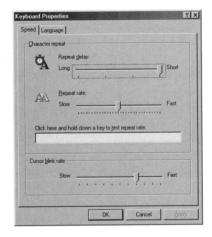

Typing with the United States-International Keyboard Layout

The Windows 98 character set consists of many more characters than those you can peck out on the keyboard. Symbols such as £ and ¢, and foreign letters such as ä and ç are all part of the Windows ANSI character set. If you need to access these characters only occasionally, it's best to use the Character Map accessory (Start | Programs | Accessories | Character Map). For those who use these symbols regularly, however, Windows 98 provides a way to type them directly on the keyboard.

The trick is that Windows 98 supports various keyboard layouts. In particular, it supports a layout called United States-International that augments the normal keys with many new symbols. To switch to this layout, follow these steps:

1. In the Keyboard Properties dialog box, select the Language tab.

2. In the Language list, highlight the English (United States) item.

3. Click the Properties button. Windows 98 displays the Language Properties dialog box.

4. In the Keyboard layout drop-down list, select United States-International (see Figure 8.10).

FIGURE 8.10.

Use the Language Properties dialog box to choose the United States-International keyboard layout.

5. Click OK to return to the Keyboard Properties dialog box.

6. Click OK or Apply.

7. Follow the prompts onscreen when Windows 98 asks you for your source CD-ROM or disks.

Table 8.1 outlines the changes this new layout makes to your keyboard. The Ctrl+Alt column means that you hold down Ctrl and Alt and press the key; the Ctrl+Alt+Shift column means that you hold down Ctrl, Alt, and Shift and press the key.

Table 8.1. Keyboard changes with the United States-International layout.

Key	Ctrl+Alt	Ctrl+Alt+Shift	Key	Ctrl+Alt	Ctrl+Alt+Shift
1	?	1	I	í	Í
2	2	N/A	O	ó	Ó
3	3	N/A	P	ö	Ö
4	¤	£	[	«	N/A
6	··	N/A	]	»	N/A
7	´	N/A	\	¬	¦
8	p	N/A	A	á	Á
9	´	N/A	S	ß	§
0	´	N/A	D	u	q
-	¥	N/A	L	ø	Ø
=	¥	÷	;	T	°
Q	ä	Ä	Z	æ	Æ
W	-	-	C	©	¢
E	é	É	N	ñ	Ñ
R	®	N/A	M	µ	N/A
T	w	t	<	ç	Ç
Y	ü	Ü	?	¿	N/A
U	ú	Ú			

RIGHT ALT EQUALS CTRL+ALT

Rather than holding down both Ctrl and Alt, you can use the right Alt key by itself.

8

CUSTOMIZING THE
MOUSE AND
OTHER DEVICES

Besides the layout changes shown in Table 8.1, Windows 98 also sets up several so-called "dead keys." These are keys that do nothing until you press another key. When you do, Windows 98 inserts the second key with an accent. Table 8.2 lists the dead keys. Note that, in each case, you press and release the dead key (such as ˜) and then press and release the other key (such as N). If you want to type a particular dead key itself, press the key and then press the spacebar.

Table 8.2. Dead keys used with the United States-International layout.

Dead Key	Accent Created	Example
˜ (tilde)	Tilde	Press ˜ and then N to get ñ.
' (back quote)	Grave accent	Press ' and then A to get à.
^ (caret)	Circumflex	Press ^ and then E to get ê.
" (quotation mark)	Diaeresis	Press " and then I to get ï.
' (apostrophe)	Acute accent	Press ' and then E to get é.

Working with Keyboard Languages

If you need to write documents in different languages, or even if you need to use multiple languages in a single document, Windows 98 can make your life a lot easier. That's because no matter what kind of keyboard you have, Windows 98 supports keyboard layouts for various languages.

To add another keyboard language to Windows 98, follow these steps:

1. Display the Language tab in the Keyboard Properties dialog box.
2. Click the Add button. The Add Language dialog box, shown in Figure 8.11, is displayed.

FIGURE 8.11.

Use the Add Language dialog box to select the keyboard language you want to add.

3. Use the Language drop-down list to select the language you want to work with.
4. Click OK to return to the Keyboard Properties dialog box.
5. If you want to set the new language as the default for your applications, highlight the language and then click Set as Default.
6. Use the Switch languages group to set the shortcut key for switching from one language to another.

7. If you leave the Enable indicator on taskbar check box activated, you can switch languages from the taskbar (explained after these steps).

8. Click OK or Apply.

9. Follow the prompts onscreen when Windows 98 asks you for your source CD-ROM or disks.

After you add a second keyboard language, Windows 98 displays a language indicator in the taskbar's information area. Clicking this indicator displays a pop-up list of the available languages, as shown in Figure 8.12. Click the language you want to use. (You can also cycle between languages by pressing the shortcut key you specified in the Keyboard Properties dialog box; the default is Left Alt+Shift.)

FIGURE 8.12.

Use the taskbar's language indicator to choose the language in which you want to type.

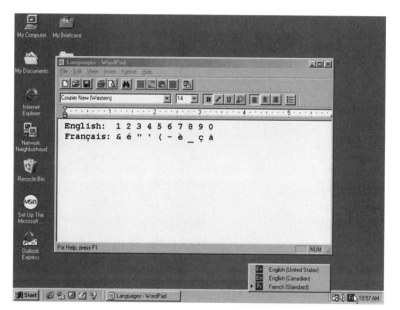

8

CUSTOMIZING THE
MOUSE AND
OTHER DEVICES

MULTILANGUAGE SUPPORT

If you installed the Multilanguage Support component when you installed Windows 98 (or by using the Add/Remove Programs Wizard), you can use WordPad to write documents in the Baltic, Cyrillic (Bulgarian, Belarusian, and Russian), Greek, Turkish, and Central European (Czech, Hungarian, Polish, and Slovenian) languages. You also need to add the appropriate keyboard language. Use the taskbar to switch to the keyboard language you want to use; then open WordPad's Font dialog box and choose the language (or language group) from the Script drop-down list.

CHANGING THE KEYBOARD DRIVER

The General tab on the Keyboard Properties dialog box enables you to change your keyboard driver. I provide the general steps for changing hardware drivers in Chapter 11.

Using the Microsoft Natural Keyboard

If you have the Microsoft Natural Keyboard (or a compatible keyboard), you have access to a wealth of Windows 98 shortcuts. In particular, the ⊞ key saves lots of wear and tear on your wrists and fingers. Used by itself, this key opens the Start menu, which is a lot easier than pressing the tough-to-reach Ctrl+Esc key combination. But you also can use it in various key combinations to gain quick access to many Windows 98 features. Table 8.3 summarizes these key combinations.

Table 8.3. The Microsoft Natural Keyboard—the key.

Key	Action
⊞	Opens the Start menu
⊞+A	Opens the Accessibility Options (if installed)
⊞+C	Opens the Control Panel
⊞+E	Opens the Explorer
⊞+F	Finds a file or folder
Ctrl+⊞+F	Finds a computer
⊞+I	Opens the mouse properties
⊞+K	Opens the keyboard properties
⊞+L	Logs on and off Windows
⊞+M	Minimizes all
Shift+⊞+M	Undoes minimize all
⊞+P	Opens the Print Manager
⊞+R	Displays the Run dialog box
⊞+S	Enables or disables the Caps Lock key
⊞+V	Views the Clipboard
⊞+F1	Displays Windows Help
⊞+Break	Displays the system properties
⊞+Spacebar	Displays this list of shortcuts
⊞+Tab	Activates open programs in order

For good measure, the Microsoft Natural Keyboard also includes an Application key. It has a picture of a little pull-down menu. Pressing this key activates the context menu for the current object.

IntelliType Options

The Microsoft Natural Keyboard also comes with version 1.1 of Microsoft's IntelliType software. Installing IntelliType adds an extra Options tab to the Keyboard Properties dialog box, as shown in Figure 8.13. (You also get the Pointer Activity tab, which contains the mouse-related Sonar, PointerWrap, SnapTo, and Vanish options discussed earlier.) Here's a review of the new options found on this tab:

FIGURE 8.13.

The IntelliType keyboard software adds an extra Options tab to the Keyboard Properties dialog box.

Windows Logon/Logoff: When activated, this options enables you to display the Windows Logon dialog box by pressing both keys on your keyboard. Note, however, that this option is available only in Windows NT and Windows for Workgroups.

Key Locks: These check boxes specify the state of the Num Lock, Caps Lock, and Scroll Lock keys at system startup. Activating a check box tells Windows 98 to activate the corresponding key at boot time.

Sounds: This drop-down list lets you assign sounds to keyboard events. A number of sound schemes are available.

Disable CAPS LOCK while in Windows: If you activate this check box, Windows 98 ignores the Caps Lock key while you're working in Windows. This is an excellent idea, because it prevents accidental activation of Caps Lock and long runs of all-uppercase letters. If you find that you do need Caps Lock turned on, press the key three times in succession.

Calibrating a Game Controller

Nothing takes the joy out of playing certain kinds of games more than a joystick that's out of whack. If you use a joystick or other game controller for your Windows 98–based games, you want to calibrate it so that Windows 98 understands its features (range of motion, throttle, rudder, and so on). Here are the steps to follow to calibrate a game controller:

1. Select Start | Settings | Control Panel and select the Game Controllers icon. Windows 98 displays the Game Controllers dialog box, shown in Figure 8.14.

FIGURE 8.14.

Use the Game Controllers dialog box to customize your joystick.

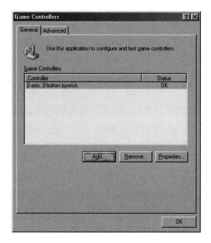

2. If your game controller is not listed, click Add, highlight the type of game controller you use, and then click OK.

3. If you have multiple game controllers, use the Game Controllers list to select the one you want to calibrate.

4. Click Properties to display the Game Controller Properties dialog box.

5. Click the Calibrate button. The Calibration dialog box for the selected game controller appears.

6. You now work through a series of dialog boxes that sets various properties of the joystick (such as its center position, as shown in Figure 8.15, and its range of motion). In each, perform the requested action, press a joystick button, and click Next >.

7. When the calibration is complete, click Finish to return to the Game Controller Properties dialog box.

8. To test your calibration, display the Test tab, shown in Figure 8.16.

9. Move the joystick and press its buttons to test the calibration, and then click OK.

Figure 8.15.

To calibrate your joystick, you run through a series of dialog boxes like this one.

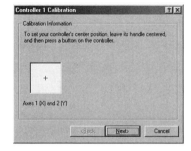

Figure 8.16.

Use this dialog box to test your calibration.

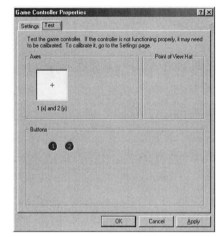

8

Customizing the Mouse and Other Devices

Summary

This chapter took you through various options for customizing your input devices in Windows 98. For the mouse, you learned how to set options such as the double-click speed, pointers, and tracking speed. You also learned about the new options found in IntelliPoint 2.0. For the keyboard, I showed you how to set the delay and repeat rate, how to use the United States-International keyboard layout and keyboard languages, and how to use the Microsoft Natural Keyboard. You also learned how to calibrate a game controller in Windows 98.

Here's a list of chapters where you'll find related information:

■ Windows 98's Accessibility Options contains a number of mouse- and keyboard-related tools. I tell you about them in Chapter 7, "Setting Accessibility Options, User Profiles, and More."

■ To learn how to install device drivers, see Chapter 11, "Device Advice: Dealing with Devices in Windows 98."

Performance Tuning: Optimizing Memory and Disk Access

IN THIS CHAPTER

Speed, it seems to me, provides the one genuinely modern pleasure.

—Aldous Huxley

In Chapter 1, "Preparing for the Windows 98 Installation," I spent some time musing about why our workaday computer chores seem to take just as long as they ever did, despite the fact that our hardware is, generally speaking, bigger, better, and faster than ever. The answer to this apparent riddle is related to Parkinson's Law of Data: Data expands to fill the space available for storage. On a more general level, Parkinson's Law could be restated as follows: The increase in software system requirements is directly proportional to the increase in hardware system capabilities. A slick new chip is released that promises a 30 percent speed boost; software designers, seeing the new chip gain wide acceptance, add extra features to their already bloated code to take advantage of the higher performance level; then another new chip is released, followed by another software upgrade—and the cycle continues *ad nauseum* as these twin engines of computer progress lurch codependently into the future.

So how do you break out of the performance deadlock created by the immovable object of software code bloat meeting the irresistible force of hardware advancement? By optimizing your system to minimize the effects of overgrown applications and to maximize the native capabilities of your hardware. Learning how to optimize memory, hard disks, and devices is the key to unleashing your system's performance potential, and that's exactly what I'll show you how to do in this chapter.

Before discussing those tools, you should know that Microsoft claims Windows 98 should be faster than Windows 95 and should consume fewer resources. Here's why:

- The number of chores Windows 98 performs at startup and shutdown have been reduced or even eliminated in some cases. This should result in faster startups and shutdowns for most machines.

- The Windows 98 Memory Manager module has been optimized. Microsoft claims the new Memory Manager uses less memory and smaller swap files.

- The Windows 98 Memory Manager also includes a utility called Winalign. This tool runs during the Windows 98 Setup, and its purpose is to realign the clusters within a file so that they begin on certain predetermined boundaries. This enables the Memory Manager to optimize how these files are loaded into memory.

- Windows 98 supports the Intel MMX chip via DirectX 5.0. This should supply a noticeable speed increase in some graphics-intensive applications, particularly if you don't have a good 3D graphics accelerator in your system.

- Disk Defragmenter does a better job of optimizing your hard disk. In particular, Disk Defragmenter can monitor the programs you use most often and arrange the clusters of those programs so they are contiguous and thus easier to find and load.

Windows 98 and Memory: A Primer

Entire books can be (and, indeed, have been) written about the relationship between Windows and memory. What it all boils down to, though, is quite simple: The more memory you have, the happier Windows (and most of your programs) will be. However, not everyone can afford to throw 64 megabytes of memory at their problems. We have to make do with less, and that, in essence, is what this chapter is all about. Later, I'll show you some ways to fight back if a lack of memory is slowing Windows 98 to a crawl.

The Move to 32 Bits

Windows 98 simplifies things (relatively speaking) by moving from the 16-bit segmented memory addressing that shackled DOS for so many years to the full 32-bit addressing associated with 80386 and higher processors. 32 bits can be arranged in 2^{32}, or 4,294,967,296, different ways, which gives programs an address space of 4GB. Not only that, but the 80386 and higher processors handle data in 32-bit pieces. This means that programmers no longer have the 64KB segment restrictions. Instead, they're free to reference any memory location in the full 4GB address space directly (with certain restrictions, as you'll see later). This is called a *flat memory space*. (Technically, they still use the segment/offset model; however, the segment register always points to the beginning of the address space.) Data is also no longer restricted to 64KB, but can be as large as 4GB. This new memory model is called a *flat memory model*, or sometimes a *linear addressing model*.

32-BIT APPLICATIONS

To take full advantage of Windows 98's "32-bitness," however, you need to use 32-bit applications. Sixteen-bit programs still must use the old segmented memory model, so they remain inherently inefficient. That's not to say, though, that the move to 32-bit programs will result in instant speed increases. If the program always works with small data (less than 64KB), a 32-bit program won't process this data any faster. However, 32-bit programs will likely be better bets in the long run because of the Win32 advantages, such as preemptive multitasking and multithreading. (Win32 is the application programming interface (API) that developers use to create 32-bit applications.)

How Windows 98 Handles Memory

One of the big breakthroughs with Windows 98 is that it uses this flat memory model. All that messing about with extended, expanded, upper, and high memory is, more or less, a thing of the past.

A 4GB address space is, obviously, a huge amount of memory, and few systems will be stocked with anything approaching that figure. Machines with 8MB and 16MB are currently the norm, so how do we reconcile the massive difference between the size of the address space and the size of physical RAM? The Windows 98 solution to this disparity is called virtual memory management.

Understanding Windows 98's Virtual Memory Management

To overcome the discrepancy between addressable memory and physical memory, Windows 98 uses a concept called *virtual memory*. Regardless of how much RAM is actually installed on your system, Windows 98 lets each application think it has the entire 4GB address space to deal with. In reality, Windows 98 uses up the physical RAM first, and then, if more memory is needed, it uses hard disk locations as though they were memory locations.

To understand how this process works, you need to know a bit more about the 80386 (and higher) processors. The 80386 looks at memory in 4KB chunks called *pages*. The processor divides the entire address space into the 4KB pages and assigns pages as needed. When you begin running programs and opening documents, the processor assigns pages that correspond to physical RAM. The processor uses a *page table* to keep track of which piece of data is in which page, which process the page belongs to, whether the data has changed, and so on.

The key is that the pages can be moved to a different location simply by changing the appropriate entry in the page table. In particular, pages can be moved *outside* physical memory and stored temporarily in a special file on the hard disk. This file—it's called a *swap file* or a *paging file*—is set up to emulate physical memory. If you open enough programs or data files so that physical memory is exhausted, the swap file is brought into play to augment memory storage.

Demand Paging and the Virtual Memory Manager

Windows 3.*x* also used a swap file to "extend" physical RAM, so the idea of virtual memory is nothing new. Windows 98, however, has vastly improved its virtual memory management by implementing a demand-paged virtual memory model similar to the one used by Windows NT.

Demand paging is an efficient algorithm for swapping program code and data between physical RAM and the paging file. After physical RAM has been used up, the Virtual Memory Manager (part of the Windows 98 Kernel) begins to manage the paging file. Here's how the entire process works:

1. At first, the Virtual Memory Manager loads code and data into physical RAM. (The mapping of virtual addresses from the program's address space to the physical pages in the computer's memory is handled by the Memory Pager.)

2. A program requests code or data that can't fit inside physical RAM.

3. The Virtual Memory Manager uses the processor's built-in least-recently used (LRU) routine to determine which memory pages haven't been used for the longest time.

4. These pages are checked to see whether the data they contain has changed. (Changed pages are often called *dirty* pages.)

5. If the data has changed, the Virtual Memory Manager swaps these LRU pages out to disk and increases the size of the paging file to compensate. If the data hasn't changed, the pages are made available without being swapped to disk.

6. The freed-up pages are used for the new code or data.

7. Steps 2 through 6 are repeated, as necessary, while you work with the program.

8. When you close a program or document, the Virtual Memory Manager removes related code and data from both physical RAM and the paging file. It also fills in freed-up physical RAM pages with pages from the paging file.

In Windows 3.*x*, you had two swap file choices: You could either use a permanent swap file that remained on your hard drive whether or not Windows was running, or you could create a temporary swap file that was deleted each time you exited Windows. In both cases, however, the swap file was static: Its size remained constant no matter which operations the system was running.

Windows 98 improves this situation by using a dynamic swap file. As you saw in the preceding steps, the Virtual Memory Manager enlarges the paging file as you work with applications and data, and it shrinks the paging file as you shut down your programs and close documents. This technique makes the most efficient use of your hard disk, and it eliminates the guesswork involved in deciding how big to make the paging file. (As you'll soon see, though, you can still set maximum and minimum sizes.)

The Windows 98 Memory Map

The 4GB virtual address space isn't made available in its entirety to your applications. For example, certain areas are reserved for system processes, and other areas are used as private address space for Win32 applications. The diagram in Figure 9.1 shows how the virtual address space looks from an application's point of view. Here are some notes about this diagram:

- The area from 0–1MB is used for virtual DOS machines (VDMs) and real-mode device drivers.

- The area between 1MB and 4MB is rarely used.

- Memory locations from 4MB to 2GB are mapped to the private address space of Win32 applications. Each running 32-bit program thinks that it has the entire 2GB space available, and it can't see any other running 32-bit application. This prevents Win32 programs from compromising each other's memory locations.

- Between 2GB and 3GB, Windows 98 runs the core system components (User, GDI, and Kernel), DLLs and OLE objects shared by multiple applications, and the virtual machine that houses all running Win16 applications.

■ Addresses between 3GB and 4GB are reserved for all the ring 0 components: Configuration Manager, Installable File System Manager, Virtual Machine Manager, and the virtual device drivers.

FIGURE 9.1.

Windows 98's memory map.

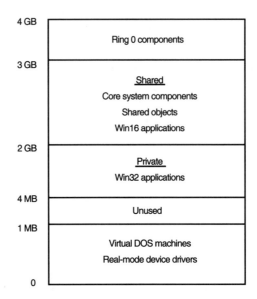

VCACHE: The Protected-Mode Disk Cache

In Windows 3.*x*, you probably used a 16-bit real-mode driver named SMARTDrive as a disk cache. Windows uses the *cache*—an area of memory the size of which is user-selected (and fixed) via the command that loads SMARTDrive—to store frequently used bits of program code and data. This technique improves performance because Windows can often load code and data directly from the cache rather than the much slower hard disk.

In Windows 98, the VFAT file system now works with a new disk cache: VCACHE. The VCACHE driver offers the following improvements over SMARTDrive:

■ VCACHE is a 32-bit protected-mode virtual device driver (VCACHE.VXD), so it's faster and uses no conventional memory.

■ The VCACHE driver uses an improved algorithm that makes caching faster and more intelligent, resulting in greater "hits" (a *hit* is when the driver requests a piece of data that already exists in the cache).

■ VCACHE works with CD-ROMs and network redirectors as well as regular disks.

■ The memory pool used by VCACHE is dynamic and adjusts itself according to the total memory available and the processes that are running.

System Resources in Windows 98

One of the biggest frustrations with Windows *3.x* was its inefficient use of system resources. You could have megabytes of free memory, but you'd still get Out of memory errors because Windows had run out of system resources. These resources are memory areas—called *heaps*—devoted to the User and GDI components. They hold the data structures used for windows and menus (for User), brushes, pens, and fonts (for GDI), and other resources created by applications (such as toolbars).

The resource data structures are stored in these segments as they're needed, so the percentage of free system resources was just the percentage of free memory available on the heap. (Actually, the percentage of free system resources reported in Program Manager's About dialog box was the *lower* of the values for the User and GDI heaps.)

The problem was that Windows *3.x* used 16-bit heaps, so their size was restricted to a single 64KB segment. This is quite small, so it wasn't hard to run out of resources and receive an Out of memory complaint.

Windows 98 provides greatly improved resource management. The major change was in moving all the User component's system resources into a 32-bit heap, where storage area is now measured in gigabytes instead of kilobytes. As well, some of the GDI's data structures have been moved into a 32-bit heap, although, for compatibility reasons, about half the data structures remain in the 16-bit heap. To give you an idea of the improvement, Table 9.1 compares the resource limits in Windows 3.1 to those now available in Windows 98. (The note "All in a 64KB segment" means that the resource must fit within the 64KB segment allotted to the appropriate component—User or GDI. Because the segment also contains other resources, there is no way to specify an exact limit for these resources.)

Table 9.1. System resource limits in Windows 3.1 versus Windows 98.

Resource	Windows 3.1	Windows 98
Windows menu handles	About 299	32KB
Timers	32	Unlimited
COM and LPT ports	4 per type	Unlimited
Items per list box	8KB	32KB
Data per list box	64KB	Unlimited
Data per edit control	64KB	Unlimited
Regions	All in a 64KB segment	Unlimited
Physical pens and brushes	All in a 64KB segment	Unlimited

9

OPTIMIZING MEMORY AND DISK ACCESS

continues

Table 9.1. continued

Resource	Windows 3.1	Windows 98
Logical pens and brushes	All in a 64KB segment	All in a 64KB segment
Logical fonts	All in 64KB segment	750 to 800
Installed fonts	250 to 300	1,000
Device contexts	200	16KB

Besides providing larger heaps to store the system resources, Windows 98 is also much better at freeing system resources for programs that forget (or refuse) to clean up after themselves. When Windows 98 sees that a particular Win32-based process has ended, it automatically checks for resources that remain allocated and removes them from the heap. Win16 applications are a slightly different story, however. Some Win16 programs *intentionally* leave their system resources allocated so that they can be used by shared DLLs, or even other programs. In this case, Windows 98 waits until you exit *all* your Win16 applications before it frees up the resources.

Performance Tuning: General Considerations

Now that you've seen some of the nuts and bolts of Windows 98, it's time to put all this information to good use and tune Windows 98 for optimal performance. Of course, you've just seen that Windows 98 has plenty of built-in features that offer superior performance over Windows 3.*x* right out of the box. These include the 32-bit Kernel, the flat memory model, preemptive multitasking and multithreading for Win32 applications, a 32-bit disk cache and file system, and improved handling of system resources. At the beginning of the chapter I outlined several features that should give Windows 98 a performance edge over Windows 95.

Besides these improvements, Windows 98 also has a number of self-tuning features which ensure that a reasonable level of performance is maintained at all times:

- The virtual memory paging file is expanded or contracted dynamically.
- The memory footprint of the disk cache is changed dynamically.
- Setup examines your system and (hopefully) adjusts the Windows 98 configuration to best suit your system.
- Plug and Play ensures that Windows 98 always knows your current configuration and can easily adjust to device changes (assuming that these devices are Plug and Play–compatible, that is).

Windows 98 also includes several tools you can use to monitor and optimize various settings. These tools include System Monitor (discussed next), Resource Monitor (see the later section

"Optimizing Memory"), and Disk Defragmenter (see the later section "Optimizing Disk Access"). You can use the Task Scheduler and Tune-Up Wizard (both covered in Chapter 17, "Wielding the Windows 98 System Tools") to perform many optimization tasks automatically.

Using System Monitor

Before you get too involved with optimizing your system, it will help to have some way of monitoring your progress (and seeing whether your system needs any tuning in the first place). One of the best (albeit advanced) tools for this is System Monitor. Assuming that System Monitor is installed, select Start | Programs | Accessories | System Tools | System Monitor. You see the System Monitor window, shown in Figure 9.2.

FIGURE 9.2.

Use the System Monitor to keep an eye on various system processes.

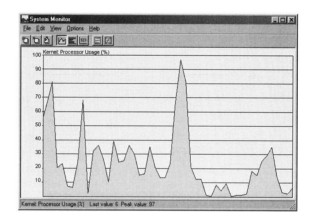

System Monitor's job is to provide you with real-time reports on how various system processes are performing. The idea is that you should configure System Monitor to show the processes you're interested in (swap file size, free memory, and so on) and then keep System Monitor running while you perform your normal chores. By examining the System Monitor readouts from time to time, you gain an appreciation of what is "typical" on your system. Then, if you run into performance problems, you can check System Monitor to see whether you've run into any bottlenecks or anomalies.

Setting Up System Monitor

By default, System Monitor shows only the Kernel Processor Usage setting, which tells you the percentage of time the processor is busy. To add another setting to the System Monitor window, follow these steps:

1. Select Edit | Add Item or click the Add Item button in the toolbar. The Add Item dialog box, shown in Figure 9.3, appears.

FIGURE 9.3.

Use this dialog box to choose the settings you want to track with System Monitor.

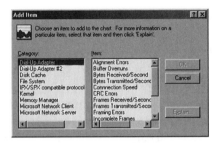

2. Use the Category list to highlight one of the following categories (not all of which are shown in Figure 9.3):

   Dial-Up Adapter: Tracks a number of parameters related to Dial-Up Networking connections.

   Disk Cache: Tracks settings related to the swap file.

   File System: Tracks file system performance (reads and writes).

   IPX/SPX compatible protocol: Tracks packet performance using NetWare's IPX/SPX protocol.

   Kernel: Tracks Kernel performance, including processor usage, the number of active threads, and the number of active virtual machines.

   Memory Manager: Tracks a large number of memory-related settings, including allocated memory, cache size, and swap file size.

   Microsoft Client for NetWare Networks: Tracks network performance via Microsoft's NetWare client.

   Microsoft Network Client: Tracks network performance via the Microsoft network client.

   Microsoft Network Server: Tracks network server performance.

SYSTEM MONITOR'S SETTINGS

I discuss the individual items in the Disk Cache, File System, and Memory Manager categories later in this chapter.

---

3. Use the Item list to highlight the setting you want to monitor. (If you need more information about the item, click the Explain button.)

4. Click OK.

System Monitor also gives you several customization options:

- You can change how you view the data. The default view is a line chart that shows the progress of each setting over time. If you're more interested in the current value, you might prefer either the bar chart view (select View | Bar Charts or click the Bar Charts toolbar button) or the numeric view (select View | Numeric Charts or click the Numeric Charts toolbar button).

■ To adjust the frequency with which System Monitor updates its charts, select Options | Chart, select an update interval in the Options dialog box, and click OK.

■ To adjust the color and scale of a particular chart, select Edit | Edit Item or click the Edit button in the toolbar. Highlight the item you want to edit and click OK. Use the Chart Options dialog box to select a different color and enter a new scale; then click OK.

To remove settings from the System Monitor window, select Edit | Remove Item or click the Remove Item button in the toolbar. In the Remove Item dialog box, highlight the item you want to remove and click OK.

Examining Performance Properties

Another tool you can use to monitor and improve performance is the Performance tab in the System Properties dialog box. To check it out, use either of the following techniques:

■ Right-click My Computer (either on the desktop or in Explorer) and click Properties.

■ Select Start | Settings | Control Panel and open the System icon in the Control Panel folder.

In the System Properties dialog box that appears, select the Performance tab, shown in Figure 9.4. The Performance status group shows the current status of several crucial settings, including physical memory, free system resources, file system, virtual memory, and disk compression. If the last three are all 32-bit, Windows 98 declares your system to be "configured for optimal performance," as shown in Figure 9.4.

FIGURE 9.4.

The Performance tab summarizes the current performance settings of your computer and offers tools for changing these settings.

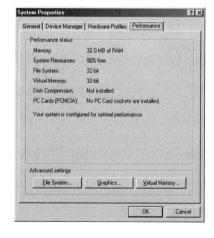

Otherwise, the Performance tab shows which elements of your system aren't configured optimally. For example, Figure 9.5 shows the Performance tab when real-mode drivers are being used for two CD-ROM drives. (You learn about MS-DOS compatibility mode in Chapter 10, "Getting the Most Out of Device Manager and Hardware Profiles.") You can use the buttons in the Performance tab (File System, Graphics, and Virtual Memory) to control various performance-related settings, as I'll show you later in this chapter.

FIGURE 9.5.

This is the version of the Performance tab you see when your system isn't configured optimally.

General Performance Tuning Suggestions

Before we get to some specific optimization techniques for memory and disk access, let's look at a few issues that affect performance in more general ways:

Processor: Although Windows 98 will run on machines equipped with an Intel (or compatible) processor from the 80386SX to the Pentium II, the performance you get depends greatly on the processor. The 80386SX, for example, runs Windows 98 pathetically slow due to its 16-bit internal data registers. The 80386DX is better, but because it was optimized for 16-bit code, Windows 98 is no speed demon. Windows 98 comes into its own only with the 80486 processor, thanks to the 486's 32-bit optimization. In fact, everything else being equal (memory, clock speed, and so on), the 80486 delivers performance close to that of a garden variety Pentium. The Pentium's real advantage over the 486 is that it's available in much higher clock speeds (300MHz, with faster processors planned in the near future). The Pentium Pro won't run Windows 98 much faster than a regular Pentium (given the same clock speed). That's because the Pentium Pro chokes those chunks of 16-bit code that still exist within Windows 98.

Data bus: The right data bus can make a tremendous difference in performance under Windows 98. Older ISA and VL bus machines cause CPU bottlenecks due to their typically poor throughput. The PCI bus, however, when combined with Windows 98's miniport drivers (explained in the Chapter 10) handles data at maximum speed with no CPU bottlenecks. PCI buses are also Plug and Play–compliant, which is another big advantage under Windows 98.

Hard disk access time: Unless you have scads of physical RAM in your machine, or just play FreeCell all day long, Windows 98 will spend a good chunk of its time paging code and data to and from the swap file. Although no hard disk even remotely approaches the speed of RAM, having the fastest hard disk you can afford will greatly improve paging performance. Note too that Windows 98 loves a large hard disk because it poses no restrictions on the size of the swap file.

Video hardware and drivers: Windows 98 is a graphical user interface, so its performance is in large measure dictated by your graphics hardware. Video accelerator cards can make a huge difference in display performance by removing some of the graphics burden from the shoulders of the CPU. Also, be sure to use the appropriate Windows 98 mini-driver for your video adapter. The new drivers offer much faster performance than do their Windows 3.*x* ancestors.

Protected-mode drivers: For maximum device performance, you should use protected-mode drivers wherever possible. With real-mode drivers, Windows 98 must switch out of its native protected mode and operate in virtual 8088 mode (sometimes several times in a single operation), which is very time-consuming from the processor's point of view.

Optimizing Memory

Memory is the lifeblood of your PC, and it is, by far, the single most important factor affecting your computer's performance. The minimum memory requirement for Windows 98 is 16MB, but I've found that this level of memory provides only minimally acceptable performance. If what you're really after is a system that will let you work in a high-end word processor, handle large spreadsheet files, send and receive email, access material on a CD-ROM, and surf the Internet, 16MB just won't cut the electronic mustard. A more realistic minimum would be 24MB if you want to squeeze any kind of performance out of Windows 98. If your needs are more high-end—manipulating large graphics files, working with video, heavy database querying—you should be thinking 64MB and up.

Whatever amount of RAM you have crammed into your system, though, you can use some techniques to optimize that memory for top performance. The next few sections take you through these techniques.

9

OPTIMIZING
MEMORY AND
DISK ACCESS

Using System Monitor to Track Memory Settings

System Monitor is a great tool for tracking memory usage and identifying where memory problems might be occurring. This section takes a closer look at the various memory-related settings you can track with System Monitor.

System Monitor's Memory Manager Settings

System Monitor's Memory Manager category is chock-full of important settings that track various memory processes. Table 9.2 provides a summary of these settings to help you decide which ones to monitor.

Table 9.2. System Monitor's Memory Manager settings.

Setting	Description
Allocated Memory	The total number of bytes allocated to applications and system processes. This is the sum of the Other Memory and Swappable Memory settings.
Discards	The number of pages discarded per second from memory. (These are pages where the data hasn't changed. They're discarded rather than swapped because the data already exists on the hard disk.)
Disk Cache Size	The current size, in bytes, of the disk cache.
Instance Faults	The number of instance faults per second.
Locked Memory	The amount of allocated memory, in bytes, that is locked (that can't be swapped out to disk) by applications or the operating system.
Locked Non-Cache Pages	The number of pages outside the swap file that are locked.
Maximum Disk Cache Size	The largest size possible for the disk cache, in bytes.
Mid Disk Cache Size	The purpose of this setting is unknown.
Minimum Disk Cache Size	The smallest size possible for the disk cache, in bytes.
Other Memory	The amount of allocated memory, in bytes, that can't be stored in the swap file. This includes code from Win32 DLLs and executable files, memory-mapped files, non-pageable memory, and disk cache pages.

Setting	Description
Page Faults	The number of page faults per second.
Page-ins	The number of pages swapped from the page file to physical RAM per second.
Page-outs	The number of pages swapped from physical RAM to the page file per second.
Pages Mapped from Cache	The total number of pages swapped from the page file to physical RAM.
Swapfile Defective	The number of defective bytes in the swap file. These defective bytes are caused by bad sectors on the hard drive.
Swapfile In Use	The number of bytes currently being used in the swap file.
Swapfile Size	The current size, in bytes, of the swap file.
Swappable Memory	The number of bytes allocated from the swap file. This value includes locked pages.
Unused Physical Memory	The total amount of free physical RAM, in bytes. (This setting was called Free Memory in Windows 95.)

Using System Monitor to Troubleshoot Memory Issues

Here are a few ideas on how to use System Monitor to investigate and narrow down to particular memory-related performance problems:

- If you're monitoring the Kernel: Threads setting, watch for applications that create new threads and then don't release them. Although Windows 98 does a good job of reclaiming these "memory leaks" after you exit the application, the threads remain lost while the program is running. You can free up memory by stopping and restarting the program occasionally.

- If your system seems slow, keep an eye on the Discards and Page-outs settings. High values for these items might mean that system memory is having trouble handling the load and that you might have to add more physical memory.

- If your system feels slow, watch the Page Faults setting. A high value might mean that you're using an application that requires more memory than your system can deliver.

- Locked memory can't be paged to the swap file. If you find that the Locked Memory value is always a large percentage of the Allocated Memory setting, inadequate free memory might be affecting performance. Also, you might be running an application that locks memory unnecessarily.

Managing the Swap File

The less RAM you have in your system, the more important Windows 98's virtual memory features become. That's because if you're dealing with a relatively small amount of physical RAM, Windows 98 can still create a swap file and therefore enable you to open many more programs than you could otherwise. No matter how much RAM you have, however, Windows 98 will still create a swap file and will still use it for paging data blocks. To make this process as efficient as possible, you need to optimize your swap file. The next couple of sections show you how to do just that.

Some Swap File Notes

Here are some ideas to bear in mind for maximum swap file performance:

Use the hard disk with the most free space. The best way to ensure top swap file performance is to make sure that the hard disk containing the swap file has lots of free space. This extra space gives the swap file enough room to expand and contract as needed. (If you want to use a different hard disk for your swap file, I'll show you how to do this in the next section.)

Use the hard disk with the fastest access time. If you have multiple physical hard disks on your system, make sure that the swap file is using the disk that has the fastest access time.

Track the swap file size. The System Monitor's Memory Manager: Swap file size setting shows you the current size of the swap file. If you see that this size is approaching the amount of free space left on the disk, you should free up some disk space to ensure that the swap file has complete flexibility.

Defragment the swap file's hard drive. Unlike the Windows 3.x swap file, the Windows 98 swap file can occupy noncontiguous clusters. However, this fragmentation slows down the swap file operation (not substantially, but a little). For best results, keep the disk drive containing the swap file defragmented (as described later in this chapter).

Use an uncompressed hard disk. If you're using a protected-mode driver for a compressed disk, Windows 98 can store the swap file on the compressed drive (again, unlike Windows 3.x). You see a small performance degradation if you do this, however, so it's best to use an uncompressed drive for the swap file.

Windows 98 compacts the swap file. Have you ever heard hard drive activity when you're not using your computer? It might seem like your system is possessed, but it's really just Windows 98 performing some housekeeping chores. In particular, Windows 98 begins compacting your swap file as soon as you haven't used your computer for a minute.

Don't use a network drive. Avoid placing your swap file on a network drive. Access to these drives is usually slow, so your swap file's performance will suffer correspondingly.

Changing Swap File Settings

As I mentioned earlier, virtual memory is one of Windows 98's self-tuning features. The system uses a highly sophisticated algorithm to determine the optimum parameters for the swap file, so in nearly all cases you won't have to change a thing. (This is a welcome relief from the constant swap file fiddling we had to perform in Windows 3.*x*.)

At times, however, you might need to adjust some swap file settings. For example, you might want to change the hard disk used by the swap file. Here are the steps to follow to make adjustments to the swap file:

1. Open the System Properties dialog box and select the Performance tab, as described earlier.

2. Click the Virtual Memory button. Windows 98 displays the Virtual Memory dialog box, shown in Figure 9.6.

FIGURE 9.6.

Use the Virtual Memory dialog box to adjust the swap file settings.

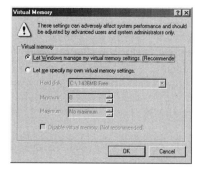

3. Activate the Let me specify my own virtual memory settings option. The controls below this option become available.

4. Use the Hard disk drop-down list to specify a different hard disk.

5. Use the Minimum spinner to set the smallest possible size, in megabytes, for the swap file.

6. Use the Maximum spinner to set the largest possible size, in megabytes, for the swap file.

9

OPTIMIZING MEMORY AND DISK ACCESS

WATCH YOUR MAXIMUM

If you set the Maximum value equal to the amount of free space on the hard disk, Windows 98 assumes that it can always use all the available free space. So if you free up space on the disk down the road, Windows 98 will increase the maximum swap file size accordingly. If this isn't what you want, be sure to set the Maximum to a value that's less than the current free space on the disk.

7. If you'd prefer to disable the swap file, activate the Disable virtual memory (Not recommended) check box.

> **DON'T DISABLE VIRTUAL MEMORY**
>
> Disabling virtual memory is a sure way to send Windows 98's performance down the tubes. If you're running out of disk space, you're better off deleting files or compressing the hard disk to create more room.

8. Click OK. Windows 98 prompts you to restart your system.

Optimizing System Resources

The changes made to the system resources in Windows 98—especially moving the User resources to a 32-bit heap—have resulted in dramatically better resource management. You start with a higher percentage of resources free (typically over 90 percent, as compared to about 80 percent in Windows 3.*x*), and you can open many more applications and document windows before the resources start to hit stress levels. Still, Windows 98's resources aren't infinite, so there are limits to what you can do. It still pays to monitor your resources and take steps to conserve resources wherever possible.

Using the Resource Meter

In Windows 3.*x*, you could keep an eye on your free system resources by displaying Program Manager's About dialog box (Help | About Program Manager). Also, there was no shortage of utilities that would display the current health of your system's resources and warn you when they were getting low.

Windows 98 has improved resource monitoring in two ways:

- Windows 98 now warns you when your system resources get too low.
- Windows 98 includes a Resource Meter utility that gives you a visual readout of the current state of the system resources.

To try out Resource Meter, select Start | Programs | Accessories | System Tools | Resource Meter. If this is the first time you're starting Resource Meter, you see a dialog box that just states the obvious: that Resource Meter itself will use up a few system resources. To avoid this dialog box in the future, activate the Don't display this message again check box and then click OK.

When the Resource Meter loads, it adds an icon to the taskbar's information area that gives you a visual representation of the system resource status. The green bars indicate free system resources, and the "level" goes up and down as you open and close applications, windows, and objects. You can get an exact figure for User resources, GDI resources, and System resources (the lower of the User and GDI values) by using either of the following techniques:

■ Hover the mouse pointer over the Resource Meter icon for a second or two to display a banner showing the individual resource percentages.

■ Double-click the Resource Meter icon to display the Resource Meter dialog box, which shows a bar chart for each resource percentage (see Figure 9.7).

FIGURE 9.7.

Double-click the Resource Meter icon in the toolbar to display a graphical representation of your free system resources.

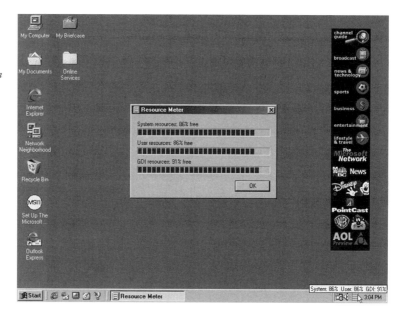

So what do these numbers mean in the real world? Well, as long as the bars in the Resource Meter icon are green, you're fine: This means that Windows 98 has plenty of resources available. As the bar inches downward, however, keep an eye out for a color change:

■ When the bars change to yellow, the free resources have dropped below about 34 percent. You should exercise caution at this point and avoid opening more applications or windows. Run through some of the techniques discussed in the next section for saving system resources.

■ When the bars change to red, the free resources have dropped to 15 percent or less. This is very dangerous territory, and you should immediately start shutting down applications.

When the free resources drop to 10 percent or less, you see the dialog box shown in Figure 9.8. (Note that this dialog box appears whether or not you have the Resource Meter running.) Your system is in imminent danger of hanging, so you must start closing applications to avoid losing data. It's interesting to note just how many applications and windows are running in Figure 9.8. No less than 46 windows are open, including several Internet Explorer windows and DOS sessions. Clearly, this is vastly superior to what we could accomplish in Windows 3.*x*.

(Note, however, that your mileage may vary. Figure 9.8 was produced on a machine with 32MB of memory which, although not outrageous these days, is still not your ordinary Windows 98 machine.)

FIGURE 9.8.

Windows 98 warns you when your free system resources drop to 10 percent or less.

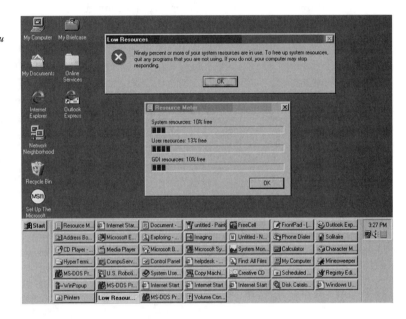

Saving System Resources

If you find that your system resources are getting low, here are some ideas that will send the Resource Meter bar up:

- Close any applications you won't be using for a while.
- If your applications support multiple open documents, close files you aren't using.
- Run DOS applications full-screen rather than in a window.
- Turn off application objects you don't use, such as toolbars, rulers, and status bars.
- Minimize any running applications you aren't using.
- Turn off desktop wallpaper and animated cursors.

Miscellaneous Ideas for Optimizing Memory

To finish your look at optimizing memory, here are a few random ideas that create more memory and give your programs more room to roam:

Run only the programs you need. Each running program usurps some physical RAM, so the more programs you have open, the more paging Windows 98 will have to do.

Minimize your network services. Network services—clients and protocols—use up memory even when you're not logged on to your network. To minimize this footprint, run only one network client, and use only those protocols you really need.

Use system resources wisely. Remember that system resource heaps exist in memory, so saving resources saves overall memory. Follow the guidelines from the preceding section to keep your resource use in check.

Make sure that your system's RAM cache is enabled. RAM caches are small processor-based memory areas that store frequently used processor instructions, and they can increase performance tremendously. If your system feels slow, enter your BIOS setup program the next time you reboot, and make sure that its RAM cache isn't disabled. Depending on your BIOS, the RAM cache might be called an "L1 cache," an "internal cache," or a "system memory cache."

Delete the contents of the Clipboard. When you cut or copy a selection in a Windows application, the program stores the data in an area of memory called the Clipboard. If you're working with only a few lines of text, this area remains fairly small. Cutting or copying a graphics image, however, can increase the size of the Clipboard to several hundred kilobytes or more. If you've run out of memory, a large Clipboard might be the problem. To release this memory, try one of the following methods:

- If you have an application running, highlight a small section of text (a single character will do) and select Edit | Copy. This action replaces the current Clipboard with a much smaller one.

- Select Start | Programs | Accessories | Clipboard Viewer. When the Clipboard Viewer window appears, select Edit | Delete to clear the contents of the Clipboard.

Buy more memory. The ultimate way to beat the low-memory blues, of course, is simply to add more memory to your system. Unlike Windows 3.*x*, which couldn't care less if your system had more than 16MB of RAM, Windows 98 can take advantage of every last megabyte in your system. I've run Windows 98 on a machine with 64MB, and it absolutely soars. Contact your computer manufacturer to find out the best kind of memory to add to your system.

Optimizing Disk Access

Memory and hard disk access are the "Twin Towers" of Windows 98 performance. Memory, as you've just seen, is where you spend most of your productive computer life. However, keeping your hard disk tuned and optimized benefits three areas:

Storage: Given a finite amount of hard disk space, you want to optimize not only the amount of data that can be stored, but also how the data is stored.

Program loading: Your applications are started from the hard disk, so a fast, efficient disk will load programs more quickly.

> **Paging and caching:** Windows 98 uses dynamic paging files and caching, so a well-tuned disk will increase performance in these crucial areas.

The next few sections take you through various techniques for optimizing hard disk access.

Optimizing Cluster Size

When it comes to hard disk inefficiency, one of the biggest culprits is the capacity of the disk. That might sound strange, but it's true: The bigger the hard disk, the greater the waste. This section explains what I mean and shows you how to reduce this inefficiency. In particular, you'll learn later how Windows 98's new FAT32 file system can make hard disk inefficiency a thing of the past.

VFAT and Clusters

To see why large hard disks are inherently inefficient, you need to understand how VFAT, Windows 98's file system, stores files. When you format a disk, the disk's magnetic medium is divided into small storage areas called *sectors*, which usually hold up to 512 bytes of data. Hard disks typically contain hundreds of thousands of sectors, so it would be just too inefficient for Windows 98 to deal with individual sectors. Instead, Windows 98 groups sectors into *clusters*, the size of which, as you'll see, depends on the size of the disk.

Still, each hard disk has tens of thousands of clusters (up to 65,536), so some sort of "file filing system" is necessary to keep track of everything. Every formatted disk comes with its own built-in filing system called the File Allocation Table, or FAT for short. The FAT contains a 16-bit entry for every cluster on the disk, and these entries can assume any of the values shown in Table 9.3.

Table 9.3. Values for each FAT entry.

Entry	Description
0	The cluster is available to store data.
nn	This value indicates the cluster number that contains the next part of the file.
BAD	The cluster contains one or more bad sectors. The file system won't use this cluster for storage.
EOF	The cluster represents the end of the file.
Reserved	The cluster is to be used only by Windows 98.

How does the FAT know where the file begins? For each file on the disk, the FAT maintains an entry in a *file directory*, a sort of table of contents for your files. Table 9.4 lists the contents of each entry in the file directory. (Note that this is the VFAT—Virtual File Allocation Table—version of the file directory, which is slightly different from the one used by DOS and Windows 3.*x*. VFAT serves as a protected-mode go-between for applications and the disk's FAT.)

Table 9.4. The structure of each file directory entry in Windows 98.

Field	Size
Filename	8 bytes
Extension	3 bytes
Attributes (archive, hidden, and so on)	1 byte
Reserved (these bytes aren't used)	6 bytes
Date the file was last modified	2 bytes
Exclusive access handle	2 bytes
Time the file was created	2 bytes
Date the file was created	2 bytes
Starting cluster number in the FAT	2 bytes
File size in bytes	4 bytes

WHERE ARE THE LONG FILENAMES?

You might be wondering how Windows 98 implements long filenames if the directory entry for each file has room for only the traditional 8.3 name. The answer is that in Windows 98, the directory structure shown in Table 9.4 is only for each file's initial directory entry. VFAT also keeps track of several other directory entries for each file, and it's in these secondary entries that the long filenames are stored.

For our purposes, the key item is the starting cluster number. This 16-bit value tells VFAT the number of the cluster where the file begins. When VFAT needs to open a file, it follows these steps:

1. It looks up the file in the file directory.
2. It uses the file's directory entry to get the starting cluster number.
3. It looks up the cluster number in the FAT.
4. If the cluster entry points to another cluster number, there is still more of the file to read, so VFAT repeats step 3.

   If the cluster entry is EOF, the entire file has been read, so VFAT is done.

For example, Figure 9.9 shows a simplified version of the file directory and FAT. The file LETTER.DOC, for instance, has a starting cluster number of 100. When VFAT checks the FAT entry for cluster 100, it sees that the entry contains the value 101. This tells VFAT that it will find the next portion of the file in cluster 101. So now it moves to the entry for cluster 101 and finds that the entry contains EOF. This tells VFAT that the file ends within this cluster, so it knows that clusters 100 and 101 contain the entire file (this is called a cluster chain).

9

OPTIMIZING
MEMORY AND
DISK ACCESS

FIGURE 9.9.

The relationship between the file directory and the FAT.

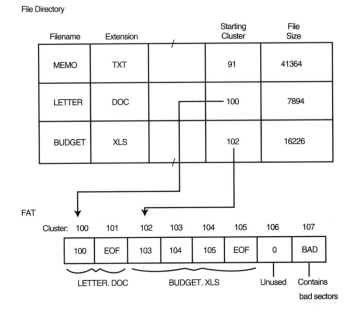

The Relationship Between Disk Size and Cluster Size

One of the hard disk facts of life is that every formatted disk, from 40MB pip-squeaks to 4GB behemoths, can't have any more than 65,536 clusters. Why? Recall that the FAT entries for each cluster are 16 bits long. This means that the largest possible cluster number is 65,536, so that's the maximum number of clusters on any hard disk. (Note that FAT32 and non-FAT partitions such as NTFS and HPFS don't have this restriction.) This means that the larger the hard disk, the larger the cluster size, as shown in Table 9.5.

Table 9.5. The relationship between disk size and cluster size.

Disk Size	Cluster Size
16–127MB	2,048 bytes
128–255MB	4,096 bytes
256–511MB	8,192 bytes
512–1023MB	16,384 bytes
1024–2047MB	32,768 bytes
2048–4191MB	65,536 bytes

HARD DISKS UNDER 16MB

Hard disks with capacities less than 16MB are anomalies and don't quite fit this pattern. These disks use a 12-bit FAT, so they have cluster sizes of 4096 bytes.

The key point is that VFAT always allocates entire clusters when storing files. For example, assume that the files shown in Figure 9.9 exist on a 200MB hard drive that therefore uses a cluster size of 4096 bytes. The file size of LETTER.DOC is 7894 bytes, but it takes up two whole clusters, or 8192 bytes. This means that the second cluster has an extra 298 bytes of wasted space. This wasted space is called *cluster overhang*. 298 bytes isn't anything to worry about, but suppose that LETTER.DOC was stored on a 550MB disk. This disk uses 16,384-byte clusters, which means LETTER.DOC could be housed in a single cluster. However, the cluster overhang jumps to a whopping 5,490 bytes. Put LETTER.DOC on a 1GB drive, and the overhang leaps to a little over 24KB, over three times the size of the actual file!

Think this is a bad example because LETTER.DOC is such a small file? Think again. Suppose you store a 100KB file on a 1GB drive that uses 32KB clusters. The file's first three clusters hold 96KB, but the remaining 4KB sits in the last cluster, wasting 28KB in cluster overhang.

Checking Cluster Overhang

If you're wondering how much space is being wasted on your hard disk due to cluster overhang, there's an easy way to figure it out. In a DOS session, change to the root folder of the drive you want to check and then enter the following DOS command:

```
dir /s/a/v
```

The /A parameter tells DIR to find hidden and system files, and the /S parameter tells DIR to run through the drive's subfolders. However, it's the /V parameter that helps you with cluster overhang. This switch tells DIR to display a few extra numbers: the size of each file, the amount of space allocated to each file, the total size of all the files, and the total amount allocated to all the files. Here's an example of such a listing:

```
C:\dir /s/a/v

 Volume in drive C is HARD DRIVE
 Volume Serial Number is 3441-1201

Directory of C:\
File Name      Size    Allocated  Modified           Accessed  Attrib

SUHDLOG  DAT   5,166    32,768    01-01-98 12:13p    12-18-96  RH        SUHDLOG.DAT
BOOTLOG  TXT  26,942    32,768    02-10-98  3:37p    03-04-97  H    A    BOOTLOG.TXT
COMMAND  COM  93,812    98,304    01-01-98 11:11a    03-28-97       A    COMMAND.COM
BOOTLOG  PRV  26,942    32,768    02-08-98  6:10p    02-08-97  H    A    BOOTLOG.PRV
CONFIG   SYS     823    32,768    01-01-98  5:55p    03-28-97       A    CONFIG.SYS
MSDOS    SYS   1,653    32,768    01-01-98  1:43p    03-25-97       A    MSDOS.SYS
CONFIG   DOS     845    32,768    01-01-98 11:41a    12-18-96       A    CONFIG.DOS
```

9

OPTIMIZING
MEMORY AND
DISK ACCESS

```
AUTOEXEC DOS      429   32,768   01-01-98 11:23a  12-18-96      A   AUTOEXEC.DOS
etc.
Total files listed:
   3,017 file(s)    326,412,057 bytes
     481 dir(s)     388,005,888 bytes allocated
                    844,464,128 bytes free
                  1,259,044,864 bytes total disk space,  32% in use
```

With this data in hand, calculating cluster overhang becomes a simple two-step procedure:

1. Subtract the bytes value from the bytes allocated value.

2. Divide the difference calculated in step 1 by the bytes allocated value.

In the preceding example, the difference between the bytes value and the bytes allocated value is 61,593,831 (388,005,888 minus 326,412,057), and dividing 61,593,831 by 388,005,888 gives a cluster overhang of just under 16 percent.

Partitioning for More Efficient FAT16 Disks

The massive amounts of cluster overhang in large hard disks is clearly inefficient, but what can be done? Well, it turns out that cluster size is determined not by the overall capacity of the hard disk, but by the size of each *partition* on the hard disk. So if you create a 200MB partition on a 1GB disk, the partition will use cluster sizes of 4096 bytes. The secret to increased storage efficiency on FAT16 partitions is to chop up your hard disk into smaller partitions. How small? That depends on how you use your computer:

- If your data consists mostly of small files, use small partitions (127MB or less).

- If you work with very large files (such as graphics, video, or music files), use big partitions to give yourself room to store these files. Cluster overhang is less an issue on massive data files (for example, greater than 1MB).

- Remember that many applications usurp huge amounts of disk real estate, so you need partitions big enough to hold them. A 127MB partition, for example, isn't large enough to store a complete installation of Microsoft Office.

- Make sure that the partitions you use are a bit less than the changeover point for cluster sizes. Partitioning a disk to 127MB gives you 2KB clusters, but adding a mere megabyte to the partition bumps the drive up to 4KB clusters.

- Ideally, you should have separate partitions for programs and data, using a larger partition for the programs and a smaller partition for the data. An added advantage of this technique is that backing up your data is easier.

- Remember that each partition creates a new drive letter. Dividing a 1GB disk into a dozen small partitions might enable efficient storage, but finding what you want in all those drives can be difficult. ("Let's see…did I store that budget file on drive F or drive N?")

After you've decided on the partition sizes you need, you use Windows 98's FDISK program to repartition a hard disk. I show you how to wield FDISK in Chapter 15, "Disk Driving: The Windows 98 Disk Utilities."

Cluster Sizes and FAT32

Back in 1981, when Bill Gates was asked about the 640KB memory constraint in the original IBM PC architecture, he said, "640K ought to be enough for anybody." In fact, a case could be made that the entire history of the PC involves someone saying that "*x* ought to be enough for anybody" and then a few years later saying "*x* just doesn't cut it anymore." Hard disk size is a good example. When the FAT file system was modified a few years ago to accommodate disks with up to 2GB capacity, such a vast number seemed laughably large at the time. (After all, it wasn't that long before that DOS 4.0 had finally broken the 32MB barrier!) Now, however, 2GB disks are *de rigueur* on even modest systems and notebooks (and can be purchased for less than 10 cents a megabyte), and disks with 4GB and even 9GB capacities aren't all that unusual.

So, once again, we're at an architectural crossroads in the PC industry:

- Until now, manufacturers had been handling large (over 2GB) hard disks by splitting them into multiple partitions.
- As you've seen, the FAT system is extremely wasteful at large partition sizes.

To get us past this crossroads and into the next era, Microsoft has updated the FAT portion of the file system to the new FAT32 architecture. This is one of the key new features found in Windows 98. How does FAT32 help? Here's a summary:

Smaller cluster sizes: Instead of the massive 32KB clusters used in large FAT16 partitions, FAT32 uses only 4KB clusters in partitions up to 8GB. Table 9.6 shows the full range of cluster sizes used in FAT32. This will improve storage efficiency on the vast majority of systems and should free up large amounts of disk space automatically.

Table 9.6. The relationship between disk size and cluster size in FAT32.

Disk Size	Cluster Size
16MB to 8GB	4,096 bytes
8–16GB	8,192 bytes
16–32GB	16,384 bytes
Over 32GB	32,768 bytes

9

OPTIMIZING
MEMORY AND
DISK ACCESS

Support for larger hard disks: Officially, FAT32 can handle hard disks that have a capacity of up to 2 terabytes (2,048GB). Strangely, however, the math suggests a different maximum capacity. The "32" in FAT32 means that the cluster numbers used in directory entries are now 32-bit values. Four of those bits are reserved for future use, so this means that the file system can track 268,435,456 (2 to the power of 28) distinct values, which, at 32,768 bytes per cluster, yields an 8TB limit. Why the discrepancy? That's a good question and it's one I haven't been able to answer.

DO YOU KNOW THE ANSWER?

If you know why FAT32 supports only 2TB disks when the math says it should support 8TB disks, please e-mail me to put my curiosity out of its misery. (You'll find my e-mail address in the Introduction. If you don't have e-mail, you can write to me care of Sams.) The first reader with the right answer gets a free copy of one of my books.

Improved robustness: FAT32 implements three new features that should improve the reliability of the file system: a movable root directory (useful for avoiding corrupt disk areas), the ability to use the backup copy of the FAT (FAT16 maintained two copies of the FAT but could use only one of them), and an internal backup copy of some critical FAT data structures.

Flexible partitioning: Unlike FAT16, FAT32 imposes no restrictions on the number of directory entries in a partition's root folder, and it allows the root to be located anywhere on the hard drive. These features mean that it's possible to resize a FAT32 partition dynamically without losing data. Windows 98 includes just such a tool: the Drive Converter.

Although Microsoft took great pains to avoid upsetting the file system apple cart with FAT32, any major change in this critical area is going to break a few applications and be cause for a few caveats. Here are a few notes to bear in mind when working with FAT32:

- The change from a 16-bit to a 32-bit cluster numbering scheme should have no effect on mainstream applications. Disk utilities are another story, however. Because these programs expect a 2-byte cluster value, they won't work with FAT32. You need to get updated versions of your favorite utilities before you use them on your FAT32 drives.

- Windows 98 comes with updated versions of its disk utilities, including the real-mode FDISK, FORMAT, SCANDISK, and DEFRAG commands and the protected-mode Format, ScanDisk, and Disk Defragmenter applets.

- DriveSpace 3 does not work with FAT32.

- Existing file systems, including FAT16 and the NTFS used in Windows NT, aren't compatible with FAT32, so FAT32 drives won't be visible locally. (You can see them across network connections, however.) This also means that you can't dual-boot on a FAT32 partition.

- Don't expect large changes in file system performance under FAT32. Although an improved caching system helps performance, this benefit is offset by the larger number of clusters that the system must deal with.

Converting a Partition to FAT32

As I mentioned in the last section, Windows 98 comes with a utility to convert existing FAT16 partitions into FAT32 partitions. This utility also looks for incompatible virus checkers and disk utilities that might be running, gives you a chance to make a backup, and will optimize the new partition. Here are the steps to follow:

1. Select Start | Programs | Accessories | System Tools | Drive Converter (FAT32).

2. The initial Drive Converter dialog box gives you an overview of the conversion process. Click Next > to continue. Drive Converter prompts you to choose the drive you want to convert, as shown in Figure 9.10.

FIGURE 9.10.

Use this Drive Converter dialog box to choose the drive you want to convert.

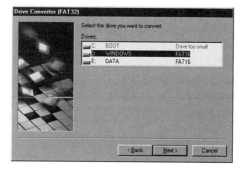

3. Select the drive you want to convert to FAT32 and click Next >.

4. Drive Converter warns you that the new FAT32 drive will not be accessible from other operating systems. Click OK.

5. Drive Converter now checks for incompatible virus programs and disk utilities. If Drive Converter finds any incompatible programs, it displays a list and gives you further instructions. Click Next > when you're ready to continue.

6. Drive Converter gives you an opportunity to back up your files. If you want to take advantage of this, click the Backup button. When that's done and you're back with Drive Converter, click Next >.

7. Click Next >. Drive Converter reboots your machine in MS-DOS mode and then performs the conversion. Along the way, you see a long checklist of tasks that Drive Converter is performing. The entire process shouldn't take more than a couple of minutes.

8. When it's done, Drive Converter reboots your computer again, loads Windows 98, and reports that the conversion was successful. Click Next >.

9. Click Finish to launch Disk Defragmenter. See "Overcoming File Fragmentation with Disk Defragmenter," later in this chapter.

To see for yourself that your drive was converted, right-click the drive in My Computer or Explorer and then click Properties. In the properties sheet that appears, the File system value will now read FAT32, as shown in Figure 9.11.

FIGURE 9.11.

After converting your drive, the properties sheet for the drive now tells you that the file system is FAT32.

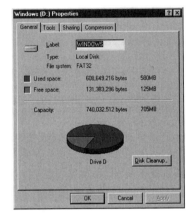

A Spring Cleaning for Your Hard Drive

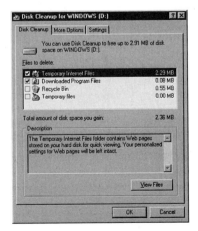

New to 98

You can improve your hard drive performance by making sure there are no unused files and programs cluttering the drive. In the past, cleaning this debris meant scouring the drive for old and unused files, temporary files not cleaned up by applications, and so on. Windows 98 takes the drudgery out of this chore by automating the cleanup process.

To try this out, open the properties sheet for the drive you want to work with. As you saw earlier in Figure 9.11, this sheet includes a Disk Cleanup button. Clicking this button displays the Disk Cleanup Manager, as shown in Figure 9.12. The Disk Cleanup tab lists various categories of files that Disk Cleanup Manager can safely delete, along with the expected disk space to be recovered. Activate the check boxes for the categories you want to remove and then click OK. When Disk Cleanup Manager asks whether you're sure, click Yes.

FIGURE 9.12.

The new Disk Cleanup Manager automates the tedious chore of removing unneeded files from your system.

CLEANING COMPONENTS AND APPLICATIONS

Disk Cleanup Manager also has a More Options tab with three groups:

Windows setup: Click the Clean Up button in this group to display the Add/Remove Programs Properties dialog box with the Windows Setup tab selected. You can then remove unneeded Windows 98 components, as described in Chapter 2, "From Disc to Disk: Installing Windows 98."

Installed programs: Click the Clean Up button in this group to display the Add/Remove Programs Properties dialog box with the Install/Uninstall tab selected. You can then uninstall applications you no longer use. See Chapter 18, "The Ins and Outs of Installing and Uninstalling Programs," for the details.

FAT32 conversion: If this drive is still using the FAT16 file system, you can click the Convert button to launch the Drive Converter.

Using Protected-Mode Drivers

In Windows 3.*x* (except Windows 3.0), there was an obscure, hard-to-find option called FastDisk that enabled a 32-bit disk driver and greatly improved hard disk performance. Windows 98 brings 32-bit disk performance out of the shadows and into the light by defaulting to a 32-bit protected-mode driver for most hard disks. However, Windows 98 might be using a 16-bit real-mode driver for your hard disk if you're using Stacker or if Setup didn't have a replacement for your existing driver when you upgraded.

To find out, examine the Performance tab in the System Properties dialog box. In the Performance status group, check the File System line:

■ If it says 32-bit, Windows 98 is using the 32-bit driver.

■ If it says Some drives are using MS-DOS compatibility mode, Windows 98 is using a real-mode driver for one of your disks.

In the latter case, the Performance tab also shows a list of disks that are using the real-mode drivers, as shown in Figure 9.8. If your system feels sluggish, this is probably the reason. When Windows 98 accesses data on a disk that's using a real-mode driver, Windows 98 must switch out of protected mode, access the data in real mode, and switch back into protected mode. All this mode switching exacts a heavy price in terms of hard disk performance. There are two solutions:

■ Check to see whether you're loading the real-mode driver at startup in either CONFIG.SYS or (less likely) AUTOEXEC.BAT. If so, try commenting out the lines that load the drivers (by adding REM and a space to the left of the lines). Restart Windows 98 and check the Performance tab to see whether a protected-mode driver is being used.

■ If Windows 98 doesn't have the correct protected-mode driver, contact the manufacturer of the hard disk or the company that made your system to see whether it has a Windows 98 driver available.

Enabling Hard Drive DMA Support in Windows 98

One of the new features in Windows 98 is support for hard drive Direct Memory Access (DMA) for IDE drives. Systems that can take advantage of this feature (you must be using the default Windows 98 bus mastering IDE controller drivers), can access the hard drive directly, without having to use up processor cycles. Depending on your system, this can result in a slight performance improvement (as well as reduced overhead for the processor, of course). To make sure this feature is activated, follow these steps:

1. Right-click My Computer and then choose Properties to display the System Properties dialog box.

2. Activate the Device Manager tab.

3. Open the Disk drives branch, highlight your IDE hard drive, and click Properties.

4. In the properties sheet that appears, select the Settings tab and then activate the DMA check box, as shown in Figure 9.13.

5. Click OK to return to the System Properties dialog box and then click OK again.

6. When Windows 98 asks whether you want to restart your computer, click Yes.

FIGURE 9.13.

Make sure that Windows 98's hard drive DMA support is activated.

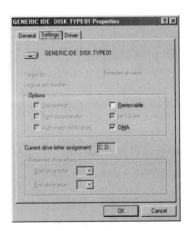

WINDOWS 98 ALSO SUPPORTS CD-ROM DMA

Windows 98 can also implement DMA on CD-ROM drives. To make sure DMA is activated for your CD-ROM, follow the steps outlined in this section (except that you need to open the CDROM branch in Device Manager).

Making Cache Adjustments

Disk caches are memory areas (*buffers*) that store recently used or frequently used bits of program code and data. If a program requests some data, Windows 98 checks the cache to see whether the data is in the cache. If it is, it's moved into main memory extremely quickly, thus improving performance.

The disk cache not only holds in memory code and data that's used frequently, but it also "reads ahead" to get the clusters that are next to the ones just read. The cache also "writes behind" by holding changed data in the buffer until the system is idle and then writing the data to disk.

VCACHE is the Windows 98 disk caching replacement for SMARTDrive (although SMARTDrive still exists and can be used to optimize DOS application performance; see Chapter 23, "DOS Isn't Dead: Unleashing the DOS Shell"). VCACHE is dynamic, which means that Windows 98 tailors the cache size to suit the current system load. (VCACHE and the dynamic swap file work together on this project.) This dynamic behavior is the best way to manage the cache optimally, so there's no need—and no way—to mess around with different cache sizes, as you could do with SMARTDrive. That's not to say, however, that VCACHE isn't configurable. It is, and I'll show you how to configure it a bit later in this section.

Adjusting the Hard Disk Cache

To make some adjustments to the hard disk cache, follow these steps:

1. In the Performance tab, select File System to display the File System Properties dialog box.

2. Make sure that the Hard Disk tab is selected, as shown in Figure 9.14.

FIGURE 9.14.

Use the Hard Disk tab to adjust some hard disk cache parameters.

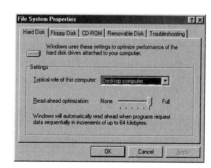

3. In the Typical role of this computer drop-down list, select one of the following options:

   Desktop computer: This option is for standalone machines, network clients, and notebook computers running on AC power. In each case, the computer should have at least 8MB of RAM. Windows 98 uses moderate settings for the cache size and write-behind operations. Specifically, VFAT tracks the 32 most recently used folders and the 677 most recently used files. This setting consumes about 10KB of memory.

Mobile or docking system: This option is for notebook computers running on batteries, docking stations, and desktop machines that use less than 8MB of RAM. Windows 98 uses conservative settings for the cache size and write-behind operations. This ensures that the disk cache is cleaned out regularly. In this case, VFAT tracks the 16 most recently used folders and the 337 most recently used files. This setting usurps only about 5KB of memory.

Network server: This option is for network servers with plenty of RAM that spend most of their time accessing the disk. Windows 98 assumes that the computer uses an uninterruptible power supply (UPS). Windows 98 uses aggressive settings for the cache size and write-behind operations. For this setting, VFAT tracks the 64 most recently used folders and the 2,729 most recently used files (using about 40KB of memory in the process). This greatly increases performance, but with added risk: If a power failure shuts down the machine, data could easily be lost (hence the need for a UPS).

4. Use the Read-ahead optimization slider to specify the maximum size of VCACHE's read-ahead buffer. In most cases, you get the best performance with this option set to Full.

5. Click OK to return to the System Properties dialog box.

6. Click Close. Windows 98 prompts you to restart your computer.

7. Click Yes.

Adjusting the CD-ROM Cache

VCACHE also maintains a separate cache that works with CD-ROM drives to improve performance. Again, you can configure some parameters for the CD-ROM cache, as described in the following steps:

1. In the Performance tab, select File System to display the File System Properties dialog box.

2. Select the CD-ROM tab, shown in Figure 9.15.

FIGURE 9.15.

Use the CD-ROM tab to adjust parameters for the CD-ROM cache.

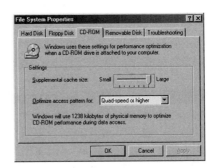

3. Use the Supplemental cache size slider to set the size of the CD-ROM cache. Note that this cache is used only while you're working with your CD-ROM applications, so it shouldn't affect how much memory is available to your other programs.

4. The Optimize access pattern for drop-down list sets the optimal cache size based on the speed of your CD-ROM and the amount of physical RAM in your system. On the low end, for example, if you have a single-speed drive and less than 8MB of RAM, the cache is set to 64KB; on the high end, if you have a quad-speed or higher drive and 12MB or more of RAM, the cache size is set to 1238KB.

5. Click OK to return to the System Properties dialog box.

6. Click Close. Windows 98 prompts you to restart your system.

7. Click Yes.

WRITE-BEHIND CACHING AND REMOVABLE DRIVES

If you have a removable drive (such as a ZIP or Jaz drive), you can use the Removable Disk tab to enable write-behind caching for your removable drives (which Windows 98 disables by default). To do this, activate the Enable write-behind caching on all removable disk drives check box.

Overcoming File Fragmentation with Disk Defragmenter

Windows 98 comes with a utility called Disk Defragmenter that's an essential tool for tuning your hard disk. Disk Defragmenter's job is to eliminate *file fragmentation* from your hard disk.

File fragmentation is one of those terms that sounds scarier than it actually is. It simply means that a file is stored on your hard disk in scattered, noncontiguous bits. This is a performance drag because it means that Windows 98, when it tries to open such a file, must make several stops to collect the various pieces. If a lot of files are fragmented, it can slow even the fastest hard disk to a crawl.

Why doesn't Windows 98 just store files contiguously? Recall that Windows 98 stores files on disk in clusters, and that these clusters have a fixed size, depending on the disk's capacity. Recall too that Windows 98 uses the FAT to keep track of each file's whereabouts. When you delete a file, Windows 98 doesn't actually clean out the clusters associated with the file. Instead, it just places a 0 in the appropriate FAT cluster entries to reflect that the file's clusters are now available.

To see how fragmentation occurs, let's look at an example. Suppose that three files are stored on a disk—FIRST.TXT, SECOND.TXT, and THIRD.TXT—and that they use up four, three, and five clusters, respectively. Figure 9.16 shows how they might look on the disk.

9

OPTIMIZING
MEMORY AND
DISK ACCESS

FIGURE 9.16.

Three files before fragmentation.

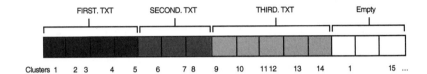

If you now delete SECOND.TXT, clusters 5, 6, and 7 become available. But suppose that the next file you save—call it FOURTH.TXT—takes up five clusters. What happens? Well, Windows 98 starts at the beginning of the FAT and looks for the first available clusters. It finds that 5, 6, and 7 are free, so it uses them for the first three clusters of FOURTH.TXT. Windows continues and finds that clusters 13 and 14 are free, so it uses them for the final two clusters of FOURTH.TXT. Figure 9.17 shows how things look now.

FIGURE 9.17.

A fragmented file.

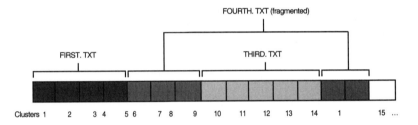

As you can see, FOURTH.TXT is stored noncontiguously—in other words, it's fragmented. Although a file fragmented in two pieces isn't that bad, it's possible for large files to get split into dozens of blocks.

FRAGMENTATION FOILS THE CACHE

Fragmented files not only take longer to open, but they also defeat the operation of the read-ahead portion of the cache. That's because the cache assumes that the next cluster in the chain is the one most likely to be accessed next. If the file is badly fragmented, chances are the next cluster won't belong to the file.

Getting Started with Disk Defragmenter

The Disk Defragmenter accessory works by physically rearranging the files on your hard disk so that each file has its clusters stored contiguously. Before using Disk Defragmenter, you should perform a couple of housekeeping chores:

- Delete any files from your hard disk that you don't need. Defragmenting junk files only slows down the whole process. Windows 98's Disk Cleanup Manager is perfect for this (see the section "A Spring Cleaning for Your Hard Drive," earlier in this chapter).

- Check for file allocation errors and other disk problems by running ScanDisk (as described in Chapter 17).

DEFRAGMENTATION CAVEATS

Don't use the DEFRAG utility that shipped with DOS 6.x, because it doesn't understand long filenames. Also, don't use Disk Defragmenter on drives compressed with Stacker or SuperStor, network drives, CD-ROM drives, or drives created with the DOS commands ASSIGN, JOIN, and SUBST.

Running Disk Defragmenter

To launch Disk Defragmenter, select Start | Programs | Accessories | System Tools | Disk Defragmenter. You see the Select Drive dialog box, shown in Figure 9.18. To start the defragment, use the Which drive do you want to defragment? drop-down list to choose a drive and click OK.

FIGURE 9.18.

Use this dialog box to select the drive you want to defragment.

NOTE

It's possible to avoid the Select Drive dialog box and begin defragmenting a drive right away. In Windows Explorer or My Computer, right-click the drive you want to defragment, click Properties, and then display the Tools tab in the dialog box that appears. Click the Defragment Now button.

Disk Defragmenter starts tidying up your hard disk and displays the dialog box shown in Figure 9.19 to keep you apprised of its progress.

FIGURE 9.19.

Disk Defragmenter displays this dialog box to show you the progress of the defragmentation.

If you'd like to see a visual representation of the Disk Defragmenter's labors, click the Show Details button.

When Disk Defragmenter finally finishes its chores (it might take up to an hour, depending on the size of your disk, how cluttered it is, and how fast your computer is), your computer beeps, and Disk Defragmenter displays a dialog box telling you that the defragmentation is complete and asking whether you want to quit Disk Defragmenter. If you do, click Yes; otherwise, click No to return to the Select Drive dialog box.

HOW OFTEN SHOULD YOU DEFRAGMENT?

How often you defragment your hard disk depends on how often you use your computer. If you use it every day, you should run Disk Defragmenter about once a week. If your computer doesn't get heavy use, you probably need to run Disk Defragmenter only once a month or so.

Rather than trying to remember this yourself, you can use a couple of Windows 98 tools to schedule regular optimizations: the Maintenance Wizard and the Scheduled Tasks folder. I cover both these utilities in Chapter 17.

Disk Defragmenter Settings

To change the defragmenting options, click Settings in the Select Drive dialog box to display the Disk Defragmenter Settings dialog box, shown in Figure 9.20. Here's a summary of the controls:

Rearrange program files so my programs start faster: When this check box is activated, Disk Defragmenter tracks the applications you use most frequently. Disk Defragmenter will then use this information to store the program files for these applications contiguously and in the most optimal part of the disk. This should improve application load times and overall application performance.

Check drive for errors: When this check box is activated, Windows 98 checks for file and folder errors before starting the defragmentation. If you've already run ScanDisk, you should deactivate this check box to save time.

I want to use these options: If you want to use the options you've chosen each time you run Disk Defragmenter, select Every time I defragment my hard drive. To use the selected options now but return to the default options the next time you run Disk Defragmenter, select This time only.

When you're done, click OK to return to the Disk Defragmenter dialog box.

FIGURE 9.20.
Use this dialog box to set some advanced Disk Defragmenter options.

Using Disk Defragmenter from the Command Line

For an extra level of control over how Disk Defragmenter performs its duties, you can start the program either by using the Run dialog box or by using the DOS prompt and including one or more command-line parameters. The command that starts Disk Defragmenter is `defrag`. It uses the following syntax:

```
defrag [d: ¦ /all] [/noprompt] [/concise ¦ /detailed]
```

Here's an explanation of each parameter:

`d:`	The drive letter of the disk you want to defragment.
`/all`	Defragment all (local) hard disk drives.
`/noprompt`	Bypass confirmation dialog boxes.
`/concise`	Show the defragmentation progress only (no details; see Figure 9.19). This is the default.
`/detailed`	Display the Show Details view.

Summary

This chapter showed you how to give Windows 98 a tune-up by optimizing memory, hard disk access, the CD-ROM cache, and more. You'll find more information related to these issues in the following chapters:

- For hardware-related performance issues, see Chapter 10, "Getting the Most Out of Device Manager and Hardware Profiles."

- You can use the Registry for some performance tuning. I show you how in Chapter 13, "A Few Good Hacks: Some Useful Registry Tweaks."

- For more data on the Windows 98 file system, including instructions on how to compress disks to get more space, see Chapter 15, "Disk Driving: The Windows 98 Disk Utilities."

- To learn about backing up files, try out Chapter 16, "Working with a Net: The Windows 98 Backup Utility."

- I cover ScanDisk, the Maintenance Wizard, the Scheduled Tasks folder, and lots more in Chapter 17, "Wielding the Windows 98 System Tools."
- I talk a bit about optimizing printing in Chapter 21, "Prescriptions for Perfect Printing."
- To get the best performance out of your DOS programs, see Chapter 23, "DOS Isn't Dead: Unleashing the DOS Shell."
- The two chapters in Part V, "Unleashing Multimedia: The Sights and Sounds of Windows 98," contain tips and techniques for optimizing multimedia.

Getting the Most Out of Device Manager and Hardware Profiles

> *Man is a shrewd inventor, and is ever taking the hint of a new machine from his own*
> *structure, adapting some secret of his own anatomy in iron, wood, and leather, to some*
> *required function in the work of the world.*
>
> *—Ralph Waldo Emerson*

Emerson's concept of a "machine" was decidedly low-tech ("iron, wood, and leather"), but his basic idea is still apt in these high-tech times. Man has taken yet another "secret of his own anatomy"—the brain—and used it as the "hint of a new machine"—the computer. And although even the most advanced computer is still a mere toy compared to the breathtaking complexity of the human brain (Deep Blue notwithstanding), some spectacular advancements have been made in the art of hardware in recent years.

One of the hats an operating system must wear is that of an intermediary between you and your hardware. Any OS worth its salt has to translate incomprehensible "devicespeak" into something you can make sense out of, and it must ensure that devices are ready, willing, and able to carry out your commands. Given the sophistication and diversity of today's hardware market, however, that's no easy task. The good news is that Windows 98 brings to the PC world an unprecedented level of interaction with hardware. From its basic architecture to the advanced device management tools it provides, Windows 98 is built from the ground up to make your hardware travails trivial. Did Microsoft achieve this laudable goal? Not really, no. But it's a huge improvement over the primitive tools that existed in previous versions of Windows, so, if nothing else, it will make your hardware chores easier. This chapter provides you with an introduction to Windows 98's hardware support and provides detailed coverage of Device Manager and hardware profiles. I cover specific hardware devices in Chapter 11, "Device Advice: Dealing with Devices in Windows 98."

Working with the Device Manager

Windows 98 stores all its hardware data in the Registry, but it provides the Device Manager to give you a graphical view of the devices on your system. To display the Device Manager, use either of the following techniques:

- Select Start | Settings | Control Panel and open the System icon in the Control Panel window.
- Right-click My Computer and click Properties in the context menu.

In the System Properties dialog box that appears, select the Device Manager tab, as shown in Figure 10.1. Device Manager's default display is a treelike outline that lists various hardware classes (CD-ROM, Disk drives, and so on).

To see the specific devices, click the plus sign (+) to the left of a device class or highlight the class and press the + key on the keyboard's numeric keypad. For example, opening the Disk drives class displays all the disk drives attached to your computer, as shown in Figure 10.2.

FIGURE 10.1.

The Device Manager shows you a visual representation of all the devices on your system.

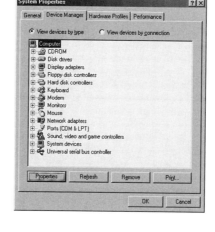

FIGURE 10.2.

Opening a hardware class shows you the specific devices within that class that are attached to your computer.

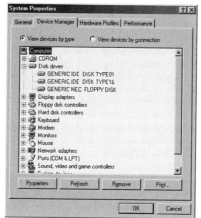

If you like, you can also view the devices according to the component to which they're connected by activating the View devices by connection option button. This is handy, for example, if you want to see the devices attached to your SCSI controller.

Viewing Devices by IRQ, I/O Port, and DMA Channel

One of the major problems associated with device management has always been knowing which of your system's hardware resources were being used, and by which device. This is particularly true of limited resources such as IRQs and DMA channels. One of Device Manager's most powerful features is its capability of showing you a list of your devices according to the hardware resources they use. To try this, highlight the Computer item at the top of the list and then click the Properties button. You see the Computer Properties dialog box, shown in Figure 10.3. Use the option buttons at the top of the dialog box to select the type of resource you want to view. (The Memory option shows you which areas of upper memory are being used by your devices.)

10

DEVICE MANAGER AND HARDWARE PROFILES

FIGURE 10.3.

Use the Computer Properties dialog box to view your devices by specific resources.

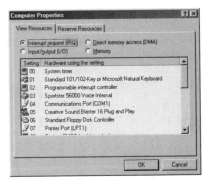

RESERVING RESOURCES

If your system has legacy devices and you plan to install a Plug and Play device, there's a chance the Plug and Play device will end up using a resource that belongs to one of the legacy peripherals. To prevent this from happening, Device Manager lets you reserve the resources used by your legacy devices so that they can't be assigned to a different device. In the Computer Properties dialog box, select the Reserve Resources tab. For each resource you want to reserve, use the option buttons to activate the appropriate resource type, click Add, enter the resource value, and click OK.

Printing a System Report

Device Manager's hardware listing and the capability of viewing devices by resource are among the highlights of the Windows 98 package. However, Device Manager won't do you a lick of good if you're having some kind of hardware problem that prevents you from starting Windows 98. That might never happen, but just in case it does, you should print a hard copy of the device data. Here's how you do so:

1. If you want a printout of only a specific hardware class or device, use the Device Manager list to highlight the class or device.

2. Click the Print button to display the Print dialog box, shown in Figure 10.4.

FIGURE 10.4.

You can get a printout of your system's device information.

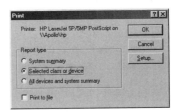

3. In the Report type group, select one of the following report options:

System summary: A summary of resource usage on your system: IRQs, I/O ports, DMA channels, and upper memory.

Selected class or device: The driver and resource data for the highlighted hardware class or device.

All devices and system summary: Both the summary of resource usage on your system and the driver and resource data for every device.

4. To make printer adjustments, click Setup, select the options you want from the Print Setup dialog box, and click OK.

5. Click OK to print the report.

Removing a Device

If your computer has a Plug and Play BIOS and you remove a device, the BIOS informs Windows 98 that the device is no longer present. Windows 98, in turn, updates its device list in the Registry, and the peripheral no longer appears in the Device Manager tab.

If you don't have a Plug and Play BIOS, but the device you're removing is Plug and Play–compliant, Configuration Manager figures out that the device is missing and updates Windows 98 accordingly.

If you're removing a legacy device, however, you need to tell Device Manager that the device no longer exists. To do that, highlight the device in the Device Manager tab and click the Remove button. If you've defined multiple hardware profiles (as described later, in the "Setting Up Hardware Profiles" section), Windows 98 will ask whether you want to remove the device from all the profiles or just from a specific profile. Select the appropriate option. When Windows 98 warns you that you're about to remove the device, click OK.

DON'T FORGET TO REMOVE THE DEVICE

If you remove a device from the Device Manager, you must also remove the physical device from your system. Otherwise, either the BIOS or Windows 98 will just detect the device again, or the device's resources won't be freed for other devices to use.

Viewing Device Properties

Each device listed in the Device Manager has its own properties sheet. You can use these properties sheets not only to learn more about the device (such as the resources it's currently using), but also to make adjustments to the device's resources, change the device driver, alter the device's settings (if it has any), and make other changes.

10

DEVICE MANAGER AND HARDWARE PROFILES

To display the properties sheet for a device, display the device in the Device Manager tab, and then either double-click the device or highlight the device and click Properties. Figure 10.5 shows the properties sheet for a sound card. The General tab tells you the name of the device and its hardware class, the manufacturer's name, and the hardware version (if known). The Device status group tells you whether the device is working properly. You use the Device usage group to add and remove devices from hardware profiles (see "Setting Up Hardware Profiles" later in this chapter).

FIGURE 10.5.

The properties sheet for a sound card.

Besides this general information, a device's properties sheet includes a wealth of other useful data. Depending on the device, the properties sheet can also tell you the resources used by the device, the device driver, and miscellaneous settings specific to the device. I cover each of these items in the next few sections.

Viewing and Adjusting a Device's Resources

To view the resources being used by the device (if any), select the Resources tab, shown in Figure 10.6. The two-column list shows you the resource type on the left and the resource setting on the right. If you suspect that the device has a resource conflict, check the Conflicting device list to see whether any devices are listed. If the list displays only `No conflicts`, the device's resources aren't conflicting with another device.

If, however, you do have a conflict, you need to change the appropriate resource. Some devices have multiple configurations, so one easy way to change resources is to select a different configuration. To try this, use the Setting based on drop-down list to select a different configuration.

FIGURE 10.6.

*The Resources tab
outlines the resources
used by the device.*

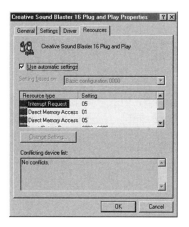

Otherwise, you need to play around with the resource settings by hand. Here are the steps to follow to change a resource setting:

1. In the Resource type list, highlight the resource you want to change.

2. Deactivate the Use automatic settings check box, if it's activated.

3. For the setting you want to change, either double-click it or highlight it and click the Change Setting button. You see an Edit dialog box similar to the one shown in Figure 10.7.

FIGURE 10.7.

*Use this dialog box to
change an IRQ. Other
resources display similar
dialog boxes.*

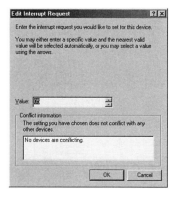

4. Use the Value spinner to select a different resource. Watch the Conflict information group to make sure that your new setting doesn't step on the toes of an existing setting.

5. Click OK to return to the Resources tab.

6. Click OK. If Windows 98 asks whether you want to restart your computer, click Yes.

10

**DEVICE MANAGER
AND HARDWARE
PROFILES**

Changing Drivers via the Device Manager

New to 98

In a device's properties sheet, you can click the Driver tab's Driver File Details button to see the current driver (or drivers) associated with the device.

If you need to change the driver (for example, if you've obtained an updated driver from the manufacturer), you can do it from Device Manager. In the Driver tab, click the Upgrade Driver button to start the Upgrade Device Driver Wizard. Click Next > and the Wizard displays a dialog box with two options:

> **Search for a better driver than the one your device is using now:** Choose this option to have Windows 98 search your disk drives or even the Internet for a more recent driver. If you have a disk from the manufacturer, insert it into the appropriate drive now.

> **Create a list of all the drivers in a specific location, so you can select the driver you want:** Choose this option to select a driver from a list of the devices that Windows 98 can work with.

Click Next > to proceed.

If you asked Windows 98 to search for a better driver, the Wizard displays the dialog box shown in Figure 10.8. Activate the appropriate check boxes and then click Next >. If you activated the Microsoft Windows Update option, Windows 98 connects to the Windows Update site on the Internet. The first time you do this, Windows 98 installs a "download agent" to help you download and install drivers. (Note, too, that you must register your copy of Windows 98 before you can access the online driver updates.) If the Wizard finds a better driver, follow the instructions onscreen to install and configure the driver.

FIGURE 10.8.

Select the locations the Wizard should search for a newer driver.

If you opted to select the driver you want from the Windows 98 list, you see a dialog box similar to the one shown in Figure 10.9.

FIGURE 10.9.

Use this dialog box to pick the new driver for the device.

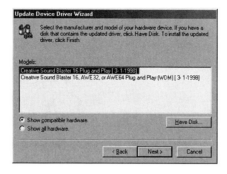

There are three ways to proceed from here:

- If the new device driver you want is shown in the Models list, highlight it and click OK.

- If you don't see the device, activate the Show all hardware option to display the full list of available drivers, as shown in Figure 10.10. Highlight the appropriate device manufacturer in the Manufacturers list, highlight the driver you want in the Models list, then click OK.

FIGURE 10.10.

Activating Show all hardware displays Windows 98's complete list of drivers for this hardware class.

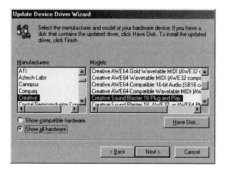

- If you have a disk from the manufacturer, insert the disk and then click the Have Disk button. In the Install from Disk dialog box, enter the appropriate drive and folder in the Copy manufacturer's files from box and click OK. Windows 98 displays a list of possible device drivers in the Select Device dialog box. Highlight the driver you want to install and click OK.

At this point, Windows 98 will likely ask whether you want to restart your computer. Click Yes to reboot and put the new driver into effect.

Adjusting Device Settings

Some devices have a Settings tab in their properties sheet that lets you set various options specific to the device (see Figure 10.11). For a CD-ROM drive, for example, you can specify the

drive letter to use and whether the drive runs the Windows 98 AutoPlay feature. For a SCSI controller, you can add any command-line parameters or switches the driver might need.

Figure 10.11.

For some devices, you can use the Settings tab to adjust various device parameters.

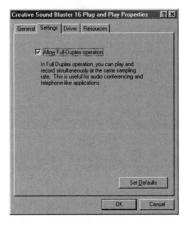

DETECTING FLAWED PENTIUM CHIPS

If you have an older Pentium, one of the most useful Settings tabs is the one for the numeric data processor. You might recall the big Pentium scandal of late 1994, when it was discovered that the Pentium chip had a bug that produced arithmetic errors in certain (rare) conditions. Windows 98 can check for these faulty Pentium CPUs and optionally disable the numeric data processor until you can get an upgraded chip. To see whether your CPU has this bug, open Device Manager's System devices tree, display the properties sheet for the Numeric data processor, and select the Settings tab. If your CPU is flawed, you see the following message in the Diagnostics group:

```
The numeric processor in this computer can sometimes
compute inaccurate results when dividing large numbers.
```

To disable the coprocessor, activate the Never use the numeric data processor option.

Enabling IRQ Steering in Windows 98

Windows 98 supports IRQ steering on PCI machines. To make sure that this support is enabled on your machine, follow these steps:

1. In Device Manager, open the System devices branch.
2. Highlight PCI bus and then click Properties.
3. In the properties sheet that appears, activate the IRQ Steering tab, shown in Figure 10.12.

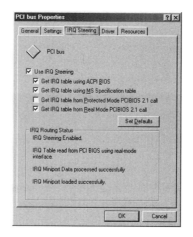

FIGURE 10.12.

Use the IRQ Steering tab to activate IRQ steering on your OSR2 machine.

4. Activate the Use IRQ Steering check box.

5. To determine the tables used by Windows to program the IRQ steering, check one or more of the following:

   Get IRQ table using ACPI BIOS: Activate this check box to allow the PCI bus to get the IRQ table via the ACPI (Advanced Configuration and Power Interface) BIOS.

   Get IRQ table using MS Specification table: Activate this check box to have Windows 98 itself construct the IRQ table.

   Get IRQ table from Protected Mode PCIBIOS 2.1 call: Activate this check box to allow the PCI bus to get the IRQ table directly from the PCI BIOS (that is, without using Windows 98 as an intermediary) via a protected mode call.

   Get IRQ table from Real Mode PCIBIOS 2.1 call: Activate this check box to allow the PCI bus to get the IRQ table directly from the PCI BIOS via a real mode call.

6. Click OK to return to the System Properties dialog box.

7. Click OK.

8. When Windows 98 asks whether you want to restart your computer, click Yes.

Setting Up Hardware Profiles

In most cases, your hardware configuration will remain relatively static. You might add the odd new device or remove a device, but these are permanent changes. Windows 98 merely updates its current hardware configuration to compensate.

In some situations, however, you might need to switch between hardware configurations regularly. A good example is a notebook computer with a docking station. When the computer is undocked, it uses its built-in keyboard, mouse, and display; when the computer is docked, however, it uses a separate keyboard, mouse, and display. To make it easier to switch between these different configurations, Windows 98 lets you set up a hardware profile for each setup. It then becomes a simple matter of your selecting the profile you want to use at startup; Windows 98 handles the hard part of loading the appropriate drivers. (See also "Notes About Hot-Docking and Hardware Profiles," later in this chapter.)

YOU DON'T NEED PROFILES WITH PLUG AND PLAY

You don't need to bother with hardware profiles if your computer has a Plug and Play BIOS and you're using Plug and Play devices. Plug and Play detects any new hardware configuration automatically and adjusts accordingly. For example, Plug and Play supports hot-docking of a notebook computer: While the machine is running, you can insert it into, or remove it from, the docking station, and Plug and Play handles the switch without breaking a sweat.

Creating a New Hardware Profile

Before creating a new hardware profile, run the Add New Hardware Wizard (see the next chapter) to install the drivers you need for all the hardware you'll be using. If the hardware isn't currently installed, that's OK; just be sure to specify the appropriate devices by hand in the Add New Hardware Wizard. The important thing is to make sure that all the drivers you need are installed.

After that's done (and you've rebooted to put the changes into effect), display the System Properties dialog box and select the Hardware Profiles tab. On most systems, you see a single profile named `Original Configuration`, as shown in Figure 10.13. This profile includes all the installed device drivers. The idea is that you create a new profile by making a copy of this configuration, and then you tell Windows 98 which devices to include in each profile.

FIGURE 10.13.
The Hardware Profiles tab lists the currently defined profiles.

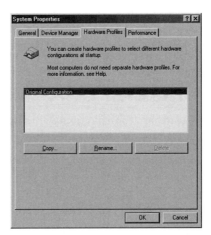

To make a copy of the profile, click the Copy button, enter a name for the new profile in the Copy Profile dialog box, and click OK.

If you want to rename a profile, highlight the profile, click Rename, enter the new name in the Rename Profile dialog box, and click OK. For example, on my notebook machine I renamed `Original Configuration` to `Undocked` to go along with the new `Docked` profile I created, as shown in Figure 10.14.

FIGURE 10.14.

Here, I've added a new profile and renamed the original profile.

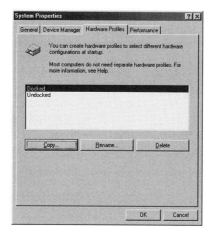

Adding and Removing Devices in a Hardware Profile

Now that you have multiple profiles in place, you need to tell Windows 98 which devices go with which profile. Return to the Device Manager tab and open the properties sheet for a device you need to adjust (see Figure 10.15).

In the General tab's Device usage group, you may see one or more of the following three choices, depending on the device:

> **Disable in this hardware profile**: If you activate this check box, Windows leaves the device in the current hardware profile, but the device is disabled.

> **Remove from this hardware profile**: Activate this check box to take the device out of the current hardware profile.

> **Exists in all hardware profiles**: Use this check box to add or remove a device from all your profiles—even new profiles that you create later on.

Dealing with Ambiguous Profiles

How does Windows 98 know which profile to use? Generally, it goes by the current hardware configuration. For example, if you have a Docked hardware profile that uses an external keyboard, Windows 98 will use this profile at startup if it detects an attached keyboard.

FIGURE 10.15.

The properties sheet for each device lets you include or exclude the device from each profile.

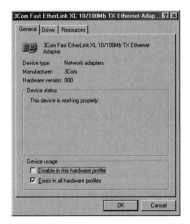

Note, however, that all the devices in a profile must match the physical devices present in the system before Windows 98 will use a profile automatically. If there is some ambiguity (that is, the physical devices don't match the devices specified in the profile), Windows 98 will display a menu of hardware profiles at startup. This menu will be similar to the following example:

```
Windows cannot determine what configuration your computer is in.
Select one of the following:

  1. Undocked
  2. Docked
  3. None of the above

Enter your choice:
```

In this case, you need to select the hardware profile you want Windows 98 to use.

Notes About Hot-Docking and Hardware Profiles

I'll be discussing PC Card devices in the next chapter, and you'll see that they are an innovative solution to the problem of notebook expandability, but they're not a total solution. For one thing, most notebooks have only a small number of PC card sockets (usually one or two), so the number of devices you can have plugged in at any one time is limited. For another thing, many devices still are available only as cards designed for bus slots (such as video capture cards).

If you need multiple devices attached to your notebook, or if you need a device that's not available in the PC card format, an excellent compromise is the *docking station*. These are platforms into which you can slide your notebook and thus create a full-fledged desktop machine. The notebook provides the guts—the CPU, the memory, the hard drive—and the docking provides everything else—drive bays; bus slots; and ports for an external monitor, keyboard, mouse, printer, modem, and so on.

If your notebook has a Plug and Play BIOS, Windows 98 supports *hot-docking*: inserting your notebook into, and removing it from, the docking station while Windows 98 is still running.

The first time you try this, the Plug and Play BIOS alerts Windows 98 of the hardware change. The Configuration Manager takes over, examines the new hardware configuration, and installs the appropriate drivers. When that's done, Windows 98 establishes a new hardware profile (usually called Dock 1) for the docked computer. You can then enable and disable devices in each profile.

As I mentioned earlier, I have two profiles on my notebook: Docked and Undocked. When the machine is docked, I use (among other things) an external mouse; when the machine is undocked, I use the notebook's built-in mouse. Each mouse, however, uses a different device driver: Standard Serial Mouse for the external mouse, and Standard PS/2 Port Mouse for the built-in mouse. To tell Windows 98 which driver to use in which profile, I use each device's properties sheet to disable the appropriate profile, as descried earlier.

Another advantage you get with a Plug and Play notebook BIOS is the Eject PC command. You can find this command on the Start menu while your notebook is docked. Selecting the command tells Windows 98 to unload the drivers used in the undocked profile. When that's done, Windows 98 either prompts you to undock your notebook or does it for you (if your docking station has an automatic undocking feature).

Summary

This chapter introduced you to Windows 98's hardware features. I showed you how to work with Device Manager to view devices, print a system report, and view device properties. You also saw how to use Device manager to change drivers, adjust device settings and resources, and create hardware profiles.

I deal with hardware issues in plenty of other locations in this book. Here's a list of those places:

- I discuss the Add New Hardware Wizard as well as specific devices in Chapter 11, "Device Advice: Dealing with Devices in Windows 98."
- The Device Manager gets all its hardware info from the Registry. To see where this valuable data is stored, see Chapter 12, "Getting to Know the Windows 98 Registry."
- I cover printers in Chapter 21, "Prescriptions for Perfect Printing."
- Multimedia hardware tidbits are sprinkled throughout Part V, "Unleashing Multimedia: The Sights and Sounds of Windows 98."

10

DEVICE MANAGER AND HARDWARE PROFILES

Device Advice: Dealing with Devices in Windows 98

IN THIS CHAPTER

Man will never be enslaved by machinery if the man tending the machine be paid enough.

—Karel Capek

This chapter changes the view from the forest of Windows 98's hardware support you saw in Chapter 10, "Getting the Most Out of Device Manager and Hardware Profiles," to the trees of specific devices. In this view, you deal with many different kinds of devices, including disk drives, graphics adapters, monitors, PC Cards, and much more. I also provide instructions for using your computer's Advanced Power Management features, and you also learn a few hardware troubleshooting techniques.

Adding New Hardware

You've seen how the Windows 98 Setup program made hardware installation a breeze by detecting your devices automatically. You can get the same level of convenience after Windows 98 is installed by running the Add New Hardware Wizard. This Wizard essentially just runs the Detection Manager again with a few extra bells and whistles thrown in. If you'd prefer to specify the new device, or if you have a disk from the manufacturer, the Add New Hardware Wizard also lets you install individual devices by hand.

In either case, though, you need to display the Add New Hardware Wizard. To do that, select Start | Settings | Control Panel and then open the Add New Hardware icon in the Control Panel folder. Windows 98 displays the first of the Add New Hardware Wizard's dialog boxes. Click Next > to continue. The next few sections take you through the rest of the process.

The Plug and Play Phase

The Windows 98 version of the Add New Hardware Wizard uses a slightly different *modus operandi* than its Windows 98 predecessor. Specifically, the new Wizard first performs a check for any new Plug and Play devices installed on your system. The next wizard dialog box that appears tells you that it will perform this search, so click Next >.

If the Wizard finds one or more new Plug and Play devices, you see various messages onscreen telling you that Windows has found a new device and is installing the software for it. You may be prompted to insert your Windows 98 CD-ROM during this process. Depending on the device, the Wizard may then display a list of the installed devices and present you with two options:

> **Yes, I am finished installing devices:** Activate this option and click Next > to exit the Add New Hardware Wizard.

> **No, I want to install other devices:** Activate this option and click Next > to install a non–Plug and Play device.

If the Wizard found new Plug and Play devices, but there are problems with those devices, you see the dialog box shown in Figure 11.1. To install one of these devices, highlight it, click Next >, and then click Finish. Windows 98 then displays the properties sheet for the device, which includes an explanation of the problem. See "Device Manager as a Troubleshooting Tool" later in this chapter.

FIGURE 11.1.
If the Wizard finds new
Plug and Play devices,
you see this dialog box.

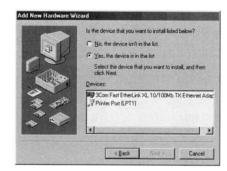

If you don't want to install any of the listed Plug and Play devices, activate the No, the device isn't in the list option and click Next >. In the dialog box that appears, you choose the Add New Hardware Wizard method you want to use for specifying legacy devices:

> **Yes (Recommended):** Choose this option to have the Wizard detect your hardware automatically.

> **No, I want to select the hardware from a list:** Choose this option to specify the device manually. This method is best if you know exactly which device you're dealing with or if you have the appropriate driver on disk.

When you've made your choice, click Next > to continue. The next two sections take you through both methods.

Automatically Detecting New Devices

If you elected to have the Add New Hardware Wizard detect your devices automatically, the next dialog box that appears warns you that your computer might stop responding. Click Next > to begin the detection progress. Note that the Wizard checks all your hardware, so this process will take a few minutes.

When the Wizard has completed its labors, it tells you whether it found any new devices. (It also tells you whether a device has been removed.) If the Wizard did find new hardware, click the Details button to display a list of the devices. Click Finish. Depending on the device, you might need to run through a configuration process. Follow the instructions onscreen and reboot when prompted.

Specifying New Devices Manually

Rather than going through the lengthy detection process, you might prefer to specify your new hardware manually. This is particularly true if you have a disk from the manufacturer that contains the drivers for the device. If you selected No in the second Add New Hardware Wizard dialog box, clicking Next > displays a list of hardware classes, as shown in Figure 11.2.

FIGURE 11.2.

If you elected to specify a device manually, the Wizard displays this list of hardware classes.

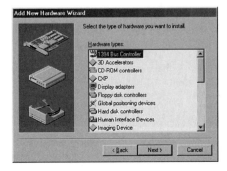

Here are the steps to follow to specify a device manually:

1. In the Hardware types list, highlight the hardware class for your device and click Next >. The Wizard displays the Select Device dialog box with a list of the manufacturers and models that Windows 98 knows about for the hardware class. For example, Figure 11.3 shows the dialog box that appears for the Network adapters class.

FIGURE 11.3.

The device list for the Network adapters class. Other hardware classes display similar lists.

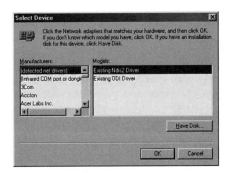

2. If, after you highlight the appropriate device manufacturer in the Manufacturers list, the driver you want appears in the Models list, highlight it and skip to step 6.

3. If you have a disk from the manufacturer, insert the disk and then click the Have Disk button.

4. In the Install from Disk dialog box, enter the appropriate drive and folder in the Copy manufacturer's files from box and then click OK. Windows 98 displays a list of possible device drivers in the Select Device dialog box.

5. Highlight the driver you want to install.

6. Click OK to return to the properties sheet.

7. Click OK. Windows 98 asks whether you want to restart your computer.

8. Click Yes to reboot and put the new driver into effect.

Working with CD-ROM Drives

CD-ROM drives are a big part of the multimedia revolution. Now that 5 1/4-inch floppy drives have been relegated to the dustbin of computer history, CD-ROM drives have moved in and taken their place. In fact, the vast majority of new systems sold today come with a CD-ROM drive. This critical mass of drives convinced multimedia developers to release their new titles on CD-ROM and, with hundreds of megabytes to play with, many of these titles are truly spectacular. (Games such as Myst and encyclopedias such as Encarta come to mind.) The quality of these applications, the reduced price, and a constant increase in performance (double-speed drives begat quad-speed, quad-speed begat six-speed, six-speed begat eight-speed, and on and on) convinced even more people to add CD-ROM drives to their systems.

Windows 98 and CD-ROMs

Windows 98 supports CD-ROM drives with a 32-bit protected-mode driver named VCDFSD.VXD (the CDFS stands for CD-ROM File System). This driver replaces MSCDEX.EXE, the real-mode driver used in previous versions of DOS and Windows. If a line loading MSCDEX.EXE already existed in AUTOEXEC.BAT when you installed Windows 98, the Setup program comments out the line and adds VCDFSD.VXD to its list of protected-mode drivers to load at startup. If you've added a CD-ROM drive since installing Windows 98, you need to run the Add New Hardware Wizard (in automatic mode) to detect the drive and load VCDFSD.VXD. (The exception to this is if your CD-ROM drive is attached to a SCSI controller. In this case, Windows 98 will detect the drive automatically at startup.)

With CDFS, you should notice improved performance from your CD-ROM drive. Not only is CDFS faster than the old real-mode driver, but it also boasts improved multitasking abilities and works with VCACHE (the protected-mode cache driver) to create a separate (and dynamic) pool of cache memory to help optimize CD-ROM performance. I showed you how to make adjustments to the CD-ROM cache in Chapter 9, "Performance Tuning: Optimizing Memory and Disk Access."

The AutoPlay Feature

Windows 98 continually performs a number of chores in the background. One of these chores is to use the CDVSD.VXD driver to constantly poll your CD-ROM drive to see whether a new disc has been inserted. If it finds a new disc, it alerts Explorer to update the Folders pane, and then it looks for a file named AUTORUN.INF. This file gives Windows 98 instructions on what to do with the CD-ROM. For example, here's the AUTORUN.INF file from the Windows 98 CD-ROM:

```
[autorun]
OPEN=AUTORUN\AUTORUN.EXE
ICON=AUTORUN\WIN98CD.ICO
```

The OPEN line tells Windows 98 the name and location of an executable file. When Windows 98 detects this line, it runs the file automatically. In most cases, the executable either loads a Setup program or starts the applications.

If the disc is an audio CD, Windows 98 starts playing it automatically. ("Play" is the default action for the AudioCD file type.)

If you'd prefer that Windows 98 not run the AutoPlay executable when you load a disc, just hold down the Shift key. Windows 98 will still update Explorer, but it will ignore the OPEN line in AUTORUN.INF.

For a more permanent solution, follow these steps:

1. Open the System Properties dialog box and display the Device Manager tab.
2. Open the CD-ROM hardware class.
3. Highlight your CD-ROM and click Properties.
4. Display the Settings tab.
5. Deactivate the Auto insert notification check box.
6. Click OK to return to the System Properties dialog box.
7. Click OK. When Windows 98 asks whether you want to restart your computer, click Yes.

DVD: Welcome to the Next Level

Although CD-ROMs will be around for a long time, the writing is on the wall, and it says *DVD*. DVD stands for Digital Versatile Disc (or sometimes Digital Video Disc), and it's the end result of a long battle to settle on the new standard for digital media. Supported by all the major players in the electronics industry, DVD promises previously unheard-of levels of performance, storage, and compatibility. The first units began shipping in the spring of 1997. They play not only the new consumer video titles in DVD format (hundreds of movies will be released throughout 1997), but also today's audio CDs, CD-ROMs, laserdiscs, and the new DVD-ROM format (which supports MPEG-2 digital video). The latter promises up to 4.7GB (yes, *gigabytes*) of the same kind of data that we see on regular CD-ROMs, with the performance of an eight-speed CD-ROM drive. This technology also supports "double-layered" discs that can pack a walloping 8.5GB, which is the equivalent of about 13 of today's CD-ROMs. When the DVD format hits its full stride in 1998, discs will be able to store 17GB and will be writable and erasable.

Windows 98 supports DVD drives via an update in the CD-ROM driver. In fact, Windows 98 lists DVD drives under Device Manager's CD-ROM hardware class, as shown in Figure 11.4. Note, however, that you won't be able to install a Windows 98 DVD driver or the DVD Player unless Windows detects that you have a DVD decoder card that is supported by Windows 98. Note, too, that Windows 98 also implements a new file system called the Universal Disk Filesystem, or UDF. This is the file system used by DVD movies.

Device Advice: Dealing with Devices in Windows 98

Chapter 11

273

11

Dealing with
Devices in
Windows 98

Figure 11.4.

*Windows 98 supports
DVD drives via the
CD-ROM driver, so
DVD drives are listed
in the CD-ROM class.*

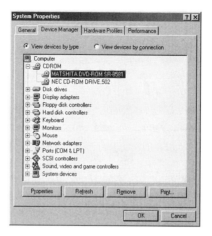

Getting Great Graphics

Your computer's display is what you look at all day long, so you need to be comfortable with what you see. This is especially important for multimedia applications. To get the most out of these titles, you need graphics hardware that can handle the blizzard of data produced by the bitmaps, videos, and animations that are de rigueur in modern multimedia. Mainstream business applications also can benefit from a strong graphics system. After all, Windows 98 is a graphical operating system, so even day-to-day chores can create quite a graphics workload.

If you upgraded from Windows 3.*x*, you will notice an immediate graphics speed boost. Microsoft revamped the graphics subsystem to provide greater performance as well as enhanced reliability. For one thing, some of the data structures used by the graphics device interface (GDI) were converted to 32-bit, thus making better use of system resources. Also, the GDI gained a new engine for controlling output to the screen. It's called the Device Independent Bitmap (DIB) engine, and it includes 32-bit code that takes advantage of features found in 386-and-higher processors to generate highly optimized generic drawing routines for everything from lowly 4-bit graphics devices to 24-bit powerhouses. Microsoft claims that this new engine can almost double the performance of even unaccelerated graphics adapters.

The display driver architecture was upgraded as well. In Windows 3.*x*, manufacturers had to write monolithic drivers that included not only the specific implementations of their hardware, but also the basic instructions for drawing to the screen. Now, however, the graphics subsystem uses the universal driver/mini-driver model found in the rest of Windows 98's hardware architecture. The universal driver supplied by Microsoft handles the basic interaction with the GDI and the DIB engine, while mini-drivers handle the device-specific functionality.

Beyond these internals, the attractiveness and performance of your computer's display is a function of two components: the graphics adapter and the monitor. I examine both of these components in the next few sections.

Understanding Graphics Adapters

The *graphics adapter* (also known as the *video adapter, graphics card,* or *video card*) is the internal component in your system that generates the output you see on your monitor.

Accelerated Graphics Adapters

It used to be that graphics adapters relied on the CPU to handle most of the dirty work of graphics processing. However, most graphics adapters sold today are *accelerated*. This means that they come with a graphics coprocessor that assumes most of the graphics duties from the CPU, including time-consuming tasks such as drawing lines and circles. The coprocessor is specially designed to handle these tasks, so not only do screens update faster, but the CPU is relieved of a massive processing burden. For the most part, as far as graphics are concerned, all that remains for the CPU is to send the basic instructions to the graphics card about what to draw and where.

Local Bus Adapters

Most graphics adapters are designed to work with *local bus* systems—usually the VL-Bus for 486 systems and the PCI bus for Pentiums. A local bus is a high-speed data pathway that provides a direct link between the CPU and the adapter's video circuitry. This way, the CPU can send its graphics instructions directly to the adapter without having to go through the slower expansion bus. Local bus systems make a huge difference in graphics performance. There are two reasons for this:

- A local bus is designed to work at higher speeds. Whereas an ISA bus is designed for 8.33MHz operation, the VL-Bus and PCI bus typically operate at 25MHz or 33MHz.
- Both the VL-Bus and PCI bus have 32-bit data paths, compared to the 16-bit data path of the ISA bus.

Display Resolution

Display resolution is a measure of the sharpness of an onscreen image. Resolution is expressed as the number of pixels displayed horizontally by the number of pixels displayed vertically. For example, 640×480 resolution means that there are 640 pixels across the image and 480 pixels down the image. Because most screen objects have a fixed size in pixels, the resolution determines how large or small an object appears, and therefore how much apparent room you have onscreen.

For example, suppose that you have a dialog box onscreen that is 160 pixels wide and 120 pixels tall. In a 640×480 resolution, this dialog box would take up 1/16th of the desktop area. If you switched to 800×600 resolution, however, the dialog box's dimensions would remain the same, so the dialog box would end up usurping only 1/25th of the desktop. At 1024×768, the same dialog box would fit into a mere 1/40th of the screen.

You can use the various resolutions supported by your graphics adapter to enlarge or shrink the desktop. If you move to a higher resolution, objects appear smaller, so, in a virtual sense, you end up with more room. In turn, this lets you either display more windows or make your existing windows larger. Before adjusting the resolution, however, you should keep the following points in mind:

- The higher the resolution, the smaller your text will appear. You need to trade extra screen real estate for text readability. (Many applications also let you "zoom" their window contents larger or smaller. In addition, don't forget that you can scale Windows 98's system fonts. See Chapter 6, "Customizing the Taskbar, Start Menu, and Display.")

- In most cases, you also need to trade color depth for resolution. Unless you have lots of video memory on your graphics adapter, the higher the resolution, the fewer colors you can display (more on this in the next section).

- You need to match the resolution produced by the graphics adapter to that supported by your monitor. For one thing, monitors have a maximum supported resolution, so you won't be able to exceed that. For another, the size of the monitor determines the maximum comfortable resolution: The smaller the monitor, the smaller the resolution you should use. Here are my maximum resolution suggestions for various monitor sizes:

Monitor Size	Suggested Maximum Resolution
13 inches	640×480
14 inches	800×600
15 inches	800×600
17 inches	1024×768
21 inches	1600×1200

Recall from Chapter 6 that you control the resolution via the Settings tab in the Display Properties dialog box. Use the Desktop area slider to adjust the dimensions. In most cases, you should be able to set the new resolution on-the-fly (that is, without having to restart Windows 98).

Color Depth

Color depth determines the number of colors (that is, the *color palette*) available to your applications and graphics. Color depth is expressed either in bits or total colors. The bits value specifies the number of bits each pixel can use to display a color. In the simplest case—a 1-bit display—each pixel could use only two colors: If the bit were 0, the pixel would show black; if the bit were 1, the pixel would show white.

The higher the number of bits, the more combinations a pixel can assume, and the more colors you have available. The minimum realistic color depth is 4-bit, which produces 16 colors in each pixel (becausee 2 to the power of 4 equals 16). Table 11.1 lists the fundamental color depths.

Table 11.1. Fundamental color depths.

Bits	Colors
4	16
8	256
15	32,268
16	65,536 (High Color)
24	16,777,216 (True Color)

If you're just working with mainstream business applications, 256 colors is plenty. In multimedia applications, however, you might need to jump up to 16-bit to get the best-looking output. (If you're working with photographic-quality images, you need to use 24-bit for faithful reproduction.)

To adjust the color depth, open the Display Properties sheet, select the Settings tab, and use the Color palette drop-down list to select the depth you want. Again, Windows 98 enables you to put the new setting into effect immediately in most cases.

Data Width

When the graphics adapter gets some data, it usually shuffles it around between various components on the board. To speed up this part of the process, adapter manufacturers have been increasing the width of the data path (which generally refers to the path between the adapter's processor and its frame buffer—the on-board graphics memory). Although you still see 32-bit adapters on the market, the new standard is a 64-bit data width, so that's the minimum you should look for in an adapter. Some manufacturers are even shipping 128-bit adapters, but they show a speed boost only at higher color depths (at least 16-bit).

Video Memory

The resolution you can display and the number of colors available at that resolution are both a function of the amount of video memory that's installed on your graphics adapter. (Unlike system RAM, video RAM has nothing to do with performance.) To understand why, consider that the current state of each pixel on your screen has to be stored somewhere in memory. A screen displayed at 640×480 will have 307,200 pixels and therefore will need 307,200 memory locations. However, each pixel also requires a particular number of bits, depending on the color depth. At a 4-bit depth, those 307,200 pixels use 1,228,800 bits, or 153,600 bytes (150KB).

> In general, you use the following formula to calculate the amount of video memory required by a particular resolution and color depth: *Horizontal × Vertical × Bits / 8*

Here, *Horizontal* is the horizontal resolution, *Vertical* is the vertical resolution, and *Bits* is the number of bits in the color depth. Table 11.2 lists various resolutions and color depths and shows the memory required to support each combination. (The Adapter Memory column tells you the amount of memory that needs to be installed in the graphics adapter.)

Table 11.2. Adapter video memory requirements for various resolutions and color depths.

Resolution	Color Depth in Bytes	Actual Memory	Adapter Memory
640×480	4-bit	153,600	256KB
640×480	8-bit	307,200	512KB
640×480	16-bit	614,400	1MB
640×480	24-bit	921,600	1MB
800×600	4-bit	240,000	256KB
800×600	8-bit	480,000	512KB
800×600	16-bit	960,000	1MB
800×600	24-bit	1,440,000	2MB
1024×768	4-bit	393,216	512KB
1024×768	8-bit	786,432	1MB
1024×768	16-bit	1,572,864	2MB
1024×768	24-bit	2,359,296	4MB
1280×1024	4-bit	655,360	1MB
1280×1024	8-bit	1,310,720	2MB
1280×1024	16-bit	2,621,440	4MB
1280×1024	24-bit	3,932,160	4MB
1600×1200	4-bit	960,000	1MB
1600×1200	8-bit	1,920,000	2MB
1600×1200	16-bit	3,840,000	4MB
1600×1200	24-bit	7,680,000	8MB

Besides the amount of RAM installed on the graphics adapter, the type of RAM can also affect performance. Four types are available:

DRAM (Dynamic RAM): This type of RAM is cheap, so it's used on most low-end graphics adapters. However, it's slow (because the information within the RAM must be constantly updated), and it can't be read from and written to at the same time.

VRAM (Video RAM): As its name implies, this type of RAM is optimized for graphics operations and is much faster than DRAM. (Unlike DRAM, the adapter can read and write to VRAM simultaneously.) However, adapters that utilize VRAM chips tend to be expensive.

EDO (Extended Data Out) DRAM: This type of RAM is slightly faster than conventional DRAM, so it's slowly becoming the standard on low-end adapters.

WRAM (Window RAM): This type of RAM, although still relatively rare, offers many advantages over VRAM. For one thing, it incorporates special graphics features that let the adapter process graphics faster. For another, because it uses fewer components, it will be cheaper than VRAM (at least in the long run).

Installing a Graphics Adapter Driver

Windows 98 ships with mini-drivers for many of the most popular graphics adapters, and the Setup program should install the appropriate driver for you. Even if your adapter doesn't come with a Microsoft driver, it's likely that the manufacturer has released its own mini-driver designed to work with Windows 98. (Check the vendor's Internet site or BBS to find out.) So although your old adapter drivers will probably work under Windows 98, you should take advantage of the newer drivers if they're available. Here are four good reasons to upgrade from your current Windows 3.*x* driver to a Windows 98 driver:

- Windows 98's 32-bit drivers are faster and more reliable than the older drivers.
- Windows 3.1 drivers don't support on-the-fly resolution and color depth changes.
- Windows 3.1 drivers don't support animated cursors.
- Windows 3.1 drivers don't support Energy Star power-saving features.

INSTALL A NEW ADAPTER IN VGA MODE

If you're installing a new graphics adapter, you should always place Windows 98 in VGA mode before doing so. All graphics adapters can handle plain-vanilla VGA, so you're less likely to run into problems. First, follow the steps listed next to change the driver to Standard VGA. Instead of rebooting, however, shut down your system and install the new graphics adapter. Then restart Windows 98 and follow the steps listed next once again to install the correct driver for the new adapter.

Here are the steps to follow to install an adapter driver:

1. Open the Display Properties dialog box and select the Settings tab.
2. Click the Advanced button. The adapter's advanced properties sheet appears.
3. In the Adapter tab, click the Change button. Windows 98 launches the Upgrade Device Driver Wizard, which I explained in detail in Chapter 10.
4. Follow the Wizard's dialog boxes to install your new driver and then reboot your system.

Device Advice: Dealing with Devices in Windows 98

CHAPTER 11

279

11

DEALING WITH
DEVICES IN
WINDOWS 98

TROUBLESHOOTING: IF YOUR VIDEO DISPLAY IS GARBLED

You might find that your display is a mess when you reboot after installing a new video driver. This probably means one of three things:

- ■ You installed the wrong driver.
- ■ The driver you're using is corrupt.
- ■ The display resolution or color depth is beyond the capacity of the driver.

If this happens, you need to shut down your computer and restart in safe mode (as described in Chapter 3, "Start Me Up: Controlling Windows 98 Startup"). How do you shut down if you can't see anything onscreen? Here are the keyboard techniques to use:

If the logon dialog box is displayed, press Ctrl+Alt+Delete and then press Alt+S to select the Shut Down command.

If you're in Windows 98, press Ctrl+Esc, then press U, then S, then Enter.

When Windows 98 restarts, you can troubleshoot the problem (by, for example, selecting a different video driver).

Windows 98 and Your Monitor

Your monitor shows the end result of all the pixel pushing done by the graphics adapter, so it's no less an important component. This section gives you a few pointers to bear in mind when shopping for a monitor, shows you how to change the monitor type, and gives you the steps to follow to implement Windows 98's multiple-monitor support.

Changing the Monitor Type

If you change your monitor and it's Plug and Play–compatible, Windows 98 should detect it automatically the next time you restart your machine. However, in some cases Windows 98 may not detect the monitor properly and will, instead, list it as "Unknown Monitor." If this happens, follow these steps to ensure that Windows 98 detects your monitor:

1. Open the Display Properties dialog box and select the Settings tab.
2. Click the Advanced Properties button. The Advanced Display Properties dialog box appears.
3. Select the Monitor tab, shown in Figure 11.5.
4. Activate the Automatically detect Plug & Play monitors check box.
5. Click OK to return to the Display Properties dialog box.
6. Click OK to return to the desktop.
7. Restart your computer. Windows 98 should now detect your monitor.

Figure 11.5.

Use the Monitor tab to change the current monitor.

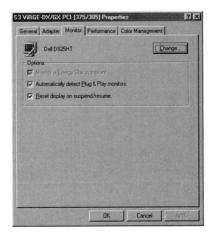

If your new monitor is not Plug and Play–compliant, here's how to let Windows 98 know about it:

1. Display the Monitor tab, as described previously.
2. Click the Change button.
3. Use the Upgrade Device Driver Wizard to select your new monitor.

Activating Your Monitor's Energy-Saving Features

Although improvements have been made in monitor power consumption, most displays are still the energy hogs of your system. As an aid to reducing monitor power appetites, many newer monitors support the VESA Display Power Management Signaling (DPMS) specification. Using the video adapter, a software driver sends a signal to the monitor that can either blank the screen (standby mode) or turn off the monitor.

I'm assuming, of course, that your system supports power management. Specifically, you need two things:

■ An Energy Star–compliant monitor that supports the VESA DPMS specification.

■ A video driver that uses either the Advanced Power Management (APM) 1.1 BIOS interface with support for device "01FF" (which isn't supported by every APM 1.1 BIOS), or the VESA BIOS Extensions for Power Management (VBE/PM). Windows 98 supports the APM 1.2 BIOS.

If your monitor meets the Energy Star requirements, make sure its energy-saving features are enabled by activating the Monitor is Energy Star compliant check box in the Monitor tab of the Advanced Display Properties dialog box (refer to Figure 11.5), if Windows 98 hasn't done so already.

After you've done this, activate the Screen Saver tab in the Display Properties dialog box, and you'll see that the Power button is enabled. Clicking this button displays the Power Management Properties dialog box, which enables you to specify the settings you want to use for conserving power on your system.

Enabling Windows 98's Multiple-Monitor Support

It used to be that the constant lament among Windows power users was a never-ending lack of hard disk space. You'd upgrade your disk and six months later it would be bursting at the seams once again. Now, however, multigigabyte drives can be had for a song, and storage solutions such as the Jaz drive and its 1GB disks offer virtually limitless storage.

New to **98**

So what's the pet peeve of today's Windows user? Probably a lack of screen space. I thought I was set for life when I moved up to a 21-inch monitor and a Matrox Millenium card that can display 16 million colors at 1280×1024 resolution. Now, however, I find my desktop is as crowded as ever what with my word processor, email, browser, and who knows what else on the go at once.

So it will come as no surprise that one of my favorite new features in the Windows 98 package is the built-in support for multiple monitors. With two or more graphics adapters installed in your computer and a monitor attached to each card, Windows 98 provides you with an expanded desktop. This enables you to move windows from one monitor to another, display a different set of desktop icons on each monitor, move the taskbar between monitors, have Active Desktop items visible on one monitor while you work on the other, and much more. Best of all, after you've installed your second graphics adapter, enabling multiple-monitor support takes just a couple of mouse clicks.

Multiple-monitor support is easy to set up, but only if you have the right hardware. The primary graphics adapter can be any PCI card running on a Windows 98 or later driver. For the secondary graphics adapter, however, Windows 98 is a bit more finicky. It must also be a PCI card, and it must use one of the following graphics chipsets:

ATI Mach64

ATI Mach64 GX

ATI Rage 1 & 2 (VT & greater)

Cirrus 5436, 7548, 5446

ET6000

S3 764V+ (765), Trio 64V2

S3 Aurora (S3M65)

S3 ViRGE

After you install the second graphics adapter and attach the monitor, Windows 98 should recognize the adapter at startup, install the necessary drivers, and then reboot. When Windows 98 restarts, the secondary monitor should display the following message:

```
If you can read this message, Windows has successfully
initialized this display adapter.

To use this adapter as part of your Windows desktop, open
the Display option in the Control Panel and adjust the
Settings on the Monitors tab.
```

When Windows 98 loads, right-click the desktop and click Properties to get to the Display Properties dialog box. You see that the Settings tab now has a modified interface, as shown in Figure 11.6.

FIGURE 11.6.

With multiple graphics adapters in your system, the Settings tab uses this revised interface.

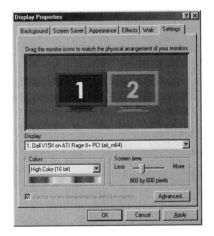

To enable your second monitor/card combination, select it in the Display list (or click the monitor icon) and then activate the Extend my Windows desktop onto this monitor check box. (Windows 98 will now display a Compatibility Warning dialog box, which lets you know that some programs don't support the multiple display feature.)

As you can see in Figure 11.6, the Monitors tab shows two monitors, labeled "1" and "2." Monitor 1 represents your main display, and monitor 2 is your secondary display. You can customize the monitors by using the following techniques:

- To adjust the display resolution, color depth, and so on, first use the Display list to select the monitor/card you want to work with. You can then use the other controls to adjust the display properties.

- To adjust the relative position of the two windows, drag the monitor representations in the Monitors tab.

When you click OK to return to the desktop, your multiple-monitor setup is ready to roll. Go ahead and drag objects (including the taskbar) from one window to another. Figures 11.7 and 11.8 attempt to illustrate the basic multiple-monitor concept. Figure 11.7 shows the view on Monitor 2, and Figure 11.8 shows the view on Monitor 1. Notice how the Control Panel window overlaps both views.

FIGURE 11.7.
This is the view from the second monitor.

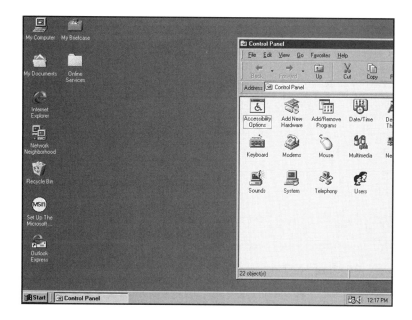

FIGURE 11.8.
This is the view from the first monitor.

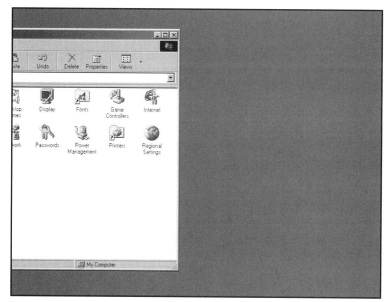

Working with PC Card (PCMCIA) Devices

One of the problems that caused notebooks to be relegated to a lower status on the PC totem pole was their lack of expandability. Desktop systems had all kinds of bus slots and drive bays that intrepid hobbyists and power users could use to augment the capabilities of their systems. Notebook configurations, however, were generally set in stone; what you bought was what you got.

That all changed with the advent of the Personal Computer Memory Card International Association (PCMCIA) and the standards it developed for notebook expansion boards. These standards let notebook manufacturers add small slots (called *sockets*) to their machines that would hold credit card–sized expansion modules for memory cards, hard disks, CD-ROMs, modems, network adapters, SCSI controllers, tape backups, and more. PCMCIA cards are also part of the Plug and Play standard, which means you can insert and remove cards while your computer is running (this is called *hot-swapping*).

PCMCIA cards are now known as PC Card devices, and I'll use both terms interchangeably in this section.

Windows 98 and PC Cards

Windows 98 supports two PCCard standards:

PC Card 16: These are 16-bit cards.

PC Card 32: These are 32-bit cards and are also known as CardBus devices.

Setup should detect your notebook's PC Card socket automatically and install the appropriate protected-mode device drivers. Windows 98 also supports real-mode and protected-mode PC Card drivers from third-party vendors, but you lose some of the Plug and Play capabilities (such as hot-swapping).

Besides the PC Card socket, Windows 98 also needs drivers for the individual PC Card devices inserted into the slots. A PC Card device driver can be implemented in three ways:

- For PC Cards that don't require device-specific functionality, Windows 98 uses a universal Plug and Play PC Card device driver. This driver can handle hot-swapping and dynamic configuration, and it can receive configuration information from Windows 98 without knowing what kind of card is in the PC Card socket.

- For devices such as modems and hard disks, Windows 98 can use generic device drivers for the particular hardware class.

- To implement device-specific functionality (such as memory-mapped I/O for network adapters or SCSI controllers), vendors can provide mini-drivers to supplement the standard universal PC Card driver.

Inserting a PC Card Device

Because PC Card devices are hot-swappable, inserting them is a no-brainer: With Windows 98 still running, just slide the card into one of your notebook's PC Card slots. If you've used and configured the card before, Windows 98 beeps the speaker, and the card is available for use immediately. You see the PC Card (PCMCIA) Status icon appear in the taskbar's system tray, as shown in Figure 11.9.

FIGURE 11.9.
When you insert a PC Card device, the PC Card (PCMCIA) Status icon appears in the system tray.

PC Card (PCMCIA) Status icon

If this is the first time you've inserted the card, Windows 98 gets right to work loading and configuring the appropriate drivers, as shown in Figure 11.10. Depending on the device, you might need to fill in a dialog box or two. If Windows 98 doesn't have a driver for the device, it prompts you for an installation disk from the manufacturer.

FIGURE 11.10.
When you insert a PC Card for the first time, Windows 98 loads and configures the appropriate driver automatically.

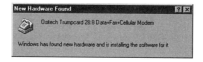

Removing a PC Card Device

Although PC Card devices are hot-swappable, you shouldn't just yank a device out of its slot. For example, if your device is a network adapter, pulling the card out without warning could cut off another user while he or she is using one of your files. Also, Windows 98 might not be able to reallocate the card's resources correctly. If you do happen to pull a card out of its slot prematurely, Windows 98 displays the warning dialog box shown in Figure 11.11.

FIGURE 11.11.
Windows 98 displays this dialog box if you remove a PC Card device without warning.

Before removing any PC Card device, you should tell Windows 98 to stop the device. The easiest way to do this is to click the PC Card (PCMCIA) Status icon in the system tray. Windows 98 then displays a menu of commands that stop each of the PC Card devices installed on your system. Click the command that corresponds to the device you want to stop. After a few seconds, Windows 98 displays a dialog box to let you know that it's safe to remove the device.

Alternatively, you can stop PC Card devices via the PC Card properties sheet. To display this dialog box, use either of the following methods:

■ Double-click the taskbar's PC Card (PCMCIA) Status icon.

■ In Control Panel, open the PC Card (PCMCIA) icon.

Figure 11.12 shows the PC Card (PCMCIA) Properties dialog box that appears. To stop a device, highlight it and click the Stop button. Again, Windows 98 displays a dialog box to let you know that it's safe to remove the device.

FIGURE 11.12.

You can also stop a PC Card device by using this dialog box.

Setting PC Card Properties

The PC Card (PCMCIA) Properties dialog box has a few other settings you can work with. In particular, the Socket Status tab, shown in Figure 11.12, has two check boxes:

Show control on taskbar: If you deactivate this check box, Windows 98 removes the PC Card (PCMCIA) Status icon from the system tray.

Display warning if card is removed before it is stopped: If you deactivate this check box, Windows 98 won't display the warning dialog box shown in Figure 11.11 when you remove a PC Card device.

In the Global Settings tab, you can use the Card services shared memory to determine the memory range used by your PC Card devices. The Windows 98 card services (device drivers) use a common pool of memory. Normally, this memory window is managed automatically by Windows 98. If, however, you have a device that doesn't work—despite having the correct drivers loaded and support for the PC Card socket enabled—the notebook is probably using the wrong memory window.

To change this, deactivate the Automatic selection check box and then use the Start, End, and Length text boxes to define the new memory window. Microsoft recommends a Start value of 100,000 or higher.

> **TROUBLESHOOTING: PC CARD DEVICE DOESN'T WORK**
>
> If you've adjusted the memory range in the Global Settings tab and your device still doesn't work, a conflicting IRQ might be the problem. Open Device Manager, display the properties sheet for the device, and change its IRQ value.

The Global Settings tab also has a Disable PC Card sound effects check box. If you activate this control, Windows 98 won't beep the speaker each time you insert a PC Card device.

Setting Up an Infrared Device

Many of the latest notebook computers come with a built-in infrared (IR) port. This port acts like both a serial port and a parallel port, and you can use it to transfer files and send print jobs. (For sending print jobs, you need a printer—such as the HP LaserJet 5MP—with an IR port. You can find more on this topic in Chapter 21, "Prescriptions for Perfect Printing.") You can also purchase infrared devices that attach to a serial port. In all cases, the device acts much like a serial port in that it sends data one bit at a time. However, instead of using electrical signals (high current and low current) to represents the 1s and 0s of binary data, IR devices manipulate infrared light waves.

Windows 98 has built-in support for infrared devices via IrDA (Infrared Data Association) drivers. Windows 98 includes support for both Serial Infrared (SIR) devices and Fast Infrared (FIR) devices. How you initialize this support depends on whether Windows 98 recognized your IR device during Setup.

New to
98

If Windows 98 recognized your device, you see an Infrared icon in the taskbar's system tray. Double-click this icon, select the Options tab in the Infrared Monitor dialog box that appears, and then activate the Enable infrared communication check box.

If Windows 98 did not recognize your device during Setup, you need to follow these steps:

1. Run the Add New Hardware Wizard. When the Wizard asks to search for new hardware, select No and click Next >.

2. In the list of hardware types that appears, highlight Infrared devices and click Next >. Windows 98 runs the Add Infrared Device Wizard.

3. Click Next >. The Wizard displays a list of infrared manufacturers and models, as shown in Figure 11.13.

4. Select the appropriate manufacturer and model and then click OK:

   SIR device: Highlight Microsoft in the Manufacturers list and then select Standard Infrared Serial (COM) Port in the Infrared Devices list. The Wizard will next prompt you for the transceiver type. Make your selection, click Next >, and head for step 5.

FIGURE 11.13.

Use this dialog box to select your IR device.

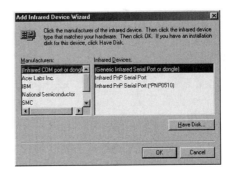

FIR device: Select one of the other devices listed. The next dialog box asks whether you want to use the default settings for the device. It's usually best to leave the default I/O addresses as is, so you should make sure the Use defaults option is activated, click Next >, and skip to step 7.

5. Now the Wizard wonders about the port to which the SIR device is physically connected. Make your choice and click Next >.

6. The next dialog box prompts you to specify simulated ports for the infrared serial and printer ports. If the default ports don't conflict with any devices on your system, click Next >. Otherwise, activate the Change ports option, use the text boxes to specify new ports, and click Next >. Windows 98 loads the IrDA drivers, sets up the simulated IR serial and parallel ports, and displays the last of the Add Infrared Device Wizard dialog boxes.

7. Click Finish.

8. Activate the Enable infrared communication check box, as described earlier.

Your IR port is now ready to go. Note that Windows 98 adds an infrared icon to the system tray. The icon you see depends on whether the driver has another IR port in its sights. If no other port is in range, you see the icon shown in Figure 11.14. If the port finds another IR device, the icon changes to the one shown in Figure 11.15.

FIGURE 11.14.

The infrared icon when no other IR device is within range.

Infrared icon (no device in range)

FIGURE 11.15.

The infrared icon when another IR device is within range.

Infrared icon (device in range)

INFRARED RANGE

For IR devices to recognize each other, their ports must be facing each other, and they should be no closer than 6 inches and no farther than 3 feet to 9 feet (depending on the device).

YOU NEED TO REINITIALIZE THE PORT WHEN YOU RESTART

The IR port isn't initialized automatically each time you restart Windows 98. To crank it up again, you need to open the Control Panel's Infrared icon, as described in the next section. To save this step each time you restart Windows 98, add a shortcut for the Infrared icon to your StartUp folder (see Chapter 14, "File and Folder Tricks and Techniques," for details).

Adjusting the IrDA Driver's Properties

The IrDA driver has a properties sheet called the Infrared Monitor that you can use to modify the behavior of the driver. To display the Infrared Monitor, use either of the following methods:

- Double-click the infrared icon in the taskbar.
- Display the Control Panel and open the Infrared icon.

Either way, the Infrared Monitor dialog box, shown in Figure 11.16, appears. The Status tab tells you how many devices are within the port's range and the names of those devices.

FIGURE 11.16.

Use the Infrared Monitor to adjust the properties for the IrDA driver.

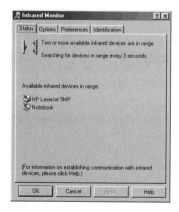

The Options tab, shown in Figure 11.17, gives you the following settings:

Enable infrared communications: Activate this check box to enable the IrDA driver.

Search for and provide status for devices within range: When this check box is activated, the IrDA driver checks for IR ports within its range. Use the Search every *x* seconds spinner to determine the interval between checks.

Limit connection speed to: If you find that your communications are unreliable at the default driver speed, activate this check box and select a lower speed from the drop-down list.

Install software for Plug and Play devices within range: When this option is activated, Windows 98 automatically installs the appropriate drivers for any Plug and Play devices that fall within the IrDA driver's range.

If you want to return these settings to their default values, click the Restore Defaults button.

FIGURE 11.17.

Use the Options tab to set various options for the IrDA driver.

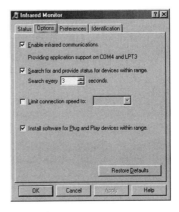

The Preferences tab, shown in Figure 11.18, contains various settings related to Infrared Monitor. You have the following choices:

Display the Infrared Monitor icon on the taskbar: This check box toggles the taskbar's infrared icon on and off.

Open Infrared Monitor when communication is interrupted: If you keep this check box activated, the Infrared Monitor appears automatically if any IR communications are interrupted. You can then use Infrared Monitor to change settings and (hopefully) get the communication reestablished.

Play sounds when available devices come within range and when communication is interrupted: When this check box is activated, Infrared Monitor plays a sound when a device comes into range or moves out of range, or if communications are interrupted.

FIGURE 11.18.

*The Preferences tab
controls various
Infrared Monitor
settings.*

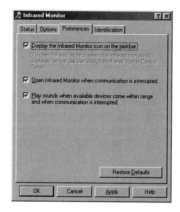

Finally, the Identification tab lets you enter a name and a short description for the computer. This data is used to identify your computer to other devices that establish an infrared connection with your machine.

Transferring Files Via an Infrared Connection

Windows 98 comes with a new utility for transferring files from one computer to another via their infrared ports. This utility is called Infrared Transfer, and you use it to transfer files by running either of the following methods:

New to 98

■ Highlight the file or files you want to send and then select the File | Send To | Infrared Recipient command.

■ Highlight the file or files you want to send, right-click the files, and then click Send To | Infrared Recipient in the shortcut menu.

Assuming that a good infrared connection exists between the two devices, Infrared Transfer will send the file or files immediately. Note that on the receiving computer, Windows 98 creates a new folder called My Received Files on the boot drive. The sent files are stored in this folder.

If your computer has established an infrared connection to two or more devices, you see the Select Device dialog box shown in Figure 11.19. In this case, click the device to which you want to send the file.

FIGURE 11.19.

*You see this dialog box
if you have an infrared
connection to multiple
devices.*

Note, too, that when the transfer is complete in this case, Windows 98 leaves the Infrared Transfer window onscreen, as shown in Figure 11.20. To send another file from here, highlight the remote device, click Send Files, and then pick out the file or files in the dialog box that appears. You can also use this window to display your My Received Files folder by clicking the Received Files button. When you're done, select File | Close to exit Infrared Transfer.

FIGURE 11.20.

You can use the Infrared Transfer window to send more files or view your received files.

Power Management in Windows 98: OnNow and ACPI

New to 98

Why can't a computer be more like a toaster? When you want to make toast, you just toss in a slice of bread and push a lever down. The toaster turns on instantly, toasts the bread, ejects the slice when it's done, and then turns itself off. Computers, on the other hand, take forever to start up and remain on even when we haven't used them for a while. If computers are going to become a ubiquitous part of everyday life, they must become more like appliances.

That, in a nutshell, is the goal of OnNow Design Initiative. OnNow is a new PC platform that affects all aspects of the machine: applications, the operating system, device drivers, system buses, and hardware devices. An OnNow-compliant machine would sport the following features:

- The computer turns on and is immediately available for use when the user throws the power switch.
- The computer turns itself off when it hasn't been used for a specified amount of time. Here, "off" means the PC is consuming as little power as possible, but windows remain open and data remains safe.
- The computer can respond automatically to certain "wakeup events," such as an incoming fax or email, or a timed event triggered by an application (such as a reminder displayed by a personal information manager).
- All internal and external devices support power management and can have their power state changed by the operating system.

This systemwide approach is ambitious, to say the least. For OnNow to work properly, a system requires each of the following five power management components to be in place:

Power management at the OS level: The operating system must be responsible for coordinating all power management chores between the applications, device drivers, and devices. Windows 98 is the first operating system capable of performing this coordination function.

Power management at the API level: For applications to take advantage of OnNow, they need to be able to access the power management system. Windows 98 supports application programming interface (API) functions that enable developers to access an abstract power management layer without having to know the specifics of the computer's hardware.

Power management at the device-driver level: To achieve fine-tuned control over the power state of any device, the operating system needs to be able to interact with the power management functions of each device via the appropriate device driver. Windows 98's Win32 Driver Model (WDM) is designed to support this functionality.

Power management at the BIOS level: The operating system must be able to control and poll devices on a systemwide basis, which means power management must be implemented at the BIOS level. Windows 98 supports the Advanced Configuration and Power Interface (ACPI), which provides a standard hardware interface for power management. ACPI also supports Plug and Play mechanisms, so ACPI replaces the Plug and Play BIOS.

Power management at the bus level: The operating system must be able to communicate with the system devices, and this communication runs across the system buses. The newest specifications for PCI, USB, and IEE 1394 buses support the OnNow initiative.

The fly in the OnNow ointment is that hardware support is still limited. However, OnNow has broad industry support, so over the next few years the computer-as-toaster goal will surely be met.

Understanding Advanced Power Management

Until OnNow becomes a reality, Windows 98 also supports the older Advanced Power Management (APM) scheme. APM is a specification developed by Microsoft and Intel that lets the operating system, the applications, the BIOS, and the system hardware work cooperatively to manage power and extend notebook battery life. For example, APM lets notebooks go into suspend mode, which shuts off the machine but preserves the operating system's current state. When you turn the machine back on, your programs and documents appear immediately, exactly as they were when you initiated suspend mode.

Windows 98 has built-in support for APM-enabled computers, and it can work with either the APM 1.0 or the APM 1.1 specification. What's the difference? APM 1.1 gives Windows 98 more control over the machine's power management services:

- With an APM 1.1 machine, Windows 98 can force the APM BIOS to wait indefinitely until Windows has prepared the running programs and drivers for suspend mode. With APM 1.0, the BIOS just waits for a predetermined time after it has received the suspend request and then shuts down, regardless of the operating system's current state.
- Windows 98 can reject requests for suspend mode on APM 1.1 systems.
- APM 1.1 provides Windows 98 with more accurate reports on the remaining battery life.

Windows 98 also supports APM 1.2, which includes the wake-on-ring feature for modems and the capability of handling multiple batteries. Windows 98 also supports the powering down of inactive PC Card modems and hard disk spin-down. (The latter feature puts the hard disk into low-power mode after it has been idle for a specified amount of time.)

Windows 98 supports a couple of APM settings. To work with these settings, follow these steps:

1. Launch the Control Panel's System icon.
2. In the System Properties dialog box, select the Device Manager tab.
3. Open the System devices branch, highlight Advanced Power Management support, and click Properties.
4. In the properties sheet that appears, select the Settings tab. The Settings tab contains two APM options:

   Force APM 1.0 mode: Activate this check box if you're having trouble initiating suspend mode or using any of the APM features. The BIOS in some laptops doesn't support APM 1.1 correctly, so moving Windows 98 down to APM 1.0 might solve your problem.

   Disable power status polling: Activate this command to tell Windows 98 to stop querying the APM BIOS about the current state of the battery. You should do this only if the keyboard or mouse stops responding while you're working in a DOS session. Activating this check box removes the power meter icon from the system tray.

If you change any of these settings, you need to restart your computer.

Monitoring Battery Life

A certain level of anxiety is always involved with running your notebook on its batteries, especially if no AC is in sight. You know that you have only a limited amount of time to get your work done (or play your games, or check your email, or whatever), so the pressure's on. To help change road worriers back into road warriors, most notebooks support some kind of power management. This means that the system conserves battery life by shutting down system components after the computer has been idle for a specified interval. Depending on the system, the power management BIOS might do the following:

- Reduce the brightness of the display or turn it off.
- Stop the hard drive from spinning.
- Slow down the processor and/or put it into "sleep" mode.
- For Pentium machines, shut off the CPU cooling fan.

On most machines, the power management feature and the specified idle time are controlled through the BIOS setup program. Your system might also have a utility program for controlling these settings.

When power management is enabled, Windows 98 displays a power meter icon in the taskbar's system tray, as shown in Figure 11.21. (This is assuming, of course, that your notebook is operating on battery power.)

FIGURE 11.21.
When your notebook is running on batteries, Windows 98 displays a power meter icon in the taskbar.

Power meter icon

When the notebook battery is fully charged, the power meter is completely yellow. As battery power is used up, the power meter's "level" decreases. For example, if the battery power is down to half, the power meter displays as half yellow, half gray. To see the current level, you have two options:

- Point your mouse at the power meter icon. Windows 98 displays a banner showing the percentage of battery life available.
- Double-click the power meter icon to display the Power Meter dialog box. Note, too, that you can use the Show power meter on taskbar check box to toggle the power meter icon on and off.

Windows 98 implements two battery alarms:

New to
98

Low: This alarm is set off when the power level reaches 5 percent. Windows 98 displays a warning message.

Critical: This alarm is set off when the power level reaches 3 percent. Windows 98 displays a warning message and puts the computer in Standby mode.

To control the power levels at which these alarms are displayed, open the Control Panel's Power Management icon and then select the Alarms tab, shown in Figure 11.22.

FIGURE 11.22.
Use the Alarms tab to set options for the battery alarms.

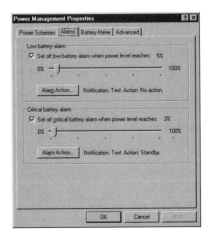

In both groups, you can perform the following actions:

- Use the check box to toggle the alarm on and off.
- Use the slider to set the power level at which the alarm is set off.
- Click the Alarm Action button to configure the alarm. Windows 98 displays the Alarm Actions dialog box. Figure 11.23 shows the dialog box for the critical alarm. You have the following options:

  Sound alarm: Activate this check box to have Windows 98 beep your computer's speaker when the alarm is triggered.

  Display message: Activate this check box to have Windows 98 display a warning message when the alarm is triggered.

  When the alarm goes off, the computer will: Use this list to choose the action taken by Windows 98 when the alarm is triggered: Standby or Shutdown.

  Force standby or shutdown even if a program stops responding: Activate this check box to tell Windows 98 to go ahead and implement the specified action even if a running program no longer responds to the system.

FIGURE 11.23.
Click the Alarm Actions button to see a dialog box like this one.

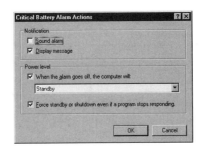

Working with Power Management Properties

Windows 98 has a few power management properties you can manipulate. To check them out, run the Control Panel and open the Power Management icon to display the Power Management Properties dialog box.

The Power Schemes tab, shown in Figure 11.24, enables you to define the intervals after which Windows 98 puts the computer in standby mode (power consumption is reduced for all possible components) and turns off the monitor and hard disk. Notebook computers have options for both Plugged in and Running on batteries states. To work with these settings you have two choices:

- Use the Power schemes list to choose one of Windows 98's predefined power schemes.

- Use the drop-down lists in the Settings for *x* power scheme group to select the intervals you want. To save these intervals as a power scheme, click Save As, enter a name for your scheme, and then click OK.

FIGURE 11.24.
Use the Power Schemes tab to set a power management scheme for your computer.

There are two more power management properties available on the Advanced tab:

Show power meter on taskbar: This check box toggles the taskbar's power meter icon on and off.

Prompt for password when computer goes off standby: Activate this check box to have Windows 98 prompt you for a password when you reactivate the computer from standby mode.

Drivers for Other Devices

Windows 98's device driver list is truly impressive. It includes protected-mode drivers for just about any class of hardware you can think of. The next few sections discuss Windows 98's driver support for specific device classes and show you the basic steps for updating or installing new drivers in each class.

Communications Device Drivers

The monolithic communications driver from Windows 3.x—COMM.DRV—has been replaced by a new driver in Windows 98: VCOMM. (Actually, Windows replaced COMM.DRV with an entirely new communications architecture, of which VCOMM is a major part.) The VCOMM driver, which loads as part of VMM32.VXD, gives applications a protected-mode interface for accessing communications ports and modems, as detailed here:

> **Communications port drivers:** VCOMM isn't a driver for communications ports (serial and parallel ports) per se, but rather it calls specific port drivers that then access the I/O ports directly. For serial ports, VCOMM calls SERIAL.VXD; for parallel ports, VCOMM calls LPT.VXD; for third-party communications products, manufacturers can write mini-drivers that VCOMM can call to access the ports. (In Windows 3.x, the manufacturer would have to write a monolithic driver that covered the entire communications subsystem.)

> **Modem drivers:** VCOMM uses a universal modem driver (UNIMODEM.VXD) that covers the entire AT command set. Applications can then use this driver (via VCOMM) to dial, answer, and configure modems without using AT commands directly. All that each modem manufacturer must supply is a mini-driver that specifies the modem's AT command set variations and enhancements.

To install a modem in Windows 98, select Start | Settings | Control Panel, and then open the Modems icon in the Control Panel folder. If this is the first time you've selected this icon, Windows 98 runs the Install New Modem Wizard, which takes you through the installation procedure. Otherwise, the Modems Properties dialog box appears, from which you can add or remove modems. Both procedures are covered in full in Chapter 26, "Getting Started with Modem Communications."

Keyboard Device Drivers

Windows 98 replaced the Windows 3.x keyboard driver—KEYBOARD.DRV—with a virtual keyboard driver—VKD.VXD—that loads as part of VMM32.VXD. To specify a different keyboard device, use either of the following techniques:

- Select Start | Settings | Control Panel and then open the Keyboard icon in the Control Panel folder. In the Keyboard Properties dialog box, select the General tab and click the Change button.

- In Device Manager, open the properties sheet for the keyboard, select the Driver tab, and click Change Driver.

Mouse Device Drivers

In Windows 3.*x*, mouse support was provided by two different drivers: a driver for Windows-based applications, and a separate driver for DOS-based applications. Both were real-mode drivers. Windows 98 uses a virtual mouse driver called VMOUSE.VXD to provide mouse support for both Windows and DOS programs. VMOUSE is a universal driver, and Windows 98 uses mini-drivers to implement functionality for specific mouse devices. For example, if you have a Microsoft mouse (or one that's compatible), the mini-driver is MSMOUSE.VXD; for a Logitech mouse, Windows 98 uses LMOUSE.VXD.

If you need to change your mouse driver, use either of the following techniques:

- Select Start | Settings | Control Panel and open the Mouse icon in the Control Panel folder. In the Mouse Properties dialog box, select the General tab and click the Change button.

- In Device Manager, open the properties sheet for the mouse, select the Driver tab, and click Change Driver.

Printer Device Drivers

Windows 98's universal driver/mini-driver architecture is based on the driver model used for printers in Windows 3.*x*. So it should come as no surprise that this printing model was maintained in Windows 98 and upgraded to an enhanced protected-mode version. The drivers in the new printing subsystem have many new features, including these:

- Bidirectional communications with printers

- Improved background spooling and the use of enhanced metafile (EMF) spooling for non-PostScript documents, which reduces the time between sending the data to the printer and returning to your application

- Improved conflict resolution when DOS and Windows applications attempt to print simultaneously

- Deferred printing support that lets notebook users send print jobs to the queue and then print them later (for example, when they arrive at the office)

- Point and Print support that lets network users install printer drivers simply by accessing shared network printers

These and many other Windows printing features are covered in Chapter 21.

To add a printer driver, select Start | Settings | Printers and then open the Add Printer icon in the Printers folder. The Add Printer Wizard guides you through the steps (as explained in Chapter 19, "Sharing Data in Windows 98: The Clipboard and OLE").

11

DEALING WITH
DEVICES IN
WINDOWS 98

SCSI Controller Device Drivers

Unlike Windows 3.*x*, Windows 98 comes with SCSI controller support built right into the operating system. A protected-mode driver (called the *SCSI layer*) provides the universal driver support, and then each manufacturer writes mini-drivers (called *miniport drivers*) for its specific devices.

You work with SCSI controller device drivers (that is, the miniport drivers) via the Device Manager. Under the SCSI controller hardware class, highlight the controller, open its properties sheet, select the Driver tab, and click the Change Driver button.

Scanner and Digital Camera Device Drivers

Getting images into digital form is now easier than ever thanks to two graphics gadgets that have become more affordable: image scanners and digital cameras. The good news is that Windows 98 understands both types of devices. In most cases, you can just install whatever software came with your scanner or camera, connect the cable, and then run the software to bring your images into Windows 98.

On the other hand, Windows 98's Kodak Imaging program is conversant with many popular scanner and digital camera formats, so you can use it as a one-stop digital imaging shop. To do so, you must have a TWAIN (Technology Without Any Interesting Name) device driver installed. The TWAIN standard implements a communications protocol and application programming interface (API) that enables imaging software to interact with scanners and other image acquisition devices.

To enable TWAIN support in Windows 98, either install the software that came with your scanner or use the Add New Hardware Wizard to install a new imaging device. The latter technique launches the Scanner and Camera Installation Wizard which enables you to either install one of Windows 98's built-in scanner data sources (such as the Kodak DC120 digital camera) or supply a manufacturer's disk.

You can test your scanner by following these steps:

1. In Control Panel, launch the Scanners and Cameras icon. Windows 98 displays the Scanners and Cameras Properties dialog box.

2. Highlight your scanner and then click Properties.

3. In the properties sheet that appears, click the Test Scanner or Camera button.

From Windows 98's point of view, there isn't any difference between a scanner and a digital camera. Both are "scanners" that you use to acquire images from an external source. So whether you're using a scanner or digital camera, the basic steps you follow to acquire an image are the same:

1. Select Start | Programs | Accessories | Imaging.

2. If you have more than one imaging device, select File | Select Scanner to display the Select Scanner dialog box, highlight the device you'd like to use, and then click OK.

3. Either select the File | Scan New command, or click the Scan New button in the toolbar.

4. What happens next depends on what device you're using. Basically, Windows 98 loads up whatever software the device uses to scan an image. For example, Figure 11.25 shows the window that appears for the Kodak DC120 digital camera. In most cases, you can perform at least the following functions:

   ■ Take one or more pictures in the camera and send them to your computer.

   ■ Delete one or more pictures from the camera.

   ■ Take a new picture and send it to your computer.

   ■ Access other camera functions, such as the focus, shutter speed, and flash.

FIGURE 11.25.

You use this window to acquire images using the Kodak DC120 digital camera.

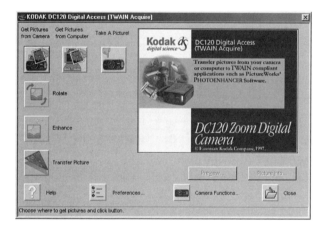

Troubleshooting Hardware Headaches

As you've seen, Windows 98's support for hardware of all stripes is vastly improved over what was found in Windows 3.*x*. From Plug and Play to the universal driver/mini-driver architecture, hardware has never been so easy for non-Macintosh users. Still, that doesn't mean hardware is foolproof; far from it. Things still can, and will, go wrong, so you need to perform some kind of troubleshooting. (Assuming, that is, that you're not just dealing with a part that has kicked the electronic bucket.) Fortunately, Windows 98 also has some handy tools to help you both identify and rectify hardware ills.

Troubleshooting with the Performance Tab

If your system feels sluggish, it might be because Windows 98 is being dragged down by 16-bit real-mode drivers. To find out, open the System Properties dialog box and select the Performance tab. If your system is fine, Windows 98 will show Your system is configured for optimal performance. Otherwise, you may see something like the Performance tab shown in Figure 11.26. Here, Windows 98 is complaining that the FLASHPT driver (a SCSI controller driver loaded in `CONFIG.SYS`) is forcing Windows 98 to operate all disk drives in MS-DOS compatibility mode, which causes a sizable performance hit. The solution here is to remove the driver from `CONFIG.SYS` and let Windows 98 use its 32-bit SCSI driver. (Note too that an updated, 32-bit miniport driver for the SCSI controller will also likely need to be installed.)

FIGURE 11.26.

Check the Performance tab to see whether your system is experiencing any problems.

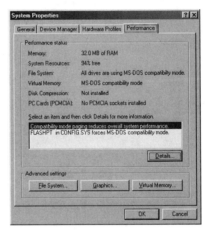

Device Manager as a Troubleshooting Tool

Device Manager's capability of listing devices and letting you change their resources is impressive enough. But this handy utility is also a powerful troubleshooting tool. To see what I mean, check out the Device Manager tab shown in Figure 11.27. See how the icon for the Creative Labs Sound Blaster 16 device has an exclamation mark (!) icon superimposed on it? This tells you that there's a problem with the device.

FIGURE 11.27.

The Device Manager uses icons to warn you if there's a problem with a device.

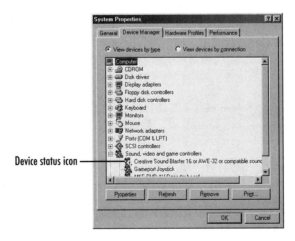

Device Advice: Dealing with Devices in Windows 98

CHAPTER 11

303

11

DEALING WITH
DEVICES IN
WINDOWS 98

If you examine the device's properties, as shown in Figure 11.28, the Device status area tells you a bit more about what's wrong. As you can see in Figure 11.28, the problem here is that the device is using a resource that conflicts with another device.

FIGURE 11.28.

*The Device status area
tells you if the device
isn't working properly.*

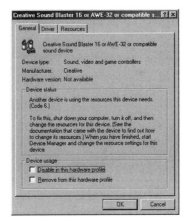

To fix this, head for the Resources tab. When there's a resource conflict, the Conflicting device list tells you which resource is causing the problem and which device is conflicting, as shown in Figure 11.29. In this case, you'd change the resource setting for one of the devices to resolve the conflict.

FIGURE 11.29.

*If there's a resource
conflict, Device
Manager supplies the
details in the
Conflicting device list.*

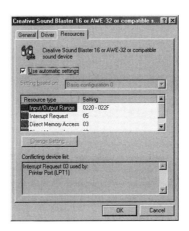

In all, Device Manager uses three different icons to give you an indication of the device's current status:

- A black exclamation mark (!) on a yellow field tells you that there's a problem with the device.

- A red x tells you that the device is disabled or missing.

■ A blue i on a white field tells you that the device's Use automatic settings check box (on the Resources tab) is deactivated and that at least one of the device's resources was selected manually. Note that the device might be working just fine, so this icon doesn't indicate a problem. If the device isn't working properly, however, the manual setting might be the cause. (For example, the device might have a DIP switch or jumper set to a different resource.)

Troubleshooting Protected-Mode Driver Problems

In Chapter 3, I showed you a general procedure for troubleshooting Windows 98 startup. In one of the scenarios, I told you to boot Windows 98 in step-by-step mode and then to click No when you got to the Load all windows drivers? prompt. If Windows 98 started properly, that meant you have a problem with a protected-mode driver.

To resolve this problem, restart Windows 98 in Safe mode, display the System Properties dialog box, and select the Device Manager tab. For all the hardware classes shown here, disable each device listed under each class:

Display adapters

Floppy disk controllers

Hard disk controllers

Keyboard

Mouse

Network adapters

PCMCIA socket

Ports

SCSI controllers

Sound, video, and game controllers

You disable a device by displaying its properties sheet, activating the Disable in this hardware profile check box, and clicking OK. Note that Windows 98 asks whether you want to restart the computer. Don't click Yes until you've deactivated the last device.

When you're done, restart your computer. Now use Device Manager to reenable the devices you disabled earlier one at a time, in the following order:

COM ports

Hard disk controllers

Floppy disk controllers

Other devices

For each device, display its properties sheet, deactivate the Disable in this hardware profile check box, click OK, and click Yes when Windows 98 asks whether you want to shut down your computer.

Restart your computer. If Windows 98 won't start, you've found the culprit. You need to remove the device, reinstall the driver, or install an updated driver.

Summary

This chapter took you through a few device specifics in Windows 98. I began by showing you how to use the Hard New Hardware Wizard. From there, you learned about CD-ROM drives, DVD players, graphics adapters, monitors, PC Card devices, infrared devices, and much more. I also showed you how to work with Windows 98's power management features. I finished by taking you through the Windows 98 hardware troubleshooting features.

I deal with hardware issues in plenty of other locations in this book. Here's a list of those places:

- I discussed Device Manager and hardware profiles in Chapter 10, "Getting the Most Out of Device Manager and Hardware Profiles."

- The Device Manager gets all its hardware information from the Registry. To see where this valuable data is stored, see Chapter 12, "Getting to Know the Windows 98 Registry."

- I cover printers in Chapter 21, "Prescriptions for Perfect Printing."

- Multimedia hardware tidbits are sprinkled throughout Part V, "Unleashing Multimedia: The Sights and Sounds of Windows 98."

- If you're interested in modems and the Windows 98 communications architecture, head for Chapter 26, "Getting Started with Modem Communications."

Getting to Know the Windows 98 Registry

CHAPTER 12

IN THIS CHAPTER

> *It is almost everywhere the case that soon after it is begotten the greater part of human wisdom is laid to rest in repositories.*
>
> —*G.C. Lichtenberg*

As you've learned throughout this book, a big part of unleashing Windows 98 involves customizing the interface and the accessories either to suit your personal style or to extract every last ounce of performance from your system. For the most part, these customization options are handled via the following mechanisms:

- Control Panel
- The properties sheets for individual objects
- Program menu commands and dialog boxes
- Command-line switches

But there is another, even more powerful mechanism you can use to customize Windows 98: the Registry. No, it doesn't have a pretty interface like most of the other customization options, and many aspects of the Registry give new meaning to the word arcane, but it gives you unparalleled access to facets of Windows 98 that would be otherwise out of reach. This chapter introduces you to the Registry and its structure, and it shows you how to make changes to the Registry by wielding the Registry Editor. With all that behind you, you'll be ready to start customizing Windows 98 at will, which is what you'll do in Chapter 13, "A Few Good Hacks: Some Useful Registry Tweaks."

A Synopsis of the Registry

When you change the desktop wallpaper using Control Panel's Display icon, the next time you start your computer, how does Windows 98 know which wallpaper you selected? If you change your video display driver, how does Windows 98 know to use that driver at startup and not the original driver loaded during Setup? In other words, how does Windows 98 "remember" the various settings and options either that you've selected yourself or that are appropriate for your system?

The secret to Windows 98's prodigious memory is the Registry. The Registry is a central repository Windows 98 uses to store anything and everything that applies to the configuration of your system. This includes hardware settings, object properties, operating system settings, and application options. It's all stored in one central location, and, thanks to a handy tool called the Registry Editor, it's yours to play with (carefully!) as you see fit.

A Brief History of Configuration Files

It wasn't always this way. In the early days of DOS and Windows (version 1!), system data was stored in two humble files: CONFIG.SYS and AUTOEXEC.BAT, those famous (or infamous) Bobbsey twins of configuration files.

When Windows 2.0 was born (to little or no acclaim), so too were born another couple of configuration files: WIN.INI and SYSTEM.INI. These so-called *initialization files* were also simple text files. It was WIN.INI's job to store configuration data about Windows and about Windows applications; for SYSTEM.INI, life consisted of storing data about hardware and system settings. Not to be outdone, applications started creating their own INI files to store user settings and program options. Before long, the Windows directory was festooned with dozens of these INI garlands.

The air became positively thick with INI files when Windows 3.0 rocked the PC world. Not only did Windows use WIN.INI and SYSTEM.INI to store configuration tidbits, but it also created new INIs for Program Manager (PROGMAN.INI), File Manager (WINFILE.INI), Control Panel (CONTROL.INI), and more.

It wasn't until Windows 3.1 hit the shelves that the Registry saw the light of day, albeit in a decidedly different guise from its Windows 98 descendant. The Windows 3.1 Registry was a database used to store registration information related to OLE (object linking and embedding) applications.

Finally, Windows for Workgroups muddied the configuration file waters even further by adding a few new network-related configuration files, including PROTOCOL.INI.

The Registry Puts an End to INI Chaos

This INI inundation led to all kinds of woes for users and system administrators alike. Because they were just text files in the main Windows directory, INIs were accidents waiting for a place to happen. Like sitting ducks, they were ripe for being picked off by an accidental press of the Delete key from a novice's fumbling fingers. There were so many of the darn things that few people could keep straight which INI file contained which settings. There was no mechanism to help you find the setting you needed in a large INI file. And the linear, headings-and-settings structure made it difficult to maintain complex configurations.

To solve all these problems, the Windows 95 designers decided to give the old Windows 3.1 Registry a promotion, so to speak. Specifically, they set it up as the central database for all system and application settings. The Registry maintains this structure in Windows 98.

Here are some of the advantages you get with this revised Registry:

■ The Registry files (discussed in the next section) have their hidden, system, and read-only attributes set, so it's much tougher to delete them accidentally. Even if a user somehow managed to blow away these files, Windows 98 maintains backup copies for easy recovery.

■ Not only does the Registry serve as a warehouse for hardware and operating system settings, but applications are free to use the Registry to store their own configuration morsels, instead of using separate INI files.

■ If you need to examine or modify a Registry entry, the Registry Editor utility gives you a hierarchical, treelike view of the entire Registry database (more on this topic later).

■ The Registry comes with tools that enable you to search for specific settings and to query the Registry data remotely.

That's not to say that the Registry is a perfect solution. Many of its settings are totally obscure, it uses a structure that only a true geek could love, and finding the setting you need is often an exercise in guesswork. Still, most of these problems can be overcome with a bit of practice and familiarity, which is what this chapter is all about.

Your Old Configuration Files Still Work

Although the Registry appropriates the function of all those old initialization and startup files, it doesn't shoulder the entire configuration file burden by itself. Windows 98 still recognizes and works with the settings in WIN.INI and SYSTEM.INI to maintain compatibility with 16-bit applications that are hard-wired to use these files for configuration data. Also, you still need CONFIG.SYS and AUTOEXEC.BAT if you have hardware that requires real-mode drivers or software that requires specific DOS settings (such as an environment variable or the PATH statement). Of course, 16-bit programs can still use their private INI files.

Understanding the Registry Files

If you installed Windows 98 on a fresh partition, Setup creates the Registry and uses it to store, among other things, the options you chose in the Setup Wizard's dialog boxes and the hardware information gleaned by the Detection Manager during the hardware detection phase. (Recall that if you upgrade over Windows 95, Setup uses the same Registry files.)

To create the Registry, Setup actually creates two files: USER.DAT and SYSTEM.DAT. These are hidden, system, read-only files that sit in your main Windows folder. Each file takes care of different aspects of the Registry, as described in the next couple of sections.

The Registry, Part I: USER.DAT

The USER.DAT file is designed to store user-specific information. It tracks the following data:

■ Wallpaper, color scheme, mouse options, accessibility options, and other Control Panel settings

■ Desktop icons

■ Start menu folders and shortcuts

■ Explorer configuration

■ Settings for the Windows 98 accessories

■ Network connections and passwords

Each time you exit Windows 98, the system makes a backup copy of USER.DAT. This is another hidden, system, read-only file, and it's called USER.DA0. This backup is handy if USER.DAT becomes corrupted.

If you're the sole user of your computer, your system will have only one USER.DAT file. If, however, you enabled user profiles (as discussed in Chapter 7, "Setting Accessibility Options, User Profiles, and More"), Windows 98 creates a USER.DAT file in each user subfolder. (You find these subfolders in the \Windows \Profiles\ folder.)

The Registry, Part II: SYSTEM.DAT

The SYSTEM.DAT file is designed to store system-specific information. Among other things, it keeps track of the following settings:

■ The various hardware classes that Windows 98 recognizes

■ The devices attached to your machine in each hardware class

■ Resources (IRQs, I/O ports, DMA channels) used by each device

■ Plug and Play information gleaned from the Plug and Play BIOS or Plug and Play devices

■ Protected-mode device drivers loaded at startup

■ Internal Windows 98 settings

■ Settings for specific 32-bit applications

Each time you exit Windows 98, the system makes a backup copy of SYSTEM.DAT. This is another hidden, system, read-only file, and it's called SYSTEM.DA0. This backup is handy if SYSTEM.DAT becomes corrupted. The root folder of your boot driver has yet another version of SYSTEM.DAT: SYSTEM.1ST. This is the original Registry created by Windows 98 Setup. It's useful as a last-resort backup if SYSTEM.DAT and SYSTEM.DA0 are out of commission.

Starting the Registry Editor

Unlike CONFIG.SYS, AUTOEXEC.BAT, and the INI files, the Registry files are binary, so you can't edit the Registry with a regular text editor. That's not a problem, though, because Windows 98 ships with a utility that lets you view, edit, and delete existing Registry values and even create new Registry values. This utility, called the Registry Editor, is your ticket into the otherwise inaccessible world of the Windows 98 Registry.

12

THE WINDOWS
98 REGISTRY

As you can imagine, the Registry Editor is a powerful tool, and it's not something to be wielded lightly. For that reason, the Setup program doesn't install a shortcut for the Registry Editor on any of the Start menus. To crank up the Registry Editor, you must use either of the following techniques:

■ Select Start | Run, type regedit in the Run dialog box, and click OK.

■ In Explorer, highlight your main Windows 98 folder and open the file named Regedit.exe.

CREATE A REGISTRY EDITOR SHORTCUT

If you think you'll be using the Registry Editor regularly, you should consider adding a shortcut for it either on the Start menu or on the desktop. See Chapter 6, "Customizing the Taskbar, Start Menu, and Display."

When the Registry Editor loads, you see the window shown in Figure 12.1.

FIGURE 12.1.

Running REGEDIT.EXE *opens the Registry Editor.*

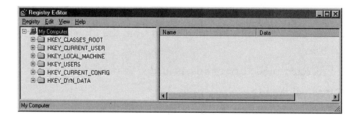

Examining the Structure of the Registry

The Registry Editor window looks a lot like the Explorer window, and it works in basically the same way. The left side of the Registry Editor window is similar to Explorer's Folders pane, except that rather than folders, you see *keys*. For lack of a better phrase, I'll call the left pane the *Keys pane*.

Navigating the Keys Pane

The Keys pane, like Explorer's Folders pane, is organized in a treelike hierarchy. The six keys that are visible when you first open the Registry Editor are special keys called *handles* (which is why their names all begin with HKEY). These keys are referred to collectively as the Registry's *root keys*. I'll tell you what to expect from each of these keys later (see the section called "The Registry's Root Keys").

These keys all contain subkeys, which you can display by clicking the plus sign (+) to the left of each key, or by highlighting a key and pressing the plus-sign key on your keyboard's numeric keypad. When you open a key, the plus sign changes to a minus sign (–). To close a key, click the minus sign or highlight the key and press the minus-sign key on the numeric keypad. (Again, this is just like navigating folders in Explorer.)

You often have to drill down several levels to get to the key you want. For example, Figure 12.2 shows the Registry Editor after I've opened the HKEY_LOCAL_MACHINE key and then opened five more subkeys to get to the WinbootDir key. Notice how the status bar tells you the exact path to the current key, and that this path is structured just like a folder path.

12

THE WINDOWS 98 REGISTRY

Current key   Settings pane

FIGURE 12.2.

You often have to dig deep to get to the keys you want to work with.

Keys pane

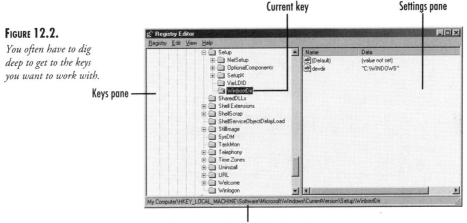

The status bar shows the full path to the key

Adjusting the Size of the Registry Editor Panes

To see all the keys properly, you likely have to increase the size of the Key pane (and, probably, the Registry Editor window as a whole). To adjust the size of the panes, use either of the following techniques:

- Drag the split bar that separates the panes to the right or left.
- Select View | Split, use the left- and right-arrow keys to adjust the split bar's position, and press Enter.

Registry Settings

If the left side of the Registry Editor window is analogous to Explorer's Folder pane, the right side is analogous to Explorer's Contents pane. In this case, the right side of the Registry Editor window displays the settings contained in each key (so I'll call it the *Settings pane*). The Settings pane is divided into two columns: The Name column tells you the name of each setting in the currently selected key (analogous to a filename in Explorer), and the Data column tells you the value of each setting (you can think of this as analogous to the contents of a file).

In Figure 12.2, for example, the `WinbootDir` key has two settings: `Default` (which isn't set) and `devdir`. The value of the latter is `c:\windows`. (This setting tells you the name of the main Windows 98 folder.)

Registry key settings can be either of the following types:

Strings: In this case, the value is always surrounded by quotation marks (as in the `devdir` example).

Binary numbers: In this case, the value is a set of hexadecimal digits.

The Registry Editor differentiates between these two types by displaying a different icon to the left of the setting name. For example, take a look at Figure 12.3. This key shows various settings for the folder used by Internet Explorer to cache its files. As you can see, some of the settings are strings (for example, `Directory`) and some are binary (for example, `Paths`).

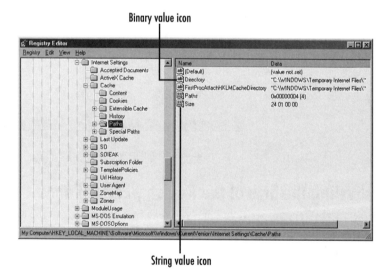

FIGURE 12.3.

Registry Editor displays a different icon for strings and binary values.

> ### DWORD VALUES
>
> A special class of binary values—called DWORD (double word) values—are 32-bit hexadecimal values arranged as eight digits. For example, 11 hex is 17 decimal, so this number would be represented in DWORD form as 0x00000011 (17). This value represents 4 bytes of data; because a "word" in programming circles is 2 bytes, these are "double word" values.

The Registry's Root Keys

The root keys are your Registry starting points, so you need to become familiar with what kinds of data each key holds. The next few sections summarize the contents of each key.

The HKEY_CLASSES_ROOT Key

The HKEY_CLASSES_ROOT key contains the same data that the Windows 3.1 Registry showed: file extensions and their associations, as well as applications and their OLE and DDE (Dynamic Data Exchange) information. There are also keys related to shortcuts and other interface features.

The top part of this key contains subkeys for various file extensions. You see .bmp for BMP (Paint) files, .doc for DOC (WordPad) files, and so on. In each of these subkeys, the Default setting tells you the name of the registered file type associated with the extension. (I discuss registered file types in Chapter 14, "File and Folder Tricks and Techniques.") For example, in Figure 12.4 I've highlighted the .txt subkey, which, as you can see, is associated with the txtfile file type.

FIGURE 12.4.

The extension subkeys in HKEY_CLASSES_ROOT tell you the file type associated with the extension.

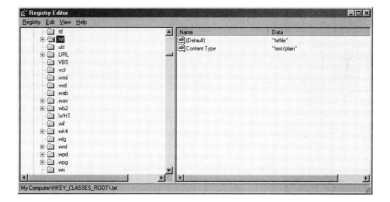

These registered file types appear as subkeys later in the HKEY_CLASSES_ROOT branch. If you scroll down, you eventually come across the txtfile subkey, as shown in Figure 12.5. The Registry keeps track of various settings for each registered file type. In particular, the shell subkey tells you the actions associated with this file type. (I added the Open_with_WordPad action by hand; check out the preceding chapter for details.)

FIGURE 12.5.

The registered file type subkeys specify various settings associated with each file type, including its defined actions.

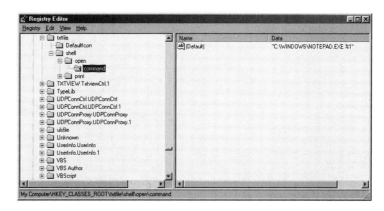

CLSID SETTINGS

Some registered file type subkeys have CLSID subkeys (check out the Wordpad.Document.1 file type for an example). These are OLE class IDs, and they're 32-character strings. Each of these strings points to a subkey of the HKEY_CLASSES_ROOT\CLSID key, which tells you the OLE implementation for that class. I talk more about class IDs in Chapter 19, "Sharing Data in Windows 98: The Clipboard and OLE."

The HKEY_CLASSES_ROOT key is actually a copy (or an *alias*, as these copied keys are called) of the following HKEY_LOCAL_MACHINE key:

HKEY_LOCAL_MACHINE\Software\Classes

The Registry creates an alias for HKEY_CLASSES_ROOT to make these keys easier for applications to access and to improve compatibility with Windows 3.1 programs.

The HKEY_CURRENT_USER Key

If you've set up multiple user profiles on your computer, the HKEY_CURRENT_USER key contains data that applies to the user that's currently logged on. In other words, it contains the settings from the USER.DAT file in the user's profile folder. (If you don't have multiple user profiles, HKEY_CURRENT_USER is the same as HKEY_USERS.)

HKEY_CURRENT_USER contains user-specific settings for Control Panel options, network connections, applications, and more, as you can see in Figure 12.6. Note that HKEY_CURRENT_USER is an alias for the subkey of HKEY_USERS that corresponds to the current user. For example, if the current user is Biff, HKEY_CURRENT_USER is the same as HKEY_USERS\Biff.

FIGURE 12.6.

The
HKEY_CURRENT_USER *key*
controls settings for the
current user.

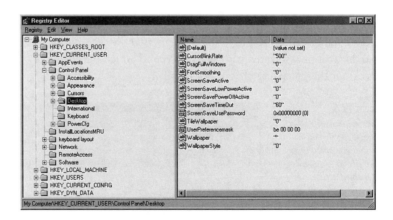

Here's a summary of the settings contained in the various HKEY_CURRENT_USER subkeys:

AppEvents: Sound files that play when particular system events occur (such as maximizing of a window).

Control Panel: Settings related to certain Control Panel icons.

InstallLocationsMRU: A list of the drives and folders that were most recently used (MRU) to install software or drivers.

keyboard layout: The keyboard layout as selected via Control Panel's Keyboard icon.

Network: Settings related to mapped network drives.

RemoteAccess: Settings related to Dial-Up Networking. (This branch only appears after you have created a Dial-Up Networking connection.)

Software: User-specific settings related to installed applications. Most 32-bit programs use this key to save their user-specific settings instead of using WIN.INI or private INIs.

The HKEY_LOCAL_MACHINE Key

The HKEY_LOCAL_MACHINE key is SYSTEM.DAT. It contains non–user-specific configuration data for your system's hardware and applications, as you can see in Figure 12.7.

FIGURE 12.7.

The HKEY_LOCAL_
MACHINE *key contains
non–user-specific
settings for devices and
programs.*

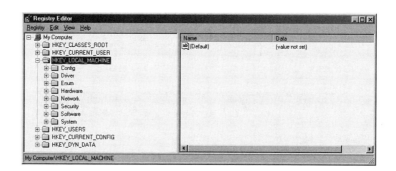

Let's run through the various HKEY_LOCAL_MACHINE subkeys:

Config: Contains subkeys for each hardware profile defined on your system. The subkey name is a unique identifier assigned to each profile (for example, 0001). To find out which profile is current, you have to head to the following subkey:

HKEY_LOCAL_MACHINE\System\CurrentControlSet\control\IDConfigDB

The CurrentConfig setting gives you the identifier of the current profile. The names of each profile are stored in the various FriendlyName settings (for example, FriendlyName0001). The current configuration is aliased by the HKEY_CURRENT_CONFIG key (see the section "The HKEY_CURRENT_CONFIG Key," later in this chapter).

Enum: Contains the data gathered by the Windows 98 bus enumerators. Enum contains subkeys for each hardware class, and each hardware class has subkeys for the installed devices in that class. Each device subkey has various settings related to the device, including its description, its driver, and its hardware ID.

Hardware: Contains subkeys related to serial ports and modems (used by HyperTerminal), as well as the floating-point processor.

Network: Contains a Logon subkey with various settings related to the network logon, including the user name and whether the logon was validated by a network server.

Security: Contains a Provider subkey that specifies the domain under which network security is administered.

Software: Contains computer-specific settings related to installed applications. Most 32-bit programs use this key to save their computer-specific settings instead of using WIN.INI or private INIs. The Classes subkey is aliased by the HKEY_CLASSES_ROOT key. The Microsoft subkey contains settings related to Windows 98 (as well as any other Microsoft products you have installed on your computer).

System: Contains subkeys and settings related to Windows 98 startup, including the following ones in the CurrentControlSet\control subkey: installable file systems (FileSystem subkey), a list of the installed Windows 98 files (InstalledFiles subkey), printers (Print subkey), the time zone (TimeZoneInformation subkey), and a list of the drivers loaded from VMM32.VXD (VMM32Files subkey).

DON'T EDIT THE SERVICES SUBKEY

The HKEY_LOCAL_MACHINE\System\CurrentControlSet\Services subkey contains settings related to the Windows 98 device arbitrators, static descriptions of hardware devices, virtual device drivers, and more. Don't make any changes to these values in the Registry Editor. Only Windows 98 should manage these keys.

The HKEY_USERS Key

The HKEY_USERS key contains settings for Control Panel options, network connections, applications, and more. If you haven't enabled user profiles on your machine, HKEY_USERS has only one subkey, .Default, that contains the same settings as HKEY_CURRENT_USER.

If you have enabled user profiles, HKEY_USERS always has three subkeys: the .Default and Software subkeys, and a key for the current user, as shown in Figure 12.8 (the Biff subkey). The settings in the .Default subkey are applied to users logging in for the first time, and the subkey for the current user is the same as HKEY_CURRENT_USER. If you want to see a list of all the user profiles, check out the following key:

HKEY_LOCAL_MACHINE\Software\Microsoft\Windows\CurrentVersion\ProfileList

FIGURE 12.8.
The HKEY_USERS *key contains configuration settings for the current user and a "default" user.*

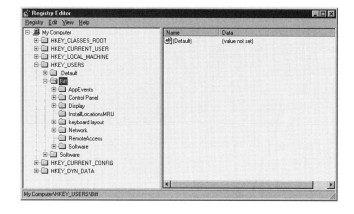

The HKEY_CURRENT_CONFIG Key

The HKEY_CURRENT_CONFIG key contains settings for the current hardware profile, as shown in Figure 12.9. If your machine uses only one hardware profile, HKEY_CURRENT_CONFIG is an alias for HKEY_LOCAL_MACHINE\Config\0001. If your machine uses multiple hardware profiles, HKEY_CURRENT_CONFIG is an alias for HKEY_LOCAL_MACHINE\Config\Current, in which Current is the numeric identifier of the current hardware profile. This identifier is given by the Current setting in the following key:

HKEY_LOCAL_MACHINE\System\CurrentControlSet\control\IDConfigDB

As with HKEY_CLASSES_ROOT, the HKEY_CURRENT_CONFIG alias makes it easier for applications to access the settings in this key.

FIGURE 12.9.
HKEY_CURRENT_CONFIG *is an alias for a subkey of* HKEY_LOCAL_MACHINE\Config.

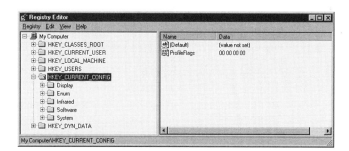

The HKEY_DYN_DATA Key

The Registry files (USER.DAT and SYSTEM.DAT) are updated when you shut down Windows 98, when you restart Windows 98, and at regular intervals while you're running Windows 98. (Also, if an application makes a change to the Registry, it can force an update of the Registry files.) This is called flushing the Registry data to the hard disk.

However, some data needs to remain in RAM (that is, it must be dynamic) at all times for fast access. This data is stored in the HKEY_DYN_DATA key, shown in Figure 12.10. HKEY_DYN_DATA contains two subkeys:

Config Manager: This subkey contains a RAM-based listing of the Windows 98 Plug and Play (PnP) hardware tree. The HKEY_DYN_DATA\ConfigManager\Enum key contains a subkey for each PnP device on the system, and each device has settings for its hardware ID, status, and any problems the device might be having.

PerfStats: This subkey contains performance statistics for the system's network components. You can view these statistics in real time via the System Monitor utility.

FIGURE 12.10.

The HKEY_DYN_DATA *key contains data that must remain in RAM for fast access.*

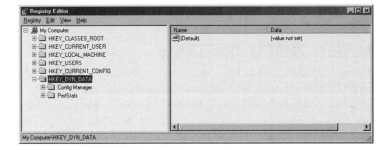

OTHER SYSTEM MONITOR STATISTICS

You find the rest of the System Monitor's performance statistics in the following key:

HKEY_LOCAL_MACHINE\System\CurrentControlSet\control\PerfStats\Enum

---

Summarizing the Structure of the Registry

The various aliases used by the Registry might make it easier for applications to access and write Registry data, but they do little to aid human comprehension. To help you while you navigate the Registry, here's a summary of the various root keys and how they relate to each other:

- HKEY_USERS is USER.DAT.
- HKEY_CURRENT_USER is an alias for either HKEY_USERS\.Default (if user profiles haven't been activated) or HKEY_USERS*UserName* (if user profiles have been activated), in which *UserName* is the user name of the current user.
- HKEY_LOCAL_MACHINE is SYSTEM.DAT.
- HKEY_CLASSES_ROOT is an alias for HKEY_LOCAL_MACHINE\Software\Classes.
- HKEY_CURRENT_CONFIG is an alias for HKEY_LOCAL_MACHINE\Config*Current*, in which *Current* is the numeric identifier for the current hardware profile (0001 if you're using only the original hardware profile).
- HKEY_DYN_DATA holds Registry data that must remain in RAM for fast access.

Figure 12.11 illustrates these relationships.

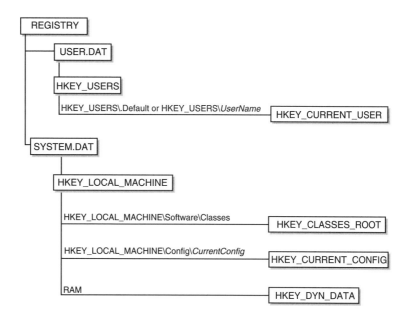

FIGURE 12.11.
*The relationships
between the Registry
files and the root keys.*

Working with Registry Entries

Now that you've had a look around, you're ready to start working with the Registry's keys and settings. In this section, I'll give you the general procedures for basic tasks, such as modifying, adding, renaming, deleting, and searching for entries, and more. These techniques will serve you well in Chapter 13, when I take you through some specific Registry modifications.

Changing the Value of a Registry Entry

Changing the value of a Registry entry is a simple matter of finding the appropriate key, displaying the setting you want to change, and editing the setting's value. Unfortunately, finding the key you need isn't always a simple matter. Knowing the root keys and their main subkeys, as described earlier, will certainly help, and the Registry Editor also has a Find feature that's invaluable (I'll show you how to use it later).

To illustrate how this process works, let's work through an example: changing the desktop wallpaper via the Registry. (As you'll see, it's much easier to change the wallpaper by using Control Panel. This simple example, however, serves to illustrate the basic technique for altering Registry settings.)

First, use the Keys pane to display the key you want to work with, and then highlight it. The key's settings will appear in the Settings pane. For the example, select the following key:

HKEY_CURRENT_USER\Control Panel\desktop

Now open the setting (in the example, it's the Wallpaper setting) for editing by using any of the following techniques:

- Highlight the setting name and either select Edit | Modify or press Enter.
- Double-click the setting name.
- Right-click the setting name and select Modify from the context menu.

The dialog box that appears depends on the value type you're dealing with. If the value is a string (as it is in our example), you see the Edit String dialog box, shown in Figure 12.12. Use the Value data text box to enter a new string or modify the existing string. For the wallpaper example, enter the full pathname for the bitmap you want to use as the wallpaper (for example, `c:\windows\Carved Stone.bmp`). When you're done, click OK. (Depending on the bitmap you entered, you might also need to change the value of the `TileWallpaper` setting. Use 1 for tiled or 0 for centered.)

FIGURE 12.12.

You see the Edit String dialog box if you're modifying a string value.

If the setting is a binary value, you see an Edit Binary Value dialog box like the one shown in Figure 12.13. For binary values, the Value data box is divided into three columns:

Starting byte number: The values in the first column tell you the sequence number of the first byte in each row of hexadecimal numbers. This sequence always begins at 0, so the sequence number of the first byte in the first row is `0`. There are 8 bytes in each row, so the sequence number of the first byte in the second row is `8`, and so on. These values can't be edited.

Hexadecimal numbers (bytes): The middle column displays the setting's value, arranged in rows of eight hexadecimal numbers, in which each number represents a single byte of information. These values are editable.

ANSI equivalents: The third column shows the ANSI equivalents of the hexadecimal numbers in the middle column. For example, the first byte of the first row is the hexadecimal value `42`, which represents the letter B. The values in this column are also editable.

When you're finished editing the value, click OK.

Edited settings are written to the Registry right away, but the changes might not go into effect immediately. In many cases, you need to exit the Registry Editor and then restart Windows 98. If you have user profiles activated on your machine, or if your machine is on a network, the easiest way to put Registry changes into effect is to select the Start | Log Off *User* command, where *User* is the name of the current user.

FIGURE 12.13.

You see the Edit Binary Value dialog box if you're modifying a binary value.

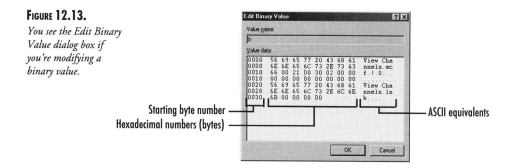

Starting byte number

Hexadecimal numbers (bytes)

ASCII equivalents

If you don't have user profiles activated or a network connection, you need to restart Windows 98 by selecting Start | Shut Down and activating the Restart option. Remember, however, that you can get a faster restart by holding down the Shift key when you click the OK button. This method bypasses the cold reboot and merely restarts Windows 98.

Other Registry Entry Techniques

Nearly all the modifications you make to Registry entries will involve modifying the value of an existing setting. Just so you know, however, you can also rename, add, and delete keys and settings. Here are the basic techniques:

Renaming a key or setting: Highlight the key or setting and select Edit | Rename (or press F2), or right-click and select Rename from the context menu. Make your changes in the text box and press Enter.

Adding a key or setting: Highlight the key in which you want to add the subkey or setting. Select File | New or right-click the key and select New from the context menu. In the cascade menu that appears, select Key, String Value, Binary Value, or DWORD Value.

Deleting a key or setting: Highlight the key or setting and select Edit | Delete (or press Delete), or right-click and select Delete from the context menu. When the Registry Editor asks you to confirm the deletion, click Yes.

Finding Registry Entries

The Registry contains only six root keys, but these root keys contain hundreds of subkeys. And the fact that some root keys are aliases for subkeys in a different branch only adds to the confusion. If you know exactly where you're going, the Registry Editor's treelike hierarchy is a reasonable way to get there. If you're not sure where a particular subkey or setting resides, however, you could spend all day poking around in the Registry's labyrinthine nooks and crannies.

To help you get where you want to go, the Registry Editor has a Find feature that lets you search for keys, settings, or values. For example, in Chapter 13 I'll demonstrate how to change

12

THE WINDOWS 98 REGISTRY

the default icon for the standard desktop icons. The appropriate keys are tough to find, however, because they use those confusing 32-digit class IDs. If you want to change the Recycle Bin icon, for example, there's no "Recycle Bin" key that lets you do it. Let's run through a Find example in which you search for some kind of Recycle Bin–related key that will let you change the icon:

1. In the Keys pane, highlight My Computer at the top of the pane (unless you're certain of which root key contains the value you want to find; in this case, you can highlight the appropriate root key instead).

2. Select Edit | Find or press Ctrl+F. The Registry Editor displays the Find dialog box.

3. Use the Find what text box to enter your search string. You can enter partial words or phrases to increase your chances of finding a match. In this example, you enter recycle.

4. In the Look at group, activate the check boxes for the elements you want to search. For most searches, you want to leave all three check boxes activated.

5. If you want to find only those entries that exactly match your search text, activate the Match whole string only check box.

6. Click the Find Next button. The Registry Editor highlights the first match.

7. If this isn't the item you want (in our example, the Registry Editor first highlights the Recycle Bin Cleaner setting), select Edit | Find Next (or press F3) until you find the setting or key you want.

When the Registry Editor finds a match, it displays the appropriate key or setting. Note that if the matched value is a setting name or data value, Find doesn't highlight the current key. This is a bit confusing, but just remember that the current key always appears at the bottom of the Keys pane.

Importing and Exporting Registry Files

If you will be making major changes to keys or settings, you should make a backup copy of the Registry. One easy way to do this is to select Registry | Export Registry File to bring up the Export Registry File dialog box. Select a location for the exported file, enter a name, and choose whether you want to export All (the entire Registry) or just the Selected branch. When you're ready, click Save.

EXPORT THE ENTIRE REGISTRY FOR GLOBAL CHANGES

You might sometimes need to make changes throughout the Registry. For example, if you want to move an application to a different folder, you need to update all references to the application's folder. The easiest way to do this is to export the entire Registry, load the resulting REG file into WordPad or some other word processor, and then use the Replace function to make your changes. (For obvious reasons, I highly recommend that you make a backup of the Registry before attempting this procedure.)

BACKING UP THE REGISTRY

The new Windows 98 Backup tool enables you to include the Registry files in your backup set. See Chapter 16, "Working with a Net: The Windows 98 Backup Utility."

New to
98

The Export Registry File command is also useful if you want to send Registry data to a different machine. In this case, however, you probably don't want to export the entire Registry, because the other machine probably won't have the same hardware configuration.

The file created during the export is a Registration file with a `.REG` extension. You can import a REG file into your Registry by selecting File | Import Registry File, highlighting the REG file in the Import Registry File dialog box that appears, and clicking Open.

12

THE WINDOWS
98 REGISTRY

FASTER WAYS TO IMPORT REG FILES

You also can import a REG file by double-clicking it, by highlighting it in Explorer and selecting File | Merge, or by right-clicking it and selecting Merge from the context menu.

WATCH FOR APPLICATION REG FILES

Many applications ship with their own REG files for updating the Registry. Unless you're sure that you want to import these files, avoid double-clicking them. They might end up overwriting existing settings and causing problems with your system.

Using REG Files to Modify the Registry

REG files are usually generated by exporting some or all of the Registry from within the Registry Editor. However, the resulting file is a simple text file, so there's nothing to stop you from creating REG files from scratch. Why would you want to do this? Well, suppose you wanted to add or update a Registry setting on a remote user's machine. You could access the computer's Registry Editor directly, or you could use Windows 98's remote Registry feature. But what if you need to update a dozen systems? or a hundred? Clearly, in this situation a "hands-on" approach just isn't practical. Instead, you could create the appropriate REG file, email it to the remote users, and instruct them to launch the file and thus update the Registry automatically.

Here's the general structure to use when building your REG files:

```
REGEDIT4
[REGISTRY_KEY]
"SettingName1"="string"
"SettingName2"=hex:value
etc.
```

Here are some notes about this structure:

- The top of the file is always REGEDIT4 followed by a blank line.
- The REGISTRY_KEY is the full path of the Registry key that contains the setting (or settings) you want to modify. You can specify multiple keys if necessary.
- The settings you want to add or modify are listed below the [REGISTRY_KEY] line. In each case, you enter the name of the setting, in double quotation marks, followed by an equals sign (=).
- For string values, enter the value you want to set enclosed in double quotation marks.
- For hexadecimal values, enter hex: followed by the value. If the setting requires multiple hex values, separate them with commas.

Here's an example of a typical REG file:

```
REGEDIT4
[HKEY_LOCAL_MACHINE\Software\Microsoft\Windows\CurrentVersion]
"RegisteredOrganization"="Logophilia Limited"
"InstallType"=hex:03,00
```

Printing the Registry

The Registry Editor enables you to print either the entire Registry or a selected key. Highlight the key you want to print (if necessary) and select File | Print. In the Print dialog box that appears, select whether you want to print the entire Registry or just the selected key, choose your other print options, and click OK.

AVOID PRINTING THE ENTIRE REGISTRY

You might want to think twice about printing the entire Registry, because it consumes more than 100 pages!

Troubleshooting the Registry

The Registry is obviously a crucial component, and you should take no chances with it. Export backup copies of the full Registry regularly, especially if you'll be making significant changes to the Registry's settings, and store a backup copy on a floppy disk in case your hard disk goes up in flames.

If the Registry itself gets corrupted, however, you might not be able to start Windows 98. This section looks at a few Registry-related problems that can occur and shows you how to fix them.

You made a change to the Registry, and now Windows 98 won't boot.

Because the Registry is such a central part of Windows 98, editing any of the settings isn't a task to be taken lightly. One false move and Windows 98 might refuse to play with you any more. If this happens, you can recover by exporting the Registry to a text file, editing the text file to fix the problem, and importing the changes back into the Registry.

How do you do all this if you can't get into Windows 98, much less run the Registry Editor? You use the real-mode version of the Registry Editor (REGEDIT.EXE). Note that you can start the real-mode version of the Registry Editor only by rebooting to the command prompt (either by selecting Safe mode command prompt only from the Windows 98 Startup menu or by rebooting with the Windows 98 Startup disk in drive A). You find REGEDIT.EXE either in your main Windows folder or on your Windows 98 Startup disk.

When you get to the DOS prompt, you first need to run REGEDIT.EXE to export the Registry to a REG text file. Here's the syntax:

```
regedit [/L:system] [/R:user] [/E] filename.reg
```

/L:*system*	Specifies the location of SYSTEM.DAT.
/R:*user*	Specifies the location of USER.DAT.
/E *filename.reg*	Exports the Registry to *filename.reg*.

For example, if you made a change to a key that's part of SYSTEM.DAT, you can export this section of the Registry to a file named SYSTEM.REG with the following command (assuming that C:\WINDOWS is your main Windows 98 folder):

```
regedit /l:c:\windows\system.dat /e c:\system.reg
```

Now use any text editor to load the SYSTEM.REG file, find the change you made that caused Windows 98 to crash, and save the file.

Your next step is to import the REG file back into the Registry by using the following REGEDIT syntax:

```
regedit [/L:system] [/R:user] [/S] filename.reg
```

/L:*system*	Specifies the location of SYSTEM.DAT.
/R:*user*	Specifies the location of USER.DAT.
/S	Bypasses the confirmation dialog box.
filename.reg	Specifies the name of the modified REG file.

In this example, you enter the following command:

```
regedit /l:c:\windows\system.dat c:\system.reg
```

Restart your computer to put the changes into effect.

Your Registry is corrupted, and your system won't boot.

If your Registry goes down for the count, it might bring your system down along with it. To recover, you need to get rid of the existing Registry files (SYSTEM.DAT and USER.DAT) and use the Registry backups (SYSTEM.DA0 and USER.DA0) in their place.

The first thing you need to do is insert your Windows 98 Startup disk (or any bootable floppy) and reboot. When you get to the A:\ prompt, change to the drive where Windows 98 is installed and then change to the main Windows 98 folder. For example, if your main Windows 98 folder is C:\WINDOWS, enter the following two commands:

```
c:
cd\windows
```

Both SYSTEM.DAT and SYSTEM.DA0 are hidden, read-only, system files, so you need to turn off these attributes with the following two commands:

```
attrib -h -r -s system.dat
attrib -h -r -s system.da0
```

Now you must delete SYSTEM.DAT and rename SYSTEM.DA0 to SYSTEM.DAT:

```
del system.dat
ren system.da0 system.dat
```

Finally, reset the hidden, read-only, and system attributes for SYSTEM.DAT with the following command:

```
attrib +h +r +s system.dat
```

You need to repeat this procedure for USER.DAT and USER.DA0. When you're done, remove the bootable floppy and restart your system. Your Registry is restored to the state it was in the last time you successfully restarted Windows 98.

Your Registry is corrupted, and you need to restore it from an exported REG file.

If the Registry is corrupted badly enough, you need to replace it entirely with an exported REG file. The real-mode version of the Registry Editor can do this for you if you use the following syntax:

```
regedit [/C] filename.reg
```

/C *filename.reg* replaces the entire contents of the existing Registry with *filename.reg*.

If the REG file is named REGBACK.REG, you'd use the following command to do it:

```
regedit /c regback.reg
```

When you start your computer, the Windows 98 Startup menu is displayed automatically, and the following message appears:

```
Warning: Windows has detected a registry/configuration error.
Choose Safe mode, to start Windows with a minimal set of drivers.
```

This error indicates that the Registry files are either missing or corrupted. You need to boot Windows 98 in Safe mode.

Windows 98 first tries to restore the Registry from its backup copies (SYSTEM.DA0 and USER.DA0). You see the Registry Problem dialog box with an explanation of the problem. Click the Restore From Backup and Restart button.

If Windows 98 can restore the backups, it prompts you to restart your computer. Click Yes to reboot.

If Windows 98 can't restore the backups, it suggests that you shut down your system and reinstall Windows 98. Although you might have to reinstall Windows 98 as a last resort, you can still try two other things:

- If you have a backup copy of the Registry files on floppy disk in the form of a REG file, you can use it to create a new Registry, as described earlier.

- Delete SYSTEM.DAT (you need to remove its hidden, read-only, and system attributes first) and then copy SYSTEM.1ST from your root folder to SYSTEM.DAT in your main Windows 98 folder. (Again, you need to adjust the attributes before you can copy SYSTEM.1ST.)

- Reboot to the command prompt and check MSDOS.SYS. Make sure that the WinDir and WinBootDir settings point to the correct folder (that is, your main Windows 98 folder, which is where the Registry files are stored).

During the hardware detection phase of the Windows 98 installation, Setup displays the following error message:

```
SDMErr(80000003): Registry access failed.
```

This error message tells you that the Registry is damaged. To fix this problem, follow these steps:

1. Restart your computer, and when you see the Starting Windows 98... message, press F8 to display the Windows 98 Startup menu.

2. Select the Safe mode command prompt only option.

3. When you get to the DOS prompt, enter the following command (if REGEDIT complains about missing data, ignore it):

   ```
   regedit /e reg.txt
   ```

4. Enter the following command to regenerate the Registry's internal data structures:

   ```
   regedit /c reg.txt
   ```

5. Restart your computer and then try Setup again.

Summary

This chapter gave you an introduction to one of Windows 98's most important components: the Registry. I gave you a short history of configuration files, from CONFIG.SYS and AUTOEXEC.BAT to the INI madness that characterized Windows 3.*x.* I then showed you how Windows 98 improved the situation by consolidating configuration data into a single structure: the Registry. You then took a tour of the Registry structure using the Registry Editor, and I showed you how to use the Registry Editor to work with the Registry entries.

You'll put this newfound knowledge to good use in Chapter 13, where I show you a number of tricks and secrets that take advantage of the Registry to modify Windows 98. Here's a list of a few other chapters that contain related information:

■ You'll find lots more information on Windows 98 startup in Chapter 3, "Start Me Up: Controlling Windows 98 Startup."

■ Many of the Registry values are generated by Windows 98's customization features. I discuss many of these features in Chapters 5 through 7.

■ For a broad look at Windows 98 memory features, as well as how to use the System Monitor, see Chapter 9, "Performance Tuning: Optimizing Memory and Disk Access."

■ To better understand the Registry's hardware-related keys, head for Chapter 10, "Getting the Most Out of Device Manager and Hardware Profiles."

■ You'll learn how to back up the Registry's files in Chapter 16, "Working with a Net: The Windows 98 Backup Utility."

■ In Chapter 19, "Sharing Data in Windows 98: The Clipboard and OLE," I talk about the Registry's OLE-related keys (including the CLSID keys) and settings.

CHAPTER 13

A Few Good Hacks: Some Useful Registry Tweaks

> *A little knowledge that acts is worth infinitely more than much knowledge that is idle.*
>
> —*Kahlil Gibran*

An old Scottish proverb says that "fine words butter no parsnips." Chapter 12, "Getting to Know the Windows 98 Registry," presented plenty of fine words (if that's not too immodest a thing to say) about the Registry and how you work with it, but now it's time to butter a Registry parsnip or two. In other words, you're well versed in the theory of the Registry, so now you need to get up to speed with the practice. What kinds of things can you do with the Registry? In particular, what kinds of things can you do with the Registry that can't be done via the Control Panel, Explorer, or any of the applets? That's what this chapter is all about. I'll show you a fistful of practical Registry techniques that lets you customize Windows 98 in undreamed-of ways.

Working with File Types and Applications

You begin your look at Registry tricks by examining a few techniques that will give you more control over file types and applications.

Customizing the New Menu

In Chapter 14, "File and Folder Tricks and Techniques," I show you how to create new file types and modify existing ones. One of Windows 98's handiest features is the New menu, which lets you create a new file without working within an application. In Explorer, just select File | New, or right-click inside the Contents pane and select New, to display the menu shown in Figure 13.1. From there, just select a command to create a new instance of that particular file type.

FIGURE 13.1.

The New menu lets you create new documents without opening an application.

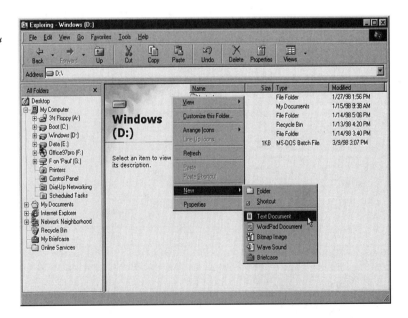

You'll see in Chapter 14 that Windows 98 recognizes more than 100 file types, but the New menu lists only seven by default (installed applications may add more). What mechanism determines whether a file type appears on the New menu? The Registry, of course. Start the Registry Editor and open the HKEY_CLASSES_ROOT key. As I mentioned in Chapter 12, the first 150 or so subkeys of HKEY_CLASSES_ROOT are the file extensions that Windows 98 recognizes. Most of these keys contain only a Default setting that takes on either of the following values:

■ If the extension is registered with Windows 98, the Default value is a string pointing to the file type associated with the extension. For example, the Default value for .bat is batfile (batch file).

■ If the extension isn't registered with Windows 98, the Default value isn't set.

A few of these extension keys, however, also have subkeys. For example, open the .bmp key and you see that it has a subkey named ShellNew, as shown in Figure 13.2. This subkey is what determines whether a file type appears on the New menu. Specifically, if the extension is registered with Windows 98 and it has a ShellNew subkey, the New menu sprouts a command for the associated file type.

FIGURE 13.2.
The ShellNew *subkey controls whether a file type appears on the New menu.*

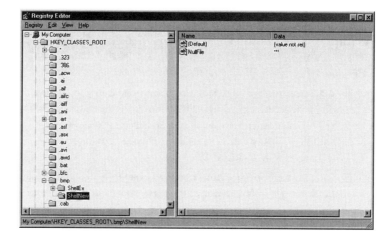

The ShellNew subkey always contains a setting that determines how Windows 98 creates the new file. Four settings are possible:

NullFile: This setting, the value of which is always set to a null string (" "), tells Windows 98 to create an empty file of the associated type. Of the six file types (excluding Folder and Shortcut) that appear on the New menu, three use the NullFile setting: Text Document (.txt), Bitmap Image (.bmp, see Figure 13.2), and Wave Sound (.wav).

FileName: This setting tells Windows 98 to create the new file by making a copy of another file. Windows 98 has a special folder to hold these "template" files. This folder, called ShellNew, is hidden, so you must activate Explorer's Show all files option to view it, as shown in Figure 13.3. On the New menu, only the WordPad Document (.doc) file type uses the FileName setting, and its value is winword.doc. (Recall that the default file type for WordPad is a Word for Windows 6 document.) To see this value, you need to open the following key:

```
HKEY_CLASSES_ROOT\.doc\Wordpad.Document.1\ShellNew
```

Figure 13.3.

The ShellNew folder holds templates used by the New menu to create new documents.

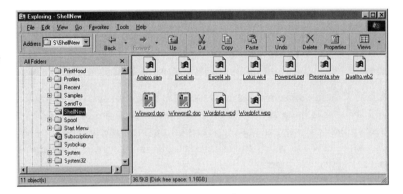

ABOUT ShellNew AND THE FileName SETTING

Here are a few notes about the ShellNew key's FileName setting:

■ Although the ShellNew menu contains quite a few templates, only the WordPad documents are registered with Windows 98. In other words, the Registry does have a key for .xls (Excel), for example, in HKEY_CLASSES_ROOT, and this key has a ShellNew subkey with a FileName setting that points to Excel.xls; but XLS files aren't registered with Windows 98.

■ The FileName setting doesn't have to point to a file in the ShellNew folder. It can point to a file in any folder as long as you include the file's full pathname.

■ If you check out the .doc key in HKEY_CLASSES_ROOT, you note that it has three subkeys—Word.Document.6, WordDocument, and Wordpad.Document.1—and each has a ShellNew subkey. Why isn't there a New menu command for each document type? Because Windows 98 sets up a New menu command only for registered file types (Wordpad.Document.1, in this case).

Command: This setting tells Windows 98 to create the new file by executing a specific command. This command usually invokes an executable file with a few parameters. The New menu's Briefcase item uses this setting. If you check the ShellNew subkey for .bfc in HKEY_CLASSES_ROOT, you see the following value for the Command setting:

```
C:\windows\rundll32.exe syncui.dll,Briefcase_Create %1!d! %2
```

Data: This setting contains a binary value, and when Windows 98 creates the new file, it copies this binary value into the file.

Adding File Types to the New Menu

To make the New menu even more convenient, you can add new file types for documents you work with regularly. For any file type that's registered with Windows 98, you follow a simple three-step process:

1. Add a ShellNew subkey to the appropriate extension key in HKEY_CLASSES_ROOT.

2. Add one of the four settings discussed in the preceding list (NullFile, FileName, Command, or Data).

3. Enter a value for the setting.

In most cases, the easiest way to go is to use NullFile to create an empty file. The FileName setting, however, can be quite powerful because you can set up a template file containing text and other data.

Using Multiple New Menu Commands for a Single Application

For a given extension, Windows 98 lets you have only one New menu command. But what if you want to use the same application to create multiple kinds of new documents? For example, you might have a WordPad file that you use as a template (such as a daily to-do list). It would be nice to be able to create new WordPad documents that either are empty or use this template.

To accomplish this task, you need to set up a new, registered file type for the template, complete with its own extension, and set up a ShellNew key for this new type. Here are the basic steps to follow:

1. Use Explorer's View | Folder Options command to create a new file type that's associated with the application (see Chapter 14 for details). For a to-do list, you could create a TDL extension associated with WordPad.

2. Copy the template file into the ShellNew folder and rename it so that it has the extension you just registered. For example, if your WordPad file is named TODOLIST.DOC, rename it TODOLIST.TDL.

3. In the Registry Editor, find the new extension in HKEY_CLASSES_ROOT and add the ShellNew subkey.

4. Add the FileName setting and use the name of the template file in ShellNew.

Deleting File Types from the New Menu

Many Windows 98 applications like to add their file types to the New menu. (Microsoft Office alone adds five commands to the New menu.) If you find that your New menu is getting overcrowded, you can delete some commands to keep things manageable.

To do this, you need to find the appropriate extension in the Registry and delete the `ShellNew` subkey.

DETERMINING THE CORRECT FILE EXTENSION

If you're not sure which extension is associated with the New menu command you want to delete, you could search the Registry all day looking for it. An easier way is to just use the command to create a new document in any Explorer folder and see the resulting extension. Remember, though, that to see extensions in Explorer you need to select View | Options and deactivate the Hide MS-DOS file extensions for file types that are registered check box.

A MORE CAUTIOUS APPROACH

Instead of permanently deleting a `ShellNew` subkey, you can tread a more cautious path by simply renaming the key (to, for example, `ShellNewOld`). This will still prevent Windows 98 from adding the item to the New menu, but it also means that you can restore the item just by restoring the original key name.

Creating Application-Specific Paths

When you install a 32-bit application, it uses the Registry to store the path to its executable file. This means that you can start any 32-bit application simply by entering the name of its executable file, either in the Run dialog box or at the prompt in a DOS session. You don't need to spell out the complete pathname. For example, the executable filename for Backup is `Msbackup.exe`, so you could type `msbackup` and press Enter to start it.

This pathless execution is handy, but in the following two situations it doesn't work:

16-bit applications: These older programs don't store the paths to their executables in the Registry.

Documents: As you'll learn in Chapter 14, you can double-click a document in Explorer, and Windows 98 starts the associated application and loads the document. However, you can't load a document just by typing its filename in the Run dialog box or at the DOS prompt (unless the document is in the current folder).

To solve both these problems, you can add a path to an executable file (an application-specific path) or to a document (a document-specific path) into the Registry by hand.

In the Registry Editor, open the following key:

```
HKEY_LOCAL_MACHINE\Software\Microsoft\Windows\CurrentVersion\App Paths
```

As you can see in Figure 13.4, the `App Paths` key has subkeys for each installed 32-bit application. Each of these subkeys has one or both of the following settings:

Default: This setting spells out the path to the application's executable file. All the `App Paths` subkeys have this setting.

Path: This setting specifies one or more folders that contain files needed by the application. An application first looks for its files in the same folder as its executable file. If it can't find what it needs there, it checks the folder or folders listed in the `Path` setting. Not all `App Paths` subkeys use this setting.

FIGURE 13.4.

The `App Paths` *key contains path information for all installed 32-bit applications.*

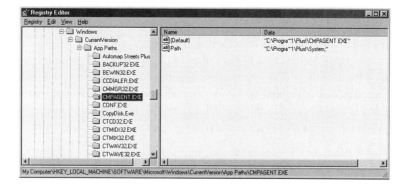

To create an application-specific path, highlight the `App Paths` key, create a new subkey, and assign it the name of the application's executable file. For example, if the program's executable filename is `OLDAPP.EXE`, name the new subkey `OLDAPP.EXE`. For this new subkey, change the `Default` setting to the full pathname for the executable file.

Actually, you don't have to give the new `App Paths` subkey the name of the executable file. You can use any name you like as long as it ends with `.EXE` and doesn't conflict with the name of an existing subkey. Why does it have to end with `.EXE`? Unless you specify otherwise, Windows 98 assumes that anything you enter in the Run dialog box or at the DOS prompt ends with `.EXE`. So by ending the subkey with `.EXE`, you need to type only the subkey's primary name. For example, if you name your new subkey `OLDAPP.EXE`, you can run the program by typing `oldapp`.

You create document-specific paths the same way. (Note, however, that the document's file type must be registered with Windows 98.) In this case, though, the `Default` setting takes on the full pathname of the document. Again, if you want to load the document just by typing its primary name, make sure that the new `App Paths` subkey uses the `.EXE` extension. For example, you can see in Figure 13.5 that I've created a subkey called `TODO.EXE` that points to `E:\Data\Documents\ToDoList.doc`. To launch this document, I need only type `todo` in the Run dialog box or at the DOS prompt.

13

SOME USEFUL
REGISTRY TWEAKS

FIGURE 13.5.

*An example of a
document-specific path.*

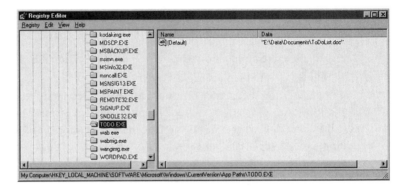

Instead of creating a path for a specific document, you might prefer to set up a path that points to an entire folder of documents. For example, it's usually a good idea to create separate folders for your data files. This technique makes it easier to find your data files and to back them up. Suppose, for example, that you store all your WordPad documents in a folder named E:\Data\Documents. Ideally, you'd like to be able to launch any of the documents in this folder just by typing its name in the Run dialog box or at the DOS prompt.

No problem. In the App Paths key, highlight the subkey that corresponds to the application you use to work with the documents. Modify the Path setting (if it has one; if not, you need to create a Path setting) to include the full pathname of the folder that contains the documents. Be sure to end the pathname with a semicolon (;). For example, Figure 13.6 shows a Path setting added to the WORDPAD.EXE subkey that points to G:\Data\Documents.

FIGURE 13.6.

*You can add a path
that points to a folder
full of documents.*

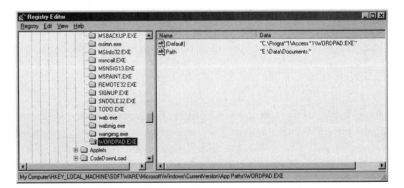

Associating Multiple Extensions with One Application

In Chapter 14 I'll show you how to register new file types with Windows 98. This lets you set up an association between an extension and an application. For example, to handle the

README.1ST text files that come with some programs, you could associate the .1ST extension with Notepad. This creates a new 1ST file type.

The problem with this approach, however, is that it involves re-creating the wheel by having to set up certain actions—such as Open and Print—for the new file type. In the 1ST file type, for example, the actions you set up are identical to those that are already set up for the Text Document file type. It would be better if you could just augment an existing file type with a new extension, such as adding the .1ST extension to the existing Text Document file type.

You know this is possible because if you look through the list of file types (in Explorer, select View | Folder Options and activate the File Types tab), you see that several file types have multiple extensions. The Movie Clip file type, for example, has several extensions, including .MPEG and .MPG. Unfortunately, there's no way you can use the File Types tab to add an extension to an existing file type.

However, you can do this via the Registry. Here are the steps to follow:

1. In the Registry Editor, open HKEY_CLASSES_ROOT.

2. Find the extension subkey for the file type you want to work with. For the Text Document file type, for example, find the .txt subkey.

3. Make a note of the value of the extension subkey's Default setting. For example, the Default setting for the .txt subkey is txtfile.

4. Highlight HKEY_CLASSES_ROOT and add a key for the new extension. In the 1ST extension example, you'd add a key named .1st.

5. For this new key, change the Default setting to the value you noted in step 3, as shown in Figure 13.7.

13

SOME USEFUL
REGISTRY TWEAKS

FIGURE 13.7.

To associate an extension with an existing file type, you need to add the extension to the Registry.

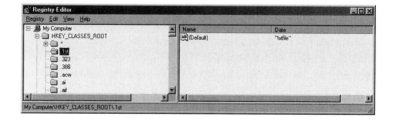

After you've created this new key, it becomes available to Windows 98 immediately. To see for yourself, check out the file type in the File Types tab. You should see the new extension in the File type details group, as shown in Figure 13.8.

FIGURE 13.8.

The new extension shows up in the File Types tab.

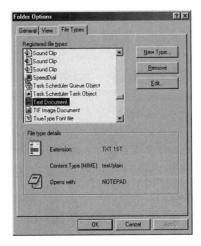

Modifying Windows 98's Desktop Icons

The default icons that populate the Windows 98 desktop are handy, but they can be annoyingly difficult to work with. For example, if you don't use My Computer, Network Neighborhood, or Recycle Bin, there's no way to delete them from the desktop. Also, you can rename all the desktop icons except for the Recycle Bin, which stubbornly refuses all renaming attempts.

Fortunately, all these problems are overcome easily with a few simple tweaks of the Registry. The next few sections show you some tricks for modifying the desktop icons.

Changing the Desktop Icons

If you're getting a bit a tired of seeing the same old icons on your desktop, changing these icons is a nice way to give Windows 98 a quick facelift. You learned in Chapter 6, "Customizing the Taskbar, Start Menu, and Display," that you can use the Icons tab of the Display Properties dialog box to change the icons for My Computer, Network Neighborhood, and the Recycle Bin. For the other desktop icons, you need to use the Registry.

Each desktop icon has a subkey in the following key:

`HKEY_LOCAL_MACHINE\SOFTWARE\Classes\CLSID`

`CLSID` is short for class ID, and each Windows 98 object has its own unique class ID. These are long, 16-byte values that consist of 32 hexadecimal digits arranged in an 8-4-4-4-12 pattern, surrounded by braces ({}). For example, the `CLSID` for My Computer is {20D04FE0-3AEA-1069-A2D8-08002B30309D}, so this is My Computer's Registry key:

`HKEY_LOCAL_MACHINE\SOFTWARE\Classes\CLSID\{20D04FE0-3AEA-1069-A2D8-08002B30309D}`

Table 13.1 lists the `CLSID` values for all the desktop icons.

Table 13.1. CLSID values for the desktop icons.

Desktop Icon	CLSID
My Computer	{20D04FE0-3AEA-1069-A2D8-08002B30309D}
My Documents	{450D8FBA-AD25-11D0-98A8-0800361B1103}
Internet Explorer	{3DC7A020-0ACD-11CF-A9BB-00AA004AE837}
Network Neighborhood	{208D2C60-3AEA-1069-A2D7-08002B30309D}
Set Up The Microsoft Network	{4B876A40-4EE8-11D1-811E-00C04FB98EEC}
Recycle Bin	{645FF040-5081-101B-9F08-00AA002F954E}
My Briefcase	{85BBD920-42A0-1069-A2E4-08002B30309D}

Each desktop icon key contains various subkeys. In particular, you'll find a subkey named `DefaultIcon` that determines the icon used by each object. By changing the `Default` setting in the `DefaultIcon` subkey, you can define new icons for your desktop.

The `DefaultIcon` subkey's `Default` setting always uses the following general value:

IconFile,IconNumber

Here, *IconFile* is the name of a file (plus the path, if the file isn't in the main Windows 98 folder or its System subfolder) that contains one or more icons. Most of the desktop icons use the file `SHELL32.DLL`.

IconNumber is an integer that specifies which icon to use in `IconFile`, in which the first icon is 0. For example, the Network Neighborhood's `DefaultIcon` setting is this:

`shell32.dll,17`

To change the icon, either specify a different icon number in the existing icon file or use a different icon file altogether.

How do you know which files contain which icons? The best way to browse icon files is to create a shortcut, open its properties sheet, select the Shortcut tab, and click the Change Icon button. In the Change Icon dialog box that appears, shown in Figure 13.9, use the File name text box to enter the name of an icon file (such as a DLL, an EXE, or an ICO file) and then press Tab. If you're not sure about which file to try, click the Browse button and choose a file in the dialog box that appears. Here are a few suggestions:

`C:\WINDOWS\SYSTEM\SHELL32.DLL`

`C:\WINDOWS\SYSTEM\PIFMGR.DLL`

`C:\WINDOWS\SYSTEM\USER.EXE`

`C:\WINDOWS\EXPLORER.EXE`

```
C:\WINDOWS\MORICONS.DLL

C:\WINDOWS\PROGMAN.EXE
```

FIGURE 13.9.

Use the Change Icon dialog box to browse the available icons in an icon file.

After you've opened a file, use the Current icon box to browse the available icons. If you see an icon you want to use, you can get its icon number by counting from the first icon, starting at 0, until you get to the icon. Note that you must count *down* each column and work your way across the columns.

Deleting the Recycle Bin

You can delete most of the desktop icons by right-clicking an icon and then clicking Delete. (For the My Documents folder, right-click and then click the Remove from Desktop command.) Unfortunately, both the My Computer icon and the Network Neighborhood icon are permanent fixtures on the desktop, and so they can't be deleted. (However, I'll show you how to hide the Network Neighborhood icon a bit later.)

That just leaves the Recycle Bin, which can only be deleted by using the Registry. All you have to do is delete the appropriate subkey in the CLSID key:

HKEY_LOCAL_MACHINE\SOFTWARE\Classes\CLSID\{645FF040-5081-101B-9F08-00AA002F954E}

Click the desktop and then press F5 to refresh the icons. The Recycle Bin will turn into a folder icon, which you can then delete normally.

EXPORT THE RECYCLE BIN KEY FIRST

Just in case you change your mind down the road, you should export the Recycle Bin's CLSID key before deleting it. To do so, highlight the key and then select Registry | Export Registry File.

Editing the Icon InfoTips

In Windows 98, when you point at any of the System Folder desktop icons, a banner called an InfoTip appears with a brief description of the icon. For example, Figure 13.10 shows the InfoTip that appears when you point at the Internet Explorer icon.

New to **98**

The InfoTip text is stored in the Registry, so you can edit the text to, for example, give further instructions to new users. To work with the InfoTip text, find the CLSID key for the desktop icon. As shown in Figure 13.10, you see an InfoTip setting. Just edit this string value to customize the InfoTip.

FIGURE 13.10.

Each desktop icon has an InfoTip setting that holds the InfoTip text.

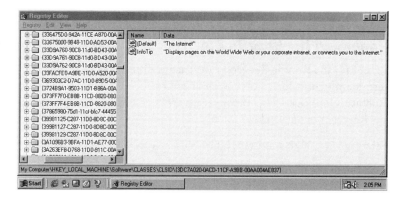

13

SOME USEFUL
REGISTRY TWEAKS

Hiding the Network Neighborhood

Although you can't delete the Network Neighborhood, you can hide it from view by creating a new Registry entry. First, use the Registry Editor to head for the following key:

```
HKEY_USERS\.Default\Software\Microsoft\Windows\CurrentVersion\Policies\Explorer
```

Create a new DWORD value named NoNetHood. If you assign the value 1 to this setting, Windows 98 hides the Network Neighborhood icon. (You need to restart Windows 98 to put this into effect.) To display the Network Neighborhood icon again, set NoNetHood to 0.

Saving Your Desktop Configuration

Have you ever carefully arranged your desktop icons, only to find that Windows 98 has reverted to its previous state? This is frustrating (and, thanks to its intermittent behavior, puzzling), but there is a workaround.

In the Registry Editor, head for the following key:

```
HKEY_CURRENT_USER\Software\Microsoft\Windows\CurrentVersion\Policies\Explorer
```

If you don't see a setting named NoSaveSettings, go ahead and add it as a binary value. Edit this new setting and enter the following value:

```
00 00 00 00
```

With this setting in place, Windows 98 will save your current desktop arrangement each time you shut down or reboot. Exit the Registry Editor, adjust your icons as necessary, and then restart Windows 98.

To tell Windows 98 not to save the desktop arrangement at shutdown, return to the Registry Editor and then change the NoSaveSettings value to the following:

```
01 00 00 00
```

Renaming the Recycle Bin

Except for the Recycle Bin, you can rename all the desktop icons. If the name "Recycle Bin" just doesn't cut it for you, you can assign this icon a new name—Trash Can, Garbage Pail, Rubbish Heap, Last Stop Before Deletesville, or whatever—via the Registry. First, head for the Recycle Bin's CLSID key:

```
HKEY_CLASSES_ROOT\CLSID\{645FF040-5081-101B-9F08-00AA002F954E}
```

To change the name, edit the Default setting for this key. Note, too, that clearing the title from this setting will display the Recycle Bin with no name. To see the change, click the desktop and then press F5 to refresh it.

Using the Registry to Fiddle with Files

Let's turn our attention now to some Registry techniques that operate on files. The next five sections introduce you to various Registry keys that change the way you work with files in Windows 98.

Adjusting Explorer's Refresh Rate

Windows 98 does a pretty good job of updating the Explorer window whenever you use another application to add, delete, or rename files. It sometimes misses some file updates, however, especially if the changes were made at the DOS prompt or with a DOS application. You can always update the Explorer display to show the latest information by selecting View | Refresh or by pressing F5. If, however, you want to make Explorer *really* diligent about keeping its display up-to-date, head for the following Registry key:

```
HKEY_LOCAL_MACHINE\System\CurrentControlSet\control\Update
```

You see a setting named UpdateMode, which controls the Explorer refresh rate. To set this rate at its fastest, change the value of UpdateMode to 0.

Removing the Arrows from Shortcut Icons

If you use shortcuts regularly, you know that Windows 98 displays a small arrow in the lower-left corner of the shortcut icon. If you normally leave "Shortcut to" as part of the shortcut's name, you might prefer not to see the arrow. To tell Windows 98 not to add the arrow to your shortcuts, display the following Registry key:

HKEY_CLASSES_ROOT\lnkfile

In the Settings pane, find the IsShortcut setting and rename it (to, say, IsShortcutNot). Exit the Registry Editor to put this change into effect. (You don't need to restart Windows 98.)

Customizing the System Icons

Most of the Windows 98 system icons—such as those that appear in the Start menu and the default icons that Explorer uses for unknown file types and DOS applications—can be customized. To understand how, let's run through an example. First, use the technique I showed you earlier to browse the icons in Shell32.dll. As you can see in Figure 13.11, the first icon (icon 0) is the one Windows 98 uses in folder windows to display files with unregistered types. Suppose, instead, you want Windows 98 to display the chip icon, which is the one at the top of the fourth column (icon number 12).

FIGURE 13.11.

The SHELL32.DLL *file contains a couple of suitable replacements for the shortcut arrow.*

Icon 12

Icon 0

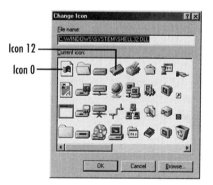

To accomplish this replacement, follow these steps:

1. Use the Registry Editor to display the following key:

   HKEY_LOCAL_MACHINE\SOFTWARE\Microsoft\Windows\CurrentVersion\explorer

2. In the Shell Icons subkey, create a new string value setting named 0. This number corresponds to the position in Shell32.dll of the icon we want to replace.

3. Change the value of the 0 setting to shell32.dll,*n*, in which *n* is the number of the replacement icon you want to use. For this example, you enter shell32.dll,12, as shown in Figure 13.12.

FIGURE 13.12.

You customize the system icons by adding new settings to the Shell Icons *key.*

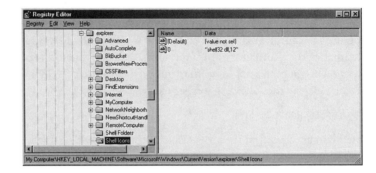

Implementing this change isn't as straightforward as logging on again or restarting Windows 98. The problem is that Windows 98 stores all its system icons in a hidden file named ShellIconCache (you find it in your main Windows 98 folder). The change you just made to the Registry doesn't update this file, and neither does a restart of Windows 98.

To put the change into effect, open the properties sheet for the desktop, select the Appearance tab, and choose Icon from the Item drop-down list. Modify the Size value (it doesn't matter what number you choose), and click Apply. This action refreshes the ShellIconCache file and updates the system icons. Return the Icon item to its original size (you might also need to select Windows Standard from the Scheme drop-down list) and click OK to return the icons to their normal size.

As you might have guessed by now, you can use a similar technique to customize any of Windows 98's system icons. Use the Change Icon dialog box to get the appropriate number for the system icon in Shell32.dll (remember to start counting at 0) and create a string value setting for that number in the Shell Icons key. Change this setting to the icon file and icon number you want to use as a replacement.

To get you started, here are the setting names to use for the icons in the Start menu:

Command	Setting Name
Programs	19
Favorites	43
Documents	20
Settings	21
Find	22
Help	23
Run	24
Log Off	44
Suspend	25

Command	Setting Name
Eject PC	26
Shut Down	27

Using a Bitmap File's Own Image as Its Icon

Because bitmap files are associated with Paint, they're displayed in Explorer with Paint's icon. Wouldn't it be nice if, rather than the generic Paint icon, each bitmap file used its own image as its icon? With the Registry, all things are possible.

Open the following Registry key:

```
HKEY_CLASSES_ROOT\Paint.Picture\DefaultIcon
```

The `Default` setting for this key should have the following value:

```
C:\Progra~1\Access~1\MSPAINT.EXE,1
```

This is telling Windows 98 to use the generic Paint icon. Change this setting to `%1`. With this value, each BMP file uses its built-in icon handler to generate its own icon. This technique is normally used with EXE files that have icons imbedded inside them. Because a BMP file doesn't have an embedded icon, it just uses its own image.

After you've changed the `Default` setting, the new value goes into effect immediately. Switch to Explorer and select View | Refresh to update the display. For each BMP file, the contents of the file are used as the icon, as shown in Figure 13.13.

FIGURE 13.13.

BMP files generating their own icons.

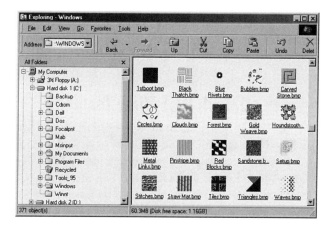

Clearing the MRU List in the Run Dialog Box

One of the features I hated most about Windows 3.*x* was the inability of the Run commands in Program Manager and File Manager to remember commands you entered previously. Thankfully,

13

SOME USEFUL
REGISTRY TWEAKS

Windows 98 remedied that bit of brain-deadness by building a memory into the Start menu's Run command. This "memory" is actually the following Registry key:

`HKEY_CURRENT_USER\Software\Microsoft\Windows\CurrentVersion\Explorer\RunMRU`

Here, MRU stands for Most Recently Used. As you can see in Figure 13.14, this key is just a list of commands that have been entered into the Run dialog box. Notice how each command is assigned a letter. The MRUList setting at the bottom determines the order in which commands appear by arranging these letters in the order you entered each command.

FIGURE 13.14.

The list of commands in the Run dialog box is given by the RunMRU Registry key.

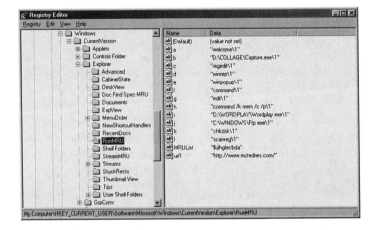

The Run feature will remember up to the last 26 commands you entered (because there are 26 letters in the alphabet). That's a lot of commands to wade through, so you might want to clear the MRU list from time to time and start fresh. To do so, delete every one of the lettered settings in the RunMRU key, as well as the MRUList setting (don't touch the (Default) setting, however).

Changing the Default Web View Templates

In Chapter 5, "Web Integration and the Active Desktop," I showed you how Windows 98 uses HTT files as templates for various folder Web views. For example, the file `\Web\Folder.htt` is used as the default template to display any folder in Web view. The name and location of these template files are stored in the Registry. This means you could create a custom HTT file, store it in a separate location (such as a shared folder on a server), and then change the appropriate Registry setting to point to that file.

For example, the default path and filename for the folder template is given by the `PersistMoniker` setting in the following Registry key (see Figure 13.15):

`HKEY_CLASSES_ROOT\Directory\shellex\ExtShellFolderView\`
➥`{5984FFE0-28D4-11CF-AE66-08002B2E1262}`

FIGURE 13.15.

The Registry stores the default path and filename for the folder Web view templates.

Edit the `PersistMoniker` setting to point to the new location and filename.

For Control Panel, edit the `PersistMoniker` setting in the following key:

```
HKEY_CLASSES_ROOT\CLSID\{21EC2020-3AEA-1069-A2DD-
08002B30309D}\shellex\ExtFolderViews\</DIV><DIV>{5984FFE0-28D4-11CF-AE66-
➥08002B2E1262}<DIV>
```

For My Computer, edit the `PersistMoniker` setting in the following key:

```
HKEY_CLASSES_ROOT\CLSID\{20D04FE0-3AEA-1069-A2D8-
08002B30309D}\shellex\ExtFolderViews\</DIV><DIV>{5984FFE0-28D4-11CF-AE66-
➥08002B2E1262}</DIV>
```

Customizing the Windows 98 Interface

As you learned in Chapter 12, Windows 98 uses the Registry to store the current values of the various Control Panel settings. Of course, you can use the Registry Editor to edit these values directly, although you usually are better off using the dialog boxes and controls that the Control Panel icons give you.

Plenty of customization keys and settings in the Registry, however, can't be modified via the Control Panel. The next few sections show you a few of them.

Creating a Desktop Pattern Without a Mouse

In Chapter 6, I showed you how to create your own desktop pattern. Unfortunately, you have to use a mouse to create a custom pattern in the desktop properties sheet. The Registry, however, lets mouse-averse users create a cool pattern (albeit not quite as intuitively).

The secret to doing this can be found in the following Registry key:

```
HKEY_CURRENT_USER\Control Panel\desktop
```

When you apply a pattern to the desktop, this key contains a `Pattern` setting that's a string value consisting of eight numbers. These digits are a numeric representation of the pattern.

For example, consider the Circuits pattern shown in Figure 13.16. As you can see, the `Pattern` setting represents this pattern with the string `82 41 132 66 148 41 66 132`. To see how Windows 98 derives these numbers, recall that each pattern is an 8×8 array of pixels. Each pixel is either "on" (that is, black) or "off" (that is, the desktop color). The following grid shows the On/Off values that make up the Circuits pattern:

Off	On	Off	On	Off	Off	On	Off
Off	Off	On	Off	On	Off	Off	On
On	Off	Off	Off	Off	On	Off	Off
Off	On	Off	Off	Off	Off	On	Off
On	Off	Off	On	Off	On	Off	Off
Off	Off	On	Off	On	Off	Off	On
Off	On	Off	Off	Off	Off	On	Off
On	Off	Off	Off	Off	On	Off	Off

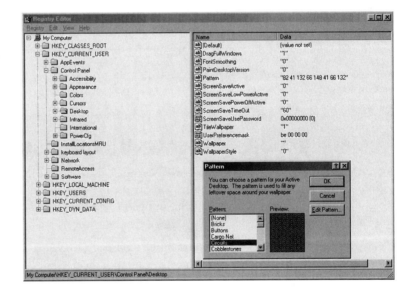

Figure 13.16.

Desktop patterns are represented in the Registry as a string of numbers.

In computing circles, however, "on" is usually represented by a 1, and "off" is usually represented by a 0. So you can rewrite the preceding grid as the following series of 1s and 0s:

```
01010010
00101001
10000100
01000010
10010100
00101001
01000010
10000100
```

Each of these rows, however, can be read as a binary number. Now try this little experiment:

1. Select Start | Programs | Accessories | Calculator.

2. Select View | Scientific to display the Scientific view (if it's not already displayed).

3. Activate the `Bin` option.

4. Enter the first row—`01010010`—into the readout.

5. Activate the `Dec` option. The binary number you entered changes to `82` in decimal format. If you look back at Figure 13.15, you'll see that `82` is the first number of the `Pattern` setting.

If you repeat steps 3 through 5 for the other rows, you see that their decimal equivalents are all in the `Pattern` setting. In other words, the `Pattern` setting uses decimal values to represent the binary nature of the pattern.

So to create your own pattern, you need only adjust the `Pattern` setting. The best way to do this is to create an 8×8 grid, fill it with 1s and 0s in a pattern that looks interesting, and use Calculator to convert the resulting binary numbers in decimal values that you can use with the `Pattern` setting

Disabling Window Animation

One of the pet peeves many new users had with Windows 3.*x* was that they would click a window's Minimize button (accidentally or otherwise) and the window would "disappear." They didn't realize that it was still there, just minimized as an icon at the bottom of the screen.

To help these users, Microsoft decided to "animate" windows as they were minimized to the taskbar. In other words, when you click the Minimize button in Windows 98, the window's title bar flashes quickly, and then you see the window retreating to the taskbar. (You get the same show when you restore the window from the taskbar.) This is called window animation, and it's a real help to novice users because they can follow the window down to the taskbar.

The rest of us, however, know where the window goes when we click the Minimize button, so we don't need to bother with the animation. To have your windows snap into place, you can turn off window animation by using the Registry.

The place to be is the following key:

```
HKEY_CURRENT_USER\Control Panel\desktop\WindowMetrics
```

Create a new string value setting called `MinAnimate`, and then change the value of this setting to 0. Exit the Registry Editor and restart Windows 98 (or log on again) to set up the change.

Playing with Button Shadows

In Chapter 6 I showed you how to use the desktop properties sheet to modify Windows 98's colors. A few objects can't have their colors modified with this method. They're in the Registry, however, so you can work with them there.

Windows 98's 3D objects appear with either a "raised" or a "sunken" effect. Command buttons, for example, appear raised, whereas text boxes appear sunken. These effects are achieved by small strips of color around each object. On the top and left side of a raised object are, for example, a strip of light gray and a strip of white; on the bottom and right side are a strip of dark gray and a strip of black. Sunken objects use an opposite color scheme. These colors are controlled by settings in the following Registry key:

```
HKEY_CURRENT_USER\Control Panel\Colors
```

THE Colors SUBKEY MIGHT NOT APPEAR

The Colors subkey appears only if you've modified Windows 98's colors via the desktop properties sheet. If you don't see the Colors subkey, open the desktop properties sheet, select the Appearance tab, change the color of any object, and click Apply. Change the color back and click OK. When you're back in the Registry, select View | Refresh to see the Colors subkey.

As you can see in Figure 13.17, this key has many settings that hold the RGB color values of various objects. In particular, four settings control the color of the strips around 3D objects. Table 13.2 lists these settings and shows their default values. For something a bit different, you can reverse the raised and sunken objects by using the values in the Reversed column of the table. Figure 13.18 shows the result (you need to restart Windows 98 to put the new colors into effect).

FIGURE 13.17.

The Colors key uses RGB values to store the color of various Windows 98 objects.

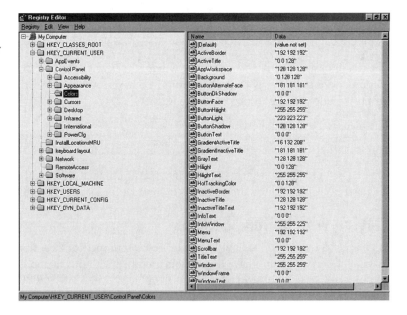

Table 13.2. Color settings for 3D objects.

Setting	Default	Reversed
ButtonDkShadow	0 0 0 (black)	255 255 255
ButtonHiLight	255 255 255 (white)	0 0 0
ButtonLight	223 223 223 (light gray)	128 128 128
ButtonShadow	128 128 128 (dark gray)	223 223 223

FIGURE 13.18.

An interesting effect created by switching the color values for the settings that create 3D objects.

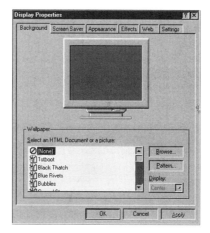

What do you do if you want to try other colors, but you don't know the appropriate RGB values? Windows 98 has a color picker that can help you. Open the desktop properties sheet, select the Appearance tab, drop down either Color list, and click Other. The Color dialog box is displayed. Click a color you like and then use the Red, Green, and Blue text boxes to make a note of the RGB value.

Getting Better Double-Clicking

In Chapter 8, "Customizing the Mouse, Keyboard, and Other Input Devices," I showed you how to customize various aspects of your electronic rodent. In particular, I showed you how to modify the double-click speed so that Windows 98 is better able to recognize your double-clicks. If Windows 98 is still balking at some of your double-clicks, or if you're administering novice users who are complaining about this situation, the problem might not be the double-click speed. You see, Windows 98 actually uses two criteria to differentiate between a double-click and two single-clicks:

- ■ The time between the two clicks (the double-click speed).

- ■ The distance between the two clicks. If you move the mouse more than a few pixels between each click, Windows 98 interprets the action as two single-clicks. I'll call this the "double-click distance."

The latter criterion is often the real cause of misinterpreted double-clicks for novice users who are still a little unsteady with the mouse. To give them more room to maneuver, you can use the Registry to increase the double-click distance. Begin by highlighting the following key in the Registry Editor:

```
HKEY_CURRENT_USER\Control Panel\desktop
```

Now create two new string value settings: `DoubleClickHeight` and `DoubleClickWidth`. These settings specify how far the mouse pointer is allowed to travel (in pixels) between each click. I'd suggest starting with values of 10 for each setting and experimenting from there.

Setting the Number of Lines Scrolled with the IntelliMouse Wheel

If you have an IntelliMouse—the mouse with the wheel in the middle—Windows 98 enables you to scroll up and down within a list or window by rotating the wheel forward and back. The default number of lines scrolled is three with each discrete movement of the wheel. To change the number of lines, head once again to the following key in the Registry Editor:

```
HKEY_CURRENT_USER\Control Panel\desktop
```

Create a new string value called `WheelScrollLines` and set it to the number of lines you want to scroll. You need to restart Windows 98 (or log on again) to put this into effect.

Customizing Some Setup Settings

To finish this look at Registry tricks and secrets, I'll close with a couple of techniques for modifying some of the settings you specified during Setup.

Changing Your Registered Name and Company Name

During the Windows 98 installation process, Setup may have asked you to enter your name and, optionally, your company name. (If you upgraded from Windows 95, this data was recorded when you ran the Windows 95 Setup program.) These "registered names" appear in several places as you work with Windows 98:

- If you right-click My Computer and select Properties (or open the System icon in Control Panel), your registered names appear in the General tab of the System Properties dialog box.

- If you select Help | About in just about any Windows 98 accessory or folder, your registered names appear in the About dialog box.

- If you install a 32-bit application, the installation program uses your registered names for its own records (although you usually get a chance to make changes).

With these names appearing in so many places, what do you do if you change one of the names? Why, head for the Registry, of course. In particular, make tracks to the following key:

```
HKEY_LOCAL_MACHINE\SOFTWARE\Microsoft\Windows\CurrentVersion
```

This key has two settings that store your registered names: `RegisteredOrganization` and `RegisteredOwner`. Use these settings to tell Windows 98 that you want to use different registered names.

Changing the Windows 98 Source Path

When you install Windows 98, Setup makes a note of the disk drive you used for the source CD-ROM or floppy disks. Later, when you add new Windows 98 applets or adjust your hardware, Windows 98 prompts you to insert a source disk in the same drive. You might, however, need to change this source path:

■ You might have used floppies for the original installation and now have the CD-ROM.

■ You might have used the CD-ROM originally, but now your CD-ROM is using a different disk drive.

■ You might have copied the Windows 98 source files to a hard disk or Zip disk.

For all these situations, you can let Windows 98 know that the source path has changed. In the Registry Editor, highlight the following key:

`HKEY_LOCAL_MACHINE\SOFTWARE\Microsoft\Windows\CurrentVersion\Setup`

Find the `SourcePath` setting and change it to the new path. For example, if you installed Windows 98 originally from floppies in drive A, the `SourcePath` setting will be `A:\`. If you now have the CD-ROM and your CD-ROM drive is drive D, change SourcePath to `D:\WIN95`.

Summary

This chapter put your hard-won knowledge from Chapter 12 to good use by showing you a few practical tips and tricks for modifying the Registry. I showed you how to customize the New menu, create application-specific paths, modify the desktop icons, change various file settings, customize the Windows 98 interface, and make a couple of post-Setup alterations. All in all, not a bad day's work.

I'll be using the Registry throughout the rest of this book, but here are a couple of related chapters you might want to check out:

■ The TweakUI utility offers an easier front-end for some Registry changes. I tell you about it in Chapter 6, "Customizing the Taskbar, Start Menu, and Display."

■ For a refresher course in Registry theory and techniques, Chapter 12, "Getting to Know the Windows 98 Registry," is the place to be.

■ To learn about file types, see Chapter 14, "File and Folder Tricks and Techniques."

III

PART

IN THIS PART

Unleashing Files, Folders, and Disks

File and Folder Tricks and Techniques

CHAPTER

14

Is not the whole world a vast house of assignation of which the filing system has been lost?

—Quentin Crisp

Education might take as its foundation the three Rs (reading, 'riting, and 'rithmetic), but for Windows 98, it's the three Fs: files, folders, and floppy (or fixed) disks. When you're not slaving away in your applications, you'll spend a good chunk of your Windows 98 life working with at least one of these "f-words."

This chapter covers two of those three topics: files and folder. I'll begin with a few basics for those who are new to Windows Explorer. From there, I'll head into some unabashed ringing of bells and blowing of whistles in Windows Explorer, followed by detailed looks at a few other Windows 98 tools, including Find and the Recycle Bin.

First, a Few File and Folder Fundamentals

If you're new to Windows or if you upgraded to Windows 98 from Windows 3.*x*, you need to spend some time with Windows Explorer so the two of you can get to know each other. After all, as a Windows power user, you'll find that Windows Explorer is one of the most indispensable tools in the Windows 98 package. To that end, this section gives you a quickie introduction to Windows Explorer and runs through a few basic techniques.

The first thing we need to get clear is that in Windows 98 the differences between Windows Explorer—the file management tool—and Internet Explorer—the Web browser—are blurred. That is, each program is capable of displaying both local resources (disks and folders) and remote resources (Web pages on an intranet or the Internet).

To demonstrate this, launch both programs and display drive C, as follows:

- For Windows Explorer, select Start | Programs | Windows Explorer. Figure 14.1 shows Windows Explorer displaying the contents of drive C.
- For Internet Explorer, click The Internet on the desktop or select Start | Programs | Internet Explorer | Internet Explorer. In the Address toolbar, type c:\ and press Enter. Figure 14.2 shows Internet Explorer displaying drive C.

Internet Explorer is useful for quick views of local folders and for simple file maintenance chores. However, Windows Explorer offers a more comprehensive and easily navigated view of your computer, and it also offers more file management tools. So this chapter focuses exclusively on Windows Explorer (which I'll refer to as just "Explorer" throughout the rest of this chapter).

FIGURE 14.1.

Windows Explorer displaying the contents of drive C.

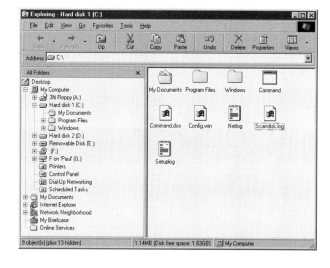

FIGURE 14.2.

The Internet Explorer Web browser can also display local resources, such as drive C shown here.

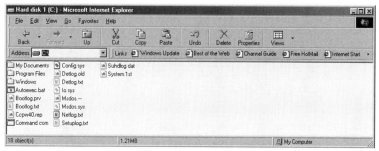

Exploring the Explorer Window

On the surface, Explorer's layout is reminiscent of File Manager. The window is split in two: On the left, Explorer's All Folders list is comparable to File Manager's directory tree, and on the right, Explorer's Contents list is basically the same as File Manager's contents list. There are, however, two significant differences between the two:

■ File Manager's drive icons are gone. Instead, the All Folders list in Explorer includes disk drives (as well as a few other goodies, such as the Network Neighborhood).

■ Explorer isn't a Multiple Document Interface (MDI) application. So, unlike with File Manager, you can't open multiple windows for different drives or folders. This sounds like a drawback, and it feels like one at first if you're used to the File Manager's way of doing things. But Explorer's All Folders list has some slick navigation options that render the lack of multiple window support moot. And, besides, if you *really* need to open a second window, you can always start a second copy of Explorer.

Navigating the All Folders List

The job of the All Folders list is to display (and let you work with) all the folders to which your system has access. Remember that the desktop is the main folder for your system. If you think of the desktop as a sort of "root" folder, it makes sense that Explorer shows a "Desktop" folder at the top of the All Folders list. From there, the Desktop folder's subfolders branch out in that multilevel, "upside-down tree" layout that you might be used to from File Manager.

THE DESKTOP DIFFERENCE

In this section, I want to distinguish between the desktop proper and the Desktop's folder in Explorer. To do this, I use "desktop" when I'm speaking of the actual desktop (as I've done throughout this book), and I use "Desktop" when I'm speaking of the folder.

The first "branch" is the My Computer folder. It shows, among a few other things, the various disk drives attached directly to your machine (either attached physically or attached via a network connection). Yes, this is the same My Computer folder that appears if you click My Computer on the desktop, but in a slightly different guise. Below My Computer, the Desktop folder's other first-level branches include a few more folders, depending on what's installed on your system. (At the very least, you see the My Documents and Recycle Bin folders.)

Navigating among the visible folders is straightforward: Either click a folder or use the up- and down-arrow keys to move through the folders. Whenever you highlight a folder, its contents (subfolders and files) appear automatically in the Contents list.

Explorer's default All Folders list displays the subfolders for both My Computer and drive C. To open any other folders, either click the plus sign (+) to the left of the folder name, or highlight the folder and press the plus sign on the keyboard's numeric keypad. The plus sign then changes to a minus sign (–) to indicate an open branch. Closing a folder is just as easy: Either click the minus sign or highlight the folder and press the minus sign key on the numeric keypad.

EXPLORER'S PLUS SIGNS CAN BE DECEIVING

Explorer is a bit lazy; it doesn't check all the folders associated with disk drives to see whether they have subfolders. (Actually, this is to save time when Explorer starts.) This means that it places a plus sign beside every folder (except the ones that are open, of course). If you click a plus sign for a drive or folder that doesn't have any subfolders, Explorer clues in and simply removes the plus sign.

Here's a summary of a few more techniques you can use to navigate folders:

- To display the parent of the current folder, either click the Up button in the toolbar or select Go | Up One Level.

- To return to the previous folder you viewed, either click the Back button or select Go | Back.

- To return to any previously viewed folder, click the Back button's arrow to drop down a list of the folders you've visited, as shown in Figure 14.3. Then click the folder you want to display.

FIGURE 14.3.

Drop down the Back button's list to return to a previously viewed folder.

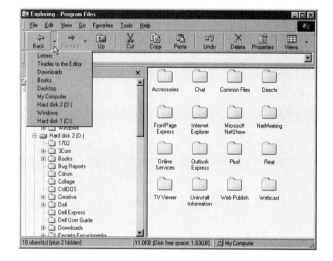

- After you've gone back to a folder, you can use the Forward button to head in the opposite direction. To move ahead to the next folder, either click the Forward button or select Go | Forward. You can also click the Forward button's arrow to see a list of folders.

- The File menu also keeps track of the last few folders you visited. To head for a recent folder, pull down the File menu and select one of the folder names that appear near the bottom of the menu.

- You can set up commonly accessed folders as "favorites." To do this, display the folder, select Favorites | Add to Favorites, and then click OK in the dialog box that appears. To navigate to that folder, pull down the Favorites menu and select the folder name. (Note, too, that in Windows 98 the Favorites folder is also available from the Start menu. See Chapter 33, "Exploring the Web with Internet Explorer," to learn more about the Favorites folder.)

14

FILE AND FOLDER TRICKS AND TECHNIQUES

Working with the Contents List

The job of the Contents list is to show you what's inside whatever folder is currently highlighted in the All Folders list. This means you see not only the files that the folder contains, but all its subfolders as well. When you first open Explorer, the Contents list shows the contents of drive C.

For example, Figure 14.4 shows the Contents list with the Windows folder highlighted. The first 30 or so items are subfolders (as evidenced by their folder icons), and the rest of the entries are files. (The icon that Explorer displays depends on the file and, in the case of documents, the program used to create the file.) Notice, too, that the status bar supplies you with a few tidbits of information:

- The number of objects (subfolders and files) in the folder
- The number of hidden objects
- The number of megabytes used by the files (this value doesn't count the files in the subfolders)
- The amount of free space left on the drive

FIGURE 14.4.

The contents of the Windows folder.

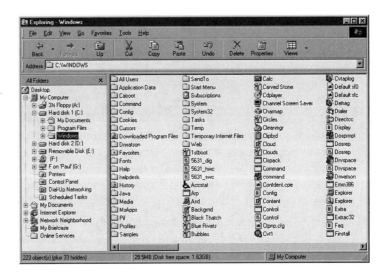

Are you wondering why most of the files in Figure 14.4 don't have an extension? That's because, by default, Explorer hides the extensions for file types that are "registered" with Windows 98 (which is similar to the file associations you might have worked with in File Manager). For example, BMP files are registered (associated) with the Paint accessory. So instead of showing the .BMP extension, Explorer displays each BMP file with the Paint program's icon. In Figure 14.4, take a look at the files named Black Thatch, Blue Rivets, and Bubbles (BMP files all) to see what I mean.

The Contents list layout you see in Figure 14.4 is called the *List view* because it shows a simple columnar list of the folder's contents. You can adjust this view to show more items or to show more detail about each item. Both the View menu and the Views toolbar button offer the following choices:

Large Icons: This view increases the size of the folder and file icons to make them easier to see and displays them across the pane.

Small Icons: In this view, Explorer also displays the objects across the Contents list, but it uses much smaller icons to fit more into the pane.

List: This is the default view for Explorer.

Details: As shown in Figure 14.5, the Details view displays the folder's objects in a single column, and for each item, Explorer shows you the size, type, and date and time the object was created or last modified.

FIGURE 14.5.

The Contents list using the Details view.

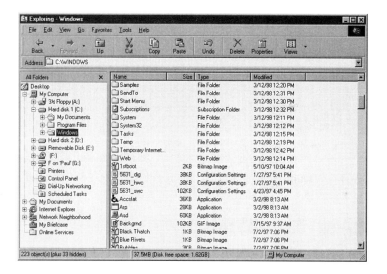

Selecting Multiple Files and Folders

You'll be learning many advanced techniques for dealing with files and folders later in this chapter. For now, though, the next few sections take you through some fundamentals.

To select a single file or folder, use one of the following methods:

■ If Web integration is on, point at the file until it is highlighted. (I described Web integration and how to turn it on and off in Chapter 5, "Web Integration and the Active Desktop.")

■ If Web integration is off, click the file.

New to **98**

If you need to work with multiple files or folders (which, to save some verbiage, I'll just call *objects* throughout this chapter), Explorer has various techniques you can exploit.

With the mouse, you can use three methods to select multiple objects (note that all these techniques apply to the Contents list only):

■ To select noncontiguous objects, hold down the Ctrl key while you select each object.

■ To select contiguous objects, select the first object, hold down the Shift key, and select the last object.

■ You can also select a group of objects by "boxing" them with the mouse. Move the mouse pointer to the right of the first object's name (make sure that it's not over the object's name or icon) and then drag the mouse down and to the left. As you're dragging, Explorer displays a dotted-line box, and every object that falls at least partially within that box gets highlighted. When all the objects you need are highlighted, release the mouse button.

Here's how to select multiple objects from the keyboard (press Tab and Shift+Tab to move between panes):

■ To select every object in the current folder, either run the Edit | Select All command or press Ctrl+A.

■ To select noncontiguous objects, use the arrow keys to highlight the first object and then hold down Ctrl. For each of the other objects you want to select, use the arrow keys to highlight the object (actually, it's not a true highlight, just a dotted-line box) and then press the Spacebar. When you're done, release Ctrl.

■ To select contiguous objects, highlight the first object, hold down Shift, and use the arrow keys to highlight the other objects.

Copying Files and Folders

One of the things that often has former Windows 3.*x* people scratching their heads when they start using Explorer is that the File menu has no Copy command (as it did in File Manager). Instead, in keeping with Windows 98's OLE-centric architecture, you copy files and folders by using a copy-and-paste technique, as though the object were a chunk of data (which is exactly how OLE views a file). That is, you make a copy of an object by copying it to the Clipboard, selecting the destination, and pasting the object from the Clipboard.

Given this background, it makes more sense then that the Copy command is on Explorer's Edit menu. Here's how to copy an object:

1. Select the object or objects you want to copy.

2. Run the Edit | Copy command.

FASTER COPYING

You can also send the selected objects to the Clipboard by pressing Ctrl+C, by clicking the Copy button in the toolbar, or by right-clicking any selected object and choosing Copy from the context menu.

3. Move to the destination folder.
4. Select Edit | Paste.

FASTER PASTING

You can also paste the copied objects from the Clipboard by pressing Ctrl+V, by clicking the Paste button in the toolbar, or by right-clicking inside the destination folder and choosing Paste from the context menu.

Moving Files and Folders

Moving an object is similar to copying it. In this case, though, you "cut" the object to the Clipboard and paste it to the destination folder:

1. Select the object or objects you want to move.
2. Run the Edit | Cut command.

FASTER CUTTING

You can also cut the selected objects by pressing Ctrl+X, by clicking the Cut button in the toolbar, or by right-clicking any selected object and choosing Cut from the context menu.

3. Move to the destination folder.
4. Select Edit | Paste.

Copying and Moving with Drag-and-Drop

For most copy and move operations, you might find that using the mouse to drag the selected objects to their destination folder is much easier. First make sure that the destination folder is available in Explorer's All Folders list. (In other words, if the destination folder is a subfolder, open its parent folder so that the destination is visible.) Select the objects you want to copy or move and then use the All Folders list to bring the destination folder into view. (Be sure to use the All Folders list's scroll bars to do this; otherwise, your objects will no longer be selected.)

Depending on whether you want to copy or to move the objects, you might need to hold down a key before you start dragging:

- If you're dragging the objects to a folder on the same drive, Explorer assumes that you're moving the objects. To make Explorer copy the objects, hold down Ctrl while dragging. (When you're copying an object, Explorer appends a small plus sign (+) to the mouse pointer.)

- If you're dragging the objects to a folder on a different drive, Explorer assumes that you're copying the objects. To make Explorer move the objects, hold down Shift while dragging.

- If you're dragging an executable file, Explorer assumes that you want to create a shortcut. To copy the file, hold down Ctrl; to move the file, hold down Shift. (Explorer signifies that it will create a shortcut by appending a small box with an arrow inside it to the mouse pointer.)

Hold down the appropriate key (if any), drag the objects to the destination folder, and drop them.

DRAG-AND-DROP CONVENIENCES

I show you a few techniques for making drag-and-drop easier later in this chapter. See "Drag-and-Drop Revisited."

Renaming Files and Folders

One of Windows 98's nice features is that you can rename objects "in place." In other words, instead of using some sort of "Rename" dialog box (as with File Manager), you just edit the file or folder name directly. To try this, select the object and then select File | Rename.

Explorer creates a text box around the object's name, complete with insertion-point cursor. You can then use the standard text box techniques (arrow keys, Backspace, Delete, and so on) to edit the name. When you're done, press Enter.

FASTER RENAMING

You can also rename an object by selecting it and pressing F2, or by right-clicking the object and choosing Rename from the context menu.

Deleting Files and Folders

Deleting objects you no longer need is easy: Just highlight the objects and then select File | Delete. When Windows 98 asks you to confirm the deletion, click Yes.

FASTER DELETING

You can also delete the selected objects by pressing Delete, by clicking the Delete button in the toolbar, or by right-clicking any selected object and choosing Delete from the context menu. Another handy technique is to drag the object from Explorer and drop it on the Recycle Bin icon.

USE NEW DIALOG BOXES FOR FILE CHORES

If you're using 32-bit applications designed for Windows 95 or Windows 98, these programs come with powerful new Open and Save As dialog boxes. These dialog boxes are like scaled-down versions of Explorer. For example, you can use them to rename files by pressing F2 when a file is highlighted. Also, you can right-click a file and use the context menu to copy, cut, and delete files.

Exploiting Explorer: Shortcut Keys, Customizations, and More

These basic techniques will serve you well in most of your Explorer expeditions, but they represent only the tiniest fraction of what Explorer can do. To help you unleash the true power of Explorer, this section takes a more in-depth look at the program, tells you what options are available, and runs through some techniques that will enable you to exploit Explorer's most valuable resources.

The Expedited Explorer

If your job requires working with a computer regularly, chances are you don't make your living performing file maintenance and management tasks. Instead, your computer productivity is more likely measured by how many memos, letters, spreadsheets, databases, presentations, or graphics you crank out in a day. Because unglamorous file chores usually do little to enhance this core productivity, you want to get them over with as soon as possible so that you can get back to doing some real work. To that end, the next few sections show you a few tools and techniques that will help put file finagling in the fast lane.

14

FILE AND FOLDER
TRICKS AND
TECHNIQUES

The Economical Explorer Keyboard

If you don't feel like reaching all the way over to your mouse, or if you're just an old keyboard die-hard like me, you'll be happy to know that there's no shortage of keyboard time-savers for Explorer. Table 14.1 lists them all.

Table 14.1. Explorer keyboard shortcuts.

Key	What It Does
+	Opens the next level of folders below the current folder. Use the + on the numeric keypad.
−	Closes the current folder. Use the − on the numeric keypad.
*	Opens all levels of folders below the current folder. Use the * on the numeric keypad.
Alt+Enter	Displays the properties sheet for the selected objects.
Alt+F4	Closes Explorer.
Alt+left arrow	Takes you back to a previously displayed folder.
Alt+right arrow	Takes you forward to a previously displayed folder.
Backspace	Takes you to the parent folder of the current folder.
Ctrl+A	Selects all the objects in the current folder.
Ctrl+arrow key	Scrolls up, down, left, or right (depending on the arrow key used) without losing the highlight on the currently selected objects.
Ctrl+C	Copies the selected objects to the Clipboard.
Ctrl+V	Pastes the most recently cut or copied objects from the Clipboard.
Ctrl+X	Cuts the selected objects to the Clipboard.
Ctrl+Z	Reverses the most recent action.
Delete	Sends the currently selected objects to the Recycle Bin.
F2	Renames the selected object.
F3	Displays the Find dialog box with the current folder as the default.
F4	Opens the Address toolbar's drop-down list.
F5	Refreshes the Explorer window. This is handy if you've made changes to a folder via the command line or a DOS program and you want to update the Explorer window to display the changes.
F6	Cycles the highlight among the All Folders list, the Contents list, and the Address toolbar. Tab does the same thing.
Shift+Delete	Deletes the currently selected objects without sending them to the Recycle Bin.

Key	What It Does
Shift+F10	Displays the context menu for the selected objects.
Tab	Cycles the highlight among the All Folders list, the Contents list, and the Address toolbar. F6 does the same thing

MICROSOFT NATURAL KEYBOARD SHORTCUTS

If you have a Microsoft Natural Keyboard (or a compatible keyboard), the Windows logo key (⊞) gives you two Explorer-related shortcuts: Press ⊞+E to start Explorer; press ÿ+F to display the Find dialog box.

DON'T FORGET THE CONTEXT MENUS

Another way to get quick access to many Explorer commands and features is to right-click the selected object (or objects) and select the command you need from the context menu that appears. I'll show you a couple of ways to customize an object's context menus later in this chapter.

Customizing Explorer's Folder Options

The Windows 98 version of Explorer is quite a bit more "customizable" than its Windows 95 predecessor. To view the available customization options, select View | Folder Options and then activate the View tab in the Folder Options dialog box (see Figure 14.6) that appears.

New to 98

14

FILE AND FOLDER TRICKS AND TECHNIQUES

FIGURE 14.6.

Use the Folder Options dialog box to set up Explorer to suit your taste.

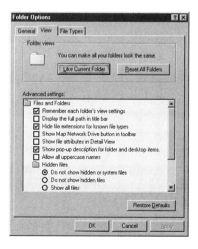

The buttons in the Folder views group enable you to set up a common view for all your folders. The idea is that you first use Explorer's View menu commands to set up the current folder the way you want. Once that's done, display the View tab and click the Like Current Folder button. This tells Windows to apply the current view to all your folders. To revert to the default folder view, click Reset All Folders.

Here's a rundown of the various options that reside in the Advanced Settings list:

Remember each folder's view settings: When this check box is activated, Windows 98 monitors the folder windows you open and keeps track of the view settings (Large Icons, Details, and so on) that you specify. The next time you open a folder window, Windows 98 uses these saved view settings to display the folder's contents.

Display the full path in title bar: If you activate this check box, Explorer displays in the title bar the full path—the drive, the parent folders, and the name—of the current folder. Otherwise, Explorer just displays the name of the current folder.

Hide file extensions for known file types: This check box toggles file extensions on and off for file types that are registered with Windows 98.

FILE TYPES AND FILE EXTENSIONS

A registered file type is a species of file that Explorer, in a sense, "understands." In other words, Explorer knows what program to use to open the file if you click the file. For example, Explorer uses Notepad to open a file if that file's type is text. How does Explorer know what type of file it's dealing with? It's nothing too sophisticated: Explorer just looks at the file's extension. If the extension is .TXT, Explorer treats the file as a text file. (I'll discuss all this in greater detail later in this chapter; see the section "Working with File Types.")

When Explorer sees that a file is one of its registered types, it hides the extension. This is consistent with Windows 98's document focus: Don't worry about the application that creates a document; just worry about the document itself. So all you need to do is click a filename, and Explorer handles the dirty work of finding the appropriate application, launching it, and loading the document. The extension is unnecessary, and it makes the Explorer display seem less intimidating for beginners. In the absence of the extension, however, Explorer does give you two hints about the file type:

■ Each file type has its own icon, and Explorer displays the appropriate icon for the file's type to the left of the filename.

■ If you use the Details view, the Type column tells you the file's type.

YOU CAN'T CHANGE EXTENSIONS

Hiding the file extensions does, however, have one major drawback: Explorer won't let you change the extension. For example, files ending with .DOC are registered with WordPad.

Suppose that you have a file named README.TXT that you'd prefer to open in WordPad (for example, because the file is too big for Notepad's britches). All you have to do is rename the file to README.DOC, right? Not so fast. If file extensions are hidden, Explorer displays README.TXT as just README. If you change this to README.DOC, Explorer actually renames the file to README.DOC.TXT, and Notepad remains the default application!

If you want to rename a file's extension, you have to deactivate the Hide file extensions for known file types check box to force Explorer to display the extensions. Note, however, that if you change the extension for a registered file type, Explorer displays a warning dialog box. You need to click Yes to continue with the rename. (I'll show you how to create new file types later.)

Show Map Network Drive button in toolbar: If you activate this check box, Explorer adds two new buttons to the toolbar. Click the Map Network Drive button to map the current network resource as a drive on your system. Click the Disconnect Network Drive button to unmap a network resource. See Chapter 29, "Working with Network Resources."

Show file attributes in Detail View: Activating the check box adds an extra Attributes column to the Detail view. This column displays letters that represent the attributes for a folder or file: *R* for read-only, *H* for hidden, *A* for archive, and *S* for system.

CHANGING ATTRIBUTES

To change the attributes of a folder or file, either highlight the file and select File | Properties, or right-click the file and click Properties in the context menu. In the properties sheet that appears, use the various Attributes check boxes to set or remove attributes. For example, to remove the hidden attribute from a file, deactivate the Hidden check box. Click OK when you're done.

Show pop-up description for folder and desktop items: I mentioned in Chapter 13, "A Few Good Hacks: Some Useful Registry Tweaks," that some Windows 98 icons—particularly those on the desktop and in the Control Panel—have an associated InfoTip that pops up when you point at them. This check box toggles those InfoTips on and off.

Allow all uppercase names: When this check box is deactivated, Explorer displays all uppercase filenames with only the first letter as uppercase. To display all uppercase filenames, activate this check box.

Hidden files: These three options determine which files Explorer displays:

Do not show hidden or system files: This option prevents Explorer from displaying files that have their hidden or system attribute set.

Do not show hidden files: This option prevents Explorer from displaying files that have their hidden attribute set.

Show all files: This option tells Explorer to display all files.

FILES ARE HIDDEN GLOBALLY

The Hidden files options apply not only to Explorer, but to all your Windows applications. In other words, if hidden or system files aren't displayed in Explorer, they also won't appear in the Open dialog box of any Windows applications.

Hide icons when desktop is viewed as Web page: This check box toggles the desktop's icon layer on and off. That is, when this option is activated, Windows 98 removes the desktop icons when you view the desktop as a Web page.

Smooth edges of screen fonts: If you activate this check box, Windows 98 smoothes the jagged edges of large fonts, which makes them more readable. You need to have your display set up with a color depth of at least high color (16 bits) to use this feature.

Show window contents while dragging: This check box toggles full-window drag on and off. When it's deactivated, Windows 98 shows only the outline of any window you drag with the mouse (by dragging the title bar); if you activate full-window drag, however, Windows 98 displays the window's contents while you're dragging. You need a fast video card to make the full-window drag feature worthwhile.

Sorting Files and Folders

By default, Explorer arranges the objects in the Contents list in ascending alphabetical order, with folders first, followed by files. To change this sort order, select View | Arrange Icons or right-click an empty part of the Contents list and click Arrange Icons in the context menu. The cascade menu that appears gives you five choices:

by Name: This is the default sort order.

by Type: This option sorts the objects in ascending alphabetical order by file type, with folders first.

by Size: This option sorts the objects in ascending numerical order by file size, with folders first.

by Date: This option sorts the objects in ascending order by the last modified date, with folders first.

Auto Arrange: When activated, this command sorts the objects automatically if you move them, add new objects, or resize the window. This command is available only in the Large Icons and Small Icons views.

Notice that each of these commands sorts the objects only in ascending order. What if you'd prefer a descending sort? For example, you might want to sort the objects by last modified date in descending order to show the most recently modified files at the top of the list.

To do this, you need to put Explorer in Details view. As shown in Figure 14.7, Details view displays column headings at the top of the Contents list: Name, Size, Type, and Modified. To sort the objects on a particular column, click the column's heading. For example, clicking the Size heading sorts the objects in ascending order by file size. How do you get a descending sort? Just click the same column heading again.

FIGURE 14.7.

Use the column headings in Details view to sort the Contents list.

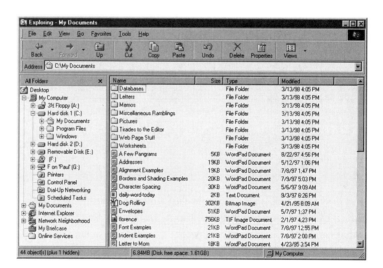

14

FILE AND FOLDER
TRICKS AND
TECHNIQUES

Working with the Details View Columns

When working in Details view, mouse users get a couple of bonus customization techniques:

- To rearrange the columns, drag the column headings left or right.
- To adjust the width of a column, point the mouse at the right edge of the column's heading. The pointer will change to a two-headed arrow. Now drag the pointer left (to get a narrower column) or right (to get a wider column).

Drag-and-Drop Revisited

Explorer's cut-and-paste (or copy-and-paste) file management metaphor takes getting used to, but it makes sense after a while. Still, in most cases, it's usually faster to drag an object from one location and drop it on another. Explorer's drag-and-drop rules can be confusing, however, so Table 14.2 runs through them one more time for good measure.

Table 14.2. Explorer's default drag-and-drop behavior.

Operation	Mouse Pointer While Dragging	Comments
Copy		If the source and destination folders are on the same disk, Explorer copies the object.
Move		If the source and destination folders are on different disks, Explorer moves the object.
Executable file		If the object is an executable file, Explorer creates a shortcut in the destination folder.

You can also force Explorer to copy or move an object or to create a shortcut for any object:

- ■ Hold down Ctrl while you drop the object to force a copy operation.
- ■ Hold down Shift while you drop the object to force a move operation.

If you don't feel like memorizing any of this information, you can perform a special drag instead. In this case, you use the right mouse button to drag the object. When you drop it on the destination folder, Explorer displays the context menu shown in Figure 14.8 (the default action is shown in bold). Now just click the action you want.

SPECIAL-DRAG WITH THE LEFT MOUSE BUTTON

If your mouse doesn't have a right mouse button, or if your right mouse button is broken, you can still do the special drag. Just hold down both Ctrl and Shift and drag the object while holding down the left mouse button. Note that in this case, the default action is always to create a shortcut.

FIGURE 14.8.

If you right-drag an object, Explorer displays this context menu when you drop the object on its destination.

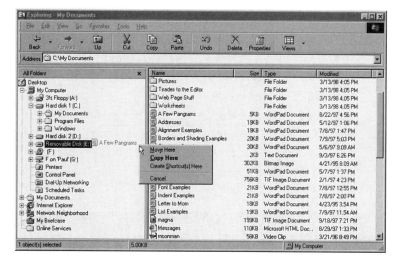

Here are a few drag-and-drop tidbits that should make your object copying and moving a bit easier:

- Don't forget that you can cancel a drag at any time by pressing Esc.

- It's possible to drag and scroll at the same time. For example, what do you do if you drag an object into the All Folders list and then realize you can't see the destination folder? Instead of canceling, drag the object to either the top or the bottom of the All Folders list (depending on where the destination folder is). Explorer either scrolls the folders down (if you're at the top of the pane) or scrolls the folders up (if you're at the bottom of the pane).

- Windows 98's Explorer also enables you to open folder branches in mid-drag. To open a branch, drag the file over to the branch to highlight it. After a couple of seconds, Explorer opens the branch.

- Unlike File Manager, Explorer doesn't let you open two child windows and drag between them. The All Folders list is quite flexible, so you shouldn't need to use multiple windows for drag-and-drop. If you feel more comfortable doing it that way, however, feel free to start a second copy of Explorer and arrange them side-by-side.

- One handy feature that's missing from Windows 98 is the capability of dragging an object onto the taskbar. You get the next best thing, however. If you have a folder window minimized on the taskbar, you can drag an object from Explorer and then let the mouse pointer hover over the folder window's taskbar button for a couple of seconds. Windows 98 then opens the folder window so that you can drop the object into the folder.

New to 98

14

FILE AND FOLDER TRICKS AND TECHNIQUES

HOW DO YOU OPEN A FOLDER WINDOW?

You can use several methods to open a folder in its own window:

■ In Explorer, right-click the folder and select Open from the context menu.

■ Use My Computer to open the folder.

■ Create a desktop shortcut for the folder and open the shortcut. (For more on short-cuts, see "Can I Get There from Here? Working with Shortcuts," later in this chapter.)

■ Select Start | Run to display the Run dialog box, type the folder's full pathname in the Open text box, and click OK.

DRAGGING A FOLDER TO THE RUN DIALOG BOX

If the Run dialog box is open, dragging a folder from Explorer and dropping it anywhere on the Run dialog box pastes the folder's full pathname into the Open text box.

Easier File Finagling with the Send To Command

Copying or moving a file or folder is usually a three-step process: Copy (or cut) the object to the Clipboard, head to the destination folder, and paste the object from the Clipboard. Drag-and-drop is much easier, but it still requires that you have the destination folder in view.

For certain file operations, Explorer offers a method that's much easier than the Clipboard or drag-and-drop: the Send To command. To try this, highlight an object in the Contents list and select File | Send To. You can also right-click an object in the Contents list and then select Send To from the context menu. As you can see in Figure 14.9, the cascade menu that appears offers several possible locations. The choices depend on which Windows 98 components you have installed, but you'll at least see commands for your floppy disks. Selecting a floppy disk from this menu sends a copy of the file to that disk. (Of course, you need to make sure that you have a disk in the drive before you try this.) If you'd prefer to move the file to the floppy disk, hold down Shift while selecting the command from the Send To menu.

An interesting point about the Send To command is that the contents of the Send To cascade menu are shortcut files. For example, if you have a 3½ Floppy (A) command in your Send To menu, this command is just a shortcut to floppy drive A. Selecting this command is identical to dragging the object and dropping it on drive A in the All Folders list.

Now here's the real kicker: The contents of the Send To menu—the shortcut files—come from a special SendTo folder that runs off your main Windows folder. To see for yourself, open the Windows folder and select the SendTo folder, as shown in Figure 14.10. Sure enough, there's a shortcut file for each Send To menu item.

FIGURE 14.9.

The Send To command offers an easy method of copying files to floppy disks and other locations.

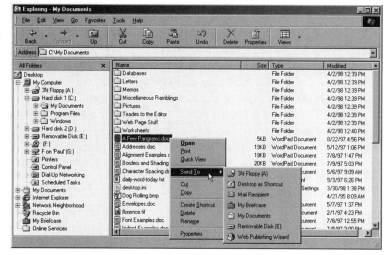

FIGURE 14.10.

The Send To menu items are just shortcut files in the SendTo folder.

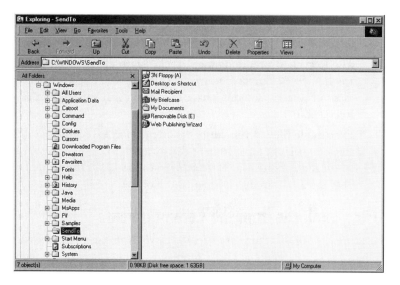

14

FILE AND FOLDER
TRICKS AND
TECHNIQUES

The great thing about this arrangement is that you're free to add your own shortcuts to this folder, and they'll appear on the Send To menu. For example, if you use an Upload folder to store files before sending them out via modem, you could create a shortcut to that folder in the SendTo folder. Similarly, if you like to include shortcuts to programs in your Start menu folders, include these folders in the Send To menu. You could do the same thing for disk drives, network drives, and any other location you use to store files.

SEND TO USES DRAG-AND-DROP RULES

Bear in mind that Send To uses the same rules for copying and moving objects (including executable files) that drag-and-drop does. For example, if the object and the Send To menu item (or, more specifically, the file or folder pointed to by the Send To shortcut) are on the same drive, Send To *moves* the object. Similarly, executable files are always sent to shortcuts. If you want to force a particular operation, use the same Ctrl, Shift, or Ctrl+Shift tricks I showed you earlier for drag-and-drop.

There's no reason why you have to restrict the Send To commands to just folders and disk drives, however. Because you can create shortcuts for just about anything in Windows 98, you can populate the SendTo folder with any number of interesting destinations. I'll talk more about this when I discuss shortcuts in detail later (see "Can I Get There from Here? Working with Shortcuts"), but for now, here are a few examples:

Printers: If you add a printer shortcut to the Send To menu, you can print a document just by sending it to the printer. You find your installed printers in the Printers folder.

The Recycle Bin: Adding the Recycle Bin to the Send To menu is handy if you can't see the Recycle Bin icon on your desktop. It also offers one advantage over deleting files in Explorer: You don't have to confirm that you want to send the object to the Recycle Bin.

Executable files: If you create a shortcut to an executable file on the Send To menu, Explorer will open a document that's sent to the underlying application. For example, if you add a shortcut to Notepad, you can send a text file (even one that doesn't have a .TXT extension) to the shortcut, and Notepad opens with the document loaded.

Using Explorer from the Command Line

For extra control over how Explorer starts, you can use a few command-line options in the Run dialog box or from the DOS command prompt. Here's the syntax:

```
explorer [/n],[/e],[/root,folder,[subobject]],[/select]
```

Here's a summary of the various switches and parameters:

/n	Opens a new Explorer window.
/e	Starts Explorer in Explorer view (that is, with both the All Folders list and the Contents list); if you omit /e, Explorer starts in Open view (that is, with only the Contents list, as with My Computer).
/root,*folder*	Specifies the *folder* that will be the root of the new Explorer view. (In other words, this folder will appear at the top of the All Folders list.)

subobject	Specifies the folder (of which *folder* must be the parent) that will be displayed in the Contents list. For example, if the root is `C:\WINDOWS` and you want the displayed folder to be `C:\WINDOWS\SYSTEM`, use `C:\WINDOWS\SYSTEM` for *subobject*.
`/select`	Specifies that the *folder* specified as the root should be highlighted in the Folders list. If you don't include this switch, the *subobject* folder is highlighted instead.

For example, if you want to open Explorer with `C:\WINDOWS` as the root and you want the `C:\WINDOWS\SYSTEM` folder displayed in the Contents list, use the following command:

```
explorer /n,/e,/root,c:\windows,c:\windows\system
```

DISPLAY THE DESKTOP AS THE ROOT

You can open an Explorer window with the desktop as the root by using the following Explorer command (don't miss the comma at the end):

```
explorer /root,
```

Can I Get There from Here?
Working with Shortcuts

I've mentioned shortcuts a few times in this book, and you saw earlier how shortcuts are invaluable for enhancing the Send To menu. In your quest to unleash Windows 98, you'll find yourself using shortcuts constantly, so it's time we took a step back and looked a little more closely at these handy files. This section explains shortcuts in more detail, runs through all the possible methods of creating them, and shows umpteen ways to put shortcuts to good use.

What Is a Shortcut?

If you used any flavor of Windows 3.*x*, shortcuts will already be familiar to you: They're just like program items (icons) in a Program Manager group. In other words, a shortcut is a pointer to an object, such as an executable file or a document. If it points to an executable, clicking the shortcut starts the underlying program; if it points to a document, clicking the shortcut starts the application associated with the document *and* loads the document (assuming, that is, that the document type is registered with Windows 98—see "Working with File Types" later in this chapter for more info). And, as with a program item, because a shortcut only points to another object (a program or document), you can safely delete a shortcut without affecting the underlying object.

14

FILE AND FOLDER TRICKS AND TECHNIQUES

A very important difference exists, however, between a Windows 98 shortcut and a Program Manager icon: The shortcuts themselves are *files*. (They use the .LNK—for *link*—extension.) This means you can create shortcuts in any folder, and you're free to move or copy shortcuts anywhere you like, including the desktop. (About the only place that's off-limits is the taskbar.)

Also, shortcuts are much more flexible than program items because shortcuts can point to many more object types. So, yes, they can point to executable files and documents, but they can also point to disk drives, folders, printers, and a whole host of useful objects (I'll show you lots of examples a bit later).

When you create a shortcut, you notice that Windows 98 adds an arrow to the lower-left corner of the icon. This is to remind you that the shortcut *points to* another file. Windows 98 also adds the phrase "Shortcut to" to the name of the underlying object. You can rename shortcuts the same way you rename files, so you can delete this extra phrase, if you like.

Methods of Creating Shortcuts

Shortcuts are an important part of the Windows 98 interface, so there's no shortage of methods you can use to create them. Here's a summary:

- Unless you hold down Ctrl (for copy) or Shift (for move), dropping a dragged executable file always creates a shortcut that points to the executable. Note that this applies only to executable files that use the .EXE and .COM extensions; it doesn't work with files with the .BAT (batch) extension.

- To create a shortcut for any dragged file, hold down Ctrl and Shift when you drop the file. In the context menu that appears, select Create Shortcut(s) Here.

- Right-drag a file and, after you drop it on its destination, select Create Shortcut(s) Here from the context menu.

- Right-click a file or folder and select Create Shortcut on the context menu to create a shortcut in the same folder. You can then drag this shortcut to the appropriate destination.

- Copy a file to the Clipboard, highlight the destination, and select Edit | Paste Shortcut.

- In Explorer, highlight a folder and select File | New | Shortcut. (You can also right-click an empty part of the Explorer Contents list and select New | Shortcut from the context menu.) Explorer displays the Create Shortcut dialog box, shown in Figure 14.11. Enter the command line for the underlying file (or use the Browse button) and click Next >. Enter a name for the shortcut and click Finish.

NEW DESKTOP SHORTCUTS

To create a new shortcut on the desktop, right-click an empty part of the desktop and select New | Shortcut from the context menu.

FIGURE 14.11.

*Use the Create Shortcut
Wizard to create a new
shortcut.*

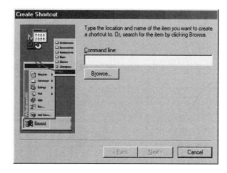

Telling Windows 98 Not to Add Shortcut To

One of the many things Microsoft is working on in its research labs is the problem of how to make software adapt automatically to the needs and preferences of individual users. In Office 97, for example, the Office Assistant watches what you do and occasionally offers help based on your actions.

A bit of this behavior also made it into Windows 98. Specifically, if you start deleting the Shortcut to prefix in your shortcut names, Windows 98 eventually clues in and stops adding Shortcut to for future shortcuts. How does this work? The secret lies inside the Registry at the following key:

```
HKEY_CURRENT_USER\Software\Microsoft\Windows\CurrentVersion\Explorer
```

Here you need to add a new binary setting called link and set the value of link to 00 00 00 00. (I showed you how to create and edit Registry settings in Chapter 12, "Getting to Know the Windows 98 Registry.") Restart Windows 98 (or log off and then back on) and the system will no longer add the "Shortcut to" prefix.

14

FILE AND FOLDER
TRICKS AND
TECHNIQUES

THE TWEAKUI POWER TOY CAN DO IT, TOO

You can also use the TweakUI utility to prevent Windows 98 from adding Shortcut to to your shortcut names. In TweakUI (see Chapter 6, "Customizing the Taskbar, Start Menu, and Display"), display the Explorer tab and then deactivate the Prefix Shortcut to on new shortcuts check box.

Working with Shortcut Properties

As I mentioned earlier, a shortcut is really a LNK file. This means that, like any file object, a shortcut has properties you can manipulate. To view these properties, highlight the shortcut file in Explorer and select File | Properties. You can also right-click the shortcut icon and select Properties from the context menu. In the properties sheet that appears, the General tab gives you basic file information: location, name, size, attributes, and so on. The really interesting stuff is in the Shortcut tab, shown in Figure 14.12.

Figure 14.12.

Use the Shortcut tab to manipulate various properties for a shortcut file.

Here's an explanation of each control that appears on the Shortcut tab:

Target: This text box gives you the full pathname of the object that's linked to the shortcut. If the shortcut points to a document, you might want to adjust the target so that a different application opens the file. In Figure 14.12, for example, I could force WordPad to open the TODOLIST.TXT file by appending the path to WordPad to the front of the target, like so:

```
"C:\Program Files\Accessories\Wordpad.exe" "C:\My Documents\To-Do List.txt"
```

WATCH OUT FOR LONG FILENAMES

I had to put quotation marks around the WordPad path. That's because the path includes a space and the Target box won't accept names that include spaces. You either have to surround the path with quotation marks or use the DOS versions of the name. In the preceding example, the DOS name would look like this

```
C:\PROGRA~1\ACCESS~1\WORDPAD.EXE C:\MYDOCU~1\TO-DOL~1.TXT
```

Start in: If your shortcut starts an application, this text box sets the application's default folder.

Shortcut key: Use this text box to assign a key combination to the shortcut. The default key combo is Ctrl+Alt+*character,* in which *character* is any keyboard character key you press while this text box has the focus. If you prefer a key combination that begins with Ctrl+Shift, hold down both Ctrl and Shift and then press a character; for a Ctrl+Alt+Shift combination, hold down all three keys and then press a character. To help you remember the key combination, you might want to include it as part of the shortcut's name.

Run: If the shortcut starts an application, this drop-down list determines how the application window appears. Select Normal window, Minimized, or Maximized.

Find Target: This command button opens a folder window and highlights the target file or folder. This provides you with a quick way to get to the target object (for example, to make a copy of it).

Change Icon: Use this command button to assign a different icon to the shortcut. (The little arrow in the lower-left corner remains in place, however.) Clicking this button displays the Change Icon dialog box, shown in Figure 14.13. For other icon collections, try the following files (the first one is a hidden file):

```
C:\WINDOWS\SYSTEM\PIFMGR.DLL
C:\WINDOWS\MORICONS.DLL
C:\WINDOWS\PROGMAN.EXE
```

FIGURE 14.13.

Use the Change Icon dialog box to select a different icon for a shortcut.

If You Move, Rename, or Delete the Target

You've just seen that a shortcut points to a specific target. What happens, however, if you move, rename, or delete that target? Let's find out.

If you move or rename the target, Windows 98 tries to find the correct target the next time you invoke the shortcut. Because other files might have the same name as the missing target, Windows 98 doesn't search for the filename. Instead, it uses the original target's size, type, and the date and time it was created, because these attributes are unlikely to be the same for any other file. While it's searching, you see the Missing Shortcut dialog box, shown in Figure 14.14.

FIGURE 14.14.

Windows 98 displays this dialog box when searching for a target that you've moved or renamed.

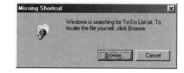

14

FILE AND FOLDER
TRICKS AND
TECHNIQUES

If Windows 98 finds the target, it updates the shortcut and opens the object. If it can't find the target, Windows 98 makes an educated guess and displays a Problem with Shortcut dialog box similar to the one shown in Figure 14.15. If this is the correct target, click Yes; if it's not the correct target, click No, invoke the shortcut again, click the Browse button in the Missing Shortcut dialog box, and use the Open dialog box that appears to select the target.

Figure 14.15.

Windows 98 displays this dialog box if it can't find the original target.

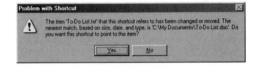

TARGET TROUBLES

Windows 98 doesn't do a good job of finding targets that have been moved to a different drive. Also, if the target exists on a mapped network drive and the drive's letter changes, Windows 98 won't find the target.

If you delete the target, Windows 98 will, of course, fail to find it. In this case, you should click No in the Problem with Shortcut dialog box and then delete the shortcut.

A Cornucopia of Shortcut Ideas and Techniques

Shortcuts are extremely handy time-savers, and you'll find endless uses for them. To get you started, the next few sections run through a few ideas for using shortcuts.

Folders

If you have a favorite folder you often view or use for file storage, a shortcut to the folder is an easy way to work:

- To view the contents of the folder, double-click the shortcut. Windows 98 displays a folder window (similar to the kind you see in My Computer) showing the objects inside the folder.
- If you want to move or copy objects to the folder, just drag them from Explorer (or My Computer) and drop them on the shortcut icon.

If the folder has subfolders, you might prefer to display the folder in "Explorer" view (that is, with the All Folders list and the Contents list). To do this, open the properties sheet for the shortcut, select the Shortcut tab, and add `explorer.exe /e,` (include the comma) to the front of the `Target` value. For example, if the current target is `c:\windows`, the new target should be this:

```
explorer.exe /e,c:\windows
```

Of course, you're free to use any of the Explorer command-line switches that we looked at earlier.

The Start Menu

In Chapter 6 I showed you how to customize your Start menu by adding and removing items in the Start Menu folder. The Start menu itself is easy to customize: You just drag items onto the Start button. However, to add items to the Start menu's subfolders (Programs, Accessories, and so on), you need to display these folders in Explorer. If you plan on using this technique regularly, you can make your life easier by creating desktop shortcuts for the Start menu's subfolders. This way, you get fast access to these folders, and you can add items to them just by dragging them from Explorer and dropping them on the appropriate shortcut.

EACH USER HAS A START MENU FOLDER

If you've set up user profiles on your system (as described in Chapter 6), note that each user gets his or her own Start Menu folder. For example, if you have a user named Biff, you can customize his Start menu by adding shortcuts to the `C:\Windows\Profiles\Biff\Start Menu` folder (assuming that `C:\Windows` is your main Windows 98 folder).

Note that, for each user, the Profiles folder also contains Desktop and SendTo subfolders.

The StartUp Folder

Even if you don't plan on remaking all the Start menu's folders in your own image, there's one folder you almost certainly want to customize: the StartUp folder. This folder controls the objects that appear on the StartUp menu and that, more importantly, load automatically each time you start Windows 98. The path for the StartUp folder is `C:\Windows\Start Menu\Programs\StartUp`.

BYPASSING STARTUP FILES

To tell Windows 98 not to load your StartUp folder objects at boot time, hold down Shift while Windows 98 starts.

Disk Drives

The Macintosh desktop displays an icon for each disk drive on the computer. To give your system a Mac-like feel, create shortcuts for your disk drives on the desktop. The default drag-and-drop operation for a disk drive is to create a shortcut, so you don't have to hold down any keys or right-drag.

One of the nice things about having this shortcut is that you can work with the shortcut as though it were the actual drive. For example, you can right-click a floppy drive shortcut and use the commands on the context menu to format or copy a disk that's in the drive. (These operations are discussed in Chapter 15, "Disk Driving: The Windows 98 Disk Utilities.")

Computers on Your Network

If you're running Windows 98 on a network, you can create shortcuts for those computers that appear in the Network Neighborhood. This applies even to computers you connect to via Dial-Up Networking. In the latter case, invoking the shortcut dials your modem automatically. The default drag-and-drop operation for a computer is to create a shortcut, so you don't have to hold down any keys or right-drag.

Executable Files

Shortcuts to executable files give you an easy way to launch the application (especially if you create a keyboard shortcut). But there's more to an executable shortcut than that. In particular, you can drag a document from Explorer and drop it on the shortcut. As long as the application knows how to deal with the document, the application starts and it displays the document.

This is a useful technique for those file types that don't have a default application. For example, if you want to open CONFIG.SYS in Notepad, normally you have to start Notepad, select File | Open, display all files, and select CONFIG.SYS. If, however, you have a shortcut to NOTEPAD.EXE on your desktop (or wherever), all you have to do is drag CONFIG.SYS and drop it on the shortcut. Notepad starts and it loads CONFIG.SYS automatically.

Documents

Creating document shortcuts is useful only if the document's file type is registered with Windows 98. In this case, clicking the shortcut starts the registered application and loads the document automatically. In Windows 98, this technique works for TXT (text) files, DOC (WordPad document) files, BMP (bitmap) files, HT (HyperTerminal) files, and more. I'll talk about registered file types in detail later, in the section "Working with File Types."

THE DOCUMENTS MENU

Another quick way to open a document is to select Start | Documents. The cascade menu that appears contains shortcuts to the last 15 documents you worked with in any of your applications. Selecting one of these shortcuts opens the appropriate applications and loads the document. These shortcuts are stored in the \Windows\Recent folder, so you can always add and remove Document menu shortcuts by hand.

Document Scraps

For applications that support OLE (object linking and embedding), you can create desktop shortcuts to bits of text or part of a graphics image. Just highlight the data you want to use, drag it from the application, and drop it on the desktop. (The default drag-and-drop operation for an OLE object is to create a shortcut, so you don't have to hold down any keys or right-drag.) Windows 98 creates an OLE object—called a *document scrap*—on the desktop. You can then drop this scrap inside another document or double-click it to start the source application and load the scrap.

Printers

Printers are common shortcuts because they can be quite handy. For one thing, the shortcut gives you easy access to a particular printer so that you can manipulate any pending print jobs (more on this topic in Chapter 21, "Prescriptions for Perfect Printing"). For another, you can drag a document from Explorer and drop it on the printer shortcut, and Windows 98 then prints the document automatically. Use the Printers folder to drag a printer onto the desktop (or wherever). The default drag-and-drop operation for a printer is to create a shortcut, so you don't have to hold down any keys or right-drag.

Control Panel Icons

If you have any Control Panel icons you use regularly, creating a shortcut to the icon is much faster than having to display the Control Panel folder. (I showed you other methods of getting easier access to Control Panel icons in Chapter 6.) To create the shortcuts, drag the icons from the Control Panel folder and drop them on the desktop. The default drag-and-drop operation for a Control Panel icon is to create a shortcut, so you don't have to hold down any keys or right-drag.

Web Sites

If you have Internet Explorer installed, you can easily create desktop shortcuts to the Web sites you visit most often. Just use Internet Explorer to display the site, and then select File | Create Shortcut (or right-click the page and select Create Shortcut from the context menu). I explain how to use Internet Explorer in Chapter 33.

Working with File Types

I've mentioned *file types* a couple of times in this chapter, so perhaps it's time to take a closer look at them. A file is an object, so it has various properties, including its name, its size, and the date and time it was created. The extension part of the filename determines another property: the *file type*. For example, a file with the extension .TXT is a text document, and a file with a .BMP extension is a bitmap.

The file type, in turn, defines which actions you can use with the file. A text document, for example, has two actions: Open, which displays the document in Notepad, and Print, which sends the document to the Windows 98 default printer. (Technically, the Print action opens Notepad, loads the document, selects File | Print, and closes Notepad. This all happens in the blink of an eye.) Each file type has a default action that runs when you perform any of the following actions on a document of that file type:

- Click the document (if Web integration is on).
- Highlight the document and press Enter.

- Pull down the File menu and select the command in bold.

- Right-click the document and, in the context menu that appears, select the command in bold.

For a text file, the Open action is the default. Any other actions associated with the file type appear below the default action on either the File menu or the context menu. For a text file, you see a Print command below the Open command.

File types that have associated actions are said to be *registered* with Windows 98 (because this data is stored in the Registry). If you used Windows 3.*x*, this whole idea is very similar to File Manager's file associations, but Windows 98's file types are much more powerful.

To see the list of Windows 98's registered file types, in Explorer, select View | Folder Options to display the Folder Options dialog box, and then select the File Types tab. As you can see in Figure 14.16, the Registered file types list contains the icons and names for each registered file type. When you highlight one of these items, the File type details group shows the extensions associated with the file type and the application that opens the file type (if any).

FIGURE 14.16.

The File Types tab displays a list of Windows 95's registered file types.

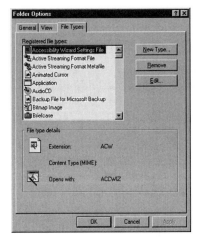

When working with file types, you can take the following actions:

- Use a different file type to open a document.

- Modify the existing actions for a file type. For example, you could tell Windows 98 to open text files in WordPad rather than Notepad.

- Create new actions for an existing file type. For example, you could define a secondary application to use for displaying a file type (such as WordPad for text files).

■ Create new file types and assign actions for the new type. For example, many applications ship with files named README.1ST. You could create a new file type for files that use the .1ST extension and then assign an Open action that uses Notepad to view these files.

Each of these techniques is discussed in the following sections.

Using a Different File Type to Open a Document

Most file types have an Open action that defines the default application that Windows 98 should use to display the file. Sometimes, however, the default application isn't the one you want to use. For example, if you have a text file that you know is too large for Notepad, you'd be better off loading it in WordPad instead. Here are the steps to follow to open a file with a different application:

1. In Explorer, highlight the document you want to open.

2. Hold down Shift and either select File | Open With or right-click the document and select Open With from the context menu. The Open With dialog box, shown in Figure 14.17, appears.

FIGURE 14.17.

Use the Open With dialog box to choose the application you want to use to open the file.

3. In the Choose the program you want to use list, highlight the application you want to use to open the file.

4. If you want to use this application for this file type all the time, activate the Always use this program to open this type of file check box.

5. Click OK. Windows 98 uses the selected program to open the file.

Modifying Actions for an Existing File Type

If an existing file type uses an action you don't like, it's easy enough to change it. For example, if you deal with large text files, Notepad is a pain because it just doesn't have the horsepower to handle anything too large. WordPad can handle such files, however, so you might want to change the Open action for text files to use WordPad instead. Here's how you'd do it:

1. In the File Types tab, use the Registered file types list to highlight the file type you want to change.

2. Click the Edit button. An Edit File Type dialog box similar to the one shown in Figure 14.18 appears.

FIGURE 14.18.

The Edit File Type dialog box lists the existing actions for the selected file type.

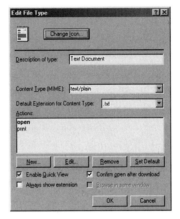

3. The Actions list displays the available actions for this file type. (Note that the "open" action is equivalent to the old file associations used in Windows 3.*x*.) Highlight the action you want to change and then click Edit. An editing action dialog box similar to the one shown in Figure 14.19 appears.

FIGURE 14.19.

Use this dialog box to change the selected action.

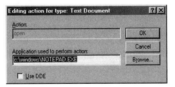

4. In the Application used to perform action text box, enter the full pathname of the application you want to use. If you're not sure, click Browse, highlight the appropriate executable file in the Open With dialog box, and click Open.

USE QUOTATION MARKS ON NAMES WITH SPACES

If the pathname of the executable file contains a space, be sure to enclose the path in quotation marks, like so:

```
"C:\Program Files\Accessories\Wordpad.exe"
```

Also, if you'll be using documents that have spaces in their filenames, add the "%1" parameter after the pathname:

```
"C:\Program Files\Accessories\Wordpad.exe" "%1"
```

The %1 part tells the application to load the specified file (such as a filename you click), and the quotation marks ensure that no problems occur with multiple-word filenames.

THE PRINT ACTION NEEDS THE PRINT SWITCH

If you're changing the Print action, be sure to include the /P switch after the application's pathname, like this:

```
"C:\Program Files\Accessories\Wordpad.exe" /P
```

5. Click OK to return to the Edit File Type dialog box.
6. Click Close to return to the File Types tab.

Creating New Actions for an Existing File Type

Instead of replacing an action's underlying application with a different application, you might prefer to create new actions. In our text file example, you could keep the default Open action as it is and create a new action—called, for example, Open with WordPad—that uses WordPad to open a text file. When you highlight a text file and pull down the File menu, or right-click a text file, the menus that appear will show both commands: Open (for Notepad) and Open with WordPad (for WordPad). Follow these steps to create a new action for an existing file type:

1. In the File Types tab, use the Registered file types list to highlight the file type you want to change.
2. Click the Edit button to display the Edit File Type dialog box.
3. Click New. The New Action dialog box, shown in Figure 14.20, appears.

FIGURE 14.20.

Use the New Action dialog box to set up a new action for a file type.

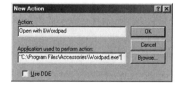

4. Use the Action text box to enter a name for the new action.

14

FILE AND FOLDER TRICKS AND TECHNIQUES

ASSIGNING AN ACCELERATOR KEY

In the Action text box, if you precede a letter with an ampersand (&), Windows 98 designates that letter as the menu accelerator key. For example, as shown in Figure 14.20, entering Open with &WordPad defines W as the accelerator key. You can then press this letter's key to select the command on either the File menu or the context menu (see Figure 14.21).

5. In the Application used to perform action text box, enter the full pathname of the application you want to use. If you're not sure, click Browse, highlight the appropriate executable file in the Open With dialog box, and click Open.

6. Click OK to return to the Edit File Type dialog box. The new action appears in the Actions list.

7. If you want to make the new action the default, highlight it and click the Set Default button.

8. Click Close to return to the File Types tab.

As I said, the new action appears both in the context menu for the file type and in the File menu when you highlight a document of the file type. For example, Figure 14.21 shows the context menu that appears for a text file after you've added the Open with WordPad action.

EASIER DISK DEFRAGMENTING

Interestingly, Windows 98 has a file type for disk drives. This enables you to set up actions for the drive. In particular, you can create a Defragment action that runs Disk Defragmenter (C:\WINDOWS\DEFRAG.EXE) on the drive.

Creating a New File Type

Windows 98 defines over 100 file types, but that isn't nearly enough to cover every possible extension. For example, no actions are defined for files that use the .DOS extension, such as CONFIG.DOS or AUTOEXEC.DOS. It would be handy to associate these text files with Notepad. Similarly, you might want to use nonstandard extensions in some of your files. For example, if you use both Word for Windows and Word for DOS, you might want to use the extension .WIN for files created with Word for Windows and the extension .DOS for files created with Word for DOS.

To satisfy all these needs, Windows 98 lets you define new file types and create actions for them. I'll show you two methods: a simple method of creating a new file type with just an Open action, and a more advanced method of creating a new file type with multiple actions.

FIGURE **14.21.**
*New actions appear on
the context menu for
the file type.*

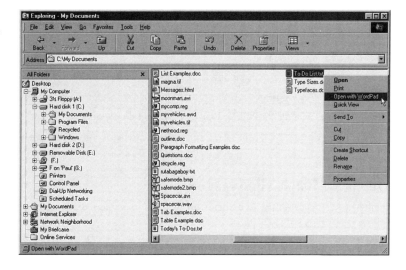

CREATE A NEW FILE TYPE FOR WORDPAD

If you use Word for Windows, the .DOC extension is associated with Word rather than
WordPad. If you like to create small notes in WordPad, it's a pain to double-click these files
and have them open (slowly) in Word. Instead, you should create a new file type for
WordPad documents (using an extension of, say, .PAD or .WPD).

CREATE A TEMPLATE FOR WORDPAD

To create a template file in WordPad, follow these steps:

1. Open a new file in WordPad.

2. Make any changes you want to include in the template, such as font size and style,
   margin settings, and so on.

   Note that if you want to change the default font, you must type some text into the
   template and then assign the font.

3. Save the file with a name that will easily identify the template, such as WordPad
   Courier TEMPLATE.TPL.

4. In Explorer, select View | Folder Options.

5. On the File Types tab, click the New Type button.

6. Type a description of the template in the Description Of type box.

7. In the Associated extension box, type tpl.

continues

14

FILE AND FOLDER
TRICKS AND
TECHNIQUES

continued

8. Click the New button.

9. In the Action box, type open.

10. In the Application used to perform action box, enter the complete path for WordPad.

11. Click OK until the Folder Options dialog box closes.

When you double-click a file that has a .TPL extension, the file will be opened in WordPad.

Creating a Simple File Type

If all you want is to set up an association between a particular file extension and an application, follow these steps:

1. In Explorer, highlight a file that contains the extension you want to use as the new file type.

2. Either select File | Open With or right-click the file and select Open With from the context menu. You then see the Open With dialog box, shown earlier in Figure 14.17.

3. In the Choose the program you want to use list, highlight the application you want to use to open this file type.

4. Activate the Always use this program to open this type of file check box and click OK.

Windows 98 uses the selected program to open the file, and it also creates a new file type with a single action: Open. The default name for the new file type is *EXT* File, in which *EXT* is the file extension (for example, WIN File). To change this description, display the File Types tab, highlight the file type, click Edit, and enter a new description in the Description of type text box.

Creating a More Advanced File Type

If you need to define more than just the Open action (such as the Print action) for a new file type, you need to use the File Types tab. Here are the steps to follow:

1. In the File Types tab, click the New Type button. The Add New File Type dialog box appears.

2. Set up your new file type using the following controls, as necessary (see Figure 14.22 for an example):

   Description of type: Use this text box to enter a description for the new file type. (This is the text that will appear in the Registered file types list and in the Type column of Explorer's Details view.)

   Associated extension: Use this text box to enter the extension for the file type.

Content Type (MIME): Use this drop-down list to specify the Internet content type. For example, if you're setting up Windows 98 to handle AIFF sound files, you select the audio/aiff item.

Default Extension for Content Type: This control lists the extensions that correspond with the Content Type you chose, as well as the value you entered in the Associated extension text box. In most cases, you select the associated extension.

FIGURE 14.22.

Use this dialog box to define your new file type.

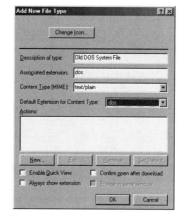

3. Click New. The New Action dialog box appears.

4. Use the Action text box to enter a name for the new action.

5. In the Application used to perform action text box, enter the full pathname of the application you want to use. If you're not sure, click Browse, highlight the appropriate executable file in the Open With dialog box, and click Open. (Remember to add the /P switch for the Print action.)

6. Click OK to return to the Edit File Type dialog box. The new action appears in the Actions list.

7. If you want to make the new action the default, highlight it and click the Set Default button.

8. Repeat steps 3 through 7 to define other actions.

9. Click Close to return to the File Types tab.

Finding File Needles in Hard Disk Haystacks

With multi-gigabyte hard disks selling for a couple of hundred dollars on the street, the days of king-size hard disk storage at a pint-size price are upon us. Recall from Chapter 1, "Preparing for the Windows 98 Installation," however, that Parkinson's Law of Data ensures us that data expands to fill the space available. So, yes, our hard disks are massive, but they also contain massive numbers of files. Misplacing a file under these conditions can be a real problem because finding it among thousands of files becomes a chore. To help out, Windows 98 has a Find utility that can search for files (or folders) by name, date, size, or even content. The next few sections describe all of Find's features.

Starting Find

To get the Find utility cranked up, you can use three methods:

- To search in a particular folder or disk drive, highlight the folder or disk drive in Explorer, and then either select Tools | Find | Files or Folders or right-click the folder or disk drive and select Find from the context menu. (You can also press F3.)
- To search the entire Desktop folder, click an empty part of the desktop and press F3.
- Select Start | Find | Files or Folders. (If you have a Microsoft Natural Keyboard or a compatible, press ⊞+F.)

In each case, the Find window, shown in Figure 14.23, is displayed.

FIGURE 14.23.

Use the Find window to scope out files or folders on your system.

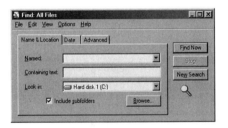

Searching by Name, Text, and Location

The Find window's Name & Location tab enables you to search for files by name and by the text they contain. It also enables you to specify the drive or folder in which to search.

Use the Named combo box to enter a filename specification for the file or files you want to find. (After you've run some searches, you can use the drop-down list to select previous filename specifications.) If you're looking for a specific file, enter the complete name using the following guidelines:

- If the file contains a space, enclose the filename in quotation marks (for example, "Letter To Mom.doc").
- If you want to search for multiple files, separate each name with a space, comma, or semicolon.
- Find's filename searches aren't case-sensitive, so don't worry about whether you use upper- or lowercase.
- Although I keep using the word "file," remember that you can use Find to search for folder names as well.

If you're not sure of the exact filename, or if the name is a long one, Find is happy to accept partial names. For example, an entry of `fig` will find files named `CONFIG.SYS`, `CHAPTER1_FIGURE57.BMP`, and `FIG.NEWTON`. Notice how Find matches files that contain `fig` anywhere in the name.

To give your searches extra flexibility, the Named combo box also accepts wildcard characters. As with DOS wildcards, you use the question mark (?) to substitute for a single character and the asterisk (*) to substitute for multiple characters. Table 14.3 shows you several examples of these wildcards in action.

Table 14.3. Wildcard character examples.

Named Text	Which Filenames It Matches
`*.txt`	Filenames that have the extension `.TXT` and any primary name (for example, `BOOTLOG.TXT`, `LETTER.TXT`).
`memo.*`	Filenames that have `memo` as the primary name and any extension (for example, `MEMO.TXT`, `MEMO.DOC`).
`chapter1*.bmp`	Filenames that have a primary name that begins with `chapter1` and a `.BMP` extension (for example, `CHAPTER1.BMP`, `CHAPTER1_FIGURE57.BMP`, `CHAPTER1_NOTES.BMP`).
`*log.txt`	Filenames that have a primary name that ends with `log` and have a `.TXT` extension (for example, `BOOTLOG.TXT`, `SETUPLOG.TXT`, `LOG.TXT`).
`*.*`	Filenames that have any primary name and any extension (that is, all files).
`?o?ato.doc`	Filenames that have the extension `.DOC` and have primary names that are exactly six characters long, in which the first and third letters can be any character, the second character is `o`, and the fourth through sixth characters are `ato` (for example, `POTATO.DOC`, `TOMATO.DOC`, but not `POTATOE.DOC`).
`????.dbf`	Filenames that have a primary name that is exactly four characters long and have the extension `.DBF` (for example, `DATA.DBF`, `BOOT.DBF`).
`?ales*.doc`	Filenames that have the extension `.DOC` and have a primary name that begins with any character followed by `ales` (for example, `SALESMAN.DOC`, `BALES_OF_HAY.DOC`).

14

FILE AND FOLDER TRICKS AND TECHNIQUES

To narrow your search even further, you can use the Containing text box to enter a word or phrase contained in the file. If you enter multiple words, note that Find will match files that contain only *all* the words. (That is, Find uses a Boolean "and" search technique.)

After you've filled in the Named and Containing text boxes, use the Look in box to enter the drive or folder you want to use for the search. If you want to search multiple drives or folders, separate them with semicolons:

```
c:\windows;d:\data
```

If you want Find to search not only the specified folder, but also all its subfolders, activate the Include subfolders check box.

Searching by Date

If you know, more or less, when the file was created or when it was last modified, you can narrow your search criteria even further. Select the Date tab to display the controls shown in Figure 14.24. To enter date criteria, select the Find all files created or modified option. The following controls become active:

> **Between:** Activate this option to enter a date range in the two text boxes.
>
> **During the previous *x* month(s):** Activate this option to narrow the search to the previous number of months you enter in the spinner.
>
> **During the previous *x* day(s):** Activate this option to narrow the search to the previous number of days you enter in the spinner.

FIGURE 14.24.

Use the Date tab to search for files by date.

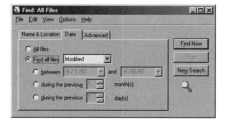

Advanced Searching

Finally, the Advanced tab, shown in Figure 14.25, enables you to search for files by type or size. Here are your choices:

> **Of type:** This drop-down box contains a list of all the registered file types.
>
> **Size is:** Use these controls to specify a file size. In the drop-down list, select either At least or At most; in the spinner, enter a value in kilobytes.

Running the Search

Okay, you're ready to go. Click the Find Now button and Find goes to work. As the search progresses, Find displays any matching files at the bottom of the window. When it's done, the status bar shows you the number of files found, as shown in Figure 14.26.

FIGURE 14.25.

Use the Advanced tab to search by file type, file content, or file size.

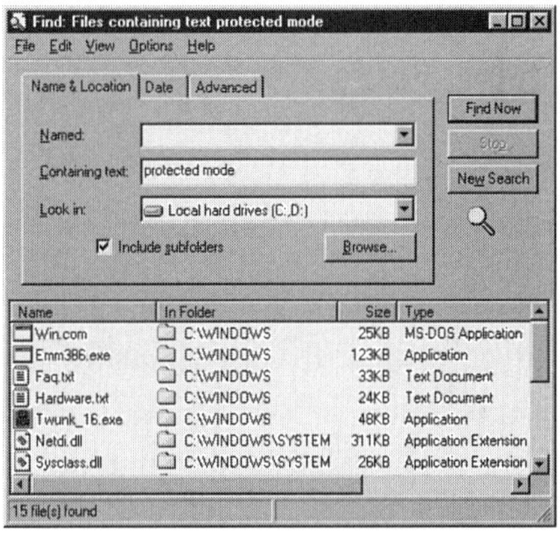

FIGURE 14.26.

Find displays the matching files at the bottom of the window.

The area where Find displays the matching files is like a scaled-down version of Explorer. You can select files, cut or copy files to the Clipboard, delete or rename files, drag-and-drop files, and do just about anything you can do in Explorer. If you want to open the folder that contains a specific file, highlight the file and select File | Open Containing Folder.

If you think you might want to reuse the search criteria later, select File | Save Search. Find adds a file to your desktop of type Saved Search (with the `.FND` extension). Clicking this file redisplays the Find window with your search criteria entered automatically.

Trash Talk: Understanding the Recycle Bin

In the early days of the PC revolution, accidentally deleted files were gone for good, and no amount of cursing, groaning, or bellyaching would get them back.

Then some genius realized that when DOS deleted a file, it didn't actually delete the file's contents. Instead, it just changed the file's name so that the first letter began with a lowercase Greek sigma, and it changed all the file's FAT entries to 0 (to indicate that these clusters could be used by another file). Thus was born the "undelete" command, which could restore a deleted file by restoring the FAT entries and the original first character of the filename.

The problem, however, was that if you didn't undelete the file quickly, some other file would come along and use up some of the deleted file's clusters, and the file would be unrecoverable.

So the next stage in the evolution of undelete was a separate directory used to hold deleted files. A deleted file was simply moved from its original directory to a hidden directory. Undeleting the file became a trivial matter of moving the file back to its original location.

Which brings us to the state of the art in undeletion technology: the Windows 98 Recycle Bin. The Recycle Bin works by setting up hidden folders named Recycled on each of your disk drives. When you delete a file, the Recycle Bin moves the file to the appropriate Recycled folder. When you restore a file, the Recycle Bin moves it back to its original folder. The next few sections discuss the Recycle Bin in more detail.

Sending a File or Folder to the Recycle Bin

When you decide to blow away a file or folder, Windows 98 gives you lots of choices on how to proceed. Here's the rundown:

- Highlight the file or folder and select File | Delete.
- Press the Delete key.
- Right-click the file or folder and select Delete from the context menu.
- Highlight the file or folder and click the Delete button in the toolbar.
- Drag the file to the Recycle Bin icon on the desktop or the Recycle Bin folder.

For the first four methods, Windows 98 displays a dialog box asking you to confirm that you want to send the file or folder to the Recycle Bin, as shown in Figure 14.27. If you're sure, click Yes; otherwise, you can bail out by clicking No.

FIGURE 14.27.

When you delete a file, Windows 98 displays this dialog box to ask for confirmation.

FLOPPY AND NETWORK DRIVE DELETIONS ARE PERMANENT

If you delete a file from a floppy disk or a network drive, Windows 98 does not send the file to the Recycle Bin (even if you drop the file on the Recycle Bin icon). Instead, Windows 98 deletes the file permanently.

BYPASSING THE RECYCLE BIN

If you're sure you won't ever need to restore the file, you can delete a file or folder permanently (that is, without placing it in the Recycle Bin) by holding down the Shift key while you delete it. What happens if you use this technique and then decide that you need the file restored? Are you out of luck? Maybe not. You can try using the DOS UNDELETE command to recover the file. I'll show you how this works in Chapter 23, "DOS Isn't Dead: Unleashing the DOS Shell."

Restoring a File from the Recycle Bin

It's axiomatic in computer circles that there are two kinds of users: those who have accidentally deleted the wrong file, and those who will. When this happens to you, it's nice to know that the Recycle Bin is there to bail you out.

Actually, before learning how to restore files from the Recycle Bin, you should know that there's an easier way. If the deletion was the last action you performed, you can reverse it by selecting Edit | Undo Delete, or by right-clicking an empty part of the Contents list and selecting Undo Delete from the context menu.

The Undo command applies only to the last action you performed, however, so Undo Delete might no longer be available by the time you realize your mistake. No problem, though. You can still recover the file or folder by following these steps:

1. Display the contents of the Recycle Bin either by highlighting the Recycle Bin folder in Explorer or by double-clicking the Recycle Bin icon on the desktop.

2. Highlight the file or folder you want to restore.

3. Select File | Restore, or right-click the file or folder and select Restore from the context menu. Windows 98 restores the file or folder to its original location.

CLEANING OUT THE RECYCLE BIN

The Recycle Bin contents take up disk space, of course. If you need to free up some disk real estate, you have a couple of choices. If you want to expunge one or more Recycle Bin objects permanently, highlight it and select File | Delete, or right-click it and click Delete. When Windows 98 asks whether you want to delete the object, click Yes. Alternatively, you can clean out the Recycle Bin entirely either by highlighting the Recycle Bin folder and selecting File | Empty Recycle Bin, or by right-clicking the Recycle Bin icon and selecting Empty Recycle Bin from the context menu.

14

FILE AND FOLDER
TRICKS AND
TECHNIQUES

Setting Recycle Bin Properties

To give you a measure of control over how the Recycle Bin operates, various properties are available for you to work with. To check out these properties, either highlight the Recycle Bin and select File | Properties, or right-click the Recycle Bin icon and select Properties from the context menu. You see a Recycle Bin Properties dialog box similar to the one shown in Figure 14.28.

FIGURE 14.28.

Use this dialog box to set some Recycle Bin properties.

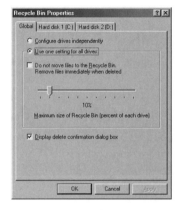

For starters, you need to decide whether you want to configure the Recycle Bin settings for each drive independently or globally (assuming, of course, that your system has multiple drives). For example, if you have a drive that's perilously low on disk space, you probably want to configure the drives independently so that you can tailor the amount of disk space that the Recycle Bin uses.

If you want to configure the drives globally, activate the Global tab's Use one setting for all drives option button. You can then manipulate two settings that apply to all your hard disk drives:

> **Do not move files to the Recycle Bin. Remove files immediately when deleted:** Activate this option to bypass the Recycle Bin for all deletions.
>
> **Maximum size of Recycle Bin (percent of each drive):** This slider controls the maximum amount of hard disk acreage that the Recycle Bin usurps on all the drives. The default is 10 percent, which is probably a bit high (100MB on a 1GB drive!). Note, however, that the lower the value, the fewer files the Recycle Bin can store.

If you prefer to configure the drives separately, activate the Configure drives independently option button and then use the various drive tabs to adjust the settings for each drive.

Finally, the Global tab also has a Display delete confirmation dialog check box. If you deactivate this option, Windows 98 doesn't prompt you for confirmation when you select the Delete command or press the Delete key.

When you're done, click OK to put the settings into effect.

Summary

This chapter took a long, hard look at working with files and folders in Windows 98. I began by showing you a number of basic file and folder techniques. From there, I gave a few pointers for unleashing Explorer. Then you learned about working with shortcuts and file types, finding files and folders, and understanding the Recycle Bin. For related information, here are some chapters to check out:

- Various Registry tricks affect files and shortcuts. I showed you a few in Chapter 13, "A Few Good Hacks: Some Useful Registry Tweaks."
- Disk operations such as formatting, copying, compressing, and partitioning are the subject of Chapter 15, "Disk Driving: The Windows 98 Disk Utilities."
- I show you how to make backups of your files in Chapter 16, "Working with a Net: The Windows 98 Backup Utility."
- To learn how to keep your files safe from harm, check out Chapter 17, "Wielding the Windows 98 System Tools."
- To learn how to perform file maintenance from the DOS prompt, see Chapter 23, "DOS Isn't Dead: Unleashing the DOS Shell."
- For network-related file and folder info, see Chapter 29, "Working with Network Resources."

14

FILE AND FOLDER TRICKS AND TECHNIQUES

CHAPTER 15

Disk Driving: The Windows 98 Disk Utilities

IN THIS CHAPTER

Never let a computer know you're in a hurry.

—Anonymous

I concentrated on files and folders in the last chapter, but Windows 98 has plenty of goodies for disk drives as well. This chapter looks at Windows 98's various disk-related commands and utilities.

Formatting a Floppy Disk

Floppy disks come in two standard sizes: 5 1/4-inch and 3 1/2-inch. The 5 1/4-inch disks are the veterans of the PC wars. They've been around, in one form or another, since the days of the earliest PCs. They come in two capacities: double-density and high-density. (Actually, the term *double-density* is relatively meaningless in this day and age. It originates from the old days of computers—way back in the 1980s—when there were such things as *single-density* disks. You often see double-density disks referred to as *low-density* or *regular-density*.) The 5 1/4-inch double-density disks have a storage capacity of 360KB, and the high-density variety can store 1.2MB.

Although 3 1/2-inch disks are relatively new kids on the floppy drive block, they're now the true "standard" (at least until the next one comes along). They come in three capacities: double-density, high-density, and the new (and still rare) extended-density disks. Double-density disks store up to 720KB, high-density disks store 1.44MB, and extended disks can pack a whopping 2.88MB of data. You can't, of course, just stick any old piece of plastic in a disk drive and expect it to read and write information. Even official I-bought-'em-at-the-local-Radio-Shack floppy disks need to be set up first so that information can be properly stored on the disk.

It's like the difference between a pegboard and an ordinary piece of wood. Buying new disks (unless the box says they're "preformatted") is like buying a bunch of flat, featureless pieces of wood. You can try all day to stick pegs in them, but they'll just fall off. What you need to do is "format" the wood so that it has proper holes for the pegs.

This pegboard analogy can also help explain the difference between double-density and high-density disks. Picture two pegboards: one with large holes and one with smaller holes. The large-holed board can hold a certain number of pegs, but because the holes in the other board are smaller, it can hold even more pegs. So a double-density disk is like the board with large holes: It has fewer "pegs" (fewer *tracks per inch*, technically) on which to place data than a high-density (small-holed) disk. This also helps explain why you can't format double-density disks as high-density. All disks use a magnetic field to hold their data. High-density disks must use a *lower* field strength than double-density because the data, like the holes in the small-holed peg-board, are closer together. If high-density disks didn't use the lower field strength, the various magnetic bits would start moving around because of mutual attraction and repulsion. Not good! This is exactly what happens, though, when you format a double-density disk as high-density. The tracks are placed close together, but the disk's stronger magnetic field eventually trashes the data.

When you need to format a floppy disk, follow these steps:

1. Insert the disk you want to format.

2. In Explorer, right-click the drive containing the disk and select Format. (Don't highlight the drive first, or Windows 98 won't let you format the disk.) Alternatively, you can highlight the drive in My Computer and select File | Format. In either case, the Format dialog box, shown in Figure 15.1, appears.

FIGURE 15.1.

Use the Format dialog box to select your formatting options.

3. Use the Capacity drop-down list to select the appropriate capacity for the disk.

4. In the Format type group, select one of the following options:

    Quick (erase): This option removes all the files from the disk, but it doesn't check the disk for bad sectors. You can use this option only on disks that have been previously formatted.

    Full: This option removes all the files from the disk and checks the disk for bad sectors. Use this option for new disks and for older disks that you suspect might have bad sectors.

    Copy system files only: This option copies only the Windows 98 system files to the disk: IO.SYS, MSDOS.SYS, DRVSAPCE.BIN, and COMMAND.COM. The disk then becomes bootable. Any existing files on the disk remain intact.

5. The Other options group contains the following controls:

    Label: Use this text box to enter a label for the disk (11 or fewer characters).

    No label: Activate this check box to disable the Label check box. Any existing label will be deleted.

    Display summary when finished: If this check box is activated, Windows 98 displays a summary dialog box when the format is complete. This dialog box tells you the total disk space, the total bytes in bad sectors, the size of each cluster, and a few other disk statistics.

    Copy system files: Activate this check box to copy the system files to the disk after it has been formatted. This will make the disk bootable.

6. Click Start. Windows 98 formats the disk.

7. If you activated the Display summary when finished check box, the Format Results dialog box appears when the format is complete. Click OK to return to the Format dialog box.

8. Click Close.

1.44MB? NO, NOT REALLY

In the Format Results dialog box, Windows 98 will show that a 1.44MB floppy has 1,457,664 bytes total disk space. If you divide this value by 1,048,576 (the number of bytes in a megabyte), you end up with 1.39. In other words, the true capacity of a "1.44MB" floppy disk is actually 1.39MB.

You can also use the Format command to format a hard disk. In this case, though, when you click Start, Windows 98 displays the warning dialog box shown in Figure 15.2. If you're sure you want to continue, click OK.

FIGURE 15.2.

Windows 98 warns you that formatting a hard disk will erase all the data on the disk.

After formatting the hard disk, note that it will no longer be set up to accept long filenames, because when you format the drive, you wipe out the information cache that Windows 98 stores on each drive. This cache contains data about the drive, including whether it supports long filenames. To restore the long filename capability for the drive, you have two choices:

- Restart your computer.
- Highlight the drive in Explorer or My Computer and then select View | Refresh (or press F5).

Copying a Floppy Disk

If you need to make a copy of a floppy disk, Windows 98 is up to the task. Here are the steps you need to follow:

1. Insert the disk you want to copy (this is the source disk). If your system has a second drive of the same type, insert the disk you want to use for the copy (this is the destination disk) in the other drive.

2. Highlight the source disk drive and select File | Copy Disk, or right-click the source disk drive and select Copy Disk from the context menu. Windows 98 displays the Copy Disk dialog box, shown in Figure 15.3.

FIGURE 15.3.

Use the Copy Disk dialog box to make a copy of a floppy disk.

3. The Copy from box lists the floppy and removable drives on your system. Highlight the drive that contains the source disk.

4. The Copy to box also lists the floppy and removable drives on your system. Highlight the drive you want to use for the destination disk. Make sure that this drive uses disks of the same type as the source disk. If your system has two drives of different types, you can use the same drive for the copy procedure. (For example, suppose that drive A is 3 1/2-inch and drive B is 5 1/4-inch, and you want to copy a 3 1/2-inch disk. You can select the 3 1/2-inch drive (drive A) in both Copy from and Copy to.)

5. Click Start. Windows 98 reads the data from the source disk. If you're using the same drive for the copy, Windows 98 prompts you to insert the destination disk.

6. Insert the destination disk and click OK. Windows 98 copies the data to the destination disk.

7. When the copy is complete, click Close.

Viewing Disk Properties

Disks are objects in the Windows 98 scheme of things, so they have their own properties and actions. You've just seen a couple of actions—Format and Copy Disk—but what about a disk's properties? To check them out, either highlight a disk and select File | Properties, or right-click a disk and click Properties in the context menu. You see a properties sheet similar to the one shown in Figure 15.4. The General tab shows you the disk's label, its type, the amount of used and free space, the total capacity, the drive letter, and a pie chart comparing used and free space.

FIGURE 15.4.

The properties sheet for a disk drive.

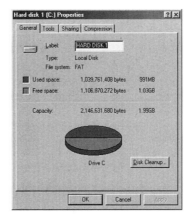

15

DISK DRIVING:
THE WINDOWS 98
DISK UTILITIES

Selecting the Tools tab displays the controls shown in Figure 15.5. This handy tab lets you keep track of when you last performed certain maintenance chores on this disk:

Error-checking status: This group tells you how long ago you last ran ScanDisk on this disk. If you want to run ScanDisk now, click the Check Now button. (I explain how ScanDisk works in Chapter 17, "Wielding the Windows 98 System Tools.")

Backup status: This group tells you when you last backed up files from this disk. To perform a backup now, click the Backup Now button. (See Chapter 16, "Working with a Net: The Windows 98 Backup Utility," to learn how to perform backups.)

Defragmentation status: This group tells you when you last defragmented the files on this disk. Click Defragment Now to start Disk Defragmenter for this disk. (I showed you how to use Disk Defragmenter in Chapter 9, "Performance Tuning: Optimizing Memory and Disk Access.")

FIGURE 15.5.

Use the Tools tab to monitor when you last performed maintenance on the disk.

TROUBLESHOOTING: CONSTANT FLOPPY DRIVE ACCESS

If you've performed any floppy disk–based file chores recently, you may have noticed that Windows 98 constantly attempts to access your system's floppy drive whenever you run any kind of file maintenance (saving, renaming, opening, and so on).

This stubborn and annoying behavior is caused by the Documents menu. The problem is that the Documents menu probably still lists the floppy disk file you worked on earlier. Every time you do something to a file, Windows 98 updates the Documents menu, which includes verifying that the floppy disk is still in place.

You can correct this problem by clearing the Documents menu (as described in Chapter 6, "Customizing the Taskbar, Start Menu, and Display").

Compressing Disks with DriveSpace

Although hard disks have been getting bigger and cheaper over the years, they haven't kept pace with the ever-fatter programs that developers have been throwing at us. As a result, we have a new corollary to Murphy's Law: No matter how huge your hard disk seems today, you'll wish it was twice as big six months from now. Rather than dipping into your savings yet again, you can squeeze more storage space out of your current disk by using DriveSpace, Windows 98's disk compression program.

Disk compression is based on a complex mathematical algorithm (called the Lempel-Ziv algorithm) that searches a file for redundant character strings and replaces them with small tokens. Let's look at a simple example. Consider the following phrase:

```
It was the best of times, it was the worst of times, it was the age of wisdom,
it was the age of foolishness.
```

To compress this quotation, the program starts at the beginning and looks for at least two consecutive characters it has already seen. In this case, the first such match is the `t` and the following space at the end of the word `best`; this matches the `t` and the following space seen earlier at the end of the word `It`. So now the program replaces the match with a token, something like this (I use an asterisk to represent the various tokens):

```
I*was the bes*of times, it was the worst of times, it was the age of wisdom,
it was the age of foolishness.
```

The program chugs along, finding small redundancies (for example, the `es` in `times` matches the `es` seen earlier in `bes*`). Then it hits the jackpot: Larger phrases such as `it was the`, `of times`, and `age of` are repeated, and these can all be replaced by tokens. Finally, you end up with something that looks like this:

```
I***b******wors******w*dom******fool*hn*s
```

(Again, I'm using a single asterisk token for all the replacements. A compression program uses separate tokens.) It looks strange, but the program has reduced the original string from 110 characters to 42. To decompress such data, all the program has to do is translate the tokens back to their original form. It's all handled by a mathematical formula, and it's quite safe.

How DriveSpace Works

DriveSpace can create more room to roam on your hard disk in two ways:

- By compressing both the existing files and the remaining free space on the disk
- By compressing only the remaining free space on the disk and creating a new compressed drive from this free space

If You Compress Files and Free Space

If you elect to compress the files and free space, DriveSpace works through the following procedure (assuming that you're compressing drive C):

1. The disk's drive letter is changed from C to H (or, if H is already used, the first free drive letter), and the drive is hidden (this is optional). This new drive letter is used as the host of the compressed data.

2. DriveSpace compresses the files on drive H and concatenates them into a single file. This is called the compressed volume file (CVF). This file is usually named DRVSPACE.000.

3. The CVF's file attributes are set to hidden, read-only, and system.

4. Windows 98 assigns the original disk's drive letter (C) to the CVF.

In other words, your system looks very much the same after compression as it did before: You use the same drive letter to work with your data, and your files and folders are still intact and unchanged. The only difference is that you now have much more free hard disk space on the drive. (You might also notice a very slight decrease in hard disk performance, because Windows 98 now must uncompress files as you work with them.)

This method takes quite a while, but you end up with the maximum amount of storage capacity on your disk. For example, suppose that you have a 200MB hard disk that contains 100MB of files and, therefore, 100MB of free space. Assuming an average compression ratio of 2:1, you should be able to fit 200MB of compressed data into the space formerly used by your 100MB of uncompressed files, and you should be able to fit 200MB of new compressed data into the space formerly used by the 100MB of uncompressed free space. Thus, your total storage capacity for the disk is up to 400MB.

COMPRESSION RATIO

The compression ratio of a file is the ratio of the size of the uncompressed file to its compressed size. For example, a file that is 10,000 bytes uncompressed and 5,000 bytes compressed has a compression ratio of 2:1. Some files—especially text, database, and graphics files—achieve high compression ratios because they tend to have many redundant character strings. On the other hand, executable files and Help system files have relatively few redundant character strings, so their compression ratios are usually much lower.

If You Compress Free Space Only

Instead of compressing your existing files, you can elect to compress only the remaining free space on the disk (or part of the free space). In this case, DriveSpace turns the free space into a separate disk drive (for example, drive D) with a storage capacity of approximately double the original free space. This new capacity is only a guess on DriveSpace's part, however; it assumes an average compression ratio of 2:1. The real compression ratio (and therefore the actual number of megabytes you can store on the new drive) depends on the files you place on the drive.

This method is faster, but you end up with less storage capacity than with the other method. For example, consider the 200MB disk with 100MB of files and 100MB of free space. Again, assuming an average compression ratio of 2:1, you end up with two drives: one that has 100MB of uncompressed files and no free space, and one that has 200MB of free space. Your total storage capacity, therefore, is 300MB.

Managing the CVF

After a drive has been compressed, DriveSpace uses a device driver to manage the CVF. When you start your computer, a real-mode driver (DRVSPACE.BIN) is loaded to make the CVF available during the real-mode portion of the startup. When Windows 98 switches to protected mode, DRVSPACE.BIN is unloaded and the protected-mode driver (DRVSPACX.VXD) takes over.

Is it safe to put all your file eggs in one CVF basket? Absolutely. The algorithms used to compress and decompress files are bulletproof, and even in the unlikely event that something does go wrong, DriveSpace has built-in safeguards designed to keeps things in order. The chances of corrupting your data are no different than they are in using uncompressed files.

WINDOWS 98 SUPPORTS OTHER COMPRESSION SCHEMES

Windows 98 also supports the DoubleSpace compression that was used in DOS 6.0. In this case, the real-mode driver used at startup is DBLSPACE.BIN (although, in protected mode, DRVSPACX.VXD is used to manage both kinds of compressed drives). Windows 98 also supports (in real mode) the third-party compression schemes Stacker, SuperStor, and AddStor.

Compressing Files and Free Space

If you want to compress both the files and the free space on your disk, start DriveSpace by selecting Start | Programs | Accessories | System Tools | DriveSpace. You see the DriveSpace window with a list of the disk drives on your system, as shown in Figure 15.6.

Figure 15.6.

Use the DriveSpace window to select the drive you want to compress.

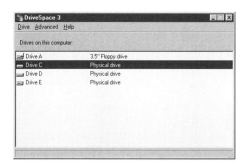

To compress a drive, highlight it in the Drives on this computer list and then select Drive | Compress. At this point, one of two things will happen:

> **If the drive capacity is less than 1GB:** You see the version of the Compress a Drive dialog box shown in Figure 15.7. The box on the left shows the current free space and used space; the box on the right shows the free space and used space after compression.

FIGURE 15.7.

You see this dialog box if the capacity of the drive is less than 1GB.

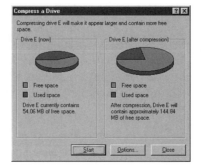

> **If the drive capacity is greater than 1GB:** You see the version of the Compress a Drive dialog box shown in Figure 15.8. DriveSpace can't create a compressed drive that's larger than 2GB, so it compresses just enough of the drive that the resulting drive has 2GB of storage. It then creates the remaining (uncompressed) free space on the host drive. You can run DriveSpace again later to compress the remaining free space into a new drive.

FIGURE 15.8.

You see this dialog box if your drive is greater than 256MB but has less than 500MB of files.

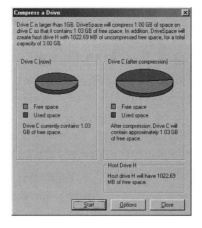

Before starting the compression, you might want to adjust a few compression settings. To view these settings, click the Options button to display the Compression Options dialog box, shown in Figure 15.9. You can work with the following controls:

Drive letter of host drive: Use this drop-down list to change the drive letter that DriveSpace assigns to the host drive. H is usually the default letter, but you can use any unassigned letter for the host drive.

Free space on host drive: This text box specifies the amount of uncompressed free space used on the host drive. Increasing this number reduces the space available for the CVF; decreasing this number (if possible) increases the amount of space available for the CVF. You can't decrease this number below 2MB, and you can't decrease it if the compressed drive is already at the 1GB maximum size.

Hide host drive: Activate this check box to set the hidden attribute of the host drive. You want to leave this check box deactivated if the host drive has more than the minimum amount of free space (2MB). This way, you can still see and work with the host drive in Explorer.

When you're done, click OK to return to the Compress a Drive dialog box.

FIGURE 15.9.

Use this dialog box to adjust various compression settings.

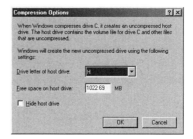

To begin the compression, click the Start button. You might see the Create Startup Disk dialog box, which asks whether you want to create a startup disk. Click Yes to create the disk or No to continue.

Now you may see the Are You Sure? dialog box, which offers to back up your files. If you want to do a backup, click Back Up Files and then use the Microsoft Backup utility to perform the backup. (See Chapter 16.) Otherwise, click Compress Now.

DriveSpace checks the drive for errors and then starts the compression. Note that DriveSpace might need to restart your computer if you're compressing the drive that contains the Windows 98 system files. In this case, Windows 98 starts with a minimal configuration so that DriveSpace can compress all the files safely. DriveSpace restarts Windows 98 when it's finished.

15

DISK DRIVING: THE WINDOWS 98 DISK UTILITIES

When DriveSpace has completed its labors, it returns you to the Compress a Drive dialog box and shows the free space now contained in the drive. Click Close. If DriveSpace prompts you to restart your computer, click Yes.

Compressing Free Space Only

If you want to compress only the free space on your drive, follow these steps:

1. Select Start | Programs | Accessories | System Tools | DriveSpace to display the DriveSpace window.

2. Use the Drives on this computer list to highlight the drive you want to use.

3. Select Advanced | Create Empty. The Create New Compressed Drive dialog box, shown in Figure 15.10, appears.

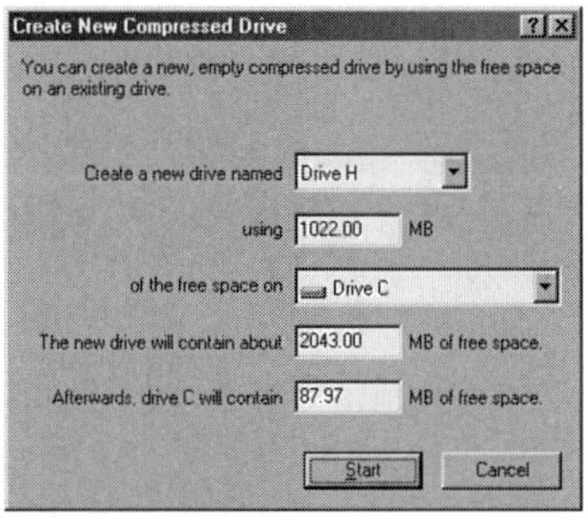

FIGURE 15.10.

Use this dialog box to set the parameters for your new compressed drive.

4. You can adjust the following controls:

    Create a new drive named: Use this drop-down list to select an unused drive letter for the new drive.

    using: This text box specifies the amount of uncompressed free space you want to use for the new drive. Because DriveSpace can't work with drives any larger than 2GB, the maximum value you can enter is about 1022MB (DriveSpace assumes a 2:1 compression ratio).

    of the free space on: Use this drop-down list to change the drive you want to use, if necessary.

    The new drive will contain about: Alternatively, use this text box to specify how much free space you want on the new drive.

    Afterwards, drive *X* will contain: Use this text box to specify how much free space you want to keep on the original drive.

5. Click Start.

6. If DriveSpace asks you about a startup disk, click Yes or No, as appropriate. DriveSpace checks the drive for errors and then creates the new drive. When it's done, you're returned to the Create New Compressed Drive dialog box.

7. Click Close. If Windows 98 asks whether you want to restart your computer, click Yes.

Modifying the Size of a Compressed Drive

If you want to change the size of a compressed drive or the host drive, you can do so by following these steps:

1. Select Start | Programs | Accessories | System Tools | DriveSpace to display the DriveSpace window.

2. Use the Drives on this computer list to highlight the compressed drive you want to adjust.

3. Select Drive | Adjust Free Space. DriveSpace displays the Adjust Free Space dialog box, shown in Figure 15.11.

FIGURE 15.11.

Use this dialog box to adjust the amount of free space on a compressed drive or host drive.

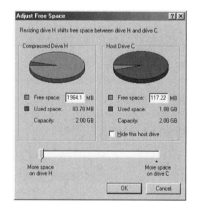

4. Move the slider to the left to create more space on the compressed drive; move the slider to the right to create less space on the compressed drive (that is, more space on the host drive).

5. Click OK. DriveSpace adjusts the size and displays a dialog box showing you the new size.

6. Click OK. If Windows 98 asks whether you want to restart your computer, click Yes.

15

DISK DRIVING:
THE WINDOWS 98
DISK UTILITIES

Working with Compression Settings

The Windows 98 version of DriveSpace compresses files in the CVF on-the-fly as you save them. DriveSpace uses three kinds of compression:

Standard compression: This is the same compression method used with regular DriveSpace.

HiPack compression: This option gives you a higher compression ratio (10 or 20 percent higher).

UltraPack compression: This option gives you the highest compression ratio possible. This is available only through the Compression Agent. (See the next section, "Using the Compression Agent.")

A few more options are also available for DriveSpace 3. To see them, select Advanced | Settings to display the Disk Compression Settings dialog box, shown in Figure 15.12. These settings control the on-the-fly compression used by DriveSpace 3. You have the following options:

HiPack compression: This option activates on-the-fly HiPack compression.

Standard compression: This option activates on-the-fly standard compression.

No compression, unless drive is at least x % full: This option turns off the on-the-fly compression. If the used space on the disk rises above the percentage entered in the text box, standard compression is activated.

No compression (fastest): This option deactivates on-the-fly compression. This increases the performance of your system, because DriveSpace will save files without using compression. If you elect to go this route, be sure to use Compression Agent (discussed in the next section) to compress your files while you aren't using your computer.

FIGURE 15.12.

Use this dialog box to set various options for DriveSpace compression.

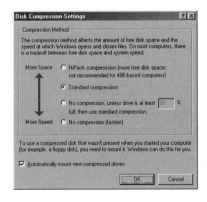

Using the Compression Agent

After you've upgraded your compressed drives (or created new compressed drives) with DriveSpace 3, you can start using the Compression Agent to manage on-the-fly compression. Follow these steps to set up Compression Agent:

1. Select Start | Programs | Accessories | System Tools | Compression Agent. If you have multiple compressed drives, the Select Drive dialog box appears.

2. Select the compressed drive you want to recompress and click OK.

3. If the drive you're working with was compressed using an earlier version of DriveSpace, the Compression Agent displays a dialog box asking whether you want to run DriveSpace 3. Click Yes and then upgrade the compressed drive. (See the next section, "Upgrading to DriveSpace 3.")

4. In the Compression Agent window, click Settings to display the Compression Agent Settings dialog box, shown in Figure 15.13.

FIGURE 15.13.

Use this dialog box to choose the compression method that you want Compression Agent to use.

5. Choose the files you want Compression Agent to compress using UltraPack:

   Do not UltraPack any files: Choose this option to bypass UltraPack compression for optimum compression/decompression performance.

   UltraPack all files: Choose this option to achieve the maximum amount of compressed disk space.

   UltraPack only files not used within the last x days: Choose this option to have Compression Agent use UltraPack only on older files (which, presumably, you don't access very often).

6. If you didn't elect to use UltraPack compression on all your files, choose an option from the Do you want to HiPack the rest of your files? group:

   Yes: Choose this option to use HiPack compression on the non-UltraPack files.

   No: Choose this option to bypass compression on the non-UltraPack files.

7. Compression Agent will reduce the compression level on files you've access recently to improve performance. However, you can set a drive free space threshold at which Compression Agent no longer reduces the compression level. The default is 20MB, but you can adjust that by clicking Advanced and adjusting the spin box in the Advanced Settings dialog box that appears. Click OK when you're done.

8. If you want to specify compression settings for a specific file, folder, or file type, click Exceptions and then click Add in the dialog box that appears. In the Add Exceptions dialog box, choose a file, folder, or file extension; select a compression method and then click Add. Click Cancel until you return to the Compression Agent Settings dialog box.

9. Click OK. Compression Agent asks whether you want to use these settings when compression is invoked via the Task Scheduler.

10. To use these settings, click Yes. Otherwise, click No.

11. Click Start. Compression Agent goes to work recompressing the drive. The Compression Agent window displays the progress of the operation.

12. When it's done, a dialog box is displayed to ask whether you want to recompress another drive. If you do, click Yes and repeat steps 4 through 9; otherwise, click No to return to the Compression Agent dialog box.

13. Click Exit.

Upgrading to DriveSpace 3

Windows 98's DriveSpace 3 is an enhanced version of the DriveSpace component found in Windows 95. (DriveSpace 3 was part of the OSR2 package, however.) As you've seen, it supports compressed drives up to 2GB (compared to the 512MB maximum in the original DriveSpace), but it also compresses files about 20 times faster and comes with the HiPack and UltraPack options for squeezing even more data onto a disk.

To take advantage of these DriveSpace 3 features, you need to upgrade any drives that were compressed using the original DriveSpace. Here are the steps to follow:

1. Highlight the compressed drive you want to upgrade.

2. Select Drive | Upgrade. DriveSpace examines the drive and then displays the Upgrade a Drive dialog box, shown in Figure 15.14.

FIGURE 15.14.
You see this dialog box when you upgrade a compressed drive.

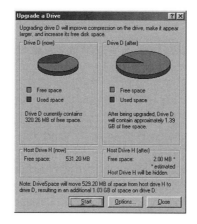

3. Because DriveSpace 3 supports larger compressed volumes, it will likely attempt to compress all the free space on the drive. If this isn't what you want, click Options to display the Upgrade Options dialog box. Use the Reserved space on host text box to specify the amount of uncompressed free space you want and then click OK.

4. Click Start.

5. If DriveSpace asks you about creating a startup disk, click Yes or No, as appropriate.

6. If you want to back up the drive, click Back Up Files.

7. Click Upgrade Now. DriveSpace checks the drive for errors and then performs the upgrade. When it's done, you're returned to the Upgrade a Drive dialog box.

8. Click Close. If Windows 98 asks whether you want to restart your computer, click Yes.

Uncompressing a Drive

If you decide you don't want to use compression any longer, it's easy enough to remove it. Here are the steps to follow:

1. Select Start | Programs | Accessories | System Tools | DriveSpace to display the DriveSpace window.

2. Use the Drives on this computer list to highlight the compressed drive you want to adjust.

3. Select Drive | Uncompress. DriveSpace displays the Uncompress a Drive dialog box.

4. Click Start. DriveSpace might ask whether you want to back up your files.

5. If you want to do a backup, click Back Up Files.

6. Click Uncompress Now to start uncompressing the files.

15

DISK DRIVING:
THE WINDOWS 98
DISK UTILITIES

7. If your system has no other compressed drives, DriveSpace will display a dialog box asking you whether you want to remove the compression driver from memory. That's a good idea, so click Yes. When the operation is complete, DriveSpace returns you to the Uncompress a Drive dialog box.

8. Click Close. If Windows 98 asks whether you want to restart your computer, click Yes.

Partitioning a Disk

In Chapter 9, I showed you how the size of a hard disk can have a tremendous effect on storage efficiency, thanks to a phenomenon called *cluster overhang*. Generally speaking, the smaller the hard disk, the more efficiently it stores data (provided, that is, that most of your data exists in relatively small files).

Here, "hard disk size" really means *partition size*, a partition being just a subset of the total hard disk storage space. For example, a 1200MB hard disk could be broken up into four partitions, each one 300MB in size. In FAT16, this partitioning would reduce the cluster size from 32KB for the full disk to 8KB for each partition. (Remember, though, that Windows 98's new FAT32 file system reduces cluster overhang by supporting smaller cluster sizes on larger hard disks.)

When working with partitions, you need to keep the following concepts in mind:

Primary partition: This is the first partition (drive C).

Active partition: This is the bootable partition. Its boot sector tells the ROM BIOS at startup that this partition contains the operating system's bootstrap code. The active partition is usually the same as the primary partition.

Extended partition: This is the hard disk space that isn't allocated to the primary partition. For example, if you have a 1.2GB disk and you allocate 300MB to the primary partition, the extended partition is 900MB. You can then subdivide the extended partition into logical DOS drives (see the next paragraph).

Logical DOS drive: This is a subset of an extended partition. For example, if the extended partition is 900MB, you could create three logical DOS drives, each with 300MB, and they would use drive letters D, E, and F. You can assign up to 23 logical DOS drives to an extended partition (letters D through Z).

To adjust partition sizes, you use the FDISK utility from the command line. You can use FDISK in a number of ways, but two scenarios are most common:

■ You break up a large partition into two or more smaller partitions.
■ You partition a new hard disk.

Here are the general steps to follow if you need to break up an existing partition into smaller partitions (the exact FDISK steps will be explained later):

1. FDISK will destroy all the files on the disk during partitioning, so be sure to back up your important files before beginning.

2. Make sure that you have a bootable floppy disk that contains the FORMAT utility. The Windows 98 Startup disk is ideal.

3. Select Start | Shut Down, activate Restart in MS-DOS mode, and click Yes.

4. At the DOS prompt, type `fdisk` and press Enter.

5. Delete all your partitions, starting with the extended DOS partition (if you have one).

6. Create a new primary partition, a new extended partition, and new logical drives in the extended partition.

7. Exit FDISK, insert the bootable disk, and reboot the computer.

8. When you get to the `A:\` prompt, use the FORMAT utility to format each of the new drives. Be sure to add the `/S` switch when you format the active partition. This switch adds the system files to the boot drive.

9. Reinstall Windows 98, as described in Chapter 2, "From Disc to Disk: Installing Windows 98."

10. Restore your backed-up data.

Here are the general steps to follow if you need to set up partitions on a new disk (again, the exact FDISK steps will be explained later):

1. Insert a bootable disk that contains both `FDISK.EXE` and `FORMAT.COM` and reboot the computer.

2. At the `A:\` prompt, type `fdisk` and press Enter.

3. Create a new primary partition, a new extended partition, and new logical drives in the extended partition.

4. Exit FDISK, insert the bootable disk, and reboot the computer.

5. When you get to the `A:\` prompt, use the FORMAT utility to format each of the new drives. Be sure to add the `/S` switch when you format the primary partition. This switch adds the system files to the boot drive.

6. Install Windows 98, as described in Chapter 2.

When you start FDISK, you may see a long message and the following prompt:

```
Do you wish to enable large disk support (Y/N)..........?
```

You see this message if your system has a hard disk larger than 512MB. FDISK is basically asking whether you want to use FAT32 on partitions larger than 512MB. If you do, press Y and Enter to enable FAT32; otherwise, press N and Enter to use FAT16. If you decide to use FAT32, please note the following:

- If you create a partition that's less than 512MB, Windows 98's Format utilities will format the partition as FAT16.

- If you create a partition that's greater than 512MB, Windows 98's Format utilities will format the partition as FAT32.

THE FAT32 CONVERTER

Don't forget that Windows 98 enables you to convert FAT16 partitions to FAT32. You learned how to use the FAT32 Converter utility in Chapter 9.

Now you see the FDISK Options screen, which includes the following menu:

```
Current fixed disk drive: 1

Choose one of the following:

1. Create DOS partition of logical DOS Drive
2. Set active partition
3. Delete partition of Logical DOS Drive
4. Display partition information

Enter choice: [1]
```

If you have two or more hard drives, you also see the following option:

```
5. Change current fixed disk drive
```

Use this option to change the current fixed disk drive (that is, the drive you'll be working with), if necessary. If you're not sure, use the Display partition information command to display information about the current disk.

When you're done with FDISK, press Esc to get back to the prompt.

Creating a Primary Partition

The following steps show you how to create a primary DOS partition in FDISK:

1. At the FDISK Options screen, press 1 and Enter. FDISK displays the following menu:

```
1. Create Primary DOS Partition
2. Create Extended DOS Partition
3. Create Logical DOS Drive(s) in the Extended DOS Partition

Enter choice: [1]
```

2. Press 1 and Enter. FDISK takes a moment or two to examine the disk and then displays the following prompt:

```
Do you wish to use the maximum available size for a Primary DOS Partition
and make the partition active (Y/N)....................? [Y]
```

3. If you want to use the entire drive as your primary partition, press Y and Enter. FDISK creates the partition and returns you to the DOS prompt.

   If you don't want to use the entire drive as your primary partition, press N and Enter. FDISK prompts you as shown here:

```
Total disk space is 2046 Mbytes (1 Mbyte = 1048576 bytes)

Maximum space available for partition is 2046 Mbytes (100%)

Enter partition size in Mbytes or percent of disk space (%) to
create a Primary DOS Partition...............................: [1204]
```

4. Type the number of megabytes you want to use for the primary partition and press Enter. FDISK creates the partition.

5. Press Esc to return to the FDISK Options screen.

6. Press 2 and Enter. FDISK prompts you to enter the number of the partition you want to make active (bootable).

7. Press 1 and Enter (assuming that you want to boot from drive C).

8. Press Esc to return to the FDISK Options screen.

Creating an Extended Partition and Logical DOS Drives

After you've set up the primary partition, you can create an extended partition and divide it into logical DOS drives by following this procedure:

1. At the FDISK Options screen, press 1 and Enter. FDISK displays the following menu:

```
1. Create Primary DOS Partition
2. Create Extended DOS Partition
3. Create Logical DOS Drive(s) in the Extended DOS Partition

Enter choice: [1]
```

2. Press 2 and Enter. FDISK takes a moment or two to examine the disk and then displays the following prompt:

```
Total disk space is 2046 Mbytes (1 Mbyte = 1048576 bytes)
Maximum space available for partition is  1646 Mbytes (80%)

Enter partition size in Mbytes or percent of disk space (%) to
create an Extended DOS Partition...............................: [ 1646]
```

3. If you want to use the rest of the disk as your extended partition, press Enter. Otherwise, type the number of megabytes you want to use for the extended partition and then press Enter. FDISK creates the partition.

> ## USE ALL AVAILABLE SPACE FOR THE EXTENDED PARTITION
>
> You probably want to use all the remaining disk space for your extended partition. If you don't, the disk space left out of the extended partition won't be available to DOS (that is, Windows 98). The only time you'll want to use less space for the extended partition is if you plan on using this space for another operating system (such as NT, OS/2, or Linux).

4. Press Esc. FDISK tells you that no logical drives are defined and displays the following prompt:

```
Total Extended DOS Partition size is  1646 Mbytes (1 MByte = 1048576 bytes)

Maximum space available for logical drive is  1646 Mbytes (100%)
Enter logical drive size in Mbytes or percent of disk space (%)...[ 1646]
```

5. Type the number of megabytes you want to use for the logical drive and press Enter.

6. Repeat step 5 until you've allocated all the available space to logical drives.

7. Press Esc to return to the FDISK Options screen.

Deleting an Extended Partition

Here are the steps to follow to delete an extended partition in FDISK:

1. At the FDISK Options screen, press 3 and Enter. FDISK displays the following menu:

```
1.  Delete Primary DOS Partition
2.  Delete Extended DOS Partition
3.  Delete Logical DOS Drive(s) in the Extended DOS Partition
4.  Delete Non-DOS Partition

Enter choice: [ ]
```

2. Press 3 and Enter. FDISK displays a list of the logical DOS drives—including their drive letters, volume labels, and sizes—and the following prompt:

```
Total Extended DOS Partition size is  1846 Mbytes (1 Mbyte = 1048576 bytes)

WARNING! Data in a deleted Logical DOS Drive will be lost.
What drive do you want to delete.............................? [ ]
```

3. Type the drive letter and press Enter. FDISK prompts you to enter the volume label for the drive.

4. Type the volume label and press Enter. FDISK, ever cautious, asks whether you're sure.

5. Press Y and Enter.

6. Repeat steps 3 through 5 to delete the other logical DOS drives.

7. Press Esc twice to return to the FDISK Options screen.

8. Press 3 and Enter.

9. Press 2 and Enter. FDISK displays the partition data for the disk and the following prompt:

```
Total disk space is 2046 Mbytes (1 Mbyte = 1048576 bytes)

WARNING! Data in the deleted Extended DOS Partition will be lost.
Do you wish to continue (Y/N)................? [N]
```

10. Press Y and Enter.

11. Press Esc to return to the FDISK Options screen.

Deleting a Primary Partition

Here are the steps to follow to delete a primary partition in FDISK:

1. At the FDISK Options screen, press 3 and Enter to display the following menu:

```
1.  Delete Primary DOS Partition
2.  Delete Extended DOS Partition
3.  Delete Logical DOS Drive(s) in the Extended DOS Partition
4.  Delete Non-DOS Partition

Enter choice: [ ]
```

2. Press 1 and Enter. FDISK displays the disk's partition information and the following prompt:

```
Total disk space is 2046 Mbytes (1 Mbyte = 1048576 bytes)

WARNING! Data in the deleted Primary DOS Partition will be lost.
What primary partition do you want to delete..? [1]
```

3. Press Enter. FDISK prompts you to enter the volume label for the drive.

4. Type the volume label and press Enter. FDISK asks whether you're sure.

5. Press Y and Enter.

6. Press Esc to return to the FDISK Options screen.

Summary

This chapter continued your look at the Windows 98 file system by showing you a few techniques for working with disks. You learned how to format a floppy disk, copy a disk, and view disk properties. I also showed you how to wield Windows 98 disk compression and how to use FDISK to partition a disk. Here are a few chapters that contain related information:

■ I discuss various techniques for optimizing disk access—including converting FAT16 partitions to FAT32—in Chapter 9, "Performance Tuning: Optimizing Memory and Disk Access."

■ I showed you how to work with file and folders in Chapter 14, "File and Folder Tricks and Techniques."

■ To learn how to use Windows 98's new Backup program, see Chapter 16, "Working with a Net: The Windows 98 Backup Utility."

15

DISK DRIVING:
THE WINDOWS 98
DISK UTILITIES

■ I show you how to create an emergency startup disk, as well as how to use ScanDisk and a few other disk-related utilities in Chapter 17, "Wielding the Windows 98 System Tools."

■ To learn how to perform file maintenance from the DOS prompt, see Chapter 23, "DOS Isn't Dead: Unleashing the DOS Shell."

Working with a Net: The Windows 98 Backup Utility

IN THIS CHAPTER

CHAPTER 16

In theory, theory and practice are the same thing; in practice, they're not.

—*Anonymous*

That old saw applies perfectly to data backups. In theory, backing up data is an important part of everyday computing life. After all, we know that our data is valuable to the point of irreplaceability, and we know that there's no shortage of ways that a hard disk can crash: power surges, rogue applications, virus programs, or just simple wear and tear. In practice, however, backing up our data always seems to be one of those chores we'll get to "tomorrow." After all, that old hard disk seems to be humming along just fine, thank you—and anyway, who has time to work through the couple of dozen floppy disks you need for even a small backup?

When it comes to backups, theory and practice don't usually converge until that day you start your system and you get an ugly `Invalid system configuration` or `Hard disk failure` message. Believe me, losing a hard disk that's crammed with unsaved (and now lost) data brings the importance of backing up into focus real quick. To avoid this sorry fate, you have to find a way to take some of the pain out of the practice of backing up. Fortunately, you can do two things to make backups more painless:

- Use the revamped Backup accessory that comes with Windows 98. This program has a few nice features that make it easy to select files for backup and to run backups regularly.

- Practice what I call real-world backups. In short, these are backups that protect only your most crucial files.

To help you get through your backup chores, Windows 98 comes with a new and much improved Backup utility. (It's actually a version of the backup software that comes with Seagate drives.) The interface is better set up for power users to select the options they need. For novices, Backup has several Wizards that take them through complex operations such as backup and restore. There are also many new options (including the welcome ability to back up and restore Registry files) and built-in support for SCSI tape drives and many other backup devices.

This chapter shows you how to use new Backup and explains real-world backups in more detail.

Starting Backup

Assuming that you've installed the Backup accessory, select Start | Programs | Accessories | System Tools | Backup to get the show on the road.

Backup first checks your system to see whether you have any backup devices installed. If you don't, Backup displays a dialog box asking whether you want to run the Add New Hardware Wizard to install a device. If you do have a backup device on your system, click Yes and use the wizard to specify the device. Otherwise, click No to continue.

Each time you start Backup, you see the dialog box shown in Figure 16.1. You have the following choices:

Create a new backup job: If you activate this option and click OK, the program launches the Backup Wizard to take you step-by-step through the process of creating a backup job. In this case, see the section, "Using the Backup Wizard to Define a New Backup Job," later in this chapter. If you prefer to set up the new backup job yourself, click Cancel and see "Creating a Backup Job by Hand," also later in this chapter.

Open an existing backup job: If you've already defined a backup job, activate this option and click OK. In the Open Backup Job dialog box that appears, highlight the backup job you want to work with and then click Open.

Restore backed up files: If you've already run a backup job, activate this option and click OK to restore files from that backup job. See "Restoring Backed-Up Data," later in this chapter.

FIGURE 16.1.

Backup presents you with this dialog box at startup.

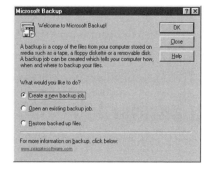

Some Thoughts on Real-World Backups

Before getting down to business, you need to ask yourself which files you want to include in the backup job. Your first inclination might be to back up all your drives just to be safe. This is fine if you have lots of room on your destination drive, whether it's a tape drive, another hard drive, or a network drive.

But what if you're backing up to a location with limited free space or even to floppy disks? Although Backup can compress your backed-up files so that they consume only about half their normal volume, that can still add up to hundreds of megabytes on a big system. And even a small hard disk contains enough data to fill a few dozen floppy disks. Shuffling that many disks in and out of your machine every time you do a backup will get old in a hurry. For these limited situations, you need to take a real-world approach to backups:

■ The problem with a full backup is that it includes all your program files. Presumably, however, you have these files on disk somewhere, so why include them in a backup? If necessary, you can always reinstall your programs (and even Windows 98 itself).

■ If you're going to leave out your program files, however, you should seriously consider making backup copies of your program disks. You have to do it only once, and you probably can do it only for your most important programs. (I showed you how to copy disks in Chapter 15, "Disk Driving: The Windows 98 Disk Utilities.")

■ All the energy you put into backing up should go toward protecting your documents and data because, unlike your programs, these are usually irreplaceable. To make life easier, you should create separate folders to hold only your documents (or use Windows 98's My Documents folder). That way, adding these documents to the backup job is an easy matter of selecting the folder.

■ Take advantage of Backup's three different backup types:

Full: Backs up all the files in the backup job.

Differential: Backs up only those files that have changed since the last full backup.

Incremental: Backs up only those files that have changed since the last full or differential backup.

Your overall backup strategy might look something like this:

1. Perform a full backup of all your documents once a month or so.
2. Do a differential backup of modified files once a week.
3. Do an incremental backup of modified files every day.

Defining a Backup Job

In Backup lingo, a *backup job* is a file that defines your backup. It includes three things:

■ A list of the files you want to include in your backup

■ The Backup options you selected, including the type of backup you want to use

■ The destination drive and folder for the backed-up files

You can either use the Backup Wizard to create a backup job (see the next section), or you can create the backup job right from the Microsoft Backup window (see "Creating a Backup Job by Hand," later in this chapter).

Using the Backup Wizard to Define a New Backup Job

Windows 98's Backup program contains several wizards that take you through various backup-related operations. The Backup Wizard's role is to help you set up a new backup job. You start this Wizard using either of the following methods:

■ In the startup Microsoft Backup dialog box, activate Create a new backup job and click OK.

■ In the Microsoft Backup window, select Tools | Backup Wizard.

Either way, you see the first of the Wizard's dialog boxes, which offers you two choices:

Back up My Computer: Activate this option and click Next > to perform a complete backup of all local hard drives.

Back up selected files, folders, and drives: Activate this option and click Next > to choose the files you want to include in the backup job.

If you elected to back up only selected files, you use the next Wizard dialog box to choose those files. The dialog box that appears is reminiscent of the Explorer window, with one important difference: In the Backup window, all the disk drives, folders, and files have a check box next to them. The basic idea is that you activate the appropriate check box for each drive, folder, and file that you want to include in the backup. Figure 16.2 shows an example. Click Next > to move on.

FIGURE 16.2.

Use this Wizard dialog box to choose the drives, folders, and files to include in the backup job.

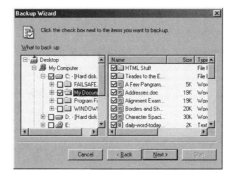

The Wizard next asks whether you want to back up All selected files or New and changed files. Make your choice and click Next >.

The Wizard next asks you which of the selected files you want to back up:

All selected files: If you choose this option, every one of the files you selected is included in the backup job.

New and changed files: If you choose this option, only new files and files that have been modified since the last backup are included in the backup job.

The Wizard next wonders where you want the selected files backed up. Depending on your system, you see one or both of the following:

File: Select this option to back up your files to a single QIC backup file. The Wizard adds an extra text box so that you can specify the name and location of this backup file.

Backup Device: Select this option (the name of which varies depending on the backup device you have installed) to use your backup device as the destination.

Click Next > to continue.

Now the Wizard presents you with the following options:

Compare original and backup files to verify data was successfully backed up: If you activate this check box, Backup checks each backed-up file against its original to make sure that the backup archived the file without any errors. Note that activating this option effectively doubles the backup time.

Compress the backup data to save space: If you activate this check box, Backup compresses the backed-up files. The backed-up files will take up approximately half the space of the originals.

Click Next > to move to the Wizard dialog box shown in Figure 16.3. Use the text box to enter a name for your new backup job.

FIGURE 16.3.

Enter a name for the new backup job.

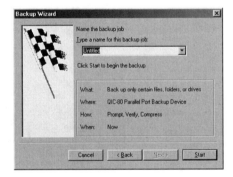

You're now ready to get the backup process under way. Click Start and Backup goes to work. Backup may ask you for a unique name for the backup media. If so, enter a name and click OK.

During the backup process, you see the Backup Progress window, shown in Figure 16.4. When the operation is complete, Backup displays a dialog box to let you know. Click OK and then click OK in the Backup Progress window. (For the latter, you can also click Report to see a summary report for the backup operation.)

Creating a Backup Job by Hand

The Backup Wizard is a boon for new users who might be intimidated by all of Backup's options. If you want a bit more control over the process of defining a backup job, however, you need to bypass the Wizard and set up the job by hand. To do this, you use the Microsoft Backup window, shown in Figure 16.5.

FIGURE 16.4.

This dialog box shows the progress of the backup operation.

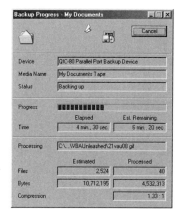

FIGURE 16.5.

Use the Microsoft Backup window to define your backup job by hand.

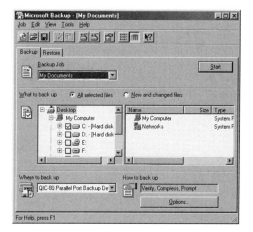

Here are the steps to follow to define a backup job:

1. If you want to adjust an existing backup job, select it using the Backup Job list.

2. Select the backup type: All selected files or New and changed files.

3. Use the folder and file lists to activate the check boxes for the drives, folders, and files you want to include in the backup job.

4. Use the Where to back up list to choose a backup device or a backup file.

5. Click Options to set the backup job options. (See the next section, "Working with the Backup Job Options.")

6. Select Job | Save. If you're creating a new backup job, enter a name in the Save Backup Job As dialog box and then click Save.

7. Click Start to perform the backup.

When the backup operation is complete, you can see a report by selecting the View | Report command and then selecting either View or Print.

DISPLAYING FILE TOTALS

To see the number of files included in the backup job and the total number of bytes involved, select View | Selection Information.

Working with the Backup Job Options

Backup has various options you can work with, and the options you choose are stored with each backup job. To view the options, either click Options in the Backup tab or select Job | Options. Backup displays the Backup Job Options dialog box, shown in Figure 16.6. The next few sections discuss each tab in this dialog box.

FIGURE 16.6.

Selecting Job | Options displays this dialog box.

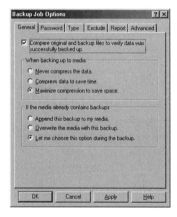

The General Options

In the General tab, use the Compare original and backup files to verify data was successfully backed up check box to toggle the verification process on or off.

The When backing up to media group contains the following three options:

Never compress the data: Activate this option to turn off Backup's compression setting.

Compress data to save time: This option compresses the data, but doesn't use full compress, which speeds things up a bit.

Maximize compression to save space: If the backup media is low on space, activate this option to use full compression on the backed up files. This reduces the size of the backup, but takes longer.

The If the media already contains backups group contains these option buttons:

Append this backup to my media: This option adds your backup to the existing backups on the media.

Overwrite the media with this backup: Activate this option to replace the old backup data with your new backup data.

Let me choose this option during the backup: When this option is activated, Backup prompts you to append or overwrite the existing backup.

Setting a Backup Password

If you're backing up to a network drive or other public location, you can protect your backup from snoops by activating the Protect this backup with a password check box in the Password tab. Enter your password in both the Password and Confirm password text boxes.

Setting the Backup Type

You use the Type tab (see Figure 16.7) to choose the type of backup you want to run. Activate either the All selected files option or the New and changed files only option. If you activate the latter, select either Differential backup type or Incremental backup type.

FIGURE 16.7.

Use the Type tab to choose the backup type.

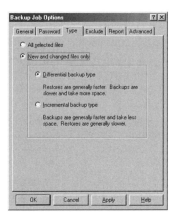

Excluding Files from the Backup Job

Besides letting you select individual drives, folders, and files, Backup also has an Exclude feature that enables you to exclude files based on the file type. Here are the steps to follow:

1. In the Exclude tab, click Add to display the Add Exclude dialog box, shown in Figure 16.8.

2. The Registered type list displays all the registered file types known to Windows 98. (See Chapter 14, "File and Folder Tricks and Techniques," for an in-depth discussion of file types.) To exclude one of these types, activate the Registered type option button and then highlight the file type in the list.

3. Alternatively, you can exclude files with any other extension by activating the Custom type option and then entering the three-letter extension in the text box.

4. Click OK. Backup returns you to the Exclude tab and adds the chosen file type to the list.

5. Repeat steps 1 through 4 to exclude other file types.

FIGURE 16.8.

Use this dialog box to exclude particular file types from the backup job.

Setting the Report Contents

You saw earlier that Backup can display a post-backup report that summarizes what happened during the operation. To specify the data included in this report, use the check boxes in the Report tab, shown in Figure 16.9.

Note, too, that this tab also contains the Perform an unattended backup check box. When this option is activated, you can run this backup job without prompts. This is handy if you use Task Scheduler to schedule overnight backup jobs. (See Chapter 17, "Wielding the Windows 98 System Tools.")

FIGURE 16.9.

The Report tab enables you to specify the data included in Backup's report.

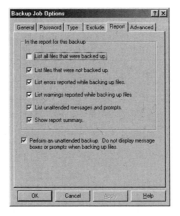

Backing Up the Registry

One of the most welcome improvements the Windows 98 Backup offers is the ability to include the Registry files as part of the backup job. (This was a glaring omission in the Windows 95 Backup program.) Whether the Registry files are included is controlled by the Back up

Windows Registry check box in the Advanced tab. Make sure this check box is activated to include the Registry in your backup job.

Working with Backup Media

If you have a backup device attached to your computer, Backup offers several commands for working with the device media. If you select the Tools | Media command, Backup displays a submenu with the following commands:

Identify: This command displays the name of the device and the name of the media (see Figure 16.10).

Initialize: This command erases the media and prepares it for new data. Backup will ask you to confirm that you want to erase the data.

Format: This command formats QIC media so that it can hold files. Because this operation erases any existing data on the media, Backup asks you to confirm that you want to format the media.

Retension: This command performs a fast forward and rewind on tape media to remove slack and produce even tensioning on the tape.

Rename: This command changes the name associated with the media.

FIGURE 16.10.

Running the Identity command displays this dialog box.

Setting Backup Preferences

You can use the Preferences dialog box, shown in Figure 16.11, to set some Backup options that apply to all backup jobs. To display this dialog box, select the Tools | Preferences command. Here's a summary of the check boxes:

Show startup dialog box when Microsoft Backup is started: This check box toggles the startup dialog box on and off.

Back up or restore the registry when backing or restoring the Windows directory: When this check box is activated, Backup automatically selects the Registry files for backup if you include your main Windows 98 folder as part of a backup job.

Show the number and size of files before backing up, restoring and comparing data: When this check box is activated, Backup displays a dialog box showing the number of files in the backup job and the total number of bytes represented by those files.

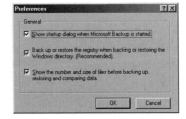

Restoring Backed-Up Data

If some unforeseen disaster should occur, you need to restore your data from the backups. As with backing up, you can either use a Wizard or restore by hand.

Using the Restore Wizard

Backup has another Wizard that takes you step-by-step through the process of restoring previously backed-up data. You start this Wizard using either of the following methods:

■ In the startup Microsoft Backup dialog box, activate Restore backed up files and click OK.

■ In the Microsoft Backup window, select Tools | Restore Wizard.

In the first of the Wizard's dialog boxes, use the Restore from list to select the source of the backup job and then click Next >.

The Wizard then displays a list of the backups found on the media. Activate the check boxes beside each backup job you want to restore and then click OK.

Now the Wizard creates a list of the drives, folders, and files in the chosen backup jobs. When it's done, it displays the dialog box shown in Figure 16.12. Activate the check boxes beside the items you want to restore and then click Next >.

The Wizard next asks where you want the files restored. You can select either Original Location or Alternate Location. If you choose the latter, a new text box appears so that you can specify the new location. Click Next > when you're ready to proceed.

FIGURE 16.12.

Use this Wizard dialog box to choose the data you want to restore.

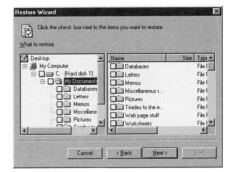

Now the Wizard asks what it should do if a file with the same name already exists in the restore destination (see Figure 16.13). Here are your choices:

> **Do not replace the file on my computer**: If you activate this option, Backup won't replace any files on the destination drive or folder with backed-up files that have the same name.

> **Replace the file on my computer only if the file is older**: If you activate this option, Backup replaces files on the destination drive or folder only with backed-up files of the same name that have a later date.

> **Always replace the file on my computer**: If you activate this option, Backup replaces any files on the destination drive or folder with backed-up files that have the same name.

FIGURE 16.13.

Use this dialog box to let the Wizard know how it should replace existing files.

Click Start to get the restore operation under way. Backup will prompt you to insert the media for the backup. Insert the media, if necessary and then click OK.

The Restore Progress window appears during the restore operation. When Backup is done, it displays a dialog box to let you know. Click OK and then click OK in the Restore Progress window. (Note that you can also click Report to see a summary report for the restore operation.)

Restoring Backed-Up Data by Hand

If you prefer the direct approach, you can bypass the Restore Wizard and opt to run the restore operation manually. Here are the required steps:

1. In the Microsoft Backup window, select the Restore tab, shown in Figure 16.14.

FIGURE 16.14.

Use the Restore tab to restore data from a backup job.

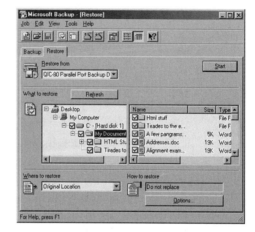

2. Use the Restore from list to select a backup source.
3. Use the folder and file lists to activate the check boxes for the drives, folders, and files you want to include in the restore.
4. Use the Where to restore list to choose the destination (Original Location or Alternate Location).
5. Click Options to set the backup job options. (See the next section, "Working with the Restore Options.")
6. Select Job | Save to save your settings.
7. Click Start to perform the restore.

Working with the Restore Options

You can set a few options for the restore operation. To view these options, either click Options in the Restore tab or select Job | Options. Backup displays the Restore Options dialog box, shown in Figure 16.15.

FIGURE 16.15.
Selecting Job | Options
displays this dialog box.

Restore uses a simpler set of options than does Backup, so I can run through the tabs quickly:

The General tab: Use the options in the When restoring files that already exist group to set what Backup does if it comes across a file that already exists during the restore. The available options are identical to those you saw earlier with the Restore Wizard.

The Report tab: The contents of the Restore report are determined by the check boxes you activate in the Report tab.

The Advanced tab: Whether the Registry files are included in the restore is controlled by the Restore Windows registry check box.

Summary

This chapter showed you how to use the new and improved Backup utility that comes with Windows 98. After a brief discussion of "real-world" backups, I showed you how to create backup jobs both by using the Backup Wizard and by hand from the Microsoft Backup window. You also learned a few techniques for working with backup media and for creating Emergency Recovery disks. I closed by showing you how to restore backed-up data.

Here's a list of chapters where you'll find related information:

■ I explain the Registry files in detail in Chapter 12, "Getting to Know the Windows 98 Registry."

■ You'll learn how to create an emergency startup disk in Chapter 17, "Wielding the Windows 98 System Tools."

■ If you perform a full backup, Windows 98's new System Recovery utility can restore your entire system, even if you have to format your hard disk. I'll show you how to use System Recovery in Chapter 17.

■ Chapter 17 is also the place to learn how to use other utilities (such as ScanDisk and the Maintenance Wizard) that can prevent system problems.

Wielding the Windows 98 System Tools

CHAPTER

17

He is safe from danger who is on guard even when safe.

—Publilius Syrus

Computer problems, like the proverbial death and taxes, seem to be one of those constants in life. Whether it's a hard disk giving up the ghost, a power failure that trashes your files, or a virus that invades your system, the issue isn't whether something will go wrong, but when will it happen.

Instead of dealing with these difficulties only after they occur (what I call pound-of-cure mode), you need to get your system prepared in advance (ounce-of-prevention mode). This chapter shows you various Windows 98 utilities and techniques that can help you do just that. In particular, I'll show you how to use all the new utilities that come with the Windows 98 package, including Registry Scan, System File Checker, System Troubleshooter, Microsoft System Information Utility, the Maintenance Wizard, the Task Scheduler, and System Recovery.

Creating an Emergency Boot Disk

When most computers are switched on, the startup BIOS code first runs the Power-On Self Test and then looks for a disk in drive A. If it finds a disk, the BIOS code checks for a boot sector and, if one is present, boots the system via the floppy to get you to the A:\ prompt. If there's no disk in drive A, the system tries to boot via the active hard disk partition. If your hard disk dies or if Windows 98 refuses to run, you can use a bootable floppy disk to bypass the hard disk and regain control of your system. Windows 98 gives you two methods of creating bootable floppy disks:

- You can use the Format command to either copy the necessary system files to an already formatted disk or format a disk to make it bootable. I showed you how to do this in Chapter 15, "Disk Driving: The Windows 98 Disk Utilities."
- You can create a Windows 98 startup disk.

When you install Windows 98, the Setup program asks whether you want to create a startup disk, which is a bootable disk that contains various files you can use to troubleshoot problems. No system should be without a bootable disk of some kind, so if you skipped the startup disk during setup, you can still create it from within Windows 98.

THE SYSTEM RECOVERY UTILITY

The perfect complement to an emergency boot disk is the new System Recovery utility. See "Getting Your System Back on Its Feet with System Recovery," later in this chapter.

To do this, open the Control Panel and launch the Add/Remove Programs icon. Activate the Startup Disk tab and then click the Create Disk button. While Windows 98 prepares the startup files, insert a disk in drive A. (Make sure that it's either a new disk or a disk that doesn't contain any files you need.) When you see the Insert Disk dialog box, click OK.

Table 17.1 lists the files Windows 98 adds to the Startup disk.

Table 17.1. Windows 98 Startup disk files.

File	Description
ASPI2DOS.SYS	A real-mode driver for Adaptec SCSI adapter models AIC-6260/6360/6370
ASPI4DOS.SYS	A real-mode driver for Adaptec SCSI adapter models AHA-154X/1640
ASPI8DOS.SYS	A real-mode driver for Adaptec SCSI adapter models AIC-75XX/78XX
ASPI8U2.SYS	A real-mode driver for Adaptec SCSI adapter models AIC-789X
ASPICD.SYS	An Adaptec SCSI CD-ROM driver
AUTOEXEC.BAT	A batch file that runs automatically at startup
BTCDROM.SYS	A Mylex/BusLogic SCSI CD-ROM driver
BTDOSM.SYS	A Mylex/BusLogic real-mode SCSI driver
COMMAND.COM	A real-mode command interpreter
CONFIG.SYS	A text file containing instructions for loading device drivers at startup
DRVSPACE.BIN	A real-mode driver for compressed disks
EBD.CAB	A cabinet file that contains a number of DOS utilities
EBD.SYS	A utility for the Startup disk
EXTRACT.EXE	A utility for extracting files from a compressed cabinet (CAB) file
FDISK.EXE	A utility for partitioning a disk
FINDRAMD.EXE	A utility that locates an installed RAM drive
FLASHPT.SYS	A BusLogic FlashPoint real-mode SCSI driver
HIMEM.SYS	An extended memory manager utility
IO.SYS	A Windows 98 system file
MSDOS.SYS	A Windows 98 startup file
OAKCDROM.SYS	A generic IDE CD-ROM driver
RAMDRIVE.SYS	A utility that sets up a temporary disk drive in RAM
README.TXT	A file that explains the features of the Emergency Boot Disk
SETRAMD.BAT	A batch file that sets the drive letter for the RAM drive

To save room on the disk, Windows 98 compresses a number of useful DOS utilities into the EBD.CAB cabinet file. Table 17.2 lists the files stored inside this cabinet.

Table 17.2. Files stored in EBD.CAB.

CHKDSK.EXE	A real-mode utility for scanning and repairing a disk
DEBUG.EXE	A utility for testing and debugging executable files
EDIT.COM	A text editor for making changes to configuration files
EXTWRAP.EXE	Another utility for extracting files from a cabinet
FORMAT.COM	A utility used to format a disk
MSCDEX.EXE	A utility that loads support for a CD-ROM drive
SCANDISK.EXE	A utility for scanning and repairing a disk
SCANDISK.INI	A configuration file for ScanDisk
SYS.COM	A utility for transferring Windows 98 system files to a disk
UNINSTAL.EXE	A utility for uninstalling Windows 98 (if you installed over an existing version of Windows)

When you perform a floppy boot with the Startup disk, a RAM drive is created and then the contents of the EBD.CAB file are extracted into this RAM drive.

You probably have a few hundred kilobytes left over on the disk, so to make this a true emergency disk, you should include any other diagnostic or repair utilities you might have. If you want access to your system devices (such as a different SCSI controller or removable hard disk), you should include the necessary device drivers on the disk as well.

TROUBLESHOOTING: YOUR BOOT DISK WON'T BOOT

If your system won't boot from the disk but you're sure that the disk is bootable, check your computer's CMOS settings. Some systems let you bypass the floppy disk boot sector check and boot from the hard drive first. In this case, you need to access your computer's setup program and change this setting so that the computer attempts to boot from drive A first.

Understanding CD-ROM Support in the Windows 98 Startup Disk

Notice in Table 17.1 that Windows 98 Startup disks include a welcome new addition: CD-ROM drivers. OAKCDROM.SYS is a generic IDE driver that should work with most IDE drives, and the disk also includes drivers for Adaptec and Mylex/BusLogic SCSI CD-ROM drives. The Windows 98 startup disk also comes with the necessary support files for the CD-ROM driver: MSCDEX.EXE to load the real-mode CD-ROM extensions, CONFIG.SYS to load the appropriate driver, and AUTOEXEC.BAT to load MSCDEX.EXE.

When you boot from this disk, you see the following menu:

```
Microsoft Windows 98 Startup Menu
=================================


    1. Start computer with CD-ROM support.
    2. Start computer without CD-ROM support.
    3. View the Help file.
Enter a choice
```

Press the number of the menu option you want to run and then press Enter

This menu comes from a few specialCONFIG.SYS commands

```
[menu
menuitem=CD, Start computer with CD-ROM support
menuitem=NOCD, Start computer without CD-ROM support
menuitem=HELP, View the Help file
menudefault=CD,3
menucolor=7,

[CD
device=himem.sys /testmem:of
device=oakcdrom.sys /D:mscd00
device=btdosm.sy
device=flashpt.sy
device=btcdrom.sys /D:mscd00
device=aspi2dos.sy
device=aspi8dos.sy
device=aspi4dos.sy
device=aspi8u2.sy
device=aspicd.sys /D:mscd00

[NOCD
device=himem.sys /testmem:of

[HELP
device=himem.sys /testmem:of

[COMMON
files=1
buffers=1
dos=high,um
stacks=9,25
devicehigh=ramdrive.sys /E 204
lastdrive=
```

The [menu] item is a *block header* that specifies you're creating a startup menu. The next fe sections discuss the commands and structure used in this CONFIG.SYS file

The CONFIG.SYS MENUITEM Command

You use a series of MENUITEM commands to define the menu options. Here's the general format:

MENUITEM=*block*, [*menutext*]

Here, *block* is the name of a configuration block (which I'll define soon), and *menutext* is an optional description that will appear as the menu option. (If you leave out *menutext*, Windows 98 uses *block* instead.)

Some notes about MENUITEM:

■ The *block* parameter can be up to 70 characters long, but it can't include spaces or any of the following characters:

\ / , ; = [ ]

■ The *menutext* parameter can also be up to 70 characters long, but it can include any characters that strike your fancy.

■ You can't have more than nine MENUITEM commands in a menu block.

The CONFIG.SYS MENUCOLOR Command

The MENUCOLOR command defines the text and background colors for the startup menu. Here's the general format:

MENUCOLOR=*x*, [*y*]

Here, *x* is the text color and *y* is the optional background color. Table 17.3 lists the available values for both parameters.

Table 17.3. Available color values for the MENUCOLOR command.

Value	Color	Value	Color
0	Black	8	Gray
1	Blue	9	Bright blue
2	Green	10	Bright green
3	Cyan	11	Bright cyan
4	Red	12	Bright red
5	Magenta	13	Bright magenta
6	Brown	14	Yellow
7	White	15	Bright white

The CONFIG.SYS MENUDEFAULT Command

The MENUCOLOR command defines a default choice for the startup menu. The general format is as follows:

```
MENUDEFAULT=block, [timeout]
```

In this case, *block* is a block name used in a MENUITEM command, and *timeout* is an optional number of seconds that Windows 98 waits before selecting the default choice automatically. The following are some MENUDEFAULT notes:

- If you don't enter a value for *timeout*, DOS waits patiently until you press Enter.
- You can enter a *timeout* value between 0 and 90 seconds. If you enter 0, DOS selects the default choice automatically.

CONFIG.SYS Configuration Blocks

After you have your menu definition in place, you need to set up *configuration blocks* for each menu item. A configuration block is just a collection of related CONFIG.SYS commands. When you select an option from the startup menu, Windows 98 runs only the commands in the corresponding block.

A configuration block always begins with a block header, which is the name of the block enclosed in square brackets. You then place each block command below the header. The startup disk CONFIG.SYS file has four menu options, and they invoke the IDE, ADAPTEC, MYLEX, and NOCD configuration blocks. The IDE block, for example, contains the following DEVICE line:

```
DEVICE=OAKCDROM.SYS /D:mscd001
```

This command loads the IDE CD-ROM device driver. The /D parameter defines a name for this device driver.

Also notice that the startup CONFIG.SYS includes a [COMMON] block. [COMMON] is a special configuration block that is used to specify drivers and commands that run no matter which startup option you choose.

Handling Menu Options in AUTOEXEC.BAT

The final step in setting up these startup options is to modify AUTOEXEC.BAT to handle your different CONFIG.SYS configurations. When you select a startup menu option, Windows 98 places the name of the corresponding configuration block in an environment variable named %CONFIG%. So, in AUTOEXEC.BAT, all you need to do is check the value of %CONFIG% to see whether real-mode CD-ROM support is required.

To do this, the startup disk `AUTOEXEC.BAT` file first extracts the contents of the `EBD.CAB` cabinet file to the RAM disk. It then checks for CD-ROM support using the following lines:

```
IF "%config%"=="NOCD" GOTO QUIT
LH %ramd%:\MSCDEX.EXE /D:mscd001 /L:%CDROM%
GOTO QUIT

:QUIT
```

If the user selects menu option 4 (No CD-ROM support), the `CONFIG` environment variable is set to `NOCD`. The `IF` command checks to see whether `%CONFIG%` is equal to `NOCD`:

- If it is, the `GOTO QUIT` command runs, which means the batch file skips down to the `:QUIT` label.
- If it's not, a CD-ROM driver was loaded, so `AUTOEXEC.BAT` loads the `MSCDEX.EXE` (Microsoft CD-ROM Extensions) program from the RAM disk for real-mode CD-ROM support.

Here's the syntax for `MSCDEX`:

```
MSCDEX /D:driver [/E] [/K] [/S] [/V] [/L:letter] [/M:buffers]
```

`/D:driver`	Specifies the CD-ROM device driver. Here, `driver` is the same name that you specified with the `/D` switch on the CD-ROM driver's `DEVICE` line in `CONFIG.SYS`.
`/E`	Enables the CD-ROM driver to use expanded memory (if it's available).
`/K`	Specifies that the CD-ROM driver is encoded in Kanji.
`/S`	Enables sharing of the CD-ROM drive over a network.
`/V`	Loads `MSCDEX` in verbose mode, which displays memory statistics at startup.
`/L:letter`	Specifies the drive letter to use for the CD-ROM drive.
`/M:buffers`	Specifies the number of sector buffers to use.

The values you use for these switches depend on the CD-ROM device. See your drive's documentation.

Preventing and Repairing Hard Disk Errors with ScanDisk

An old ad for Steve Gibson's SpinRite hard disk utilities said it all: "Hard disks die." That's a stark message but, let's face it, an honest one. Just consider everything that a modern hard disk has to put up with:

General wear and tear: If your computer is running right now, its hard disk is spinning away at between 5,400 and 10,000 revolutions per minute. That's right, even though you're not doing anything, the hard disk is hard at work. Because of this constant activity, most hard disks simply wear out after a few years.

The old bump-and-grind: Your hard disk includes "read/write heads" that are used to read data from and write data to the disk. These heads float on a cushion of air just above the spinning hard disk platters. A bump or jolt of sufficient intensity can send them crashing onto the surface of the disk, which could easily result in trashed data. If the heads happen to hit a particularly sensitive area, the entire hard disk could crash.

Power surges: The current that is supplied to your PC is, under normal conditions, relatively constant. It's possible, however, for your computer to be assailed by massive power surges (for example, during a lightning storm). These surges can wreak havoc on a carefully arranged hard disk.

Power outages: If a power outage shuts down your system while you're working in Windows, you will almost certainly lose some data, and you might (in extremely rare cases) lose access to your hard disk as well.

Viruses: Unfortunately, computer viruses are all too common nowadays. Although some of these viruses are benign—they display cute messages or cause characters to "fall off" the screen—most are downright vicious and exist only to trash your valuable data (more on this topic later).

Bad programming: Some not-ready-for-prime-time software programs can end up running amok and destroying large chunks of your hard disk in the process. Luckily, these rogues are fairly rare these days.

So what can you do about it? Well, backing up your files regularly and keeping a bootable emergency disk nearby are good places to start. But Windows 98 also comes with a program called ScanDisk that can check your hard disk for problems and repair them automatically. It might not be able to recover a totally trashed hard disk, but it can at least let you know when a hard disk might be heading for trouble.

ScanDisk performs a battery of tests on a hard disk, including looking for invalid filenames, invalid file dates and times, bad sectors, and invalid compression structures. In the hard disk's file system, ScanDisk also looks for the following errors:

- Lost clusters
- Invalid clusters
- Cross-linked clusters

FAT BACKGROUND

Many of the problems that ScanDisk looks for are related to the File Allocation Table (FAT). I introduced you to this data structure in Chapter 9, "Performance Tuning: Optimizing Memory and Disk Access."

Understanding Lost Clusters

A *lost cluster* (also sometimes called an *orphaned cluster*) is a cluster that, according to the FAT, is associated with a file, but that has no link to any entry in the file directory. Lost clusters are typically caused by program crashes, power surges, or power outages.

If ScanDisk comes across lost clusters, it offers to delete them or convert them to files in the drive's root folder with names like FILE0000.CHK and FILE0001.CHK. You can take a look at these files to see whether they contain any useful data and then try to salvage the data. Usually, however, these files are unusable, and most people just delete them to save the disk space.

Understanding Invalid Clusters

An *invalid cluster* is one that falls under one of the following three categories:

- A FAT entry that refers to cluster 1. This is illegal because a disk's cluster numbers start at 2.
- A FAT entry that refers to a cluster number larger than the total number of clusters on the disk.
- A FAT entry of 0 (which normally denotes an unused cluster) that is part of a cluster chain.

In this case, ScanDisk asks whether you want to convert these "lost file fragments" to files. If you say yes, ScanDisk truncates the file by replacing the invalid cluster with an EOF marker and then converts the lost file fragments to files. These are probably the truncated portion of the file, so you can examine them and try to piece everything back together. More likely, however, you just have to trash these files.

Understanding Cross-Linked Clusters

A *cross-linked cluster* is a cluster that has somehow been assigned to two different files (or twice in the same file). Figure 17.1 shows a diagram of a FAT with a couple of cross-linked files. In this case, both BADFILE.DBF and NOGOOD.DOC contain FAT entries that refer to cluster 101, so they're cross-linked. BADFILE.DBF also has two FAT entries that refer to the same cluster (103), which is also a cross-link error.

FIGURE 17.1.
Files with cross-linked clusters.

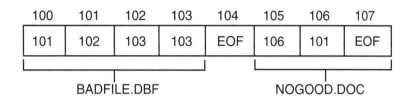

File Allocation Table

100	101	102	103	104	105	106	107
101	102	103	103	EOF	106	101	EOF

BADFILE.DBF   NOGOOD.DOC

ScanDisk offers to delete the affected files, copy the cross-linked cluster to each affected file, or ignore the cross-linked files altogether. In most cases, the safest bet is to copy the cross-linked cluster to each affected file. This way, at least one of the affected files should be usable.

Getting ScanDisk Ready

To get ScanDisk up and running, select Start | Programs | Accessories | System Tools | ScanDisk. You see the ScanDisk window shown in Figure 17.2.

FIGURE 17.2.
The main ScanDisk window.

Use the Select the drive(s) you want to check for errors list to highlight the drive or drives you want ScanDisk to check. If you select a floppy drive, be sure to insert a disk in the drive before proceeding.

The Type of test group contains two options that determine how ScanDisk checks the disks:

Standard: This test checks for FAT problems, invalid filenames, invalid file dates and times, and compression errors. On most drives, this test should take only a few seconds.

Thorough: This test runs the Standard test and then checks the surface of the disk for bad sectors. Depending on the size of the disk, this test can take an hour or two.

Setting Surface Scan Options

If you select the Thorough test, ScanDisk enables the Options button. Clicking this command button displays the Surface Scan Options dialog box, shown in Figure 17.3. Here's a summary of the controls in this dialog box:

Areas of the disk to scan: The option buttons in this group determine which parts of the physical disk will be checked. The *system area* is where the master boot record and other system structures are stored. Although ScanDisk won't be able to fix errors in this area, an indication that errors exist might be a sign that your hard disk is about to fail. The *data area* is the area where your files and folders are stored on the disk. If ScanDisk finds a bad sector here, it can relocate the data to a safe part of the disk and mark the sector as bad so that no programs will use it in the future.

Do not perform write-testing: ScanDisk normally checks for bad sectors by reading each sector and then writing the data back to the disk. If this read/write cycle is performed successfully, the sector is good. To speed up the surface scan, you can activate this check box. This tells ScanDisk not to write the data back to the disk.

Do not repair bad sectors in hidden and system files: Some programs expect certain hidden and system files to be stored in specific clusters. If any part of these files is moved, the program might no longer function properly. If you activate this check box, ScanDisk won't move any bad sectors it finds in hidden and system files. (Of course, if a hidden or system file contains a bad sector, the program that needs the file might not work anyway, so you should probably leave this option deactivated.)

Click OK when you're done to return to the ScanDisk window.

Figure 17.3.

Use this dialog box to set options for Scan-Disk's Thorough test.

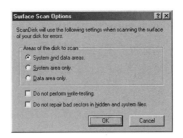

Setting Advanced Options

ScanDisk has a few advanced options that determine its default behavior. To view these options, click the Advanced button in the ScanDisk main window to display the ScanDisk Advanced Options dialog box, shown in Figure 17.4.

FIGURE 17.4.

Use this dialog box to modify ScanDisk's default behavior.

Here's a rundown of the various settings you can work with in this dialog box:

Display summary: The options in this group determine whether ScanDisk Always or Never displays a summary at the end of the check. This summary shows the total disk space, the number of bytes used, the size of each cluster (or *allocation unit*, as ScanDisk calls a cluster), the number of bad sectors, and the repairs that were made, if any. If you want to see this summary only if ScanDisk finds a problem, activate the Only if errors found option.

Log file: ScanDisk normally creates a file named SCANDISK.LOG in the drive's root folder. This file contains a log of the scan, including errors that were found and the steps that were taken to repair them. You have three choices:

    Replace log: ScanDisk creates a new SCANDISK.LOG file each time you check the drive.

    Append to log: ScanDisk adds the data from the current check to the end of the existing SCANDISK.LOG file.

    No log: ScanDisk doesn't log the progress of the check.

Cross-linked files: The options in this group determine how ScanDisk handles cross-linked files, as described earlier.

Lost file fragments: The options in this group determine how ScanDisk handles lost and invalid clusters, as described earlier.

Check files for: These check boxes specify a few file tests ScanDisk can run:

> **Invalid file names:** ScanDisk tests the name of each file for validity. If a name is invalid (if, for example, it contains an illegal character), ScanDisk attempts to fix the name.

> **Invalid dates and times:** ScanDisk tests the date and time stamp of each file and attempts to fix any invalid entries it finds.

> **Duplicate names:** ScanDisk checks folders to see whether they contain multiple files with the same name.

Check host drive first: Compressed drive errors are usually caused by problems on the host drive. If you're checking a compressed drive, activate this check box to force ScanDisk to check the compressed drive's host drive first.

Report MS-DOS mode name length errors: When this check box is activated, ScanDisk tells you if it finds files with illegal DOS names.

When you've made your selections, click OK to return to the ScanDisk window.

Starting the Test

Your final chore before letting ScanDisk do its thing is to decide how you want the program to handle any errors it finds. If you'd prefer to be informed of the error so that you can decide what to do about it, leave the Automatically fix errors check box deactivated. If, instead, you want ScanDisk to handle everything, activate the Automatically fix errors check box. This tells ScanDisk to use the settings in the Advanced Options dialog box to handle disk errors.

To get the ScanDisk show on the road, click the Start button. ScanDisk starts checking the disk, and the progress meter at the bottom of the window tells you how it's doing. If ScanDisk comes across an error (and if you didn't activate the Automatically fix errors check box), you see a dialog box similar to the one shown in Figure 17.5. Choose the option you prefer and click OK. (If you need more data before making your decision, click the More Info button.)

Figure 17.5.

If ScanDisk trips over a disk error, it displays a dialog box like this one.

RUNNING SCANDISK FROM EXPLORER

You can run ScanDisk on a specific drive by using Windows Explorer (or My Computer). Right-click the drive and then click Properties in the context menu. In the properties sheet that appears, display the Tools tab and then click Check Now in the Error-checking status group.

Running ScanDisk at Startup

Unrepaired disk problems can cause endless headaches on your system, so it's a good idea to run ScanDisk regularly. The easiest way to do this is to create a ScanDisk shortcut in the StartUp folder. The ScanDisk executable file is SCANDSKW.EXE, and you find it in your main Windows 98 folder. To make ScanDisk easier to use, SCANDSKW.EXE can take a few command-line parameters:

```
scandskw drive: [/a] [/n] [/p]
```

drive:	Specifies the drive or drives you want to check.
/a	Checks all your local, nonremovable hard disks.
/n	Starts and shuts down ScanDisk automatically.
/p	Prevents ScanDisk from correcting any errors it finds.

Enter these parameters in the shortcut's properties sheet by selecting the Shortcut tab and using the Target text box. For example, if you want ScanDisk to check drives C and D and shut down automatically, you use the following command line in the Target text box:

```
c:\windows\scandskw.exe c: d: /n
```

There is a new feature in Windows 98 that runs ScanDisk automatically after a bad shutdown (for example, if the system power is switched off before you exit Windows 98) or if Windows 98 detects one or more bad sectors on your hard disk. In this case, you see a message similar to the following at startup:

```
Windows was not properly shut down. One or more of your disk drives
may have errors on it. Press any key to run ScanDisk on these drives...
```

When you press a key, Windows 98 runs the real-mode version of ScanDisk. (Note, too, that you can modify MSDOS.SYS to change the behavior of the automatic scan. See Chapter 3, "Start Me Up: Controlling Windows 98 Startup," for details.)

> **YOU CAN USE WINDOWS 98'S SCANDISK WITH DOS 6.X**
>
> If you've dual-booted to DOS 6.x and you need to check a disk for errors, you can run the real-mode version of Windows 98's ScanDisk. The executable file is SCANDISK.EXE, and you find it in Windows 98's Command subfolder.

Protecting System Files with Registry Scan

At startup, Windows 98 automatically checks the Registry files for corruption and creates backup copies of these files. The utility that performs these tasks is called Registry Scan and it comes in two flavors:

> **SCANREG:** This is the real-mode version of Registry Scan, and it's located in the Command subfolder of your main Windows 98 folder.

> **SCANREGW:** This is the protected-mode version of Registry Scan, and it's located in your main Windows 98 folder.

Here's the syntax:

```
SCANREG [/BACKUP] [/RESTORE] [/AUTORUN] [/COMMENT]
SCANREGW [/BACKUP] [/RESTORE] [/AUTORUN] [/FIX] [/COMMENT]
```

/BACKUP	Forces a backup of the system files.
/RESTORE	Restores the previous day's backup.
/AUTORUN	Runs SCANREG without prompting. This is the switch used by Registry Scan during the Windows 98 startup.
/FIX	Attempts to fix a Registry error if no backup copy is available.
/COMMENT="text"	Adds text to the CAB file used to store the backups.

Registry Scan gathers the Registry files—SYSTEM.DAT and USER.DAT—as well as WIN.INI and SYSTEM.INI and stuffs them into a CAB file. The names of these CAB files take the form RB00x.CAB, where x is the backup number, and they're stored in the Sysbckup subfolder of your main Windows 98 folder. Note that Registry Scan makes only a single backup each day.

The command run by Registry Scan at startup is governed by the ScanRegistry setting in the following Registry key:

```
HKEY_LOCAL_MACHINE\SOFTWARE\Microsoft\Windows\CurrentVersion\Run
```

Here's the default ScanRegistry value (assuming C:\Windows is the main Windows 98 folder):

```
c:\windows\scanregw.exe /autorun
```

Note that Windows 98 runs the protected-mode version of Registry Scan. If this fails, Windows 98 defaults to the real-mode version in an attempt to solve the problem.

ADD SCANREG.EXE TO YOUR STARTUP DISK

I'd recommend adding the real-mode SCANREG.EXE to your Windows 98 startup disk. That way, if a Registry problem prevents you from booting Windows 98, you can boot to the startup disk and run SCANREG /RESTORE to restore the last backup.

Some Registry Scan settings are controlled via the SCANREG.INI file in your main Windows 98 folder. Here's a summary of the settings you can adjust within this file:

Backup: Registry Scan backs up the configuration files when this value is set to 1. Set this to 0 to skip the backup.

Optimize: This setting determines whether Registry Scan optimizes the Registry files. Set this value to 1 to perform the optimization; set this value to 0 to skip the optimization.

MaxBackupCopies: This setting determines the maximum number of backup copies Registry Scan creates. The default is 5.

BackupDirectory: You use this setting to change the default folder used to store the Registry Scan CAB files.

Files: Use these lines to specify additional system files to include in the backup. (You need to delete the semicolon at the beginning of the line to "uncomment" the line.) Separate multiple filenames with commas. Note, too, that you can use the following special *directory codes* instead of actual folder names:

Use	To specify
10	The main Windows 98 folder
11	The System subfolder of the main Windows 98 folder
30	Your system's boot folder (usually c:\)
31	Your system's boot host folder (usually c:\)

For example, the following line tells Registry Scan to include CONTROL.INI from the main Windows 98 folder as part of the backup:

```
Files=10,control.ini
```

Although Windows 98 runs Registry Scan at startup automatically, you can run it from the DOS command line or the Run dialog box any time you like. To force a backup of the system files, be sure to use the /BACKUP switch. Otherwise, Windows 98 will ask whether you want to back up the system again. In this case, click Yes.

17

WIELDING THE
WINDOWS 98
SYSTEM TOOLS

Using System File Checker

Windows will often act strange or go down for the count because of a corrupted or missing system file, or because a crucial system file has been replaced with an older version by a brain-dead installation program. (Note that these system files include not only the programs used by Windows 98, but also support files such as those that use the extensions `.DLL`, `.OCX`, `.SYS`, `.VXD`, and so on.)

To help prevent these kinds of problems, and to recover from them if they happen, you can use Windows 98's new System File Checker utility. This program takes a snapshot of your system's configuration. It can then use that snapshot as a base from which to compare future configurations. If System File Checker detects corrupted, missing, or replaced system files, it can restore your system to a previously stable configuration.

To run System File Checker, select Start | Programs | Accessories | System Tools | System Information. In the Microsoft System Information window, select Tools | System File Checker. (I discuss the Microsoft System Information utility a bit later in this chapter.) You see the window shown in Figure 17.6.

FIGURE 17.6.

This window appears when you launch System File Checker.

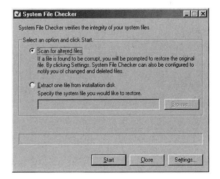

System File Checker Options

Before using System File Checker to scan your system, you might want to examine the program's available options. To do so, click the Settings button to display the System File Checker Settings dialog box shown in Figure 17.7. When you finish working with this dialog box, click OK to return to the System File Checker window.

The Settings tab contains the following controls:

> **Back up file before restoring:** These options determine what System File Checker does before restoring a configuration file:
>
> > **Always back up before restoring:** Activate this option to force System File Checker to make a backup copy of the existing system file before restoring the original file.

Prompt for backup: Activate this option to have System File Checker ask you whether it should make a backup copy of the existing file.

Never back up before restoring: Activate this option to force System File Checker not to make a backup copy of the existing file.

Default backup location: This option displays the folder to which System File Checker backs up the existing files before restoring the originals. Click Change to specify a different backup folder.

Log file: System File Checker can maintain a log of its activities. The log file is named `Sfclog.txt`, and it's stored in your main Windows 98 folder. You can examine the log by clicking the View Log button. The options in the Log file group determine how System File Checker works with this log file:

Append to existing log: Activate this option to have System File Checker add the log from the current session to the log file.

Overwrite existing log: Activate this option to have System File Checker start a new log file each time.

No log: Activate this option to bypass logging.

Check for changed files: If you activate this check box, System File Checker looks for system files that have changed.

Check for deleted files: If you activate this check box, System File Checker looks for system files that have been deleted.

FIGURE 17.7.

Use this dialog box to configure System File Checker.

You use the Search Criteria tab, shown in Figure 17.8, to specify the folder and file types that System File Checker should examine. The Select the folders you want to check list displays the folder(s) that System File Checker examines. Use the following buttons to adjust this list:

Add Folder: To add another folder to the list, click this button and then use the Browse for Folder dialog box to choose the folder you want.

Remove: Click this button to remove the currently highlighted folder from the list. When System File Checker asks whether you're sure, click Yes. System File Checker will then ask whether you want to keep the data about this folder in case you want to check it again later. Click Yes to keep the data or No to delete it.

Include Subfolders: This button toggles whether System File Checker also checks in a folder's subfolders. The list's Subfolder column tells you whether subfolders are being checked.

The Select the file types you want to check list displays all the file types (file extensions) that System File Checker will examine. You use the following buttons to massage this list:

Add Type: To add a new file type to the list, click this button, enter a file type specification (such as `*.dat`) in the dialog box, and then click OK.

Remove: Click this button to remove the currently highlighted file type from the list. When System File Checker asks whether you're sure, click Yes. When System File Checker asks whether you want to keep the data about this file type, click Yes to keep the data or No to delete it.

FIGURE 17.8.

The Search Criteria tab specifies the folders and file types checked by System File Checker.

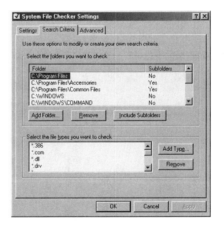

The controls in the Advanced tab, shown in Figure 17.9, enable you to work with the database files used by System File Checker. These files contain the data used by System File Checker to verify the integrity of the system files. The default database is stored in the file `Default.sfc` in your main Windows 98 folder. If you prefer to use a different database file (because, for example, you want to leave `Default.sfc` with your original Windows 98 configuration data), click Create, enter a name for the new file, and click Save.

If System File Checker has updated its database and you'd prefer to return `Default.sfc` to the data from the original Windows 98 installation, click the Restore defaults button.

FIGURE 17.9.

Use the Advanced tab to work with the System File Checker database files.

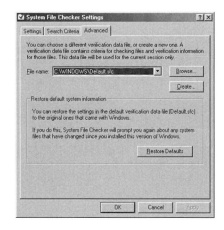

Scanning System Files for Errors

After you've configured System File Checker to your liking, make sure Scan for altered files is activated in the System File Checker window and then click Start.

As System File Checker goes about its duties, you may see various dialog boxes whenever the program detects a problem. For example, if System File Checker detects a corrupted file, you see the File Corrupted dialog box shown in Figure 17.10. Here's a rundown of the options you can work with:

Update verification information: Choose this option if you're sure there isn't a problem and you want System File Checker to revise its database accordingly.

Restore file: If you choose this option, System File Checker displays the Restore File dialog box, shown in Figure 17.11. Use the Restore from text box to enter the path to your Windows 98 installation files, make sure the Save file in text box displays the correct destination, and then click OK.

Ignore: Choose this option to ignore the problem.

FIGURE 17.10.

You see this dialog box if System File Checker detects a corrupted system file.

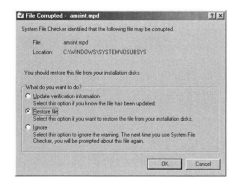

FIGURE 17.11.

Use the Restore File dialog box to extract a system file from your Windows 98 installation files.

If you activated the Check for changed files option, you may see a File Changed dialog box like the one shown in Figure 17.12. In this case, System File Checker also shows extra data for the original and existing files: the data and time stamp, the size, and the version number. You also get an extra Update verification information for all changed files option. Choose this option to tell System File Checker to use the Update verification information option for all future changes.

FIGURE 17.12.

You see a dialog box like this one if System File Checker detects a file change.

When the check is complete, System File Checker displays the Finished dialog box to let you know. You can click Details to see a summary of the changes made.

Extracting Files with System File Checker

You can also use System File Checker to extract files from your original Windows 98 installation files. Here are the steps to follow:

1. In the System File Checker window, activate the Extract one file from installation disk option.

2. Use the File to extract text box to enter the name of the file you want to work with. (Or click Browse to pick out the file using the Select File to Extract dialog box.)

3. Click Start. System File Checker displays the Extract File dialog box, which is identical to the Restore File dialog box shown in Figure 17.11.

4. Use the Restore from text box to enter the path to your Windows 98 installation files.

5. Use the Save file in text box to enter the destination folder for the extracted file.

6. Click OK.

7. When System File Checker reports that the file has been successfully extracted, click OK.

Avoiding Device Driver Failures with Automatic Skip Driver

If your computer hangs at startup, there are many possible causes (see Chapter 3's "Troubleshooting Windows 98 Startup" section). However, one of the most common startup woes is a device driver that fails to load, either because the driver is missing or corrupted or because the associated device is defective.

To help prevent these kinds of startup snags, Windows 98 offers the Automatic Skip Driver (ASD) utility. ASD checks the startup logs and looks for devices that failed to start. It then offers to skip those devices on subsequent startups.

To run ASD, either launch Asd.exe from your main Windows 98 folder, or select Start | Run, type asd, and then click OK. (You can also open the Microsoft System Information utility and select Tools | Automatic Skip Driver Agent.) After ASD has checked your system, it will display a list of the potential startup trouble spots (if any) and give you a chance to skip those problem areas on subsequent startups.

Using the Microsoft System Information Utility

Adequate information is one of the keys to both keeping a system healthy and trouble-shooting a system should something go awry. To that end, it helps to have as much data as possible about the state of the system's hardware, software, and other inner workings. Device Manager can help, but for a truly comprehensive look at what's happening inside your system, you can't beat the new System Information (SI) utility that comes with Windows 98.

To try out this utility, select Start | Programs | Accessories | System Tools | System Information to display the window shown in Figure 17.13. The System Information pane on the left presents you with a list of categories. The pane on the right displays the data associated with each category.

FIGURE 17.13.

Windows 98's System Information utility tells you everything you always wanted to know about your system.

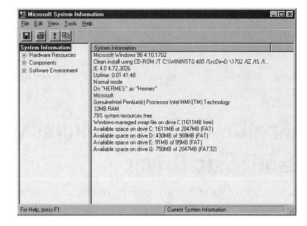

The top-level System Information item displays some basic data about your system. Here's a summary of what you find in the other major categories:

Resources: These categories display information on the hardware resources used by your computer. These hardware resources include DMA usage, I/O ports, and IRQ lines.

Components: These categories display specific information about the devices attached to your computer. These categories include Multimedia, Display, and Network. There's also a History category that provides you with a chronological account of the changes you've made to your system.

Software Environment: These categories are devoted to the programs, applets, and device drivers on your system. You can find out all the device drivers installed (including version numbers and descriptions), the 16-bit and 32-bit modules that are loaded, the tasks that are currently running, the programs that run at startup, and much more.

You can also perform the following tasks within the SI window:

■ To save this data to an SI file (an MSInfo file with an .NFO extension), select File | Save.

■ To export the data to a text file, select File | Export.

■ To print the data, select File | Print.

■ To run one of Windows 98's system tools, pull down the Tools menu and select the program you want to run.

Protecting Long Filenames

You shouldn't use pre-Windows 95 disk utilities on VFAT volumes—they'll destroy your long filenames. If you have a favorite utility you hate to give up, your best bet is to upgrade to a version designed to work with Windows 95 or Windows 98.

If a 32-bit version of the utility doesn't exist, or you can't upgrade for some reason, there is a way to keep using the program, but it's a bit of a pain. You need the Windows 98 CD-ROM and the `LFNBK.EXE` file that you find in the `\tools\reskit\file\lfnback\` folder.

LFNBK is the Windows 98 real-mode Long Filename Backup program. The idea behind LFNBK is to back up not your files, but the names of your files. In other words, for each file on a disk, LFNBK records both the short 8.3 filename and the long filename in a file named `LFNBK.DAT`, and it then removes the long filename. This enables you to run your old disk utility without mishap. You can then use LFNBK to restore the long filenames. To use LFNBK, copy it from the CD-ROM to your main Windows 98 folder.

Before you can use LFNBK, you must tell Windows 98 to stop tunneling long filenames. Tunneling is a process that Windows 98 uses to preserve long filenames when files are used by 16-bit applications. When these programs write a file to disk (during, for example, a save), they write only the file's 8.3 filename. Windows 98 recognizes this fact and tacks the file's long filename onto its directory entry.

Unfortunately, tunneling will prevent LFNBK from doing its job, so you must disable tunneling by following these steps:

1. Right-click My Computer, select Properties, and select the Performance tab.
2. Select File System and, in the File System Properties dialog box that appears, select the Troubleshooting tab.
3. Activate the Disable long name preservation for old programs check box and then click OK.
4. When Windows 98 asks whether you want to restart your computer, click Yes.
5. While your computer reboots, hold down Ctrl so that you eventually see the Startup menu.
6. Run the Command prompt only option.

You're now ready to run LFNBK. Here's the syntax:

```
lfnbk [/v] [/b ¦ /r ¦ /pe] [/nt] [/force] [/p] [drive]
```

/v	Reports actions onscreen (verbose mode).
/b	Backs up and removes long filenames on the disk.
/r	Restores previously backed-up long filenames.
/pe	Extracts errors from the backup database.
/nt	Doesn't restore backup dates and times.
/force	Forces LFNBK to run, even in unsafe conditions.

/p	Finds long filenames but doesn't convert them to 8.3 filename aliases. This switch reports the existing long filenames, along with the associated dates for file creation, last access, and last modification of the file.
drive	Indicates the letter of the drive you want to work with.

For example, to back up and remove long filenames on drive D, you enter the following command:

```
lfnbk /b d
```

LFNBK reports the number of directories and files it processed, as well as the number of long filenames it found and removed.

With long filenames removed and safely stowed in `LFNBK.DAT`, you can now run your disk utility. When you're done, run LFNBK with the `/r` switch to restore the long filenames. For drive D, here's the command to run:

```
lfnbk /r d
```

Restart your computer and boot into Windows 98 normally. Use the procedure described earlier to deactivate the Disable long name preservation for old programs check box and reenable tunneling.

Scheduling Maintenance Tasks with Task Scheduler

The key to keeping your system in fine fettle is to run your maintenance programs—Backup, ScanDisk, or whatever—regularly. Placing shortcuts for these programs in your Windows 98 Startup folder is one way to ensure regularity. Performing a large backup or a Thorough ScanDisk check, however, might not be the most productive way to start your day.

Ideally, it would be nice to be able to set up a schedule so that these chores not only run at regular intervals, but also run in the evening or overnight when you won't be using your machine. Well, I'm happy to report that Windows 98 comes with a great little program called Task Scheduler that will do exactly that.

Starting Task Scheduler

To see what Task Scheduler is all about, display its window by selecting Start | Programs | Accessories | System Tools | Scheduled Tasks. Figure 17.14 shows the window that appears. The five columns give you the name of the scheduled task, the time it's scheduled to run, the last time it started and ended, and the status of the last result.

FIGURE 17.14.
The Scheduled Tasks window.

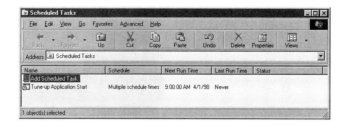

Adding a New Scheduled Task

Although you use it most for system maintenance utilities, you're free to schedule any Windows application, macros, DOS programs, or even batch files.

To create a new scheduled task, open the Add Scheduled Task item. This launches the Add Scheduled Task Wizard. The first dialog box just presents an overview, so click Next > to proceed.

The Wizard scours your Start menu and displays a list of all the programs in a dialog box. Click the program that you want to schedule. If the item you want to schedule isn't in this list, click Browse, use the Select Program to Schedule dialog box to choose the program, and then click Open. When you're ready to move on, click Next >.

Now the Wizard prompts you for a name and to choose the frequency with which this task is to be run (see Figure 17.15). Enter a name, select a schedule option, and then click Next >.

FIGURE 17.15.
Enter a name and frequency for the new task.

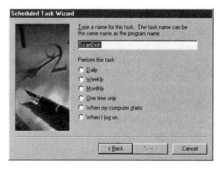

The next dialog box that appears depends on the schedule you chose for your task. For example, Figure 17.16 shows the Wizard dialog box that shows up if you choose the Daily schedule. Specify the exact schedule you want and then click Next >.

Now the last Wizard dialog box appears. Note that this dialog box has an Open the advanced properties of the task when I click Finish check box. If you activate this check box and click Finish, the Wizard opens the properties sheet for the task. See "Modifying a Scheduled Task's Properties," later in this chapter.

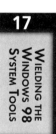

FIGURE 17.16.

The next Wizard dialog box enables you to set up a specific schedule for the task.

Working with Scheduled Tasks

Here are a few techniques you can use to work with the scheduled tasks:

- If you'd prefer to run the scheduled task right away, either highlight the task and select File | Run, or right-click it and select Run from the context menu.

- If a task is running, you can stop it by selecting File | End Scheduled Task.

- To remove a task, either highlight it and select File | Delete, or right-click it and select Delete from the context menu. When Task Scheduler asks you to confirm, click Yes.

- To suspend all the scheduled tasks, select Advanced | Pause Task Scheduler. To resume operations, select Advanced | Continue Task Scheduler.

- If you no longer want to use Task Scheduler at all, select Advanced | Stop Using Task Scheduler. To enable Task Scheduler, select Advanced | Start Using Task Scheduler.

Modifying a Scheduled Task's Properties

Each scheduled task has various properties that control the program's executable file, how it runs, which folder it runs in, and more. To view and modify these properties, either highlight a scheduled task in the Scheduled Tasks window and select File | Properties, or right-click the task name and select Properties from the context menu. Figure 17.17 shows an example of the properties sheet that appears.

The Task Tab

Here are the properties you get to play with on the Task tab:

Run: This is the name of the executable file that starts the program. If the program isn't in the main Windows 98 folder (or its Command subfolder), you need to use the full pathname of the executable file.

ADD PROGRAM SWITCHES

The Run text box is a good place to add any switches or parameters for the task. As you can see in Figure 17.17, I added the /A and /N switches to make ScanDisk check all local hard disks and to quit when it's done (as described earlier in this chapter).

Start in: This specifies the drive and folder that the program should use as its default.

Comments: Use this text box to enter your own comments or notes regarding the task.

Enabled (scheduled task runs at specified time): This check box toggles the task on and off.

FIGURE 17.17.

The properties sheet for the scheduled ScanDisk program.

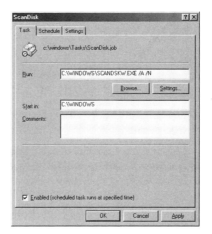

The Schedule Tab

You can use the Schedule tab to change the task's schedule. Use the Schedule Task list to choose the frequency with which you want the task to run, then use the controls that appear (which vary depending on the frequency you selected) to set the specifics of the schedule.

If you'd like to set up two or more schedules for a task, activate the Show multiple schedules check box. This adds a new list box to the top of the Schedule tab, as shown in Figure 17.18. Click New to start a new schedule.

Figure 17.18.

*Activating the Show
multiple schedules check
box adds a drop-down
list to the Schedule tab.*

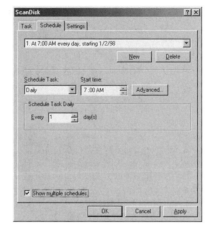

Advanced Scheduling Options

The Schedule tab also has an Advanced button that displays the Advanced Schedule Options dialog box. Here are the available options:

Start Date: Use this calendar control to set the date the task starts.

End Date: Activate this check box and then use the calendar control to set the last date this task should run.

Repeat task: If the preset schedules aren't exactly what you need, activate this check box and then use the controls to specify a custom interval:

Every: Set the interval in minutes or hours.

Until: Some programs might not shut down automatically after they complete their mission. Rather than leave these programs running, you can ensure that they shut down by activating either Time or Duration and setting a cutoff point for the task.

If the task is still running, stop it at this time: If the program is still running by the time the deadline rolls around, it might be that the program is hung or stuck. To allow for this possibility, you should leave this check box activated so that Task Scheduler shuts down the program if it's still running at the specified time.

The Settings Tab

Here's a quick look at the controls on the Settings tab, shown in Figure 17.19:

Delete the scheduled task when finished: If you want your task to run only once, activate this check box to have Task Scheduler delete it for you when the task is done.

Stop the scheduled task after *x* hours *y* minutes: Use these controls to set an upper limit on the amount of time the task can run.

Only start the scheduled task if computer is idle for: If you activate this check box, Task Scheduler won't run the task if you're still using your computer. Use the spinner to set the number of minutes your machine must be idle before the task begins.

If computer is not idle at scheduled start time, retry for up to: Use this spinner to set the number of minutes Task Scheduler will wait for idle time.

Stop the scheduled task if computer is in use: If you activate this check box, Task Scheduler shuts down the task if you start using your computer while the task is running.

Don't start scheduled task if computer is running on batteries: When this option is turned on, Task Scheduler will check to see whether your notebook is on battery power and, if it is, it won't run the task.

Stop the scheduled task if battery mode changes: When this check box is on, Task Scheduler will shut down a running task if your notebook switches from AC to batteries.

FIGURE 17.19.
The Settings tab.

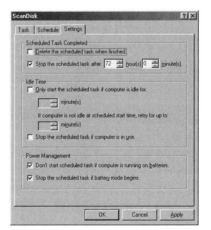

Guarding Against Viruses

Viruses are nasty little programs that live for the sheer thrill of trashing your valuable data. They're crafted in dank basements by pale, Jolt-cola–fueled miscreants—programming wizards who've succumbed to the dark side of The Force. These amoral hackers like to muddy the waters by describing their wicked offspring as "self-propagating, autonomous computer programs" and giving them innocent-sounding names such as Michelangelo and Christmas. But don't be fooled: These small slices of evil can do irreparable harm to your files. (Just so you know, many viruses have names that more directly reflect their intentions. These include Armageddon, Beast, Black Monday, Dark Avenger, and Darth Vader.)

Viruses comes in three basic flavors:

■ *File infectors*, which attach themselves to executable files and spread among other files when you run the program.

■ *Boot sector viruses*, which replace the hard disk's master boot record (or the boot sector on a floppy disk) with their own twisted version of the bootstrap code. This lets them load themselves into memory whenever you boot your system (the famous "Michelangelo" virus is one of these boot sector beasts).

■ *Trojan horse viruses*, which appear to be legitimate programs at first glance but, when loaded, proceed to viciously maul your data.

Viruses are, by now, an unpleasant fact of computing life, and you just have to learn to live with the threat. That makes it all the more puzzling why Microsoft didn't include an anti-virus utility in Windows 95 or Windows 98. Not to worry, though, quite a few Windows 98-specific anti-virus programs are on the market that will help you sleep better at night.

Boza: A Virus that Windows Can Call Its Own

In early 1996, it was announced that the first virus program designed specifically for Windows 95 had been let loose upon the world. Dubbed the *Boza* virus (after a Bulgarian liquor "so powerful that just looking at it will give you a headache"; it's also known as the *Bizatch* virus), this program infects 32-bit executable files that are in Microsoft's Portable Executable (PE) format. It uses direct calls to the Windows 95 or 98 operating system.

Boza is a simple file infector virus. If you execute a Boza-infected program, the Boza code proceeds to infect up to three other programs in the same folder. It does this by adding an extra code section to these files and then manipulating the file header so that program execution begins with the viral code. After the virus has done its dirty work, it hands control back to the original program entry point, which means that infected files appear to work as usual. Note that Boza doesn't set itself up in memory.

By itself, Boza is more annoying than destructive. (On the 30th of the month, it displays a dialog box that says "The taste of fame just got tastier! VLAD Australia does it again with the world's first Win95 virus." VLAD is an Australian virus-creation cabal.) According to virus experts, however, the Boza code is sloppily written and buggy, so it can accidentally destroy the files it infects.

Within days of the discovery of this virus, all major anti-virus firms had "Boza detectors" ready for public consumption.

Windows 98 Anti-Virus Programs

When Microsoft announced that there would be no virus protection program included with Windows 95, plenty of utilities vendors sniffed opportunity in the air. As a result, there's no lack of anti-virus programs designed specifically for Windows 95. These utilities should run fine on Windows 98. However, you should check in all cases to see whether the product supports FAT32 partitions, if you have them on your system. Here are three I recommend:

Norton AntiVirus: This is a powerful program capable of recognizing and nuking thousands of viruses (including Boza). Norton AntiVirus comes with its own scheduler and has many customization options. Regular updates are available. This program sells for $79.95. For an evaluation copy, check out the Symantec Web site at `http://www.symantec.com`.

ThunderBYTE: ThunderBYTE's anti-virus utilities are justly renowned for their speed and sophistication. For example, ThunderBYTE has a "heuristic viral analysis" technique that can recognize even unknown viruses. Version 7.0 recognizes and eradicates the Boza virus. ThunderBYTE sells for $149.95. You can get an evaluation copy at `http://thunderbyte.com`.

VirusScan: This one is an excellent utility (although a touch on the slow side) from McAfee Associates, one of the veterans of the anti-virus wars. VirusScan is loaded with options, integrates seamlessly with Task Scheduler, and can eradicate the Boza virus. A monthly update program is available. VirusScan sells for $65. You can get more information and a free evaluation copy at `http://www.mcafee.com/`.

More Virus Tips

Here are a few other tips to help keep your system virus-free:

- If your computer has a BIOS setting that disables boot-sector writes, be sure to activate this setting.

- Most viruses are transmitted from machine to machine via floppy disks, so you should always be careful about which used disks you trust in your computer. If you've inherited some old disks, you can make sure that no viruses are lurking in the weeds by formatting each disk before you use it.

- Trust no one when it comes to loading programs on your machine. Whether they come from family, friends, a BBS, or the Internet, use an anti-virus program to scan downloaded files before running anything.

- Keep your virus utility's virus library up-to-date. By some accounts, more than 100 new virus strains are released each month, and they just get nastier and nastier. Regular updates will help you keep up-to-date.

Putting It All Together with the Maintenance Wizard

New to
98

In this section, I'll examine a new utility that combines many of the items you've seen so far in this chapter and other chapters. It's called the Maintenance Wizard, and it enables you to schedule routine maintenance tasks. Specifically, this wizard creates new Task Scheduler jobs that run any of the following four utilities: DriveSpace, Scan Disk, Disk Defragmenter, and Disk Cleanup Manager. This is much easier than setting up all these utilities by hand; so although the Maintenance Wizard is designed for novice users, it's also a boon to power users.

To launch the Maintenance Wizard, select Start | Programs | Accessories | System Tools | Maintenance Wizard. In the initial dialog box, make sure the Custom - Select each maintenance setting myself option is activated and then click Next >.

Your first chore is to select a schedule for the tune-up, as shown in Figure 17.20. Assuming you leave your computer on all the time, your best bet is to select the Nights - Midnight to 3:00 AM option, because that's likely to be a time when you're not using your machine. When you've made your choice, click Next >.

FIGURE 17.20.

Use this dialog box to schedule your tune-ups.

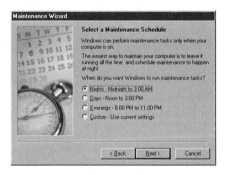

If you have one or more shortcuts in your Startup folder, the Maintenance Wizard will display the Start Windows More Quickly dialog box. This dialog box displays all your Startup folder shortcuts with check boxes. The idea is that you deactivate the check boxes for those shortcuts that you no longer want to run at startup, which will help Windows to load faster.

If you have a compressed drive on your system, you see the dialog box shown in Figure 17.21.

All the Maintenance Wizard dialog boxes are front-ends for particular system tools. For example, the Optimize Compressed Drive dialog box is a front-end for the Compression Agent utility. In every Maintenance Wizard dialog box, you see two option buttons:

Yes: Activate this option to schedule the task. In this case, Maintenance Wizard will create a new Task Scheduler job that runs the underlying system utility.

No: Activate this option to bypass the task.

FIGURE 17.21.

You see this Wizard dialog box if you have compressed drives on your system.

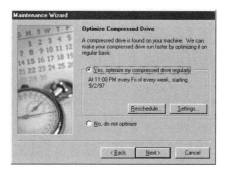

If you activate Yes, you can also work with the following buttons:

Reschedule: This button displays the Reschedule dialog box, which is just the Schedule tab from Task Scheduler's task properties sheet.

Settings: This button displays a dialog box that contains settings related to the underlying program.

Here's a summary of the rest of the Maintenance Wizard dialog boxes that will come your way:

Speed Up Programs: This dialog box is a front-end for Disk Defragmenter.

Scan Hard Disk for Errors: This dialog box enables you to schedule a ScanDisk check. Note that this is a *thorough* check, so ScanDisk also checks disk surfaces. You may want to set an earlier start time or a less-frequent schedule.

Delete Unnecessary Files: This dialog box is a front-end for the Disk Cleanup Manager. Note that the No option is selected by default. After you activate Yes, click Settings to specify what types of files Disk Cleanup Manager should delete.

The last Maintenance Wizard dialog box displays a summary of the options you chose. Click Finish to schedule the tasks. If you look at the `Scheduled Tasks` folder again, you see that each option you elected to schedule now appears as a task, as shown in Figure 17.22.

FIGURE 17.22.

The tools you choose in Maintenance Wizard appear in the `Scheduled Tasks` *folder.*

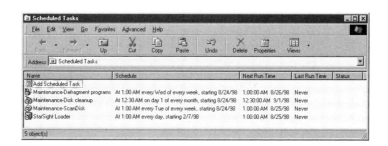

Getting Your System Back on Its Feet with System Recovery

Despite your best maintenance efforts, your system may crash hard enough that a simple recovery becomes impossible. In that case, you have no alternative but to format (or replace) your hard drive and start from scratch. However, that doesn't mean you have to laboriously reinstall Windows 98 and your applications. With some advance planning, you can use the new System Recovery utility to both reinstall Windows 98 and return your hard drive to its pre-crash state.

System Recovery consists of three pieces:

PCRESTOR.BAT: After you format your hard drive, you boot from your startup disk and then run this batch file. PCRESTOR.BAT performs several chores, but its main task is to start the Windows 98 Setup program with various switches and parameters.

MSBATCH.INF: This is an information file that specifies a number of settings and parameters used by Setup. In particular, this file tells Setup to run the System Recovery Wizard (see "How Does It Work?"). When PCRESTOR.BAT starts Setup, it tells the program to use MSBATCH.INF.

System Recovery Wizard: After Windows 98 is reinstalled, this Wizard loads automatically to take you through the rest of the recovery process, including restoring the files from your system backup.

HOW DOES IT WORK?

How is Setup able to run the System Recovery Wizard automatically? The key (literally!) can be found inside MSBATCH.INF, where you'll find the following settings:

```
[RegistrySettings]
HKLM,%KEY_RUN%,BatchReg1,,"%11%\srw.exe"
```

```
[Strings]
KEY_RUN="SOFTWARE\Microsoft\Windows\CurrentVersion\Run"
```

These settings modify the following Registry key:

```
HKEY_LOCAL_MACHINE\Software\Microsoft\Windows\CurrentVersion\Run
```

This key is used to specify programs that run automatically at startup. In this case, the program SRW.EXE—the System Recovery Wizard—is added to the key.

To use System Recovery successfully, you must assume your machine will crash one day and so make the necessary preparations. Specifically, you must follow these guidelines:

- Create a Windows 98 startup disk.
- Perform a full backup of the hard disk that contains the Windows system files.
- Your main Windows 98 folder must be C:\WINDOWS.

Running System Recovery

System Recovery is one of those tools that you hope you never use. However, if the day does come when your system needs to be recovered, you'll be glad to know that doing so takes just a few steps:

1. Boot your system using the startup disk. Make sure you enable CD-ROM support.
2. Format drive C if you haven't done so already.
3. Insert your Windows 98 CD-ROM.
4. Create a folder named WIN98 on your hard disk and then copy the Windows 98 Setup files (that is, all the files in the WIN98 folder of your Windows 98 CD-ROM) into that folder.
5. In your Windows 98 CD-ROM, head for the folder named \TOOLS\SYSREC and copy PCRESTOR.BAT and MSBATCH.INF to the root folder of the *same* hard disk that you used to create the WIN98 folder in step 4.
6. In the root folder of your hard disk, run PCRESTOR.BAT and, once you've read the welcome message, press any key. The Windows 98 Setup begins.
7. Once Setup is complete, the System Recovery Wizard loads, as shown in Figure 17.23. The initial dialog box offers an overview of the process, so click Next >. System Recovery prompts you to enter your name and company name.

FIGURE 17.23.

The System Recovery Wizard takes you through the process of restoring your system to its pre-crash state.

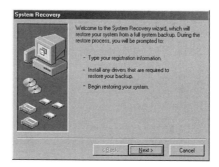

8. Enter your name and (optionally) your company name, and then click Next >. System Recovery lets you know that it is about to restore your system.
9. Insert the backup media that contains your full system backup.

10. In the final Wizard dialog box, click Finish. System Recovery launches Microsoft Backup.

11. Use Backup to restore your files, as described in Chapter 16, "Working with a Net: The Windows 98 Backup Utility." (Make sure you choose to overwrite all files.) When Backup asks if you want to restore the Registry and the hardware and software settings within the Registry, make sure you select Yes.

12. When the restore process is done, Backup will ask if you want to restart. Click Yes and your system will be completely recovered when Windows 98 restarts.

Making System Recovery More Flexible

As you've seen, System Recovery is quite rigid about a few things. For example, it will only reinstall Windows 98 into `C:\WINDOWS`, and it will only install from a hard disk. System Recovery would be a much more useful tool if it enabled you to overcome these and other limitations. However, although Microsoft does not recommend or support customized System Recovery procedures, it *is* possible to improve upon the basic process.

The reason System Recovery is so inflexible is that most of its options are set in advance within the `PCRESTOR.BAT` and `MSBATCH.INF` files. These are just text files, however, and text files can be edited, albeit with a modicum of caution and a nod to common sense. Here are a few techniques you can try:

> **To reinstall Windows into a different directory:** The installation directory is governed by the `InstallDir` setting within the `[Setup]` section of `MSBATCH.INF`. If you prefer to install Windows 98 on drive D, for example, you must modify this setting as follows:

```
InstallDir="D:\Windows"
```

> **Customizing the network logon:** If you're on a network, Setup prompts you to log on to the network during the reinstall. However, System Recovery uses a generic username of `System Recovery` and a generic workgroup name of `WORKGROUP`, which is also used as the logon domain. System Recovery also sets up a generic computer name of `Windows 98 User`. You can customize all four values using the following settings in `MSBATCH.INF`. (Note that these values assume a Microsoft Networking login):

```
[NameAndOrg]
Name="System Recovery"

[Network]
ComputerName="Windows 98 User"
Workgroup="WORKGROUP"
 [VREDIR
 LogonDomain="WORKGROUP"
```

To reinstall Windows from the CD-ROM: The reason you must reinstall Windows from a hard drive is that PCRESTOR.BAT launches Setup from a WIN98 directory that's in the same drive as PCRESTOR.BAT:

```
cd\
cd win98
setup.exe c:\restore\msbatch.inf /is /id /iq /im /id /ie /IW
```

To start Setup from another location, you must modify the first two lines. For example, if you want to run Setup from the Windows 98 CD-ROM in drive D, modify the first two lines as follows:

```
d:
cd\win98
```

Summary

This chapter showed you how to wield a few of the Windows 98 system tools to help keep your machine trouble-free. I showed you how to create an emergency boot disk (just in case), how to use ScanDisk, and how to use some new Windows 98 utilities, including Registry Scan, System File Checker, Task Scheduler, and the Maintenance Wizard. The chapter also included information on preventing viruses from invading your system. I closed with a look at yet another new Windows 98 program: System Recovery.

Here's a list of chapters where you'll find related information:

- I showed you how to use Disk Cleanup Manager in Chapter 9, "Performance Tuning: Optimizing Memory and Disk Access."

- To learn more about the Registry, check out Chapter 12, "Getting to Know the Windows 98 Registry."

- The best way to protect your investment, especially if you want to be able to use the System Recovery utility, is to back up your data regularly. See Chapter 16, "Working with a Net: The Windows 98 Backup Utility."

IV

PART

Unleashing Day-to-Day Windows 98

The Ins and Outs of Installing and Uninstalling Programs

We do not quite say that the new is more valuable because it fits in; but its fitting in is a test of its value.

—*T.S. Eliot*

For your consideration, I submit the following examples of hardware longevity: The computer I use to test software and run beta copies of programs is a trusty old 486 that has served me faithfully for over five years; I recently purchased a new laser printer, but the old LaserJet I had was four-and-a-half years young; my first notebook computer is still going strong after five years (albeit in the company of my goddaughter, to whom I donated it last year); and my fax machine will celebrate its seventh birthday later this year.

Why the litany of Methuselan machines? Because I want to compare these old hardware codgers with the software I use. To wit, of all the programs and utilities I crank up regularly, the *oldest*—an accounting package I use to track my finances—has been out of its shrink wrap for a little less than a year!

Hardware, then, is a typical high-end commodity—we buy it and then tend to hang on to it until it wears out. Software, on the other hand, is a new kind of consumer product, one that reinvents itself constantly. Thanks to cheap, frequent upgrades and an unending stream of new, innovative products, it's tough to resist the siren song of the latest and greatest.

The upshot is that we spend a not-insignificant chunk of our computing lives installing software. The designers of Windows 98, bless their fully vested hearts, understood this all too well, so they included some features in Windows 98 that make it easier to install applications. Even better, there's also support for *uninstalling* programs, just in case the two of you don't get along very well. This chapter shows you how to use Windows 98's built-in install/uninstall features, and it also shows you how to add and remove older Windows applications and DOS programs.

Practicing Safe Setups

For those who enjoy working with computers, few things are as tempting as a new software package. The tendency is to just tear into the box, liberate the source disks, and let the installation program rip without further ado. This approach often loses its luster when, after a willy-nilly installation, your system starts to behave erratically. That's usually because the application's setup program has made adjustments to one or more important configuration files and given your system a case of indigestion in the process. That's the hard way to learn the hazards of a haphazard installation.

To avoid such a fate, you should always look before you leap. That is, you should follow a few simple safety measures before double-clicking that SETUP.EXE file. The next few sections give you some precautionary tales.

Check the New Program for Viruses

If the application you're installing is from a well-known developer, if you purchased it from a reputable dealer, and if the box is unopened, you almost certainly don't have to think twice about viruses. Yes, there have been documented cases of viral code infecting a disk or two in brand-name programs, but these are *extremely* rare, to the point where worrying about it verges on the paranoid.

However, there are other situations in which it pays to be paranoid. You should check for viruses before installing if

- You ordered the program directly from an unknown developer.

- The package was already open when you purchased it from a dealer (buying opened software packages is never a good idea).

- A friend or colleague gave you the program on a floppy disk (most viruses are transmitted via floppies, but CD-ROMs can catch these bugs as well).

- You downloaded the program from the Internet or a BBS.

Ideally, your virus checker should be able to hunt down viruses even in ZIP files and other compressed archives. All the anti-virus programs I mentioned in Chapter 17, "Wielding the Windows 98 System Tools," can do this.

Make Sure You Have a Bootable Disk

It's a rare (and poorly constructed) installation program that will bring an entire system to its knees, but it can happen. An amateurish Windows 98 installer could rip apart the Registry, for example, or a dumb DOS setup program could write to a verboten memory address. Although having a bootable disk within reach is *always* a good idea, make sure you have one handy before installing any new software. To learn how to create a bootable disk and stock it with utilities and files that will let you recover gracefully, see Chapter 17 (in the "Creating an Emergency Boot Disk" section).

Understand the Effect on Your Data Files

Few software developers want to alienate their installed user base, so they usually emphasize upward compatibility in their upgrades. That is, the new version of the software will almost always be able to read and work with documents created with an older version. However, in the interest of progress, you often find that the data file format used by the latest incarnation of a program is different from its predecessors, and this new format is rarely *downward*-compatible. That is, an older version of the software will usually gag on a data file that was created by the new version.

So you are faced with the following choices:

- Continue to work with your existing documents in the old format, thus possibly foregoing any benefits that come with the new format.

- Update your files and thus risk making them incompatible with the old version of the program, should you decide to uninstall the upgrade.

One possible solution to this dilemma is to make backup copies of all your data files before installing the upgrade. That way, you can always restore the good copies of your documents if the upgrade causes problems or destroys some of your data. If you've already used the upgrade to make changes to some documents, but you want to uninstall the upgrade, most programs have a Save As command that lets you save these documents in their old format.

Back Up the Registry

If you're installing a Windows 98 application, it will write the bulk of its configuration data to the Registry. Most of these changes will be application-specific, but some installation programs also make changes to more global settings. You could end up with a system that behaves strangely or, in the worst case, doesn't behave at all!

Fortunately, as you'll see later, true Windows 98 applications have an uninstall feature that not only removes the program's files, but also purges any traces of the program from the Registry. However, programs designed for Windows 3.1 and Windows for Workgroups might also change some Registry settings in the HKEY_CLASSES_ROOT key.

So, just to be safe, you should make a backup copy of the Registry before installing any application that might fiddle with the Registry. You should do two things:

■ Use the Registry Editor's Registry | Export Registry File command to export the entire Registry to a REG (text) file (I showed you how to do this in Chapter 12, "Getting to Know the Windows 98 Registry"). As you'll see later, you can use this file to compare the Registry before and after the installation and possibly make adjustments.

■ Use Windows 98's Backup utility to make backup copies of the Registry files (see Chapter 16, "Working with a Net: The Windows 98 Backup Utility").

In Fact, Back Up All Your Configuration Files

While you're in a backing-up frame of mind, you can add an extra level of protection to your installations by backing up all your configuration files: the Registry, CONFIG.SYS, AUTOEXEC.BAT, WIN.INI, SYSTEM.INI, and so on. This is particularly important before installing 16-bit or DOS applications that routinely make changes to these files.

The best way to back up all these configuration files in one fell swoop is to use Windows 98's Registry Scan utility, described in Chapter 17. Be sure to customize the utility to back up all your configuration files.

Save Directory Listings for Important Folders

When I discuss uninstalling applications later in this chapter, you'll see that one of the biggest problems you'll face is figuring out which files the program used outside its home folder. Many 16-bit Windows applications like to add files to both the main Windows folder and the SYSTEM subfolder. Unfortunately, there's no easy method of determining which files an application inserts into these two folders. (However, as I explain later, Windows 98's Quick View accessory can help ferret out which DLLs a program uses.)

The only way to be sure is to take a "snapshot" of the current state of the main Windows 98 folder and the SYSTEM subfolder both before and after you install the software. To do this, head to the DOS prompt and run the following two commands before you install:

```
dir c:\windows /a-d /on > windir1.txt
dir c:\windows\system /a-d /on > sysdir1.txt
```

The first line runs the DIR command on C:\WINDOWS (which you should change to the path of your main Windows 98 folder) and saves it in a file named DIRWIN1.TXT. (The /a-d switch tells DIR not to display folders, and the /on switch sorts the files alphabetically by name.) The second line saves a file listing of the SYSTEM subfolder in the file SYSDIR.TXT1.

When the installation is complete, go back to the prompt and enter the following commands:

```
dir c:\windows /a-d /on > windir2.txt
dir c:\windows\system /a-d /on > sysdir2.txt
```

You can then compare WINDIR1.TXT to WINDIR2.TXT, and SYSDIR1.TXT to SYSDIR2.TXT, to see which files the setup program foisted upon your system.

One way to do this would be to open two copies of Notepad and load the contrasting files into each window. In the post-installation versions, if you delete the lines corresponding to the files that haven't changed, you end up with a list of the new files. You can then keep this list in a safe location in case you need it later while uninstalling.

Another way to compare these files is to use the DOS FC (file compare) command. I'll explain how this command works later in this chapter (see the section titled "The FC Command").

Read README Files and Other Documentation

If you do nothing else to prepare for a software installation, you should read whatever documentation the program provides that pertains to the setup. This includes the appropriate installation material in the manual, README files found on the disk, and whatever else looks promising. By spending a few minutes perusing these resources, you can glean the following information:

- Any advance preparation you need to perform on your system
- What to expect during the installation
- Information you need to have on hand in order to complete the setup (such as a product's serial number)
- Changes the install program will make to your system
- Changes to the program and/or the documentation that were put into effect after the manual was printed
- Whether the installation will make changes to configuration files, program-specific INI files, or your data files

18

INSTALLING AND
UNINSTALLING
PROGRAMS

Many programs offer to display their README files when the installation is complete, but that might be too late. On more than one occasion, I have installed a program, viewed the README file, and then groaned when I read some crucial tidbit that I should have known before the setup procedure began. (You should always assume that setup programs were coded in haste at the end of the development cycle and therefore tend to be somewhat poorly designed.)

Take Control of the Installation

Some setup programs give new meaning to the term "brain-dead." You slip in the source disk, run SETUP.EXE (or whatever), and the program proceeds to impose itself on your hard disk without so much as a how-do-you-do. Thankfully, most installation programs are a bit more thoughtful than that. They usually give you some advance warning about what's to come, and they prompt you for information as they go along. You can use this newfound thoughtfulness to assume a certain level of control over the installation. (The Windows 98 Setup program is a perfect example of a polite installer that gives you as much or as little control over the installation process as you'd like.) Here are a few things to watch for:

Choose your folder wisely: Most installation programs offer to install their files in a default folder. Rather than just accept this without question, think about where you want the program to reside. Personally, I prefer to use the Program Files folder to house all my applications. If you have multiple hard disks or partitions, you might prefer to use the one with the largest amount of free space. If the setup program lets you select data directories, you might want to use a separate folder that makes it easy to back up the data.

Use the custom install option: Like Windows 98 Setup, the best programs offer you a choice of installation options. Whenever possible, choose the Custom option, if one is available. This will give you maximum control over the components that are installed, including where they're installed and how they're installed.

Perform your own configuration file modifications: If an installation program is truly polite, it will let you know that it needs to modify one or more of your configuration files. Hopefully, you also can choose between letting the program make the modifications automatically or making the modifications yourself. If so, you should always opt for the latter so that you can change the files in a way that won't harm your system.

Comparing Files Before and After

I've mentioned three separate examples of files that you might need to compare before and after an installation:

- Registry files exported to REG text files
- Other configuration files (CONFIG.SYS, AUTOEXEC.BAT, and so on)
- Redirected file listings of your main Windows 98 folder and its SYSTEM subfolder

In each case, you compare the pre-installation version with its post-installation counterpart to see what changes were made (if any). You can use three basic methods to make these comparisons: brute force, the DOS FC command, and your word processor's compare feature.

The Brute Force Method

The most straightforward method is to load the before-and-after files into separate Notepad (or WordPad) windows and compare them line by line. This is fine for small files (such as CONFIG.SYS) or ordered files (such as the results of the DIR command I showed you earlier), but it's next to useless for a large file such as the exported Registry.

The FC Command

DOS has an FC (file compare) command that will compare two files and report on their differences. Here are the two syntaxes you can use with this command:

```
FC [/A] [/C] [/L] [/LBn] [/N] [/T] [/W] [/n] filename1 filename2
FC /B filename1 filename2
```

/A	Displays only first and last lines for each set of differences.
/B	Performs a binary comparison.
/C	Disregards the case of letters.
/L	Compares files as ASCII text.
/LBn	Sets the maximum consecutive mismatches to the specified number of lines.
/N	Displays the line numbers on an ASCII comparison.
/T	Does not expand tabs to spaces.
/W	Compresses white space (tabs and spaces) for comparison.
/n	Specifies the number of consecutive lines that must match after a mismatch.
filename1	The first file you want to compare.
filename2	The second file you want to compare.

For example, to compare the SYSTEM folder file listings I mentioned earlier, you use the following command (assuming that the files are in the root folder of drive C):

```
fc /l c:\sysdir1.txt c:\sysdir2.txt > fc.txt
```

In this case, I've redirected the output of the FC command into a file named FC.TXT. Figure 18.1 shows part of this output. Each time FC finds a difference, it displays the lines that are changed, as well as the lines before and after that are still the same. For example, FC shows the following output for SYSDIR1.TXT:

```
WINSSPI   DLL        30,416  08-11-97  11:34a  WINSSPI.DLL
WINTRUST  DLL        78,096  08-18-97   4:43p  WINTRUST.DLL
```

This is followed by the output for SYSDIR2.TXT:

```
WINSSPI   DLL        30,416  08-11-97  11:34a  WINSSPI.DLL
WINTOP    VXD        14,102  06-22-96   5:04a  WINTOP.VXD
WINTRUST  DLL        78,096  08-18-97   4:43p  WINTRUST.DLL
```

As you can see, one file has been added between WINSSPI.DLL and WINTRUST.DLL—namely, WINTOP.VXD.

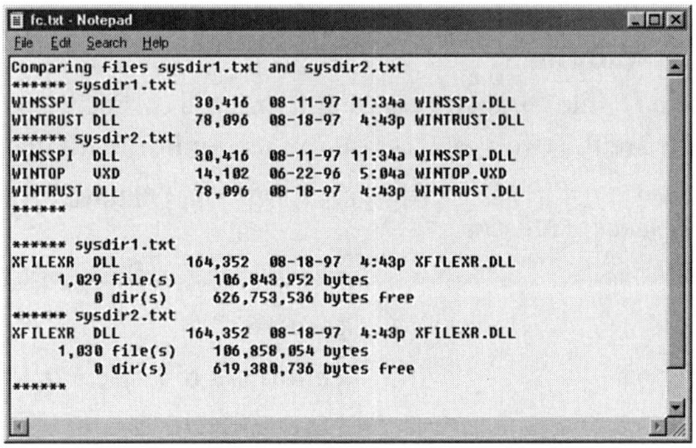

FIGURE 18.1.

The output of an FC command.

Your Word Processor's Compare Feature

Most high-end word processors have a feature that enables you to compare two files. In Word 97, for example, open the post-install file, select Tools | Track Changes | Compare Documents, and then use the Open dialog box to open the pre-install file. Word examines the documents and then inserts the changes using revision marks.

Working with the Add/Remove Programs Wizard

You've seen throughout this book that Windows 98 has a Wizard for almost every occasion. Installing applications is another one of those occasions. The Add/Remove Programs Wizard is a simple series of dialog boxes that help you find and run an application's setup program. This might sound like something that's useful only for novices, but there are good reasons to use this Wizard to launch all your installation programs. The biggest reason is that it warns Windows 98 that you're about to install an application, so the operating system can set itself up accordingly. Also, for Windows 98 applications, it ensures that the appropriate data is stored in the Registry (the program's installed components, the parameters needed to run the program successfully, the information needed to uninstall the program, and so on).

Here are the steps to follow to run the Add/Remove Program Wizard:

1. In Control Panel, open the Add/Remove Programs icon to display the Add/Remove Program Properties dialog box.

2. Click the Install button. The first of the Wizard's dialog boxes appears.

3. Insert the floppy disk or the CD-ROM that contains the installation program.

4. Click Next >. The Wizard scours your floppy disk drives and CD-ROM drives for a file named SETUP or INSTALL (with an extension of .EXE, .COM, or .BAT) and then displays the dialog box shown in Figure 18.2. If it finds an installation program, it displays the file's pathname in the Command line for installation program text box; otherwise, it leaves the text box blank.

FIGURE 18.2.

If the Wizard finds an installation program, it displays its pathname.

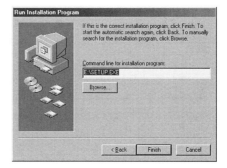

5. Edit the command line as necessary. If you're not sure, or if the program uses an installation program with a different name, you can click the Browse button, choose the install program from the Browse dialog box, and then click Open.

6. Click Finish. The Wizard launches the installation program.

7. Complete the installation normally.

If the installation program tells you to restart your computer, try to avoid letting the program do it for you. It's safer to just exit the installation program, close your running applications, and then restart the system manually.

Installing Applications

Let's now turn our attention to the three main types of applications you might need to install: 32-bit applications, 16-bit applications, and DOS applications. The next few sections discuss the installation issues involved with each type of application, as well as approaches that work best with each type.

Installing 32-Bit Applications

There are plenty of reasons to use 32-bit applications under Windows 98, including long filename support, preemptive multitasking, and protected memory space. Here are two more to add to the list: a standard installation procedure that's easy to use and the ability to uninstall applications.

Before proceeding, I should clarify that when I talk about "32-bit" applications, I'm referring specifically to applications that qualify for the Windows 95 or Windows 98 logo. In other words, I'm not talking about applications written specifically for computers running Win32s (a subset of the Win32 API) or Windows NT.

Microsoft has published a new set of requirements for the Windows 98 logo. As a recap, to qualify for the Windows 95 logo, an application must meet the following guidelines:

- It must use the Win32 application programming interface (API) and must be compiled with a 32-bit compiler that generates an executable file of the Portable Executable (PE) format.

- It must support the Windows 95 user interface as published in The Windows Interface Guidelines for Software Design. This includes using the system-defined dialog boxes and controls, registering both 16×16-pixel and 32×32-pixel icons for each file type and the application, using the system metrics for setting the size of elements within the application, using the system-defined colors, and using the right mouse button for context menus (and not for any other purpose).

- It must support long filenames and use them to display all document and data filenames in the shell, in title bars, in dialog boxes and controls, and with icons. In addition, an application should hide the extensions of filenames that are displayed within the application itself.

- It must be aware of Plug and Play events. For example, it must react to system messages that occur when a new device is attached or removed.

- It must run on Windows NT 3.5 or later. If the application uses features that are available only in Windows 95, the features must degrade gracefully in Windows NT. Conversely, if it uses features available only in Windows NT, the features must degrade gracefully in Windows 95. The application must run successfully with both Windows 95 and Windows NT, unless architectural differences between the two operating systems prevent it.

- It must support Universal Naming Conventions (UNC) names for paths.

- It must support OLE containers or objects, or both. It must also support the OLE style of drag-and-drop. An application should also support OLE Automation and compound files (with document summary information included).

- It must support simple mail enabling by using the Messaging Application Programming Interface (MAPI) or the Common Messaging Call (CMC) API. In other words, it must include some kind of "Send Mail" command that lets the user send the current document via email.

■ It must follow the Windows 95 application installation guidelines to make the application properly visible in the shell.

For Windows 98, Microsoft has put together a new set of guidelines (known as the Logo 4.0 requirements) that an application must meet to qualify for the "Designed for Windows 98" logo. Here are some of the highlights:

■ It must support the OnNow initiative and ACPI (see Chapter 11, "Device Advice: Dealing with Devices in Windows 98"). This means, for example, no nonessential hard disk activity while the computer is in sleep mode, keeping idle time activity to a minimum while a notebook computer is on batteries, support for wake-on-ring in telephony applications, and so on.

■ It must support Windows 98's multiple monitor feature. This means an application understands the virtual desktop coordinates and that each monitor can have separate resolutions and color depths.

■ It must distribute new features, particularly DLLs and other core components, via a service pack in the form of a self-extracting EXE.

■ It must use the Registry to obtain the correct language-specific folder names used on the system. In other words, the application should never assume it will deal only with English-language folder names.

■ It must provide keyboard access to all program features, and it must document that access. This ensures that disabled users who cannot manipulate a mouse can still work with the application.

■ It must expose the current keyboard focus. This enables Microsoft Magnifier (see Chapter 7, "Setting Accessibility Options, User Profiles, and More") to track and thus magnify the current keyboard context.

18

INSTALLING AND
UNINSTALLING
PROGRAMS

THE LATEST LOGO NEWS

To get the latest information about the "Designed for Windows 98" logo, keep an eye on the following Web site:

`http://www.microsoft.com/windows/thirdparty/winlogo/`

Installation Guidelines for 32-Bit Applications

Thirty-two–bit applications that qualify for the coveted Windows 98 logo have strict guidelines they must follow during installation. These guidelines are designed to make the installation easier for the user and to make sure that the application fits into the Windows 98 way of doing things (what Microsoft calls, somewhat chillingly, being a "good Windows 98 citizen"). These guidelines include the following points:

- The user should have a choice of installations, such as Typical, Compact, and Custom.

- Each step of the installation should have default choices so that users, if they want to, can work through the entire process by pressing the Enter key.

- Each floppy disk should be needed only once during the installation, and the computer should beep whenever a new disk is required.

- There should be a progress meter so that users know how far into the installation they are.

- The user should be able to cancel the installation at any time. The install program should keep track of the files copied so that it can reverse any changes made to the system in the event of a cancellation.

- The installation program should determine the user's hardware and software configuration before starting to copy files. This means determining whether the user's system has all the resources needed to run the program successfully and has enough disk space (the program should always display how much disk space it requires). The program also should check to see whether any files needed by the application (especially shared DLLs) already exist on the system. For the latter, the install program should check the version number of existing files to make sure a newer version of the file doesn't get overwritten by an older version.

- The program should not use `WIN.INI`, `SYSTEM.INI`, `CONFIG.SYS`, or `AUTOEXEC.BAT` to store configuration information.

- The program must use the Registry to store configuration options as well as the information required to uninstall the product.

What Happens to the Registry

The Registry is crucial because it identifies the application to Windows 98 and sets up functionality, such as file types, default document actions, OLE information, application-specific paths, uninstall data, and more. The next few sections run through some of the changes that a typical installation program might make to the Registry.

Version-Specific Settings

Most programs add a new subkey to `HKEY_LOCAL_MACHINE\SOFTWARE` that uses the following general format:

`HKEY_LOCAL_MACHINE\SOFTWARE\CompanyName\ProductName\Version`

`CompanyName` is the name of the vendor, `ProductName` is the name of the software package, and `Version` is the version number of the application. This key stores general information pertaining to this copy of the application.

User-Specific Settings

Most programs also add the following key:

`HKEY_CURRENT_USER\Software\CompanyName\ProductName`

This key stores user-specific preferences and generally has a number of subkeys. For example, Figure 18.3 shows the various subkeys added by Netscape Navigator. Applications used to store this data in `WIN.INI`.

FIGURE 18.3.

Applications use `HKEY_CURRENT_USER\` `Software` *to store their user-specific options and preferences.*

Application-Specific Paths

As explained in Chapter 13, "A Few Good Hacks: Some Useful Registry Tweaks," Windows 98 uses application-specific paths instead of a general PATH statement. When you enter just the primary name of an application's executable file, Windows 98 will launch the program successfully.

To set up this feature, the installation program must add a new subkey to the following key:

`HKEY_LOCAL_MACHINE\SOFTWARE\Microsoft\Windows\CurrentVersion\AppPaths`

This new subkey will have the same name as the application's executable file, and its `Default` setting will contain the full pathname to the executable. The install program might also create a `Path` setting that specifies a default folder (or folders) for the application. Netscape, for example, adds a `NETSCAPE.EXE` subkey with the following settings:

```
Default   C:\Program Files\Netscape\Navigator\Program\Netscape.exe
Path      C:\Program Files\Netscape\Navigator\Program;C:\Program
➥Files\Netscape\Navigator\System
```

Extensions and Actions

If the program creates data files with a unique extension, the installation procedure will register a new file type with Windows 98. This involves adding an extension subkey to `HKEY_CLASSES_ROOT` (the alias of `HKEY_LOCAL_MACHINE\SOFTWARE\Classes`), as well as a corresponding file type subkey. The latter will define the default icon for the file type, actions available for the file type, and a few other things. For OLE applications, a unique `CLSID` subkey will be added to `HKEY_CLASSES_ROOT\CLSID` (you'll learn more about this in Chapter 19, "Sharing Data in Windows 98: The Clipboard and OLE").

Shared DLLs

As you'll see later when you learn about uninstalling, one of Windows 98's nicest features is that it keeps track of shared DLLs—DLL files that are used (or can be used) by multiple applications. A common example is the `VBRUN300.DLL` file that's used by most programs created with Visual Basic version 3.

It's up to the installation program to check the user's system for any shared DLLs (and other components) that are required by the application. If it finds any, the installation program should increment the Registry's usage counter for each DLL. You find these usage counters in the following key:

`HKEY_LOCAL_MACHINE\SOFTWARE\Microsoft\Windows\CurrentVersion\SharedDLLs`

Figure 18.4 shows some sample entries in this key. Each setting uses a DWORD value that tells you how many applications use each DLL. For example, Figure 18.4 tells you that two applications use the file `CTRES.DLL`.

FIGURE 18.4.

Windows 98 uses the SharedDLLs *key to keep track of the number of 32-bit applications using a particular DLL file.*

Pathname of DLL file ——

Number of applications that use it ——

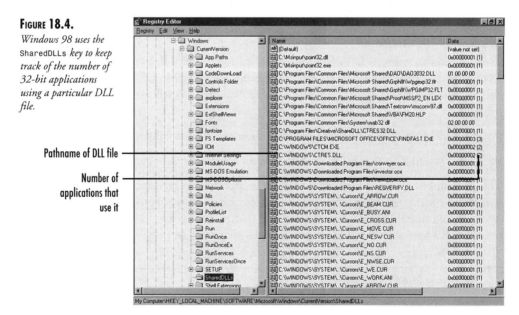

Uninstall Data

To facilitate easy removal of an application, the setup program stores uninstall information in the following Registry key:

```
HKEY_LOCAL_MACHINE\SOFTWARE\Microsoft\Windows\CurrentVersion\Uninstall
```

I'll talk more about this feature later in this chapter in the section called "Uninstalling 32-Bit Applications."

The 32-Bit Installation Procedure

Installing 32-bit applications is easy. Use the Add/Remove Programs Wizard to launch the setup program, and the installation proceeds with (generally speaking) little in the way of user input. (This depends on the complexity of the application, of course.) Many Windows 98 developers use the InstallShield SE Toolkit that's included in the Win32 Software Development Kit (SDK) to develop their installation programs. This means that most of your 32-bit programs will have a similar look and feel during installation. You know that a program is using the InstallShield Wizard if you see the dialog box shown in Figure 18.5.

DON'T FORGET AUTOPLAY

Another advantage of using 32-bit applications designed for Windows 95 or Windows 98 is that they often support the AutoPlay feature for CD-ROMs. In particular, these applications will often launch their installation programs automatically when you insert the CD.

FIGURE 18.5.

If you see this dialog box, you know that the setup program was developed using the InstallShield SE Toolkit.

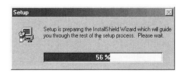

From here, the InstallShield Wizard takes you through a series of dialog boxes like the ones shown in Figures 18.6 and 18.7. Unlike with Windows 3.*x*, in the vast majority of cases you won't have to reboot after installing your 32-bit application. Because all the configuration information is stored in the Registry, Windows 98 can handle the newcomer dynamically. (The exceptions to this rule are applications that require device drivers to be loaded at startup.)

FIGURE 18.6.

The first of the InstallShield Wizard's dialog boxes.

FIGURE 18.7.

This InstallShield Wizard dialog box prompts you for a file location.

Installing 16-Bit Applications

Sixteen-bit Windows 3.*x* applications are, by definition, ineligible for the Windows 98 logo, so their installation programs don't have all the fancy features that 32-bit applications have. In particular, 16-bit install programs don't know about the Registry—or, more accurately, they know, at best, only about a small part of the Registry: HKEY_CLASSES_ROOT. Therefore, they don't support new features, such as application-specific paths, shared DLLs, and uninstall data.

Microsoft, of course, was well aware of this, so it made sure that any 16-bit application would install in Windows 98 exactly as it would install in Windows 3.*x*. To accomplish this, Microsoft made the following design decisions in Windows 98:

> **Support for older configuration files:** Most 16-bit applications store their configuration data in WIN.INI and SYSTEM.INI, and they read data from these files as well. Therefore, Windows 98 still maintains these files so as not to break 16-bit installation programs. Sixteen-bit install programs are also free to add or edit lines in CONFIG.SYS and AUTOEXEC.BAT, and Windows 98 will honor these changes.

Built-in 32-bit functionality to replace 16-bit components: Most drivers and TSRs that used to get loaded in CONFIG.SYS and AUTOEXEC.BAT are now part of the Windows 98 operating system in 32-bit versions. Sixteen-bit applications don't know this, however, so they'll often look to CONFIG.SYS and AUTOEXEC.BAT for the appropriate files. The polite ones will let you know that you're "missing" a particular component and offer to add it for you, as shown in Figure 18.8. Other, ruder install programs will just go ahead and add lines to your startup files.

FIGURE 18.8.

Here, VISIO's setup program wants to add the SHARE *command to* AUTOEXEC.BAT. SHARE *is now implemented as the VSHARE VxD, so you could ignore this request.*

CHECK YOUR STARTUP FILES AFTER INSTALLING

After installing any 16-bit application, check your CONFIG.SYS and AUTOEXEC.BAT files to see whether any extraneous lines have been added, and delete them if necessary.

A SYSTEM subfolder: Microsoft now encourages developers to store DLLs and other behind-the-scenes components in their program's main folder. However, most 16-bit applications are set up to just toss all their DLLs, font files, and whatever else into the SYSTEM subfolder of the main Windows folder. Because these install programs can't update the SharedDLLs usage counters, it's a good idea to save a DIR file listing for the SYSTEM subfolder before and after installing 16-bit applications.

Windows 98 watches the SYSTEM subfolder: Microsoft wanted to avoid letting bull-in-a-china-shop install programs overwrite newer DLLs or add useless DLLs to the SYSTEM subfolder. Therefore, while you're installing, Windows 98 keeps an eye on activity in this folder and prevents install programs from messing with any of the existing files. This is another good reason to use the Add/Remove Programs Wizard to install 16-bit applications, because it alerts Windows 98 that an installation is under-way.

DO YOU HAVE TO REINSTALL YOUR 16-BIT APPS?

If you chose to install Windows 98 in a folder separate from Windows 3.x, you might think that you have to reinstall all your 16-bit applications to get them to work from Windows 98. Actually, in many cases you won't have to. As long as you add the main Windows 3.x folder and its SYSTEM subfolder to your Windows 98 PATH, many of your 16-bit applications will run just fine. To do this, add the following line to your AUTOEXEC.BAT file:

```
PATH %PATH%;C:\WIN31;C:\WIN31\SYSTEM
```

Be sure to substitute your main Windows 3.x folder for C:\WIN31. Note that, in some cases, you might also need to add the application's folder to the PATH as well.

Installing DOS Programs

Because DOS programs (for the most part) don't bother with any Windows-related procedures, they're the simplest of all programs to install. Just fire up the Add/Remove Programs Wizard, find the installation program, and proceed from there. As usual, it's best to use this procedure and not simply install the program from Explorer or the DOS prompt. That way, Windows 98 can monitor the progress of the installation and make sure nothing untoward goes on. Also, this ensures that Windows 98 checks APPS.INF for program-specific configuration information.

You may occasionally find that a DOS-based setup program won't run under Windows 98. If this happens, you have no choice but to abandon Windows 98 and install the program using MS-DOS mode. (For details on MS-DOS mode, see Chapter 23, "DOS Isn't Dead: Unleashing the DOS Shell.")

As with 16-bit applications, you need to watch out for unnecessary changes to CONFIG.SYS and AUTOEXEC.BAT. If the program adds drivers or TSRs that have been replaced by protected-mode components in Windows 98, you need to remove the offending lines from the startup files. However, if the program will run only in MS-DOS mode, you have two choices:

- Leave the lines in CONFIG.SYS and AUTOEXEC.BAT so that they will be loaded automatically each time you reboot.

- Create "custom" CONFIG.SYS and AUTOEXEC.BAT files for the application. These files are loaded only when you run the program in MS-DOS mode. Again, see Chapter 23 to learn how to create custom startup files for a DOS program.

Installing Applications from a Network Server

If you're a system administrator and you often install software on multiple machines on your network, Windows 98 gives you a handy method for allowing users to install these applications themselves. Setting this up requires three steps:

1. On your server, create a folder for each application you want to make available. Each folder should contain the setup program and source files for the application.

2. Create an APPS.INI file that specifies where on the server each application's setup program can be found.

3. Modify the user's Registry to point to the APPS.INI file.

The next two sections expand on steps 2 and 3.

Creating an APPS.INI File

APPS.INI is an initialization file that specifies both the name of each application and the location on the server of the application's setup program. Create APPS.INI as a plain text file in a read-only folder on the server. Then open APPS.INI and enter the following section title:

```
[AppInstallList]
```

Below this heading, enter the specifics for each application using the following general format:

```
Application Name=[*]UNC-Path
```

Application Name is any descriptive name you give to the application (this is the name the users will see when they install the application). *UNC-Path* is the UNC path to the application's setup program. Here's an example:

```
Netscape Communicator=\\ZEUS\C\Applications\Netscape4\cb32e401a.exe
```

If the application's setup program doesn't support UNC paths, append an asterisk (*) to the front of the UNC path. This tells the server to temporarily map a drive letter for the application's folder.

Modifying the User's Registry

To enable the network install feature on a user's machine, you need to modify the user's Registry. Specifically, you need to launch the Registry Editor and travel to the following key:

```
HKEY_LOCAL_MACHINE\SOFTWARE\Microsoft\Windows\CurrentVersion
```

From here, select Edit | New | String Value and then name the new setting AppInstallPath. Open this new setting and, in the Edit String dialog box that appears, enter a UNC path that points to the APPS.INI file on the server. Figure 18.9 shows an example.

FIGURE 18.9.

You need to add an AppInstallPath *setting to each user's Registry.*

18

INSTALLING AND UNINSTALLING PROGRAMS

This new setting goes into effect as soon as you exit the Edit String dialog box. The result is a new Network Install tab in the Add/Remove Programs Properties sheet, as shown in Figure 18.10. This tab contains a list of all the applications you entered in your APPS.INI file. To install the application from the server, highlight it and click Install.

FIGURE 18.10.

With the AppInstallPath *setting in effect, the Add/Remove Programs Properties dialog box sprouts a new Network Install tab.*

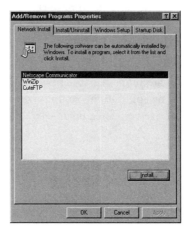

Uninstalling Applications

Applications, like the people we meet, fall into three categories: friends for life, acquaintances we deal with occasionally, and those we hope never to speak to again. Avoiding people we dislike is usually just a matter of avoiding contact with them—they'll get the hint after a while. Unlikable applications, however, just don't seem to get it. They keep hanging around like party guests who won't leave. If you have an application that's worn out its welcome, this section shows you the proper way to uninstall it so that it's out of your life forever.

Uninstalling 32-Bit Applications

One of the truly useful features you get with 32-bit Windows 98 logo-compliant applications is the ability to uninstall these programs easily. When you install one of these programs, it adds a new subkey to the following Registry key:

```
\HKEY_LOCAL_MACHINE\SOFTWARE\Microsoft\Windows\CurrentVersion\Uninstall
```

As you can see in Figure 18.11, this subkey contains two settings:

DisplayName: This setting is usually the name of the program, and it's what appears in the list of programs to uninstall that you see in the Add/Remove Programs Properties dialog box (discussed later).

UninstallString: This is the command line for the program that performs the removal. Note that it's not Windows 98 that's doing the removing. Instead, it's a program provided by the developer of the application (a sort of "anti-install" program).

FIGURE 18.11.

32-bit applications store uninstall data in the Registry.

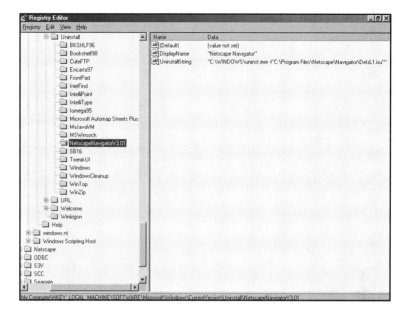

When removing an application from your system, the uninstall program does the following:

- If the application used any shared DLLs, the uninstall program decrements the appropriate usage counter in the Registry. If the usage counter for a particular file is 0, the program usually asks whether you want to delete the DLL. Because a 16-bit program might need the DLL, you should leave the file alone. However, if you're using only 32-bit applications, you can delete the file safely.

- Delete all program files related to the application. Data files will remain in place.

- Delete Start menu folders and shortcuts.

- Remove empty directories left by the application.

- Remove from the Registry all information used by the application.

To uninstall an application, open Control Panel's Add/Remove Program icon. The box in the bottom half of the Install/Uninstall tab lists the applications that you can uninstall, as shown in Figure 18.12. To remove an application, highlight it and click the Add/Remove button. A dialog box will appear, asking you to confirm the deletion. Click Yes to continue.

If the program finds a shared DLL that isn't used by another program (that is, a DLL with a usage counter at 0), you see a Remove Shared File? dialog box similar to the one shown in Figure 18.13. Click Yes or No as appropriate. You might need to repeat this process a few times.

18

INSTALLING AND
UNINSTALLING
PROGRAMS

FIGURE 18.12.

*The Add/Remove
Programs Properties
dialog box lists the
applications you can
uninstall.*

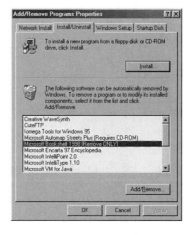

FIGURE 18.13.

*You see this dialog box
for shared DLLs with
a usage counter that's
now down to 0.*

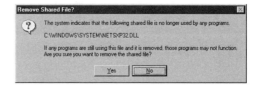

TROUBLESHOOTING: YOU CAN'T UNINSTALL A PROGRAM

When you remove a program using the Add/Remove Programs tool in Control Panel, you receive the following error message:

```
An error occurred while trying to remove <Program Name>.
Uninstallation has been canceled
```

This error occurs if a program that's listed in the Install/Uninstall tab has already been deleted manually. To remove a program from the list in the Install/Uninstall tab, delete the appropriate subkey under the following Registry key:

```
HKEY_LOCAL_MACHINE\SOFTWARE\Microsoft\Windows\CurrentVersion\Uninstall
```

Uninstalling 16-Bit Applications

Unfortunately, removing a 16-bit application from your system is much less straightforward. Unless the program comes with its own uninstall feature (and some do), you have to employ a bit of guesswork to eradicate these older programs.

The real problem with 16-bit applications is that they tend to litter the main Windows 98 folder and the SYSTEM subfolder with all kinds of extraneous files. Determining which files can be deleted is often a tricky business. Here are some ideas:

- If you used the before and after DIR snapshots that I suggested earlier, you know exactly which files the program added.

- Look for filenames that match the program. For example, many WordPerfect DLLs begin with WP.

- Check out the application's program files to see whether they have a common date and time stamp. If they do, you can check other folders for files that use the same date and time.

- Open WIN.INI and SYSTEM.INI and look for lines that refer to specific DLLs.

- Use Windows 98's Quick View accessory to get a list of the DLLs that the program uses. To do this, either highlight the executable file and select File | Quick View or right-click the executable and select Quick View from the context menu. In the window that appears, scroll down until you find a section called either Imported-Name Table or Import Table. You see a list of the DLLs that the program uses. Figure 18.14 shows the DLLs used by NETSCAPE.EXE.

FIGURE 18.14.

The Quick View accessory can tell you which DLLs an executable file uses.

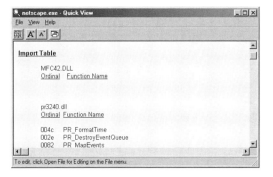

You can delete some of these files without a second thought. A private INI file is a good example. However, it's dangerous to delete DLLs and other SYSTEM folder files, because other applications might need them. There are a couple of ways to check, however.

For example, you could examine the SharedDLLs key in the Registry to see whether any 32-bit applications are using the DLLs. You could also use the Find feature (Start | Find | Files or Folders) to look for mentions of the DLL in other files. You probably just need to search the main Windows 98 folder and all its subfolders. (For example, if the DLL is named OLDAPP.DLL, search for oldapp.) You need to enter the primary name of the DLL in the Containing text box. If Find locates any executable files or other DLLs that mention the DLL in question, you can assume it's being used by another application.

If, in the end, you're still not sure about a particular DLL, just move it to another folder. Then, down the road, if a program complains that the file is missing, you can always restore it.

When all that's done, you can get rid of the rest of the program by following these steps:

1. If you want to save your data files, move them to a safe location if necessary.

2. Delete the program's main folder and all its subfolders.

3. Display Windows 98's Start Menu subfolder and delete any folders and shortcuts used by the program.

4. Scour WIN.INI and SYSTEM.INI and remove any traces of the program that you find.

5. Check the CONFIG.SYS and AUTOEXEC.BAT files for evidence of the program (such as a folder added to the PATH statement).

6. Check HKEY_LOCAL_MACHINE\SOFTWARE\Classes and delete any keys and settings related to the program (such as extension keys, file type keys, CLSID keys, and so on).

Uninstalling DOS Programs

Uninstalling DOS programs is usually more straightforward, because they tend to store all their files in one folder. This means you can remove most DOS programs with a simple four-step procedure:

1. If you have data files you want to preserve for posterity, move them to a different location if necessary.

2. Delete the program's main folder and all its subfolders.

3. Delete any shortcuts (PIFs) you might have created for the program.

4. Remove any traces of the program from CONFIG.SYS and AUTOEXEC.BAT.

Summary

This chapter showed you how to install and uninstall applications in Windows 98. I began by showing you a few tips and techniques for practicing "safe" setups. These included checking for viruses, having a bootable disk nearby, backing up configuration files, reading the documentation, and taking control of the installation. I then showed you how to wield the Add/Remove Programs Wizard. The rest of the chapter showed you how to install and uninstall 32-bit applications, 16-bit applications, and DOS programs.

Here's a list of chapters where you'll find related information:

- I covered Windows 98 installation, as well as how to add and remove Windows 98 components, in Chapter 2, "From Disc to Disk: Installing Windows 98."

- For a Registry refresher course, turn to Chapter 12, "Getting to Know the Windows 98 Registry."

- Backup is covered in Chapter 16, "Working with a Net: The Windows 98 Backup Utility."

- The System File Checker is invaluable for restoring configurations should a new program make a mess of things. Read all about it in Chapter 17, "Wielding the Windows 98 System Tools."

- For information on how best to run DOS programs, including the full scoop on PIF shortcuts, MS-DOS mode, custom configuration files, and more, check out Chapter 23, "DOS Isn't Dead: Unleashing the DOS Shell."

18

INSTALLING AND
UNINSTALLING
PROGRAMS

Sharing Data in Windows 98: The Clipboard and OLE

IN THIS CHAPTER

> *Father (eating chocolate bar): What did you learn in school today?*
>
> *Daughter (eyeing chocolate bar): Sha-a-a-a-ring.*
>
> —*Chocolate bar commercial from the '70s*

It used to be that applications operated in splendid isolation. For example, if you needed to write a memo, you'd fire up your word processor program and start hunting and pecking. If you then realized you needed a spreadsheet to complement the text, you'd shut down the word processor, load up your spreadsheet program, and start crunching numbers. The only tools you had at hand to connect these two documents were a paper clip and a "See attached" message.

Now, thanks to Windows wonders such as multitasking, the Clipboard, and OLE, applications have gone from isolation to collaboration. Not only can you have your word processor and spreadsheet applications running at the same time, but you can easily share data between them, to the point where you can actually place, for example, an entire spreadsheet inside a word processing document.

This willingness to share data between applications is one of Windows 98's best features, and it's the subject of this chapter. I'll focus on the sophisticated linking and embedding operations used with OLE.

Understanding OLE

As you probably know, you can use simple cut, copy, and paste techniques to transfer text and graphics from one application to another via the Clipboard. However, these methods suffer from three major drawbacks.

First, if the data gets changed in the original application, the document containing the copy will become out-of-date. This has two consequences:

- If you know that the data needs to be updated, you have to repeat the whole copy-and-paste procedure to get the latest version of the data.
- If you don't know that the data needs to be updated (for example, if someone else changes the original data without telling you), you are stuck with an old version of the info.

Second, what if you want to make changes to the copied data? You might be able to edit the data directly (if it's just text, for example), but more often than not you need to run the original application, change the data there, and then copy the data via the Clipboard again. However, problems can arise if you're not sure which application to use, or if you're not sure which file contains the original data.

Third, copying data between documents is often wasteful, because you end up with multiple copies of the same data. You could cut the data from the original application and then paste it, but then there would be no easy way to edit the data using the original application.

It would be nice if you didn't have to worry about the updating of your shared data. It would be nice if there were a system that would accomplish three goals:

■ If the data changes in the original application, update the copied data automatically.

■ If you want to edit the copied data, make it easy to find both the original application and the original data file.

■ Enable you to store nonnative data inside a document without having to maintain separate documents for the original data.

Happily, OLE—object linking and embedding—meets all three goals and adds a few extra conveniences to the mix for good measure. OLE is one of Microsoft's most important technologies. It can be described without hyperbole as the foundation of all Microsoft's future development efforts in operating systems, applications, and the Internet. Understanding how OLE operates, then, is crucial to understanding not only Windows 98 (which, as you'll soon see, makes extensive use of OLE internally), but also Windows 98 applications, which must support OLE in order to qualify for the Windows 98 logo.

OLE wasn't always such a big deal. Microsoft originally hoped that dynamic data exchange (DDE) would carry the data-sharing torch into the future. DDE works by establishing a communications "channel" between two applications along which data can be transferred. Unfortunately, DDE failed miserably. It was slow, flaky, and inflexible, and it was a programmer's solution to what is, really, an end-user's problem.

OLE leaped into the breach by making it easy for users to share data between applications, keep shared data updated automatically, and mix multiple data types in a single document without wasting disk space. The problem, however, was that OLE was implemented only sporadically. Because Microsoft relied on individual applications to execute OLE functionality, users could never be sure of what they were getting and whether two applications could work together. That all changed with the release of Windows 95, however, because OLE was built into the operating system. This continues in Windows 98. For example, you're working with OLE when you create a shortcut to a program or document. Not only that, but all Windows 95 or Windows 98 applications that deal with documents are guaranteed to be OLE-compliant, so you always know what you're getting.

First, Some Fundamentals

You'll spend the rest of this section exploring some important OLE underpinnings. Before diving into these theoretical waters, however, you should know about three crucial OLE concepts: *objects*, *servers*, and *containers*:

Object: In the OLE world, an object is not only data—a slice of text, a graphic, a sound, a chunk of a spreadsheet, or whatever—but also one or more functions for creating, accessing, and using that data.

Server application: The application that you use to create and edit an object. Also known as the *source application*.

Container application: The application that you use to store a linked or embedded object created with a server application. Also known as the *client application*.

With these simple fundamentals in hand, you can now take a closer look at OLE architecture. However, OLE is a large, complicated standard, and it's hideously complex to program. Lucky for you, though, unleashing OLE in Windows 98 does not require you to delve too deeply into this complexity.

Compound Documents

A *compound document* is a document that contains, along with its native data, one or more objects that were created using other applications. The key point is that the compound document's native data and its objects can have entirely different data formats. For example, a word processing document can include a spreadsheet range object or a sound clip object. The container application doesn't need to know a thing about these alien data formats, either. All it has to know is the name of the server application that created the data and how to display the data. All this information (and more) is included free of charge as part of the object, so it's readily available to the container application.

As the name *object linking and embedding* implies, you create a compound document by either linking objects to the document or embedding objects in the document. The next three sections explain linking and embedding in more depth, and then I examine four more issues related to linking and embedding: visual editing, OLE-related Clipboard formats, nested objects, and object conversion.

Understanding Linking

Linking is one of the OLE methods you can use to insert an object into a file from a container application and thus create a compound document. In this case, the object includes only the following information:

- The Registry key needed to invoke the object's server application.

- A metafile that contains GDI instructions on how to display the object. These instructions simply generate the primitives (lines, circles, arcs, and so on) that create an image of the object. These primitives are the heart of Windows' Graphical Device Interface (GDI), and they form the basis of any image you see onscreen. So the container application doesn't have to know a thing about the object itself; it just follows the metafile's instructions blindly, and a perfect replica of the object's image appears.

- A pointer to the server application file (the *source document*) that contains the original data.

Linking brings many advantages to the table, but three are most relevant to our purposes.

First, the link enables the container application to check the source document for changes. If it finds that the data has been modified, OLE can use the link to update the object automatically. For example, suppose you insert a linked spreadsheet object into a word processor document. If you revise some of the numbers in the spreadsheet sometime down the road, the object inside the document is automatically updated to reflect the new numbers. However, this updating is automatic only under certain conditions:

- If the container application is running and has the compound document open, the update is automatic.

- If the compound document isn't open when the data is changed, the object gets updated automatically the next time you open the compound document.

- Most OLE applications let you disable automatic updating either for individual documents or for the application as a whole. In this case, you need to perform the updates manually. (I'll show you how this is done later in this chapter.)

Second, because the object "knows" where to find both the server application and the source document, you can edit the object from within the container application. In most cases, double-clicking the object invokes the server and loads the appropriate source file. You can then edit the original data and exit the server application, and your object is, once again, updated automatically.

Third, because the source data exists in a separate file, you can easily reuse the data in other compound documents, and you can edit the data directly from within the server application.

Understanding Embedding

One of the problems associated with linking is that if you distribute the compound document, you also have to distribute the source document. Similarly, if you move the source document to a different drive on your system, the link breaks. (Note that Windows 98 will track the link if you move the file to a different folder on the same drive. Also, it's possible to edit the link to reflect the new location.)

Embedding solves these problems by inserting an object not only with the server's Registry information and the metafile for displaying the object, but also with the object's *data*. This way, everything you need to display and work with the object exists within the object itself. There's no need for a separate source file, so you can distribute the compound document knowing that the recipient will receive the data intact.

In fact, embedding lets you *create* server objects from within the container application. If you're working with Word for Windows, for example, you can insert a new spreadsheet object right from Word. OLE will start Excel so that you can create the new object, but when you exit Excel, the object will exist only within the Word compound document. There will be no separate Excel file.

19

**SHARING DATA IN
WINDOWS 98**

Note that many applications can operate only as OLE servers. This means that they aren't standalone applications and therefore have no way to create files on their own. They exist only to create OLE objects for compound documents. Microsoft Office ships with several examples of these applications, including WordArt and Microsoft Graph.

Should You Link or Embed?

Perhaps the most confusing aspect of OLE is determining whether you should link your objects or embed them. As you've seen, the only major difference between linking and embedding is that a linked object stores only a pointer to its data, but an embedded object stores its own data internally.

With this in mind, you should link your objects if any of the following situations apply:

■ You want to keep your compound documents small. The information stored in a linked object—the pointers to the server and source document, and the metafile—consumes only about 1.5KB, so very little overhead is associated with linking. (If you're using WordPad as the container, you can check this out for yourself. Click the object and select Edit | Object Properties, or right-click the object and select Object Properties from the context menu. The properties sheet that appears shows you the size of the object, as shown in Figure 19.1.)

FIGURE 19.1.

The WordPad properties sheet for a linked object. Notice that the linked object takes up only 1.5KB.

■ You're sure the source document won't be moved or deleted. To maintain the link, OLE requires the source file to remain in the same place. If the document gets moved or deleted, the link is broken. (Although, as I've said, most OLE applications let you reestablish the link by modifying the path to the source document.)

■ You need to keep the source file as a separate document in case you want to make changes to it later, or in case you need it for other compound documents. You're free to link an object to as many container files as you like. If you think you'll be using the source data in different places, you should link it to maintain a separate file.

■ You won't be sending the compound document via email or floppy disk. Again, OLE expects the linked source data to appear in a specific place. If you send the compound document to someone else, he or she might not have the proper source file to maintain the link.

Similarly, you should embed your objects if any of the following situations apply:

■ You don't care how big your compound documents get. Embedding works best in situations in which you have lots of hard disk space and lots of memory. For example, Figure 19.2 shows the WordPad properties sheet for an embedded object. This is the same bitmap image that was linked in Figure 19.1, but you can see that the embedded object is much larger.

FIGURE 19.2.

The WordPad properties sheet for an embedded object. Because embedded objects store their own data, they're much larger than linked objects.

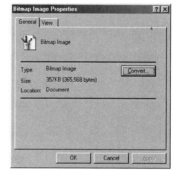

■ You don't need to keep the source file as a separate document. If you need to use the source data only once, embedding it means you can get rid of the source file (or never have to create one in the first place) and reduce the clutter on your hard disk.

■ You'll be sending the compound documents and you want to make sure the object arrives intact. If you send a file containing an embedded object, the other person will see the data complete and unaltered. If that person wants to edit the object, however, he or she needs to have the server application installed.

OLE NEEDS MEMORY

Whether you link or embed, OLE will still put a strain on your system's memory resources. Although Microsoft has made some strides in improving the efficiency of the OLE standard, the memory cost is still high. You need a minimum of 12MB of physical RAM to achieve anything approaching reasonable performance out of OLE.

Visual Editing

In the original incarnation of OLE, double-clicking an object opened a new window for the server application and loaded the source document (if the object was linked) or loaded the object's data (if the object was embedded). This process is called *open editing*.

When OLE 2.0 debuted a few years ago, it introduced the idea of *visual editing* (also known as *in-place editing*). When you double-click an embedded object, you don't see the server application in a separate window. Instead, certain features of the container application's window are temporarily hidden in favor of the server application's features. (Linked objects still use open editing.) Here's a summary of the changes that occur in the container application:

- The document window's title bar changes to tell you what kind of object you're now working with. (Not all applications do this.)

- The menu bar (with the exception of the File and Window menus) is replaced by the server application's menu bar.

- The toolbars are replaced by the server application's toolbars.

Essentially, the container application "becomes" the server application while still maintaining the object's context in the compound document. Let's look at an example. First, Figure 19.3 shows the normal Microsoft Excel window.

FIGURE 19.3.

The Microsoft Excel window before you insert an object.

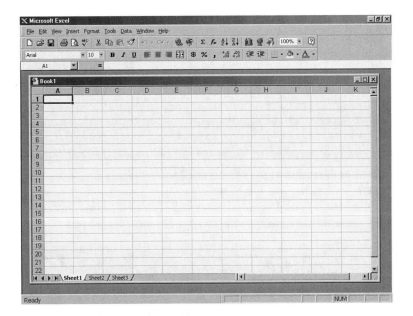

If you now insert a Microsoft Word document into Excel, OLE changes the menu bar and toolbars from Excel's to Word's, as you can see in Figure 19.4. However, the rest of the Excel interface—including the row and column headers, the underlying worksheet cells, and the sheet tabs—remain visible to give context to the embedded object. (To exit visual editing, click outside the object.)

Word's menu bar

FIGURE 19.4.

FIGURE 19.4.

During visual editing, the Excel window assumes many features of the Word window.

Word's toolbars

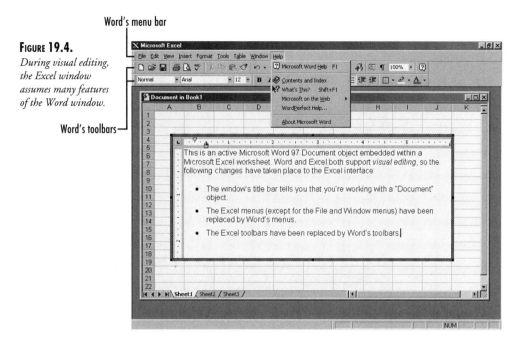

Nested Objects

After you open the server application to create or edit an object, most of the server's features become available. (During visual editing, you can't access server features that relate to files and windows; that's why the container application's File and Window menus don't change.) In particular, if the server application can also double as a container application, you have access to the server features that let you insert linked or embedded objects. In other words, you can double-click an object to activate the server application, and you can then insert a linked or embedded object inside the existing object. This is called *nesting objects*. OLE has no limit on the number of nesting levels you can use.

For example, Figure 19.5 shows a WordArt object nested inside the Word Document object that's embedded in an Excel worksheet.

Object Conversion

I mentioned earlier that if you send a compound document to another person, the recipient won't be able to edit the linked or embedded objects unless he or she has the appropriate server application. However, that's not true in all cases. OLE has a feature called *object conversion* that lets OLE servers convert objects into formats they can work with.

For example, suppose you embed an Excel worksheet into a Word document. If you then send the resulting compound document to a colleague, the recipient can read the document as long as he or she has Word. If the recipient wants to edit the embedded worksheet, however, he or she might not need Excel. All the recipient needs is a spreadsheet program that's capable of converting Excel worksheet objects into the program's native object format.

FIGURE 19.5.

OLE enables you to nest objects within objects.

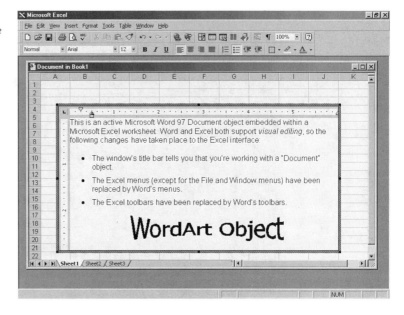

Note as well that object conversion can also be used by the server application to convert its own objects:

- To convert an existing object to a related format. In Excel, for example, you can convert a Worksheet object to a Chart object, and vice versa.

- To upgrade older objects to a new format. If a server enhances its objects with extra functionality, for example, it can use object conversion to upgrade existing objects so that they also have access to the same functions.

Working with OLE

After all that OLE theory, you're due for some hands-on techniques. To that end, I spend the rest of this chapter showing you how to put OLE to work creating compound documents. You look at several methods of both linking and embedding objects, how to edit those objects, and how to maintain links.

Linking an Object

If you have data you'd like to share between applications, and you feel that linking is the best way to go, Windows 98 gives you two methods: linking via the Clipboard, and inserting a linked file. The next two sections discuss each method. Then I'll show you how to work with and maintain your links.

Linking via the Clipboard

You know that you can use the Clipboard's cut, copy, and paste methodology to transfer static data between applications. However, the Clipboard is no slouch when it comes to OLE data transfers. If the original application is an OLE server, a cut or copy operation passes not only the selected data to the Clipboard, but also various bits of data—known as *Clipboard formats*—such as Object Descriptor, Link Source, and Link Source Descriptor. A container application can use these formats to determine whether the object on the Clipboard can be linked and to perform the actual linking.

After you place the data on the Clipboard, switch to the container application and position the cursor where you want the data to be pasted. Now select the Edit | Paste Special command to display the Paste Special dialog box, shown in Figure 19.6.

FIGURE 19.6.

Use the Paste Special dialog box to paste Clipboard data as a linked object.

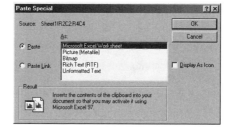

The As box lists the various formats available for the data, but you can ignore most of them. To establish a link between the container and the server, activate the Paste Link option. Usually, most of the formats will disappear, and you are left with only the object format. If you'd like the data to appear as an icon in the container document, activate the Display As Icon check box. When you're ready, click OK to paste the linked object into the container, as shown in Figure 19.7.

FIGURE 19.7.

A linked object displayed as an icon.

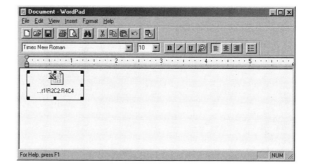

LINKING VIA DRAG-AND-DROP

You'll see later that some OLE applications let you embed objects by dragging them from a server and dropping them on a container. In theory, you can use this method to create a linked object as well by holding down Ctrl+Shift as you drop the object. However, few applications currently support this feature.

Inserting a File as a Linked Object

Instead of pasting part of a document as a linked object, you might prefer to insert an entire file as a linked object. For example, if you insert a linked Excel worksheet into a Word document, the container object will reflect *any* changes made to the original worksheet, including data added or removed, global formatting adjustments, and so on.

Also, there are situations in which you have no choice but to insert a file. For example, you can't insert part of a bitmap as a linked object; you must insert the entire file.

Here are the basic steps to follow to insert a file as a linked object:

1. In the container application, position the cursor where you want the file inserted.
2. Depending on the application, select either Insert | Object or Edit | Insert Object.
3. Select Create from File. How you do this depends on the application. In the Microsoft Office applications, for example, you select the Create from File tab, as shown in Figure 19.8. In WordPad, on the other hand, you activate the Create from File option button.

FIGURE 19.8.

The Object dialog box from Excel 97. You use the Create from File tab to insert a file object in the container.

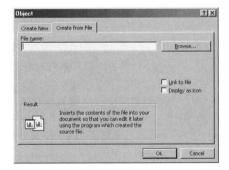

4. Enter the filename of the file you want to link. You can also click the Browse button to choose the file from a dialog box.
5. Activate the Link to file check box. (In some dialog boxes, this option is named Link.)
6. If you want the linked file to appear as an icon, activate the Display as icon check box.
7. Click OK to insert the linked file object.

Managing Links

All container applications that support object linking also give you some kind of method to manage document links. This involves updating a link so that the container displays the most recent changes, changing a link's source, determining how links are updated in the container, and breaking links you no longer need to maintain.

In most container applications, you manage links by selecting Edit | Links. You see a Links dialog box similar to the one shown in Figure 19.9 (this is the Links dialog box from WordPad). Here's a rundown of the basic link management chores you can perform:

Changing the link update method: By default, links are updated automatically. In other words, if both the source and the container are open, whenever the source data changes, the data in the container also changes. If you prefer to update the container document by hand, highlight the link and activate the Manual option.

Updating the link: If you've set a link to Manual, or if the server document isn't open, you can make sure a link contains the latest and greatest information by highlighting it and clicking the Update Now button.

Changing the link source: If you move the source document, you need to modify the link so that it points to the new location. You can do this by highlighting the appropriate link and clicking the Change Source button.

Breaking a link: If you no longer want to maintain a link between the source and the container, you can break the link. This will leave the data intact, but changes made to the original data will no longer be reflected in the container. To break a link, highlight it and click the Break Link button.

FIGURE 19.9.

Container applications that support object linking have a Links dialog box that you can use to maintain the links.

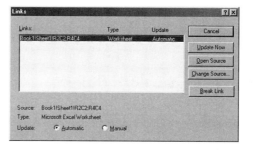

19

SHARING DATA IN WINDOWS 98

Embedding an Object

If you prefer to embed an object instead of linking it, Windows 98 gives you three or four methods to choose from (depending on the server application): the Clipboard, drag-and-drop, inserting a new embedded object, and inserting an embedded file.

Embedding via the Clipboard

Assuming that the original application is an OLE server, a cut or copied object in the Clipboard includes not only link-related formats, but also a few formats that enable a container application to embed the data (such as the Embed Source format). Again, the container application can use these formats to perform the embedding.

To embed data that's been placed on the Clipboard, switch to the container application, position the cursor where you want the data to be pasted, and select Edit | Paste Special. In the Paste Special dialog box that appears, select the object format from the As list (this format should be highlighted by default) and make sure that the Paste option is activated. Also, if you'd like the data to appear as an icon in the container document, activate the Display As Icon check box. When you're ready, click OK to paste the embedded object into the container.

Embedding via Drag-and-Drop

Server and container applications that support OLE 2 also support drag-and-drop embedding. This means you can select some data in the server document, drag the data with the mouse, and then drop it inside the container window. Most applications move the data from the source to the container, but this isn't universally true. To be sure that you're moving the data, hold down the Shift key while you drag-and-drop. If you'd prefer to copy the data, hold down Ctrl during the drag-and-drop.

DROPPING AN OBJECT ON A MINIMIZED WINDOW

Remember that you can't drop an object on a window that's been minimized. However, if you drag the object over the minimized window's taskbar button and then wait a second or two, the window will be restored automatically, and you can then drop the data inside the window.

Inserting a New Embedded Object

If the object you want to embed doesn't exist, and you don't need to create a separate file, OLE enables you to insert the new object directly into the container application. Here's how it works:

1. In the container application, move the cursor to where you want the new object to appear.
2. Depending on the application, select either Insert | Object or Edit | Insert Object. In either case, you see a dialog box similar to the one shown in Figure 19.10.

FIGURE 19.10.
*Use this dialog box
to select the type of
embedded object you
want to create.*

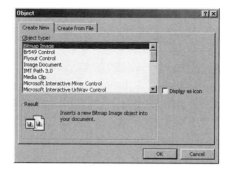

3. The Object type list displays all the available objects on your system. (Recall that
   Windows 98 generates this list by looking for all the Registry entries in
   HKEY_CLASSES_ROOT that have an Insertable subkey.) Highlight the type of object you
   want to create.

4. Click OK. Windows 98 starts the server application for the object type you selected.
   The server will appear either in place or in a separate window.

5. Create the object you want to embed.

6. Exit the server application. If you were working with the server using visual editing,
   click outside the object. Otherwise, select File | Exit & Return to *document*, where
   document is the name of the active document in the container application.

Inserting an Embedded File

You can insert an entire existing file (as opposed to an object within a file) as an embedded
object. This is useful if you want to make changes to the file from within the container without
disturbing the original. Follow these steps:

1. In the container document, position the cursor where you want to embed the object.

2. Depending on the application, select either Insert | Object or Edit | Insert Object.

3. Select Create from File. How you do this depends on the application. In the
   Microsoft Office applications, for example, you select the Create from File tab. In
   WordPad, on the other hand, you activate the Create from file option button.

4. Enter the filename of the file you want to embed. You can also click the Browse
   button to choose the file from a dialog box.

5. If you want the linked file to appear as an icon, activate the Display as Icon check box.

6. Click OK to insert the linked file object.

19

SHARING DATA IN
WINDOWS 98

Editing a Linked or Embedded Object

If you need to make some changes to a linked or embedded object, you can use the container application to launch the server application and load the object automatically. (Remember, too, that for a linked object you can always run the server application and work with the object directly.) How you do this depends on the application, but here are a few methods that work for most OLE containers:

- Double-click the object.

- Select the object, pull down the Edit menu, and then select either Linked *ObjectType* Object (for a linked object) or *ObjectType* Object (for an embedded object). In both cases, *ObjectType* is the type of object you selected (for example, Bitmap Image or Worksheet). From the cascade menu that appears, select Edit. If the server application supports visual editing, this will launch the object in place.

- Select the object, pull down the Edit menu, and then select either the Linked *ObjectType* Object command (for a linked object) or the *ObjectType* Object command (for an embedded object). In the cascade menu that appears, select Open. For servers that support the Open verb, this will launch the object in a separate window.

- Right-click the object, select either Linked *ObjectType* Object or *ObjectType* Object, and select either Edit or Open.

EDIT ISN'T ALWAYS THE DEFAULT VERB

Sometimes, when you double-click an object (such as a sound file or a video file), Windows 98 will play the object instead of editing it. In this case, you can edit the object only by using the appropriate Edit command.

Summary

This chapter showed you how to share data in Windows 98 using OLE. I gave you an extensive look at OLE theory—including compound documents, objects, linking, and embedding—and then I showed you how to put OLE to good use in your applications.

Here's a list of chapters where you'll find related information:

- To refresh your memory on some Registry basics, head for Chapter 12, "Getting to Know the Windows 98 Registry."

- You're using OLE when you cut, copy, and paste files and when you create shortcuts. I showed you how to do all these things in Chapter 14, "File and Folder Tricks and Techniques."

- I'll show you how to share data between Windows and DOS applications in Chapter 23, "DOS Isn't Dead: Unleashing the DOS Shell."

Using Fonts in Windows 98

CHAPTER 20

> *Letterforms conceal arbitrarily deep mysteries.*
>
> *—Douglas Hofstadter*

Windows has turned many otherwise ordinary citizens into avid amateur typographers. People at cocktail parties the world over are debating the relative merits of serif versus sans serif fonts, expounding the virtues of typefaces with names like Desdemona and Braggadocio, and generally just byte-bonding over this whole font foofaraw.

OK, so most of us don't take fonts to that extreme. However, we certainly appreciate what they do to jazz up our reports, spreadsheets, and graphics. There's nothing like a well-chosen font to add just the right tone to a document and to make our work stand out from the herd.

This chapter shows you how Windows 98 and fonts work together. You learn just what fonts are and how Windows 98 sees them, and then you learn a few techniques for dealing with the fonts on your system.

Fontamentals, Part I: The Architecture of Characters

Back in the days when DOS dinosaurs dominated the PC landscape, people rarely had to pay much attention to the characters that made up correspondence and memos. Outside of a measly few effects (such as making words bold), there wasn't a whole lot you could do with individual letters and symbols, so they became mere foot soldiers in any given war of words.

The advent of the graphical interface changed all that, however. With Windows, it suddenly became a snap to alter the size and shape of letters and numbers and therefore impart an entirely different atmosphere to writings. The engine behind this newfound typographical prowess was, of course, the *font*.

I always like to describe fonts as the "architecture" of characters. When you examine a building, certain features and patterns help you identify the building's architectural style. A flying buttress, for example, is usually a telltale sign of a Gothic structure. Fonts, too, are distinguished by a unique set of characteristics. Specifically, four items define the architecture of any character: the typeface, the type size, the type style, and the character spacing.

Typeface

A *typeface* is a distinctive design that is common to any related set of letters, numbers, and symbols. This design gives each character a particular shape and thickness (or *weight*, as it's called in type circles) that is unique to the typeface and difficult to classify. However, three main categories serve to distinguish all typefaces: serif, sans serif, and decorative.

A *serif* typeface contains fine cross strokes (called *feet*) at the extremities of each character. These subtle appendages give the typeface a traditional, classy look that's most often used for long stretches of text. In Windows 98, Times New Roman is an example of a serif typeface.

A *sans serif* typeface doesn't contain these cross strokes. As a result, sans serif typefaces usually have a cleaner, more modern look that works best for headings and titles. Arial is an example of a sans serif font that comes with Windows 98.

Decorative typefaces are usually special designs that are supposed to convey a particular effect. So, for example, if your document needs a fancy, handwritten effect, something like Brush Script is perfect. (Unfortunately, the Brush Script typeface doesn't come with Windows 98. However, lots of companies sell font collections that include all kinds of strange and useful fonts. Expect to pay about a dollar a font.)

Figure 20.1 shows examples of a few typefaces. As you can see, they can produce wildly different effects.

Figure 20.1.

Some sample typefaces in WordPad.

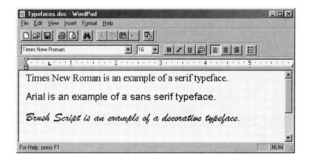

Type Size

The *type size* measures how tall a font is. The standard unit of measurement is the *point*; there are 72 points in an inch. So, for example, the letters in a 24-point font would be twice as tall as those in a 12-point font. Technically, type size is measured from the highest point of a tall letter, such as "f," to the lowest point of an underhanging letter, such as "g." (In case you're wondering, this book is laid out in a 10.5-point AGaramond font.)

Type Style

The *type style* of a font refers to extra attributes added to the typeface, such as **bold** and *italic*. Other type styles (often called type *effects*) include <u>underlining</u> and ~~strikeout~~ (sometimes called *strikethrough*). These styles are normally used to highlight or add emphasis to sections of your documents.

Character Spacing

The *character spacing* of a font can take two forms: *monospaced* or *proportional*. Monospaced fonts reserve the same amount of space for each character. For example, look at the Courier New font shown in Figure 20.2. Notice how skinny letters such as "i" and "l" take up as much space as wider letters such as "m" and "w." Although this is admirably egalitarian, these fonts tend to look like they were produced with a typewriter (in other words, they're ugly).

By contrast, in a proportional font, such as the Times New Roman font shown in Figure 20.2, the space allotted to each letter varies according to the width of the letter. This gives the text a more natural feel.

FIGURE 20.2.
Monospaced versus proportional.

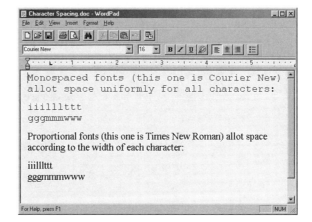

Fontamentals, Part II: Screen Fonts Versus Printer Fonts

Windows 98 also characterizes fonts by their intended output device: the screen or the printer:

- *Screen fonts* are designed to represent characters on a display screen only.
- *Printer fonts* are used by the printer to generate the characters that will appear on the printed page. Windows 98 can work with three kinds of printer fonts:

  Device fonts, which are generated by the printer hardware

  Downloadable soft fonts, which are sent to the printer during a print job

  Printable screen fonts, which can be rendered both onscreen and on the printer

Fontamentals, Part III: The Font-Rendering Mechanism

Windows 98 also categorizes fonts according to how they're rendered onscreen or on the printer. Windows 98 can work with three different font-rendering mechanisms: raster, vector, and TrueType.

Raster Fonts

With *raster fonts*, each character is represented by a bitmap pattern, something like the one shown in Figure 20.3. These simple patterns are easy to manipulate, so Windows 98 can display and print raster fonts quickly. Windows ships with five raster fonts: Courier, MS Sans Serif, MS Serif, Small Fonts, and Symbol. You can also get raster fonts by purchasing third-party products such as Adobe Type Manager, Bitstream FaceLift, and Hewlett-Packard Type Director.

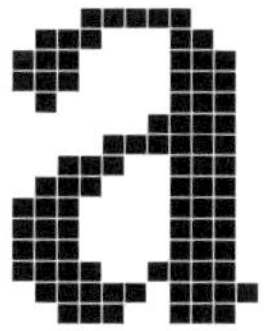

FIGURE 20.3.

The characters in raster fonts are made up of a pattern of small squares.

Raster fonts are stored in files as graphic images (or bitmaps, which is why they're also called bitmapped fonts). These files contain everything the system needs to know about the font (what styles it can display, what sizes are available, and so on). However, to show even a single character from the font, Windows 98 must load the entire file into memory.

The available representations of a given raster font are set in stone according to what's in the font file. You get only a fixed number of font sizes (for example, 8-, 10-, 12-, and 14-point) for each output device (display or printer). You can try a different size, but it must be a multiple of one of the supplied sizes (for example, 16-, 20-, or 24-point), and the resulting text usually suffers from excessive jagged lines (or "jaggies").

For each raster font, Windows 98 provides two display varieties: VGA and 8514. Each variety is identified by a letter appended to the font's filename. The VGA raster fonts have an E tacked on, so their filenames are COURE.FON, SSERIFE.FON, SERIFE.FON, SMALLE.FON, and SYMBOLE.FON. For 8514 raster fonts, the filenames have an F: COURF.FON, SSERIFF.FON, SERIFF.FON, SMALLF.FON, and SYMBOLF.FON. (You find these files in the Fonts subfolder of your main Windows 98 folder.)

Vector Fonts

Vector fonts are created from GDI (graphical device interface) functions that define an outline for each character (which is then filled in with whatever the current text color is). The big advantage of vector fonts is that they can be scaled at will to different sizes, because all Windows has to do is adjust the GDI parameters. (So these are also called *scalable* fonts.) This also saves memory, because you don't have to keep the full font family loaded. Vector fonts do have their downside, though:

- The complexity of the GDI calls tends to slow things down.
- You need separate fonts for your screen and printer.
- The character outlines tend to break down at smaller font sizes (anything smaller than 14 points or so) and thus become virtually unreadable.

Windows 98 dropped a couple of vector fonts from Windows 3.*x* and thus comes with just one example of the species: Modern.

TrueType Fonts

TrueType fonts use a newer, more sophisticated outline technology. Instead of a few hard-wired equations, TrueType fonts are displayed using a full-fledged *font management program* (called TrueType, which is where the fonts get their name). This program can produce great-looking characters at any size. For example, check out the differences between the three font types shown in Figure 20.4. The raster font (Courier) looks good in 10-point type, but it's downright hideous at 72 points. The vector font (Modern) is barely legible at the smaller size, but it looks okay scaled up to 72 points. The TrueType font (Times New Roman) passes with flying colors by looking good at both sizes.

FIGURE 20.4.

Raster, vector, and TrueType fonts compared at 10-point and 72-point sizes.

TrueType fonts look good at all type sizes (even rotated), because they are shapes that are described by their outlines. Instead of being composed of bitmaps (like raster fonts) or lines (like vector fonts), TrueType fonts consist of a series of contours.

Truly scalable characters are by no means the only advantage TrueType brings to the table, however:

- TrueType uses the same fonts for both the screen and the printer. This makes your characters truly WYSIWYG (What You See Is What You Get).
- TrueType fonts use less disk space because, for each font, you need only a single TTF file for every size, resolution, and output device. (Note, however, that most font families consist of multiple TTF files for each font effect. For example, the Arial font

family consists of four files: ARIAL.TTF (Regular), ARIALBD.TTF (Bold), ARIALI.TTF (Italic), and ARIALBI.TTF (Bold Italic).

■ TrueType fonts will print on any printer—laser or dot-matrix—that Windows supports. Other fonts are often printer-specific, so if you switch printers, you have to switch fonts.

■ Many companies have put together collections of TrueType fonts that can be had for just a few cents a font.

■ TrueType doesn't cost a dime, because everything you need is built into Windows 98.

Windows 95 came with only five TrueType font families (Arial, Courier New, Symbol, Times New Roman, and Wingdings), but the Windows 98 font collection is loaded with over two dozen, including the following new ones: Book Antiqua, Comic Sans MS, Impact, Lucida Sans, Tahoma, Verdana, and Webdings.

For comparison, Table 20.1 shows you which types of fonts can be used with the four main varieties of printers.

Table 20.1. Font types that can be used with different printers.

Type of Printer	*Raster Fonts*	*Vector Fonts*	*TrueType Fonts*
Dot matrix	Yes	No	Yes
Hewlett-Packard laser	No	Yes	Yes
PostScript	No	Yes	Yes
Plotter	No	Yes	No

Other Windows 98 Fonts

The Windows 98 user interface is mostly based on TrueType fonts, but four other fonts enter into the mix: System, Fixed, OEM (or Terminal), and DOS:

■ *System* is a proportional font used by default to draw menus, dialog box controls, and other text in Windows 98. Its font files are VGASYS.FON and 8514SYS.FON.

■ *Fixed* is a fixed-width font used in Windows 2.*x* and earlier versions as the system font (for menus and dialog boxes). Its font files are VGAFIX.FON and 8514FIX.FON.

■ *OEM* (which is also known as the Terminal font) is a fixed-width font used in various applications (such as the Clipboard). The OEM font also provides an OEM character set used by some Windows applications. Its font files are VGAOEM.FON and 8514.FON.

■ *DOS fonts* are used for displaying DOS programs. Their font files are CGA40WOA.FON, CGA80WOA.FON, and DOSAPP.FON.

20

USING FONTS IN
WINDOWS 98

Working with Fonts

Windows 98 makes it easy to work with the fonts on your system. Using a special Fonts folder, you can view individual fonts, add new fonts, and remove fonts. Windows 98 gives you two main methods of getting to the Fonts folder:

- In Explorer, highlight the Fonts subfolder of your main Windows 98 folder, as shown in Figure 20.5.

- In Control Panel, open the Fonts icon to display the folder window shown in Figure 20.6.

FIGURE 20.5.

You can work with the Fonts folder either from Explorer...

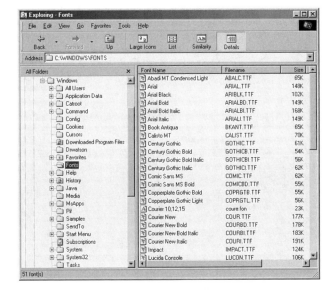

FIGURE 20.6.

...or by opening Control Panel's Fonts icon.

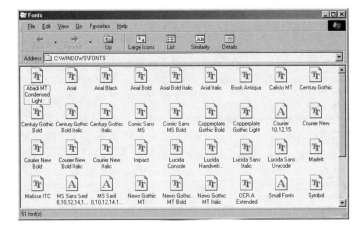

Opening a Font

The Font dialog box in most applications gives you a sneak preview of what a particular combination of typeface, type style, and type size will look like. However, it's not particularly convenient to continually select all these options, and the little preview screens show you only a few characters. A much easier way to see how a particular font looks is to open a font file directly from the Fonts folder. You can use any of the following methods:

■ Click a font file (or double-click the file if you have Web integration turned off).

■ Highlight a font file and select File | Open.

■ Right-click a font file and select Open from the context menu.

Whichever method you use, the Font Viewer application (FONTVIEW.EXE) runs and loads the font, as shown in Figure 20.7. The window displays a few font facts (such as the file size and version), shows you how each letter, each number, and a few symbols are represented in the font, and displays the font at various type sizes. If you'd like a printout of the window, click the Print button. When you're finished, click Done to return to the Fonts folder.

FIGURE 20.7.

When you open a font, the Font Viewer displays various bits of font info and a few font examples at different type sizes.

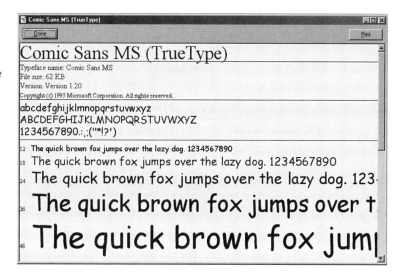

Changing the Fonts Folder View

If you have lots of fonts installed on your system, the Fonts folder will be jammed with tons of TTF and FON files. To help you manage this mess, Windows 98 offers two useful methods to filter the Fonts folder:

View | List Fonts By Similarity: This command displays the fonts according to how similar they are to a specified font. When you select this command (or click the Similarity button on the toolbar), the window changes, as shown in Figure 20.8.

Use the List fonts by similarity to drop-down list to select the comparison font. The Similarity to column tells you whether the other fonts are Very similar, Fairly similar, or Not similar.

Figure 20.8.

You can use the Fonts folder to list the fonts according to how similar they are to a given font.

View | Hide Variations (Bold, Italic, etc.): If you select this command, Windows 98 shows only the main font file. The variations (bold, italic, bold italic, and so on) are removed from the view to simplify things, as shown in Figure 20.9.

Figure 20.9.

Select View | Hide Variations to simplify the Fonts folder by removing the font variations.

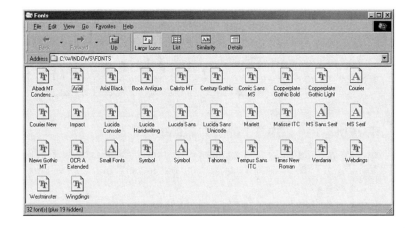

Adding New Fonts to Windows 98

As I mentioned earlier, there are all kinds of TrueType font collections on the market now. If you're feeling cramped by the paltry selection that comes with Windows 98, perhaps one of these packages can provide just the right typeface to give your documents that certain *je ne sais quoi*. Before you can use your new fonts, however, you need to add them to Windows 98. The following steps show you how it's done:

1. Display the Fonts folder.

2. Select File | Install New Font. The Add Fonts dialog box appears.

3. Insert the disk containing the font files and then select the appropriate disk drive from the Drives list. (If the font files are in a different folder, use the Folders list to select the appropriate location.) Windows reads the font names from the disk and displays them in the List of fonts box, as shown in Figure 20.10.

FIGURE 20.10.

Use the Add Fonts dialog box to select the new fonts you want to add to your system.

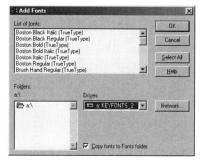

4. Use the List of fonts box to highlight the fonts you want to install. Alternatively, you can install all the fonts on the disk by clicking the Select All button.

5. Windows 98 normally likes to see the font files copied to the Fonts folder. So, in most cases, you should make sure the Copy fonts to Fonts folder check box is activated. There are three exceptions to this rule:

   ■ If hard disk space is at a premium and the font files already exist elsewhere on the hard disk. In this case, there isn't much point in creating an extra copy of each file.

   ■ If you're loading the font files from a network drive.

   ■ If you're loading the font files from a CD-ROM drive. CD-ROMs can have tens (if not hundreds) of megabytes of fonts, so it's usually impractical to load all this chaff onto your hard disk.

6. Click OK. Windows 98 installs the fonts. If you elected not to copy the fonts to the Fonts folder, Windows 98 creates shortcuts to the original files instead.

EMBEDDING FONTS

You might have problems sending files that use third-party fonts to other people because they won't have the proper font files on their system. The result is usually a mess as Windows tries to convert the fonts into something like Courier. To avoid this, you either need to stick with the standard fonts that come with Windows 98 or send the font files with your documents (along with a note telling the recipients that they need to install the fonts; they will be very pleased, I'm sure).

Some applications (such as Microsoft PowerPoint and Microsoft Word) let you embed fonts in your documents. Embedded fonts enable others to view the file properly without having to clutter their hard drives with your fancy fonts. Over the next year or so, you'll likely see this feature included in most mainstream Windows applications.

Deleting Old Fonts

Although TrueType fonts take up considerably less disk space than the other font types, you're still looking at anywhere from 30–120KB per font file. If you have hundreds of fonts, the numbers can add up to a big chunk of hard disk acreage in a hurry. Also, all your installed fonts take up memory, whether you use them or not.

To keep a lid on both hard disk and memory usage, you should periodically clean out those font files you never use. To do this, just delete the appropriate font files from the Fonts folder.

DISABLING OLD FONTS

If you'd like to keep your old fonts around but not have them load when you start Windows 98, just move them to another folder. Windows 98 will remove the fonts from the Registry, so they won't load in the future.

Font Tips

Windows makes it easy to add unique and eye-catching fonts to all your documents. However, some restraint is called for here. Nothing looks worse than—or is as confusing as—a document with too many fonts crammed together on one page. This is known in the trade as the *ransom note look*.

Here are a few things to keep in mind when performing your font formatting chores:

■ Try to restrict your fonts to no more than a couple per document. If you need various looks, use larger sizes or different styles of the same fonts.

- A good font combination is a sans serif font for titles and headings and a serif font for the document's main body text (which is the combination used in this book).

- If you need to emphasize something, bold or italicize it in the same typeface as the surrounding text. Avoid using underlining for emphasis.

- Use larger sizes only for titles and headings. Also, avoid using anything smaller than 10 points; text that small is just too difficult to make out.

- Avoid using decorative or excessively narrow fonts for large sections of text. They're almost always hard on the eyes after a half a dozen words or so.

Using Character Map for Extra Symbols and Characters

A given typeface covers not only the letters, numbers, and symbols you can see on your keyboard, but dozens of others as well. For example, were you stumped the last time you wanted to write "Dag Hammarskjöld" because you didn't know how to get an ö character? I thought so. Well, Windows 98 gives you an easy way to get not only an ö, but a whole universe of interesting symbols.

It all begins with one of the accessories that comes with Windows 98: Character Map. To check it out, select Start | Programs | Accessories | System Tools | Character Map. You see the Character Map window, shown in Figure 20.11.

FIGURE 20.11.

The Character Map window gives you access to the full spectrum of Windows 98 characters.

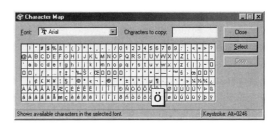

The layout is pretty simple: the squares show you all the symbols available for whatever typeface is displayed in the Font drop-down list. If you select a different typeface, a whole new set of symbols is displayed. (Webdings and Wingdings, in particular, have many interesting symbols, including astrological signs, currency symbols, and even clock faces.)

To use a symbol from Character Map in an application, you first select the symbol you want by using either of the following methods:

- Double-click the symbol.

- Highlight the symbol and click Select or press Enter.

The symbol will appear in the Characters to copy box. Feel free to select multiple characters if you like.

When you're ready, click the Copy button to copy the character (or characters) to the Clipboard. Finally, return to your application, position the cursor where you want the character to appear, and select Edit | Paste.

MULTILINGUAL FONTS

Don't forget that you can access a number of language fonts (such as Cyrillic) by installing Windows 98's Multilanguage Support. I showed you how to do this in Chapter 8, "Customizing the Mouse, Keyboard, and Other Input Devices."

Font Limitations

When you install a font, Windows 98 adds that font to the GDI and to the following Registry key:

`HKEY_LOCAL_MACHINE\SOFTWARE\Microsoft\Windows\CurrentVersion\Fonts`

Unfortunately, this puts certain restrictions on how many fonts you can install:

- The GDI reserves about 10KB for font filenames. This means that if font filenames average about 10 characters (including the period and extension), you won't be able to add any more than about 1,000 fonts to the GDI.
- The Fonts subkey in the Registry stores both the font name and the font filename. Unfortunately, Registry keys are limited to 64KB. This means that if your fonts average 40 or 45 characters for their names and 10 characters for their filenames, you won't be able to cram much more than about 1,000 fonts into the key.

So, all in all, your system is restricted to about 1,000 total fonts.

Troubleshooting Fonts

Fonts, especially TrueType fonts, are a proven technology, so their implementation is fairly straightforward. However, a few things can go wrong. This section discusses a few of the most common problems and offers some solutions.

Your Font dialog boxes show only TrueType fonts, despite the fact that you have other kinds of fonts installed on your system.

If you don't see any other kinds of fonts in your Font dialog boxes, this means that Windows 98 has been set up to show only TrueType fonts. To remedy this, display the Fonts folder, select View | Folder Options, and head for the TrueType tab, shown in Figure 20.12. Deactivate the

Show only TrueType fonts in the programs on my computer check box, and then click OK. When Windows 98 asks whether you want to restart your computer, click Yes.

FIGURE 20.12.

The TrueType tab determines whether your Font dialogs show only TrueType fonts.

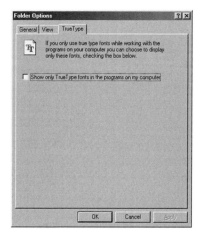

You don't see any information on your PostScript fonts in the Registry.

PostScript fonts are installed by Setup programs just as they were in earlier versions of Windows. Therefore, you still find data on PostScript fonts in WIN.INI.

You added a TrueType font and the font seems to be installed correctly, but it doesn't appear in the Fonts folder. Or, you receive the following error message:

```
The fontname TrueType font is already installed. To install a new version, first
remove the old version.
```

This behavior can occur if the Registry's Fonts key is missing or damaged. To resolve this problem, either delete the existing Fonts key and then add it back in, or add the Fonts key if it doesn't already exist. Restart your computer. Windows 98 will rebuild the font list based on the font files that exist in the Fonts folder.

The Fonts folder is missing several menu commands, including File|Open, File|Print, File|Install New Font, View|List Fonts By Similarity, and View|Hide Variations.

This problem likely means that the Fonts folder's System attribute has been turned off. To reinstate this attribute, open a DOS window, make sure you're in your main Windows 98 folder, and then enter the following command:

```
attrib +s fonts
```

Close the DOS window and restart your computer.

You can't change the font in a DOS window while running a DOS program.

This problem is probably caused by the DOS program. If the program is running in graphics mode, you won't be able to change the DOS window's font, because the program manages the font directly. If you really need to change the font, switch the DOS program to text mode if possible.

When you attempt to add a TrueType font, you receive the following error message:

`Unable to install the fontname (TrueType) font. The font file may be damaged.`

This error means that one of two things has happened:

■ The font file you're trying to install is corrupted. In this case, you need to contact the vendor for a replacement.

■ Windows 98 has reached its font limit, as described earlier. In this case, you need to delete some existing fonts before you can add more.

After installing Adobe Type Manager (ATM) to the Fonts folder, you receive the following error message when you start the ATM Control Panel:

`Invalid Fonts Directory`

As you've seen, the Fonts folder, with its extra commands and views, isn't your average folder. In particular, Fonts has its `System` attribute set, which means that although ATM can install into Fonts, it doesn't function correctly from this folder.

The solution is to use either of the following methods:

■ Create a new folder for the ATM fonts and then move the ATM fonts from the Fonts folder to the new folder. Be sure to edit the `ATM.INI` file in your main Windows 98 folder and change the path for the ATM fonts to reflect the new folder.

■ Remove the ATM fonts from the Fonts folder, remove the `ATM.INI` file from your main Windows 98 folder, and then reinstall ATM. This time, however, choose a folder other than the Fonts folder for the installation.

Summary

This chapter looked at how Windows 98 works with fonts. You began by learning some font fundamentals, including the three main classification schemes for fonts: "architectural" (typeface, type size, type style, and character spacing), output device (screen or printer), and font-rendering mechanism (raster, vector, or TrueType.) I then showed you how to view and open font files, install new fonts, delete old fonts, and troubleshoot some font woes. I even threw in some info about the Character Map accessory for good measure. For more font-related information, check out the following chapters:

■ Chapter 6, "Customizing the Taskbar, Start Menu, and Display," is the place to learn how to change the system fonts—the fonts used in the Windows 98 interface.

■ I showed you how to work with keyboard layouts and Windows 98's Multilanguage support in Chapter 8, "Customizing the Mouse, Keyboard, and Other Input Devices."

■ If you need some background on the Registry, try Chapter 12, "Getting to Know the Windows 98 Registry."

■ Fonts and printing are closely related. I'll discuss printing in Chapter 21, "Prescriptions for Perfect Printing."

■ You learn how to adjust the DOS window font in Chapter 23, "DOS Isn't Dead: Unleashing the DOS Shell."

20

USING FONTS IN
WINDOWS 98

Prescriptions for Perfect Printing

> *The moment a man sets his thoughts down on paper, however secretly, he is in a sense writing for publication.*
>
> —*Raymond Chandler*

Remember when all this high-falutin' computer technology was supposed to result in the proverbial "paperless office" of tomorrow? Clearly, tomorrow never came. If anything, we're awash in more paper than ever since computers took over. It's just like all the other pipe dreams from those "here's-what-the-future-will-bring" flicks from the '50s. By the time the '90s roll around, they assured us, we'll all have endless leisure hours to spend rocketing around in flying cars. As someone once said, we always overestimate change in the long term and underestimate it in the short term.

I suspect one of the reasons for this plenitude of paper is that we all have a real need for hard copy. For one thing, it just feels good to create something tangible, something we can literally get our hands on. For another, I don't think we trust our computers fully. Electronic files, with their unfortunate tendency to get wiped out by the merest power surge or an accidental press of a Delete key, seem so fragile. Printouts, on the other hand, seem heartier and, well, *safer.*

So I say if we're going to be printing fools, we might as well be wise printing fools. Happily, as this chapter will show you, such wisdom is fairly easy to come by thanks to Windows 98's easy and consistent approach to printing. You begin with some printing basics, and then you graduate to some intermediate and advanced techniques that will help you unleash Windows 98 printing.

Installing a Printer with the Add Printer Wizard

Windows 98 is the control freak of the computer world. It has to know absolutely *everything* about your machine and whatever peripherals—especially printers—are along for the ride. This isn't a bad thing, though, because it actually makes your life easier. How? Well, for example, in the anarchic world of DOS, every program has its own particular printing agenda. Although there's nothing wrong with such digital individualism, the downside is that you have to perform the rigmarole of setting up your printer for every DOS program.

Windows 98, though, is different, because it performs the printing drudgery itself. As a result, you have to tell Windows only what kind of printer you have, and then you're in business. Windows applications handle print jobs by simply passing the buck to the printing subsystem, so there's no need to perform separate printer setups for all your programs.

As with any device, you need to install a driver in order to get Windows 98 to print properly. If you didn't do this during the Windows 98 installation, or if you have a new printer to set up, you can use the Printers folder to do it from the desktop. Here are the steps you need to follow:

1. Select Start | Settings | Printers to open the Printers folder. (You can also get to the Printers folder by opening the Printers icon in Control Panel.)

2. Open the Add Printer icon to start the Add Printer Wizard.

3. The first Wizard dialog box just gives some introductory info, so click Next > to move on.

4. If your computer is on a network, the Wizard will ask whether you want to set up a Local printer or a Network printer. Choose the appropriate option and click Next >.

5. If you chose the Network printer option, the Wizard will prompt you to enter a network path. Enter the appropriate UNC path or use the Browse button to choose the printer from a dialog box. The Wizard also wants to know whether you print from DOS programs. Select Yes or No as appropriate and click Next >.

6. The next Wizard dialog box, shown in Figure 21.1, lists the manufacturers and printers that Windows 98 supports. Use these lists to track down your printer and then highlight it. If your printer isn't in the list, you have two choices:

   ■ Check your printer manual to see whether the printer works like (emulates) another printer. If it does, see whether you can find the emulated printer in the list.

   ■ If your printer comes with a disk, click Have Disk and follow the onscreen prompts.

FIGURE 21.1.

Use this Wizard dialog box to highlight your printer.

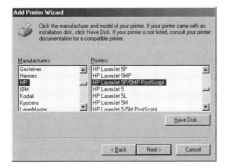

7. Click Next >.

8. The Wizard may now tell you that a driver for your printer is already installed. If so, you probably want to select the Keep existing driver option. The only time you should choose Replace existing driver is when you're having trouble printing and you think a corrupt driver may be the culprit. Click Next > after you've made your choice.

9. In the next Wizard dialog box, shown in Figure 21.2, use the Available ports list to select your printer port and then click Next >. If you've installed the Windows 98 infrared driver (as explained in Chapter 11, "Device Advice: Dealing with Devices in Windows 98"), make sure you select the infrared printing port.

Figure 21.2.

Use this Wizard dialog box to select the port your printer is attached to.

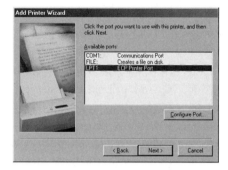

10. The next Add Printer Wizard dialog box that appears is shown in Figure 21.3. Use the Printer name text box to enter a descriptive name for the printer. If you've installed other printers, the Wizard will ask whether you want this printer to be the default for all your Windows applications. If so, activate the Yes option. Click Next > to continue.

Figure 21.3.

Use this dialog box to name your printer and, optionally, set it as the default printer.

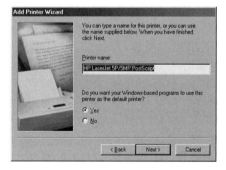

11. Finally, the Wizard asks whether you'd like to print a text page. This is a good idea, so select Yes and then click Finish.

12. Follow the onscreen prompts to insert your Windows 98 source disks.

13. After the Wizard installs the drivers, it sends the test page to the printer, and a dialog box asks whether the page printed properly. If it did, click Yes. If it didn't, select No. In this case, Windows 98 runs the Print Troubleshooter. I'll show how this works in the section "Troubleshooting Windows 98 Printing," near the end of this chapter.

When all is said and done, you are dropped off at the Printers folder. Your new printer will have its own icon, as shown in Figure 21.4.

FIGURE 21.4.

For each printer you install, an icon appears in the Printers folder.

PLUG AND PLAY PRINTERS

If you have a printer that is Plug and Play–compatible, installation is easy. Just connect the printer to your computer, turn the printer on, and restart your computer. When Windows 98 starts, it will detect the printer, query it for its device ID, and prompt you for your Windows 98 source disks.

USING MULTIPLE SETTINGS? INSTALL MULTIPLE PRINTERS

Windows 98 is happy to install as many printers as you like, even multiple copies of the same printer. Why would you want to do that? One good reason is that you can use each copy to create printers that use different settings. For example, many printers let you choose between printing on letter-size and legal-size paper. Rather than constantly changing these settings for a particular printer, you can install the printer twice and set up each one to use a different paper size. I'll show you how to work with these and other printer settings later in this chapter (see the section "Working with Printer Properties").

Removing a Printer

If you've upgraded to a new printer, you should remove your old printer to reduce clutter in the Printers folder and free some disk space.

To remove a printer, highlight it in the Printers folder and then either select File | Delete, press the Delete key, or right-click the printer and select Delete from the context menu. When Windows 98 asks whether you're sure you want to delete the printer, click Yes.

If no other printer is using some or all of the printer's files, another dialog box asks whether you want to delete these files. (You won't see this dialog box if all the printer's files are being used by another printer.) They're useless, so you might as well click Yes to get rid of them. If the printer you deleted was your default printer, another dialog box shows up to let you know. Click OK to end the process.

Printing Documents in Windows 98

One of Windows 98's principle missions in life is to give all the applications you use a reasonably consistent look and feel. This means that the vast majority of Windows applications use, for example, the same dialog box controls, the same method of selecting text, the same command for saving a file, and so on. Printing is a good example of this consistency. In most applications, with some relatively minor exceptions, you select File | Print (or in many programs, press Ctrl+P), fill out the Print dialog box that appears (see Figure 21.5), and click OK. The options in this dialog box vary between applications, but you usually see the following controls:

Name: This drop-down list tells you the name of the currently selected printer. When you first open the Print dialog box, the Name list displays the default Windows 98 printer. If you'd prefer to use a different printer (assuming you've installed more than one), select it from the list. The other fields in the Printer group give you information about the printer, such as its status and port.

Properties: This button displays a dialog box with a few options that are specific to the current printer. These options enable you to choose from various printer settings (such as selecting a paper tray).

Print to file: If you activate this check box, the document will be saved to a printer (PRN) file instead of going to the printer. When you click OK, the Print to File dialog box will appear so that you can enter the filename and select a location. See the section "Getting a 'Soft' Copy: Printing to a File" later in this chapter for more information on printing to a file.

Print range: Most applications let you print some or all of a document. In a word processor, for example, you can usually print the entire document, a range of pages, or the current selection.

Copies: You usually see a text box or spinner control for entering the number of copies you want. In some cases, you can also choose whether you want multiple copies *collated.* For example, suppose you want two copies of a three-page document. If you collate the print job, you get one copy of all three pages, followed by the second copy. If you don't collate, you get two copies of page 1, then two copies of page 2, and then two copies of page 3.

Using Drag-and-Drop to Print Files

As you've seen throughout this book, Windows 98's drag-and-drop capabilities can be extremely useful. But, to my mind, one of the best uses of drag-and-drop is to print a file without having to open the source application and load the document.

FIGURE 21.5.

Select File | Print in most applications to display the Print dialog box. The one shown here is from WordPad.

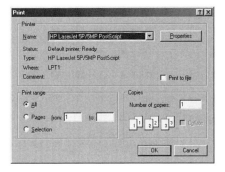

21

PRESCRIPTIONS FOR PERFECT PRINTING

All you have to do is drag the document from Explorer or My Computer and drop it on a printer icon in the Printers folder. Alternatively, you can create a shortcut for a printer (by dragging its icon from the Printers folder to the desktop) and then drop your documents on this shortcut.

With either method, the source application loads just long enough to send the document to the printer, and then it shuts down automatically.

Other Printing Methods

You've seen how Windows 98 delights in offering users a veritable cornucopia of methods to perform just about any task. Printing is no exception. Besides the two methods you've seen already, there are a few other methods you can use. Here's a rundown:

■ Many applications have a Print button on their toolbar.

■ In Explorer or My Computer, you can print a file by highlighting it and selecting File | Print or by right-clicking the file and selecting Print from the context menu.

■ If you've defined a new, printable file type, you can add the Print action to the file type's definition. (I showed you how to work with file types in Chapter 14, "File and Folder Tricks and Techniques.") In most cases, you define the Print action by entering the application's executable path, followed by the /P switch, as in the following example:

```
C:\WINDOWS\NOTEPAD.EXE /P
```

■ You can create a shortcut for a printer in the Send To folder. If you then right-click a file, select Send To from the context menu, and select the printer, Windows 98 will print the document.

Note that all these methods bypass the Print dialog box and send the document to the printer immediately.

Deferring Print Jobs

Taking advantage of Windows 98's new deferred printing feature is easy. In the Printers folder, highlight your printer and select File | Work Offline, or right-click the printer icon and select Work Offline from the context menu. Windows 98 indicates that the printer is offline by dimming the printer's icon.

You can still "print" your documents the way you normally would. Windows 98 spools the files and then stores each print job in a queue. Later, when the printer is available, just deactivate the Work Offline command, and Windows 98 will start printing the documents.

YOU CAN ALSO DEFER PRINTING BY PAUSING

If you're using a local printer, you might not see the Work Offline command on the File menu. If you still would like to defer your print jobs, you can pause the printer. See the section "Managing Print Jobs" later in this chapter for details.

Getting a "Soft" Copy: Printing to a File

What do you do if you don't have a printer? Or what if you have only a dot matrix printer and you want to print your résumé on a laser printer? If you know someone who has the printer you need, Windows 98 lets you print your document to a file. You can then transport the file to the other computer and print it from there. The other computer doesn't even need the source application.

You saw earlier that you can print to a file by activating the Print to file check box in the Print dialog box. If you'd prefer a more permanent solution, you can tell Windows 98 to print to a port named FILE instead of, for example, LPT1. To do this, use either of the following methods:

- If you haven't installed the printer (that is, the type of printer you'll eventually use to print the file), run the Add Printer Wizard as described earlier. When the Wizard asks you to specify a port, select FILE.

- For an installed printer, open the Printers folder and display the properties sheet for the printer you want to use (by highlighting the printer icon and selecting File | Properties or by right-clicking the icon and selecting Properties). Select the Details tab, and then use the Print to the following port list to select the FILE port. Click OK to put the new setting into effect.

When that's done, use any of the methods outlined earlier to print a document. When you do, you see the Print To File dialog box, shown in Figure 21.6. Enter the filename, choose a location, and click OK.

Prescriptions for Perfect Printing

CHAPTER 21

557

21

PRESCRIPTIONS
FOR PERFECT
PRINTING

FIGURE 21.6.

Use the Print To File dialog box to enter the name of the file you want to print to.

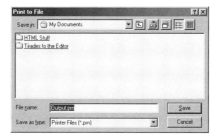

After the document has been "printed" to the file, what happens next? Now you copy the file to a floppy disk, head to where the printer is located, and copy the file to the other computer. To print the file, start up a DOS session and enter the following generic command:

```
COPY /B filename port
```

The /B switch tells DOS to print a binary file, `filename` is the name of your file, and `port` is the port the printer is attached to. For example, if your file is named PRINT.PRN, and the printer is attached to LPT1, you enter the following:

```
COPY /B print.prn lpt1
```

I'm assuming that the file is in the current folder. If it isn't, you need to include the drive and folder with the filename.

Managing Print Jobs

The printing subsystem is one of those unassuming components that does its job quietly and without a lot of fanfare. In most cases, you can just let it go about its business, safe in the knowledge that your printing chores are in the hands of a competent professional. But what if you need to cancel a print job in progress or pause the printing while you insert some paper? For these situations, Windows 98 lets you interrupt the printing subsystem's peace and quiet so that you can manipulate various aspects of the print job.

In Windows 3.*x*, you used Print Manager to mess around with your print jobs. In Windows 98, however, each printer is given its own status window. To open this window, use any of the following techniques:

- In the Printers folder, click the printer's icon, select File | Open, or right-click the icon and select Open.
- Double-click the Printer icon in the taskbar's system tray. This icon appears while the printing subsystem is spooling the file, so you have only a few seconds (depending on the size of the job) in which to do this.

Figure 21.7 shows an example of a printer window. It lists each pending print job and tells you the name of the document, its current status, the document's owner, the progress of the print job, and the date and time it began.

FIGURE 21.7.

Each printer window shows the current print jobs for the printer.

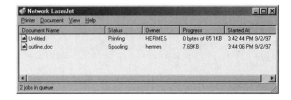

Pausing a Print Job

If you need to add paper to your printer or change the ribbon or toner cartridge, you can tell the printing subsystem to hold its horses. Just select Printer | Pause Printing. When you're ready to roll again, deactivate Printer | Pause Printing to resume the print jobs. (The Pause Printing command is also available in the Printers folder.)

You can also pause individual documents. Highlight the document you want to delay and either choose Document | Pause Printing or right-click the document and choose Pause Printing from the context menu. Select one of these commands again to deactivate it and resume the print job.

Canceling a Print Job

If you accidentally print the wrong file, or if you simply change your mind, you can delete a file from the queue. Highlight the appropriate document in the printer window and then select Document | Cancel Printing, press Delete, or right-click the document and select Cancel Printing from the context menu.

If you want to get rid of all the pending print jobs, select Printer | Purge Print Documents.

SEND PRINT JOBS TO THE RECYCLE BIN

Another way to delete print jobs is to drag them from the printer window and drop them on the desktop's Recycle Bin icon.

Changing the Order of Print Jobs

The printing subsystem prints documents in the order it receives them. If you'd like to change this order, all you have to do is drag a print job up or down in the queue. Note, however, that you can't drag a print job higher than the currently printing document.

Working with Printer Properties

Each printer you install becomes an object in the Windows 98 shell. These printer objects have just one action—printing—but they have a boatload of properties, some of which vary from printer to printer. To view the properties sheet for an installed printer, try either of the following methods:

- In the Printers folder, highlight a printer icon and select File | Properties, or right-click an icon and select Properties from the context menu.
- In a printer's window, select Printer | Properties.

The dialog box that appears depends on the printer, but it will look something like the one shown in Figure 21.8. Here's a summary of the various tabs you might see in your printer's properties sheet:

General: Contains a few miscellaneous controls that don't fit anywhere else. See the next section, "General Properties."

Details: Lets you set various options for the printer port, printer driver, and spooler. See "Details Properties" later in this chapter.

Sharing: Sets up the printer as a shared network resource.

Paper: Contains a number of controls that let you manipulate paper-related properties (such as the paper size used in the printer). I cover this tab in the "Paper Properties" section later in this chapter.

Graphics: Determines how the printer handles graphics. The options you see depend on your printer, so I won't cover them here. Check your printer manual and the What's This? Help system for details on the available controls. (To use What's This? Help, click the question mark (?) icon in the upper-right corner of the dialog box and then click a control. Windows 98 pops up a banner that describes the control.)

Fonts: Determines how your printer works with TrueType fonts. See "Fonts Properties" later in this chapter for details.

Device Options: Contains printer-specific options, such as memory settings. Becausee the controls you see depend on the printer, I won't cover them here. Check your printer manual and the What's This? Help system for details.

PostScript: Sets various properties for PostScript printers. I discuss these options later in this chapter, in the "PostScript Properties" section.

FIGURE 21.8.

The properties sheet for a printer.

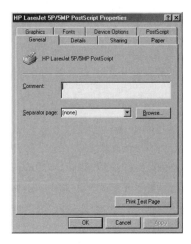

General Properties

When you first open a printer's properties sheet, you see the General tab, as shown in Figure 21.8. This tab contains the following controls:

Comment: Use this text box to add a short description of the printer. This comment appears in the Print dialog box, and it's transferred to network users who install your printer on their systems. You can use the Comment box to describe unique features of the printer (such as the paper size it's designed to handle), hours it can be accessed, and so on.

Separator page: A separator page is a sheet that prints in advance of each document you send to the printer. The idea is that this extra sheet marks the beginning of each print job, thus separating multiple printed documents. The Separator page drop-down list gives you three choices:

(none)	No separator page
Full	A graphical separator page that includes the document name, the name of the person who submitted the print job, and the date and time of the print job
Simple	A text-only separator page that gives the same information as the Full page

If you prefer, you can specify your own separator page by clicking the Browse button and choosing a WMF file from the dialog box that appears. (If you have Microsoft Office installed, you'll find a large collection of WMF files in the ClipArt subfolder.)

SEPARATOR PAGES ARE LOCAL PHENOMENA

You can assign a separator page only to a local printer (that is, a printer that's attached directly to your computer).

Print Test Page: If you've made changes to your printer's properties, you can click this button to test the new configuration by sending a page to the printer. After the test page has been sent, Windows 98 displays a dialog box that asks whether the page printed correctly. If the page showed up without any mistakes, click Yes; otherwise, click No to start the Print Troubleshooter (explained later in this chapter).

Details Properties

The Details tab, shown in Figure 21.9, is a busy screen that contains all kinds of controls. These options let you modify various aspects of the printer port, the printer driver, and the spooler.

FIGURE 21.9.

Use the Details tab to set various port and driver options.

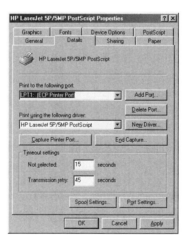

Here's the rundown of what's available in this tab:

Print to the following port: Use this drop-down list to select the port you want to use for printing. This is useful if you need to print only to files (the FILE "port," as described earlier) or if you have an infrared port and want to switch between a cable connection and the infrared connection.

Add Port: This button displays the Add Port dialog box, which lets you specify a new printer port (activate the Other option and highlight the port in the list) or a path to a network printer (activate the Network option and either enter the UNC path to the shared printer or click Browse and choose the printer from the dialog box that appears).

Delete Port: Click this button if you want to remove a port from the Print to the following port list. First, make sure that no printers are using the port. Then, in the Delete Port dialog box that appears, highlight the port and click OK.

Print using the following driver: This drop-down list contains all the printer drivers that are installed on your system. If you want to use a different driver (as long as it can work with the current printer), select it from the list. If you'd prefer to add a new driver, click the New Driver button and follow the dialog boxes that appear.

Capture Printer Port: In the same way that you can map a shared network drive or folder and have it appear as though it were a physical drive on your system, so too can you map a shared network printer and have it appear as though it were a physical printer port on your system. This is called *capturing* a printer port. To try this, click the Capture Printer Port button. In the Capture Printer Port dialog box, use the Device list to select a logical printer port (such as LPT2) and use the Path combo box to enter the network path to the shared printer.

End Capture: Click this button when you no longer want to capture a network printer as a logical port on your system. In the End Capture dialog box that appears, highlight the printer and click OK.

Not selected: This value (which is available for local printers only) determines how long Windows 98 waits before the printer signals that it's online. The default is 15 seconds. So, for example, if you submit a print job while the printer is turned off, you have 15 seconds to get the printer online before Windows 98 generates an error. If your printer takes longer than that to warm up, you might consider increasing this value.

Transmission retry: This value (which is available for local printers only) determines how long Windows 98 attempts to resend data to the printer before declaring an error. There are many reasons why Windows 98 might not be able to send data to the printer successfully: The printer's buffer might be full, there might be a paper jam or some other printer problem, or the printer might be taking a long time to process graphics or some other large chunk of data. For the latter, you might want to bump up the Transmission retry value if your print jobs are usually large or if you're using a PostScript printer (which requires extra overhead for processing fonts and other goodies).

Spool Settings: This button displays the Spool Settings dialog box, shown in Figure 21.10, which controls various aspects of the printing subsystem's spooler:

> **Spool print jobs so program finishes printing faster:** Activate this option to enable spooling. For the fastest return-to-application time, activate Start printing after last page is spooled. In this case, Windows 98 spools the entire print job before sending anything to the printer. This is the quickest method, but it uses more disk space. For a slower method that uses less disk space, try the Start printing after first page is spooled option.

Prescriptions for Perfect Printing

CHAPTER 21

563

21

PRESCRIPTIONS
FOR PERFECT
PRINTING

Print directly to the printer: Activate this option to bypass the spooler and send your print jobs right to the printer.

Spool data format: This drop-down list determines the type of format Windows 98 uses to spool the data: EMF or RAW. You read earlier in this chapter that EMF files are faster to spool, so they get you back to your application quicker. The RAW format is printer-specific, so it takes longer to spool. Choose RAW only if you're having trouble printing with the EMF format.

Enable bi-directional support for this printer: Activate this option to tell Windows 98 to use your printer's bidirectional capabilities. To bypass this feature, activate Disable bi-directional support for this printer instead.

DIRECT PRINTING

If you activate the Print directly to the printer option, you won't be able to pause your print jobs or work offline. Also note that if you've shared your printer on a network, this option will be disabled.

FIGURE 21.10.
Use this dialog box to control how Windows 98 spools your print jobs.

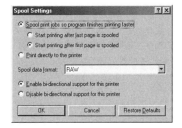

Port Settings: Clicking this button displays the Configure LPT Port dialog box. The Spool MS-DOS print jobs check box toggles spooling for DOS programs on and off. The Check port state before printing check box determines whether Windows 98 checks the current status of the port before starting a print job.

Paper Properties

The layout of the Paper tab depends on the printer driver you're working with. Figure 21.11 shows how the Printer tab looks for the LaserJet 5P/5MP driver. Here are a few options that are common to most Paper tabs:

Paper size: This is a list of the paper sizes and envelope sizes that the printer supports. You can either highlight the material your printer uses or select one of the custom icons at the end of the list. If you see an icon covered by the international "not" symbol, it means you can't use that particular size until you select another option (such as a paper tray).

Layout: These options determine how many pages of each document are printed on a single sheet of paper.

Orientation: These options specify the layout of the data on the page. With Portrait, the page is oriented so that the height of the page is greater than the width. This is the more common orientation. With Landscape, the page is oriented so that the width of the page is greater than the height.

DISPLAYING THE PAGE DIMENSIONS

To see the page's dimensions (the height and width, and where the top, bottom, left, and right margins are), move your mouse pointer over the page icon in the Orientation group and hold down the left mouse button.

Paper source: This drop-down list determines what part of the printer the paper is fed from (for example, a paper tray, envelope feeder, or manual feed). The AutoSelect Tray choice tells Windows 98 to determine the tray based on the selected paper size.

Copies: The default number of copies to use with this printer.

Unprintable Area: This button displays the Unprintable Area dialog box. You use the spinners in this dialog box to set the default margins for the printer. (If you intend to reduce one or more of these values, first check your printer manual to find out the minimum values allowed. If you enter any values below these numbers, you could end up truncating text in your printouts.)

FIGURE 21.11.

Use the Paper tab to specify various paper options for your printer.

Fonts Properties

The Fonts tab, shown in Figure 21.12, contains three options that determine how your printer works with Windows 98's TrueType fonts:

Send TrueType fonts to printer according to the font Substitution Table: If you activate this option, Windows 98 doesn't download all of a document's TrueType fonts to the printer. Instead, it substitutes a built-in printer font for some of the TrueType fonts to speed up printing. These substitutions are controlled by the Font Substitution Table. If you like, you can make changes to these substitutions by clicking the Edit the Table button. In the dialog box that appears, highlight a font and use the Printer font for drop-down to select a substitute. (Or you can select Send As Outlines to send the TrueType font without substitution.)

Always use built-in printer fonts instead of TrueType fonts: If you activate this option, Windows 98 won't download any TrueType fonts to the printer. Instead, it will select substitute fonts from the printer's built-in fonts. Note, however, that because your screen shows TrueType fonts, your printed document might look different.

Always use TrueType fonts: Activate this option to always download TrueType fonts to the printer. This might slow down the print job (but not by much), but your printouts will look exactly as they did onscreen.

Send Fonts As: This button displays the Send Fonts As dialog box. The controls in this dialog box let you determine how Windows 98 sends fonts to the printer.

FIGURE 21.12.

The Fonts tab determines how your printer works with TrueType fonts.

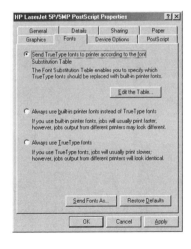

PostScript Properties

If you're using a PostScript printer, the properties sheet will have a PostScript tab, as shown in Figure 21.13. Here's a review of the available controls:

PostScript output format: This drop-down control contains a list of the various PostScript formats you can use. You probably want to use the PostScript (optimize for speed) choice most of the time. However, if you need to use Adobe Document Structuring Conventions (ADSC) or Encapsulated PostScript (EPS) format, select the appropriate choice.

PostScript header: PostScript printers use header information to set up the printer's page layout and other options before processing the print job. If you're sure the header information won't change from job to job, you can activate the Assume header is downloaded and retained option. (If you select this option, you can send new header information at any time by clicking the Send Header Now button.) For most print jobs, however, you want to activate the Download header with each print job option.

Print PostScript error information: If you're having trouble printing to a PostScript printer, make sure this check box is activated. This will force the printer to report any PostScript errors that occur (errors that Windows 98 might miss).

PostScript timeout values: These spinners determine how patient Windows 98 is with PostScript jobs. The Job timeout value specifies how long Windows 98 will wait for a print job to get to the printer before signaling an error. A value of 0 means Windows 98 will wait indefinitely. The Wait timeout value specifies how long the printer should wait for Windows 98 to send more data before terminating the print job and printing an error report.

Advanced: This button displays a dialog box filled with advanced PostScript settings. These settings include the PostScript language level, compression for bitmaps, the format used for the data, and when Ctrl+D is sent to indicate that the print job is complete.

FIGURE 21.13.

Use the PostScript tab to set various options for your PostScript printer.

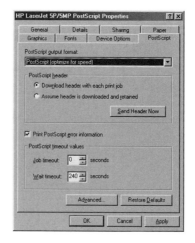

Tips for Saving Paper

As you've seen in this chapter, Windows 98 and its printing subsystem make printing so easy that you now have yet another reason to print too many documents. So, to keep your paper costs down and save a tree or two, here are some tips that will help you cut down on the amount of paper you use:

- Print a document only when you have to. Too many people print intermediate drafts or whenever they make the slightest change. With Windows' WYSIWYG (What You See Is What You Get) display, you shouldn't need a hard copy until the document is finished.

- Take advantage of the Print Preview feature. Many Windows applications have a Print Preview command that lets you see exactly what your document will look like (including things such as headers and footers, page numbers, and footnotes) when it's printed. A sneak peek at the document will save you many a reprint.

- Proofread your documents carefully before printing them. You usually need to reprint because of spelling and grammatical errors that you didn't catch until you read the printout. You can avoid this by giving a document the once-over before printing it. And, by all means, use your application's built-in spell checker and grammar checker.

- Try to maximize the print area on each page. You can do this by reducing the margins and by using smaller type sizes. Many word processors also have a feature that suppresses *widows*, which are single lines that appear by themselves at the top of the last page.

- Print only what you need. Most applications let you print a selection of text, a single page, or a range of pages. There's no point in printing the entire document if you need only a small chunk of it.

- If you print a document and then discover a small mistake (such as a spelling gaffe) on one page, just reprint the offending page.

- Distribute your documents electronically if you can. Rather than sending a printout to someone, you can send the file over a network, as an email attachment, or even via floppy disk.

- Use two-sided printing if your printer supports this feature.

- Reuse printouts you no longer need. If you're printing an unimportant document that only you will see, turn some used pages around and print on the other side. Note, however, that reused pages sometimes have a tendency to get jammed in the printer, so this suggestion may not always work for you.

Troubleshooting Windows 98 Printing

When you need hard copy, the last thing you need is for your printer to play hard-to-get. If your printer does mess up, however, Windows 98 offers a couple of troubleshooting features that might help. I discuss these features, as well as solutions to specific printer woes, in the next few sections.

Using the Print Troubleshooter

If your printer won't print anything, or if your printouts contain garbage characters or only partial data, or if printing seems to take forever, you need to do some troubleshooting. For these kinds of problems, the Windows 98 Help system has a Print Troubleshooter that can help you narrow down to the cause.

To try it, select Start | Help and choose the Contents tab in the Windows Help dialog box that appears. Open the Troubleshooting book, open the Windows 98 Troubleshooters book, and then display the Print topic. This loads the Print Troubleshooter, shown in Figure 21.14. As with Windows 98's other Troubleshooters, the Print Troubleshooter operates by asking you a series of questions. You simply activate whatever option best answers the posed question and then click Next >. The Troubleshooter will gradually narrow down to the problem and (hopefully) reach a solution.

FIGURE 21.14.

The Print Trouble-shooter asks a series of questions to help you narrow down to the printing problem.

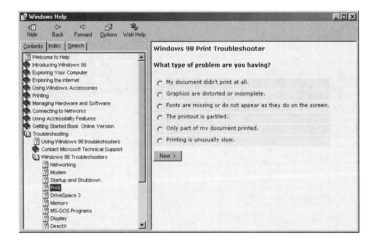

Miscellaneous Printing Perplexities

This section presents some miscellaneous printing problems (and, of course, their appropriate solutions) that might come your way.

Your printer won't print.

If your printer refuses to print, there are a number of possible reasons. Here are a few things to check out:

■ Make sure that the printer is powered up and online and that the cable connections are secure.

Prescriptions for Perfect Printing

CHAPTER 21

569

21

PRESCRIPTIONS
FOR PERFECT
PRINTING

- Make sure that the printer has paper and that there is no paper jam.

- Clear the printer's buffer by turning off the power, waiting for a few seconds, and then turning the power back on again. Given a printer that's online, properly connected, and not jammed with paper, I've found that this technique almost always convinces the printer to resume its duties once again.

- If your printer can switch between PostScript and normal operation, make sure the driver you're using matches the printer's current configuration.

- Try sending your print job directly to the printer. If this works, Windows 98 is having a problem spooling the document. You should run ScanDisk to check the integrity of the disk and file system. If Windows 98 still won't spool, you probably need to turn off spooling permanently.

- Delete the printer icon from the Printers folder and then reinstall it. This will fix any problems related to a corrupt driver or a corrupt Registry setting.

- Try printing to a file. If this works, head for the DOS prompt and try copying the PRN file to the printer port.

Your printer takes a long time to print.

If your printing seems to be taking longer than normal, here are some possible solutions:

- Make sure that spooling is enabled and that Windows 98 is spooling to EMF files.

- Make sure the drive where Windows 98 is installed isn't running low on disk space. The printing subsystem needs hard disk space to create the temporary EMF files.

- Use Disk Defragmenter to defragment the hard disk where Windows 98 is installed.

- Make sure your system resources aren't running low.

- Reinstall the printer driver or upgrade to the latest printer driver from the manufacturer.

- Make sure Windows 98 is sending TrueType fonts as outlines and not bitmaps. In the Fonts tab of your printer's properties sheet, click Send Fonts As and make sure the Send TrueType fonts as list shows Outlines.

Your printouts contain garbage characters or are missing data.

Here are a few things to look for if your printouts are faulty:

- Your printer might not have enough memory. Try printing at a lower resolution.

- Try printing directly to the printer or try spooling using the RAW format instead of the EMF format.

- If possible, try printing the document using a PostScript driver. If the document prints OK, the Windows 98 universal printer driver might be corrupted. Try extracting the file UNIDRV.DLL from the appropriate CAB file in your Windows 98 source disc.

■ Try printing just one job at a time to avoid conflicts.

■ Make sure the printable region isn't larger than what is supported by the printer.

You can't print a document because the File | Print command is dimmed.

If you can't select File | Print, you haven't yet installed a printer in Windows 98. See the earlier section "Installing a Printer with the Add Printer Wizard."

Your computer has an Extended Capabilities Port, but it doesn't show up in Device Manager.

The Windows 98 Setup program should recognize your ECP port automatically. If it doesn't, this probably means one of two things:

■ Your computer's BIOS isn't set up to use the ECP.

■ Windows 98 failed to recognize the ECP.

Either way, you need to run your computer's BIOS setup program (how you do this depends on the machine). When you're inside the program, find the setting that controls the parallel port and change it to ECP mode (if necessary). Make a note of the memory address, IRQ, and DMA channel used by the ECP. Exit the BIOS program and restart Windows 98.

You now need to run the Add New Hardware Wizard (see Chapter 11) to set up the ECP. However, you should bypass the automatic search for hardware and opt to specify the new device by hand. When the Wizard displays the list of hardware types, select Ports (COM & LPT). In the next dialog box, select Standard port types and highlight the ECP Printer Port "model" (as shown in Figure 21.15). Run through the remaining dialog boxes, but don't restart the computer when you're done.

Figure 21.15.

Use the Add New Hardware Wizard to specify the ECP by hand.

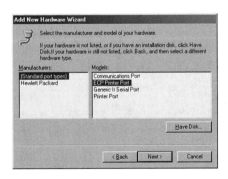

You now need to use Device Manager to set up the ECP resources. Open the System Properties dialog box and select the Device Manager tab. In the hardware tree, open Ports (COM and LPT), highlight ECP Printer Port (LPT1), and select Properties. In the Resources tab, shown in Figure 21.16, make sure the values in the Resource settings box match those used in the BIOS. If they don't, either select a different configuration or edit the individual resources by hand. (I showed you how to do this in Chapter 10.) When you're done, exit Device Manager and restart your system.

FIGURE 21.16.

Use the Resources tab to make sure that the ECP resource settings match those assigned to the ECP in the BIOS.

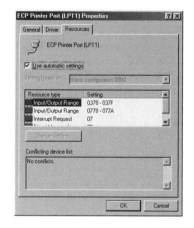

You're having trouble printing from a DOS program.

Most DOS programs should print properly using Windows 98's new spooling feature for DOS. However, if you do have problems, here are the steps required to turn off the spooling of DOS print jobs:

1. Open the Printers folder.
2. Open the properties sheet for the printer you're using.
3. Activate the Details tab.
4. Click the Port Settings button.
5. In the Configure LPT Port dialog box, shown in Figure 21.17, deactivate the Spool MS-DOS print jobs check box and click OK.

FIGURE 21.17.

If you're having trouble printing from DOS, deactivate the Spool MS-DOS print jobs option.

6. Click OK to return to the Printers folder.

Summary

This chapter took you on a tour of Windows 98 printing facilities. You learned how to install a printer driver, remove a printer, manage print jobs, and work with printer properties. I closed with a look at some printer troubleshooting issues. You'll find related information in the following chapters:

- I cover Device Manager in detail in Chapter 10, "Getting the Most Out of Device Manager and Hardware Profiles."

- The Add New Hardware Wizard is covered in Chapter 11, "Device Advice: Dealing with Devices in Windows 98."

- In case you have a printer that has an infrared port, I showed you how to install Windows 98's new infrared driver in Chapter 11.

- Network printing issues are covered in Chapter 29, "Working with Network Resources."

Portable Windows: The Briefcase and Direct Cable Connection

CHAPTER

22

A man must carry knowledge with him, if he would bring home knowledge.

—*Samuel Johnson*

It used to be that notebook computers occupied very specific and unalterable niches in the computing ecology. Sales professionals didn't leave home without them, executives on business trips routinely packed their portables, and corporate employees without a personal machine lugged a laptop home to do some extra work. In each case, though, the notebook computer—with its cramped keyboard, hard-to-read LCD display, and minuscule hard disk—was always considered a poor substitute for a desktop machine.

For many years it seemed that notebooks were doomed to remain among the lower castes in the social hierarchy of personal computers. But recent developments have caused notebooks to shed their inferiority complex. Today's luggables have impressive 800×600 (or better) displays, gigabyte-sized hard disks, and built-in sound and CD-ROMs. There's even one—the IBM ThinkPad 701C—with a keyboard that expands when you flip the cover! Add a couple of PC card slots, connectors for full-sized keyboards and monitors, maybe even a docking station, and suddenly your desktop system doesn't look so superior.

The notebook community's bid for respectability wasn't lost on the designers of Windows 98. They incorporated many notebook-specific features into the operating system, including support for power management, PC Card devices, and infrared ports. I discuss all these notebook knickknacks in Chapter 11, "Device Advice: Dealing with Devices in Windows 98."

Windows 98 also includes two features that let you exchange data between your portable and a desktop or network: Briefcase and Direct Cable Connection. I cover both these features in this chapter.

Synchronizing Laptop and Desktop with Briefcase

Previous versions of Windows refused to admit the existence of notebook computers. They simply assumed that a computer was a computer, and it really didn't matter whether your computer could be slung over your shoulder and lugged home at night.

Windows 98, however, not only knows about notebooks, but it also recognizes an important fact of portable computing life: Your notebook machine often has to use documents from your desktop machine, and vice versa. For example, if you're traveling to a client's office to make a presentation, you'll probably use your desktop computer to build the presentation, copy the files to your notebook, and take the notebook on the road. If you make any changes to these files while you're away (such as adding some annotations), you need to copy the updated files back to your desktop computer.

This apparently simple procedure is fraught with all kinds of unforeseen complications and perils:

■ If you modify only some of the documents when you're working on the notebook, how can you be sure which ones to copy to the desktop?

- What if you create a new document on the notebook?

- What if the floppy disk you're using to move the files back and forth contains other files?

- What if you make changes to the same document on both the desktop and the notebook?

These are thorny issues that until now required patience, careful planning, and often some knowledge of DOS batch files to overcome. Now, however, these problems are a thing of the past, because Windows 98 includes a feature that solves them all in one shot: Briefcase.

Briefcase works with special folders on your computer that you can use to hold the documents you transfer between your desktop and notebook computers. Instead of always copying individual documents back and forth, you usually just work with the Briefcase folders. Briefcase gets truly useful, however, when you realize that it *synchronizes* the documents on both machines automatically. If you work on a few documents on your notebook, for example, Windows 98 can figure out which ones are different, and then it lets you update the desktop by running a simple command. There's no guesswork involved and no chance of copying a file to the wrong folder.

Here are the basic Briefcase steps you follow to keep notebook and desktop files in sync:

1. After you finish working with the files on the desktop machine, copy them to a Briefcase folder and then copy the Briefcase folder to a floppy disk.

2. Insert the floppy disk into the notebook and copy the Briefcase files to the notebook's hard drive.

3. Use your notebook to work on the files. When you're done, open the floppy disk Briefcase folder and run the Update command. This action updates the floppy disk files with the changes you made on the notebook.

4. Insert the floppy disk into the desktop computer, open its Briefcase folder, and run the Update command. This action updates the hard disk files with the changed files in the floppy disk Briefcase.

The next few sections take you through each of these steps in detail.

Step 1: Copy the Files to the My Briefcase Folder

When you install Briefcase, Windows 98 adds a My Briefcase icon to the desktop. This is a special folder that supports the Briefcase features and that can be used to keep files synchronized. You can use this folder if you like, but you can also create new Briefcase folders by using either of the following techniques:

- In Explorer, highlight the folder you want to contain the Briefcase and then select New | Briefcase.

- Right-click either in Explorer's Contents pane or on the desktop and select Briefcase from the context menu.

After you complete your desktop work and decide which documents you want to work with on your notebook, you need to copy those documents to My Briefcase (or whichever Briefcase folder you want to use). Because My Briefcase has an icon on the desktop, it's easiest just to drag the files from Explorer and drop them on the My Briefcase icon. Alternatively, you can right-click each file and select Send To | My Briefcase.

The first time you copy a file to My Briefcase (or attempt to open the My Briefcase folder), you see the Welcome to the Windows Briefcase dialog box. This just gives you an overview of the Briefcase process, so you can click Finish to remove it.

The file you copy to a Briefcase folder is called a *sync copy* because Briefcase attempts to synchronize this file with the original. It does this by using a database to keep track of where the original file is located, as well its date and time stamp, size, and file type. If any of these attributes changes, Briefcase knows that the files are out of sync.

To see how the Briefcase folders work, use Explorer to display the contents of My Briefcase. As you can see in Figure 22.1, the Contents pane for a Briefcase folder is a bit different from the one you see with a regular folder. (Make sure that you have Explorer's Details view turned on.) Besides the usual Name, Size, Type, and Modified columns, Briefcase folders also show two extra columns:

> **Sync Copy In:** This column shows the drive and folder where the original document resides.

> **Status:** This column tells you the current state of each document. At first, the status is Up-to-date because you haven't done anything to the files. The status will change after you've made modifications to a file (as you'll see later).

FIGURE 22.1.

The Contents pane for a Briefcase folder has a few extra columns.

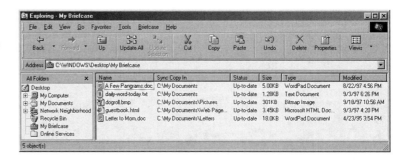

What happens if, after copying the files to My Briefcase, you make a change to one of the originals? No problem. You can either copy the modified document into My Briefcase or use Briefcase itself to update the document automatically. For example, if I make a change to the original of the file named guestbook.html and then display My Briefcase again, the Status column will tell me that the file Needs updating, as shown in Figure 22.2.

FIGURE 22.2.

If you change an original document, Briefcase tells you that the sync copy needs to be updated.

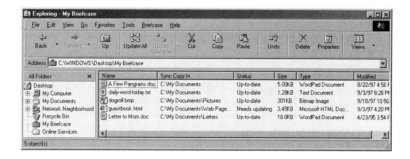

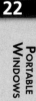

To update the file, use any of the following techniques:

- Highlight the file and select File | Update.
- Right-click the file and click Update.
- Highlight the file and click the Update Selection button in the toolbar.
- For multiple files, either highlight them all and use the preceding techniques or click the Update All toolbar button.

In each case, you see an Update dialog box similar to the one shown in Figure 22.3. The arrow shows you the direction of the update. In this case, the modified version of guestbook.html in the C:\My Documents\Web Page Stuff folder will replace the unmodified file in the Briefcase. If this is what you want, click Update. If, for some reason, you want to reverse the replacement, right-click either file and select the opposite arrow from the context menu that appears.

FIGURE 22.3.

When you run the Update command, Briefcase displays a list of the files that need updating.

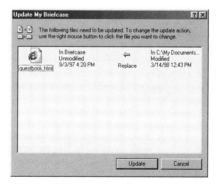

After you've copied all your documents to the Briefcase, insert a disk into one the desktop computer's floppy disk drives and then copy the My Briefcase folder to the floppy disk. If you've used this disk to copy the Briefcase before, Windows 98 asks whether you want to replace any files in the folder that have the same name. In this case, you want to click Yes to replace the files.

THE SEND TO COMMAND MOVES THE FOLDER

When putting the Briefcase on the floppy disk, you might be tempted to use the Send To command. Be warned, however: Send To moves the Briefcase folder to the floppy. To make Send To copy the folder, hold down the Ctrl key.

NEED A BIGGER BRIEFCASE?

I'm discussing the "sneakernet" Briefcase method in this section—that is, using a floppy disk to transfer files between desktop and notebook. The disadvantage of this method is that the size of your Briefcase is limited to the capacity of the floppy disk. If the files you need to transfer won't fit on a floppy, here are a few ideas:

- Compress the floppy disk (see my coverage of DriveSpace in Chapter 17, "Wielding the Windows 98 System Tools").

- If you have a ZIP drive installed on both your desktop and your notebook (or if you have an external ZIP drive that you can transfer between machines), use a ZIP disk (100MB capacity).

- Hook up your notebook to your network.

- Use Windows 98's Direct Cable Connection accessory. I discuss Direct Cable Connection later in this chapter.

Step 2: Copy the Files to the Notebook

Your next task is to get the files from the floppy disk Briefcase onto the notebook computer. Insert the disk into the notebook and then open the My Briefcase folder. As you can see in Figure 22.4, the floppy version of the My Briefcase folder has two changes:

- The paths in the Sync Copy In column include the name of the hard disk where the original files reside (Hard disk 1, in this case).

- The Status column shows Unchanged in Briefcase for each file.

Now copy the files to whatever destination you like on the notebook's hard disk. Whatever you do, don't *move* the files to the notebook, and don't move or copy the My Briefcase folder from the floppy disk. If you do, you break the link between the Briefcase files and the original files.

When you copy the files to the notebook, you're creating another sync copy, so Briefcase sets up a link between the floppy Briefcase files and the notebook files. For example, suppose that I copy all the files in my floppy My Briefcase folder to the C:\My Documents folder on the notebook. The floppy Briefcase now appears as shown in Figure 22.5. As you can see, Briefcase has set up a link to the sync copies in C:\My Documents. The Briefcase database is still keeping track of the original files, however.

FIGURE 22.4.

The floppy copy of the My Briefcase folder.

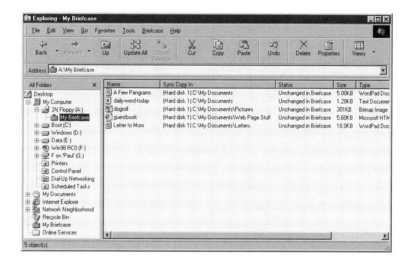

FIGURE 22.5.

When you copy the files from the floppy Briefcase to the notebook, Briefcase maintains a link between them.

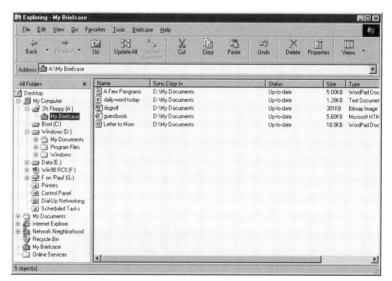

Step 3: Work on the Files and Then Update the Floppy Briefcase

With the documents now safely stowed on the notebook's hard drive, you can go ahead and work on the files. When you've completed your notebook labors, the documents you worked with are out of sync with the documents in the floppy disk Briefcase. So your next chore is to update the Briefcase on the floppy disk.

Once again, display the floppy disk's My Briefcase folder. The Status column tells you which files need updating, as shown in Figure 22.6.

Figure 22.6.

If you modified files on the notebook, the floppy Briefcase keeps track and tells you which files need updating.

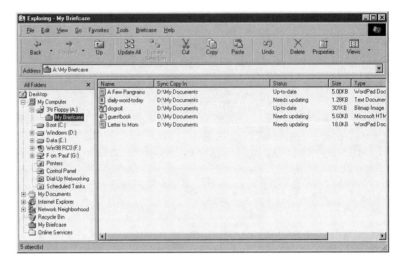

Use the techniques I outlined earlier to run the Update command and display an Update dialog box similar to the one shown in Figure 22.7. Change the replacement arrows if necessary and then click Update. Briefcase updates the files in the floppy Briefcase with the modified files on the notebook.

Figure 22.7.

Run the Update command to display this dialog box, which summarizes the files that need to be updated.

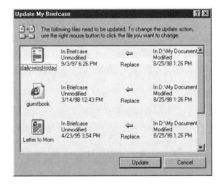

Step 4: Update the Files on the Desktop Computer

When you get back to the office, slip the floppy disk into your desktop and open the disk's My Briefcase folder. This time, Briefcase checks the floppy Briefcase files with the originals and tells you whether any files need updating, as shown in Figure 22.8. If they do, run the Update command again.

FIGURE 22.8.

When the floppy Briefcase is inserted into the desktop machine, Briefcase compares the floppy files to the originals.

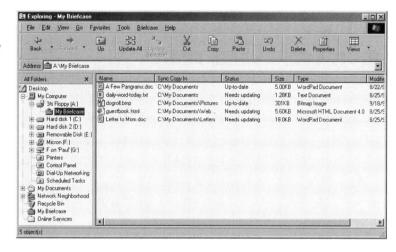

Figure 22.9 shows the three possibilities you get in the Update My Briefcase dialog box:

Replace: If only one of the files is changed, updating will cause Briefcase to replace the original file with the changed file.

Skip (both changed): If one of the original files was also modified, Briefcase offers to skip the update for that file. If you still want to go ahead with the update (that is, if you don't want to keep the changes made to one of the files), right-click the file and select the appropriate replacement direction. Otherwise, you need to skip the update, open both files in the application, and incorporate the changes by hand.

Merge: Some Windows applications (such as Microsoft Access) are programmed with *reconcilers* that let you merge two modified files. In this case, the default Update action is Merge, as shown in Figure 22.9. When you update, the application attempts to incorporate changes from both files into the original file.

FIGURE 22.9.

If both the original file and the file in the floppy Briefcase have changed, Briefcase offers to skip the update for the file.

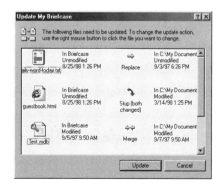

From Laptop to Desktop and Back: Direct Cable Connection

For many users, a full-blown network is overkill (and expensive overkill, to boot). If you want to just share files between a desktop machine and a notebook, it makes no sense to install network interface cards and cables and run through the whole network configuration rigmarole.

On the other hand, using floppy disks to transfer files between two machines, even with the useful synchronization features built into Briefcase, is still a relatively tedious affair.

For easier file transfers, Windows 98 provides a solution that's simpler to implement than a network connection and is less cumbersome than floppy disks: Direct Cable Connection.

Direct Cable Connection is a network client that doesn't need the usual card/cable network hardware. Instead, as its name implies, Direct Cable Connection establishes a mini-network between two computers via a special cable that connects the computers' serial or parallel ports. (Direct Cable Connection can even work with connections established through infrared ports.) One computer is designated as the *host*, and it acts as a kind of server by sharing its resources. A second computer—called the *guest*—connects to the host and can access its shared resources. Moreover, if the host is attached to a network, the guest computer can access the Network Neighborhood and therefore work with any of the shared resources on the larger network.

The rest of this chapter shows you how to work with Direct Cable Connection. You learn what kind of cable you need, how to configure the host and guest, and how to establish the connection.

Port and Cable Considerations

As I said, the hardware requirements for Direct Cable Connection are modest:

- A free serial or parallel port on each computer (the computers must use the same type of port; you can't use, for example, a parallel port on one machine and a serial port on the other). Alternatively, you can use infrared ports.

- A special cable running between the machines' ports. (Obviously, no cable is required for infrared connections.)

Before loading and configuring the Direct Cable Connection software, let's take a moment to examine these hardware requirements more closely.

Serial Ports and Null-Modem Cables

If you'll be using serial ports with Direct Cable Connection, you need to use a *null-modem* cable for the connection. Why not just use a regular serial cable? You'll learn in Chapter 26, "Getting Started with Modem Communications," that serial ports use individual wires to transmit and receive data one bit at a time. In a 9-pin serial port, pin 3 is the Transmit Data wire and pin 2 is the Receive Data wire. Because of these pin arrangements, you can't connect two serial ports with a garden-variety serial cable. Suppose you did and then tried sending data from one machine to the other. The bits would go out through the Transmit Data wire, but because there is no modem between the computers to route the signals appropriately, the other computer would receive them on *its* Transmit Data wire. Chaos, of course, would ensue.

To prevent this, use a null-modem cable instead. It uses a different pin arrangement than a regular serial cable and therefore ensures that bits sent through the Transmit Data wire on one port head for the Receive Data wire of the other port. A null-modem cable also ensures that the correct wires are used on both ends for the Request To Send (RTS) and Clear To Send (CTS) signals, as well as the Data Set Ready (DSR) and Data Terminal Ready (DTR) signals. Table 22.1 specifies how a null-modem cable translates 9-pin serial port signals between a host computer and a guest computer.

Table 22.1. Wire translations for a 9-pin-to-9-pin null-modem cable.

Host Pin	Signal	Guest Pin	Signal
2	Receive Data	3	Transmit Data
3	Transmit Data	2	Receive Data
4	Data Terminal Ready	6	Data Set Ready
5	Signal Ground	5	Signal Ground
6	Data Set Ready	4	Data Terminal Ready
7	Request To Send	8	Clear To Send
8	Clear To Send	7	Request To Send

There are also null-modem cables that work with 25-pin serial ports. Table 22.2 spells out the wire translations for a host and guest.

Table 22.2. Wire translations for a 25-pin-to-25-pin null-modem cable.

Host Pin	Signal	Guest Pin	Signal
2	Transmit Data	3	Receive Data
3	Receive Data	2	Transmit Data
4	Request To Send	5	Clear To Send
5	Clear To Send	4	Request To Send
6	Data Set Ready	20	Data Terminal Ready
7	Signal Ground	7	Signal Ground
20	Data Terminal Ready	6	Data Set Ready

22

PORTABLE WINDOWS

If you use a serial port connection, be aware that your data transfer speeds will be anything but snappy. If you have an older 8250 or 16450 UART, Direct Cable Connection's maximum theoretical throughput will be 57,600 bits per second (bps), or about 7 kilobytes per second (KBps). If you have a 16650 UART, maximum throughput doubles to 115,200 bps, or about 14KBps, which still isn't very fast compared to network cable.

Standard Parallel Ports and Cables

The main reason that serial ports are inherently slow is that they spit out data only one bit at a time. For faster data transfers with Direct Cable Connection, you should consider using a parallel port, which can handle 8 bits of data at a time. Again, you don't use the standard parallel (printer) cable, but a special cable designed for exchanging data between parallel ports. These are usually called *parallel LapLink cables* or *parallel InterLink cables.* (LapLink is a communications program that has been the standard for cable-based computer connections for many years. InterLink is the cable connection utility that comes with DOS 6.*x*.) Table 22.3 shows the wire translations that occur when you connect the parallel ports of a host and guest with one of these cables.

Table 22.3. Wire translations for a 25-pin–to–25-pin parallel cable.

Host Pin	Guest Pin
2	15
3	13
4	12
5	10
6	11
10	5
11	6
12	4
13	3
15	2
25 (Ground)	25 (Ground)

Standard parallel ports come in two varieties:

> **Unidirectional:** This type of port is designed for one-way communication between a computer and a printer. It can be used for both output and input, but this will cost you some speed. Output uses the full 8 bits of the parallel port to transfer data, so it can reach throughput speeds of about 80 to 120KBps. Input uses only 4 bits, so throughput is restricted to approximately 40 to 60KBps.

> **Bidirectional:** This type of port is designed for two-way communications between a computer and another device. Because the port can use all 8 bits for output or input, you usually achieve throughput speeds of 80 to 120KBps for all data transfers. Note that bidirectional ports have been the standard for many years, so it's likely that your system will have this type of port (if not one of the advanced parallel ports discussed in the next two sections).

A standard bidirectional parallel port is six to eight times faster than even a serial port with a 16550 UART, so you should use parallel ports for Direct Cable Connection whenever possible.

Enhanced Parallel Ports and Cables

The Enhanced Parallel Port (EPP) specification was developed jointly by Intel, Zenith Data Systems, and Xircom. It's been around since 1991. Operating at high speeds compared to standard parallel ports, an EPP offers approximately 10 times the throughput (theoretically, up to 2MBps). For these ports, you use the same parallel LapLink cables mentioned in the preceding section. Also note that both computers must have an EPP to achieve maximum throughput.

Extended Capabilities Ports and Cables

The Extended Capabilities Port (ECP) was developed by Microsoft and Hewlett-Packard in 1992. It includes the EPP specification but uses a DMA channel to ensure better multitasking. You need a cable that supports the ECP specification. ECP's performance is about equal to EPP's.

USE A UCM CABLE FOR MAXIMUM THROUGHPUT

There are actually a couple of standards in existence for ECP, so you might have trouble getting the right cable or connecting two ECP-enabled machines. To prevent these problems, you should invest in a *Universal Cable Module* (UCM) cable. These cables can auto-detect the parallel port and adjust accordingly. Also, UCM cables include special hardware logic that can increase throughput. Therefore, you can achieve maximum possible data transfer speed by connecting ECPs with a UCM cable.

Parallel Technologies makes such a cable—it's called the DirectParallel Universal Cable. Here's the address of its Web site:

```
http://www.lpt.com/lpt/
```

Configuring the Host Computer

Recall that to work with Direct Cable Connection, you must configure one computer as the host (this is usually the desktop machine) and the other computer as the guest (usually the notebook). Remember that the guest system gains access to the resources shared on the host, but not the other way around. In other words, the host computer can't work with the resources on the guest computer. Use this fact as a guide when determining which machines to use as host and guest.

You start this section of the chapter by learning how to configure the host machine, and then you move on to the guest configuration in the next section. Before performing either procedure, make sure you've connected the two machines with whatever ports and cable you've decided to use.

Step 1: Set Up Direct Cable Connection as a Host

To get started, select Start | Programs | Accessories | Communications | Direct Cable Connection. The first time you select this menu option, the Direct Cable Connection Wizard loads, and you see the first of its dialog boxes. Make sure that the Host option is activated and then click Next >.

At this point, Direct Cable Connection might display a dialog box to tell you that it needs to install the Microsoft Dial-Up Adapter. (You won't see this message if the Dial-Up Adapter is already installed.) When you click OK, Windows 98 shuts down the Direct Cable Connection Wizard and installs the Dial-Up Adapter. When this is complete, restart Direct Cable Connection, select Host, and click Next > to continue with the configuration.

The Direct Cable Connection Wizard checks the available ports on your system and displays a list of these ports, as shown in Figure 22.10. Highlight the port you want to use and click Next >.

FIGURE 22.10.

Use this Wizard dialog box to choose the port you want to use with Direct Cable Connection.

IF YOU ADD PORTS

If you add ports to your machine down the road, rerun the Direct Cable Connection Wizard. When you get to the dialog box shown in Figure 22.10, click the Install New Ports button to make the Wizard check for the new ports.

If the host computer isn't already on a network, you won't have file and print sharing set up. (File and print sharing lets you make resources such as folders, disk drives, and printers available to other computers on a network or, in this case, to the guest computer via Direct Cable Connection.) In this example, you see the dialog box shown in Figure 22.11.

FIGURE 22.11.

The Direct Cable Connection Wizard displays this dialog box if you haven't enabled file and print sharing on the host computer.

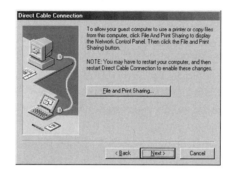

Here are the steps to enable file and print sharing:

1. Click the File and Print Sharing button to display the Network properties sheet.

2. If the File and Print Sharing button is enabled, skip to step 5. Otherwise, click Add. The Select Network Component Type dialog box appears.

3. Highlight Service and click OK. Windows 98 displays the Select Network Service dialog box.

4. Use the Manufacturers list to highlight Microsoft, use the Network Services list to highlight File and printer sharing for Microsoft Networks (see Figure 22.12), and then click OK.

FIGURE 22.12.

Use this dialog box to add the file and print sharing service.

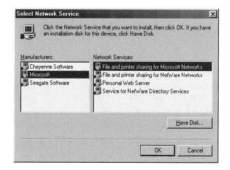

5. In the Network properties sheet, click the File and Print Sharing button.

6. In the File and Print Sharing dialog box that appears, activate the I want to we able to give others access to my files check box. If you also want to print over Direct Cable

Connection, activate the I want to be able to allow others to print to my printer(s) files check box. Click OK when you're done.

7. Click OK. When Windows 98 asks whether you want to restart your computer, click Yes.

When you're back in Windows 98, restart Direct Cable Connection and run through the Wizard's dialog boxes. You eventually see a dialog box asking whether you want the guest computer to use a password to access the host, as shown in Figure 22.13. If you do, activate the Use password protection check box, click the Set Password button, enter your password (twice) in the Direct Cable Connection Password dialog box, and click OK. Click Finish to complete the host configuration. The Wizard will then wait for a connection from the guest. Click Close if you don't want to connect right away.

FIGURE 22.13.

Use this dialog box to set up a password for Direct Cable Connection.

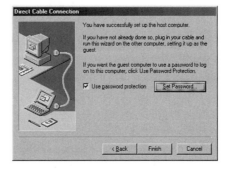

Step 2: Share Folders, Drives, and Printers

The guest computer won't be able to do very much during a connection unless you share some resources on the host machine. If you've already shared some of the host's resources for a regular network connection, you might not need to do anything else (unless you want to give the guest machine access to different resources). Otherwise, follow the instructions for sharing resources that I outline in Chapter 29, "Working with Network Resources."

Configuring the Guest Computer

Configuring the guest computer is even easier than configuring the host. Again, there are two steps: configuring Direct Cable Connection for guest duty and setting up some network properties.

Step 1: Set Up Direct Cable Connection as a Guest

You first need to move to your other computer and set it up as a Direct Cable Connection guest. Here are the steps:

1. Select Start | Programs | Accessories | Communications | Direct Cable Connection to get things off the ground.

2. In the first Direct Cable Connection Wizard dialog box, activate the Guest option and click Next >.

3. Highlight the port you want to use and click Next >.

4. Click Finish.

Step 2: Installing Network Protocols

The only other configuration chore you might have to perform on the guest computer is installing one or more network protocols, as follows:

■ If you want to share exchange data only with the host computer, make sure that the two computers have at least one common protocol. If they don't use a common protocol, you won't be able to establish a connection between the two machines. To avoid connection problems, I recommend that the common protocol be IPX/SPX.

■ If you want the guest computer to be able to access shared resources in the Network Neighborhood, make sure that the guest uses the common protocol used on the network.

See Chapter 28, "Setting Up Windows 98 for Networking," for instructions on installing protocols.

Establishing the Connection

With Direct Cable Connection configured on the host and guest computers and a cable running between their ports, you can now establish a connection between the two machines.

On the host computer, select Start | Programs | Accessories | Communications | Direct Cable Connection. In the dialog box that appears, click the Listen button. Direct Cable Connection initializes the port and then displays the dialog box shown in Figure 22.14.

FIGURE 22.14.

When Direct Cable Connection is started, the host computer waits for a connection from the guest.

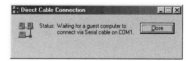

CHANGING YOUR DIRECT CABLE CONNECTION SETUP

If you need to make changes to your Direct Cable Connection configuration—for example, to switch host and guest, to use a different port, or to add new ports—click the Change button and run through the Direct Cable Connection Wizard's dialog boxes again.

On the guest computer, you also select Start | Programs | Accessories | Communications | Direct Cable Connection. In the dialog box that appears, click the Connect button.

Now the two machines exchange pleasantries along the cable. Before the connection is established, you might be asked to enter more information:

- If you're connecting to a larger network, you might be asked to enter a username and password for verification from a server.

- If the host computer is protected by a Direct Cable Connection password, you have to enter that password.

TROUBLESHOOTING: DCC AND DIAL-UP NETWORKING

When you try to connect to the host machine, you might receive the following error message:

```
Cannot connect to host computer. Make sure you have run Direct
Cable Connection on the host computer and you have connected
your cable to both computers.
```

Besides checking that the host is configured correctly and that the cables are connected securely, make sure that you don't have a Dial-Up Networking session running on a different port. Both Direct Cable Connection and Dial-Up Networking use the same network interface driver (PPPMAC.VXD), and only one instance of the driver can be loaded at a time. You won't be able to establish your connection to the host until you close the Dial-Up Networking session. (I discuss Dial-Up Networking in Chapter 30, "Remote Computing with Dial-Up Networking.")

When the two machines finally see eye-to-eye, Direct Cable Connection opens a folder window on the guest computer that shows all the shared resources on the host, as shown in Figure 22.15. If the host is attached to a larger network, the guest computer can use this window (or the Network Neighborhood) to browse and work with the network's shared resources. As I've said, however, neither the host machine nor the other network computers can see the guest.

FIGURE 22.15.

When the Direct Cable Connection session is established, the guest computer sees a folder containing the host's shared resources.

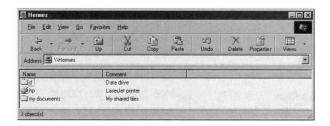

TROUBLESHOOTING: IF DCC FAILS

Direct Cable Connection might fail to establish a connection to the host. You won't receive any error messages, but the guest computer's Direct Cable Connection status window will tell you it was "Disconnected." The likely problem here is that the guest computer is also trying to log on to a network, but it has only the NetBEUI protocol installed. This confuses the NetBIOS, which in turn confuses the NetBEUI protocol, so the network logon fails. The solution is to install the IPX/SPX protocol as well.

22

PORTABLE
WINDOWS

Direct Cable Connection and Infrared Ports

If your host and guest computers have infrared ports, you can use these ports to establish a connection without having to bother with cables. When configuring the connection, note the following:

■ When the Direct Cable Connection Wizard asks you to specify a port for the connection, select the virtual serial port used by your infrared adapter. Note that infrared ports aren't identified explicitly, but only by the virtual ports they use (such as COM 4, for example).

■ Make sure you position the host and guest ports so that they're facing each other directly and are no closer together than six inches and no farther apart than three to nine feet.

■ Because the infrared serial port isn't initialized at startup, you need to enable it before starting Direct Cable Connection. To do this, display Control Panel and open the Infrared icon to display the Infrared Monitor.

After your connection is established, the Infrared Monitor will keep track of the connection by telling you the name of the computer that the guest is connected to and the current communication efficiency, as shown in Figure 22.16.

FIGURE 22.16.

During an infrared connection, the Infrared Monitor keeps tabs on the link's status.

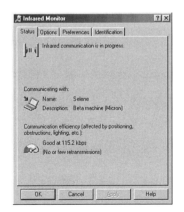

Direct Cable Connection and the Briefcase

I showed you how to use Windows 98's Briefcase feature earlier in this chapter. You saw how Briefcase took most of the guesswork out of synchronizing files between a desktop and notebook computer. However, you still had to face the drudgery of moving the Briefcase between machines via floppy disk.

To avoid this "sneakernet" situation, you can use Direct Cable Connection to transfer the files back and forth between the machines using a single Briefcase folder. Here's a rundown of the basic Briefcase procedure from a Direct Cable Connection point of view:

1. On the host machine, make sure the folder containing the files you want to work with is either shared directly or resides in a shared folder.

2. On the guest computer, connect via Direct Cable Connection and access the shared folder.

3. Copy the files to the guest computer's My Briefcase folder.

4. Use the guest computer to work on the files from within the My Briefcase folder. You don't need to have the connection established at this point.

5. When you're done, reestablish the connection, if necessary, and then open the My Briefcase folder on the guest computer.

6. Select Briefcase | Update All. This updates the host computer's files with the changed files in the guest computer's Briefcase.

Summary

This chapter showed you how to share files between a desktop and a notebook computer. I began by showing you how to use Briefcase folders to transport files to and fro and keep the versions synchronized. You then learned how to use Direct Cable Connection to set up a mini-network between two computers. The basic idea behind Direct Cable Connection is that by stringing a special cable between, for example, a desktop and a notebook computer, you can share files, folders, disk drives, and printers between them. To that end, you learned about the various serial and parallel ports you can use with Direct Cable Connection, as well as the associated cables that are designed for these ports. I then showed you how to configure the host computer and the guest computer and establish a connection. I closed with a quick look at using Direct Cable Connection with infrared ports and Briefcase.

For related information, take a look at the following chapters:

■ Chapter 11, "Device Advice: Dealing with Devices in Windows 98," is the place to go to learn how to work with other Windows 98 notebook features, such as power management and infrared devices.

■ All the network basics you need for setting up Direct Cable Connection, including installing protocols, can be found in Chapter 28, "Setting Up Windows 98 for Networking."

■ For information on network resource sharing, see Chapter 29, "Working with Network Resources."

■ To learn how to use your notebook to dial in to a network, see Chapter 30, "Remote Computing with Dial-Up Networking."

22

PORTABLE
WINDOWS

23

DOS Isn't Dead: Unleashing the DOS Shell

IN THIS CHAPTER

> **cruft together** *v* To throw together something ugly but temporarily workable.
>
> **MS-DOS** *n* A clone of CP/M for the 8088 crufted together in six weeks by hacker Tim Paterson, who is said to have regretted it ever since.
>
> from *The New Hacker's Dictionary*

In Internet circles, a *holy war* is a never-ending debate on the merits of one thing versus another, in which people use the same arguments over and over, and nobody's opinion budges even the slightest bit one way or the other. Common holy war topics include liberalism versus conservatism, pro-choice versus pro-life, and neatness versus sloppiness.

Operating systems cause frequent holy war skirmishes, with most battles pitting Macintosh against Windows, and UNIX against NT. Until recently, the mother of all operating system holy wars was DOS versus Windows, with correspondents devoting obscene amounts of time and energy extolling the virtues of one system and detailing the shortcomings of the other. But with Windows's decisive victory over DOS both technologically and in the marketplace, the DOS-devoted are heard from only rarely nowadays.

That isn't to say that DOS is dead. Far from it. DOS is alive and well and adjusting nicely to its new role as just another Windows 98 accessory. With DOS no longer the boss, it's entirely possible that you might go your entire Windows 98 career without having to fire up a DOS session. But if you do need DOS, you need to know a few things in order to get the most out of your command-line sessions. This chapter shows you how to squeeze the best and most reliable performance out of them under Windows 98.

Getting to DOS

Okay, so Windows 98 comes with DOS, and DOS comes with all kinds of internal and external commands. The next question is, how do you get to DOS so that you can work with these commands? The next few sections explain everything you need to know.

Starting a DOS Session

As you'll see in a bit, Windows 98 offers various methods of running DOS commands. One of these methods is the most obvious: Start a DOS session and run your commands from the DOS prompt. If this is your preferred method, you'll find that Windows 98 (as usual) offers umpteen different ways to get to the DOS prompt.

Starting DOS Without Exiting the Windows 98 GUI

If you want to start a DOS session without exiting the Windows 98 GUI, use any of the following methods:

- Select Start | Programs | MS-DOS Prompt.
- Launch COMMAND.COM in the root folder of your computer's boot drive.

■ Create a shortcut for COMMAND.COM on your desktop and then launch the shortcut.

■ Select Start | Run, enter command in the Run dialog box, and click OK.

STARTING YOUR DOS SESSION IN A SPECIFIC FOLDER

If you highlight a folder in Explorer before starting COMMAND.COM via Start | Run, the DOS window that appears will open in the highlighted folder.

For the last two methods, you can specify extra parameters and switches after the COMMAND.COM filename. Here's the syntax used by COMMAND.COM:

```
COMMAND [[drive:]path] [device] [/E:x] [/L:y] [/U:z] [/P] [/MSG] [/LOW]
➥[/Y [/[C¦K] command]]
```

[drive:]path	Specifies the drive and folder containing COMMAND.COM.
device	Specifies the device to use for command input and output.
/E:x	Sets *x* as the initial environment size (in bytes), in which *x* is between 256 and 32768.
/L:y	Sets *y* as the size of each internal buffer (requires /P), in which *y* is between 128 and 1024).
/U:z	Sets *z* as the size of the input buffer (requires /P), in which *z* is between 128 and 255. Set this to a higher value (the default is 127) if you plan on entering long filenames at the prompt.
/P	Makes COMMAND.COM permanent (that is, you can't quit with the EXIT command).
/MSG	Stores all error messages in memory (requires /P).
/LOW	Forces COMMAND.COM to keep its resident data in low (conventional) memory.
/Y	Steps through the batch program specified by /C or /K.
/C command	Executes the specified *command* and returns.
/K command	Executes the specified command and continues running.

An Easier Method of Opening a DOS Session in the Current Folder

I mentioned in the preceding tip that if you start COMMAND.COM from the Run dialog box, Windows 98 opens the DOS window in whichever folder is currently highlighted in Explorer. This capability is very handy, but having to open the Run dialog box and enter the command is a pain. However, you can do this another way, and after you've set it up, it takes only a couple of mouse clicks.

The secret is that a folder is a file type in Windows 98. All you need to do is create a new action for the folder file type that runs COMMAND.COM and automatically displays the correct folder. Here are the steps to follow:

1. In Explorer, select View | Folder Options, and in the Folder Options dialog box that appears, display the File Types tab.

2. Highlight Folder in the Registered file types list and then click Edit. The Edit File Type dialog box appears.

3. Click the New button. The New Action dialog box appears.

4. In the Action text box, type Open in DOS &Window (or whatever you want to name the command), and in the Application used to perform action text box, type command.com /k cd %1. The cd %1 part runs the CD (change directory) command on the current folder (see Figure 23.1).

FIGURE 23.1.

Fill in the New Action dialog box to create a new action for the Folder file type.

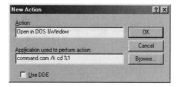

5. Click OK to return to the Edit File Type dialog box.

6. Click Close to return to the Options, and then click Close again to return to Explorer.

Now when you right-click a folder in Explorer, the context menu has an Open in DOS Window command, as shown in Figure 23.2. Clicking this command starts a DOS session in the folder.

FIGURE 23.2.

The new Open in DOS Window command starts COMMAND.COM in the current folder.

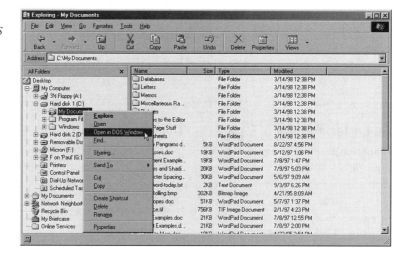

Starting a DOS Session in MS-DOS Mode

If you want to exit the Windows 98 GUI and then start your DOS session, use any of these techniques:

■ Select Start | Shut Down, activate the Restart in MS-DOS mode option, and click OK.

A FASTER WAY TO GET TO MS-DOS MODE

After you run the Restart in MS-DOS mode option the first time, Windows 98 creates a shortcut that gives you quicker access to MS-DOS mode. It's called Exit to DOS.PIF, and you find it in your main Windows 98 folder. Running this file takes you directly to the MS-DOS mode prompt, without your having to deal with the Shut Down dialog box. For even easier access, you might want to copy this shortcut to the desktop.

■ Reboot the computer, invoke the Windows 98 Startup menu, and select Command prompt only.

■ In MSDOS.SYS, add the line BootGUI=0 in the [Options] section (or edit the line if it already exists). Each time you restart your computer, Windows 98 will boot to the DOS prompt.

These methods not only shut down the Windows 98 GUI, but also take Windows 98 out of protected mode and change to MS-DOS mode (which I'll explain in more detail in a moment). To get back to the safety of the Windows 98 GUI and protected mode, type win (or exit) and press Enter at the DOS prompt.

23

DOS ISN'T DEAD:
UNLEASHING THE
DOS SHELL

What Happens When You Start a DOS Session?

When you create a new DOS session, whether you're running an instance of COMMAND.COM, a DOS command, or a DOS program, the Virtual Machine Manager kicks in and sets up a new virtual machine for the DOS session.

First, it carves out 1MB of virtual memory that the DOS session can call its own. To the DOS session, this megabyte of virtual memory will look like 640KB of conventional memory and 384KB of upper memory.

Next, the Virtual Machine Manager creates the DOS environment in which the session will operate. This environment is determined at startup and is based on the default settings and drivers used by IO.SYS. An "invisible" DOS machine is set up as though it were booted using the following CONFIG.SYS and AUTOEXEC.BAT files (assuming that Windows 98 is installed in C:\WINDOWS):

CONFIG.SYS:

```
DEVICE=C:\WINDOWS\HIMEM.SYS
DEVICE=C:\WINDOWS\IFSHLP.SYS
```

```
DEVICE=C:\WINDOWS\SETVER.EXE
DOS=HIGH
FILES=30
BUFFERS=30
STACKS=9,256
FCBS=4
LASTRIVE=Z

AUTOEXEC.BAT:

PROMPT=$P$G
PATH=C:\WINDOWS;C:\WINDOWS\COMMAND
SET TMP=C:\WINDOWS\TEMP
SET TEMP=C:\WINDOWS\TEMP
SET COMSPEC=C:\WINDOWS\COMMAND.COM
SET windir=C:\WINDOWS
SET winbootdir=C:\WINDOWS
```

Entries in your real CONFIG.SYS or AUTOEXEC.BAT are also taken into account, in the following ways:

■ If you have an entry that duplicates one of the IO.SYS settings, your entry takes precedence. For example, if your CONFIG.SYS has a FILES=60 line, the invisible DOS machine is set up with FILES equal to 60.

■ If you have any other lines in your CONFIG.SYS and AUTOEXEC.BAT files, they're incorporated into the DOS machine's environment.

The environment of this invisible DOS virtual machine acts as a kind of template on which the real DOS sessions are based. This is equivalent to "booting" each virtual machine with the preceding CONFIG.SYS and AUTOEXEC.BAT files.

Note, too, that many of the goodies available to Windows 98 applications are also available at the DOS prompt: 32-bit disk caching and file access, protected-mode drivers for the mouse, CD-ROM and other devices, multitasking, and so on.

A STARTUP BATCH FILE FOR DOS SESSIONS

Besides editing your real CONFIG.SYS and AUTOEXEC.BAT files, another way to customize each DOS session is to tell Windows 98 to run a batch file each time you start the session. I show you how this is done later.

What Happens When You Switch to MS-DOS Mode?

By their very nature, DOS programs like to monopolize a computer's resources. That's contrary to Windows 98's nature, of course, so the Virtual Machine Manager's job is to make DOS programs think they have total control over the computer. Few DOS programs see through this ruse, so they run happily ever after.

However, some DOS programs—especially DOS games—insist on full control over the computer's resources, and they won't be hoodwinked into thinking they've got it when they really don't. For these control freaks, Windows 98 can run in *MS-DOS mode*, which gives the program exclusive access to the computer.

When you switch to MS-DOS mode, the Virtual Machine Manager shuts down all running applications, unloads all protected-mode drivers, exits Windows 98, and "reboots" the system into a pure real-mode DOS environment. (Well, if you exit to MS-DOS mode from within Windows 98, it's not quite pure: A 4KB remnant of Windows 98 remains in memory.) As before, the settings created for the invisible DOS virtual machine are used to boot the new DOS session. (I tell how to customize this environment for individual DOS programs later in this chapter—see the section "Creating a Program-Specific Startup Configuration.")

The Virtual Machine Manager also runs the DOSSTART.BAT batch file, which contains the lines (if any) that Setup commented out from AUTOEXEC.BAT during installation. If it exists, you find DOSSTART.BAT in your main Windows 98 folder.

While you're in MS-DOS mode, you can't multitask applications, work with long filenames, or access protected-mode drivers.

Running DOS Commands

Although many of the Windows 98 accessories provide more powerful and easier-to-use re-placements for nearly all DOS commands, a few commands still have no Windows 98 peer. These include MEM, FDISK, and REN, as well as the many DOS prompt–specific commands, such as CLS, DOSKEY, and PROMPT.

How you run a command depends on whether it's an internal or external command, and on what you want Windows 98 to do after the command is finished.

For an internal command, you have two choices: You can either enter the command at the DOS prompt or include it as a parameter with COMMAND.COM. As you saw earlier, you can run internal commands with COMMAND.COM by specifying either the /C switch or the /K switch. If you use /C, the command executes, and then the DOS session shuts down. This is fine if you're running a command for which you don't need to see the results. For example, if you want to redirect the contents of drive C's root folder in the text file ROOT.TXT, entering the following command in the Run dialog box (for example) will do the job:

```
command.com /c dir c:\ > root.txt
```

On the other hand, you might want to examine the output of a command before the DOS window closes. In this case, you need to use the /K switch. The following command runs DIR on drive C's root folder and then drops you off at the DOS prompt:

```
command.com /k dir c:\
```

For an external command, you have three choices: Enter the command at the DOS prompt, enter the command by itself from within Windows 98, or include it as a parameter with COMMAND.COM.

A FULL PATHNAME ISN'T REQUIRED FOR DOS COMMANDS

When you use the DOS prompt or the Run dialog box to start an external DOS command, you don't need to use the command's full pathname. For example, the full pathname for MEM.EXE is C:\WINDOWS\COMMAND\MEM.EXE (assuming that the main Windows 98 folder is C:\WINDOWS), but to run this command, you need only enter mem. The reason is that the COMMAND subfolder is part of the PATH statement for each virtual DOS machine.

Entering the command by itself from within Windows 98 means launching the command's file in Explorer, entering the command in the Run dialog box, or creating a shortcut for the command. For the latter two methods, you can embellish the command by adding parameters and switches. Whichever command you run in this manner, Windows 98 adds Finished to the DOS window's title bar and leaves the window open so that you can examine the results, as shown in Figure 23.3. To close the window, press Alt+F4 or click the window's Close button.

FIGURE 23.3.

When you run an external DOS command, Windows 98 leaves the window open after the command has finished.

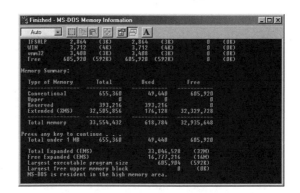

To change this behavior, you can run the command as a parameter with COMMAND.COM, as explained here:

- If you use COMMAND.COM with the /C switch (for example, command.com /c mem.exe), Windows 98 shuts down the DOS window when the external command has completed its labors.

- If you use COMMAND.COM with the /K switch (for example, command.com /k mem.exe), Windows 98 leaves the DOS window open and returns you to the command prompt when the external command is complete.

Adding Parameters and Switches to a DOS Command

If you use the DOS prompt or the Run dialog box to enter your DOS commands, you can easily tack on any extra parameters or switches you want to use to modify the command. If, however, you start an external command from Explorer, the command runs without any options. To modify how an external command operates, you can add parameters and switches by following these steps:

1. In Explorer, right-click the external DOS command you want to work with (such as Mem.exe) and then click Properties to display the properties sheet for the command.

2. Select the Program tab.

3. In the Cmd line text box, add a space after the command line, and then add your parameters and switches. Figure 23.4 shows an example.

FIGURE 23.4.

Use the Cmd line text box to append extra parameters to an external DOS command.

4. Click OK.

WINDOWS 98 CREATES A PIF FOR THE COMMAND

After you modify a DOS command's properties sheet, Windows 98 creates a PIF—a program information file—for the command. This is a separate file that has the same name as the command, but with a .PIF extension. Unfortunately, Explorer always hides the .PIF extension. You can recognize the PIF, however, if you display Explorer in Details view: The PIF says Shortcut to MS-DOS Program in the Type column. I give you complete PIF details later in this chapter (see "Understanding PIFs").

If you want to vary the parameters each time you run the command, add a space and a question mark (?) to the end of the command line, like so:

```
C:\WINDOWS\COMMAND\mem.exe ?
```

Each time you run the command (whether from Explorer or from the Run dialog box), Windows 98 displays a dialog box similar to the one shown in Figure 23.5. Use the Parameters text box to enter your switches and options, and then click OK.

FIGURE 23.5.

If you add a question mark (?) to the end of the command line, Windows 98 displays a dialog box similar to this one each time you run the command.

Working at the DOS Prompt

After you have your DOS session up and running, you can work with it more or less as you've always worked with DOS. You can run commands and DOS programs, create and launch batch files, perform file maintenance, and so on. If you're used to working with DOS 6.*x*, you'll find that the Windows 98 DOS brings a few extra goodies to the command prompt. The next few sections highlight some of the more useful ones.

DOS DELETIONS ARE DELETED!

When you're working at the DOS prompt, be warned that any files you delete aren't sent to the Recycle Bin, but are purged from your system.

Working with Long Filenames

If you've started your DOS session within Windows 98 (that is, you're not running in MS-DOS mode), the VFAT file system is still available. This means that you can work with long filenames with a DOS session.

For example, if you run the DIR command to get a listing of files in a folder, you see not only the usual data—the file's 8.3 filename, size, and date and time stamp—but also the file's long filename. Figure 23.6 shows an example.

FIGURE 23.6.

The new DIR *command shows each file's long filename.*

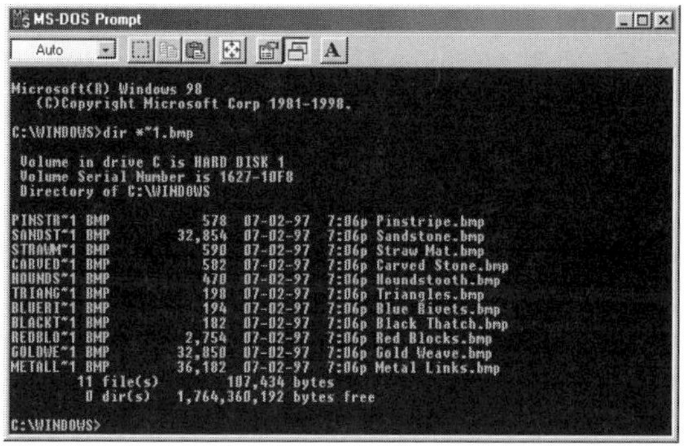

Entering Long Filenames

If you want to use long filenames in a command, however, you need to be careful. If the long filename contains a space or any other character that's illegal in an 8.3 filename, you need to surround the long name with quotation marks. For example, the following command will generate a Too many parameters error:

```
copy black thatch.bmp booby hatch.bmp
```

Instead, you need to enter this command as follows:

```
copy "black thatch.bmp" "booby hatch.bmp"
```

Note that if you use the CD command to change to a folder that has a long name, Windows 98 shows the full name in the command prompt. For example, if you change to Windows 98's Start Menu subfolder, you see the following prompt:

```
C:\WINDOWS\Start Menu>
```

Don't forget, as well, that if you need to work with commands that are longer than 127 characters, you have to adjust the input buffer length of COMMAND.COM. Recall from the COMMAND.COM syntax shown earlier that you do this by specifying the /U:z switch, where z is a number between 128 and 255 that represents the new buffer length. For example, to set the buffer to 255 characters for all DOS sessions, you add the following SHELL command to your CONFIG.SYS file (assuming that C:\Windows is your main Windows 98 folder):

```
shell=c:\windows\command.com /u:255 /p
```

Easier Ways to Work with Long Filenames

Long filenames are, of course, long, so they tend to be a pain to type at the command line. You can always use the 8.3 short names, but Windows 98 offers a few other methods for knocking long names down to size:

■ In Explorer, drag a folder or file and drop it inside the DOS window. Windows 98 pastes the name of the folder or file to the end of the command line.

■ Create application-specific and document-specific paths, as described in Chapter 13, "A Few Good Hacks: Some Useful Registry Tweaks."

■ If you're trying to run a DOS application that resides in a folder with a long name, add the folder to the PATH. This technique lets you run programs from the folder without having to specify the full pathname. (I talk about this in more detail in the next section.)

■ Use the SUBST command to substitute a virtual drive letter for a long pathname. For example, the following command substitutes drive E for the path C:\Windows\Start Menu\Programs\Accessories:

```
subst e: "C:\Windows\Start Menu\Programs\Accessories"
```

Changing Folders Faster

You probably know by now that you use the CD (change directory) command to change to a different folder on the current drive. However, DOS has always had a couple of short forms you can use to save time, and Windows 98 has added a few more.

Both DOS and Windows 98 use the dot symbol (.) to represent the current folder, and the double-dot symbol (..) to represent its parent folder. Windows 98 adds even more symbols: The triple-dot (...) represents the grandparent folder (two levels up), the quadruple-dot (....) represents the great-grandparent folder (three levels up), and so on.

Let's try to make this more concrete. Suppose that the current folder is C:\ANIMAL\ MAMMAL\DOLPHIN. You can combine the CD command and the dot notation to jump immediately to any of this folder's parent folders, as shown in Table 23.1.

Table 23.1. Combining the CD command with dot notation.

Current Folder	Command	New Folder
C:\ANIMAL\MAMMAL\DOLPHIN	CD..	C:\ANIMAL\MAMMAL
C:\ANIMAL\MAMMAL\DOLPHIN	CD...	C:\ANIMAL
C:\ANIMAL\MAMMAL\DOLPHIN	CD....	C:\
C:\ANIMAL\MAMMAL\DOLPHIN	CD..\BABOON	C:\ANIMAL\MAMMAL\BABOON

Starting Applications from the DOS Prompt

The DOS prompt isn't just for running DOS commands. You can also use it to start applications, as described in the next two sections.

Starting DOS Applications

For DOS applications, you need to either change to the drive and folder where the program resides and enter the executable file's primary name from there, or enter the executable file's full pathname from the current folder. There are two situations in which you don't have to change folders or use the full pathname:

- If the program's executable file is in the current folder
- If the folder in which the program's executable file resides is part of the PATH statement

If you enter only the primary name of an executable file, DOS first searches the current folder for a file that combines your primary name with an extension of either .COM, .EXE, or .BAT. If it doesn't find such a file, it searches the folders listed in the PATH statement. Recall that the PATH statement is a series of folder names separated by semicolons (;). The default PATH for a virtual DOS machine is this:

```
C:\WINDOWS;C:\WINDOWS\COMMAND
```

This is stored in an environment variable called PATH, so you can easily add new folders to the PATH right from the command prompt. For example, suppose you have a DOS program that resides in the C:\Program Files\Dosapp folder. To start the program without having to change folders or specify the pathname, use the following command to add this folder to the PATH statement (%path% represents the PATH environment variable):

```
set path=%path%;"c:\program files\dosapp"
```

Starting Windows Applications

The big news about starting programs from the DOS prompt is that you can also start Windows applications, launch documents, and even open folder windows. As with DOS programs, you start a Windows application by entering the name of its executable file.

This works fine if the executable file resides in the main Windows 98 folder, because that folder is part of the PATH. But most Windows 98 applications (and even some Windows 98 accessories) store their files in a separate folder and don't modify the PATH to point to these folders. Instead, as you learned in Chapter 13, the Registry has an AppPaths key that tells Windows 98 where to find an application's files. The DOS virtual machine can't use the Registry-based application paths directly, but there's a new Windows 98 DOS command that can. This command is called START, and it uses the following syntax:

```
start [/m ¦ /max ¦ /r] [/w] filename parameters
```

/m	Starts the application minimized.
/max	Starts the application maximized.
/r	Starts the application in its restored window (this is the default).
/w	Waits until the program has finished before returning to DOS.
filename	Specifies the name of the executable file or document. If you enter a document name, be sure to include the extension so that Windows 98 can figure out the file type.
parameters	Specifies options or switches that modify the operation of the program.

When you use START to launch a program, Windows 98 checks not only the current folder and the PATH, but also the Registry. For the Registry, Windows 98 looks for an AppPaths setting or a file type (if you entered the name of a document). For example, if you type wordpad and press Enter at the DOS prompt, you get a Bad command or file name error (unless you happen to be in the \Program Files\Accessories folder). If, however, you enter start wordpad, WordPad launches successfully.

The START command is also useful for opening folder windows. For example, you can open a window for the current folder by entering the following command (recall that the dot symbol represents the current folder):

start .

Similarly, the following command opens a window for the C:\Windows\Start Menu folder:

start "c:\windows\start menu"

USE THE /W SWITCH TO PAUSE BATCH FILES

The START command's /W switch is useful in batch files. If you launch a program from within a batch file by using START /W, the batch file pauses while the program runs. This lets you, for example, test for some condition (such as an ERRORLEVEL code) after the program has completed its work.

Sharing Data Between DOS and Windows Applications

DOS programs don't know about the Clipboard, so they don't support the standard cut, copy, and paste techniques. However, there are methods you can use to share data between DOS and Windows applications. I spell them out in the next few sections.

Copying Text from a DOS Application

The best way to copy text from a DOS application is to place the program in a window and highlight the text you want. The following procedure takes you through the required steps:

1. Switch to the DOS application and place it in a window (if it isn't already) by pressing Alt+Enter.

SWITCH TO TEXT MODE

If the DOS application has a graphics mode, copying a section of the screen will copy a graphic image of the text, not the text itself. If you want text only, make sure the program is running in character mode before you continue.

2. Make sure the text you want to copy is visible onscreen.

3. Use any of the following techniques to put the window into *select* mode:

   ■ Pull down the window's control menu and select Edit I Mark.

   ■ Right-click the title bar and select Edit I Mark from the context menu.

   ■ Click the Mark button on the toolbar.

4. Use the mouse or keyboard to select the data you want to copy, as shown in Figure 23.7.

FIGURE 23.7.
A DOS program with selected text.

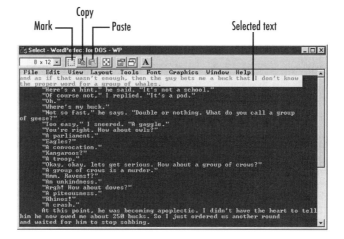

Mark ——— Copy ——— Paste ——— Selected text

5. Use any of the following techniques to copy the selected data to the Clipboard:

   ■ Pull down the window's control menu and select Edit I Copy.

   ■ Right-click the title bar and select Edit I Copy from the context menu.

   ■ Press Enter.

   ■ Click the Copy button on the toolbar.

6. Switch to the Windows application you want to use as the destination and position the insertion point where you want the copied data to appear.

7. Select Edit I Paste.

USING QUICKEDIT

If you have a lot of text to copy, you might find it easier to activate Windows 98's QuickEdit option. QuickEdit leaves the DOS window in select mode permanently so that you can select text anytime you like. (The downside, however, is that you can no longer use the mouse to manipulate the DOS program itself.) To enable QuickEdit, open the properties sheet for the DOS program, display the Misc tab, and activate the QuickEdit check box.

COPYING TEXT FULL-SCREEN

If the DOS program is running full-screen instead of in a window, you can still copy text. Pressing the Print Screen key sends all the window text—menu names, status bar text, and all—to the Clipboard.

Pasting Text to a DOS Application

If you've sent some text to the Clipboard from a Windows application (or even from another DOS application, for that matter), it's possible to copy the text into a DOS program. Make sure you've positioned the DOS program's cursor appropriately and then use any of the following techniques:

- Pull down the window's control menu and select Edit | Paste.
- Right-click the title bar and select Edit | Paste from the context menu.
- Click the Paste button on the toolbar.

TROUBLESHOOTING: YOU HAVE PROBLEMS PASTING TEXT TO DOS

You might encounter problems pasting text from the Clipboard to your DOS program. For example, you might see garbage characters, or some characters might be missing. This probably means that Windows 98 is sending the characters too fast, and the DOS program can't handle the onslaught. To solve this problem, open the DOS program's properties sheet, select the Misc tab, and deactivate the Fast pasting check box. This tells Windows 98 to hold its horses and send the characters at a slower rate.

Sharing Graphics Between DOS and Windows

Unlike with Windows-to-Windows transfers, there's no clean way to transfer graphics between Windows and DOS.

If you have a DOS graphic you'd like to place on the Clipboard, display the program in a window, adjust the window so that the image is visible, and then press Alt+Print Screen. Windows 98 will copy an image of the entire window to the Clipboard. You could then paste this image into a graphics program and remove the extraneous data.

Unfortunately, the Clipboard can't handle graphics transfers from a Windows application to a DOS program. Your only choice here is to save the image in a graphics format that the DOS program understands and then open this file in the DOS program.

Customizing the DOS Window

If you figure you'll be spending a reasonable amount of time lounging around the DOS prompt, you'll want to configure the DOS window so that you're comfortable with how it works and how it's displayed. The next few sections take you through the various options available for giving DOS a makeover. Note that although I'll be using COMMAND.COM and its MS-DOS Prompt window as an example, each technique I'll be discussing is available for any DOS program.

DOS Properties

A DOS program, like any Windows 98 object, has various properties you can manipulate to fine-tune how the program works. To display the properties sheet for a DOS program, you have three choices:

■ In Explorer, highlight the program's executable file and select File | Properties, or right-click the file and select Properties.

■ While the program's DOS window is open, click the Properties button in the toolbar (see Figure 23.8) or right-click the title bar and select Properties. (If you can't see the toolbar, right-click the title bar and activate the Toolbar command.)

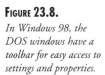

FIGURE 23.8.

In Windows 98, the DOS windows have a toolbar for easy access to settings and properties.

Full screen

Properties —— —— Font drop-down list

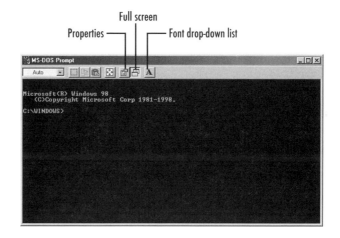

■ If the program's DOS window is open, you can get to the properties sheet from the keyboard by pressing Alt+Spacebar and selecting Properties from the control menu that appears.

TOGGLING BETWEEN FULL SCREEN AND A WINDOW

Most of the properties I'll be talking about affect the DOS program only while it's running in a window. If your program is running full-screen, press Alt+Enter to place it in a window. To change back to full-screen mode, press Alt+Enter again or click the Full Screen button in the toolbar.

Setting Program Properties

The Program tab, shown in Figure 23.9, contains various settings that control the startup and shutdown of the DOS program. The untitled text box at the top of the dialog box specifies the text that appears in the DOS window's title bar.

FIGURE 23.9.

Use the Program tab to set various properties for the DOS program's startup.

Here's a rundown of the rest of the options:

Cmd line: This text box specifies the pathname of the program's executable file. As you saw earlier, you can use this text box to add parameters and switches to modify how the program starts.

Working: Use this text box to set the application's default folder.

Batch file: This text box specifies a batch file or command to run before starting the program. This is useful for copying files, setting environment variables, changing the PATH, or loading memory-resident programs.

LOAD DOSKEY FOR THE MS-DOS PROMPT

The DOSKEY command lets you recall previous commands, edit the current command line, and create macros (multiple commands that run with a single command). To make this highly useful command available all the time in your MS-DOS prompt sessions, include the DOSKEY command in the Batch file text box of the COMMAND.COM properties sheet.

Shortcut key: Use this text box to assign a key combination to the DOS program. For launching the program, this key combination seems to work only if you create a shortcut for the program on the desktop. When the program is running, however, you can use the key combination to switch to the program quickly.

The default key combo is Ctrl+Alt+*character*, in which *character* is any keyboard character you press while this text box has the focus. If you prefer a key combination that begins with Ctrl+Shift, hold down both Ctrl and Shift and then press a character; for a Ctrl+Alt+Shift combination, hold down all three keys and press a character.

Run: If the shortcut starts an application, this drop-down list determines how the application window appears. Select Normal window, Minimized, or Maximized.

Close on exit: When you activate this check box, the DOS window closes when the program is complete. This is useful for batch files and other programs that leave the DOS window onscreen when they're done.

Advanced: This button displays a dialog box that controls various MS-DOS mode settings. I discuss these options later in this chapter (see "Running a Program in MS-DOS Mode").

Change Icon: Use this command button to assign a different icon to the program's PIF. Clicking this button displays the Change Icon dialog box.

23

DOS ISN'T DEAD:
UNLEASHING THE
DOS SHELL

Changing the DOS Window's Font Size

The font size Windows 98 uses to display text in a DOS window isn't set in stone. You're free to make the font size larger or smaller, depending on your tastes. You can adjust the size of the DOS text font in three ways:

- Select a font size from the toolbar's Font drop-down list.
- Set the font to Auto and resize the window.
- Use the program's properties sheet.

Selecting a Font Size

The easiest way to select a different font size is to use the Font drop-down list in the DOS window's toolbar. This box lists the available sizes, from 2×4 to 12×22. (The numbers represent the size of each character in the font, in pixels. The first number is the width and the second number is the height.) Windows 98 adjusts the size of the window to compensate for the new font size.

Adjusting the Size of the DOS Window

As you saw in the preceding section, Windows 98 adjusts the size of the DOS window to suit the size of the selected font. DOS windows are also sizable by hand (unlike in Windows 3.*x*). You can use the mouse to drag a border to a different location and thus resize the window.

If you select Auto from the Font drop-down list, Windows 98 compensates for the new window size by scaling the DOS text font accordingly: If you make the window smaller, the font shrinks; if you make the window larger, the font increases to compensate.

Don't expect to be able to size DOS windows as smoothly as regular windows, however. Because Windows 98 must constantly recalculate font sizes, your border dragging will occur in fits and starts. In fact, Windows 98 will often get "stuck" on a window size, and no amount of border dragging will adjust the window size. In these situations, you usually find that the lower-right corner still works, so you can use it to readjust the window and get Windows "unstuck." Also note that you won't be able to size a DOS window if it's maximized.

Setting Font Properties

Another way to select a specific font size is to use the Font tab on the DOS program's properties sheet, shown in Figure 23.10. Use the Font size list to select the font you want to use (or Auto). The Window preview area shows you how the new DOS window will appear, and the Font preview area shows you the font size you get.

FIGURE 23.10.

Use the Font tab to select the font size to use in the DOS window.

To narrow down the list of fonts, you can use the options in the Available types group:

> **Bitmap only:** Activate this option to display only the bitmap fonts in the Font size list. These are Terminal fonts, and they're the ones that don't have any symbol to the left of the font size (for example, 4 × 6).

> **TrueType only:** Activate this option to display only the TrueType fonts in the Font size list. These are Courier New fonts, and they're the ones that have the double-T symbol to the left of the font size (for example, 6 × 12).

Both font types: Activate this option to show both the bitmap and the TrueType fonts in the Font size list.

Setting Screen Properties

The properties sheet for a DOS program also includes a Screen tab, shown in Figure 23.11, that controls various aspects of the program's display.

FIGURE 23.11.

Use the Screen tab to control the appearance of the DOS program.

Here are your options:

Usage: The Full-screen and Window options determine whether the DOS program starts full-screen or in a window. The Initial size drop-down list determines the number of screen lines that appear (25, 43, or 50). This setting doesn't take effect until you restart the program.

Display toolbar: When this check box is activated, Windows 98 displays the DOS window toolbar automatically.

Restore settings on startup: When this check box is activated, Windows 98 remembers the last window position and size and restores them the next time you run the program. If you deactivate this check box, Windows 98 just uses the original settings the next time you start the program; any adjustments you make in the current session are ignored.

Fast ROM emulation: When this check box is activated, Windows 98 uses the video display VxDs to reproduce (or *emulate*) the video services (that is, writing text to the screen) that are normally the province of the ROM BIOS functions. These RAM-based VxDs are faster, so the overall performance of the DOS program's display is improved. However, if the program expects to use nonstandard ROM calls, you might see garbage characters onscreen. If so, deactivate this check box.

Dynamic memory allocation: Some DOS programs (such as WordPerfect) can operate in both text and graphics modes, but the latter requires more memory. When this check box is activated, the Virtual Memory Manager supplies memory to the program as required by the program's current mode. If you run the program in graphics mode, the VMM allocates more memory to the virtual DOS machine; if you switch the program to text mode, the VMM reduces the memory allocated to the DOS machine, which makes more memory available to other applications. If you find that your program hangs when you switch to graphics mode, it could be that the VMM can't allocate enough memory to handle the new mode. In this case, you should deactivate the Dynamic memory allocation check box to force the VMM to always supply the program with enough memory to run in graphics mode.

Some Miscellaneous Properties

To complete our look at DOS customization, let's turn our attention to the Misc tab of the DOS program properties sheet, shown in Figure 23.12. This tab contains a grab bag of options that cover a whole host of otherwise unrelated properties.

FIGURE 23.12.

The Misc tab contains an assortment of controls for customizing a DOS program.

Here's a summary of what each control contributes to the DOS program:

Allow screen saver: When this check box is turned on, Windows 98 allows your Windows screen saver to kick in while you're using the DOS program (that is, when the DOS program is in the foreground). This is probably safe for most DOS programs, but if you find that the screen saver is causing your program to hang or is causing the program's graphics to go batty, you should deactivate this check box. You should definitely clear this check box if you're using a terminal emulation program or a communications program.

QuickEdit: When this check box is active, you can select DOS text with the mouse. I explained how this works earlier in this chapter.

Exclusive mode: If you check this option, Windows 98 offers the DOS program exclusive use of the mouse. This means that the mouse will work only while you use the DOS program; it won't be available in Windows 98. You should activate this check box only if the mouse otherwise won't work in the DOS program.

Always suspend: When you activate this check box, Windows 98 doesn't supply any CPU time to a running DOS program that doesn't have the focus. (Such a program is said to be in the background.) If your DOS program doesn't do any background processing when you switch to another window, you should activate this check box. Doing so improves the performance of your other applications. This is also a good idea if a background DOS program interferes with your foreground applications. (For example, some DOS games can mess up the sound in your foreground window.) If, however, you're using the DOS program to download files, print documents, or perform other background chores, you should leave Always suspend unchecked.

Warn if still active: For safest operation, and to make sure that you don't lose unsaved data, you should always exit your DOS program completely before trying to close the DOS window. If you leave the Warn if still active box checked, Windows 98 displays the warning dialog box shown in Figure 23.13 if you attempt to shut down the program prematurely. You can force Windows 98 to close the program (if it has hung, for example) by clicking Yes.

FIGURE 23.13.

If the Warn if still active check box is activated, Windows 98 displays this warning if you try to close a DOS window before exiting the program.

Idle sensitivity: This slider determines how much CPU time Windows 98 devotes to the DOS program when the program is idle.

UNDERSTANDING IDLE SENSITIVITY

When it's multitasking applications, Windows 98 doles out to each running process fixed-sized chunks of processor cycles called *time slices*. Ideally, active applications get more time slices, and idle applications get fewer. How does Windows 98 know whether an application is idle? Windows applications send a message to the scheduler that specifies their current state. For example, an application might tell the scheduler that it's just waiting for user input (a keystroke or mouse click). In this case, Windows 98 will reduce the number of time slices for the application and redistribute them to other processes running in the background.

continues

continued

DOS programs are a different kettle of time-slice fish. In most cases, Windows 98 has no way of knowing the current state of a DOS program. (However, some newer DOS applications are Windows-aware and can send messages to the scheduler.) In the absence of keyboard input, Windows 98 just assumes that a DOS program is in an idle state after a predetermined amount of inactivity, and it then redirects time slices to other processes. The amount of time that Windows 98 waits before declaring a DOS program idle is called the idle sensitivity.

You can control the idle sensitivity for a DOS program by using the Idle sensitivity slider. The slider has a range between Low and High. Here's how to work with this slider:

Low Idle sensitivity: Windows 98 waits longer before declaring the DOS program idle. Use a Low setting to improve performance for DOS programs that perform background tasks. This ensures that, despite the lack of keyboard input, these tasks still get the time slices they need.

High Idle sensitivity: Windows 98 takes less time to declare a DOS application idle. If you know your DOS program does nothing in the background, using the High setting will improve the performance of your other running applications, because the scheduler will reallocate its time slices sooner.

Fast pasting: This check box controls the speed at which Windows 98 pastes information from the Clipboard to the DOS program. I discussed pasting data to DOS windows earlier in this chapter.

Windows shortcut keys: These check boxes represent various Windows 98 shortcut keys. For example, pressing Alt+Tab while working in a DOS program takes you to another open application. Your DOS program, however, might use one or more of these key combinations for its own purposes. To allow the program use of any of the shortcuts, deactivate the appropriate check boxes. Just so you know what you're giving up, here's a review of what each key combination does in Windows 98:

Alt+Tab	Cycles through the icons of the open applications
Ctrl+Esc	Opens the Start menu
Alt+PrtSc	Takes a screen shot of the active window and copies it to the Clipboard
Alt+Space	Pulls down the control menu for the active window
Alt+Esc	Cycles through the open applications, showing the entire window for each program
PrtSc	Takes a screen shot of the entire desktop and copies it to the Clipboard
Alt+Enter	Toggles a DOS program between a window and full-screen

Understanding PIFs

If you ran DOS programs under Windows 3.*x*, you probably became familiar with Program Information Files (PIFs) and the PIF Editor. A PIF is a file that's associated with a specific DOS program. Windows 3.*x* used PIFs to store various settings and options that controlled how DOS programs operated. For example, you'd use a PIF to tell Windows how much memory to allocate to a program.

PIFs are still alive and well in Windows 98, but their role has been expanded significantly. A particular PIF now contains settings for all the DOS program properties you learned about earlier in this chapter (screen options, fonts, and so on), as well as properties related to memory, environment, MS-DOS mode, and many more. (I'll talk about most of these other properties throughout the rest of this chapter.)

The PIF Editor is history. Instead, each DOS program has its own properties sheet with various tabs that contain the settings and options you can manipulate for the program. A separate DLL (`PIFMGR.DLL`) handles these properties and stores them in the program's PIF.

If the DOS program comes with its own PIF, Windows 98 uses the settings in this file to run the program. If you upgraded over Windows 3.*x*, any existing PIFs in your main Windows folder are upgraded to the Windows 98 format.

If no PIF exists for a DOS program, Windows 98 creates a PIF the first time you run the program, the first time you make a change to the executable file's properties, or if you create a shortcut for the program (the shortcut file is the PIF).

The PIF is (usually) stored in the same folder as the program's executable, and it uses the same primary name as the executable, but with a `.PIF` extension. (The only time Windows 98 doesn't create the PIF in the same folder as the executable is when you run the DOS program from a CD-ROM. Because Windows 98 can't create new files on a CD-ROM, it creates the PIF in its PIF subfolder—for example, `C:\WINDOWS\PIF`.)

23

DOS ISN'T DEAD: UNLEASHING THE DOS SHELL

ALWAYS USE PIFS TO START PROGRAMS

As soon as you have a shortcut PIF in place for a DOS program, always use the shortcut to start the program. That way, you ensure that Windows 98 uses the appropriate settings for the application (and not just its defaults).

As you learned earlier in this chapter, you can modify a DOS program's settings (and hence its PIF) by displaying the program's properties sheet.

CHOOSING PIFS

Explorer displays PIFs without an extension, even if you have the Hide file extensions for known file types check box turned off (select View | Folder Options | View tab to see this check box). You can recognize PIFs as follows:

- Look for the MS-DOS icon with the shortcut arrow. (This is assuming that you didn't change the icon in the DOS program's properties sheet.)
- If you're in Details view, look in the Type column for Shortcut to MS-DOS Program.

Running a Program in MS-DOS Mode

If you have a DOS program that resolutely refuses to run under Windows 98 (even full-screen), you may have no choice but to run the program in MS-DOS mode. One way to do this would be to reboot Windows 98 into MS-DOS mode (as described earlier in this chapter) and then run the program from the DOS prompt. In other cases, Windows 98 itself will start the program in MS-DOS mode if it determines that the program won't run in a DOS window. Alternatively, you can adjust the program's properties so that it runs in MS-DOS mode automatically. The next section shows you how to set this up.

Modifying a Program to Run in MS-DOS Mode

To make sure a program runs in MS-DOS mode, you need to configure its PIF. Here are the steps to follow:

1. In the program's properties sheet, select the Program tab.
2. Click the Advanced button. Windows 98 displays the Advanced Program Settings dialog box.
3. Activate the MS-DOS mode check box, as shown in Figure 23.14.

FIGURE 23.14.

Use this dialog box to tell Windows 98 to start a DOS program in MS-DOS mode.

4. If you activate the Warn before entering MS-DOS mode check box, Windows 98 displays the warning dialog box shown in Figure 23.15 each time you start the program.

FIGURE 23.15.

When you start the DOS program, you can have Windows 98 warn you that the system is about to switch to MS-DOS mode.

5. If you want Windows 98 to boot the DOS virtual machine using its default settings, keep the Use current MS-DOS configuration option activated. If you'd prefer to use a different environment for this program, activate the Specify a new MS-DOS configuration option. I'll explain how to specify the new configuration later in this chapter (see "Creating a Program-Specific Startup Configuration").

6. Click OK to return to the properties sheet.

7. Click OK.

> ### MS-DOS MODE DISABLES MOST PROGRAM OPTIONS
>
> When you activate the MS-DOS mode check box, all the options on the Font, Memory, Screen, and Misc tabs become unavailable. Windows 98 doesn't use any of these settings in MS-DOS mode. However, a few of the options on the Program tab remain enabled (the program title, the Cmd line text box, and the Close on exit check box).

Modifying DOSSTART.BAT

Earlier in this chapter, I showed you how to specify a batch file that runs each time you launch a DOS program. Unfortunately, when you activate the MS-DOS mode option, the Batch file text box becomes disabled. All is not lost, however: you can still run a batch file when Windows 98 reboots to MS-DOS mode. The secret is that, when Windows 98 switches to MS-DOS mode, it always looks for a batch file named DOSSTART.BAT in your main Windows 98 folder. If it finds this file, Windows 98 processes the batch commands before running the DOS program.

DOSSTART.BAT is usually (but not always) created by the Windows 98 Setup program during installation. This file is created if Setup comments any lines out of AUTOEXEC.BAT (such as the line that loads MSCDEX.EXE, the real-mode CD-ROM driver). These lines are then stored in DOSSTART.BAT. If Setup did not create this file, you can create it yourself.

However, you're free to add any extra commands you like, such as DOSKEY, real-mode device drivers (such as a mouse driver), a PATH statement, or a different PROMPT. If you'd like to run program-specific batch files, use the CALL command to run them from DOSSTART.BAT. For example, to run a batch file named DOSPROG.BAT, you add the following command to DOSSTART.BAT:

```
CALL DOSPROG.BAT
```

Troubleshooting MS-DOS Mode

MS-DOS mode is Windows 98 at its simplest, so not a whole lot can go wrong. Most of the problems you might encounter are related to the DOS program's not liking something about the default environment that Windows 98 uses for MS-DOS mode. You can usually fix these kinds of difficulties by specifying custom startup files for the program, as explained in the next section. However, a few other things can go haywire in MS-DOS mode. This section tells you about these problems and shows you how to solve them.

Windows 98 doesn't restart after you quit the DOS program.

Windows 98 should restart automatically after you've finished the MS-DOS mode program. If it doesn't, type win and press Enter to restart Windows 98 by hand.

When you choose the Restart the computer in MS-DOS mode option in the Shut Down Windows dialog box and click OK, you receive the following error message:

```
Invalid COMMAND.COM
```

This error usually implies that the command line in the Exit To Dos PIF is pointing to a different version of COMMAND.COM from the one loaded in RAM (or it might be pointing to a nonexistent version of COMMAND.COM).

To solve this problem, open the properties sheet for the Exit To Dos PIF and make sure that the Cmd line text box points to the version of COMMAND.COM that exists in your main Windows 98 folder (for example, C:\WINDOWS\COMMAND.COM).

When you restart Windows 98 in MS-DOS mode, or when a program runs in MS-DOS mode with the Use Current Configuration option activated, SET statements in the DOSSTART.BAT file are ignored.

Because of the way COMMAND.COM is run when you switch to MS-DOS mode, any SET statements added to DOSSTART.BAT are ignored. If you need to run SET statements for your file, you have two choices:

- Include them in AUTOEXEC.BAT. This will make them available at startup, and Windows 98 will include them as part of its default DOS environment.
- If you want the SET statements to apply only to a specific program, you need to create a custom AUTOEXEC.BAT file for that program (as explained in the next section) and include the SET statements in this custom AUTOEXEC.BAT.

There is no DOSSTART.BAT file in your main Windows 98 folder.

If you installed Windows 98 on a clean system, you might not have had an AUTOEXEC.BAT file. In this case, you might not find DOSSTART.BAT in your main Windows 98 folder. That's okay, though. You can always use Notepad to create it from scratch.

Creating a Program-Specific Startup Configuration

DOS was never a one-size-fits-all operating system. Every program had its own unique combination of device drivers, memory requirements, environment variables, and settings. Trying to satisfy all your programs' needs was time-consuming, frustrating, and, sad to say, only rarely successful. Things improved a little when DOS 6 introduced the Startup menu, which let you execute lines in CONFIG.SYS and AUTOEXEC.BAT conditionally (that is, based on the menu item you selected at startup). Unfortunately, the resulting configuration files were usually hideously complex and could be irreparably damaged by brain-dead installation programs that couldn't figure out the new structure.

Happily, Windows 98 does away with all that poppycock. You can now create custom CONFIG.SYS and AUTOEXEC.BAT files for each of the programs that you want to run in MS-DOS mode. This lets you specify only those drivers and settings that are needed by the program, thus immeasurably simplifying the configuration process (and improving the chances that your program will run successfully and reliably).

Specifying Custom CONFIG.SYS and AUTOEXEC.BAT Files

To set up your custom CONFIG.SYS and AUTOEXEC.BAT files, display the properties sheet for the program, select the Program tab, and click the Advanced button. In the Advanced Program Settings dialog box, shown in Figure 23.16, activate the Specify a new MS-DOS configuration option. The two boxes below this option become enabled:

> **CONFIG.SYS for MS-DOS mode:** This box shows the default commands used in the custom CONFIG.SYS file.
>
> **AUTOEXEC.BAT for MS-DOS mode:** This box shows the default commands used in the custom AUTOEXEC.BAT file.

CUSTOM COMMAND PROMPT CONFIGURATION

If you want to create custom CONFIG.SYS and AUTOEXEC.BAT files for the Restart the computer in MS-DOS mode? option (found in the Shut Down Windows dialog box), modify the properties for the Exit To Dos PIF.

FIGURE 23.16.

You can create custom
CONFIG.SYS *and*
AUTOEXEC.BAT *files for*
each of your MS-DOS–
mode DOS programs.

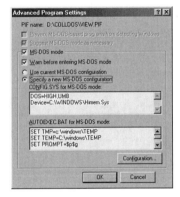

Feel free to modify these lines and add new lines as needed. Before you do, however, you might want to try the Configuration button. It displays the Select MS-DOS Configuration Options dialog box, shown in Figure 23.17. (If you've already made changes to the CONFIG.SYS and AUTOEXEC.BAT files, Windows 98 will display a warning dialog box to tell you that your changes will be overwritten. If you still want to proceed, click Yes.)

FIGURE 23.17.

Use this dialog box to
choose the CONFIG.SYS
and AUTOEXEC.BAT
settings you want to
include in your custom
configuration.

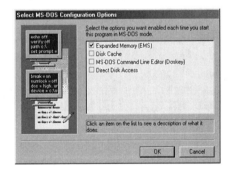

This dialog box presents a list of common items that appear in CONFIG.SYS and AUTOEXEC.BAT. The items you see depend on your system and on the DOS program, but the ones listed next are the most common (I'm assuming that the default Windows 98 folder is C:\WINDOWS):

Expanded Memory (EMS): The DOS memory manager (EMM386), which provides access to upper memory blocks (UMBs) as well as expanded memory. Activating this check box adds the following line to CONFIG.SYS:

```
DEVICEHIGH=C:\WINDOWS\EMM386.EXE
```

Disk Cache: The real-mode SMARTDrive disk cache. If your DOS program can take advantage of a disk cache, activating this check box is a must if you want top performance. (I explain how disk caches work in Chapter 9, "Performance Tuning: Optimizing Memory and Disk Access.") Activating this check box adds the following line to AUTOEXEC.BAT:

```
LOADHIGH C:\WINDOWS\SMARTDRV
```

MS-DOS Command Line Editor (Doskey): The DOSKEY command-line editor. Activating this check box adds the following line to AUTOEXEC.BAT:

LOADHIGH C:\WINDOWS\COMMAND\DOSKEY

Direct Disk Access: The LOCK command, which lets programs work with disk data structures directly. Activating this check box adds the following line to AUTOEXEC.BAT:

LOCK

USE LOCK ONLY WHEN NECESSARY

Add the LOCK command only if you're sure the program requires direct access to the disk. Many DOS programs might get confused by the extra directory entries that Windows 98 uses to track long filenames, and, given direct disk access, they might end up destroying some of your long names. Most DOS programs don't require direct disk access, so you can usually leave this option unchecked.

Note that for SMARTDrive and DOSKEY, the LOADHIGH command is added to the line only if you also included EMM386 in CONFIG.SYS. (I talk more about EMM386, LOADHIGH, upper memory blocks, and other memory optimization techniques later in this chapter.)

Activate the check boxes for the settings you want and then click OK to return to the Advanced Program Settings dialog box. You can now make any extra adjustments you need to the new settings. For example, if you know your DOS program doesn't use expanded memory, you can save an extra 64KB in the upper memory area by adding the NOEMS parameter to EMM386, like so:

DEVICEHIGH=C:\WINDOWS\EMM386.EXE NOEMS

When you're done, click OK to return to the properties sheet.

ADDING A STARTUP BATCH FILE

When you specify custom CONFIG.SYS and AUTOEXEC.BAT files, the Batch file text box on the Program tab becomes available. If you enter the pathname of a batch file in this text box, Windows 98 runs the file after it has processed the custom CONFIG.SYS and AUTOEXEC.BAT files.

ACCESSING YOUR CD-ROM DRIVE IN MS-DOS MODE

If you want access to your CD-ROM drive while in MS-DOS mode, make sure you add your CD-ROM's real-mode drivers to CONFIG.SYS and MSCDEX.EXE to AUTOEXEC.BAT. See Chapter 17, "Wielding the Windows 98 System Tools," for the details.

23

DOS ISN'T DEAD: UNLEASHING THE DOS SHELL

What Happens When You Run the Program

When you configure a DOS program to use custom CONFIG.SYS and AUTOEXEC.BAT files, Windows 98 goes through a much more elaborate process to run the program in MS-DOS mode.

When you start the program, Windows 98 first goes through the usual MS-DOS mode routine: shutting down programs, unloading device drivers, and so on. It then renames the current CONFIG.SYS and AUTOEXEC.BAT files to CONFIG.WOS and AUTOEXEC.WOS (the .WOS extension stands for, presumably, Windows Operating System). Then Windows 98 creates the new CONFIG.SYS and AUTOEXEC.BAT files for the DOS program.

For CONFIG.SYS, it takes the lines you specified in the Advanced Program Settings dialog box and tacks on one more line at the beginning:

```
DOS=SINGLE
```

This is the signal for your computer to reboot in MS-DOS mode. For AUTOEXEC.BAT, Windows 98 uses the lines you specified in the Advanced Program Settings dialog box and appends the following lines to the end:

```
REM
REM The following lines have been created by Windows. Do not modify them.
REM
drive:
CD \folder
CALL program
C:\WINDOWS\WIN.COM [/W ¦ /WX]
```

drive, *folder*, and *program* are the drive letter, folder name, and filename, respectively, of the DOS program's executable file. I explain the WIN.COM switches in a moment.

Windows 98 then performs a cold reboot of your system. After the computer's power-on self test (POST) is complete, you see the following message:

```
Windows 98 is now starting your MS-DOS-based program.
```

The system then processes the new CONFIG.SYS and AUTOEXEC.BAT files. In particular, the AUTOEXEC.BAT file changes to the drive and folder where the executable file resides, and then it uses the CALL command to run the file.

When you're done with the program, the last line of AUTOEXEC.BAT is executed. This line runs WIN.COM with either the /W switch or the /WX switch. Both switches tell Windows 98 to restore CONFIG.SYS from CONFIG.WOS and AUTOEXEC.BAT from AUTOEXEC.WOS. The difference is in how Windows 98 restarts.

Windows 98 uses the /W switch if the Close on exit check box (found on the Program tab of the DOS program's properties sheet) is deactivated. In this case, Windows 98 displays the following prompt:

```
Press any key to continue...
```

When you press a key, Windows 98 restarts.

Windows 98 uses the /WX switch if the Close on exit check box is activated. In this case, Windows 98 restarts immediately.

USE MS-DOS MODE TO DUAL-BOOT WITH WINDOWS 3.*X*

If you have Windows 3.x in a separate folder, you can dual-boot between the two systems. Instead of booting to Windows 3.x via the Startup menu, however, you can do it directly from Windows 98. Just create a new shortcut PIF for the Windows 3.x version of WIN.COM and set it to run in MS-DOS mode. For best performance, you'll probably want to create custom CONFIG.SYS and AUTOEXEC.BAT files. In AUTOEXEC.BAT, make the following adjustments:

- ■ Include the SMARTDrive disk cache.
- ■ Adjust the PATH statement to include the Windows 3.x folder.
- ■ Add the command NET START if you are starting Windows for Workgroups in a networked environment.

Optimizing Memory for DOS Applications

If you run only Windows applications, especially 32-bit applications, you may never have to worry about memory. More accurately, you might worry about the total amount of memory in your system (the more, the merrier), but you never have to worry about how that memory is managed. Windows 98's Virtual Memory Manager takes care of all the dirty work of memory paging, disk caching, and so on. (I described how this works in Chapter 9.)

This is also true for DOS programs, although to a lesser extent. As long as you run the DOS program under Windows 98 (either in a window or full-screen), the Virtual Memory Manager will still take care of the virtual memory supplied to the DOS virtual machine. No matter what kind of memory the program needs—conventional, extended, expanded, or whatever—the VMM can dish it out. However, there are two ways you can manipulate memory for DOS programs run under Windows 98:

- ■ You can adjust the program's memory properties.
- ■ You can maximize the amount of conventional memory available in the DOS virtual machine.

These methods are discussed in the next two sections. Then, I'll talk about optimizing memory for programs that run in MS-DOS mode.

Adjusting Memory Properties

For DOS programs that don't run in MS-DOS mode, the properties sheet has a Memory tab that enables you to manipulate various memory-related settings used by the Virtual Memory Manager, as shown in Figure 23.18.

FIGURE 23.18.

Use the Memory tab to customize the memory usage for a DOS program.

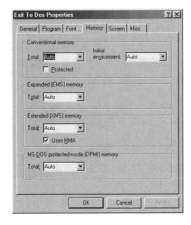

Here's a rundown of the available controls:

Conventional memory: The Total drop-down list specifies the amount of conventional memory (in kilobytes) supplied to the DOS program's virtual machine. (Recall that conventional memory is defined as the first 640KB of memory.) If you leave this value at Auto, the VMM handles the memory requirements automatically. However, it doesn't always do a good job. For example, if you run a DOS command, the VMM carves out a full 640KB of memory for the DOS virtual machine. Because most DOS commands run happily in much less, you're either wasting precious physical memory or unnecessarily paging to the swap file. You can specify a smaller value (for example, 160KB) and save memory resources. Before changing this value, check the documentation for your DOS program to find its minimum memory requirement.

Initial environment: This drop-down list specifies the size (in bytes) of the DOS environment. The environment is a small memory buffer that holds the DOS environment variables, which are settings used to control certain aspects of DOS and DOS programs. For example, the PATH, the PROMPT, and the values of all SET statements are part of the environment. If you're using the Batch file text box to run SET statements or add folders to the PATH, you might want to increase the size of the environment. You shouldn't need a value any larger than 1024 bytes.

DISPLAYING THE ENVIRONMENT

To see the contents of the environment while you're in a DOS session, type set and press Enter.

Protected: While your DOS program is running, small chunks of Windows 98 come along for the ride in the system memory area. These include IFSHLP.SYS (the real-mode file system helper) and part of VMM32 (the Virtual Memory Manager).

If the DOS program is ill-behaved, it might accidentally overwrite part of the system area and cause Windows 98 to crash. To prevent this, activate the Protected check box to write-protect the system memory area.

Expanded (EMS) memory: The Total drop-down list specifies the amount of expanded memory (in kilobytes) supplied to the program. If you know your program doesn't use expanded memory, you can set this value to None. If you set this value to Auto, Windows 98 will supply the program with whatever it needs. If you prefer to set a limit on the amount of expanded memory the program uses, select a specific value (1024KB should be plenty for most programs).

TROUBLESHOOTING: EXPANDED MEMORY SETTING IS UNAVAILABLE

If there is no Total drop-down list in the Expanded (EMS) memory group, your system isn't set up to use expanded memory. In other words, you're loading EMM386 in CONFIG.SYS with the NOEMS parameter, like so:

```
C:\WINDOWS\EMM386.EXE NOEMS
```

If you need expanded memory, you either have to delete the NOEMS parameter from CONFIG.SYS or create a custom CONFIG.SYS that doesn't include the NOEMS parameter.

Extended (XMS) memory: If your DOS program can make use of extended memory, use the Total drop-down list to specify the amount of extended memory (in kilobytes) that the VMM allocates to the program. Again, use Auto to allow the VMM to allocate extended memory automatically. However, virtual memory is mapped by the VMM as extended memory, so your programs might end up grabbing all the available virtual memory for themselves! Setting a limit of, for example, 1024KB will prevent this from happening.

Uses HMA: This check box determines whether the DOS program has access to the high memory area (HMA). The HMA is the first 64KB of extended memory. Programs can use it to load device drivers. By default, Windows 98 uses the HMA for DOS, so it's unavailable to your programs. However, you can free up the HMA by making sure your CONFIG.SYS file includes the following three lines at the top:

```
C:\WINDOWS\HIMEM.SYS
C:\WINDOWS\EMM386.EXE
DOS=UMB
```

(I'm assuming here that C:\WINDOWS is your main Windows 98 folder.) Also, feel free to add the NOEMS parameter to EMM386 if your DOS programs don't need expanded memory.

MS-DOS protected-mode (DPMI) memory: This Total drop-down list specifies the amount of DOS protected-mode memory (in kilobytes) that is supplied to the program. Use Auto to let the VMM configure this type of memory automatically.

23

DOS ISN'T DEAD: UNLEASHING THE DOS SHELL

Optimizing Conventional Memory

By itself, Windows 98 does a pretty good job of clearing out the conventional memory area. This is thanks to its protected-mode device drivers, which operate in extended memory. However, if you use any real-mode drivers or TSRs, these will reside in conventional memory. Because most DOS programs like to use conventional memory to do their thing, you have less room for these programs to operate. If things are really bad, the programs might refuse to run at all.

Upper Memory Blocks

To make sure that your DOS programs have enough memory to operate correctly, you need to optimize conventional memory by moving device drivers and other RAM interlopers into the upper memory area (the area between 640KB and 1MB). The UMA is normally the province of the BIOS and video buffers. However, it's never completely filled in. There are always gaps—called upper memory blocks (UMBs)—that aren't used by the system. You can take advantage of this fact to move device drivers out of conventional memory and into the UMBs.

A Benchmark: The MEM Command

To measure your progress, you need to have some way of determining how much memory you have available at any time. Happily, DOS provides just the tool: the MEM command. For a quick-and-dirty listing, just run MEM without any parameters. For something more detailed, use the /C switch, like so (the /P switch just pauses the output):

```
mem /c /p
```

You see a report that looks something like this:

```
Modules using memory below 1 MB:
  Name        Total          Conventional      Upper Memory
  --------    ----------     ----------         -----------
  MSDOS       17,840 (17K)   17,840 (17K)       0  (0K)
  ASPI2DOS     9,680  (9K)    9,680  (9K)       0  (0K)
  ASPICD      11,648 (11K)   11,648 (11K)       0  (0K)
  HIMEM        1,168  (1K)    1,168  (1K)       0  (0K)
  ASPI2HLP       592  (1K)      592  (1K)       0  (0K)
  IFSHLP       2,864  (3K)    2,864  (3K)       0  (0K)
  SETVER         832  (1K)      832  (1K)       0  (0K)
  WIN          3,568  (3K)    3,568  (3K)       0  (0K)
  vmm32        1,008  (1K)    1,008  (1K)       0  (0K)
  MSCDEX      41,008 (40K)   41,008 (40K)       0  (0K)
  COMMAND      7,408  (7K)    7,408  (7K)       0  (0K)
  DOSKEY       4,688  (5K)    4,688  (5K)       0  (0K)
  Free       552,896 (540K) 552,896 (540K)      0  (0K)
Memory Summary:
  Type of Memory    Total        Used         Free
  --------------    ----------   ----------   ----------
  Conventional        655,360      102,464      552,896
  Upper                     0            0            0
  Reserved            393,216      393,216            0
  Extended (XMS)   15,728,640      229,376   15,499,264
```

```
-----------------   ----------   ----------   ----------
Total memory        16,777,216      725,056   16,052,160
Total under 1 MB       655,360      102,464      552,896
Total Expanded (EMS)             16,220,160      (15M)
Free Expanded (EMS)              16,220,160      (15M)
Largest executable program size     552,880     (540K)
Largest free upper memory block           0       (0K)
MS-DOS is resident in the high memory area.
```

The report from the MEM command contains lots of information, but you can break it down into five areas:

Modules using memory below 1 MB: This is a listing of programs (modules) currently in memory—including both conventional memory and upper memory. The last line (Free) tells you how much free memory you have in both areas. Your goal is to maximize these values.

Memory Summary: This is a summary of the total memory (used plus free) for each of the five major memory areas: conventional, upper, reserved (adapter RAM/ROM), extended, and expanded.

Largest executable program size: This value tells you the largest DOS program you can run in the current setup. Increasing this number means you can load larger programs and more data.

Largest free upper memory block: To get this number, MEM scans upper memory and looks for the largest gap. This is important, because you can't load a TSR or device driver into upper memory if there is no block large enough to accommodate it.

> **YOU NEED A MEMORY MANAGER FOR UMBS**
>
> MEM reports a value of 0 for the largest UMB if no memory manager is loaded.

MS-DOS is resident in the high memory area: By default, Windows 98 loads DOS into the HMA and leaves only a 17KB MS-DOS stub behind. This saves about 60KB.

Loading Modules into Upper Memory Blocks

As you saw in the sample MEM listing just shown, a few real-mode drivers (such as ASPI2DOS.SYS, ASPICD.SYS, and MSCDEX.EXE) are usurping space in conventional memory, as well as some Windows 98 objects (such as IFSHLP.SYS and SETVER.EXE). This brings the total free space down to 540KB, which isn't enough for many DOS programs (which often require 600KB or more). To increase this number, you need to load as many device drivers as you can into UMBs.

To accomplish this, you first need to add the following lines to the top of your CONFIG.SYS file:

```
DEVICE=C:\WINDOWS\HIMEM.SYS
DEVICE=C:\WINDOWS\EMM386.EXE NOEMS
DOS=HIGH,UMB
```

USE THE RAM PARAMETER FOR EXPANDED MEMORY

If your DOS programs need expanded memory, substitute the RAM parameter for the NOEMS parameter in the EMM386.EXE line. Note, however, that this will reduce the amount of free upper memory by 64KB. This 64KB chunk is the page frame that EMM386 uses to swap data to and from expanded memory.

HIMEM.SYS is the DOS extended memory manager. EMM386.EXE is the DOS device driver that manages the upper memory area. The command DOS=HIGH,UMB loads DOS into the high memory area and tells EMM386 to make upper memory blocks available for storing device drivers and TSRs. (Why do you have to load DOS into the HMA if Windows 98 already does so? Because if you used only the command DOS=UMB, this would nullify the DOS=HIGH command that IO.SYS uses to load DOS high.)

The next step is to modify CONFIG.SYS so that, for each of your device drivers (except HIMEM.SYS and EMM386.EXE), you change the word DEVICE to DEVICEHIGH. For example, my CONFIG.SYS file used to look like this:

```
DEVICE=ASPI2DOS.SYS /D /Z
DEVICE=ASPICD.SYS /D:ASPICD0
```

Now it looks like this:

```
DEVICE=C:\WINDOWS\HIMEM.SYS
DEVICE=C:\WINDOWS\EMM386.EXE NOEMS
DOS=HIGH,UMB
DEVICEHIGH=ASPI2DOS.SYS /D /Z
DEVICEHIGH=ASPICD.SYS /D:ASPICD0
```

Finally, edit AUTOEXEC.BAT to include the word LOADHIGH (or just LH) at the beginning of each line that runs a memory-resident program:

```
LOADHIGH C:\WINDOWS\COMMAND\DOSKEY.COM
LOADHIGH C:\WINDOWS\COMMAND\MSCDEX.EXE /D:ASPICD0 /L:H /M:12 /S
```

When you've completed these steps, reboot your computer to put the changes into effect and run MEM again. Here's my new listing:

```
Modules using memory below 1 MB:
    Name        Total          Conventional      Upper Memory
    --------   --------------  --------------    ----------------
    SYSTEM     17,872  (17K)    9,984  (10K)      7,888   (8K)
    HIMEM       1,168   (1K)    1,168   (1K)          0   (0K)
    EMM386      4,320   (4K)    4,320   (4K)          0   (0K)
    WIN         3,568   (3K)    3,568   (3K)          0   (0K)
    vmm32      80,640  (79K)    1,472   (1K)     79,168  (77K)
    COMMAND     7,408   (7K)    7,408   (7K)          0   (0K)
    ASPI2DOS    9,680   (9K)        0   (0K)      9,680   (9K)
    ASPICD     11,648  (11K)        0   (0K)     11,648  (11K)
    ASPI2HLP      592   (1K)        0   (0K)        592   (1K)
    IFSHLP      2,864   (3K)        0   (0K)      2,864   (3K)
    SEIVER        832   (1K)        0   (0K)        832   (1K)
```

```
    MSCDEX     41,008   (40K)        0    (0K)     41,008   (40K)
    DOSKEY      4,688    (5K)        0    (0K)      4,688    (5K)
    Free      627,200  (613K)  627,200  (613K)          0    (0K)
Memory Summary:
    Type of Memory      Total         Used         Free
    ---------------   ----------   ----------   ----------
    Conventional         655,360       28,160      627,200
    Upper                158,368      158,368            0
    Reserved             393,216      393,216            0
    Extended (XMS)    15,570,272      140,640   15,429,632
    ---------------   ----------   ----------   ----------
    Total memory      16,777,216      720,384   16,056,832
    Total under 1 MB     813,728      186,528      627,200
    Largest executable program size            627,184   (612K)
    Largest free upper memory block                  0    (0K)
    MS-DOS is resident in the high memory area.
```

EMM386 has moved the device drivers and TSRs into upper memory, and there is now 613KB free, which is more than respectable. Notice, however, that there is no room left in upper memory. That's because VMM32 (literally) grabs whatever is left of free upper memory for its own devices. However, as you add or remove drivers in CONFIG.SYS and AUTOEXEC.BAT, VMM32 adjusts its upper memory footprint accordingly. Note, though, that you won't be able to load TSRs into upper memory from the DOS prompt.

Optimizing MS-DOS Mode Memory

To optimize memory for MS-DOS mode programs, you follow basically the same procedure I showed you in the last section. In this case, however, you can either edit the real CONFIG.SYS and AUTOEXEC.BAT files (to optimize the default MS-DOS mode environment) or your custom CONFIG.SYS and AUTOEXEC.BAT files (to optimize the environment for specific DOS programs).

Troubleshooting DOS Difficulties

This section runs through a few problems you might encounter when running DOS commands or DOS programs.

When you double-click a shortcut for an MS-DOS–based program, you receive the following error message:

```
Cannot find the file 'Path.' Make sure that the file
exists on your system and that the path and filename
are correct.
```

Shortcuts for DOS programs are stored in PIFs rather than LNK files, and the maximum length for a command line in a PIF is 62 characters. Therefore, you receive the preceding error message if the program's command line is longer than 62 characters.

You can work around this problem in several ways:

■ Add the program's folder to the PATH so that you have to enter only the executable filename in the command line.

■ Use SUBST to create a virtual drive that points to the program's folder. You can then use this virtual drive in place of the folder's path in the command line.

■ Create a batch file that launches the program and then create a shortcut for the batch file.

■ Reinstall the program to a folder with a shorter path and then create a shortcut to the new location.

While working at the DOS prompt, you can't create files with names longer than 127 characters.

By default, the DOS command line is limited to 127 characters, so you won't be able to create filenames any longer than that. (In fact, your filenames will be less than that because the total length of the command line also includes whatever command you're using.)

To increase the command-line character limit, use the /U switch with COMMAND.COM. For example, the following line increases the maximum number of characters in a command line to 250:

```
c:\windows\command.com /u:250
```

You can use this switch while you're opening a DOS session or while you're running a command. To make this change available to all DOS virtual machines, enter the following line in CONFIG.SYS:

```
shell=c:\windows\command.com /u:250
```

When you restart your computer, you receive the following error message:

```
Bad or missing Command Interpreter
Enter name of Command Interpreter (for example, C:\Windows\Command.com)
```

This error message indicates that COMMAND.COM is missing or has become corrupted. If you've moved COMMAND.COM from the main Windows 98 folder, you need to restore it. Otherwise, reboot your system with the Windows 98 Startup disk in drive A. When you get to the A:\ prompt, enter the following command:

```
sys c:
```

If drive C is compressed, however, you must use the SYS command on the host drive. For example, if the host drive is drive H, use the following command instead:

```
sys h:
```

When that's done, remove the Startup disk and reboot the computer.

While using the standard VGA driver, your computer hangs when you start a DOS session.

This problem indicates that the video adapter in your system requires special support to run an MS-DOS command-prompt session reliably. Some video adapters require special support in Windows 98 to run DOS sessions without hanging. This support is installed when you use the correct driver for the display adapter. If you use the standard VGA video driver, however, Windows 98 doesn't install any adapter-specific support.

If you want to run a standard display type (640×480 or 800×600 resolution with 16 colors), you should select the proper video driver for the video adapter installed in your computer rather than the standard VGA driver.

The COPY command incorrectly copies files with plus signs (+) in their names.

The COPY command has a little-known property called concatenation that lets you combine two or more files into a third file. For example, suppose that you have three files named JAN.TXT, FEB.TXT, and MAR.TXT. You can combine all three files into a single file named 1STQTR.TXT by using the following command:

```
copy jan.txt+feb.txt+mar.txt 1stqtr.txt
```

When COMMAND.COM sees a plus sign in a COPY command, it concatenates the files. If you have a plus sign in a filename, therefore, COMMAND.COM assumes that you're trying to concatenate. For example, consider the following command:

```
copy black+white.txt gray.txt
```

Here, you're trying to copy the file named BLACK+WHITE.TXT to the file GRAY.TXT. But COMMAND.COM thinks you're trying to concatenate two files—BLACK and WHITE.TXT—into GRAY.TXT. To make your intentions clear, enclose the file with the plus sign in quotation marks, like so:

```
copy "black+white.txt" gray.txt
```

Files with long names aren't copied when you use the XCOPY command.

First, make sure that you're not in MS-DOS mode. If you're not, display the properties sheet for the DOS prompt, activate the Program tab, and click the Advanced button to display the Advanced Program Settings dialog box. Deactivate the Prevent MS-DOS–based programs from detecting Windows check box and click OK.

I talked about the other options in the Advanced Program Settings dialog box in the earlier section "Running a Program in MS-DOS Mode."

When you use the MORE command with a document that has a long filename, you receive the following error message:

```
Invalid file name in command line
```

Unfortunately, the MORE command doesn't support long filenames. If you need to use MORE, either specify the 8.3 alias for the file or use a redirection symbol to display the file. For example, to display the file named long Filename.txt and pause the output after each screenful, use the following command:

```
more < "long filename.txt"
```

23

DOS ISN'T DEAD:
UNLEASHING THE
DOS SHELL

You can't move or resize a DOS window with the mouse.

If you can't use the mouse to drag a DOS window's title bar or borders, the DOS application likely is using the mouse in exclusive mode. As you learned earlier, this means that only the DOS program can use the mouse. Because the title bar and borders are part of Windows 98, they're off-limits.

To turn off exclusive mode, press Alt+Spacebar to pull down the DOS window's control menu, and select the Properties command. When the program's properties sheet appears, you have your mouse pointer back. Head for the Misc tab, and deactivate the Exclusive mode check box in the Mouse group. The mouse is now available to Windows 98. Click OK and then move or resize the window.

Summary

This chapter showed you a few techniques for working with the DOS shell. You learned various methods for starting DOS sessions and running commands. At the DOS prompt, I showed you how to work with long filenames, start programs (including Windows applications), undelete files, and customize the DOS screen. I also showed you how to optimize DOS applications under Windows 98. After some introductory remarks about PIFs, I showed you how to set up a DOS program to run in MS-DOS mode. Then you learned how to really leverage MS-DOS mode by creating custom CONFIG.SYS and AUTOEXEC.BAT files for each program. I then took you through a conventional memory optimization session.

Here are a few places to go in this book for more DOS data:

- I showed you how to install and uninstall DOS programs in Chapter 18, "The Ins and Outs of Installing and Uninstalling Programs."

- Windows 98 has a couple of DOS TCP/IP utilities. I tell you about them in Chapter 31, "Implementing TCP/IP for Internet and Intranet Connections."

- Windows 98 also has a few Internet-related DOS commands. I cover those in Chapter 32, "Windows 98 and the Internet."

Unleashing Multimedia: The Sights and Sounds of Windows 98

V

PART

DirectX and
Windows 98 Video

CHAPTER 24

IN THIS CHAPTER

> *The essential is to excite the spectators. If that means playing Hamlet on a flying trapeze or in an aquarium, you do it.*
>
> —*Orson Welles*

The English language is a veritable factory of new words and phrases. Inventive wordsmiths in all fields are constantly forging new additions to the lexicon by blending words, attaching morphemic tidbits to existing words, and creating neologisms out of thin air. Some of these new words strike a chord in popular culture and go through what I call the "cachet-to-cliché" syndrome. In other words, the word is suddenly on the lips of cocktail party participants and water-cooler conversationalists everywhere, and on the fingertips of countless columnists and editorialists. As soon as the word takes root, however, the backlash begins. Rants of the if-I-hear-the-word-*x*-one-more-time-I'll-scream variety start to appear, the Unicorn Society includes the word in its annual list of phrases that should be stricken from the language, and so on.

The word *multimedia* went through this riches-to-rags scenario a couple of years ago. Buoyed by the promise of media-rich interactive applications and games, techies and non-techies alike quickly made multimedia their favorite buzzword. It didn't take long, however, for the bloom to come off the multimedia rose.

Part of the problem was that when multimedia first became a big deal in the early '90s, the average computer just wasn't powerful enough to handle the extra demands made on the system. Not only that, but Windows' support for multimedia was sporadic and half-hearted. That's all changed now, however. The typical PC sold today has more than enough horsepower to handle basic multimedia, and Windows 98 has a number of slick new features that let developers and end-users alike incorporate multimedia seamlessly into their work. So now, instead of railing uselessly against overuse of the word *multimedia,* people can get down to the more practical matter of creating exciting multimedia-based documents.

This chapter kicks off your look at Windows 98 multimedia by focusing on two important multimedia components: DirectX and digital video.

Windows 98 and Multimedia

Over the years, advances in multimedia software technology have coincided with advances in multimedia hardware technology. Graphics accelerator boards, 16-bit audio cards, increasingly fast CD-ROM drives, video capture cards, and local bus technologies all served to make the PC an attractive multimedia platform.

However, Windows-based multimedia suffered from two glaring problems:

- All this new hardware was still difficult to set up, thanks to the rigors of setting IRQs and other configuration parameters.
- Except for the basic multimedia subsystem included in Windows 3.1, Microsoft relied on third-party developers, OEMs, and end-users to implement, distribute, and install new features.

Windows 95 solved these problems by making it easier to install and upgrade hardware and by incorporating all key multimedia technologies in the base operating system. Windows 98 goes even further by adding support for streaming video, OpenGL, digital scanners and cameras, broadcast architecture, MMX chips, the USB and IEEE 1394 buses, and DVD. (See Chapter 4, "What's New and Noteworthy in Windows 98," for a complete list of the new multimedia marvels that come with Windows 98.)

In other words, Windows 98 brings together all the necessary components for a successful multimedia experience.

DirectX 5.0: The Future of Windows Multimedia

All this doesn't mean that Microsoft and the rest of the PC community are resting on their multimedia laurels. Far from it. Standards and technologies continue to evolve, and Microsoft continues to aggressively pursue its stated goal of making Windows the best platform for all types of multimedia.

To that end, Microsoft has built a new family of multimedia components that are designed to give developers unprecedented, yet controlled, access to the system hardware components that most affect multimedia performance. This new family of technologies is called *DirectX*. It was made available to developers in early 1996 as part of the Windows 95 Game Software Development Kit (which gives you an idea of who Microsoft is trying to woo with DirectX). Each DirectX component is a collection of application programming interface (API) functions that developers can call with their applications.

Windows 98 includes the latest incarnation of DirectX—DirectX 5.0—which means that all the DirectX components are now an integral part of the operating system.

To understand the DirectX 5.0 model, it helps to divide the system into four layers, as shown in Figure 24.1:

Hardware/Network Layer: This layer is where the multimedia devices reside, including graphics accelerator cards, sound cards, input devices, network pipes, and so on.

DirectX Foundation Layer: This is the layer that provides the basic multimedia services for graphics, sound, and input devices. See the next section, "The DirectX Foundation Layer."

DirectX Media Layer: This layer deals with the "media" part of multimedia. As such, it provides API functions for things such as animation and streaming audio and video. See "The DirectX Media Layer," later in this chapter.

Component Layer: This layer consists of ActiveX controls and applications that take advantage of the DirectX API function to provide multimedia services to the user. Windows 98 examples include NetMeeting, NetShow, and the ActiveMovie control.

FIGURE 24.1.

DirectX 5.0 divides the
multimedia system into
a hierarchy of four
distinct layers.

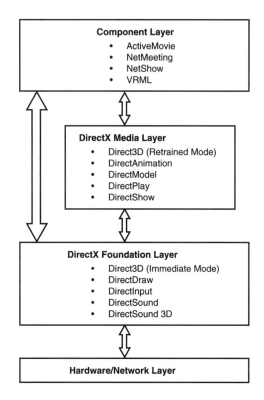

The DirectX Foundation Layer consists of the following four components:

The DirectX Foundation Layer

The DirectX Foundation Layer consists of the following four components:

- DirectDraw
- Direct3D (immediate mode)
- DirectSound and DirectSound 3D
- DirectInput

DirectDraw

DirectDraw is an API that effectively replaces the Display Control Interface that came with Windows 95. DirectDraw lets applications control display hardware directly, including today's ultra-fast 2D graphics accelerator boards. It's important to note that DirectDraw, like all DirectX technologies, isn't a set of high-level functions. Instead, it uses OLE's Component Object Model to implement a device-independent interface. Applications can use this interface to access hardware directly and thus take full advantage of the device's capabilities. DirectDraw and all the DirectX components provide this functionality without sacrificing compatibility with existing applications and drivers.

DirectDraw's mandate is to give applications consistent, safe, and extremely quick routines that provide a full range of 2D services, including bitmap composition and animation. To accomplish this, DirectDraw provides two essential features:

Direct manipulation of video display memory: In a sense, DirectDraw is a memory management utility, because it provides functions for allocating, moving, transforming, and freeing display memory.

Direct manipulation of display hardware management services: The DirectDraw hardware abstraction layer (HAL) exposes unique display hardware functionality, including stretching, overlaying, texture mapping, rotating, mirroring, and so on.

These services result in extremely fast performance, the likes of which were previously available only by using assembly language code that was fine-tuned to specific hardware.

HARDWARE ABSTRACTION AND HARDWARE EMULATION IN DIRECTX

All the DirectX APIs sit on top of a hardware abstraction layer (HAL) that insulates the developer from the specifics of a multimedia device. For example, the HAL can query a device to find out its hardware configuration and performance capabilities, thus allowing the application to tailor its feature set to match the device.

The hardware emulation layer (HEL) works alongside the HAL. In this case, though, the HEL uses software routines to emulate any features that aren't present in a particular device. This lets developers write their applications without worrying about hardware features because they know these features will be present, either physically or via emulation.

Direct3D (Immediate Mode)

Like DirectDraw, Direct3D is an OLE COM-based API. In this case, however, Direct3D is designed to deliver device-independent, highly optimized, software-based implementations of real-time 3D rendering services and enable transparent access to 3D hardware acceleration. Direct3D is based on the Reality Lab technology that Microsoft obtained when it purchased RenderMorphics in 1995.

The *immediate mode* API is a collection of routines for developers who require more control over 3D objects and scenes, and who require direct (yet device-independent) access to 3D accelerator boards (such as Creative Labs' 3D Blaster). This API makes it much easier for developers to port existing 3D applications (especially games) to the Windows 98 platform.

There is also a new Direct3D file format. This new file format makes it easy for developers to store meshes, textures, animation sets, and user-definable objects. In turn, this common format makes it easier to exchange 3D data between applications.

As with all DirectX technologies, Direct3D ensures device independence by implementing a hardware abstraction layer that insulates developers from the specifics of 3D accelerators. And a hardware emulation layer provides software-based emulation of any 3D hardware capabilities not present in the physical 3D device.

DIRECT3D VERSUS OPENGL

OpenGL is an extremely precise, high-performance 3D technology that's used mostly in high-end CAD/CAM, modeling, animation, simulation, and scientific visualization applications. OpenGL is now available to developers of Windows 98 applications, but it requires equally precise and powerful 3D hardware. So, for now, Microsoft provides two levels of 3D support: Direct3D for mainstream 3D applications and games, and OpenGL for sophisticated applications that require the highest degree of accuracy.

DirectInput

The DirectInput API provides an OLE interface that lets applications directly access analog and digital joysticks for user interaction. Extended capabilities also provide support for variations such as rudder pedals, flight yokes, steering devices, and virtual-reality headgear. Each device can use up to 6 axes of movement, a point-of-view hat, and 32 buttons.

DirectInput also supports alternative input devices that track positions with absolute coordinate systems, such as digitizing tablets, light pens, and touch screens.

DirectInput offers developers the following features:

Low-latency support: This ensures that joysticks and other "fast-twitch" game input devices maintain the fastest possible response times.

Input device querying: DirectInput can query a joystick or other device to determine its capabilities. Also, programs can process a joystick's position and button information by querying the joystick.

Support for multiple devices: DirectInput can simultaneously monitor either 2 analog joysticks that track up to 4 axes of movement and use up to 4 buttons, or 4 analog joysticks that track 2 axes of movement and use up to 4 buttons. For digital joysticks, DirectInput can support up to 16 devices, each with up to 6 axes of movement and up to 32 buttons.

DirectSound and DirectSound 3D

The DirectSound API provides an OLE interface for audio devices. This interface provides applications with the following services:

Direct access to audio devices: In the device-independent fashion of the other DirectX APIs, DirectSound hides the details of audio device specifics through its HAL and provides consistent device support by using a HEL to substitute software equivalents for audio features that might be missing from the user's hardware.

Low-latency mixing of audio streams: If an application creates two or more audio streams, DirectSound mixes these streams and writes the results to the main sound buffer (that is, the buffer that's used by the audio device to play sounds). Low latency means that the application's sound is processed without delay (technically, the delay is less than 20ms), so the user hears the sound immediately.

3D effects: DirectSound 3D enables developers to add a third dimension to their sound effects and thus "move" sounds within a simulated 3D space, create Doppler effects, and so on.

Hardware acceleration: DirectSound lets applications take full advantage of any hardware acceleration features found in the audio device.

DirectSound uses an audio device driver that has been modified by the developer to support the DirectSound HAL. (These revised audio drivers will still work with non-DirectSound applications, however.) Note that features such as low-latency mixing and hardware acceleration are available only if a DirectSound driver is present.

The DirectX Media Layer

The DirectX Media Layer consists of the following five components:

- Direct 3D (retained mode)
- DirectAnimation
- DirectModel
- DirectPlay
- DirectShow

Direct 3D (Retained Mode)

The *retained mode* API is a collection of routines that support basic, high-level 3D services, such as 3D object manipulation and 3D scene manipulation, as well as advanced services such as keyframe animation. Previously, incorporating these features into an application required sophisticated graphics programming. Now, a developer can use these features with a few simple API calls.

DirectAnimation

DirectAnimation is designed to integrate multiple media types—such as text, 2D and 3D graphics, sound, and streamed media—into a timeline format that enables animated effects. DirectAnimation is built from DirectX Foundation Layer components such as DirectDraw, DirectSound, and Direct3D.

24

DIRECTX AND
WINDOWS 98
VIDEO

The key feature of DirectAnimation is that it's implemented as both a set of API functions and as runtime control (which is included with Windows 98). Developers can use the DirectAnimation functions to build animation into ActiveX controls and applications without breaking a sweat. However, Web page authors can also add animation to their pages by inserting the runtime control.

DirectModel

DirectModel is a 3D graphics toolkit designed specifically with huge 3D models in mind. DirectModel enables scientists and engineers who work with massive 3D data sets containing millions of polygons to interact and manipulate these models in real time. DirectModel uses sophisticated geometry simplification and culling algorithms that enable it to support interactive rendering. Note that DirectModel is designed to extend existing 3D technologies such as OpenGL.

DirectPlay

The DirectPlay API is an OLE interface that simplifies connectivity between applications over communications links. Designed specifically for multiplayer games, DirectPlay gives developers an easy way to connect players either over a network or via modem. Specifically, DirectPlay lets applications connect in a way that's independent of the underlying transport hardware, network protocol, or online service. It does this by implementing a simple send/receive communications model that has been optimized for game play.

DirectShow

DirectShow (formerly ActiveMovie 2.0) enables developers to deliver high-quality audio and video streams across the Internet or a corporate intranet. As with DirectAnimation, DirectShow is implemented as both a set of API functions and as an ActiveX control (the ActiveMovie control, which is available in the Windows 98 package).

DirectShow supports all the most popular media types, including WAV and MIDI sound files and AVI, MPEG, and QuickTime video files.

Understanding Digital Video

Although other computer platforms (notably the Macintosh) could work with digital video earlier, for the Windows crowd the big moment came in 1992 with the release of Video for Windows (VfW) 1.0. As long as you installed a video capture card in your machine, you could hook up a camcorder or VCR to your computer. VfW came with a utility called VidCap that would take the incoming video, digitize it, and save the result to a file on your hard disk. You could then use VfW's VidEdit program to manipulate the digitized video frame-by-frame, just as your word processor manipulates text word-by-word.

Even if you weren't into editing video, VfW was a milestone because it came with a runtime module and driver that let anyone view digital movies created in the VfW format (AVI).

This isn't to say that VfW was a complete success, however. Hardware limitations and the sheer newness of the technology placed major limitations on the VfW file format. For one thing, the video window was restricted to a puny 160×120 pixels, making it a mere 1/16th of a basic VGA (640×480) screen. This led critics to dub VfW files "dancing postage stamps."

Another problem was that VfW playback limped along at 15 frames per second (fps), which, compared to the "full motion" rate of 30fps used by videotape, made some digital videos look jerky.

Finally, compression technology was still in its infancy, so VfW files took up huge amounts of hard disk space. Even VfW's tiny window and low frame rate still usurped almost 17MB per minute! And that figure doesn't include the audio soundtrack that was part of each VfW file, which could easily add megabytes-per-minute to the total.

VfW 1.0 was far from perfect, but most people in the industry quickly realized the massive potential for this technology. As a result, there was a flurry of activity from vendors involved in all aspects of the digital video revolution: Capture cards were beefed up with features, improved compression technology allowed more data to fit into less space, new and improved sound cards made it easier to capture the audio portion of a video, and local bus graphics let PCs keep up with the demands made on them by massive video files.

Of course, Microsoft kept improving Video for Windows itself. In 1993, VfW 1.1 was released to great fanfare. The "dancing postage stamp" was gone, replaced by a more substantial 320×240 window operating at a more-than-respectable frame rate of 24fps. (However, proving that you can't please all of the people all of the time, some killjoys were still unimpressed with VfW 1.1's achievements. They called the new quarter-screen window a "dancing credit card.")

VfW reached yet another milestone in Windows 95. Not only was VfW built into the operating system, but its 32-bit architecture and the inclusion of some of the best compressor/decompressor drivers in the business brought playback up to full screen (640×480) and full motion (30fps). Best of all, you didn't need extra hardware or some high-end graphics behemoth of a computer to get all this. Windows 95 provided excellent video quality on mainstream desktop machines (486 and higher).

In Windows 98, Microsoft has moved beyond VfW and now uses DirectShow (described earlier) to handle all its video needs.

The Various Video Formats

Video clips come in many formats, but only a few are of any interest to Windows 98 users. Here's a summary of the video formats you're likely to come across in your video travels:

> **Active Streaming Format (.ASF):** ASF is Microsoft's next-generation digital video technology. ASF allows multiple objects (such as audio objects, video objects, bitmaps, URLs, HTML pages, and programs) to be combined and stored in a single synchronized multimedia stream.

Motion Picture Experts Group (.MPG): The MPEG-1 format was designed for playback of NTSC quality video from CD-ROM–based media. It achieves extremely high compression ratios (up to 1.8Mbps) with excellent playback quality. The later MPEG-2 standard provides higher playback resolutions as well as interlacing for broadcast TV and high-definition TV.

Video for Windows (.AVI): This is the standard VfW format that was supported by Windows over the years, and it has become the standard format for Windows digital video in general. (AVI, in case you're wondering, stands for Audio Video Interleave.)

QuickTime for Windows (.MOV): QuickTime is the digital video format developed by Apple. It's the standard format for Macintosh users, but it's only recently made inroads on the Windows side of things with the release of QuickTime for Windows. The big advantage of QuickTime's MOV files is that they can be used on both Mac and Windows machines without alteration. Therefore, because so many video production houses are Mac shops, there are lots of MOV files out there.

Animation Formats (.FLC or .FLI): Some video clips aren't digitized video at all, but instead are animations. The animation standard is the FLC (or sometimes FLI) format developed by AutoDesk. To view FLC files, you need a third-party player. Auto-Desk has a Windows version of its AAPlay viewer (AAWIN.EXE, shown in Figure 24.6) that's available directly from AutoDesk or in many locations on the Internet.

Video Compression Schemes

If there were no limit to hard disk capacity, all digital video clips would be captured as raw footage and, provided you had a fast enough processor and a reasonable graphics adapter, there would be no concerns about video quality and tiny window sizes. Hard disks, however, are decidedly not infinite, so video files have to be literally cut down to size. Four factors determine the overall size of a video file:

The color depth of the images: Everything else being equal, 8-bit images take up only a third as much space as 24-bit images.

The size of the video playback window: A clip designed for a 320×240 window will be one-fourth the size of a clip that is designed to run full-screen (640×480).

The frame rate: Full-motion videos (30fps) pack twice as much information into a given amount of time than do videos playing at 15fps.

The quality of the sound: A video file incorporates synchronized audio as well as video. And, as with video, the higher the quality of the audio, the bigger the audio stream.

Quality-conscious video producers typically try to maximize as many of these variables as they can, so they capture their footage with as much data as possible. They then use some kind of compression technology to put the squeeze on the massive video files before distributing them. When you play a video clip, Windows 98 checks the compression used in the file and then calls the appropriate driver to handle the decompression.

Video compression is one of the most crucial components of digital video because it can have a huge impact on the quality of the resulting file. In general, compression involves trade-offs between file size and image quality. That's because most compression schemes are *lossy*, which means that some redundant information is discarded during the compression process. The higher the compression ratio, the more data that gets lost and the more the image degrades. On the other hand, lower compression ratios improve quality, but at the cost of larger files that might require a fast CPU to decompress.

However, the compression ratio isn't the only characteristic that a video producer must be concerned with. The compression scheme itself is an important consideration as well. If an AVI file is compressed with a codec that Windows 98 doesn't recognize, you won't be able to play that video. Happily, Windows 98 ships with drivers for many of the most popular codecs in use today (including Cinepak, Indeo, MPEG-4, RLE, TrueMotion, and Microsoft Video 1), so this is less of a concern for producers.

Unleashing Video in Windows 98

Now that you understand a bit about digital video, let's turn to more practical matters. The next three sections talk about playing video files, checking out AVI file properties, and setting up your system for maximizing video performance.

Using the ActiveMovie Control to Play Video Clips

Playing videos in Windows 98 is usually straightforward. In most cases, you use one of the following methods:

New to **98**

- Many CD-ROM applications have their own video players built in, so you can play video clips right from the application.

- For AVI files, you can use the Media Player (Start|Programs|Accessories|Entertainment|Media Player) and select Device|Video for Windows.

- As mentioned earlier, to view video clips not supported by Windows 98 (such as FLI or FLC files), you need to install a third-party player.

- Use the ActiveMovie control (discussed next).

24

DIRECTX AND WINDOWS 98 VIDEO

The ActiveMovie control (`AMOVIE.OCX`) supports all the most popular video (and audio) formats, and it's the default for AVI, MPG, QT, MOV, and other video files. To view a video clip using ActiveMovie, use any of the following techniques:

- Select Start|Programs|Accessories|Entertainment|ActiveMovie Control, and then select the video file using the Open dialog box that appears.

- In Windows Explorer or My Computer, either launch the video file or right-click the file and click Play in the context menu.

- If the ActiveMovie window is already open, drag a video file from Windows Explorer or My Computer and drop it inside the ActiveMovie window.

Figure 24.2 shows the ActiveMovie in action.

FIGURE **24.2.**

*In Windows 98, you
use the ActiveMovie
control to play most
video files.*

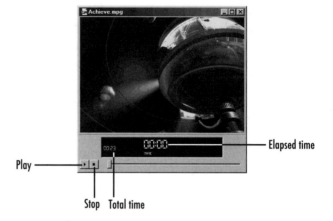

Controlling the ActiveMovie Control

The ActiveMovie control presents a very simple interface. Here's a summary of the various techniques you can use to work with that interface:

- To launch a video clip, either click the Run button, press Ctrl+R, or right-click the window and click Play in the context menu (see Figure 24.3).

- To pause a running movie, either click the Pause button, press Ctrl+P, or right-click the window and click Pause in the context menu.

- To stop a running movie, either click the Stop button, press Ctrl+S, or right-click the window and click Stop in the context menu.

- To move to a specific part of the video, drag the trackbar's slider left or right.

- To toggle the control panel (the area that holds the video controls) on and off, right-click the window and click Controls in the context menu.

- To toggle the display panel (the area that shows the elapsed time and total time) on and off, right-click the window and click Display in the context menu.

- To switch the display to frames, right-click the window and click Frames in the context menu. To return to the time display, right-click the window and click Time in the context menu.

- If you want to save the video file with a different name or location, right-click the window and click Save As in the context menu.

Working with ActiveMovie Properties

ActiveMovie is an ActiveX control, so it has a number of properties you can work with. To view these properties, right-click the ActiveMovie window and click Properties in the context menu. Figure 24.4 shows the properties sheet that appears.

FIGURE 24.3.
Right-click the ActiveMovie window to access a few extra commands.

Pause ———— ———— Trackbar

FIGURE 24.4.
Use this dialog box to set properties for the ActiveMovie control.

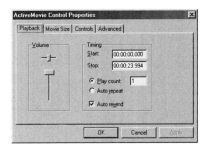

In the Playback tab, use the Volume group to adjust the audio portion of the show: the top slider controls the balance, and the bottom slider controls the volume.

The Timing group determines how much of the video is played and how often. This group offers the following options:

Start: Use this text box to set the starting position for the video. The format for this setting is *hh.mm.ss.ddd*, where *hh* is the hours, *mm* is the minutes, *ss* is the seconds, and *ddd* is the thousandths of a second.

Stop: Use this text box to set the ending position for the video. Again, you use the *hh.mm.ss.ddd* format.

Play count: If you activate this option, you can use the text box to set the number of times the video is repeated.

Auto repeat: If you activate this option instead of Play count, ActiveMovie repeats the clip until Pause or Stop is selected.

Auto rewind: When this check box is activated, ActiveMovie returns the clip to the position specified in the Start box whenever the clip ends or you select Stop.

Figure 24.5 shows Movie Size tab, which offers two controls that determine the size of the playback window:

Select the movie size: This drop-down list gives you various relative window sizes. Original size is the default size specified in the file's properties. Your other options are Double original size, various screen fractions (1/16, 1/4, and 1/2), or Maximized. Note, however, that if you increase the original window size, the quality of the video might degrade considerably.

Run full screen: If you activate this check box, ActiveMovie uses the entire screen to display the video (not even the taskbar will appear). To stop a clip that's playing full-screen, click the mouse or press any key.

FIGURE 24.5.

The Movie Size tab controls the size of the ActiveMovie playback window.

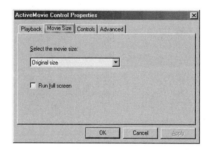

The Controls tab, shown in Figure 24.6, contains various options for customizing the ActiveMovie display panel and control panel:

Display panel: This check box toggles the display panel on and off.

Control panel: This check box toggles the control panel on and off.

Position controls: When this check box is activated, the control panel gains a few extra controls for changing the current video position. See Figure 24.7 and Table 24.1.

Selection controls: When this check box is activated, the control panel gains two extra controls that enable you to mark selected portions of the video for playback. Again, see Figure 24.7 and Table 24.1.

Trackbar: This check box toggles the trackbar on and off.

Colors: Use the Foreground and Background buttons to set the colors used in the display panel.

Table 24.1. Extra position and selection controls for the ActiveMovie window.

Control Name	Shortcut Key	Description
Previous	Ctrl+Shift+Left arrow	Go back to the previous mark.
Rewind	Ctrl+Left arrow	Rewind the media.

Control Name	Shortcut Key	Description
Forward	Ctrl+Right arrow	Fast-forward the media.
Next	Ctrl+Shift+Right arrow	Jump ahead to the next mark.
Start Selection		Mark the current spot as the playback beginning.
End Selection		Mark the current spot as the playback ending.

FIGURE 24.6.

Use the Controls tab to customize the ActiveMovie window's Display panel and Control panel.

FIGURE 24.7.

ActiveMovie sprouts a few extra controls if you activate the Position controls and Selection controls check boxes.

Previous
Rewind
Forward
Next
End Selection
Start Selection

Finally, the Advanced tab, shown in Figure 24.8, displays a list of filters that are available on your system for video playback. In the ActiveMovie architecture, *filters* are components that control and process the media stream. ActiveMovie uses various filters configured into a *filter graph*. For example, the MPEG filter graph uses the following filter components:

Source filter: Reads the media data from the disk.

Splitter transform filter: Separates the video and audio into separate streams.

Video transform filter: Decompresses the video stream.

Audio transform filter: Decompresses the audio stream.

Video rendering filter: Displays the video stream in the ActiveMovie window.

Audio rendering filter: Sends the audio stream to the sound card.

In some cases, you can click Properties to set various aspects of the filter's behavior.

FIGURE 24.8.

Use the Advanced tab to display or configure filter properties.

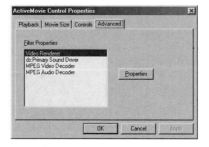

Tips for Top Video Performance

Of all the mainstream applications you use, digital video probably puts the most strain on your system's resources. The constant stream of pixels and sounds, and the need to decompress both types of media simultaneously and on-the-fly, can bring even the most powerful system to its knees. To help, here are a few tips that enable your machine to achieve peak video performance:

- Except for MPEG, the codecs used by most video clips don't require a killer machine. However, most codecs do have a minimum system requirement, usually a 33MHz 486. Obviously, anything over this minimum system will improve playback quality.

- Local bus graphics make a huge difference when displaying individual bitmaps, so you can imagine that they're a must for video clips that in effect display anywhere from 15 to 30 bitmaps a second.

- Memory is like manna from heaven for any application, but it's crucial for video. The more memory you have, the greater the portion of a huge video file that can be loaded into RAM. Consider 32MB the absolute minimum for any kind of serious video work.

- Speaking of memory, you should, if possible, max out your graphics adapter's on-board memory. An adapter with 4MB or even 8MB of video memory will sail through a typical video clip.

- Adjust your display settings so that you're using 24-bit color depth. And, to reduce the burden on the graphics adapter, drop the resolution down to 640×480. This will not only speed things up, but it will also make videos that run in smaller windows (320×240, for example) appear larger.

- Videos place an enormous burden on your CPU at the best of times, so you can imagine that they don't react well to sharing the CPU with other applications. Your clips will play at their best rate if no other applications are running.

■ Keep your hard disk defragmented. Video files run fastest when they're stored (and therefore accessed) contiguously.

■ Keep the drivers for your graphics adapter and codecs up-to-date. The latest drivers are usually the fastest ones, so you get an easy speed boost this way.

■ If you'll be working with a lot of video clips, consider investing in a video accelerator card. These cards have special video circuitry that will let you view your clips at larger sizes and greater color depths.

Windows 98 and the Broadcast Architecture

New to **98**

One of the most intriguing technologies included in the Windows 98 package is the *Broadcast Architecture*. This is a set of tools and components that enable PCs to accept broadcast signals from just about any network source, including cable, wireless cable, MBONE, satellite (DSS and DirectTV), Ethernet, ISDN, ADSL, and traditional television networks. Broadcast Architecture follows a standard client/server model, where a broadcast-enhanced computer becomes the *broadcast client* that is capable of receiving and displaying signals sent by a *broadcast server*.

What can you do with a machine set up to take advantage of Broadcast Architecture? Some very interesting things:

■ You can watch standard TV programs.

■ You can view TV program listings and use them to select the programs you want to watch.

■ You can watch *enhanced* TV programs that combine Web pages and standard TV programs.

■ You can listen to standard radio broadcasts.

■ You can listen to enhanced radio broadcasts that combine Web pages and standard radio programs.

■ You can watch *Webcasts*, which are Web-based multimedia broadcasts.

■ You can interact with the stream via a separate *back channel* (usually a modem hooked up to a telephone line).

■ Databases, software updates, and other computer data can be "pushed" to the broadcast client in the background.

What makes this list so interesting is that Broadcast Architecture expands the overall model for content delivery by setting up the broadcast client as an all-purpose receiver that can handle many different types of data streams seamlessly.

Broadcast Architecture enables existing broadcast television signals to be augmented with extra data in the form of Web pages, ActiveX controls, applets, and more. For example, you can call up player statistics during a sporting event. Similarly, if you're watching an MTV video, you can display the name of the song and data related to the band.

24

DIRECTX AND
WINDOWS 98
VIDEO

The mechanism behind this is the *vertical blanking interval.* This is a slice of time in which the broadcast signal isn't visible on the screen because it's being repositioned to the top of the screen to start a new scan. Extra data can be piggybacked inside this interval and downloaded to the computer. It's estimated that current technology can download data via the VBI at approximately 100Kbps, which approaches ISDN-level bandwidth.

In some cases, digital data can be delivered via the broadcast pipe, which allows richer content than can be crammed into a telephone line for a modem connection. For example, existing broadcast streams have a bandwidth of up to 6Mbps, compared with just 56Kbps maximum for high-end modems—a 100-fold increase.

It's also important to note that Microsoft has gone out of its way to build the Broadcast Architecture on a foundation of standard technologies. These include TCP/IP, HTML, ActiveX, MPEG-2, DirectShow, and the COM interface. This makes it easier to implement Broadcast Architecture on both the client side and the server side, because most of the components required to make this new broadcast model work are known quantities.

Hardware Requirements

So just what is a "broadcast-enhanced" computer exactly? It's a PC that contains the appropriate hardware and software for displaying broadband analog and digital broadcasts.

On the hardware side, you need the following:

Computer: Pentium 120MHz or faster processor with a PCI bus.

RAM: 16MB or better.

Monitor: For nearby viewing, a 17-inch monitor capable of 800×600 resolution with a noninterlaced refresh rate of 60Hz. For distant viewing, at least a 27-inch SVGA monitor capable of 640×480 resolution with a noninterlaced refresh rate of 60Hz. Note, too, that the monitor should have phosphors with matching persistence, which will minimize flicker.

Graphics adapter: Must be capable of MPEG-2 compression and SVGA-level video. For TV signals, it must include a cable television tuner that supports NTSC or PAL signals. (The ATI All-In-Wonder card is a good example that works flawlessly with Broadcast Architecture.)

Input: For distant viewing, a wireless keyboard and mouse.

Sound card: Should be stereo-ready and Sound Blaster–compatible.

Modem: Minimum 28.8Kbps for back channel uploads.

Configuring WebTV for Windows

The bulk of the Broadcast Architecture subsystem operates invisibly behind the scenes. Your link to much of what Broadcast Architecture has to offer is the WebTV for Windows application. WebTV consists of two components:

WebTV for Windows HTML Browser: This is a customized version of the Internet Explorer Web browser. It's used mostly to display the Program Guide components, which are ActiveX controls that enable you to work with broadcast channels.

Video ActiveX Control: This component is used to display the video and audio stream for whatever broadcast channel you select from the Program Guide. If the stream contains enhanced content, the control is hosted within another instance of the Internet Explorer browser to display the extra content.

Note, too, that you must have Windows 98 set up to access the Internet (see Chapter 32, "Windows 98 and the Internet"). Assuming you have your hardware set up correctly and a connection to the Internet established, you start WebTV by using either of the following techniques:

- Select Start|Programs|Accessories|Entertainment|WebTV for Windows.
- Click Launch WebTV for Windows in the taskbar's Quick Launch toolbar.

WebTV takes a few seconds to initialize, and then it displays the Welcome screen. Follow these steps to configure WebTV:

1. Click Next to display the Get TV Listings screen.
2. To download the program listing for your area, click the G-GUIDE link. Internet Explorer loads and takes you to the TV Program Listing Web site.
3. Enter your ZIP code or postal code. The Web page will then display a list of broadcast areas or cable providers.
4. Click the provider you want to use to receive program listings. The Web page then prompts you to download the listings to your computer.
5. Click Download. Internet Explorer downloads the data. The Status window shows you the progress of the download. Note that this may take quite some time if you have a slow connection.
6. When the Status window displays Success! to indicate a successful download, return to the WebTV screen.
7. Click Next. WebTV displays the Program Guide Tour screen.
8. When the tour is complete, click Next.
9. Click Finish in the final screen to get to the Program Guide.

Operating the Program Guide

The basic setup of WebTV's Program Guide is shown in Figure 24.9. The bulk of the screen is taken up with program listings, which show the available channels (numbers and call letters) on the left and the programs themselves arranged in a time line. The area on the right side of the screen shows a preview of the currently selected channel and other data related to the program (such as a description and the program's rating, if it has one).

Figure 24.9.

The Program Listings screen.

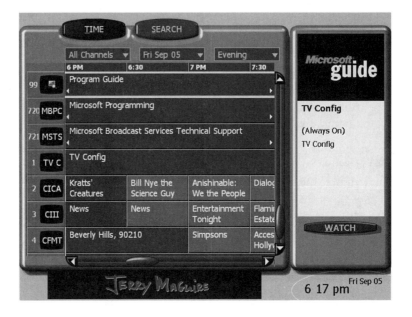

Here's a summary of the techniques you can use to work with the Program Guide:

- ■ To preview a running program, use the vertical scrollbar to bring the channel into view and then click the program.

- ■ To get information about a program that isn't running, use both scrollbars to display the program and then click it.

- ■ To watch a program, click it and then click Watch.

GETTING BACK TO THE PROGRAM GUIDE

When you're watching a program, you can return to the Program Guide by pressing F10 to display the toolbar and then clicking the Guide button.

Setting a Reminder

If you would like WebTV to remind you to watch a future program, click the program and then click the Remind button. WebTV displays the Remind dialog box, shown in Figure 24.10. You have the following options:

Once: If you activate this option, WebTV reminds you once and then deletes the reminder.

Every: If you activate this option, use the drop-down list to select a reminder frequency (the day of the week, every day, or every week).

No Reminder: Activate this option to delete an existing reminder for this program.

x **minutes before show starts:** Use this list to specify the number of minutes before the selected time that you want the reminder to appear.

Change channel automatically for recording: If you activate this check box, WebTV changes to the appropriate channel when the program begins. This saves you the effort, and it's also handy if you have your tuner card attached to a VCR for taping.

FIGURE 24.10.

Use this dialog box to set up a reminder to watch a show.

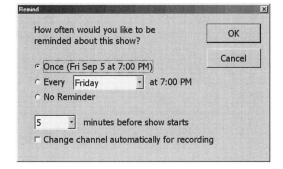

Using the Search Feature

The Program Guide has a useful Search feature that enables you to view programs by category or to search for a work in the program's title. To activate the Search interface, click the Search button near the top of the screen. Figure 24.11 shows the revised layout that appears. Here's how you use this interface:

■ Use the Categories list to select the appropriate category for the show you want to find.

■ Use the drop-down lists above the program names to restrict the number of days of programs you want to view and to sort the programs by time or title.

■ To search for a show by name, enter your search text in the Search For box and click Search.

Changing the Channels Displayed in the Program Guide

By default, the Program Guide displays all the available channels. If you want to remove some channels you never bother with, follow these steps:

1. Press F10 to display WebTV toolbar.

2. Click the Settings buttons. WebTV displays the Settings dialog box, shown in Figure 24.12.

3. If you want to see all the channels, activate the Show all option. Otherwise, activate Show only and then use the check boxes in the list to choose which channels you want to view.

24

DIRECTX AND
WINDOWS 98
VIDEO

FIGURE 24.11.

*Program Guide's
Search interface.*

4. If your cable provider has a new channel, you can add it to the Program Guide by clicking Add channel, entering the channel number in the dialog box that appears, and then clicking OK.

5. Note, as well, that you can also use the Show closed captioning check box to toggle the display of closed captioning on and off.

6. Click OK to put the new settings into effect.

FIGURE 24.12.

*Use this dialog box to
choose which channels
appear in the Program
Guide.*

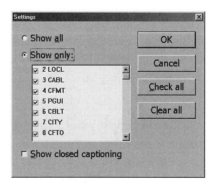

Watching a Program

After you select the program you want to watch, it's time to do some channel surfing. WebTV is designed to support remote control devices, such as the Gateway 2000 Destination remote control.

If you don't have such a device, you can still control WebTV via your keyboard. Table 24.2 lists the various keys and key combinations that you can use.

Table 24.2. Keystrokes you can use to control WebTV.

Keystroke	Description
0–9	Used for entering channel numbers. If you enter a 1- or 2-digit number, you need to press Enter as well. If you enter a 3-digit number, WebTV changes the channel without having to press Enter.
F6	Toggles WebTV between its normal full-screen mode and its windowed mode.
F10	Displays WebTV toolbar.
Arrow keys	Scrolls up and down in the Program Guide.
⊞+v	Toggles mute on and off.
⊞+Ctrl+v	Turns up the volume.
⊞+Shift+v	Turns down the volume.
⊞+Ctrl+Shift+z	Shows the Program Guide (grid view).
⊞+Ctrl+Alt+z	Tunes the channel up.
⊞+Ctrl+Alt+Shift+z	Tunes the channel down.
⊞+Ctrl+Alt+Shift+g	Recalls the last channel.

It's possible to remap some of these keystrokes using the Registry. Open the Registry Editor (as described in Chapter 12, "Getting to Know the Windows 98 Registry") and head for the following key:

`\HKEY_LOCAL_MACHINE\Software\Microsoft\TV Services\Explorer\RemoteKeys`

This key has several settings, but only three are relevant to program watching:

Setting	Value
CHANNELDOWN	5a 80 80 80 80 00 00 00 00
CHANNELUP	5a 80 80 80 00 00 00 00 00
RECALL	47 80 80 80 80 00 00 00 00

These binary values determine which keys must be pressed to activate the feature. You interpret the values as follows:

24

DIRECTX AND
WINDOWS 98
VIDEO

```
key ▦ Ctrl Alt Shift 00 00 00 00
```

key	This byte is the hexadecimal value of the uppercase letter you want to use as part of the key combination.
▦	This byte determines whether you include the ▦ key in the key combination. If this is set to 80, include the ▦ key; if it's set to 00, don't use the key.
Ctrl	This byte determines whether you include the Ctrl key in the key combination. If this is set to 80, include the Ctrl key; if it's set to 00, don't use Ctrl.
Alt	This byte determines whether you include the Alt key in the key combination. If this is set to 80, include Alt; if it's set to 00, don't use Alt.
Shift	This byte determines whether you include the Shift key in the key combination. If this is set to 80, include the Shift key; if it's set to 00, don't use the Shift key.

For example, the following values set CHANNELDOWN to Ctrl+Alt+Z, CHANNELUP to Ctrl+Alt+X, and RECALL to Ctrl+Alt+R:

Setting	*Value*
CHANNELDOWN	5a 00 80 80 00 00 00 00 00
CHANNELUP	58 00 80 80 00 00 00 00 00
RECALL	52 00 80 80 00 00 00 00 00

The key combinations used with WebTV volume are set in the following Registry key:

```
\HKEY_LOCAL_MACHINE\SOFTWARE\Microsoft\TV Services\Explorer\RemoteKeys\WakeupKeys
```

There are three settings:

Setting	*Value*
Mute	56 00 10 00
VolumeDown	56 01 10 00
VolumeUp	56 10 10 00

Here's how you interpret these values:

```
key Ctrl Shift ▦ Alt 00
```

For *Ctrl*, *Shift*, ▦, and *Alt*, a 1 means you include the key in the key combination and a 0 means you don't include the key. For example, the key combination for VolumeUp is ▦+Ctrl+v (56 is the hexadecimal value for the letter V).

Here are some customized settings (note that you need to restart Windows 98 to put these new settings into effect):

Setting	Value	Key Combination
Mute	4D 10 01 00	Ctrl+Alt+M
VolumeDown	44 10 01 00	Ctrl+Alt+D
VolumeUp	55 10 01 00	Ctrl+Alt+U

For your customization convenience, Table 24.3 lists the hexadecimal values for the letters A to Z.

Table 24.3. Hexadecimal values for the letters A through Z.

Letter	Hexadecimal	Letter	Hexadecimal
A	41	N	4E
B	42	O	4F
C	43	P	50
D	44	Q	51
E	45	R	52
F	46	S	53
G	47	T	54
H	48	U	55
I	49	V	56
J	4A	W	57
K	4B	X	58
L	4C	Y	59
M	4D	Z	5A

24

DIRECTX AND
WINDOWS 98
VIDEO

Viewing Web-Based Video with NetShow

New to
98

Microsoft puts the ASF video format through its paces with the NetShow Player that comes with Windows 98. NetShow is essentially an ActiveX control that supports *media streaming*. This means that NetShow uses special codecs that enable it to decode incoming media streams on-the-fly. The result is that you can view content-rich media with only a few seconds delay. This is a far cry from having to load a large video file that, if you're accessing it from the Web, could take minutes or even hours to download. And there are no storage worries with NetShow because the player doesn't save the incoming stream in permanent storage. It buffers the incoming data, plays it, and then tosses it in the bit bucket.

NetShow is also capable of both unicast and multicast content delivery. *Unicast delivery* means that a separate copy of the ASF file is sent to each client that asks for it. The advantage to this approach is that after the entire stream is received, the user can then replay the media and, in some cases, rewind and fast forward to specific sections. The disadvantage to this approach is that each stream usurps a large chunk of network bandwidth.

Multicast delivery, on the other hand, means that a single copy of the ASF stream is sent out to multiple clients. This is closer to the television broadcast model, because you use the NetShow player to "tune in" to whatever stream the server is sending out. This is very efficient in terms of bandwidth, but you lose the VCR-like features of the unicast model.

Using these two basic content delivery mechanisms, NetShow enables multimedia developers to build five types of streaming media:

Audio only: Using an audio codec such as MPEG Layer 3, NetShow can play high-quality stereo audio streams that include simple voice output, converted WAV and MIDI files, and music clips.

Illustrated audio: These streams play an audio track synchronized with images such as bitmaps, photos, video stills, or even PowerPoint slides.

ASF video file: This is a separate file stored on the NetShow server. The server comes with tools for converting AVI or QuickTime files to the ASF format, as well as for capturing live images from a camcorder or VCR and saving them as ASF.

Live audio and video feed: This is a stream that captures a live event (such as a radio or television feed) and broadcasts it in real time.

Application: Developers can embed events within the NetShow stream, and a script on a Web page can then capture those events and perform appropriate actions. For example, the stream can tell the script to change the text shown in the Web page, and thus provide a form of closed captioning.

One of the nice things about NetShow is that content creators can specify the required bandwidth for their stream. If they know, for example, that most people using the stream will be viewing it over a fast network connection, they can ramp up the quality of both the audio and video accordingly. Conversely, they can reduce the content quality so that the stream is available to modem surfers at 14.4Kbps or 28.8Kbps.

To get started with NetShow, dial the following address into Internet Explorer:

```
http://www.microsoft.com/netshow/
```

The page that appears gives you a bit of background about NetShow. From there, click the Gallery link to get to the NetShow Gallery page, which includes NetShow samples, pointers to upcoming live events, past events, and much more.

Each NetShow extravaganza is presented inside the NetShow Player, which comes in three different guises:

>   **Separate NetShow Player for video:** In some cases, activating a show displays a new NetShow Player window like the one shown in Figure 24.13.

FIGURE 24.13.

Sometimes the NetShow Player shows up as a separate window like this one.

>   **Separate NetShow Player for audio only:** This is basically the same as the NetShow Player in Figure 24.14, except there's no video portion.

>   **Embedded NetShow player:** Many NetShow-enhanced Web pages have the NetShow Player built in, as shown in Figure 24.14.

FIGURE 24.14.

In most cases, the Web "theater" includes the NetShow Player as part of the page.

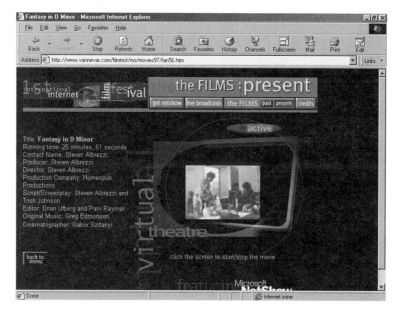

Troubleshooting Video Woes

I finish this chapter by examining some video problems, troubleshooting techniques, and solutions to specific problems.

Reinstalling a Video Codec

If you have trouble with a specific codec, removing the codec and then reinstalling it will often solve the problem. Follow these steps to remove a video codec:

1. In Control Panel, open the Multimedia icon and select the Devices tab.

2. Open the Video Compression Codecs tree and highlight the codec you want to remove (see Figure 24.15).

FIGURE 24.15.

In the Devices tab of the Multimedia Properties dialog box, highlight the codec you want to remove.

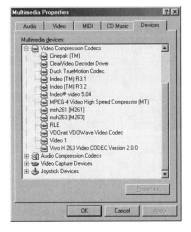

3. Click the Properties button.

4. In the codec properties sheet that appears, click Remove.

5. When Windows 98 asks whether you're sure, click Yes and then click OK in the next two dialog boxes. (Windows 98 will tell you to restart the system. You can ignore this.)

6. Close the Multimedia Properties dialog box to return to Control Panel.

To reinstall the codec, follow these steps:

1. In Control Panel, open the Add New Hardware Wizard.

2. Click Next > and then click Next > again to let Windows 98 search for Plug and Play devices.

3. When the Wizard asks whether you want Windows to search for your hardware, activate No and then click Next >.

4. In the Hardware types list, highlight the Sound, video and game controllers item and click Next >.

5. In the Manufacturers list, highlight the appropriate item. For example, highlight SuperMatch for Cinepak, highlight Intel for Indeo, or highlight Microsoft Video Codecs for RLE or Video 1 (see Figure 24.16).

FIGURE 24.16.

Highlight the codec manufacturer and model.

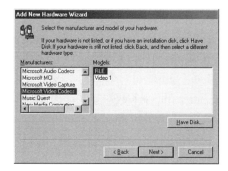

6. In the Models list, highlight the codec you want to install and click Next >.

7. Click Finish and follow the onscreen prompts for inserting your Windows 98 source disks.

8. When Windows 98 asks whether you want to restart your system, click Yes.

Miscellaneous Video Ills

This section takes you through a few specific problems related to Windows 98 video and AVI files.

When you attempt to play a QuickTime (.MOV) file, ActiveMovie displays the following error message:

```
Cannot play back the video stream: no suitable decompressor could be found.
```

Although ActiveMovie theoretically supports QuickTime files, it will choke on some files that were created on a Macintosh computer. The problem is that the Mac uses audio and video codecs that aren't supported by ActiveMovie. You use QuickTime for Windows to view these files. If you have Web access, try the following site:

```
http://quicktime.apple.com/
```

You have trouble playing an AVI file using a third-party program.

If a third-party program won't play an AVI file, there are a few things you can try.

First, see whether you can play the file either by double-clicking it in Explorer or by using Media Player. If the file plays, the problem lies with the third-party program. You need to contact the vendor's tech support department.

If you can't play the file from Explorer or Media Player, the file might be corrupted. Try playing another AVI file that uses the same codec. If the second AVI file won't play, there's probably a problem with the codec driver, so you should try removing and then reinstalling the codec. If the second file does play, the original file is probably damaged. Either reinstall it or contact the vendor for a replacement.

24

DIRECTX AND WINDOWS 98 VIDEO

If you can't play any AVI file, the MCI video device might be disabled. To enable this device, follow these steps:

1. Open Control Panel's Multimedia icon and select the Devices tab.

2. Open the Media Control Devices tree.

3. Highlight Motion Video Device and select Properties.

4. In the properties sheet that appears (see Figure 24.17), activate the Use this Media Control device option and then click OK.

FIGURE 24.17.

Make sure the Use this Media Control device option is activated.

5. Click OK and then restart Windows 98 to put the change into effect.

An AVI file plays poorly (that is, the motion is jerky or the sound is intermittent).

These kinds of playback problems are usually related to window size. As described earlier in this chapter, adjust the playback window to the original size for the clip. If you still have a problem, try using a window that's smaller than the original.

Another reason that an AVI file might play poorly is if you run it over a network. You get much better performance if you copy the file to your local hard drive.

An AVI file plays poorly from a CD-ROM drive.

If video clip playbacks are jerky or have breaks in the sound when you run them from a CD-ROM drive, the AVI file's playback rate probably is greater than the throughput of the CD-ROM drive. For example, if the AVI file is designed to be played at 200KBps and your CD-ROM is only rated at 150KBps (single-speed), you won't be able to improve the playback. In this case, you need to copy the AVI file to your hard drive and run it from there.

If your CD-ROM drive's throughput should be greater than the file's playback rate (for example, if you have a 300KBps drive and a 200KBps file), you might need to perform some CD-ROM optimization to improve the throughput. See Chapter 9, "Performance Tuning: Optimizing Memory and Disk Access," for details.

The colors in a video clip appear washed out or blocky.

A video file's colors won't display properly if the current color depth is less than the color depth of the video file. Check the video file's properties to see the inherent color depth of the file. Then adjust the color depth of your graphics adapter to match or exceed this value. For example, if the file uses 256 colors, set your graphics adapter to 256 colors or more.

If the colors still don't look right, try removing and reinstalling the graphics adapter driver, or even upgrading the driver to the latest version available from the manufacturer.

When you attempt to play an AVI file in Windows 98, you receive an error message similar to the following:

```
Video not available, cannot find x decompressor.
```

If *x* is one of the codecs that comes with Windows 98, this error means that Windows 98's video compression isn't installed. Here are the steps to follow to install video compression:

1. In Control Panel, click the Add/Remove Programs icon.
2. Select the Windows Setup tab.
3. In the Components list, highlight Multimedia and click Details.
4. Activate the Video Compression check box and click OK.
5. Click OK and then follow the onscreen prompts to insert your Windows 98 source disks.

If the decompressor that Windows 98 can't find is part of a third-party codec, you need to contact the manufacturer to get a copy of the appropriate codec and then install it. Here are the steps to follow to install a third-party codec:

1. In Control Panel, open the Add New Hardware Wizard.
2. Click Next > and then click Next > again to let Windows 98 search for Plug and Play devices.
3. When the Wizard asks whether you want Windows to search for your hardware, activate No and click Next >.
4. In the Hardware types list, highlight the Sound, video and game controllers item and click Next >.
5. Insert the disk containing the codec.
6. Click the Have Disk button and follow the onscreen prompts.

Summary

This chapter looked at DirectX 5.0 and Windows 98 video. After a brief introduction to Windows 98 and multimedia, I took you through the entire DirectX 5.0 family. I then examined various video formats and explained video compression schemes. In a more practical vein, I showed you how to play video clips in Windows 98, examine video clip and playback properties, and improve video performance. From there, you learned about a few new Windows 98 video goodies: the Broadcast Architecture, WebTV for Windows, and the NetShow Player. I closed with a look at some video troubleshooting issues.

Here's a list of chapters where you'll find related information:

- Many of the factors that affect video performance also affect system performance as a whole. I talk about this in Chapter 9, "Performance Tuning: Optimizing Memory and Disk Access."
- For information on graphics adapters and CD-ROM drives, see Chapter 11, "Device Advice: Dealing with Devices in Windows 98."
- Sound is a big part of video files, and I tell you all about how Windows 98 works with sound in Chapter 25, "Windows 98 Audio Features."
- For more about the Internet Explorer World Wide Web browser, see Chapter 33, "Exploring the Web with Internet Explorer."

Windows 98 Audio Features

Most people have ears, but few have judgment; tickle those ears, and depend upon it you will catch their judgments, such as they are.

—*Lord Chesterfield*

When I put together multimedia presentations, videos, and animations, the graphics are what make the audience "ooh" and "aah" during the playback. However, I've often found that what most people comment on *after* the show is, surprisingly, the soundtrack: the music and sound effects that accompany the visuals. It seems that adding bells and whistles (literally) to multimedia makes a big impact on people.

I'm not certain why this happens, but I'm sure that part of the reason has to do with our ears. The ear is a fine and sensitive instrument, attuned to nuance on the one hand, but shamelessly craving novelty on the other. How else do you explain, in a society supposedly in love with the visual image, the relentless popularity of radio after all these years?

I'm guessing that another reason audio is such an important part of multimedia is that most people are used to their computers being, if not voiceless, at least monotonic. Most mainstream applications are content to utter simple beeps and boops to alert you to an error or otherwise get your attention. Multimedia, however, with its music and unusual sound bites, can provide quite a jolt to people who aren't used to such things.

In other words, there's no reason to think of sound as the poor cousin of flashy videos and graphics. To help you get the biggest bang for your sound buck, this chapter examines audio fundamentals, Windows 98's sound features, and a few troubleshooting procedures, just in case you're hearing the sound of silence.

A Review of Audio File Formats

Just as video clips come in different file flavors (see Chapter 24, "DirectX and Windows 98 Video," for details), so too are there various formats for audio clips. Windows 98 and its audio applets support the following sound file formats:

Waveform audio (.WAV): This is the standard Windows digital audio format created via the PCM technique. All Windows-based sound applications can play WAV files, and each WAV file will sound the same no matter which sound application you use to play it.

Musical Instrument Digital Interface (.MID or .RMI): These are nonwaveform files that store musical instructions instead of waveform amplitudes. Sound cards that support MIDI have various synthesized instruments built into their chips. A MIDI file's instructions specify which instrument to play, which note to play, how long the note should be held, and so on.

Audio Interchange File Format (.AIF and .AIFF): This format began life on the Apple Macintosh. It supports 16-bit 44.1KHz stereo sound files.

Sun Audio Format (.AU): This is the standard UNIX audio format, so it's the standard audio format used on most of the Internet.

Note that the ActiveMovie control (discussed in Chapter 24) is the default "application" for all these formats except WAV. For the latter, the default application is Sound Recorder (discussed later in this chapter).

Audio Codecs

As their quality increases, sound files take up a progressively bigger chunk of your hard disk. To help reduce the load, codecs are used to compress digitized audio and then decompress it for playing. Windows 98 comes with a number of 32-bit codecs. Here's a list of the Microsoft codecs:

Adaptive Delta Pulse Code Modulation (ADPCM): This codec works by storing the differences between consecutive PCM samples. This allows ADPCM to store audio data in just 4 bits, which is a 4:1 compression ratio over 16-bit audio. This codec reproduces low frequencies well but tends to distort high frequencies. However, these distortions are barely noticeable at higher sampling frequencies.

Consultative Committee for International Telephone and Telegraph (CCITT) G.711 A-Law and μ-Law: Provided for compatibility with current Telephony Application Programming Interface (TAPI) standards. These codecs are supported by many hardware configurations but offer only a 2:1 compression ratio (from 16 bits to 8 bits per sample).

DSP Group TrueSpeech Software: This codec offers high compression rates for voice-oriented sound, which makes it a good codec to use when recording voice notes.

Groupe Special Mobile (GSM) 6.10: This codec offers real-time compression, which makes it a good choice for recording voice snippets with Sound Recorder. GSM gives you only a 2:1 compression ratio, but it lets you select from a relatively large range of sampling frequencies.

Interactive Multimedia Association (IMA) ADPCM: This is similar to ADPCM, because it gives you a 4:1 compression ratio over 16-bit audio. The advantage of IMA ADPCM is that it takes a little less time to compress files.

PCM Converter: This codec is included for use with older Sound Blaster and other 8-bit sound cards. It lets these cards play 16-bit audio clips. This codec also can convert the sampling frequency to a different rate for cards that don't support the original rate used to digitize a sound wave.

THE INSTALLED CODECS DEPEND ON THE SOUND CARD

Because not all sound cards support all these codecs, the number of codecs that Setup foists upon your system depends on the sound card you have installed.

Audio Hardware: What to Look for in a Sound Card

Technically, it isn't necessary to have a sound card installed on your system if all you want to do is play WAV files. (See "Installing the PC Speaker Driver" later in this chapter to learn how to set up your computer to play sounds without a sound card.) However, you definitely want to invest in some audio hardware if you need or want any of the following: high-quality audio, external speakers connected to your system, the ability to record sounds, audio compression, or MIDI support.

If you're in the market for a sound card, here are a few options and features to look for:

Compatibility: One of the most important considerations when buying a sound card is whether your applications will be able to recognize and work with the card. Unfortunately, there are no universal standards for sound cards to ensure compatibility. However, there is a de facto standard: the Sound Blaster, made by Creative Labs. This was the first sound card to ship in mass-market quantities, so almost every application that uses sound will work with any card that bills itself as "Sound Blaster–compatible."

Playback features: To play sounds on your system, check out the card's DAC. It should support at least the highest levels of digitized sound that you plan on using. For example, if you have applications that use CD-quality audio, the card's DAC should support sampling frequencies up to 44.1KHz, 16-bit sample depth, and stereo.

Sampling features: If you plan on recording audio, check the features supported by the card's analog-to-digital converter (ADC). The ADC features you get will depend on the level of recording quality that suits your needs. If all you want to do is voice annotations, a cheap 11KHz, 8-bit, mono ADC is all you need. For music and other sounds, it doesn't cost a whole lot more to move up to a 44.1KHz, 16-bit, stereo ADC.

Compression: Most cards support some kind of built-in audio compression. The codec used depends on the sound card, but the vast majority of cards support at least one of the codecs recognized by Windows 98. This is especially true if the card is Sound Blaster–compatible. If you're using some other card, you should check the codecs it uses to make sure they're among the set supported by Windows 98.

Device drivers: Make sure the card comes with drivers for Windows 98. Although the Add New Hardware Wizard offers dozens of sound card drivers, you're usually better off with the latest drivers from the manufacturer.

CD-ROM interface: Many stereo sound cards also operate your CD-ROM drive. You need to be careful, though: Some sound cards support only CD-ROM drives that use a proprietary controller, such as the Mitsumi interface or the Sony interface. If your CD-ROM doesn't work with these controllers, the sound card won't be able to operate the drive. It's best to look for sound cards that have a generic interface, such as a SCSI port or an IDE port.

FM synthesis versus wavetable synthesis: FM synthesis cards imitate musical instruments by using a mathematical approximation of the instrument's sound. For better instrumental imitations, buy a card that uses wavetable synthesis. These cards have ROM chips that contain digital recordings (samples) of real instruments.

Digital signal processor: Many of the latest sound cards come with a digital signal processor (DSP) chip. This chip augments the card's basic features by adding extra goodies, such as on-the-fly audio compression, voice mail, "surround sound" audio, and more.

Cable connectors: Besides the CD-ROM interface discussed earlier, all sound cards have several mini-plug connectors for various types of cables:

- *Line Out* connector: For cable connections from the sound card to an external device, such as a pair of speakers, a headphone set, or a stereo receiver. Some cards provide two RCA-style connectors for connecting to the left and right channels of a stereo system.

- *Speaker/Headphone Out* connector: For amplified cable connections from the sound card to a pair of speakers or a headphone set. In this case, you don't need an AC power source for the speakers, because the sound card connector provides up to 4 watts of power.

- *Line In* connector: For cable connections from an external sound source to the sound card. External sound sources include stereo system components, CD-ROM drives, synthesizers, and microphones. This lets you record audio from the external source.

- *Microphone* connector: For cable connections from an external microphone to the sound card. As opposed to the Line In connector, these connectors typically record in mono, which is fine for voice recordings.

- *Joystick/MIDI Adapter* connector: For cable connections from the sound card to a joystick or a MIDI adapter. The latter is used to control a MIDI device, such as a MIDI-compliant keyboard.

- *Internal CD-ROM sound* connector: For cable connections from an internal CD-ROM drive to the sound card. This lets you hear audio from your internal CD-ROM drive.

MIDI support: Besides the MIDI connector mentioned earlier, you need a few other features if you plan on working with MIDI files. These features include General MIDI support, polyphony, MIDI streams, and wavetable synthesis.

Plug and Play: Many of the latest sound cards are compliant with the Plug and Play standard, meaning that after you install them, Windows 98 will recognize and configure the card automatically. This is a huge benefit, because sound cards have always been notoriously difficult to install due to the fact that they usually require specific IRQ, DMA, and memory addresses.

External accessories: To get the most for your audio dollar, look for cards that come bundled with extras, such as a microphone and headphones. Most sound cards also come with audio clips and programs for playing sounds, recording and editing digital audio, composing MIDI music, converting text to speech, and more. The latest-and-greatest sound card accessory is telephony software that lets your computer act as a sophisticated telephone, with answering machine capabilities, voice mailboxes, speed dial, and much more. Some even come with Internet-based phone software.

INSTALLING SOUND CARDS

Many sound cards aren't Plug and Play–compliant, so Windows 98 won't be able to assign interrupts and DMA channels automatically. Ideally, you should install these cards before you install Windows 98. If you're installing the card with Windows 98 already on your machine, use the card's software to assign the appropriate resources. This software usually sets up a line or two in CONFIG.SYS or AUTOEXEC.BAT that specifies these resources, so you should leave these lines in place.

Installing the PC Speaker Driver

If you're just looking for basic sound capabilities (that is, the ability to play WAV files), you don't need to shell out a couple of hundred bucks on a fancy sound card. Instead, Microsoft has a PC Speaker driver that lets WAV files be played, with adequate fidelity, through your computer's built-in speaker. This section tells you how to obtain and install the PC Speaker driver.

Getting Your Hands on the PC Speaker Driver

The PC Speaker driver comes in a self-extracting archive file named SPEAK.EXE. You find SPEAK.EXE on various Internet sites, as well as on the following Microsoft sites:

CompuServe: GO MSL and then select Access the Software Library. Perform a filename search for SPEAK.EXE and then download the file.

Microsoft Download Service (MSDL): Dial 425-936-6735 to connect to MSDL, search for SPEAK.EXE, and then download it.

FTP: Connect to ftp.microsoft.com, change to the Softlib/Mslfiles directory, and then get SPEAK.EXE.

When you have the file, open it to extract its contents (AUDIO.TXT, LICENSE.TXT, OEMSETUP.INF, SPEAKER.DRV, and SPEAKER.TXT). When the utility asks whether you want to extract the files, press Y.

Installing the PC Speaker Driver

Here are the steps to follow to install the PC Speaker driver:

1. In Control Panel, open the Add New Hardware icon.
2. Click Next > and then click Next > again to have the Wizard search for Plug and Play devices.
3. When the Wizard asks whether you want Windows to search for new hardware, activate the No option and click Next >.
4. In the Hardware types list, highlight Sound, video and game controllers and click Next >.
5. Click the Have Disk button.
6. In the Install From Disk dialog box that appears, type the pathname of the folder containing the extracted PC Speaker files and click OK.
7. The Select Device dialog box that appears should display Sound Driver for PC-Speaker in the Models list. Click OK.
8. Click Finish. You may now see a dialog box asking you for the location of the `speaker.drv` file.
9. Make sure the Copy files from box shows the name of the folder containing the PC Speaker files, and then click OK. The PC-Speaker Setup dialog box, shown in Figure 25.1, appears.

FIGURE 25.1.

Use this dialog box to configure the PC Speaker driver.

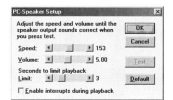

10. Adjust the settings and click Test to make sure the driver is working properly.
11. When Windows 98 asks whether you want to restart your system, click Yes.

ACCESSING THE PC SPEAKER DRIVER'S SETTINGS

To access the PC-Speaker Setup dialog box later, open Control Panel's Multimedia icon and select the Devices tab. Open the Audio Devices tree, highlight Audio for Sound Driver for PC-Speaker, and click Properties. In the properties sheet that appears, click Settings.

MEDIA PLAYER DOESN'T WORK WITH THE PC SPEAKER DRIVER

You can't use Media Player to play sounds using the PC Speaker driver. You have to use the Sound Recorder accessory.

Sounding Off: Playing Sounds in Windows 98

You'll find that playing sounds in Windows 98 is straightforward. In most cases, you use one of the following methods:

- Many CD-ROM applications have their own audio players built in, so you can play audio clips right from the application.

- To play sound clips not supported by Windows 98, you need to install a third-party player.

- For WAV files, the default application is Sound Recorder (select Start | Programs | Accessories | Entertainment | Sound Recorder). In the Sound Recorder window that appears, select File | Open to open the WAV file you want to hear. Now click the Play button (see Figure 25.2).

FIGURE 25.2.

You can use the Sound Recorder accessory to play WAV files.

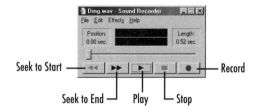

- For WAV and MIDI files, you can use the Media Player (select Start | Programs | Accessories | Entertainment | Media Player). In the Media Player window, select Device | Sound or Device MIDI Sequencer.

- For all other sound files, open the file and Windows 98 will run the ActiveMovie control. See Chapter 24 to learn how to work with the ActiveMovie control.

DRAG-AND-DROP AUDIO PLAYING

You can also play an audio clip by dragging the sound file from Windows Explorer and dropping it on ActiveMovie, Sound Recorder, or Media Player (depending on the sound file type).

DEALING WITH MULTIPLE AUDIO DEVICES

Windows 98 is happy to let you have more than one audio playback device installed on your system. However, you might want to set up one of these devices as the default. To do this, first open Control Panel's Multimedia icon. In the Audio tab of the Multimedia Properties dialog box, use the Preferred device list in the Playback group to choose the playback device you want to use as the default.

Turning It Up (or Down): The Volume Control

Controlling the volume of your audio is crucial. During playback, you might want to turn the volume down if you're in a public place where you don't want to disturb others nearby. If you have no such worries, you might want to crank up a particularly good audio CD. During recording, setting the right input levels can make the difference between recording high-quality audio and distorted noise.

Windows 98's Volume Control lets you set not only overall volume for all audio, but also specific volume settings for individual audio sources. To display the Volume Control, use any of the following techniques:

- Double-click the Volume icon in the taskbar's system tray.
- In the Media Player, select Device | Volume Control.
- Select Start | Programs | Accessories | Entertainment | Volume Control.

Adjusting Audio Sources

Whichever method you use, you see the Volume Control window, shown in Figure 25.3. The Volume Control box on the left is a master control for all audio sources. The other boxes control individual audio sources. In each case, you can make the following adjustments:

- To adjust the volume, drag the appropriate Volume slider up or down.
- To turn the sound off, activate the appropriate Mute button (or, in the case of the master Volume Control, activate the Mute all button).
- To adjust the balance between the left and right speakers, drag the Balance slider right or left.

A FASTER MASTER VOLUME CONTROL

If you want to adjust the volume for, or mute, all audio sources, here's a quick way to do so: Click the Volume icon in the taskbar's system tray. A small window appears with a Volume slider and a Mute button.

Figure 25.3.

Use the Volume Control accessory to adjust the volume levels of your audio playback and recording.

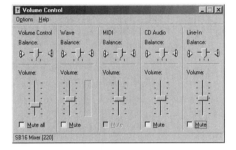

Determining the Sources That Appear in Volume Control

When you open the Volume Control, you might not see all the audio sources displayed in Figure 25.3. To control the sources that Volume Control displays, select Options | Properties to open the Properties dialog box, shown in Figure 25.4. In the Adjust volume for group, select the type of sources you want to see: Playback, Recording, or Other. In the Show the following volume controls list, activate the check boxes for the sources you want to display. When you're done, click OK.

Figure 25.4.

Use this dialog box to customize the sources that are displayed in the Volume Control window.

ADVANCED VOLUME CONTROL SETTINGS

If you select either Recording or Other in the Properties dialog box, a new Volume Control command becomes available: Options | Advanced Controls. Activating this command adds an Advanced button to the Volume Control window. Clicking this button enables you to set, among other things, the bass and treble levels for recordings (assuming that your sound card supports these settings).

Giving Windows 98 a Voice: Assigning Sounds to Events

As you work with Windows 98, you hear various sounds emanating from your speakers. These sounds always correspond to particular events. There's that relaxing, New Age–like music when you start Windows 98; there's the short, sharp shock of a sound when a warning dialog box pops up; and there's a nice little chime when you exit Windows 98.

If you're getting tired of the same old sounds, however, Windows 98 lets you customize what you hear by assigning different WAV files to these events. There also are a couple of dozen other events to which you can assign sounds. This section shows you how it's done.

Working with Sound Schemes

The sounds assigned to various Windows 98 events comprise a sound scheme. To view the current scheme, go to Control Panel and open the Sounds icon. You see the Sounds Properties dialog box, shown in Figure 25.5.

FIGURE 25.5.

Use the Sounds Properties dialog box to change the current Windows 98 sound scheme.

Here's a rundown of the various controls in this properties sheet:

Events: This list displays a number of Windows 98 events, including four that apply to the various types of dialog boxes displayed by Windows 98 and Windows applications: Asterisk, Critical Stop, Exclamation, and Question. If an event has a sound icon beside it, this means a WAV file is currently assigned to that event.

Name: This drop-down list shows you the name of the WAV file that's assigned to the currently highlighted event. You can use the Browse button to select a different WAV file (or just use the Name drop-down list to select a WAV file from Windows 98's Media subfolder), and you can use the Details button to view the properties sheet for the current WAV file.

Preview: Click the Play button to hear how the WAV file shown in the Name box will sound.

Schemes: This drop-down list displays the currently selected sound scheme.

You can use three methods to work with sound schemes:

■ To change the current sound scheme, highlight items in the Events list and change the associated WAV file.

■ To use a different sound scheme, select it from the Schemes drop-down list.

■ To create your own sound scheme, first associate WAV files with the various system events you want to hear. Then click Save As, enter a name for the new scheme, and click OK.

SOUND SCHEMES ON THE WINDOWS 98 CD-ROM

The Windows 98 CD-ROM ships with a few predefined sound schemes (such as Jungle, Musica, and Robotz). If you don't see these schemes in the Schemes box, you need to install them.

Adding New Sound Events via the Registry

You might have noticed that the Events list includes entries for opening and closing both Sound Recorder and Media Player. If you want to assign sounds to the opening and closing of other applications, you can do so by editing the Registry. You also can assign application-specific sounds to other items shown in the Events list. For example, if you assign a WAV file to the Minimize event, Windows 98 plays that sound every time you minimize a window (which means that you get thoroughly sick of the sound in about an hour). Using the Registry, on the other hand, you can assign a different sound to the Minimize event for different applications.

Here are the steps to follow to use the Registry to assign sounds to application-specific events:

1. Start the Registry Editor and open the following key:

   `HKEY_CURRENT_USER\AppEvents\Schemes\Apps`

2. Highlight the Apps key and select Edit | New | Key to create a new subkey.

3. Type the name of the executable file (no extension) for the application you want to work with and press Enter. For example, if you want to work with Paint, type `MSPaint` and press Enter.

4. For the new key, double-click the Default setting, enter the name of the application (for example, `Paint`), and click OK. (The name you enter is the name that appears in the Events list in the Sounds Properties dialog box.)

5. Now you need to add subkeys to the key you just created. These subkeys determine the events that will appear for this application in the Events list. Here are your choices:

   `Close`: Lets you assign a sound to closing the application.

   `Maximize`: Lets you assign a sound to maximizing the application.

   `MenuCommand`: Lets you assign a sound to selecting a menu command in the application.

   `MenuPopup`: Lets you assign a sound to pulling down a menu in the application.

   `Minimize`: Lets you assign a sound to minimizing the application.

   `Open`: Lets you assign a sound to opening the application.

   `RestoreDown`: Lets you assign a sound to clicking the Restore button after maximizing the application.

   `RestoreUp`: Lets you assign a sound to clicking the application's taskbar button after minimizing the application.

6. When you've finished adding subkeys (see Figure 25.6 for an example), exit the Registry Editor.

FIGURE 25.6.

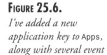

I've added a new application key to Apps, *along with several event subkeys.*

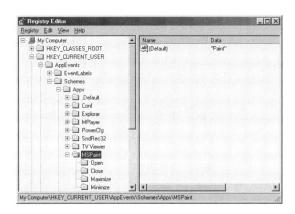

Now, when you open the Sounds Properties dialog box, your application and its events appear at the bottom of the Events list, as shown in Figure 25.7. Go ahead and assign sounds to these events.

FIGURE 25.7.

After you set things up in the Registry, the new events appear in the Sounds Properties dialog box.

Recording and Editing Sounds with the Sound Recorder

If you have a sound card capable of recording sounds (and you have a microphone attached to the sound card), you can have hours of fun creating your own WAV files. Preserving silly sounds for posterity is the most fun, of course, but you can also create serious messages and embed them in business documents. (I'll show you how in the next section.)

To get started, open the Sound Recorder as described earlier. If the Sound Recorder already has a WAV file opened, and you want to start a new file, select File | New. If you'd prefer to add sounds to an existing file, open it and find the position in the sound file where you want your recording to start. (You do this by dragging the Sound Recorder's slider.)

Setting Audio Properties

Before you start recording, you need to specify the properties you want to use for the new WAV file. These properties include the codec to use, the sampling frequency, the sample depth, and whether the new file is stereo or mono.

To set these properties, select Edit | Audio Properties to display the dialog box shown in Figure 25.8. Here's a rundown of the options in the Recording group:

Preferred Device: If you have multiple recording devices, use this drop-down list to select the device you want to use.

Advanced Properties: Clicking this button displays the Advanced Audio Properties dialog box, which contains two sliders:

Hardware Acceleration: This slider controls the amount of hardware acceleration used during the recording. If you're having trouble recording sounds, try using less acceleration.

Sample Rate Conversion Quality: This slider determines the sample rate that Sound Recorder uses to digitize the recorded sound. The higher the sample rate, the better the sound quality.

FIGURE 25.8.

Use this dialog box to set various recording options.

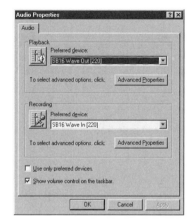

Recording a WAV File

When you're ready to start recording, here are the steps to follow:

1. With your microphone in hand, click the Record button.

2. Speak (yell, sing, whatever) into the microphone. Sound Recorder shows you the length of the file as you record. (Note that you have a maximum number of seconds to do your thing. The maximum value is a function of the audio properties you selected.)

3. When you're done, click the Stop button.

4. Check your recording by clicking the Seek to Start button and then the Play button.

5. If you don't like how your recording sounds, you can start over by clicking the Seek to Start button. (If you want to replace only part of the recording, drag the slider to the point where you want the replacement recording to start.) Then repeat steps 1 through 4.

6. If you're happy with your recording, select File | Save, enter a name and location for the file in the Save As dialog box, and click OK.

Editing a WAV File

Besides letting you record your own sounds, Sound Recorder comes with a host of interesting options for creating some really wild effects. Here's a summary:

Inserting an audio file: If you'd like to include another WAV file in your recording, position the slider where you want the other file to start. Then select Edit | Insert File, highlight the file in the Insert File dialog box, and click Open.

Mixing audio files: You can mix two or more WAV files so that they play at the same time. For example, you can combine one WAV file that contains narration with another that has soothing music. To try this, open one of the WAV files and move to where you want the second file to start. Select Edit | Mix with File, highlight the other WAV file in the Mix With File dialog box, and click Open.

PASTING THE CURRENT AUDIO FILE

If you want to insert or mix the current audio file with another file, select Edit | Copy to send the current file to the Clipboard. Open the other file, position the slider appropriately, and select either Edit | Paste Insert or Edit | Paste Mix. (Note that, if you prefer to keep the current file open, you can always start up a second copy of Sound Recorder.)

Deleting chunks of audio: If there are sections of an audio file you no longer need, Sound Recorder lets you make deletions. To delete from the beginning of the file to a specific point, position the slider appropriately and select Edit | Delete Before Current Position. To delete from a specific point to the end of the file, position the slider appropriately and select Edit | Delete After Current Position. In either case, Sound Recorder will ask you to confirm the deletion. Click OK to proceed.

Changing the volume: If you've made your WAV file too loud or too soft, select either Effects | Increase Volume (to make the sound louder by 25 percent) or Effects | Decrease Volume (to make the sound quieter by 25 percent).

Altering the playback speed: You can make your voice recordings sound like either Alvin and the Chipmunks or Darth Vader by adjusting the speed of the playback. Choose either Effects | Increase Speed (to double the speed) or Effects | Decrease Speed (to cut the speed in half).

Adding an echo...echo...echo: If you select Effects | Add Echo, Sound Recorder creates a neat echo effect that makes your WAV files sound as if they're being played in some cavernous location.

Reversing a sound: Playing a sound file backward can produce some real mind-blowing effects. To check this out, choose Effects | Reverse.

REVERSING YOUR CHANGES

If you make a mess of your WAV file, you can get back to square one by selecting File | Revert. When Sound Recorder asks for confirmation, click Yes. This returns the file to the state it was in when you last saved it.

Reinstalling an Audio Codec

If you have trouble with a specific audio codec, removing the codec and then reinstalling it will often solve the problem. Here are the steps to follow to remove an audio codec:

1. In Control Panel, open the Multimedia icon and select the Devices tab.

2. Open the Audio Compression Codecs tree (see Figure 25.9) and highlight the codec you want to remove.

FIGURE 25.9.

In the Devices tab of the Multimedia Properties dialog box, highlight the audio codec you want to remove.

3. Click the Properties button. In the codec properties sheet that appears, click Remove.

4. When Windows 98 asks whether you're sure, click Yes and then click OK in the next two dialog boxes. (Windows 98 will tell you to restart the system. You can ignore this.)

5. Close the Multimedia Properties dialog box to return to Control Panel.

To reinstall the codec, follow these steps:

1. In Control Panel, open the Add New Hardware icon.

2. Click Next > and then click Next > again to have the Wizard check for Plug and Play devices.

3. When the Wizard asks whether you want Windows to search for new hardware, activate No and click Next >.

4. In the Hardware types list, highlight Sound, video and game controllers and click Next >.

5. In the Manufacturers list, highlight the appropriate item (such as Microsoft Audio Codecs).

6. In the Models list, highlight the codec you want to install and click Next >.

7. Click Finish and follow the onscreen prompts for inserting your Windows 98 source disks.

8. When Windows 98 asks whether you want to restart your system, click Yes.

Summary

This chapter closed out your look at Windows 98 multimedia by looking at various audio features. After some audio background, including coverage of the various audio formats and codecs that Windows 98 supports, I showed you how to install the PC Speaker driver, play audio files, adjust the volume, assign sounds to events, and record new audio files.

Here's a list of chapters where you'll find related information:

■ For a more general look at hardware and device drivers, see Chapter 10, "Getting the Most Out of Device Manager and Hardware Profiles."

■ I introduced you to the Registry and the Registry Editor in Chapter 12, "Getting to Know the Windows 98 Registry."

■ Audio plays a big part in video clips. I told you all about Windows 98 video in Chapter 24, "DirectX and Windows 98 Video."

VI

PART

Unleashing Windows 98 Communications and Networking

Getting Started with Modem Communications

CHAPTER 26

There is no pleasure to me without communication: there is not so much as a sprightly thought comes into my mind that it does not grieve me to have produced alone, and that I have no one to tell it to.

—*Michel de Montaigne*

These days, the de rigueur accessory for PC fashion plates is the modem. *Everyone*, it seems, is flocking online like so many swallows to Capistrano. The Internet, of course, is the Big Thing, but folks are connecting to commercial services, bulletin boards, and other online locales in record numbers. And we're not talking only about the extroverts of the world, such as Montaigne, who just wanted to reach out and modem someone, *anyone*. No, people of all walks of life, temperaments, and levels of expertise are surfing like there's no tomorrow.

If you've upgraded from Windows 3.1, you'll see that Windows 98 has jumped on this modem bandwagon in a big way with a totally revamped communications subsystem, easier modem setup, and some decent communications applets. This chapter gives you some background in modem communications and shows you how to get your modem's mojo working. Chapter 27, "Putting Your Modem to Work," shows you how to work a couple of Windows 98 applets: Phone Dialer and HyperTerminal.

Modem-to-Modem Communications

Modem communications is one of those ideas that, after you learn a bit of background, you wonder how on earth your system actually pulls it off. I mean, you're talking about tens of thousands of bits per second busily bustling between two computers, all the while negotiating compression routines, FIFO buffers, parallel-to-serial UART conversions, modulations, and who knows what else. To combine all of these complex technologies and achieve a remarkably high level of accuracy is an amazing achievement. To help you appreciate some of the hoops your computer, serial port, and modem have to jump through to accomplish this wizardry, this section takes a closer look at just how two modems communicate with each other.

Flow Control: The Communications Traffic Cop

Modem downloads come in fast and furious, so what's your computer supposed to do if it isn't ready to receive any data? Conversely, what if you're sending data and the remote system indicates that it can't receive any more data just now? How does your modem tell the CPU to stop processing data temporarily?

These kinds of situations fall under the rubric of *flow control*, which defines how the computer and the modem communicate with each other to coordinate data exchanges and prevent overruns when one device isn't ready to receive information from the other. There are two types of flow control: software and hardware.

Software Flow Control (XON/XOFF)

With *software flow control*, the computer and modem send signals to each other that indicate whether they're ready to receive data. For example, suppose that you're downloading a file and the computer needs to pause the download briefly while it attends to some other chores. To do this, it sends to the remote system's modem a special "hold your horses" signal called *XOFF*. (In data communications circles, *X* stands for transfer, so *XOFF* means "transfer off.") XOFF is an ASCII control code character (ASCII 19 or Ctrl+S) that gets shipped out to the remote system just like any other character. When the computer decides it's okay to resume the download, it notifies the remote system by sending a signal called *XON* (which is another control code character: ASCII 17 or Ctrl+Q). Because of these two signals, software flow control is also known as *XON/XOFF flow control*.

TROUBLESHOOTING: PRESS CTRL+Q TO RESUME DATA TRANSFERS

If you find that a data transfer has halted, it might be because your system has inadvertently sent an XOFF flow control signal. Try pressing Ctrl+Q to send an XON signal. If the remote system supports software flow control, this might be enough to get the transfer going again.

Hardware Flow Control (RTS/CTS)

Because of the high overhead associated with software flow control, it becomes inefficient at data transfer rates higher than 2,400bps. For higher speeds, *hardware flow control* is a much better option. That's because instead of firing an entire character out to the remote device, hardware flow control just uses individual serial port lines to send signals. Hardware flow control uses two of these lines: RTS and CTS (which is why this method is also called *RTS/CTS flow control*).

For example, suppose your modem wants to stop the computer from sending any more data (because, for example, it has lost its Carrier Detect signal and so doesn't have a connection with the remote system). To do that, all it does is turn off its CTS (Clear To Send) signal. The computer reads that the serial port's CTS wire is off, so it stops processing data for the modem.

Similarly, the processor's willingness to accept more data from the modem is controlled by the RTS (Request To Send) wire. If the processor turns off RTS, the modem reads that the serial port's RTS wire is off, so it pauses the data transfer.

Data Bits: The Crux of the Matter

The role of the serial port's UART chip is to convert the eight parallel bits that PCs use to represent data into a series of eight consecutive bits suitable for squeezing through the serial port's TD (Transmit Data) wire.

The problem, though, is that not all computer systems use 8 bits to represent their characters. All PCs do, because they need the 8 bits to represent all 256 characters in the ASCII character set (because each bit can use one of two states—on or off, 1 or 0—and 2 to the power of 8 is 256). Most mainframe systems, however, use only 7 bits to represent characters because they recognize only the first 128 ASCII characters (2 to the power of 7 is 128). The number of bits used to represent a character is called the *data bits* setting, or the *character length*.

So one of the most important parameters when a remote system is involved is the number of data bits it uses. Problems can arise, for example, if you send 8-bit bytes to a system that knows how to deal with only 7 of them. In PC systems, fortunately, the first 128 ASCII characters have a 0 as their eighth bit, so it can be safely discarded during communication with 7-bit systems.

Start and Stop Bits: Bookends for Your Data

The data coursing through your computer is transferred from place to place at extremely high speeds by using exquisitely timed procedures to coordinate the transfers. This type of communications is called *synchronous* because it depends on timing signals.

The vagaries of modem communications, however, prevent such precise timing, so modems use *asynchronous* communications. In asynchronous communications, as long as the remote system is willing and able to receive data, the data is just sent out whenever it's ready to go.

But with no timing involved, knowing where one character ends and the next begins becomes a problem. You might think that you could just use the number of data bits. For example, if your system and the remote system both use 8-bit bytes, you could simply define every eighth bit as the starting point for each character. Unfortunately, that approach would work only in a perfect world that boasted noiseless telephone lines and error-free data transfers. In the real world, in the journey between here and there, legitimate bits can become missing, and extraneous "bits" (that is, line noises) can get tossed into the mix.

To help the receiving end delimit incoming characters, the sending system's UART tacks on extra bits on both sides of the data. At the front of the data, the UART adds a start bit that defines the beginning of each character. This is followed by the data bits, and then the UART appends a *stop bit* to mark the end of the character.

The start bit is always the same, but different systems require different length stop bits. Most systems use a single stop bit, but a few rare cases insist on two stop bits. (You also read about systems that require 1 ½ stop bits. *Half* a bit? It doesn't make sense until you remember that these "bits" I'm talking about are really electromagnetic pulses traveling along an analog carrier wave. Each pulse consumes a predefined amount of time—say, 1/14,400th of a second—so 1 ½ bits is really just 1 ½ pulses.)

At the receiving end, the UART busies itself by stripping off the start and stop bits before recombining the data bits into a full byte.

Parity: A Crude Error Check

The start and stop bits can tell the receiving modem it has received corrupted data. For example, if the modem is expecting 8 data bits but gets 7 or 9, it knows that something has gone haywire, and it can ask that the bit be retransmitted.

What if, however, a voltage spike or some line noise doesn't add or subtract bits from a character, but instead *changes* one of the existing bits? The receiving modem still gets the appropriate number of data bits, so it won't know that anything has gone awry. To cover this kind of trouble, many systems that use 7-bit characters also use *parity checking*. In this technique, an extra bit—called the *parity bit*—is added to the data bits (but before the stop bit). The parity bit is set to either 1 or 0, depending on the type of parity checking used.

> **Even parity:** In this method, you first sum all the 1s in the data bits and see whether you end up with an odd or even number. Your goal is to send out an even number of 1s, so you use (or, technically, the UART uses) the extra parity bit to ensure this. For example, suppose that the data bits are 0000111. The sum of the 1s here is 3, which is odd, so the parity bit must be set to 1 to give you an even number of 1s. The UART sends out 10000111. Similarly, suppose that your data bits are 1000001. The sum of the 1s is 2, which is even, so the parity bit can be set to 0, like so: 01000001.
>
> **Odd parity:** This is the opposite of even parity. Again, you first sum all the 1s in the data bits and see whether you end up with an odd or even number. In this case, however, your goal is to send out an odd number of 1s, and you manipulate the parity bit accordingly.

Most systems use even parity. (Two other kinds of parity—mark and space—also exist, but these are virtually obsolete.)

How does this help the receiving system check the data? Well, if it's using even parity, the receiving system's UART checks the incoming bits and adds up all the 1s. If it finds an odd number of 1s, it knows that a bit was changed en route, so it can ask for a retransmit. Of course, if a voltage spike changes several bits, the number of 1s might remain even, so the receiving UART wouldn't detect an error. Therefore, parity is only a crude error-checking mechanism.

COMMON CONNECTION SETTINGS

When setting up a connection to a remote system, you need to make sure that the three settings I've just talked about—data bits, stop bits, and parity—match the parameters expected by the remote computer. If you're not sure which settings to use, note that two combinations are the most common: 7 data bits, even parity, 1 stop bit (usually written as 7-E-1); and 8 data bits, no parity, 1 stop bit (8-N-1). The former combination is often used to connect to large online services that use mainframes (such as CompuServe); the latter works for most bulletin board systems and PC-to-PC connections.

Terminal Emulation: Fitting in with the Online World

When you use your modem to connect to a remote computer, you are, essentially, operating that computer from your keyboard and seeing the results onscreen. In other words, your computer has become a *terminal* attached to the remote machine.

It's likely, however, that the remote computer is completely different from the one you're using. It could be a mainframe or a minicomputer, for example. In that case, it isn't likely that the codes produced by your keystrokes will correspond exactly with the codes used by the remote computer. Similarly, some of the return codes won't make sense to your machine. So for your computer to act like a true terminal, some kind of translation is needed between the two systems. This translation is called *terminal emulation* because it forces your system to emulate the kind of terminal that the remote computer normally deals with.

Most communications programs give you a choice of terminal emulation methods, such as ANSI for other DOS/Windows computers, TTY for teletype terminals, or specific terminal types, such as the DEC VT100 and VT52.

File Transfers: A Matter of Protocol

Although much of your online time will be spent grazing data marketplaces and chatting with others, the most common online activity involves transferring files back and forth. When you receive a file from a remote computer, it's called *downloading*; when you send a file to a remote computer, it's called *uploading*.

For your downloads and uploads to succeed, your system and the remote system must agree on which *file transfer protocol* to use. The protocol governs various aspects of the file transfer ritual, including starting and stopping, the size of the data packets being sent (in general, the larger the packet, the faster the transfer), how errors are handled, and so on. Many different file transfer protocols are available, but as you'll see later, Windows 98 supports the following seven:

> **Xmodem:** Designed in 1977, this was the first protocol for PCs. Because it uses only a simple error-checking routine and sends data in small, 128-byte packets, Xmodem should be used only as a last resort.

> **1K Xmodem:** This is an updated version of Xmodem that uses 1,024-byte data packets and an improved 16-bit cyclic redundancy check (CRC) error-checking protocol. This makes 1K Xmodem more reliable than plain Xmodem and, as long as the telephone lines are relatively noise-free, much faster as well.

> **Ymodem:** This protocol provides all the benefits of 1K Xmodem (including 1,024-byte packets and CRC error control) but also implements multiple-file transfers and the exchange of file data, including the name and size of each file.

> **Ymodem-G:** This protocol is the same as Ymodem, except that it performs no error checking. Instead, it relies on the built-in error checking of modern modems (such as V.42 and MNP 4).

Zmodem: This is the fastest of the file transfer protocols and the most reliable. Zmodem doesn't use a fixed packet size. Instead, it adjusts the size of each packet based on the line conditions. For error checking, Zmodem uses a 32-bit CRC for enhanced reliability. Zmodem is, by far, the choice among online aficionados.

Zmodem with Crash Recovery: This version of the Zmodem protocol offers crash protection. This means that if the file transfer bails out before completing, you can restart and the Zmodem protocol resumes the transfer where it left off.

Kermit: This is a flexible protocol that can handle the 7-bit bytes used by mainframes and minicomputers. It's very slow, however, and you should avoid it if the remote machine supports any other protocol.

Configuring Serial Ports

As you've seen so far, serial ports play a vital role in modem communications. To make sure that your serial ports are ready to do their duty, you might want to set a few properties. Here's how it's done:

1. Open the Control Panel's System icon, and in the System Properties dialog box that appears, select the Device Manager tab.

2. Open the Ports (COM and LPT) branch, highlight the COM port you want to work with, and click Properties.

3. Display the Port Settings tab, shown in Figure 26.1. These drop-down lists set up default communications settings for the port. You don't need to adjust these values for your modem's port, however, because the settings you specify for the modem will override the ones you see here. You need to change these values only if you'll be attaching some other kind of device to the port.

FIGURE 26.1.

The Port Settings tab controls various communications parameters.

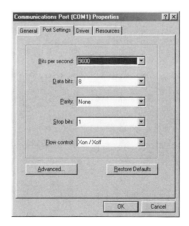

4. COM ports use interrupts to communicate with the processor. (For example, the UART uses an interrupt to let the processor know that the buffer contains incoming data.) If you have an IRQ conflict, use the Resources tab to make changes. (See Chapter 10, "Getting the Most Out of Device Manager and Hardware Profiles," for the details.)

5. Click OK and, if necessary, restart your computer.

Installing and Configuring a Modem

Before you can use Phone Dialer, HyperTerminal, or any other communications software, you need to tell Windows 98 what kind of modem you have. After that's done, you need to configure the modem to suit the types of online sessions you plan to run. To that end, the next few sections take you through the rigmarole of installing and configuring your modem.

Installing Your First Modem

The route you take to install a modem differs slightly depending on whether you've already installed a modem in Windows 98. Here are the steps to follow to install your first modem:

1. Open the Control Panel's Modems icon. The Install New Modem Wizard appears.

2. Activate the Don't run the Hardware Installation Wizard check box, and then click Next >.

3. If the modem isn't attached to your machine yet, activate the Don't detect my modem; I will select it from a list check box, and click Next >. Otherwise, leave this check box deactivated and click Next >.

4. If you have Windows 98 detect the modem, it queries your system's serial ports to see whether a modem is attached. When it's done, it displays the name of the modem it found. If this information is incorrect, click Change. Otherwise, click Next > and skip to step 6.

5. If you're selecting the modem by hand, you see the dialog box shown in Figure 26.2. Use the Manufacturers and Models lists to highlight your modem, and then click Next >. If your modem isn't in the list, you have two choices: Select Standard Modem Types in the Manufacturers list and choose a generic model; or, if you have a disk from the manufacturer, click the Have Disk button and follow the onscreen prompts.

6. The next wizard dialog box asks you to select a serial port, as shown in Figure 26.3. Highlight the appropriate port and click Next >. Windows 98 installs your modem.

7. Click Finish.

FIGURE 26.2.

If you elect to specify your modem yourself, you use this dialog box to do it.

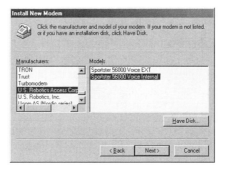

Installing Another Modem

After you've installed your first modem, Windows 98 displays the Modems Properties dialog box, shown in Figure 26.4. (You can also display this properties sheet by opening the Modems icon in Control Panel.) To install a modem from here, click the Add button and follow the steps outlined in the preceding section. (You won't have to bother with step 6, however, because Windows 98 just uses the same values that you entered for your first modem.)

FIGURE 26.3.

Use this dialog box to select the port used by your modem.

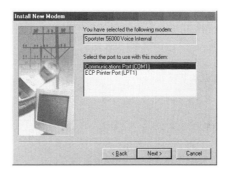

FIGURE 26.4.

The Modems Properties dialog box lists your currently installed modems.

Modifying the Modem's Dialing Properties

As you saw when you were setting up your modem, Windows 98 keeps track of various dialing properties for each modem. These properties determine how Windows 98 dials the modem. For example, the Country setting determines the country code used for long-distance calls (this is 1 in the United States and Canada), and the Area Code setting lets Windows 98 determine whether the outgoing call is long distance.

You can change these and other dialing parameters by clicking the Dialing Properties button in the Modems Properties dialog box. Figure 26.5 shows the dialog box that appears.

FIGURE 26.5.

Use this dialog box to adjust the settings that Windows 98 uses to dial your modem.

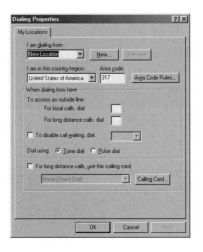

Here's a rundown of the controls in this dialog box:

I am dialing from: This list contains all the dialing locations you've defined. To learn how to define multiple locations, see "Working with Different Dialing Locations," later in this chapter.

I am in this country/region: Use this list to set the country code from which you'll be dialing.

Area code: Use this text box to set the area code from which you'll be dialing.

New to 98

Area Code Rules: This is a new button in Windows 98 and it enables you to set up 10-digit dialing and other area code customizations. Clicking this button displays the Area Code Rules dialog box (shown in Figure 26.6), which has two groups:

When calling within my area code: In some cases, the phone company requires that you use the area code even if you're calling another number within the same area code. If the call isn't a long distance number, activate the Always dial the area code (10-Digit Dialing) check box. If some of the phone number prefixes in your area code are long distance calls (and this requires the country code), click New to add the prefixes to the list.

When calling to other area codes: In some larger cities, the phone company has run out of phone numbers in the main area code. To overcome this problem, the phone company usually splits off part of the existing customers into a new area code and requires that calls between the two areas be prefaced with the appropriate area code. These aren't long-distance calls, however, so no country code is required. In this case, click New to add the area codes for which Windows 98 shouldn't dial a 1.

FIGURE 26.6.

Use this dialog box to set up 10-digit dialing.

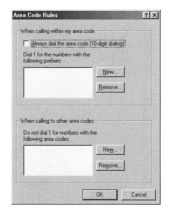

To access an outside line: Use the For local calls, dial text box to enter the code that must be dialed to get an outside line for local calls (such as 9). Use the For long distance calls, dial text box to enter the code that must be dialed to get an outside line for long distance calls (such as 8).

To disable call waiting, dial: To deactivate call waiting before making the call, activate this check box and then either enter the appropriate code in the text box or select one of the existing codes from the list.

ALWAYS DISABLE CALL WAITING

The extra beeps that call waiting uses to indicate an incoming call can wreak havoc on modem communications, so you should always disable call waiting before initiating a data call. The sequences *70, 70#, or 1170 usually disable call waiting, but you should check with your local phone company to make sure.

Dial using: Select either Tone dial or Pulse dial, as appropriate for your telephone line.

For long distance calls, use this calling card: These controls enable you to set up a calling card or long-distance carrier. This is explained in detail in the next section.

Specifying a Calling Card or Long-Distance Carrier

Although most of your phone calls are likely to be free, at times this might not be the case, and you'll want to make some other arrangements for charging the call. Two situations, in particular, might crop up from time to time:

■ You're dialing from a hotel and want to charge the call to your calling card.

■ You need to make a long-distance connection, in which case you might want to first dial the number of a long-distance carrier.

Windows 98 can handle both situations. To specify either a calling card number or a long-distance carrier phone number, follow these steps:

1. Activate the For long distance calls, use this calling card check box in the Dialing Properties dialog box.

2. Click the Calling Card button to display the Calling Card dialog box, shown in Figure 26.7.

FIGURE 26.7.

Use the Calling Card dialog box to enter a calling card number or select a long-distance carrier.

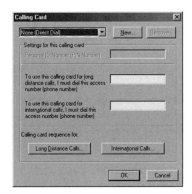

3. Use the list box to choose the type of calling card or long-distance carrier you have.

4. For a calling card, use the Personal Identification Number (PIN Number) text box to enter your PIN number.

5. Fill in the next two text boxes with the access numbers required by your calling card or carrier. The first text box is for long distance calls, and the second text box is for international calls.

6. To change the long distance dialing sequence for the calling card or carrier, click Long Distance Calls to display the Calling Card Sequence dialog box, shown in Figure 26.8. In each step, select the appropriate Dial code and use the then wait for list to specify what signal Windows 98 must wait for before continuing. Click OK when you're done.

FIGURE 26.8.

Use the Calling Card Sequence dialog box to specify the order in which Windows 98 dials the codes and phone numbers required by your calling card or carrier.

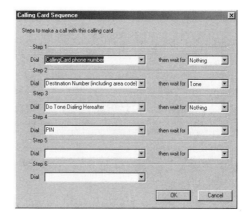

7. To change the international call distance dialing sequence, click International Calls and fill in the dialog box that appears.

8. Click OK to return to the Dialing Properties dialog box.

If your calling card or long-distance carrier doesn't appear in the list, follow these steps to add it:

1. In the Calling Card dialog box, click the New button to display the Create New Calling Card dialog box.

2. Enter a descriptive name for the calling card or carrier and then click OK. Windows 98 tells you that you must now enter the dialing rules for the card or carrier.

3. Click OK to return to the Calling Card dialog box.

4. Follow steps 4 through 8 to specify the dialing rules for your new card or carrier.

Working with Different Dialing Locations

If you have a notebook computer, you can set up multiple dialing locations. For example, you could have one location for dialing from the office that uses extra digits to access an outside line and uses your corporate calling card. You could then have a second location for home that doesn't require anything extra to access an outside line and disables your call waiting service.

WATCH FOR DIGITAL PHONE JACKS

If you travel with your notebook and use a modem to connect to the office or the Internet, watch out for the digital phone systems that are used by many hotels. Analog modems aren't compatible with digital systems, so you end up frying your modem if you attempt to connect over a digital line. Unfortunately, digital phone jacks look identical to regular analog jacks, so you need to ask the hotel staff what kind of phone jacks they use.

The location information you entered while installing your modem is stored in a location called Default Location. To set up another location, click New, enter a name in the Create New Location dialog box and click OK, and enter your dialing properties for the new location.

To choose a different location, use the I am dialing from drop-down list.

Modifying the Modem's General Properties

Your modem has all kinds of properties you can play with to alter how the device works and to troubleshoot problematic connections. To see these properties, highlight the modem in the Modem Properties dialog box, and then click the Properties button. Figure 26.9 shows the properties sheet that appears. The General tab offers the following controls:

Port: Use this drop-down list to specify the serial port you're using for the modem.

Speaker volume: This slider determines how loud your modem sounds (although not all modems support this feature). Because modems can make quite a racket, you might consider setting the volume low or even off while using it in public or in a quiet office. If adjusting this slider to its lowest setting still doesn't turn off your modem's sounds, check out "The Advanced Button" later in this chapter. The Advanced Connection Settings dialog box has an Extra Settings text box in which you can enter the ATM0 command, which mutes the modem.

Maximum speed: This setting determines the maximum throughput (in bps) that the modem can handle. This speed depends on the modulation protocol, data compression used, and a few other factors. Later, I'll show you a test you can run to determine the maximum speed for your modem (see "Testing the Modem" later in this chapter). Your modem won't necessarily use this speed. Instead, it will determine the optimum speed based on the remote system and the line conditions. If, however, you prefer that your modem connect only at this speed, activate the Only connect at this speed check box (this feature isn't supported by all modems).

FIGURE 26.9.

Use the General tab to control the modem's port, speaker volume, and maximum speed.

TROUBLESHOOTING: ADJUST THE SPEED TO YOUR UART

If you're having trouble connecting and the serial port doesn't use a 16550 UART, be sure to set the Maximum speed value to no more than 9600.

Modifying the Modem's Connection Settings

The Connection tab, shown in Figure 26.10, contains several controls that determine the modem's default behavior for connecting to remote systems. Here's a rundown of the various options:

Connection preferences: These drop-down lists determine the default values you want to use for data bits, parity, and stop bits. Note that these settings override any values you entered for the modem's serial port.

Wait for dial tone before dialing: When this check box is activated, the modem won't dial unless it can detect a dial tone, which is usually what you want. If, however, your modem doesn't seem to recognize the dial tone in your current location (if you're in a different country, for example), or if you need to dial manually, deactivate this check box.

Cancel the call if not connected within *x* secs: When this option is activated, it determines how long Windows 98 waits for a connection between your modem and a remote system to be established. If no connection is made within the allotted time, Windows 98 cancels the call.

Disconnect a call if idle for more than *x* mins: This option, when activated, determines how long Windows 98 waits for the modem to be idle before it disconnects the call. If you regularly go long intervals without modem activity, you can ignore this option. This option is invaluable, however, if you forget that you're connected or if you want to run a long file download unattended.

FIGURE 26.10.

Use the Connection tab to set up the modem's default settings for connecting to remote computers.

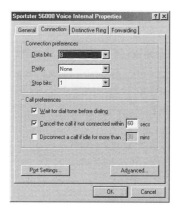

The next two sections explain the Port Settings and Advanced buttons.

The Port Settings Button

Clicking the Port Settings button displays the Advanced Port Settings dialog box, shown in Figure 26.11. The options in this dialog box control the FIFO buffers in the serial port's UART chip. The two sliders determine the level at which the UART generates interrupts for the receive and transmit buffers.

FIGURE 26.11.

The Advanced Port Settings dialog box lets you customize the FIFO buffers for a 16550 UART.

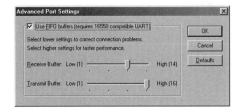

Fewer interrupts means better performance overall. For example, if you move the Transmit Buffer slider to High (16; all the way to the right), the UART won't generate an interrupt until all 16 buffers are full. Conversely, if you set the slider to Low (1), the UART generates an interrupt each time a buffer is filled. If you're having communications problems (such as dropped characters), however, a lack of interrupts might be the problem. In this case, you should move the sliders to the left to generate more interrupts.

The Advanced Button

Clicking the Advanced button displays the Advanced Connection Settings dialog box, shown in Figure 26.12. This dialog box sets up the various modem protocols, including error correction, compression, flow control, and modulation. Here's the summary:

Use error control: Activate this check box to enable the modem's built-in error-checking protocol (such as V.42 or MNP 4). Note that you must activate this option to use the three other check boxes in this group.

Required to connect: If you activate this check box, the modem uses its error-checking routine to establish a connection. If a reliable connection can't be established, the connection attempt is terminated.

Compress data: Activate this option to enable the modem's built-in data compression protocol (such as V.42bis or MNP 5). As explained earlier, you can use compression for text and binary files, but you should disable it for compressed file transfers.

Use cellular protocol: Activate this option to enable the cellular error-correction protocol. This is a feature in high-speed PC Card modems that you should use if you plan to initiate a connection via a cellular phone. This protocol helps reduce errors as the connection is transferred between cells.

Use flow control: Activate this check box to enable flow control. Select either Hardware (RTS/CTS) or Software (XON/OFF).

Modulation type: This drop-down list determines the type of modulation to use with the modem. The Standard option means the modem uses its default ITU-TSS modulation protocol. The Non-standard option usually implements whatever proprietary modulation is supported by the modem.

Extra settings: Use this text box to enter extra dialing strings to customize the modem's setup. See your modem's manual to determine the string formats to use.

Append to log: If you activate this check box, Windows 98 creates a file named Modem.log (where Modem is the name of your modem) in your main Windows 98 folder. The system monitors the calls and uses the log to keep track of connection events, status messages, and other items that might be useful during troubleshooting. Click View Log to open the log file in Notepad.

TROUBLESHOOTING: THE U.S. ROBOTICS MODEM HANGS

If you have a U.S. Robotics Sportster modem (or a model based on the Sportster, such as the Gateway TelePath), you might have experienced frequent problems with the modem's hanging during a connection. If so, you probably can fix this problem by adding the string S12=0 to the Extra settings text box.

FIGURE 26.12.

The Advanced Connection Settings dialog box lets you specify error control, flow control, modulation, and other connection-related options.

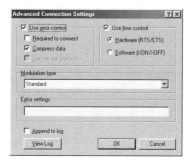

Testing the Modem

After you configure your modem, you should test it to make sure that things are working correctly. To do this, return to the Modems Properties dialog box and then select the Diagnostics tab. Highlight the port where your modem is attached, make sure that the modem is powered up, and click the More Info button.

If there's a problem with your modem, a dialog box lets you know. Otherwise, after a minute or two, you see a dialog box that tells you, among other things, the maximum speed for your modem, the UART type, and numerous internal settings.

Summary

This chapter showed you how to get started with modem communications in Windows 98. I began with an in-depth look at how modems do their thing. I then showed you how to install a modem in Windows 98 and how to configure and test the modem.

This chapter represents only the beginning of your look at Windows 98 communications. Here's what's in store in chapters to come:

- Chapter 27, "Putting Your Modem to Work," shows you how to use Windows 98's Phone Dialer and HyperTerminal accessories.

- If you're on the road, Windows 98's Dial-Up Networking feature lets you connect to your network. I provide all the particulars in Chapter 30, "Remote Computing with Dial-Up Networking."

- These days, the Internet is where the action is in communications. If you want to see what all the fuss is about, head for Chapter 32, "Windows 98 and the Internet."

Putting Your
Modem to Work

IN THIS CHAPTER

27

CHAPTER

Information is the oxygen of the modern age. It seeps through the walls topped by barbed wire, it wafts across the electrified borders.

—Ronald Reagan

With your modem now installed and configured in Windows 98, you're ready to put it to good use. To that end, this chapter gets the practical side of your modem education off the ground by showing how to use a couple of Windows 98 communications accessories. I begin by showing you how to use Phone Dialer to get your modem to dial voice calls for you. From there, I turn to more serious modem matters by showing how to use HyperTerminal to connect to bulletin board systems and online services.

Getting Your Modem to Dial Voice Calls for You

If you don't have a speed-dial phone on your desk, Windows 98 can provide you with the next best thing: Phone Dialer. This is a simple telephony application that accepts a phone number and then uses your modem to dial the number for you automatically.

To take advantage of Phone Dialer, you need to make the following arrangements with your phone cables:

- Run one phone cable from your phone to the "Phone" jack on your modem.
- Run a second phone cable from your modem's "Line" jack to the phone jack on your wall.

When that's done, you can get into Phone Dialer by selecting Start | Programs | Accessories | Communications | Phone Dialer. You see the Phone Dialer window, shown in Figure 27.1.

FIGURE 27.1.

Phone Dialer is only too happy to use your modem to dial voice calls for you.

As you can see, Phone Dialer is set up to look more or less like a telephone keypad. To dial a number, you type it in the Number to dial text box (you can also use the mouse to click the appropriate numbers in the keypad) and then click the Dial button. After a couple of seconds, you'll hear the number being dialed through your modem's speaker. Pick up the receiver and, after the modem has completed dialing, click the Talk button in the dialog box that appears. If you want Windows 98 to keep a log of the call (who you called and for how long), type the person's name in the dialog box that remains onscreen. When the call is done, click the Hang Up button.

CHANGE DIALING PROPERTIES ON-THE-FLY

The Phone Dialer uses the dialing properties you established earlier for your modem. If you want to change the properties (to use a calling card, for example), you can access the Dialing Properties dialog box from within Phone Dialer (see "Phone Dialer's Dialing Properties," later in this chapter). You can also change properties in "mid-dial," so to speak. When you click the Dial button, a Dialing dialog box appears for a couple of seconds before the dialing begins. If you click the Change Options button, Phone Dialer displays the Change Options and Redial dialog box. From there, you can click the Dialing Properties button to change the properties and then click Redial to continue with the call.

DISPLAYING THE CALL LOG

If you enter the call into the log, you can view the log later by selecting Phone Dialer's Tools | Show Log command. If you want to redial a number that's listed in the log, just double-click it.

If you want to dial the same number again later, just open the drop-down list next to the Number to dial box and select the number. No retyping is needed.

Phone Dialer's Connection Properties

Phone Dialer has a few options you can use to configure your phone dialing. For example, if you have multiple modems or multiple lines on your phone, you can tell Phone Dialer which ones to use.

To work with these options, select Tools | Connect Using to display the Connect Using dialog box, shown in Figure 27.2. Here are your options:

Line: Use this drop-down list to select the modem you want Phone Dialer to use. If you need to make changes to the modem setup, click the Line Properties button to display the modem's properties sheet.

Address: Use this drop-down list to select the phone line you want Phone Dialer to use.

Use Phone Dialer to handle voice call requests from other programs: If you activate this check box, other programs that initiate voice calls (such as the Schedule+ program that comes with Microsoft Office 95) will use Phone Dialer.

FIGURE 27.2.

Use this dialog box to select the modem or phone line to use with Phone Dialer.

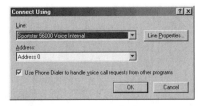

Phone Dialer's Dialing Properties

Phone Dialer also works with the dialing properties I showed you in Chapter 26, "Getting Started with Modem Communications." This is convenient because it lets you specify calling card numbers, long-distance carrier numbers, and other dialing options, which saves you from having to enter the information manually for each voice call. If you need to make changes to the dialing properties, you can do it right from Phone Dialer by selecting Tools | Dialing Properties.

Quick Connections with Speed Dial

Phone Dialer is certainly handy, but it becomes downright useful when you take advantage of the speed dialing feature. The eight buttons arranged down the right side in the Speed dial group can be programmed with frequently called numbers. You just click a programmed button, and Phone Dialer dials the number for you automatically.

Programming a Speed Dial Button

To program a speed dial button, click it to display the Program Speed Dial dialog box, shown in Figure 27.3. Use the Name text box to enter the name you want associated with the number, and use the Number to dial text box to enter the number itself. Then click the Save button to save the info, or click Save and Dial to save it and dial the number right away.

FIGURE 27.3.

Use this dialog box to program the selected speed dial button.

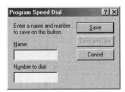

Editing Speed Dial Entries

If you want to change the name or number associated with one of the speed dial buttons, you can't just click it, because that action dials the number. Instead, select Edit | Speed Dial. In the Edit Speed Dial dialog box, shown in Figure 27.4, click the button you want to change and then use the Name and Number to dial text boxes to edit the information. Click Save when you're done.

FIGURE 27.4.

Use the Edit Speed Dial dialog box to modify your programmed speed dial entries.

Using HyperTerminal for Modem-to-Modem Connections

The Phone Dialer is a handy tool, but it's almost certainly not why you bought your modem. Instead, your modem's true raison d'être is to connect to other modems and thus propel you into the world of online services and bulletin board systems (BBSs). To do this, you need a communications program (or *terminal* program) that can operate your modem and handle the behind-the-scenes dirty work of dialing, connecting, downloading, and uploading.

In Windows 3.*x*, modem communications were handled by the Terminal accessory, a homely, Spartan program that proved to be merely adequate in everything it did. Few people liked Terminal, and even fewer actually used it, but the Windows 98 replacement—a program called HyperTerminal—should please all but the most discriminating modem jockeys. HyperTerminal is a slick, 32-bit application that integrates seamlessly with Windows 98's communications subsystem. It offers numerous improvements over Terminal, including an attractive interface, greater terminal emulation options, and support for most popular file transfer protocols, such as 1K Xmodem and Zmodem. The next few sections show you how to use HyperTerminal to set up, dial, and work with online connections.

HYPERTERMINAL AND THE INTERNET

Although I'm assuming here that you'll be using HyperTerminal to connect to online services or BBSs, you can also use it to connect to your Internet service provider if you have a dial-up account. If you have a PPP or SLIP account, however, you need to use Windows 98's Dial-Up Networking accessory, which I discuss in Chapter 30, "Remote Computing with Dial-Up Networking."

To get HyperTerminal happening, first select Start | Programs | Accessories | Communications | HyperTerminal. The HyperTerminal window, shown in Figure 27.5, appears. Note that this isn't the HyperTerminal program, but just the HyperTerminal folder, which is a subfolder of \Program Files\Accessories. This folder contains at least four icons. (You might see more icons if you have the Show all files option activated. To deactivate this option, select View | Folder Options and select the View tab in the Options dialog box.)

The Hypertrm icon leads you to the HyperTerminal program; the other icons represent pre-defined connectoids for AT&T Mail, CompuServe, and MCI Mail. In HyperTerminal, a *connectoid* is a file that defines how to connect to a remote system: the phone number, the communications settings to use, and so on. Other connectoids that you create will also appear as icons in this folder.

FIGURE 27.5.

Selecting the HyperTerminal command displays the HyperTerminal folder.

Creating a New HyperTerminal Connectoid

To create a new connectoid, you first need to start HyperTerminal. Then you set up the connectoid in three stages: defining the basic connectoid options, defining the connectoid's settings, and specifying the connectoid's modem properties.

Phase I: Defining the Basic Connectoid Options

Here are the steps to follow to get the basic connectoid options in place:

1. In the HyperTerminal folder, open the Hypertrm icon. HyperTerminal displays the Connection Description dialog box.

2. Use the Name text box to enter a descriptive name for the connectoid. Note that this entry will also serve as the primary name of the new HyperTerminal file (with the .HT extension), so you should follow Windows 98's rules for long filenames (as described in Chapter 4, "What's New and Noteworthy in Windows 98").

3. Use the Icon list to highlight an icon for the connectoid and then click OK. The Connect To dialog box, shown in Figure 27.6, appears.

4. Fill in the Country code, Area code, and Phone number for the remote system.

FIGURE 27.6.
Use the Connect To
dialog box to supply
HyperTerminal with
the dialing details for
your connectoid.

5. In the Connect using drop-down list, you have four choices:

    ■ Choose the modem you want to use for the connectoid.

    ■ If you want to use HyperTerminal to connect to a PC via a serial cable that runs between the two machines' serial ports, choose the appropriate serial port.

    ■ If your computer is part of a Virtual Private Network (VPN), select Microsoft VPN Adapter.

    ■ If the remote computer understands TCP/IP and you have the TCP/IP protocol installed on your machine (see Chapter 33, "Implementing TCP/IP for Internet and Intranet Connections"), select TCP/IP (Winsock).

6. Click OK. HyperTerminal displays the Connect dialog box, shown in Figure 27.7.

FIGURE 27.7.
You can use this dialog
box to establish the
connection or modify
the dialing properties.

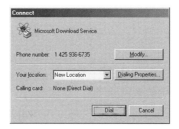

At this point, the connectoid is set up to use the default settings you defined for your modem. If you want to use those settings, you can either click Dial to connect to the remote system or click Cancel to get to the main HyperTerminal window. I suggest clicking Cancel, because then you can save the connectoid (by selecting File | Save). See "Connecting to a Remote System" later in this chapter to learn how to connect from the HyperTerminal window.

Phase II: Defining the Connectoid's Modem Properties

If you don't want to use the default modem settings, HyperTerminal lets you define alternative settings for the connectoid.

If you want to change the dialing properties for the connectoid, click the Dialing Properties button in the Connect dialog box. (If you canceled the Connect dialog box earlier, you can display it again by selecting Call | Connect.)

To change other settings (such as the connect speed and the terminal emulation), first display the properties sheet for the connectoid by using either of the following methods:

■ In the HyperTerminal window, select File | Properties.

■ In the Connect dialog box, click Modify.

Figure 27.8 shows the properties sheet that appears. The Connect To tab enables you to change the basic options (icon, country code, area code, and so on).

FIGURE 27.8.

The properties sheet for a connectoid.

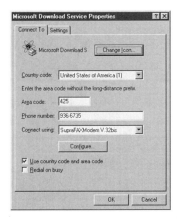

For modem-related settings, click the Configure button to display the modem's properties sheet. This dialog box offers the same settings you saw earlier in this chapter, except that a new tab named Options has been added. Here's the skinny on the controls that populate this tab:

Bring up terminal window before dialing: When this check box is activated, each time you connect to the remote system, HyperTerminal displays the Pre-Dial Terminal Screen before it dials the modem. You can use this screen to enter modem commands (see your modem manual for a list of applicable commands). You enter your commands and then click the window's Continue button.

Bring up terminal window after dialing: When this check box is activated, HyperTerminal displays the Post-Dial Terminal Screen after it connects to the remote system. Again, you can use this screen to enter modem commands.

Operator assisted or manual dial: When this option is activated, each time you connect to the remote system, HyperTerminal displays a dialog box to prompt you to dial the phone number manually. This option is useful in hotels or in other situations when you might need to speak to an operator before you can dial. When you hear the remote modem, click the Connect button in the dialog box and then hang up the receiver.

Wait for credit card tone *x* seconds: This spinner specifies how many seconds HyperTerminal should wait for a credit card tone before it continues dialing.

Display modem status: When this check box is activated, HyperTerminal displays a modem icon in the taskbar's system tray (more on this later).

Phase III: Defining the Connectoid's Settings

To finish defining the connectoid, HyperTerminal has a few other options up its electronic sleeve. To view these options, display the connectoid's properties sheet, and select the Settings tab, shown in Figure 27.9. Here's the rundown:

Function, arrow, and ctrl keys act as: These options determine how HyperTerminal reacts when you press any of the function keys, arrow keys, or Ctrl key combinations. If you activate the Terminal keys option, HyperTerminal sends the keystrokes to the remote modem; if you activate Windows keys, HyperTerminal applies the keystrokes to the Windows 98 interface.

Backspace key sends: Use these options to determine the key or key combination that HyperTerminal sends when you press Backspace. Note that Ctrl+H is the key combination that deletes the previously typed character on most UNIX systems.

Emulation: Use this drop-down list to choose the terminal emulation you want to use with the remote system. The Auto detect option tells HyperTerminal to attempt to determine the remote terminal type automatically. If you choose one of the specific terminal emulations, you can also click the Terminal Setup button to configure various aspects of the emulation. (The available options depend on the emulation.)

Telnet terminal: If you'll be using HyperTerminal as your telnet client, use this text box to enter the terminal type you want to use.

Backscroll buffer lines: This setting determines the number of lines displayed by the remote system that HyperTerminal stores in its buffer. You can scroll up or down through this buffer by using the scrollbars or the Page Up and Page Down keys.

Beep three times when connecting or disconnecting: This check box determines whether HyperTerminal beeps the speaker whenever it connects and disconnects.

ASCII Setup: Clicking this button displays the ASCII Setup dialog box, shown in Figure 27.10. These controls set various options for ASCII text you send to the remote system, as well as ASCII text you receive.

FIGURE 27.9.

Use the Settings tab to define terminal emulation and a few other options for the connectoid.

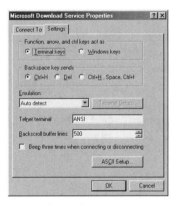

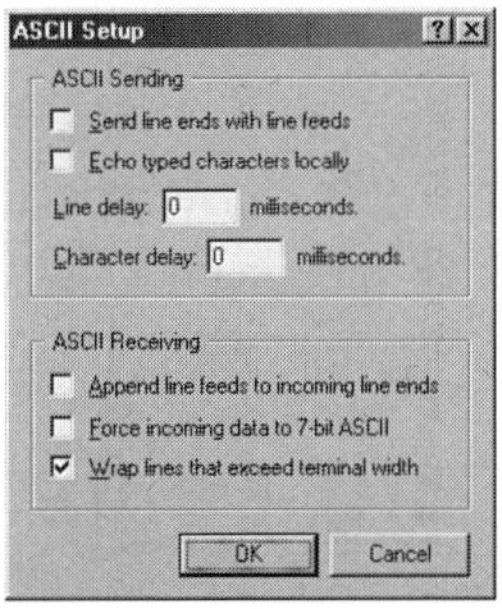

FIGURE 27.10.

Use this dialog box to set various options for incoming and outgoing ASCII text.

Connecting to a Remote System

After you have your connectoid set up to your liking, you're ready to dial in. HyperTerminal gives you a couple of methods of establishing a connection with the remote system:

- In the HyperTerminal folder, highlight the icon and select File | Connect, click (or double-click) the icon, or right-click the icon and select Connect from the context menu.

- In the HyperTerminal program, select File | Open and use the dialog box that appears to open the connectoid; then either select Call | Connect or click the Connect toolbar button, shown in Figure 27.11.

In either case, you then click the Dial button in the Connect dialog box that appears. HyperTerminal dials the modem and connects with the remote system. Text from the remote computer appears in the HyperTerminal window, as shown in Figure 27.11. The status bar tells you the length of time you've been connected, as well as indicating various connection settings. Note too that Windows 98 displays a modem icon in the taskbar's system tray after you're connected. Double-clicking this icon displays a dialog box that tells you the number of bytes sent and received during your session.

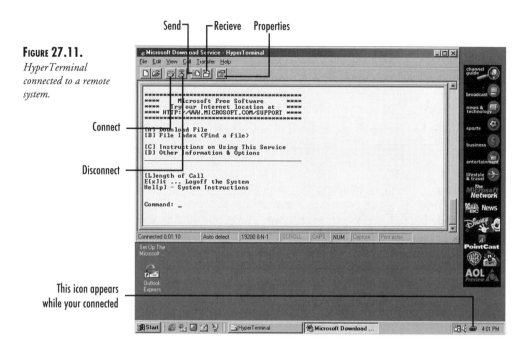

FIGURE 27.11.
HyperTerminal connected to a remote system.

Performing File Transfers

If the remote system has a file you want to download, HyperTerminal makes it easy. After you've told the online service the name of the file you want to receive or send and the protocol to use, the service says something like `Ready to send/receive file. Please initiate file transfer.` At this point, you tell HyperTerminal that a file transfer is about to take place by using one of the following techniques:

- ■ For a download, either select Transfer | Receive File or click the Receive button in the toolbar.

- ■ For an upload, either select Transfer | Send File or click the Send button in the toolbar.

- ■ For a text file upload, select Transfer | Send Text File.

(Note that, in some cases, HyperTerminal selects the appropriate command for you automatically.)

If you're downloading, the Receive File dialog box, shown in Figure 27.12, appears. In the Place received file in the following folder text box, enter the name of the folder in which you want to store the file. If you're not sure of the folder's name, click the Browse button, choose a folder in the Select a Folder dialog box that appears, and click OK to return to the Receive File dialog box. To select a protocol, drop down the Use receiving protocol list and choose the same protocol you selected in the remote system. When you're ready, click the Receive button to proceed with the transfer.

FIGURE 27.12.

Use the Receive File dialog box to select a folder in which to store the file and a protocol.

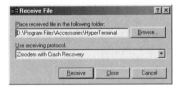

If you're uploading, either the Send File dialog box or the Send Text File dialog box appears. Select the file to send, use the Protocol drop-down list to choose the same protocol you selected in the remote system, and click Send to make it so.

Whether you're sending or receiving, HyperTerminal displays the progress of the transfer in a dialog box similar to the one shown in Figure 27.13. If, for any reason, you need to abort the transfer before it's complete, you can click the Cancel button. You can also select Skip file to bypass the current file in a multifile transfer. (The cps/bps button toggles the value in the Throughput box between characters per second and bits per second.)

FIGURE 27.13.

After you start a file transfer, HyperTerminal displays a dialog box like this one to let you know how the transfer is proceeding.

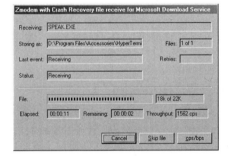

When the transfer is complete, HyperTerminal returns control to the service, and you can continue with other service options or log off.

Disconnecting from the Remote System

When you've finished working with the remote system, disconnecting is as easy as selecting Call | Disconnect or clicking the toolbar's Disconnect button.

Connecting to Another Computer

Besides the usual online services and BBS computers, you can also use HyperTerminal to connect to another PC and then chat with the remote user or send files back and forth. All that's required is that both computers be running HyperTerminal or some other terminal program and that one of the modems be set up to answer incoming calls.

To set up HyperTerminal for a PC-to-PC connection, follow these steps:

1. Create a new HyperTerminal connectoid, following these instructions:

   ■ If your computer is doing the dialing, enter the phone number of the remote PC.

   ■ If your computer is doing the answering, the phone number doesn't matter, but because HyperTerminal requires one anyway, you can just enter a bogus number.

   ■ Make sure that both computers are set up with the same connection settings (speed, data bits, emulation, and so on).

   ■ When HyperTerminal prompts you to dial, click Cancel.

2. Select File | Properties to display the properties sheet for the connectoid, and select the Settings tab.

3. Click the ASCII Setup button to display the ASCII Setup dialog box.

4. Activate the following check boxes:

   Send line ends with line feeds

   Echo typed characters locally

   Append line feeds to incoming line ends

   Wrap lines that exceed terminal width

5. Click OK to return to the properties sheet.

6. Click OK.

To make the connection, one computer dials and the other waits for the incoming call. When you see the ring indicator on the modem or hear the phone ring, type your modem's answer command and press Enter. You need to check your modem manual for the correct command, but on most modems you use either ATA or just A. (You can avoid this step if your modem supports automatic answering. If it does, check your manual to see how to set it up.)

After the connection has been established, you can send messages back and forth by typing onscreen and pressing Enter after each line. File transfers work just as I described earlier.

Entering AT Commands in HyperTerminal

If you're familiar with the AT command set, you might need to send a command or two to your modem. If so, here are the steps to follow to send commands via HyperTerminal:

1. Start HyperTerminal.

2. Enter a name for the connectoid (for example, AT Commands), select an icon, and click OK.

27

PUTTING YOUR
MODEM TO
WORK

3. In the Phone Number dialog box, use the Connect using drop-down list to choose Com*x*, where *x* is the port number to which your modem is attached, and then click OK.

4. When the port properties sheet appears, click OK. The HyperTerminal window appears.

5. Select File | Properties, activate the Settings tab, and click ASCII Setup.

6. In the ASCII Setup dialog box, activate the Send line ends with line feeds check box and make sure the Echo typed characters locally check box is deactivated. Click OK.

7. Click OK to return to HyperTerminal.

You can now enter AT commands in the terminal window. Don't forget to save your connectoid so that you can reuse it at any time.

Summary

This chapter showed you how to use two of Windows 98's communications programs. I began by showing you the ins and outs of using Phone Dialer to initiate voice calls via your modem. You also learned how to use HyperTerminal to create connectoids that enable you to dial up online services, bulletin board systems, and even other computers connected directly with a serial cable.

Here are a few more related chapters:

- I told you how to install and configure a modem in Windows 98 in Chapter 26, "Getting Started with Modem Communications."

- For remote connections requiring network access, head for Chapter 30, "Remote Computing with Dial-Up Networking."

- If you want to use your modem to connect to the Internet, read Chapter 32, "Windows 98 and the Internet."

Setting Up Windows 98 for Networking

by Paul McFedries and Peter Kuo

CHAPTER 28

IN THIS CHAPTER

Transport of the mails, transport of the human voice, transport of flickering pictures—in this century as in others our highest accomplishments still have the single aim of bringing men together.

—Antoine de Saint-Exupéry

For many years, networking was the private playground of IT panjandrums. Its obscure lingo and arcane hardware were familiar to only this small coterie of computer cognoscenti. Workers who needed access to network resources had to pay obeisance to these powers-that-be, genuflecting in just the right way, tossing in the odd salaam or two.

Lately, however, we've seen a democratization of networking. Thanks to the trend away from mainframes and toward client/server setups, thanks to the migration from dumb terminals to smarter PCs, and thanks to the advent of easy peer-to-peer setups, networking is no longer the sole province of the elite. Getting connected to an existing network, or setting up your own network in a small office or home office, has never been easier.

This chapter shows you how Windows 98 has helped take even more of the "work" out of networking. I give a bit of background on Windows 98's networking features, and then I show you how to install and configure networking components.

An Introduction to Windows 98 Networking

Let's lay some groundwork by getting a bird's-eye view of how Windows 98 does the networking thing—in particular, how Windows 98 provides networking support for Microsoft networks and NetWare networks.

Windows 98 and Microsoft Networks

Windows 98 happily interacts with Microsoft networks, which means networks that include computers running Windows NT Server, Windows NT Workstation, LAN Manager, Windows for Workgroups, Windows 95, and, of course, Windows 98. Connecting your Windows 98 machine to any of these networks gives you instant access to shared drives, folders, and printers and enables you to share your resources with the network.

Architectural Overview

To give you an appreciation for how Windows 98 and Microsoft networks interact, Figure 28.1 lays out the architectural components used by Windows 98 to implement networking in such an environment.

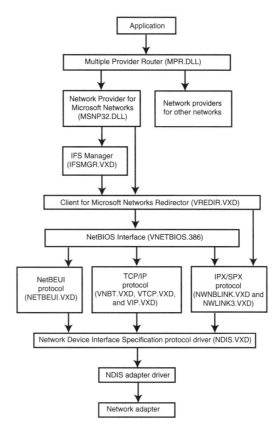

FIGURE 28.1.

*The architecture of
Windows 98
networking on a
Microsoft network.*

Here's a summary of the various layers used by Windows 98 to enable an application to communicate with a network adapter:

Multiple Provider Router: As I mentioned earlier, Windows 98 supports multiple network configurations. The service that lets Windows 98 support different networks concurrently is called the Multiple Provider Router (MPR.DLL). When an application needs a network resource, it calls the appropriate function in the WinNet32 API (or the WinNet16 API, if it's a 16-bit application). The MPR then routes the request to the appropriate network provider, which translates the request into a network-specific call.

Network Provider for Microsoft Networks: This is the network provider that is used to handle Microsoft networking requests. This provider supports operations such as browsing Microsoft networks, logging on and off Windows NT domains (including verifying passwords), and adding and removing mapped network connections.

Installable File System (IFS) Manager: If the network provider gets a request for a file system–related operation (such as mapping a network drive), it passes the request to the IFS Manager. From here, the request is passed to the redirector.

Client for Microsoft Networks Redirector: All other requests are sent directly to the Client for Microsoft Networks redirector (VREDIR.VXD). This is a 32-bit driver that provides all the mechanisms needed for an application to communicate with a remote device, including file reads and writes, print job submissions, and resource sharing. Packets are converted into the format specified by the Server Message Block (SMB) protocol used by Microsoft networks.

NETWORK NOMENCLATURE: SERVER MESSAGE BLOCK

A server message block is a packet of data that contains a request from a workstation to a server or that contains the response from the server to the workstation. SMBs are used for all communications that go through a Microsoft network, including file I/O, connecting and disconnecting remote connections, and performing any other network function the redirector needs to carry out.

NetBIOS Interface: This is the interface between the redirector and the network protocols. This interface is an API that gives the redirector a protocol-independent method of accessing the services provided by NetBEUI, TCP/IP, and other protocols.

Protocols: At this level, the request or data is converted into a packet that meets the specifications of whatever protocol the system is using (or that's required for the destination node). For example, if a message is being sent to a NetWare server, a driver converts the data into a packet suitable for transport via the IPX/SPX protocol.

Network Device Interface Specification (NDIS) protocol driver: This is a 32-bit protected-mode driver that lets the protocol driver interface with the network adapter driver.

NDIS adapter driver: This is the device driver that interacts directly with the network adapter. As with all Windows 98 hardware drivers, the NIC hardware architecture uses a universal driver/mini-driver model.

This sequence of events (from the application contacting the Multiple Provider Router to the NDIS adapter driver passing the packets to the NIC) shows you what happens when a packet is sent by an application to the network. For incoming packets, this sequence is reversed.

Notes About Microsoft Networking

To enable support for Microsoft networks, you install Windows 98's Client for Microsoft Networks component (see "Installing a Client," later in this chapter). This client provides you with 32-bit protected-mode drivers for the redirector and protocol stacks, which means that this client uses no conventional memory. The Client for Microsoft Networks lets you access shared resources on other network nodes and lets you share local resources with the network. Also, all the Windows 98 networking goodies are available through this client: user profiles, system policies, share-level security, remote administration, Dial-Up Networking, automatic reconnection of mapped resources, unified logon, recognition of long filenames on NT machines, and more.

Here are a few notes to bear in mind before setting up Windows 98 to interact with a Microsoft network:

- For easier setups, keep in mind that you can install Windows 98 on remote machines via a computer running Windows NT Server.

- If you plan on taking advantage of user profiles or system policies, you must set up Windows 98 to use the Client for Microsoft Networks as the primary network logon client.

- You can share resources with other computers on a Microsoft network only if all the machines are using a common protocol.

- You can implement user-level security by adding an account to a Windows NT domain for each user on a Windows 98 system.

- Remember that Windows 98 clients can't view or access drives that use the Windows NT file system (NTFS).

Windows 98 and NetWare Networks

NetWare is a client/server–based network operating system. This means you need to load some client software on your Windows 98 workstation to gain access to a NetWare server. Windows 98 comes with Microsoft's 32-bit NetWare client, called Client for NetWare Networks. You can get, at no charge, Novell's 32-bit NetWare client for Windows 98 (called IntranetWare Client for Windows 98, previously known as NetWare Client 32 for Windows 95) from Novell; this client software isn't included in NetWare 3.12 or IntranetWare 4.11, because Windows 98 was released after these products started shipping.

DOWNLOADING THE INTRANETWARE CLIENT

You can download the latest IntranetWare Client for Windows 98 from the Internet, free of charge, at the following sites (note that this is a 9MB+ download):

```
http://www.novell.com/download
ftp://ftp.novell.com/pub
http://support.novell.com
```

(For the latter, use the Knowledgebase search engine.) Alternatively, if you have a subscription to the Novell Support Connection (NSC) CD, the latest clients for all platforms can be found on the latest monthly update.

Microsoft's NetWare client supports NetWare 3.1*x*, and it supports NetWare 4.*x* if the server has Bindery Services enabled. If you need to access a NetWare 4 network using Novell Directory Services (NDS), you use either Novell's IntranetWare Client for Windows 98 or install the Service for NetWare Directory Services from your Windows 98 source disk (see "Installing and Configuring Network Services," later in this chapter.)

USE NOVELL'S 32-BIT CLIENTS

Although you can use Novell's 16-bit NetWare VLM clients with Windows 98, it's best to use the newer 32-bit clients, because you get much better performance and more features. Windows 98 is not compatible with VLM Client Kit version 1.21 or later.

IntranetWare Client Overview

Novell's 32-bit clients have an advanced architecture that's very different from the previous NetWare DOS Requester (the VLM-based client) design. The VLM drivers are a set of modules dynamically loaded into and unloaded from the workstation's memory by the VLM manager (VLM.EXE). In essence, they're a combination of terminate-and-stay-resident (TSR) modules and overlay programs. As a result, VLMs can be memory-hungry.

On the other hand, the new architecture used by the 32-bit clients lets the client software run in protected mode. This requires less than 4KB of conventional or upper memory while providing a larger cache. The remaining portion of the client is loaded into XMS memory. The IntranetWare Client requires HIMEM.SYS or an equivalent memory manager. The XMS memory requirement for the client is about 800KB, excluding cache memory.

Several fundamental changes were made in the design of the IntranetWare Client requester. The new requester comprises two fundamental parts: the NetWare I/O Subsystem (NIOS) and client NetWare Loadable Modules (NLMs).

The NIOS insulates the core client modules from the host operating system by providing an OS abstraction layer (much like the hardware abstraction layer used by Windows NT) that core modules can use to access system services. Instead of making OS calls to access system services, IntranetWare Client core modules make NIOS calls.

In addition, NIOS provides services to manage client NLMs, using dynamic, self-configurable parameters where possible. For example, if the number of open IPX sockets is increased, IPX.NLM dynamically allocates more memory to handle the extra sockets.

ALL "NLMS" ARE NOT ALIKE

Files used by IntranetWare Clients have the extension of `.NLM`. However, these "NLMs" are not compatible with those used by NetWare servers. Conversely, server NLMs are not compatible with IntranetWare Clients. There are some NLMs with the same name, but they are not compatible. On the other hand, the `CLIENT32.NLM` module used with Windows 98 is the same one used by the DOS/Windows Client32.

SERVER-BASED AND CLIENT-BASED NLM MODULES

There are certain things that all the NLM modules (both server-based and client-based) have in common:

- They are dynamically loadable and unloadable.
- They use the NLM executable format.
- They use `.NLM` as the file extension.
- They run in a 32-bit flat memory model.
- They allocate memory that is guaranteed not to move or be discarded.

Similar to the Microsoft 32-bit client, IntranetWare Client uses the Windows 98 Network Device Installer (NDI) and INF script files to ensure full integration with the Windows 98 environment. In addition, Novell's IntranetWare Client installation program incorporates Windows 98 property pages that have been created specifically to set IntranetWare Client configuration parameters contained in the Windows 98 Registry. IntranetWare Client saves its configuration settings in the Registry, so you can manage IntranetWare Client parameters by using Windows 98's System Policies Editor. IntranetWare Client uses Microsoft's implementation of TCP/IP, NetBIOS, WinSock, and Named Pipes, which are included in Windows 98. This means you can switch between Microsoft's NetWare client and Novell's IntranetWare client without having to change anything. Because IntranetWare Client uses the Microsoft protocol stack, it can coexist with Microsoft's Client for Microsoft Networks—a requirement if you have a mixture of NetWare and Microsoft networks in your networking environment.

Novell or Microsoft Client?

Both Novell's IntranetWare Client and Microsoft's Client for NetWare Networks perform equally well under most circumstances. However, depending on your particular network requirements and environment, you might prefer to use IntranetWare Client, because it has the following features not found in Client for NetWare Networks:

- Support for multiple NDS tree access.
- Complete Novell Directory Services access.
- A graphical user interface login utility that lets the user execute a user or system login script, update search drives, and update environment variables. Bindery and NDS connections are supported.
- Support for "deviceless" printing. That is, it's no longer necessary to use CAPTURE.EXE and to associate a printer port with a specific printer. Instead, when you set up a printer, Windows 98 writes all the printer configuration information to the Registry. To use the printer, a user simply clicks that printer's icon.
- Support for *auto-reconnect.* After a network failure has been repaired, IntranetWare Client reestablishes the entire network environment, including connections, drive mappings, printer captures, open files, and file locks. Not only does IntranetWare Client automatically detect errors and rebuild lost connections and drive mappings, it also restores open files, file locks, and other user state information. This improves the overall reliability of the client and minimizes the effects of a network failure on the end user.
- Support for *client-side caching.* To improve client performance, the requester caches files, directories, *and* file locks.
- Enhanced packet burst and LIP (Large Internet Packet) support. Both protocols have been optimized for overall network performance, including wide area network performance.
- Support for multiplexing of NCP (NetWare Core Protocol) connections. In the past, if a user had a pending request on an NCP connection, the user had to wait for a reply from that connection before using other NCP connections. IntranetWare Client can service multiple NCP connections simultaneously, without having to wait for the reply to be completed from other requests.
- Support for *packet signatures.* Packet signing means that when the client and server communicate, each one "signs" packets with a unique signature before transmitting the packet. The receiver then compares the received packet to a private key and rejects it if the signature doesn't match the key. This feature thereby precludes the possibility of an intruder forging a packet from a client or server.
- Support for login script execution if logged in from Network Neighborhood, through the use of the GUI login utility—Microsoft client performs an "attach" rather than a login, so no login scripts are executed by the Microsoft client if you log in from Network Neighborhood.
- Support for Novell's LANalyzer for Windows (a software-only protocol analyzer).

■ Support for industry standard SNMP (Simple Network Management Protocol).

■ Support for Novell's NetWare/IP environment.

■ Better integration with Windows Explorer and the Network Neighborhood.

THE NOVELL CLIENT HAS FILES NEEDED BY SOME UTILITIES

Many Novell-supplied utilities, such as NetWare Administrator (NWAdmin), and third-party NDS-aware applications, such as Cheyenne's ARCserve Manager, will not run with the Microsoft client. That's because the Microsoft client is missing some library files (DLLs), such as NWCALLS.DLL and NWNET.DLL, that are included only with the Novell client.

You can find detailed information about the installation and use of Novell's IntranetWare Client and Microsoft's NetWare Client later in this chapter.

What's New in Windows 98 Networking

Windows 98 boasts a large number of new networking features and enhancements. Here's a summary:

Novell NetWare 4.*x* client: Windows 98 includes the full client for NetWare 4.*x*, including client support Novell Directory Services. I show you how to install and configure this client later in this chapter.

NDIS 5 and ATM support: Windows 98 supports the NDIS 5 network interface, which means Windows 98 can work with Asynchronous Transfer Mode (ATM) network adapters, as well as LAN Emulation (LANE) over ATM.

Distributed Common Object Model (DCOM): DCOM extends the Common Object Model (see Chapter 19, "Sharing Data in Windows 98: The Clipboard and OLE") so that component-based applications can communicate across a network.

32-Bit Data Link Control (DLC): Windows 98 includes the 32-bit DLC protocol for accessing IBM mainframe and AS/400 computers. Although I don't discuss the DLC protocol in this book, I show you how to install network protocols later in this chapter.

Dial-Up Networking enhancements: Windows 98 incorporates several new Dial-Up Networking features, including an improved properties sheet, hands-free dial-up, support for scripting, and the ability to set up a Windows 98 machine as a dial-up server. I cover all of this in Chapter 30, "Remote Computing with Dial-Up Networking."

ISDN 1.1 Accelerator Pack: Windows 98 bundles the ISDN Accelerator pack, which enables Dial-Up Networking to work with an ISDN adapter card.

Virtual Private Networking and PPTP: Windows 98 supports the Point-to-Point Tunneling Protocol (PPTP), which enables you to establish an extended private network (called a Virtual Private Network) over a public network such as the Internet.

Multilink Bandwidth Aggregation: This is a communications feature that enables Windows 98 to combine the bandwidth from multiple lines into a single, larger, pipe.

TCP/IP improvements: The Windows 98 TCP/IP stack boasts a number of enhancements, including support for Autonet Addressing, TCP large windows, Selective Acknowledgements, Fast Retransmission, and Fast Recovery.

Windows Sockets (WinSock) 2: This is an update to the WinSock 1.1 support found in Windows 98. WinSock 2 implements a protocol-independent interface, which means it can work with protocols other than TCP/IP. It also utilizes protocol-independent name resolution, so it works not only with DNS, but also with domains such as SAP and X.500.

Resource ReSerVation Protocol (RSVP): This is a new networking protocol that Microsoft has proposed as an Internet standard. It's used to guarantee a particular level of transmission service by reserving in advance the network resources required by the transmission.

Network Installation and Configuration

When you're setting up a network, your first chore should be to install all the necessary hardware in each machine. That means adding the network adapters, running cables, and tying everything together with whatever other components you need (such as a hub if you're using a star topology).

After that's done, you need to set up Windows 98's networking components. How you do this depends on whether you're installing Windows 98 itself or adding networking to an existing Windows 98 installation:

■ If you're installing Windows 98 from scratch, be sure to choose the Custom option. If you do, the Setup Wizard will eventually display the Network Configuration dialog box, shown in Figure 28.2.

FIGURE 28.2.

When you're installing Windows 98, the Custom setup option displays the Network Configuration dialog box.

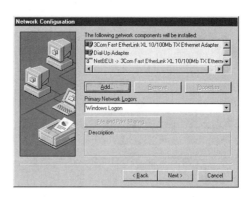

■ If Windows 98 is already installed, you need to set up the network components from within Windows 98. In this case, you open the Control Panel's Network icon to display the Network properties sheet, shown in Figure 28.3.

FIGURE 28.3.

Opening the Control Panel's Network Icon displays this dialog box.

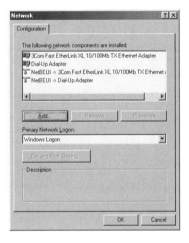

The next few sections show you how to use either dialog box to install and configure an adapter, a client, protocols, and network services. When you're done, click Next > or OK, as appropriate. (When you click OK, Windows 98 might ask you to insert your Windows 98 source discs. Follow the onscreen prompts, and when Windows 98 asks whether you want to restart your computer, click Yes.)

Installing and Configuring a Network Adapter

Windows 98 usually does a pretty good job of detecting your network hardware, particularly if your network interface card (NIC) is Plug and Play–compliant. If you're installing Windows 98, the Detection Manager should figure out your card and display it in the Network Configuration dialog box. If Windows 98 is already installed, the system should detect the new card the next time you restart.

In either case, Windows installs the appropriate device driver for the card (you might be asked to insert a Windows 98 source disk). Windows 98 comes with 32-bit protected-mode drivers for many adapter types, although you're free to use existing 16-bit drivers if Windows 98 doesn't support your card.

INTRANETWARE CLIENT NIC DRIVER SUPPORT

IntranetWare Client for Windows 98 supports ODI drivers for both 16-bit and 32-bit NICs, as well as NDIS drivers. The software supports the use of standard 32-bit ODI drivers, 16-bit DOS ODI drivers via PC32MLID.NLM (Pseudo C 32-bit Multiple Link Interface Driver), and NDIS drivers through VMLID.NLM (Virtual MLID).

Adding an Adapter

If Windows 98 didn't detect your card, or if it detected the wrong type of card, you can easily change the adapter component. If the Network dialog box shows the wrong adapter, you should first remove it by highlighting the adapter's name and then clicking the Remove button. When that's done, follow these steps to install your adapter:

1. Click the Add button to display the Select Network Component Type dialog box, shown in Figure 28.4.

FIGURE 28.4.

Use this dialog box to choose the type of network component you want to add.

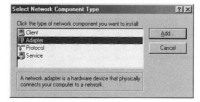

2. Highlight Adapter and then click Add. The Select Network adapters dialog box appears.

3. Use the Manufacturers list to highlight the vendor of your network card, and then use the Network Adapters list to highlight the specific card. If you don't see your NIC listed, and the card came with a disk of drivers, insert the disk, click the Have Disk button, and follow the onscreen prompts to choose the driver.

4. Click OK.

INSTALLING WITH THE ADD NEW HARDWARE WIZARD

If you're not sure which driver to install for your NIC, you can use the Add New Hardware Wizard to have Windows 98 detect your card automatically.

USING MULTIPLE ADAPTERS

If you have the room and the available resources, you can add extra adapters to a computer. Note, however, that Windows 98 supports a maximum of "only" four network adapters in a single machine.

Installing a Client

The next step is to select the network client or clients you want to use. Windows 98 comes with several clients, but you can also add third-party clients (such as Novell's IntranetWare

Client for Windows 98, discussed earlier in this chapter). The next two sections show you how to install network clients for Microsoft networks and NetWare networks.

Installing a Client for Microsoft Networks

To install the Client for Microsoft Networks, follow these steps:

1. Click the Add button to display the Select Network Component Type dialog box.
2. Highlight Client and then click Add. The Select Network Client dialog box appears.
3. In the Manufacturers list, highlight Microsoft.
4. In the Network Clients list, highlight Client for Microsoft Networks.
5. Click OK. Windows 98 adds the client to the list of network components.

Installing a Client for NetWare Networks

As mentioned earlier in this chapter, two NetWare clients are available. The Microsoft version (Client for NetWare Networks) comes with your Windows 98 package. If you need to connect to a NetWare 4.*x* network with Novell Directory Services (NDS) connections, you also need to install the Service for NetWare Directory Services, which is included with Windows 98. The Novell implementation of the 32-bit NetWare client for Windows 98 is called IntranetWare Client for Windows 98.

Installing Microsoft's NetWare Client

The steps for installing the Microsoft Client for NetWare Networks are very similar to those for the Client for Microsoft Networks, as described in the preceding section. The only difference is that when you get to the Select Network Client dialog box, highlight Microsoft in the Manufacturers list, and in the Network Clients list, highlight Client for NetWare Networks.

Installing the Microsoft Service for NDS

If you want to install the Microsoft NetWare Client update to provide NDS support, it's installed as a service rather than as a client. Here are the steps to follow:

1. Open the Network icon from the Control Panel.
2. Click the Add button to display the Select Network Component Type dialog box.
3. Highlight Service and then click Add. The Select Network Client dialog box appears.
4. In the Manufacturers list, highlight Microsoft.
5. In the Network Services list, highlight Service for NetWare Directory Services.
6. Click OK. Windows 98 adds the client to the list of network components.

Installing the 32-Bit Novell Client

As you see in this section, the installation procedure for Novell's client is slightly different and is, in some respects, easier than the procedure for installing the Microsoft client.

THE MICROSOFT CLIENT IS REMOVED

If Microsoft Client for NetWare Networks is already installed, Novell's installation program will remove it before installing the IntranetWare Client.

You can obtain the Novell client in two formats: one for floppy disk installation, and one for server (or hard disk) installation. Because of the size of the uncompressed files (over 20MB), using the server installation method is recommended. Alternatively, you can put the files on the local hard disk of your Windows 98 workstation and install from there. The following steps assume the software is located on your hard drive:

1. Obtain the IntranetWare Client files from Novell and create the installation disks, if necessary, according to its instructions.

2. Make sure the Network properties dialog box is closed.

3. Start the SETUP.EXE program from the \PRODUCTS\WIN98\IBM_ENU folder. The License Agreement dialog box appears.

4. Click Yes.

5. You now have the choice of doing a Typical install or a Custom install. The Typical selection (recommended) installs the client software as well as the Novell Remote Access Dialer. If you choose this option, skip to step 7. The Custom option enables you to select the following services to install (see Figure 28.5):

    Novell Distributed Print Services: This component enables two-way communication in real time between your workstation and your network printer.

    Novell NetWare/IP Protocol: This protocol sends and receives IPX packets in IP format. NetWare/IP enables networked applications that use only IPX to communicate over TCP/IP networks. It also provides a way for separate IPX networks to communicate across IP-based internetwork connections.

    Novell IP Gateway. This component enables WinSock applications to communicate with IP hosts through a Novell Gateway server. This enables all Internet traffic to use only one IP address on the Gateway server, significantly reducing the cost and time associated with maintaining individual workstation IP addresses.

    Novell SNMP Agent: This component enables you to monitor, from an SNMP (Simple Network Management Protocol) console, remote connections to computers running Windows 98.

    Host Resources MIB for the Novell Clients: This component is an implementation of the Host Resources MIB (Management Information Base), as defined by RFC 1514 and Novell's extensions to it. The HostMIB NLM uses the services provided by the SNMP agent. Management consoles, such as Novell's ManageWise console, can use the SNMP protocol to communicate with the HostMIB NLM to obtain information such as size of local drives and printers installed.

Network Management Responder for Windows 98: This component is an application service that returns general workstation configuration information beyond what is normally available.

Novell Target Service Agent for Windows 98: This component automatically backs up selected hard drives from a server.

Novell Remote Access Dialer: This component installs NWCAP, PhoneBook, and NWAdmin PhoneBook Snapins.

FIGURE 28.5.

The components available under the Custom installation option.

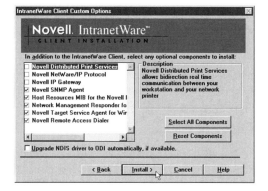

6. The Custom Options dialog box also has a check box named Upgrade NDIS driver to ODI automatically. When this option is activated, the installation program installs an ODI LAN driver if it finds one for your network adapter. If your system can't use ODI LAN drivers, the installation program disables this check box.

7. Click the Install > button to start the installation process. The necessary IntranetWare Client files are copied to the C:\NOVELL\CLIENT32 directory and subdirectories.

8. At the end of the install process, a dialog box appears with a recommendation that you set some properties for the client. You can click Yes to perform this customization now (see the next section to learn how to customize the Novell client) or click No to display the dialog box shown in Figure 28.6.

9. From here, you have three choices:

Reboot: Click this button to restart Windows 98 and log in using the new client.

Return to Windows: Click this button to shut down the installation program and return to the desktop.

Customize: Click this button to configure the client.

28

FOR NETWORKING
WINDOWS 98
SETTING UP

FIGURE 28.6.

You're presented with three options to end the installation process.

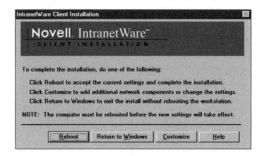

Note that the IntranetWare Client installation program also makes the following changes to your system:

- A new command is added to your Start menu for logging in to the network:
  Start | Programs | Novell | IntranetWare Login.

- The Start | Programs | Novell menu gets a new Dialup submenu, which contains two commands: Remote Access Password and Update Dial-Up Connections.

- The Network properties sheet shows two new installed components: Novell IntranetWare Client and IPX 32-bit Protocol for the IntranetWare Client. (Note that the default Windows 98 IPX/SPX-compatible Protocol remains installed. Don't remove this protocol, because it's required when using IntranetWare Client with either NDIS or ODI drivers.)

- The Primary Network Logon is changed to Novell IntranetWare Client so that when you restart Windows 98, you first see the NetWare login screen.

Configuring the IntranetWare Client

To customize the Novell IntranetWare Client, you have three ways to get started:

- When the IntranetWare Client installation programs asks whether you want to customize the client, click Yes (as described in the previous section).

- In the final Windows 98 Client installation dialog box (refer to Figure 28.6), click the Customize button.

- In the Network properties sheet, highlight the Novell IntranetWare Client components and then click Properties.

Whichever method you use, you see the Novell IntranetWare Client Properties dialog box, shown in Figure 28.7.

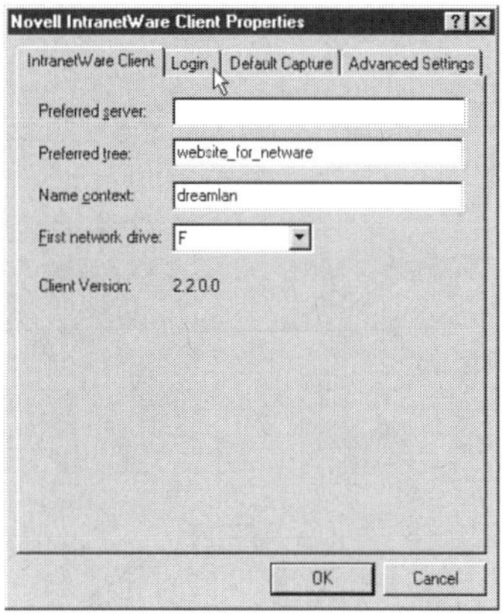

FIGURE 28.7.

This tab configures options for the general IntranetWare Client user login information.

To configure your login, use the following tabs:

IntranetWare Client: This is the tab where you specify your Preferred server (if NetWare 2.*x*/3.*x*), Preferred tree, and Name context (if NetWare 4). You also specify the DOS drive letter to be used for your First network drive; the default is F. This tab also displays the Client Version.

Login: From the Login tab, shown in Figure 28.8, you can select the type of connection (bindery or NDS) to be made by the client workstation to the NetWare server. You can also specify whether the login scripts are to be executed, whether alternative login scripts are to be used instead, and whether the results of the login scripts are to be displayed onscreen.

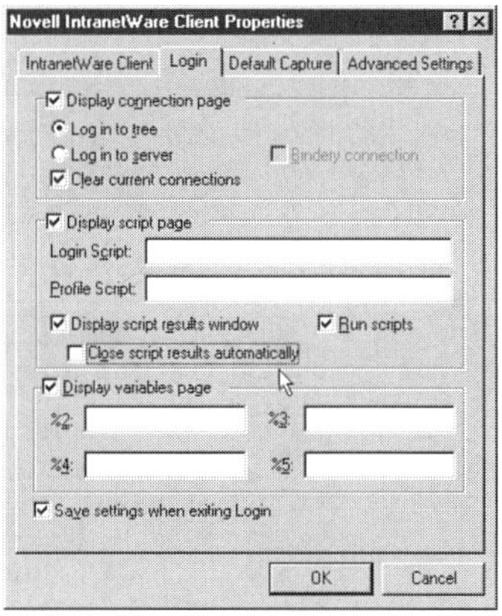

FIGURE 28.8.

The options in this tab cover the login connection and login script information.

28

SETTING UP
WINDOWS 98
FOR NETWORKING

Default Capture: This tab, shown in Figure 28.9, sets up the print capture defaults for the workstation. For example, this is where you specify whether a banner page should be printed and whether a form feed should be sent at the end of each print job.

FIGURE 28.9.

This tab defines the printer capture information.

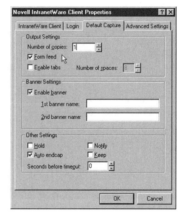

Advanced Settings: You can use this tab (see Figure 28.10) to change the various settings that might affect how IntranetWare Client functions. For example, from this sheet you can turn Packet Burst on or off. If you're accustomed to the VLM drivers and the NET.CFG file, you'll find that this sheet contains similar parameters.

FIGURE 28.10.

Use this tab to set advanced options for the IntranetWare Client.

The configuration for the Microsoft NetWare client is much simpler than that of Novell's because you have only two tabs to work through, as shown in Figure 28.11. From this properties sheet, you configure options such as the Preferred server, the First network drive, whether you want the login script to be executed during login, and so on.

Setting Up Windows 98 for Networking

CHAPTER **28**

741

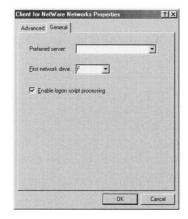

FIGURE 28.11.
*The properties sheet for
the Microsoft NetWare
Client.*

Installing and Configuring Protocols

Windows 98 will install some networking protocols automatically, depending on the client
you installed. For example, if you added the Client for Microsoft Networks, Windows 98 adds
the NetBEUI and IPX/SPX protocols. You can also add, remove, and configure protocols by
hand, as described in the next few sections.

TCP/IP PROPERTIES

To learn how to configure the TCP/IP protocol, see Chapter 31, "Implementing TCP/IP for
Internet and Intranet Connections."

Adding a Protocol

Here are the steps to follow to install another protocol:

1. From the Network properties sheet, click the Add button to display the Select
   Network Component Type dialog box.
2. Highlight Protocol and click Add. The Select Network Protocol dialog box appears.
3. In the Manufacturers list, highlight the maker of the protocol you want to use.
4. In the Network Protocols list, highlight the protocol.
5. Click OK. Windows 98 adds the protocol to the list of network components.

If you want to get rid of a protocol you don't need, simply highlight it in the list of network
components and then click the Remove button.

Binding Protocols

For Windows 98 networking to function properly, you must associate a network client with a protocol, and a protocol with a network adapter driver. These associations are called *bindings*. Windows 98 usually handles all this for you automatically. (In other words, each installed client is bound to each installed protocol, and each installed protocol is bound to each installed adapter.) However, you might prefer to remove bindings for certain components to improve performance. For example, if you've installed clients for both Microsoft and NetWare networks, but only the NetWare network will use the IPX/SPX protocol, you should remove the Microsoft networking client binding from the IPX/SPX protocol.

To work with the client bindings for a protocol, highlight the protocol in the list of network components and then click Properties. In the properties sheet that appears, select the Bindings tab, shown in Figure 28.12. This tab lists each installed client, and the clients that are bound to the protocol have their check boxes activated. To remove a client binding, deactivate its check box.

FIGURE 28.12.

You use the Bindings tab of a protocol's properties sheet to choose which clients are bound to the protocol.

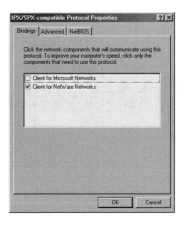

To work with the protocol bindings for a network adapter, highlight the adapter in the list of network components and then click Properties. In the properties sheet that appears, select the Bindings tab, shown in Figure 28.13. This tab lists each installed protocol, and the protocols that are bound to the adapter have their check boxes activated. To remove a protocol binding, deactivate its check box.

NetBEUI Properties

The NetBEUI protocol's properties sheet has an Advanced tab that controls a couple of NetBEUI settings. When Windows 98 is running in protected mode, these values are managed automatically, so you don't need to worry about them. If, however, you start Windows 98 using the Safe mode with network support option, these settings come into play. Here's what they mean, in case you need to make adjustments:

Maximum Sessions: This value determines the maximum number of connections to remote computers that the redirector will allow.

NCBS: These are Network Control Blocks, and the setting determines the maximum number of NetBIOS commands that can be used.

FIGURE 28.13.
You use the Bindings tab of an adapter's properties sheet to choose which protocols are bound to the adapter.

IPX/SPX Properties

The IPX/SPX-compatible protocol's properties sheet has an Advanced tab that controls various IPX/SPX settings. Six parameters are available under the Advanced tab setting:

Force Even Length Packets: Certain network card drivers want the IPX packet to have an even number of bytes. This setting forces an IPX packet to contain an even number of bytes by providing a padding byte, if necessary.

Frame Type: This specifies the frame type to which the IPX protocol is bound. By default, it's set to AUTO. If you use multiple frame types (such as Ethernet II and Ethernet 802.3) on your Windows 98 workstation and you want to have IPX bound to a specific frame type—for example, Ethernet 802.3 rather than "randomly"—use this option to specify the frame type setting.

Maximum Connections: This specifies the maximum number of concurrent IPX/SPX connections the Windows 98 workstation can have with other devices.

Maximum Sockets: This specifies the maximum number of sockets that the workstation can allocate for communications over IPX/SPX. Typically, an application uses at least one socket.

28

SETTING UP
WINDOWS 98
FOR NETWORKING

Network Address: This identifies the IPX network address. By default, the driver auto-detects the IPX number being used on the cable.

Source Routing: This parameter is useful only in a Token Ring network environment. It enables source routing capability if you have source route bridges on your network.

This properties sheet also has a NetBIOS tab, which specifies whether NetBIOS applications are to use IPX/SPX as the transport/network protocol.

IPX 32-Bit Properties

The IPX 32-bit protocol is used with IntranetWare Client. Its properties sheet contains three tabs: IPX, Advanced IPX, and SPX.

Under the IPX tab, you work with the following settings:

IPX retry count: This setting indicates the number of times the client workstation should try to find a path to a destination before timing out. The range is 0 through 65535; the default is 20.

Allow IPX access through interrupt 7Ah: When activated, this option enables DOS applications to use software interrupt 7Ah to access IPX services. It is enabled by default.

Allow IPX access through interrupt 64h: When activated, this option enables DOS applications to use software interrupt 64h to access IPX services. It is enabled by default.

IPX diagnostics enabled: When activated, this option enables the IPX diagnostic functions. It is enabled by default.

Pre-allocate VGNMA memory: When activated, this option enables the allocation of conventional memory for VGNMA (Virtual Generic Network Management Agent) operation. It is disabled by default.

Enable Source routing over NDIS: When activated, this option enables the IPX protocol to perform source routing for NDIS Token Ring and FDDI drivers. It is disabled by default.

The Advanced IPX tab enables you to input information about the primary logical board and select frame types.

The SPX tab enables you to set the following parameters:

- SPX connections
- SPX verify timeout
- SPX listen timeout
- SPX abort timeout
- Allow connection watchdogging

Installing and Configuring Network Services

The clients you install should provide all or most of the network services you need (such as sharing files and printers, the capability of browsing shared resources, and so on). Windows 98 also supports extra services that provide additional networking support.

Here are the steps to follow to install a network service:

1. In the Network properties sheet, click the Add button to display the Select Network Component Type dialog box.
2. Highlight Service and then click Add. The Select Network Service dialog box appears.
3. Use the Manufacturers list and the Network Services list to highlight the service you want to install. Alternatively, click the Have Disk button and follow the onscreen prompts to choose the service.
4. Click OK.

Establishing Your Primary Network Logon

To complete the Configuration tab of the Network properties sheet (or the Network Configuration dialog box, if you're installing Windows 98), you must choose your primary network logon. This determines both the logon dialog box you see at startup and the procedure Windows 98 uses to log you on to your network. For example, you might need to have a Windows NT Server validate your password, or you might want to run a NetWare login script.

To make sure that all this happens without incident, you need to choose an appropriate network logon. To do that, open the Primary Network Logon drop-down list and select either Windows Logon (if you don't want to log on to the network or if you're logging on to a peer-to-peer network) or the appropriate network client. (For example, if you need to process a NetWare login script, select your installed NetWare client.)

Microsoft Networking Logon Options

If you choose Client for Microsoft Networks as your primary network logon, you have a few logon options to work with. To view these options, highlight Client for Microsoft Networks in the list of components and then click Properties. The properties sheet that appears (see Figure 28.14) gives you the following controls:

Logon validation: If you're using a client/server setup, you can establish user accounts on a Windows NT server for each client. If so, you should activate the Log on to Windows NT domain check box to have the server verify each client logon. Use the Windows NT domain text box to enter the name of the domain to which your computer belongs.

Network logon options: You'll see in the next chapter that you can map a network drive so that it appears to be part of your own system. If you use lots of these connections, it can take a while for them to be reestablished each time you start Windows 98.

To speed up your restarts, activate the Quick logon option. This logs you on to the network, but it doesn't reestablish the mapped network drive connections. If you use only a few mapped network drives, you can activate the Logon and restore the network connections option instead. This option not only logs you on to the network, but also reestablishes all your mapped network drive connections automatically.

FIGURE 28.14.

The properties sheet for the Client for Microsoft Networks enables you to set various logon options.

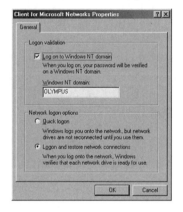

Setting Up Server Accounts

After each machine is network-ready, you can get down to business if you're setting up a peer-to-peer system. If you're going with the client/server model, however, you're not out of the woods yet. Besides setting up the server with the appropriate NOS (such as NT Server or NetWare), you need to tell the server about the client machines on the network. In other words, you need to set up accounts and passwords for each user, establish domains or workgroups, set up common directories, and so on. (A *workgroup* is a related collection of computers on the network. For example, all the computers in the Marketing department might constitute one workgroup, and all the computers in Accounting might constitute another.) How you do all this depends on the network operating system.

Identifying Your Computer

Your final network installation task is to set up your computer's network identity. If you're installing Windows 98, the Setup Wizard displays an Identification dialog box after you've clicked Next > in the Network Configuration dialog box. Otherwise, select the Identification tab in the Network properties sheet, shown in Figure 28.15.

Either way, you must enter three pieces of ID:

Computer name: This is the name other people will see when they browse the network resources. It must be unique on the network and must be 15 or fewer characters. You can't use spaces in the name, but all alphanumeric characters are fair game, as are the following symbols:

    ~ ! @ # $ % ^ & ( ) _ - { } ' .

Workgroup: In a peer-to-peer network, you organize computers into workgroups simply by giving them the same name in their respective Workgroup text boxes. (If you need to log in to a specific Windows NT Server domain, enter the name of the domain in this space.) You use the same naming rules that I outlined for the computer name.

Computer Description: You use this text box to provide a more detailed description of your computer. The description can be up to 48 characters long and can include any character except commas.

FIGURE 28.15.

Use the Identification tab to establish your computer's network identity.

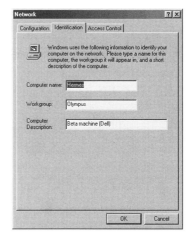

A UTILITY FOR MULTIPLE NETWORK CONFIGURATIONS

What do you do if you have to set up your computer for connections to multiple networks? I'm sorry to say that you have to repeat all the steps you just went through each time you need to connect to a different network!

If the thought of that kind of hassle scares you, you'll almost certainly want to check out NetSwitcher, a utility that enables you to set up multiple network configurations and switch between them easily. NetSwitcher was written by J.W. Hance and is available either via fax (317-575-9435) or via the Web at the following URL:

```
http://www.bysnet.com/netsw.html
```

Summary

This chapter got your Windows 98 networking education off the ground. I began by giving you an overview of Windows 98 networking and by showing you some of the new networking knickknacks that come in the Windows 98 package. From there, you learned how to install and configure network adapters, clients, protocols, and services; how to establish your primary network logon; and more.

That's a lot of material, but we're not done yet; there's a lot more networking know-how to come. Here's what to expect:

- If you have just a couple of computers, you can bypass the expense of network adapter cards and cables by using Windows 98's Direct Cable Connection. You still must set up a "network," however, and I explain how it's done in Chapter 22, "Portable Windows: The Briefcase and Direct Cable Connection."

- I show you how to access network resources, as well as share your own resources on the network, in Chapter 29, "Working with Network Resources."

- To learn how to access a network via modem, check out Chapter 30, "Remote Computing with Dial-Up Networking."

- TCP/IP is fast becoming the protocol of choice for both large and small networks. I demonstrate how to work with TCP/IP in Chapter 31, "Implementing TCP/IP for Internet and Intranet Connections."

- The Internet, of course, is *the* network. I show you how Windows 98 connects to, and works with, Internet resources in Chapter 32, "Windows 98 and the Internet."

Working with Network Resources

By Paul McFedries and Peter Kuo

IN THIS CHAPTER

CHAPTER 29

I always get back to the question, is it really necessary that men should consume so much of their bodily and mental energies in the machinery of civilized life?

—*William Allingham*

Now that your network components are installed, configured, and ready to run, you can start accessing the goodies on your network. To that end, this chapter shows you how to log on, examine the network, map network drives, and use network printers. You also get the skinny on sharing your own drives, folders, and printers with your network peers.

Accessing Network Resources

If all has gone well to this point, you are just about ready for action. Your newfound network will be up and running, and your Windows 98 machines will be able to connect to the network. Now all that remains is to log on and start looking around your net.

Logging on to the Network

With networking enabled on a Windows 98 machine, you are faced with a logon prompt each time you restart the system. One of the innovations with Windows 98 is that you can use a single unified logon for all your networks (and Windows 98 itself). The first time you start Windows 98, however, you might have to negotiate multiple logon dialog boxes. The trick to establishing the unified logon is to assign the same password for each logon.

Windows 98 Logon

If you chose the Windows Logon option as your primary network logon, you see the dialog box shown in Figure 29.1. In this case, even though the username and password are meaningful only in the context of user profiles (as explained in Chapter 7, "Setting Accessibility Options, User Profiles, and More"), you should still enter your network username so that it will be visible automatically the next time you log on to the network. (Note that the first time you start Windows 98, you need to enter your password twice.)

Figure 29.1.

You see this dialog box if you're using the Windows Logon.

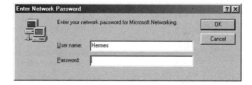

Client for Microsoft Networks Logon

If you set up the Client for Microsoft Networks to log on to a Windows NT domain, you see the dialog box shown in Figure 29.2. In this case, you need to enter the username and password defined in your account on the NT machine, and you need to make sure that the Domain text box correctly identifies the domain you belong to. When you click OK, your password is verified by the NT machine.

FIGURE 29.2.

You see this dialog box if you're logging on to a Windows NT domain.

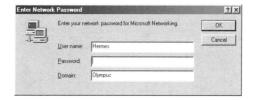

Novell IntranetWare Client Logon

When IntranetWare Client is loaded on your Windows 98 workstation, you get the graphical Novell IntranetWare Client Login when you start Windows 98, as shown in Figure 29.3. Use the Login tab to enter your username and password. The Connection tab is where you specify the name of the NDS tree or the name of a NetWare server you want to log in to and the name context if you're performing an NDS login. If you've configured this information under the IntranetWare Client properties sheets as described in Chapter 28, "Setting Up Windows 98 for Networking," you won't need to access this tab at all while logging in, unless you want to change the defaults.

LOGIN SCREEN TABS MUST BE ENABLED

You won't have access to the various tabs in the GUI screen login if they are not enabled in the IntranetWare Client Login property sheet (see Chapter 28).

FIGURE 29.3.

The GUI login of Novell IntranetWare Client.

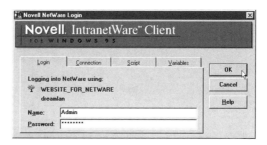

Microsoft Client for NetWare Networks Logon

If you're using the Microsoft NetWare client, the login screen will look similar to the one shown in Figure 29.4. If you're logging in using a bindery connection, just enter your username and password; if you're using an NDS connection, enter your username using the "full path" if a name context isn't set.

Figure 29.4.

The login screen of the Microsoft NetWare Client.

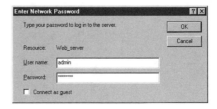

NetWare Login Scripts

When you log in to a NetWare server using either the Microsoft client or the Novell client, the various login scripts are executed. With the Novell client, if the option is selected, you can see the result of the login script execution, as shown in Figure 29.5. Both Microsoft and Novell clients support drive mapping, including search drives, in the login script processing.

Figure 29.5.

The login script result screen of IntranetWare Client.

The Network Neighborhood

If you used Windows for Workgroups, you know that one of its biggest drawbacks was that it gave you no easy way of browsing the network and checking out which shared resources were available. Windows 98 rectifies that glaring omission with the Network Neighborhood. This is a special folder that appears as part of the Windows 98 desktop. To view the Network Neighborhood, use either of the following methods:

- Open the Network Neighborhood icon on the desktop.
- In Explorer, highlight Network Neighborhood in the Folders pane.

> ### 32-BIT COMMON DIALOG BOXES ALSO DISPLAY THE 'HOOD
>
> You can also access the Network Neighborhood via the Save As and Open dialog boxes in 32-bit applications. In any Save As dialog box, open the Save in drop-down list and select Network Neighborhood; in any Open dialog box, use the Look in drop-down list instead.

The top level of the Network Neighborhood shows you the various computers that share your workgroup or domain (including your computer). As you can see in Figure 29.6, Explorer's Details view shows you not only the name of each computer, but also a descriptive Comment column (this is the text that was entered in the Computer description field in the Identification tab; see Figure 28.17 in Chapter 28).

FIGURE 29.6.

The Network Neighborhood as seen from Explorer.

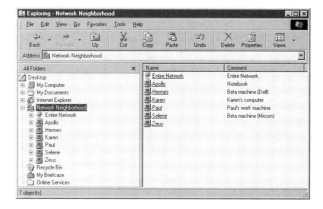

The top level of the Network Neighborhood also has an item called Entire Network. As the name implies, this item displays all the available network resources. Specifically, it shows you the workgroups and domains that compose the network. In Figure 29.7, for example, there are two workgroups: Olympus and Valhalla. These groups act as folders, so you can open them to display each group's computers.

FIGURE 29.7.

The Entire Network item displays all the workgroups and domains.

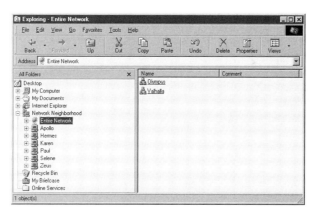

At the computer level, the Network Neighborhood shows you which resources each computer is sharing with the network. For example, Figure 29.8 shows you the resources shared by the computer named Paul, which include a couple of folders, a Jaz drive, a CD-ROM drive, and a printer.

Figure 29.8.

When you highlight a computer in the Network Neighborhood, Explorer displays the resources that the computer is sharing with the network.

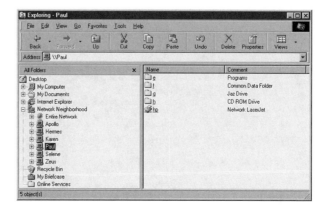

You can use any drives and folders shared by a network computer just as though they were part of your computer. If, however, the owner has assigned a password to a resource, you see a dialog box like the one shown in Figure 29.9 when you try to access the object. You won't be able to use the resource unless you know the correct password. Note, as well, that Windows 98 can create a password list. This list caches the passwords you enter for each resource, which saves you from typing the password the next time you access the resource. To cache a password, make sure that the Save this password in your password list check box is activated.

Figure 29.9.

If a resource is protected by a password, you see a dialog box like this one when you attempt to access the resource.

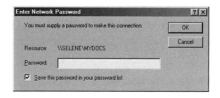

The Universal Naming Convention

If you examine Figure 29.9 closely, you see that Windows 98 uses the name \\SELENE\MYDOCS for the resource. This format, called the universal naming convention (UNC), uses the following syntax:

`\\COMPUTER\SHARE`

Here, `COMPUTER` is the name of the computer, and `SHARE` is the name given to the shared resource.

The UNC offers you several alternative methods of accessing shared network resources:

■ In the Run dialog box, enter the UNC for a shared resource to open the resource in a folder window. You can also do this from the DOS prompt by preceding the resource name with the START command (for example, `start \\selene\mydocs`).

■ In a 32-bit application's Open or Save As dialog box, you can use a UNC name in the File name text box.

■ At the DOS prompt, you can use a UNC name as part of a DOS command. For example, to copy a file named DATA.DOC to \\SELENE\MYDOCS, you use the following command:

```
copy data.doc \\selene\mydocs
```

Mapping a Network Drive

UNC names are often convenient, but they can be a bit unwieldy because you usually have to return to the Network Neighborhood to check the correct computer and share names. To avoid this hassle, you can map a shared network drive or folder to your own computer. *Mapping* assigns a drive letter to the resource so that it appears to be just another disk drive on your machine.

Connecting a Resource

To map a shared drive or folder, first use either of the following methods:

■ In Explorer or the Network Neighborhood, highlight the resource and select File|Map Network Drive.

■ In either Explorer or Network Neighborhood, right-click the resource and select Map Network Drive from the context menu.

Whichever method you choose, you see the Map Network Drive dialog box, shown in Figure 29.10. The Drive drop-down list displays the first available drive letter on your system, but you can pull down the list and select any available letter. If you want Windows 98 to map the resource each time you log on to the network, make sure that the Reconnect at logon check box is activated. When you click OK, Windows 98 adds the new drive letter to your system. (Note that you might have to enter a password at this point.)

FIGURE 29.10.
Use the Map Network Drive dialog box to assign a drive letter to a network resource.

Disconnecting a Resource

If you no longer need to map a network resource, you should disconnect it. Here are the methods you can use:

■ In Explorer or My Computer, right-click the mapped resource and select Disconnect from the context menu.

■ In My Computer, highlight the mapped resource and select File|Disconnect.

> **DON'T DISCONNECT WITH OPEN FILES**
>
> If you're using files on the mapped drive, disconnecting causes you to lose the connection to these files, and you might lose your work. Fortunately, Windows 98 displays a warning if you try to disconnect a resource in which you're using files. In this case, you should cancel the disconnect, close the files, and try again.

Accessing Resources on NetWare Networks

Both the NetWare IntranetWare Client and the Microsoft NetWare Client are tightly integrated with My Computer, Windows Explorer, and the Network Neighborhood. However, Novell's IntranetWare Client adds some extensions, so in the following subsections and the rest of this chapter, the discussion is IntranetWare Client–specific (unless otherwise noted). The overall concepts, however, apply to both IntranetWare Client and Microsoft's NetWare Client.

Browsing a NetWare Network

You can browse your NetWare network by using My Computer, Explorer, or Network Neighborhood. The easiest way is to use Network Neighborhood (bear in mind, as well, that Network Neighborhood will show NDS printers, whereas My Computer will not). Use the following steps to browse your Novell network:

1. Open Network Neighborhood to start browsing. If you're not already authenticated to the network, only the Entire Network icon is shown. If you're authenticated to the network, you see the Entire Network icon, a list of NDS trees, a list of NetWare servers, and an icon that represents your current name context, as shown in Figure 29.11.

FIGURE 29.11.

Network Neighborhood showing the Novell NetWare 4.1 network.

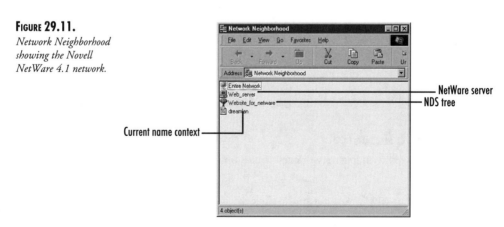

Current name context

NetWare server
NDS tree

2. Double-click the Entire Network icon, and you're presented with two options: Novell Directory Services and IntranetWare Servers.

3. Double-click Novell Directory Services. You see a list of NDS tree names.

4. Double-click a tree name. If you're authenticated to that tree, you're presented with a list of containers starting at the [Root] level. As you walk the tree, you'll see container, volume, and printer objects in a given context, as shown in Figure 29.12; you won't see other NDS objects.

Figure 29.12.

Print and file objects in an NDS context.

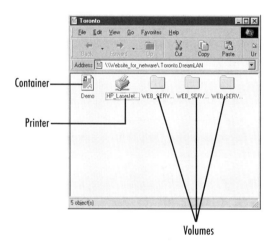

Another way to view and walk the tree is to right-click the tree and select Explore from the context menu to bring up the Explorer. Open the Novell Directory Services branch to see a list of NDS tree names. Open the IntranetWare Servers branch to see a list of servers. From there, you can open a server to see a list of volume names, and you can open a volume name to see a list of directories and files, starting at the root, as shown in Figure 29.13. Note too that you can use the Windows Explorer to explore the network printers and logical drives (created by NetWare drive mappings) as though they were local devices.

Figure 29.13.

Exploring a NetWare volume.

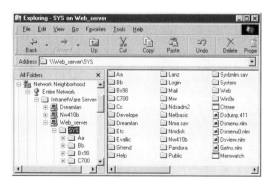

29

WORKING WITH NETWORK RESOURCES

Connecting to a NetWare Server

We have already discussed how you can log in to a NetWare server using either IntranetWare Client's GUI Login or the logon screen from NetWare Client. You can also log in to a NetWare server or a NetWare 4 NDS tree from either Explorer or Network Neighborhood by using the following steps:

1. Use either Explorer or Network Neighborhood to bring up a list of NetWare servers or NDS trees.
2. If you're using Windows Explorer, right-click the server or tree name of interest to bring up an options list. If you left-click instead of right-clicking, it's assumed that you want to authenticate to the selected server or tree, and the login dialog box appears automatically.

   If you're using Network Neighborhood, highlight the server or tree name of interest first and then right-click to bring up an options list.
3. Select either Authenticate or Login to NDS Tree. A login dialog box appears for you to enter a username and password. The Authenticate option doesn't execute any login script commands, whereas the Login to NDS Tree selection does.

To disconnect from a server or NDS tree, select Options|Logout.

Mapping a Network Drive

You can map a network drive in two ways. One is the traditional NetWare way of using the MAP.EXE command from a DOS prompt. But because Windows 98 is GUI-based, you can easily map a drive from within either Explorer or Network Neighborhood.

To try this, follow these steps:

1. Use either Windows Explorer or Network Neighborhood to locate the directory you want to map.
2. Right-click the directory and select Map Network Drive from the context menu to display the Map Drive dialog box, shown in Figure 29.14.
3. Use the Device drop-down list to select the drive letter you want to use.
4. If you want the drive to be reconnected at logon, activate the Reconnect At Logon check box.
5. If you want the drive to be map-rooted, activate the Map Root check box.
6. Click OK and the mapped drive shows up as a networked drive icon.

NetWare and Long Filenames

NetWare supports long filenames using name space. Specifically, you add either the OS/2 name space (for NetWare 4.10 and below) or the LONG name space (for NetWare 4.11 and above) to the volumes you want to support Windows 98 long filenames.

FIGURE 29.14.
Use this dialog box to map a NetWare directory to a local drive letter.

You need to perform the following steps on your NetWare 4.10 server console:

1. Enter the command LOAD OS2.NAM.

2. Add the name space to the volumes by entering the following command (in which *volumename* is the name of the volume you want to set up with long filename support):

   ADD NAME SPACE OS2 to *volumename*

3. Repeat step 2 for each volume you want to have long filename support.

4. Edit your STARTUP.NCF file and include the LOAD OS2.NAM command in the file.

You need to perform these tasks only once. The changes are made permanently to the volumes.

The steps for NetWare 4.11 and higher are similar:

1. Enter the command LOAD LONG.NAM.

2. Add the name space to the volumes by entering the following command (in which *volumename* is the name of the volume you want to set up with long filename support):

   ADD NAME SPACE LONG to *volumename*

3. Repeat step 2 for each volume you want to have long filename support.

4. Edit your STARTUP.NCF file and include the LOAD LONG.NAM command in the file.

REMOVING NAME SPACE SUPPORT

If for any reason you need to remove the name space support, use the VREPAIR.NLM that is shipped with NetWare to delete the name space.

NAME CHANGE IN NETWARE 4.11 AND ABOVE

For IntranetWare/NetWare 4.11, the OS2.NAM name space module is now called LONG.NAM. This new module provides long filename support for Windows 98, Windows NT, and OS/2 workstations.

Changing Your Password

If you ever want to change your password, you can't do it from the logon dialog box (which makes sense). Instead, you need to do it from within Windows 98. First, open the Control Panel's Passwords icon to display the Passwords Properties dialog box. The Change Passwords tab gives you two options:

> **Change Windows Password:** Click this button to change your Windows 98 logon password. You get a chance to change any of your networking passwords at the same time. This way you can keep all your passwords the same and maintain Windows 98's unified logon dialog box. In the dialog box that appears (see Figure 29.15), activate the check box beside each password you want to change and then click OK.

FIGURE 29.15.

Use this dialog box to select the passwords you want to change in addition to your Windows 98 password.

> **Change Other Passwords:** Click this button to change any of your other passwords (such as the password you use to log on to a Microsoft or NetWare network). In the list of password-protected services that appears, highlight the service you want to modify and then click the Change button.

Whichever button you click, you'll eventually see the Change Windows Password dialog box, shown in Figure 29.16. Enter your existing password in the Old password text box, enter the new password you want to use in the New password text box, and then enter the new password again in the Confirm new password text box. When you're done, click OK.

FIGURE 29.16.

Use the Change Windows Password dialog box to enter your new password (twice).

Automatic Domain Logons

By design, Windows 98 won't cache the logon password for your Windows NT domain. If security isn't an issue, there's a way to work around this:

1. Display the Passwords Properties dialog box.

2. Click Change Windows Password to get to the Change Windows Password dialog box.

3. Clear the check boxes (especially Microsoft Networking), if necessary, and then click OK.

4. Use the Old password text box to enter your current Windows logon password. Leave the New password and Confirm old password text boxes blank and then click OK.

5. When Windows 98 confirms that your password has been changed, click OK and then click Close to return to Control Panel.

6. Open Control Panel's Network icon to display the Network properties sheet.

EASY ACCESS TO THE NETWORK PROPERTIES SHEET

A quick way to open the Network properties sheet is to right-click the desktop's Network Neighborhood icon and select Properties from the context menu.

7. Double-click the Client for Microsoft Networks component. Make sure that the Log on to Windows NT domain check box is activated and that the correct domain appears in the Windows NT domain text box, and then click OK.

8. In the Primary Network Logon list, select Windows Logon and click OK.

9. Follow the onscreen prompts until Windows 95 asks you to restart your computer, and then click Yes.

10. In the logon dialog box, use the Password text box to enter your Windows NT domain password. Make sure that the Save this password in your password list check box is activated and then click OK.

From now on you'll be logged onto the NT domain when you start Windows 98, but your domain logon password will be entered automatically.

Network Printing

One of the benefits of setting up a network is that you can share peripherals among several machines. Printers are a good example of this. Any printer that's attached to a network computer can be shared with the network. This means that any users on the network can use that printer as though it was attached to their own machines. Windows 98 offers you several methods of accessing network printers; we describe them in the next three sections.

In each case, note that, thanks to Windows 98's Point and Print feature, you won't need to insert any of your Windows 98 source disks. Instead, Point and Print grabs the printer driver and any other files it needs from the network computer where the printer is installed locally. As well, Point and Print borrows the remote printer's current settings (such as paper size and page orientation) and uses them to set up the local printer. Any changes you make, however, are retained on the local computer.

After you've installed a network printer, it appears in the Printers folder along with your other printers (if any). The only difference is that a cable appears underneath the printer icon to identify this as a network printer. As with folders, printers can also be password-protected, so you might need to enter a password the first time you use the printer.

Installing a Shared Printer via the Add Printer Wizard

Chapter 21, "Prescriptions for Perfect Printing," shows you how to use the Add Printer Wizard to install a printer in Windows 98. You can use the same method to install a network printer. Here are the steps to follow:

1. Select Start|Settings|Printers to open the Printers folder. (You can also open the Printers folder by launching the Printers icon in the Control Panel.)

2. Open the Add Printer icon to start the Add Printer Wizard.

3. Click Next >.

4. Select the Network printer option and click Next >. The Wizard prompts you to enter a network path, as shown in Figure 29.17.

FIGURE 29.17.

Use the Add Printer Wizard dialog box to enter the UNC path for the network printer you want to install.

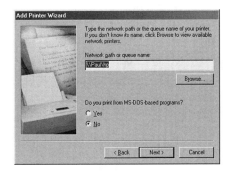

5. Use the Network path or queue name text box to enter the appropriate UNC path for the network printer you want to install. If you're not sure, use the Browse button to choose the printer from a dialog box, as shown in Figure 29.18.

6. Continue with the installation in the usual manner.

FIGURE 29.18.

If you're not sure of the printer's correct UNC path, click Browse to choose the printer from this dialog box.

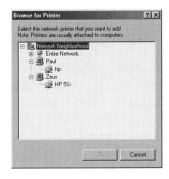

Using Point and Print with a NetWare Server

IntranetWare Client from Novell supports *deviceless* printing. In other words, it's no longer necessary to use print captures and to associate a printer port with a specific printer, as was traditionally done on the DOS/Windows 3.*x* platform. Instead, when you set up a printer, Windows 98 writes all the printer configuration information to the Registry. To use the printer, simply click the printer's icon.

Use the following steps to set up Point and Print for a network printer and store the printer information on a NetWare 3.*x* or 4.*x* server:

1. Log in to an NDS tree or NetWare server as Admin/Supervisor or an equivalent user. (This should be the tree or server where you want the path to the printer driver files to be located.)

2. In the Network Neighborhood, browse the network until you find the NetWare printer or print queue you want to set up. Right-click the queue and click Properties in the context menu.

3. In the properties sheet, select the Setup Point and Print tab, shown in Figure 29.19. (You won't see this tab if you're not logged in with the appropriate rights.)

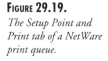

FIGURE 29.19.

The Setup Point and Print tab of a NetWare print queue.

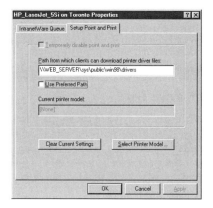

4. Ensure that the path listed under Path from which clients can download printer driver files is a valid UNC path. If it isn't correct, deactivate the Use Preferred Path check box and enter the correct path.

5. Click the Select Printer Model button.

6. Select the Manufacturer and Model from the standard print setup selection boxes as appropriate for your printer.

DISABLING POINT AND PRINT

When you activate Point and Print, the Temporarily disable point and print check box becomes available. If, sometime down the road, you need to disable Point and Print for this printer, redisplay the printer's properties sheet and activate this check box. Note that the path and printer model data remain in place, so you can easily reenable Point and Print without having to repeat the procedure outlined in these steps.

7. Click OK to copy the printer driver files.

8. After the driver files are copied, click OK to close the printer's properties sheet.

9. Make sure that the users will have at least Read and File Scan rights to the directory in which the printer driver files were copied.

To access this print queue, you now need to add the queue to the Printers folder by using the Add Printer Wizard. Follow these steps:

1. Use Network Neighborhood or Explorer to locate the print queue of interest.

2. Drag the print queue over to the Printers folder and drop it.

3. Follow the Add Printer Wizard as it prompts you to set up printing. When you're done, the Printers folder is updated to show the new printer.

Windows 98 automatically copies the printer driver files from the server to the Windows 98 SYSTEM directory.

Other Point and Print Methods

The Add Printer Wizard is only one of the methods available for installing a printer. The Point and Print feature also enables you to install a remote printer by using the following techniques:

■ In Explorer or the Network Neighborhood, either highlight a shared printer and select File|Install, or right-click the printer and select Install from the context menu.

■ In Explorer or the Network Neighborhood, drag a shared printer and drop it inside the Printers folder.

■ Drag a document and drop it on the remote printer's icon in the Network Neighborhood. When Windows 98 asks whether you want to set up the printer, click Yes. After the printer is installed, the document you dropped will print.

■ In the Run dialog box, enter the UNC path to the shared printer and click OK. When Windows 98 asks whether you want to set up the printer, click Yes.

In each case, a scaled-down version of the Add Printer Wizard appears. Follow the prompts to install the printer.

Capturing a Printer Port

In the same way that you can map a shared network drive or folder and have it appear as though it were a physical drive on your system, so too can you map a shared network printer and have it appear as though it were a physical printer port on your system. This is called *capturing* a printer port. To try this, use either of the following methods:

- Open the properties sheet for any installed printer, display the Details tab, and click the Capture Printer Port button.

- In Explorer or the Network Neighborhood, either highlight a shared printer and select File|Capture Printer Port, or right-click the printer and select Capture Printer Port from the context menu.

Then, in the Capture Printer Port dialog box, shown in Figure 29.20, use the Device list to select a logical printer port (Windows 98 automatically selects the next available port). If you're using the Details tab, you use the Path combo box to enter the network path to the shared printer. Click OK to map the printer.

FIGURE 29.20.

Use the Capture Printer Port dialog box to map a shared network printer to a logical printer port on your system.

When you no longer want to capture a network printer as a logical port on your system, follow these steps:

1. Open the properties sheet for any installed printer.
2. Display the Details tab.
3. Click the End Capture button.
4. In the End Capture dialog box that appears, highlight the port you want to release.
5. Click OK.

Windows 98 as a Server: Sharing Your Resources

In a peer-to-peer network, each computer can act as both a client and a server. So far you've seen how to use a Windows 98 machine as a client, so now let's turn our attention to setting up your system as a peer server. In Windows 98, that means enabling the file and print sharing service and then sharing individual drives, folders, and printers with the network.

Access Control: Share-Level Versus User-Level

You saw earlier that you may need to enter a password when accessing a network resource. This is called *share-level* security because it sets up protection on a resource-by-resource basis, and any user with the correct password can access the share.

If, however, you have a Windows NT or NetWare server on your network, you can implement a more robust security system known as *user-level* or *pass-through* security. In this model, access to shared resources is controlled on a user-by-user basis. In other words, when you share a resource, you also specify the users (or groups of users) who are allowed access to the resource. This information is stored on a security server (an NT or NetWare machine). When someone tries to access one of your shared resources, Windows 98 asks the security server to validate the request. The server checks the person's username and password and then checks to see whether the user is on your list of those allowed access. If that user is, the server grants the request; otherwise, the user isn't allowed to access the resource.

File and Print Sharing for Microsoft Networks

If you're using the Client for Microsoft Networks, Windows 98 comes with a 32-bit server (VSERVER.VXD) you can use to share resources with other Windows 98 machines, as well as machines running Windows NT, Windows for Workgroups, LAN Manager, and any other networks that use the SMB (Server Message Block) file-sharing protocol.

Setting Up File and Print Sharing

To enable file and print sharing on your system, first display the Network properties sheet (by opening the Network icon in the Control Panel or by right-clicking the Network Neighborhood icon and clicking Properties). Use one of the following methods to enable file and print sharing:

■ If Client for Microsoft Networks is your primary logon, click the File and Print Sharing button.

■ If Client for Microsoft Networks isn't your primary logon, click Add, highlight Service, and click Add again. In the Select Network Service dialog box, highlight Microsoft in the Manufacturers list, highlight File and printer sharing for Microsoft Networks, and click OK. When you're back in the Network properties sheet, click the File and Print Sharing button.

In the File and Print Sharing dialog box that appears, shown in Figure 29.21, you have two options:

I want to be able to give others access to my files: Activate this check box to allow sharing of drives and folders.

I want to be able to allow others to print to my printer(s): Activate this check box to allow print sharing.

Click OK to return to the properties sheet and then click OK to put the new setting into effect.

FIGURE 29.21.

Use this dialog box to turn your Windows 98 client into a peer server.

Choosing Between User-Level and Share-Level Access Control

If you're on an NT network and using the Client for Microsoft Networks, resources are secured using share-level access control by default. To switch to user-level access control, open the Network properties sheet and select the Access Control tab, shown in Figure 29.22. Activate the User-level access control option. Windows 98 should enter the name of your NT domain in the Obtain list of users and groups from text box. Windows 98 uses the server designated as the primary domain controller for your domain to get the user list. (If you like, you can enter the name of the backup domain controller instead.)

FIGURE 29.22.

Use the Access Control tab to enable user-level security on an NT network.

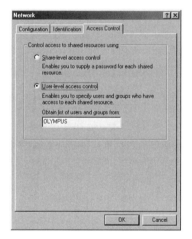

When you click OK, Windows 95 displays a message telling you that your existing shares will be removed. Click Yes to continue. When Windows 95 asks you to restart your system, click Yes.

Sharing Drives and Folders with Share-Level Access

With file sharing activated, you can share any file-related devices that are attached to your computer: hard drives, CD-ROM drives, floppy drives, and folders. To set up any of these devices as a shared resource, use either of the following techniques:

- Right-click the device and select Sharing from the context menu.
- Open the properties sheet for the device and display the Sharing tab.

If you're using share-level access control, you'll see a Sharing tab similar to the one shown in Figure 29.23. This tab contains the following options:

Not Shared: Activate this option to turn off sharing for the selected resource.

Shared As: Activate this option to share the selected resource.

Share Name: Use this text box to enter a name for the shared resource. This text appears in the Name column when others browse your computer with Explorer, and it's also the text used as part of the shared resource's UNC path. The name can be up to 12 characters long. Spaces and all alphanumeric characters are OK, as are the following symbols:

~ ! @ # $ % ^ & ( ) _ - { } ' .

Comment: Use this text box to enter a brief description of the shared resource. This text appears in the Comment column when others browse your computer with Explorer. The comment can be up to 48 characters in length.

Access Type: The options in this group determine the level of access granted to users who access the resource remotely:

Read-Only: This option lets users view only the contents of the resource; they can't modify the resource in any way. In a shared folder, for example, users can view the contained files, but they can't delete, edit, or rename existing files, and they can't add new files or subfolders. (They can, however, open a file in the shared folder and then save it to a local folder.)

Full: This option gives users complete access to all the contents within the shared resource.

Depends on Password: This option determines the level of access applied to a user, based on the password the user enters when attempting to work with the resource.

Passwords: Use the text boxes in this group to set up one or more passwords for the shared resource. The Read-Only Password text box sets the password for read-only access; the Full Access Password text box sets the password for users to get full access.

Click OK to put the settings into effect. If you entered any passwords, you're asked to confirm them. As you can see in Figure 29.24, Windows 98 appends a hand icon underneath the resource's existing icon to denote that the resource is shared.

FIGURE 29.23.
Use the Sharing tab to set up a shared resource.

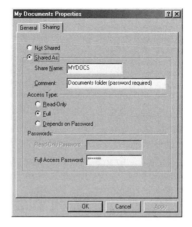

FIGURE 29.24.
Windows 98 adds a hand icon to denote a shared resource.

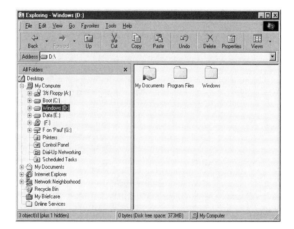

Sharing a Printer with Share-Level Access

To share a local printer when you're running share-level access control, you use an almost identical process. First, you display the Sharing tab for a printer by using either of the following methods:

- In the Printers folder, either highlight the printer and select File|Sharing, or right-click the printer and select Sharing from the context menu.
- Open the properties sheet for the printer and display the Sharing tab.

As before, you activate the Shared As option and then fill in the Share Name, Comment, and Password text boxes.

29

WORKING WITH
NETWORK
RESOURCES

Sharing a Resource with User-Level Access

If your machine is set up to provide user-level access control, you need to reshare all your previously shared resources. Let's see how user-level security affects the resource sharing procedure.

As before, open the properties sheet for the resource and then select the Sharing tab. As you can see in Figure 29.25, the Sharing tab for user-level security is a bit different. You still activate the Shared As option, and you still enter the Share Name and a Comment. However, the Access Type and Passwords groups are gone. In their place is a list box you use to add the groups and users to whom you want to give access to the resource.

FIGURE 29.25.

The Sharing tab sports a slightly different layout under user-level security.

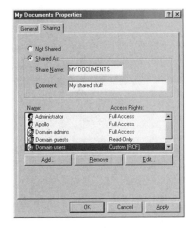

To specify which users and groups are allowed access to the resource, click the Add button to display the Add Users dialog box, shown in Figure 29.26. The Name list displays all the users and groups that are recognized as valid by the security server. This way, you're assured that the users and groups you designate for access are all legitimate and that no unauthorized user can work with the share.

FIGURE 29.26.

Use the Add Users dialog box to specify which users and groups should be allowed access to the resource.

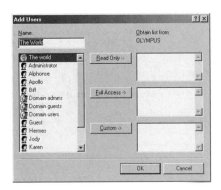

To set up the access, highlight a user or group in the Name list and then click Read Only, Full Access, or Custom. (If you're setting up access for a printer, you get only the Full Access button.) When you're done, click OK. If you added any users or groups to the Custom list, you see the Change Access Rights dialog box, shown in Figure 29.27. Use this dialog box to set up specific access rights for the users. When you're done, click OK.

FIGURE 29.27.

Use this dialog box to add specific access rights for a user.

CUSTOM ACCESS RIGHTS

To set specific access for rights for any user or group, highlight the appropriate name in the Sharing tab, click Edit, and activate the Custom Access Rights option in the Change Access Rights dialog box.

File and Print Sharing for NetWare Networks

Windows 98 supports two types of file and print sharing services. One type, as discussed earlier, is for Microsoft- and IBM-type networks. This uses the SMB protocol. The other type is for NetWare networks. It uses Novell's NCP (NetWare Core Protocol) and is supported using the NWSERVER.VXD driver.

ONLY MICROSOFT'S CLIENT SUPPORTS SHARING

The file and printer sharing for NetWare service is available only with Microsoft's Client for NetWare Networks. Therefore, if you're using Novell's IntranetWare Client, you cannot enable File and Printer Sharing for NetWare Networks service on Windows 98 workstations.

Before we show you how to enable the File and Printer sharing for NetWare Networks service, you should understand the possible implications of doing so. You need to first understand what NetWare Service Advertising Protocol (SAP) is.

29

WORKING WITH
NETWORK
RESOURCES

Service Advertising Protocol

Every NetWare service, whether it's a server, a print server, or even your RCONSOLE access (REMOTE.NLM and RSPX.NLM), advertises itself on the network every 60 seconds. This is done by the broadcasting of a SAP packet. All NetWare servers and routers listen to these SAP broadcasts and accumulate them in their internal SAP tables. Because broadcast traffic is generally restricted to the segment it's broadcast on, the routers rebroadcast the packets to the other subnets they route between so that the whole network is aware of all the services available.

As a result, every service causes SAP packets to be sent across the entire IPX network. Also, each service must be remembered by every router and server on the network. This works well for a small number of services (up to perhaps 1,000), but as the number of services increases, the bandwidth utilization due to SAP packets and the resource requirements on the routers and servers become very large.

NetWare Services Client

On a large network on which there might be hundreds or even thousands of Windows 98 workstations, it isn't practical to use SAP advertising as the method of advertising services. Instead, Microsoft created a component called NetWare Services Client (NSCL) that's used to implement browsing for large NetWare networks.

Each Windows 98 workstation is assigned to a workgroup (set in the Identification tab in the Network properties sheet). As we've said, a workgroup is a collection of related computers, and they're grouped logically, not necessarily geographically. The important thing is that they're grouped.

When an NWSERVER starts up, it registers its name and workgroup with NSCL. NSCL examines the workgroup name and locates the "master" of the workgroup. If it can't locate a master, it elects itself to be the master. The master, known as the Browse Master, advertises itself by using SAP. Any subsequent servers in the workgroup register with the master.

This scheme reduces the number of SAP packets sent out by the Windows 98 workstations. Rather than one SAP packet per Windows 98 workstation, you now have one SAP packet per workgroup.

Enabling File and Print Sharing for NetWare

The procedure to enable file and print sharing for NetWare is the same as that described earlier for Microsoft networks:

- Make sure that the Microsoft Client for NetWare Networks is your primary logon and click the File and Print Sharing button.
- If the File and Printer Sharing for NetWare service isn't already installed, it will be installed automatically.

In the File and Print Sharing dialog box that appears, you have two options:

I want to be able to give others access to my files: Activate this check box to allow sharing of drives and folders.

I want to be able to allow others to print to my printer(s): Activate this check box to allow print sharing.

Click OK to return to the properties sheet, and then click OK to put the new settings into effect.

Note that you need to configure your access control for user-level access control and specify a NetWare server name.

ENABLE BINDERY SERVICES ON NETWARE 4 SERVERS

If you provided a NetWare 4 server's name in the Obtain list of users and groups from text box, make sure that the server has Bindery Services enabled. Any usernames and group names you reference must exist in the bindery contexts of this server.

Sharing Files, Folders, and Printers

In order for other NetWare clients to be able to access your Windows 98 workstation's resources, you need to either turn on SAP or correctly configure the NSCL setup on the Windows 98 machine. To configure for SAP operation, use the following steps:

1. From the Network properties sheet, highlight File and Printer Sharing for NetWare Networks and click the Properties button.

2. In the dialog box that appears, highlight SAP Advertising in the Property list and select Enabled from the Value drop-down list.

3. Highlight Workgroup Advertising in the Property list and select Disabled from the Value drop-down list.

4. Click OK to return to the Network dialog box.

5. Click OK again to save the settings.

To use the NSCL setup, follow the preceding steps, but make sure that SAP Advertising is disabled. Then configure one Windows 98 workstation to be master and the rest to use the Enabled: may be master option.

> **VERIFYING ADVERTISING**
>
> To verify that your Windows 98 workstation is advertising, head for the MS-DOS prompt and enter either the SLIST or the NLIST SERVER /B /A command. If everything is working, you should see your computer name listed as a NetWare server. (Or you should see it listed in the Network Neighborhood.)

Accessing Files, Folders, and Printers

When the Windows 98 workstation is set up for file sharing using the SAP mode, a folder called NWSYSVOL is created in your main Windows folder and automatically shared. This folder has a subfolder named LOGIN that contains a special version of LOGIN.EXE from Microsoft. You can use this to log in to the preferred server of the Windows 98 workstation.

To access files and printers on the Windows 98 workstation, simply MAP or CAPTURE to it from your workstation as though it were a real NetWare server. The only difference is that any files you can have access to need to be placed in NWSYSVOL and any subfolders below it.

The Windows 98 workstation (actually, NWSERVER) uses the bindery of the preferred server (a real NetWare server) to look up usernames and passwords for authentication purposes. Therefore, when you're asked for a username and password, be aware of which NetWare server is the default server. If it's a NetWare 3.1*x* server, the bindery information is server-centric. On the other hand, if the preferred server is a NetWare 4 server, the NetWare 4 server must have Bindery Services enabled, and the username you specify must be located in the bindery contexts of the server—NWSERVER isn't NDS-aware.

Summary

This chapter showed you how to work with network resources in Windows 98. In your tour around Windows 98's Network Neighborhood, you learned how to log on, access network file and print resources, and share your resources with the network, using both share-level and user-level access control. Here are a few signposts that point to other network-related chapters:

- If you're using Direct Cable Connection, you need to share your resources. See Chapter 22, "Portable Windows: The Briefcase and Direct Cable Connection."

- To learn how to install and configure networking components in Windows 98, see Chapter 28, "Setting Up Windows 98 for Networking."

- To learn how to access a network via modem, check out Chapter 30, "Remote Computing with Dial-Up Networking."

CHAPTER 30

Remote Computing with Dial-Up Networking

IN THIS CHAPTER

Far folks fare well.

—English proverb

The networking techniques you've seen so far have assumed some kind of physical connection between machines. For standard peer-to-peer and client/server networks, the computers use a network card/cable package to connect to each other either directly or indirectly via a hub or router. For a Direct Cable Connection mini-network, two computers are joined at the hip via a null-modem or LapLink-style cable attached to their serial or parallel ports (or possibly via an infrared hookup).

What do you do, however, when a physical connection just isn't possible? For example, suppose that you're on the road with your notebook computer and need to access a file on your network server. Or suppose that you're working at home and need to send a file to your office machine. Is there any way to access a network in the absence of a physical connection? The answer is that for these remote predicaments, you *can* connect to a network and use its resources just as you can with a physical connection (albeit more slowly). The solution is Windows 98's Dial-Up Networking client. With Dial-Up Networking, you can establish a connection and log on to a network over phone lines by using your modem. This chapter shows you how to configure and use Dial-Up Networking, how to use Microsoft Mail with a remote connection, how to create scripts for automatic logons, how to set up your Windows 98 machine to be a Dial-Up Networking server, and more. (Note that you also use Dial-Up Networking to establish a dial-up connection to an Internet Service Provider. I'll show you how this works in Chapter 32, "Windows 98 and the Internet.")

Dial-Up Networking Fundamentals

In Chapter 26, "Getting Started with Modem Communications," I showed how your computer can exchange data with remote machines by attaching a modem to the serial port and by running a phone line to the modem. In Chapter 28, "Setting Up Windows 98 for Networking," I showed you how your computer can exchange data with machines on a network by inserting a network interface card (NIC) inside the computer and by running a network cable to the card.

Dial-Up Networking is an amalgam of these two technologies. It gives you access to a network, but a modem and phone line replace the NIC and cable. Your network access is identical to that of a machine attached directly to the network: You log on with your username and password, you can browse and use shared resources, you can share your local resources, you can access the Internet if your network has the appropriate connection, you can retrieve mail, and so on. The main difference is that, because you're using a serial port and modem as the network connection point, data transfers are much slower.

Before examining the nuts and bolts of Dial-Up Networking connectivity, let's begin with a few fundamentals. This information will help you determine the best way to configure your remote access.

For starters, you should know that three methods are available for establishing a remote dial-up session:

- You can create a Dial-Up Networking connection and then initiate that connection manually.

- You can attempt to access a network resource that is normally available via a network card. If that card isn't present (for example, if you're using an undocked notebook on the road), Windows 98 prompts you to make a dial-up connection.

- An application can use Dial-Up Networking to establish a remote session. Applications can use the Dial-Up Networking Session API to connect to a session with or without user intervention. For example, Windows 95's Windows Messaging uses these API functions to allow you to establish a remote Microsoft Mail session. (See "Configuring Microsoft Mail for Remote Sessions" later in this chapter.)

Dial-Up Networking Client Architecture

The architecture of the Dial-Up Networking client is similar to that of a regular networking client, such as the Client for Microsoft Networks or the Client for NetWare Networks. In both cases, the client packages network data into a form suitable for whatever network protocol is being used. The client then passes the data to the network adapter for transmission out to the network. In Dial-Up Networking, this process has three major architectural differences from regular networking:

Dial-Up Adapter: Instead of a physical network adapter card residing in a bus slot or PC Card slot, Dial-Up Networking uses Microsoft's *Dial-Up Adapter*, which you can think of as a "virtual" NIC. Or, more accurately, the Dial-Up Adapter turns your computer's serial port into a NIC. The driver (PPPMAC.VXD) is an NDIS 3.1 network driver to which you can bind whatever network protocols you need to use. I'll show you how to install and configure the Dial-Up Adapter later in this chapter.

Dial-Up Protocol: After the client has packaged its network requests appropriately for the underlying network protocol (which, for Dial-Up Networking, can be NetBEUI, IPX/SPX, or TCP/IP), the packets must be further modified for transmission through a serial port and along phone lines. The protocols that handle this conversion are called *dial-up protocols* (or sometimes *line protocols* or *connection protocols*).

Dial-Up Server: Instead of logging on to a network directly, Dial-Up Networking must first connect to a *dial-up server*, which then processes the network logon.

The next two sections look at dial-up protocols and dial-up servers in more detail.

Dial-Up Protocols

To ensure the safe and reliable transmission of data over phone lines between a dial-up server and a remote computer, both machines must use the same dial-up protocol. The protocol you use depends, in part, on the dial-up server. For example, you use a different protocol to connect to a NetWare server than you do to connect to an Internet service provider. The Dial-Up Networking Client supports these dial-up protocols:

- Point-to-Point Protocol
- Remote Access Service
- NetWare Connect
- Serial Line Interface Protocol
- Point-to-Point Tunneling Protocol

The Point-to-Point Protocol

The Point-to-Point Protocol (PPP) is the standard dial-up protocol used by Windows 98's Dial-Up Networking, and it's rapidly becoming (if it isn't already) the standard for all types of remote access connections. For example, most Internet service providers offer PPP access to the Internet. Part of the PPP appeal is its flexibility: It defines a standard encapsulation protocol that enables different network protocols to be transmitted across serial connections. As a result, PPP supports the three Windows 98 network protocols: NetBEUI, IPX/SPX, and TCP/IP. PPP also implements a few other useful features, such as link-quality testing, header compression, and error checking.

The Remote Access Service Protocol

The Remote Access Service (RAS) protocol is a variant of NetBEUI called *asynchronous NetBEUI* that is designed to work over slower serial links. It's used by various Microsoft operating systems, including Windows NT and LAN Manager. To use RAS, both the client and the server must be running the NetBEUI network protocol. (RAS doesn't support multiple network protocols the way PPP does.)

The NetWare Connect Protocol

NetWare servers use a proprietary dial-up protocol that's part of a product called NetWare Connect. This product adds the following features to the NetWare server:

- A proprietary Remote Access Service dial-up protocol
- Modem sharing and pooling
- Remote workstation control

NetWare Connect dial-up servers don't support software compression and can work with only the IPX/SPX network protocol.

DIAL-UP NETWORKING USES ONLY NETWARE CONNECT RAS

The Dial-Up Networking client uses only NetWare Connect's Remote Access Services. To gain access to the other NetWare Connect features, you must use Novell's NetWare Connect client software.

The Serial Line Interface Protocol

Serial Line Interface Protocol (SLIP) is a simple protocol designed to work with the TCP/IP network protocol. Until PPP came along, SLIP was the standard Internet dial-up protocol for many years. The popularity of SLIP has waned for a number of reasons, but these are the main ones:

SLIP doesn't implement error correction: Unlike PPP, SLIP performs no error checking. This keeps the packet overhead required by SLIP to a minimum (PPP, for example, includes extra packet data to handle the error checking), but it makes SLIP connections susceptible to errors on noisy phone lines. This disadvantage is mitigated somewhat by using a modem with a built-in error correction protocol.

SLIP can handle only one protocol at a time: The SLIP header doesn't include a field for specifying the network protocol, so you can't change protocol horses midstream. Whatever protocol you specify at the beginning of the connection is the one you must use throughout the session.

SLIP can't handle dynamic addressing: Under a SLIP connection, the server and client can't exchange address data, so the machines must determine each other's IP addresses in advance. This prevents you from using a feature such as Dynamic Host Configuration Protocol (DHCP) with Dial-Up Networking. (I explain IP addresses and DHCP in Chapter 31, "Implementing TCP/IP for Internet and Intranet Connections.")

SLIP doesn't support compression: The basic SLIP protocol doesn't support compression of the entire data packet. However, a different SLIP specification—called Compressed SLIP, or CSLIP—enables compression of just the IP header portion of a TCP/IP data packet.

Because of these drawbacks, you should use SLIP only for those TCP/IP dial-ups that don't support PPP.

The Point-to-Point Tunneling Protocol

The Point-to-Point Tunneling Protocol (PPTP) is designed to provide secure access to a private network by using a public network such as the Internet. The basic idea is that the remote user first establishes a connection to the Internet. Then, instead of dialing up the remote server on the private network, the user invokes Dial-Up Networking to establish an IP connection to the gateway machine. (For a complete explanation of IP, gateways, and other TCP/IP intricacies, please see Chapter 34.) The result is a *virtual private network* (VPN) where the remote user interacts with the private network exactly as though he or she was connected directly to the network and using the TCP/IP protocol.

The *tunneling* part of PPTP refers to a networking technology that allows for the encapsulation of one type of protocol within another. In this case, PPTP encapsulates PPP packets within the IP packets used on the Internet. Because it uses PPP, all network-level protocols (NetBEUI, IPX/SPX, and TCP/IP) can be transmitted, data can be encrypted and compressed, and NT domain-level security is preserved.

New to **98**

30

COMPUTING WITH DIAL-UP NETWORKING

DIAL-UP NETWORKING NEGOTIATES THE PROTOCOL

For the most part, you don't have to worry too much about the dial-up protocol, because Dial-Up Networking usually negotiates behind the scenes with the server to determine the correct protocol. PPP is the default dial-up protocol, and if the server can't handle PPP, Dial-Up Networking tries to use RAS.

Note, however, that Dial-Up Networking will not attempt to negotiate the NetWare Connect, SLIP, and CSLIP protocols. If your dial-up server requires one of these protocols, you must configure it manually (as explained later in this chapter).

Dial-Up Servers

With Dial-Up Networking, you can't just dial into any old machine willy-nilly and expect to get a connection. Rather, the remote computer must be configured as a *dial-up server*, which means that it can accept incoming calls, validate network logons, provide access to the network, and handle the intricacies of network and dial-up protocols. Clearly, not every computer—or even every network server, for that matter—has what it takes to be a dial-up server. Here's a rundown of the various dial-up servers that are supported by Windows 98 Dial-Up Networking:

Windows NT 4.0 RAS server: Windows NT 4.0 (both the Server and the Workstation) can act as dial-up servers by running the Remote Access Service (RAS). RAS lets the server run NetBEUI (and, through a process called tunneling, IPX/SPX and TCP/IP as well) over phone lines. The available dial-up protocols are PPP and, of course, RAS. Windows NT 4.0 Workstation allows only a single RAS connection at a time, but Windows NT 4.0 Server allows up to 256 simultaneous connections.

Windows NT 3.1 and Windows for Workgroups 3.11 RAS server: Both Windows NT 3.1 and Windows for Workgroups 3.11 can use RAS to act as dial-up servers using the RAS dial-up protocol. Note that because these servers run NetBEUI only, they aren't suitable for Internet connections (which require TCP/IP). You're limited to a single connection, unless you're using NT Advanced Server, which can support up to 64 simultaneous connections.

NetWare server: You can connect to a NetWare server either directly, if the server is running NetWare Connect, or indirectly via a Windows NT 3.5*x* RAS server that uses IPX/SPX to route to the NetWare server.

Shiva NetModem or LANRover server modem: These are modems designed to act as RAS servers and route IPS/SPX, TCP/IP, and AppleTalk.

UNIX server: You can use Dial-Up Networking to connect to UNIX servers to establish a TCP/IP session using the PPP, SLIP, and CSLIP dial-up protocols. Dial-Up Networking is most often used in this fashion to connect to an Internet service provider. I discuss setting up an Internet connection from a Windows 98 client in greater depth in Chapter 32, "Windows 98 and the Internet."

Windows 98 Dial-Up Networking server: You can set up a Windows 98 machine to act as a dial-up server. As with Windows NT 3.5*x* RAS, you can establish a connection using PPP or RAS and then route NetBEUI, TCP/IP, and IPX/SPX over the connection. The Windows 98 Dial-Up Networking server supports only one connection at a time.

Setting Up Windows 98 for Dial-Up Networking

Assuming that you've installed the Dial-Up Networking component on your computer, configuring Windows 98 so that it can connect to a dial-up server involves four steps:

1. Install the Dial-Up Adapter, if necessary.
2. Configure the Dial-Up Adapter.
3. Create a new Dial-Up Networking connectoid for the server.
4. Configure the connection.

The next four sections take you through each step.

Step 1: Install the Dial-Up Adapter

Windows 98 installs the Dial-Up Adapter automatically when you install Dial-Up Networking. To check that the Dial-Up Adapter is installed, open the Network properties sheet (right-click the Network Neighborhood icon and select Properties, or open the Control Panel's Network icon). Check the list of installed network components and see whether Dial-Up Adapter is among them. If, for some reason, the Dial-Up Adapter isn't installed (because you or someone else removed it, for example), here are the steps to install it:

1. In the Network properties sheet, click Add.
2. In the Select Network Component Type dialog box, highlight Adapter and click Add.
3. In the Select Network Adapter dialog box, highlight Microsoft in the Manufacturers list. You should see Dial-Up Adapter highlighted in the Network Adapters list.
4. Click OK to return to the Network properties sheet.

Step 2: Configure the Dial-Up Adapter

After the Dial-Up Adapter is installed, you need to configure it for use with the dial-up server (or servers) you plan to use. You need to perform three tasks:

■ Install the network protocols you plan to use during your dial-up sessions. I showed you how to install protocols in Chapter 28, "Setting Up Windows 98 for Networking."

■ Set various properties of the Dial-Up Adapter.

■ Configure the protocols you've bound to the Dial-Up Adapter.

30

COMPUTING WITH
DIAL-UP
NETWORKING

Setting Dial-Up Adapter Properties

To change the Dial-Up Adapter's properties, highlight Dial-Up Adapter in the list of network components and then click Properties. In the Dial-Up Adapter properties sheet that appears, select the Bindings tab, shown in Figure 30.1. (You can ignore the Driver Type tab, because Windows 98 offers only a 32-bit driver for the Dial-Up Adapter.) The Bindings tab determines which network protocols the Dial-Up Adapter can use. Activate the check box beside each protocol that is required by the dial-up server.

FIGURE 30.1.

Use the Bindings tab to specify the network protocols to use with the Dial-Up Adapter.

In the Advanced tab, shown in Figure 30.2, the Property list has four entries:

Enable Point To Point IP: Use this setting to enable or disable PPTP over this dial-up connection.

IP Packet Size: Use this setting to specify the relative size of the IP packets used by the Dial-Up Adapter.

Record a log file: If you select Yes in the Value list, Dial-Up Networking creates a text file named PPPLOG.TXT in your main Windows 98 folder and uses this file to maintain a record of each PPP session. Because maintaining the log degrades performance slightly, select Yes only if you're having trouble with your connection.

Use IPX header compression: You need to select Yes for this property only if you're connecting to a server that supports CSLIP.

After you've finished setting properties, click OK to return to the Network properties sheet.

FIGURE 30.2.

The Advanced tab controls a couple of advanced Dial-Up Adapter properties.

Setting Properties for Bound Protocols

Your final chore for configuring the Dial-Up Adapter is to modify, as needed, the properties for each protocol bound to the Dial-Up Adapter. How you do this depends on the network adapters you have installed:

- If the Dial-Up Adapter is the only adapter installed, highlight a protocol and click the Properties button.

- If you have multiple adapters installed, the Network dialog box indicates binding by using an arrow (->). For example, Figure 30.3 shows the Network dialog box with two adapters installed. Notice how the NetBEUI protocol indicates binding by using an arrow to point to each adapter. In this case, highlight a protocol bound to the Dial-Up Adapter and then click Properties.

FIGURE 30.3.

If you have multiple adapters, arrows indicate the protocol/adapter bindings.

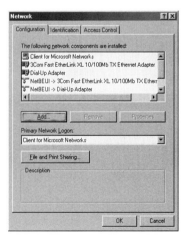

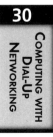

The properties you modify depend on the protocol. See Chapter 28 for more information.

SETTING TCP/IP PROPERTIES

If you'll be setting up a Dial-Up Networking connection to either an Internet service provider or a TCP/IP network, you must specify some properties for the TCP/IP protocol that's bound to the Dial-Up Adapter. I give you the goods on these settings in Chapter 33.

When you're done, click OK, and when Windows 98 asks whether you want to restart your computer, click Yes.

MORE NETWORK CONFIGURATION

If you'll be logging on to a Microsoft network or a NetWare network, and you've already set up a network connection using a regular network adapter, you can log on remotely without any trouble. That's because the Dial-Up Adapter will use your existing network settings (logon, computer identification, access control, and so on).

If, however, you've never established a regular network connection, you need to set up Windows 98 for networking. See Chapter 28 for all the gory details.

Step 3: Create a New Connectoid

You're now ready to start specifying the particulars of your Dial-Up Networking sessions. These are stored in the Dial-Up Networking folder as icons called *connectoids*. Each connectoid contains, among other things, the phone number to dial, the modem to use, and the dial-up server type.

To get started, select Start | Programs | Accessories | Communications | Dial-Up Networking. If this is your first connectoid, the Make New Connection Wizard appears and gives you a brief introduction. Click Next >.

Otherwise, you get the Dial-Up Networking folder, shown in Figure 30.4. In this case, use either of the following techniques to launch the Wizard:

- Open the Make New Connection icon.
- Select Connections | Make New Connection.

If you haven't yet installed a modem on your system, the Install New Modem Wizard steps in to take you through the procedure. I explain in Chapter 26, "Getting Started with Modem Communications," how this Wizard operates, so you might want to head there for a description.

FIGURE 30.4.

After you've created your first connection, this folder window appears when you start Dial-Up Networking.

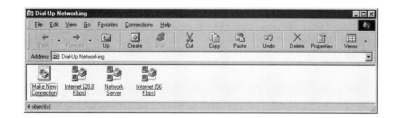

You eventually see the Make New Connection Wizard dialog box, shown in Figure 30.5. Enter a name for the connection and choose the modem you want to use. If you want to adjust any modem settings, click the Configure button. When you're ready to move on, click Next >.

FIGURE 30.5.

Use this Wizard dialog box to name your connection and select a modem.

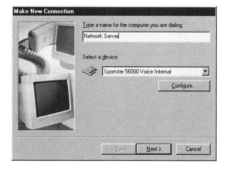

ENTERING A USERNAME AND PASSWORD

Some Internet service providers (including The Microsoft Network) require you to enter your username and password during logon. You might also have to run a command or select a menu item to choose between PPP and SLIP. To let you enter this kind of information, Dial-Up Networking can display a terminal window after the connection has been established. To set this up, click Configure in the dialog box shown in Figure 30.5. In the Modem properties sheet, select the Options tab, activate the Bring up terminal window after dialing check box, and click OK.

The Make New Connection Wizard then displays the dialog box shown in Figure 30.6. Enter the Area code, Telephone number, and Country code for the dial-up server and then click Next >. In the final Wizard dialog box that appears, click Finish. (If you bypassed installing the Dial-Up Adapter earlier, Dial-Up Networking prompts you to do so now. Click OK to install the adapter.)

FIGURE 30.6.
Use this Wizard dialog box to enter the phone number of the dial-up server.

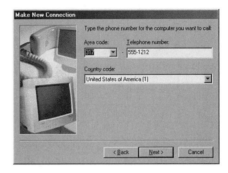

Step 4: Configure the Connectoid Properties

At this point, your Dial-Up Networking connectoid is set up with only the default properties (such as using the PPP dial-up protocol). To change these properties, highlight the connectoid's icon in the Dial-Up Networking folder, and then either select File | Properties or right-click the icon and select Properties from the context menu. You then see the dialog box shown in Figure 30.7.

FIGURE 30.7.
The properties sheet for a Dial-Up Networking connectoid.

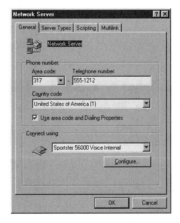

Most of the properties you see are straightforward. To change how Dial-Up Networking works with the server, activate the Server Types tab to display the dialog box shown in Figure 30.8. Here's a rundown of the controls in this dialog box:

Type of Dial-Up Server: Use this drop-down list to specify the dial-up protocol you want to use with this dial-up server.

Log on to network: When this check box is activated, Dial-Up Networking attempts to log on to the dial-up server with the username and password you use to log on to Windows 98.

Enable software compression: When this check box is activated, data transfers that are made between your computer and the server are compressed to save time.

(Note, however, that if you'll be transferring mostly files that are already compressed, activating this option degrades the performance of the connection. That's because compressing already-compressed files actually increases the file size.)

Require encrypted password: When this check box is activated, Dial-Up Networking uses encryption to send your password to the server. This is a useful security precaution that you should enable as long as the server supports it.

Require data encryption: When this check box is activated, Dial-Up Networking uses encryption to send data to the server. Again, your server must support data encryption for this option to work.

Record a log file for this connection: When this check box is activated, Dial-Up Networking maintains a log of all connection activity.

Allowed network protocols: These check boxes let you define which network protocols to use with this connectoid. Note too that for TCP/IP connections, you can click the TCP/IP Settings button to define connection-specific TCP/IP properties (see Chapter 33 for details).

FIGURE 30.8.

Use the Server Types dialog box to configure how Dial-Up Networking works with the dial-up server.

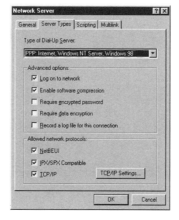

The Scripting tab enables you to specify a script that runs after the connection is established. You can use this script to watch for logon prompts and then send a username, password, or other data. See "Using the Dial-Up Scripting Tool," later in this chapter.

The Multilink tab enables you to specify additional devices to use with the connectoid. Windows 98 has built-in support for multilink PPP connections. This is a standard technology that enables you to combine the bandwidth from two or more communications links and use the extended bandwidth to improve the performance of your connection. This is called *multilink channel aggregation.* For example, if you have two modems installed and they're attached to separate telephone lines, multilink PPP will establish a connection on both lines and then manage simultaneous data transfers on the two lines. You see just a single connection, but your bandwidth has been effectively doubled.

New to **98**

30

COMPUTING WITH DIAL-UP NETWORKING

To set up the a multilink PPP connection, follow these steps:

1. Display the Multilink tab.
2. Activate the Use additional devices option.
3. Click Add to display the Edit Extra Device dialog box shown in Figure 30.9.

FIGURE 30.9.
Use this dialog box to specify additional communications devices to use with your connection.

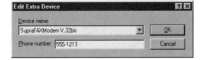

4. Use the Device name list to choose the other modem (or whatever), enter the Phone number this device should dial, and then click OK. Windows 98 adds the device to the Multilink tab, as shown in Figure 30.10.
5. Repeat steps 3 and 4 to add more devices.

FIGURE 30.10.
Windows 98 supports multiple communications links for a single connection.

Connecting to the Remote Network

You're now ready to connect to the dial-up server. Dial-Up Networking gives you various ways to proceed:

- Open the connectoid icon in the Dial-Up Networking folder.
- Highlight the icon and select Connections | Connect.
- Right-click the icon and select Connect from the context menu.

STARTING A CONNECTION FROM THE COMMAND LINE

You can start a Dial-Up Networking connection from the Run dialog box, the DOS command prompt, or a batch file by using the following command syntax:

```
rundll rnaui.dll,RnaDial connectoid
```

Here, *connectoid* is the name of the connectoid you want to run. For example, to start a connection named LAN Server, you enter the following command:

```
rundll rnaui.dll,RnaDial LAN Server
```

Note that the RnaDial and connection parameters are case-sensitive.

Dial-Up Networking displays the Connect To dialog box, shown in Figure 30.11. Enter the User name and Password that are required for logging on to the dial-up server. If you want Windows 98 to save your password and display it automatically each time you start this connection, activate the Save password check box. You can also adjust the Phone number, if necessary, and specify a different dialing location or dialing properties (see Chapter 26 for details). When you're ready to make the connection, click the Connect button.

FIGURE 30.11.

Use this dialog box to specify any last-minute settings before making the connection.

Dial-Up Networking dials the modem and then negotiates your logon with the dial-up server. (Depending on the modem settings you're using, you might see a terminal window appear so that you can enter more information.)

When you're safely connected, the Connection Established dialog box appears. If you want to track the duration of your session, double-click the Dial-Up Networking icon in the system tray to display the dialog box shown in Figure 30.12.

FIGURE 30.12.

Dial-Up Networking keeps track of the duration of the call.

TROUBLESHOOTING: PROTOCOL PROBLEMS

When you attempt to connect to the dial-up server, a dialog box might appear with the following message:

```
Dial-Up Networking could not negotiate a compatible set of network protocols
you specified in the Server Type settings. Check your network configuration
in the Control Panel then try the connection again.
```

Check your network protocols to make sure that you have at least one protocol bound to the Dial-Up Adapter that matches a protocol used by the dial-up server. Also, make sure that the dial-up protocol you're using is supported by the server.

After you're connected, your computer becomes a full peer on the network. You can then access network resources and browse the Network Neighborhood, and others on the network can see your computer as well.

After you've finished your online work, click the Disconnect button to shut down the connection.

Working with Dial-Up Networking Settings

Dial-Up Networking has a few settings that apply to all your connectoids. To get to these settings, select Connections | Settings to display the Dial-Up Networking properties sheet shown in Figure 30.13. Here are your options:

Show an icon on taskbar after connected: If you deactivate this check box, Dial-Up Networking doesn't display its icon in the system tray.

Prompt for information before dialing: If you deactivate this check box, Dial-Up Networking won't display the Connect To dialog box, shown earlier in Figure 30.11. If you never need to change the connection settings, deactivating this check box will give you one less dialog box to negotiate when connecting.

Show a confirmation dialog after connected: Deactivating this check box means that Dial-Up Networking won't show the Connection Established dialog box after a connection to the remote server has been established.

Redial: If the server is busy or down, your connection won't go through. Instead of retrying the connection manually, you can tell Dial-Up Networking to retry at regular intervals by activating this check box.

Before giving up retry *x* times: Use this spinner to specify the maximum number of redial attempts.

Between tries wait *x* mins *y* secs: Use these spinners to specify the number of minutes and seconds to pause between each retry.

Prompt to use Dial-Up Networking: When this option is activated, Windows 98 will prompt you when you attempt to access a resource that requires an established connection. For example, if you map a network drive during a Dial-Up Networking session and later attempt to access that drive while you're disconnected, Windows 98 will ask whether you want to connect.

Don't prompt to use Dial-Up Networking: Activate this option if you prefer that Windows 98 not prompt you to establish a connection.

FIGURE 30.13.

*Use this dialog box
to set some Dial-Up
Networking options
that apply to all your
connectoids.*

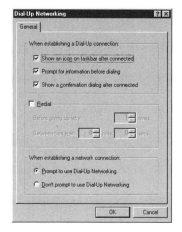

USE PROFILES TO MANAGE NOTEBOOK NICS

Suppose you have a notebook computer that uses a regular NIC (say, a PC Card adapter or an adapter in a docking station) for a direct network connection. If the NIC is part of a hardware profile—even if it's not attached to the computer—Windows 98 assumes that you want to use the NIC to establish your network connections. In this case, when you try to access a network resource, Windows 98 displays an error message instead of prompting you to use Dial-Up Networking.

To prevent this, you should create a second hardware profile that doesn't use this NIC. Then, when you're on the road, boot Windows 98 with this new profile. (See Chapter 10, "Getting the Most Out of Device Manager and Hardware Profiles," to learn how to create hardware profiles.)

30

COMPUTING WITH
DIAL-UP
NETWORKING

Using PPTP to Establish a Virtual Private Network Connection

If you want to use PPTP to establish your connection, here are the steps you follow to configure the connectoid:

1. Install Virtual Private Networking. (In the Windows Setup tab, open the Communications component and activate the check box beside Virtual Private Networking. You need to restart your computer after this protocol and the VPN adapter are installed.)

2. In the Dial-Up Networking folder, start a new connectoid.

3. In the first wizard dialog box, enter a name for the new connectoid and select Microsoft VPN Adapter in the Select a device list (see Figure 30.14). Click Next >.

FIGURE 30.14.

Make sure you select Microsoft VPN Adapter as the device for your connectoid.

4. Enter the IP address or host of the VPN server to which you want to connect, as shown in Figure 30.15. Note that this server must be set up to handle PPTP and VPN connections.

FIGURE 30.15.

Enter the host name or IP address of the VPN server.

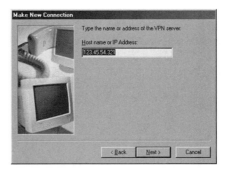

5. Click Finish.

With the connectoid ready to go, establish your Internet connection and then launch the VPN connectoid.

Configuring Microsoft Mail for Remote Sessions

Windows 95's Windows Messaging has a Microsoft Mail component that enables you to send and retrieve messages over a local area network. For those times when you want to perform email chores while you're on the road, you can set up Microsoft Mail to use a remote Dial-Up Networking connection. This section shows you how it's done.

Creating a Remote Microsoft Mail Profile

Before proceeding, you should create a new Exchange profile for your remote Microsoft Mail sessions:

1. Create a new profile by opening Control Panel's Mail icon, clicking Show Profiles, and then clicking Add. Be sure not to add the Microsoft Mail service to this profile.

2. Log on to Windows Messaging using your original profile. If Windows Messaging complains that it can't find the server (see Figure 30.16), activate the Offline option and click OK.

FIGURE 30.16.

Windows Messaging displays this dialog box if you start the program without your regular LAN connection being present.

3. Select Tools | Services to display the Services dialog box.

4. Highlight Microsoft Mail and click Copy.

5. In the Copy Information Service dialog box, highlight your remote Microsoft Mail profile and click OK.

6. Click OK to return to Windows Messaging.

7. Select Tools | Options to display the Options dialog box.

8. In the General tab, activate the Prompt for a profile to be used option and then click OK.

9. Select File | Exit and Log Off.

Setting Up Microsoft Mail's Remote Properties

With your new profile in place, restart Windows Messaging and select the remote Microsoft Mail profile you created. You now need to configure a few properties for your remote connection.

30

COMPUTING WITH
DIAL-UP
NETWORKING

The first step is to tell Windows Messaging that this profile uses a Dial-Up Networking connection to retrieve mail. To do this, select Tools | Services to display the Services dialog box, highlight Microsoft Mail, and click Properties. Windows Messaging displays the Microsoft Mail properties sheet. In the Connection tab, activate the Remote using a modem and Dial-Up Networking option, as shown in Figure 30.17.

FIGURE 30.17.

Use the Connection tab to specify that you want to use a Dial-Up Networking connection in this profile.

Next, select the Dial-Up Networking tab, shown in Figure 30.18. Here's a rundown of the available properties on this tab:

Use the following Dial-Up Networking connection: Use this drop-down list to choose the Dial-Up Networking connection you want to use for your remote Microsoft Mail sessions. Also note that you can use the Add Entry button to create a new Dial-Up Networking connection and the Edit Entry button to make changes to a connection.

When Dial-Up Networking fails to connect: These text boxes tell Windows Messaging what to do if the Dial-Up Networking connection fails. Enter the number of times to retry and the interval, in seconds, between retries.

Confirm the Dial-Up Networking connection before starting a session: These options determine whether Windows Messaging prompts you to initiate the Dial-Up Networking connection. If you select Never confirm, Windows Messaging establishes the connection automatically without prompting you for confirmation. If you select Confirm on first session and after errors, Windows Messaging asks you to confirm that you want to establish the connection only for the initial session and each time an error occurs. If you select Always confirm, Windows Messaging always prompts you to confirm the connections.

CONFIRMING THE CONNECTION GIVES YOU LOTS OF OPTIONS

As you'll see later, when Windows Messaging asks you to confirm the connection, the dialog box that appears gives you lots of options for the remote session. These options are check boxes that determine whether Windows Messaging sends mail, receives mail, updates your Microsoft Mail address list, and more. So even though it might seem like a hassle to always be asked to confirm the connection, there are advantages to doing so.

FIGURE 30.18.

Use the Dial-Up Networking tab to define how Microsoft Mail works with Dial-Up Networking.

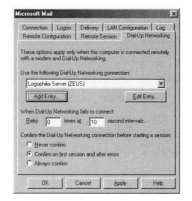

Next on the agenda is the Remote Session tab, shown in Figure 30.19. These check boxes determine when Windows Messaging starts and ends the Dial-Up Networking session:

When this service is started: If you activate this check box, the Dial-Up Networking session is initiated as soon as you start Windows Messaging.

After retrieving mail headers: If you're using Remote Mail, activating this check box tells Windows Messaging to end the Dial-Up Networking session as soon as Remote Mail has retrieved the waiting message headers.

After sending and receiving mail: When this check box is activated, Windows Messaging shuts down the Dial-Up Networking session as soon as it delivers (sends and receives) mail.

When you exit: When this check box is activated, your Dial-Up Networking session is closed when you exit Windows Messaging.

Schedule Mail Delivery: Use this button to schedule your remote Microsoft Mail sessions at regular intervals. In the Remote Scheduled Sessions dialog box that appears, click Add to display the Add Scheduled Session dialog box, shown in Figure 30.20. In the Use drop-down list, select your Dial-Up Networking connection. In the When drop-down list, select Every, Weekly on, or Once at. In the hours : minutes spinner, enter a time. Click OK until you're back in the Microsoft Mail properties sheet.

30

COMPUTING WITH DIAL-UP NETWORKING

FIGURE 30.19.

Use the Remote Session tab to specify events that start and end your remote Microsoft Mail sessions.

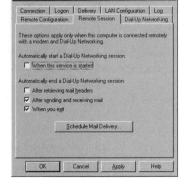

FIGURE 30.20.

The Add Scheduled Session dialog box lets you schedule a remote session at regular intervals.

Using Microsoft Mail Remotely

As you saw in the preceding section, Microsoft Mail's Dial-Up Networking session properties give you no shortage of methods for retrieving and sending mail remotely. If you specified that Windows Messaging should prompt you before establishing each connection, you see the Connect to Server dialog box, shown in Figure 30.21, whenever Windows Messaging initiates the remote session. From here, you can select a different Dial-Up Networking connection and choose which actions you want Windows Messaging to perform during the session.

FIGURE 30.21.

You see this dialog box if Windows Messaging is set up to prompt you before establishing a remote Microsoft Mail session.

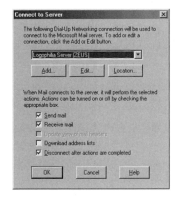

Using the Dial-Up Scripting Tool

For some dial-up servers, your logon to the remote network happens automatically. For example, if you connect to a Windows NT server on a Microsoft network, Dial-Up Networking logs you on with the username and password you enter in the Connect To dialog box. However, plenty of Dial-Up Networking connections—especially online services and Internet service providers—require further input. In this case, you usually set up the connection to display a terminal window after the connection is made. In Figure 30.22, for example, you see a connection that requires entering a username, a password, and a choice from a menu.

Figure 30.22.

For some Dial-Up Networking connections, you need to display a terminal window to enter logon data manually.

To avoid the hassle of constantly entering this extra data by hand, Windows 98 comes with a Dial-Up Scripting Tool that enables you to construct a script that enters your username, password, and other data automatically. This section shows you how to create your own scripts.

Understanding Scripts

A script is a text file (using the `.SCP` extension) that contains various commands for Dial-Up Networking to implement while making the connection. All scripts use the following structure:

```
proc main
    Enter your commands here
endproc
```

The commands you use can specify communications settings (such as the number of data bits you want Dial-Up Networking to use), control the flow of the script (such as looping through a set of commands to retry a logon), and interact with the remote system (such as waiting for a username prompt and then sending the username). You can use various commands, but four are the most common: `halt`, `delay`, `waitfor`, and `transmit`.

The `halt` Command

You use the `halt` command to shut down the script before the logon is complete. You might want to do this, for example, if the script encounters an unusual situation or if the remote server doesn't respond to a script command. (I'll show you an example in a second.)

The delay Command

The `delay` command is useful for preventing Dial-Up Networking from continuing to log on while the remote server processes other data. Here's the syntax for the `delay` command:

```
delay seconds
```

> `seconds`   The number of seconds you want Dial-Up Networking to pause.

For example, to pause the logon for 3 seconds, use the following command:

```
delay 3
```

The waitfor Command

You use the `waitfor` command to tell Dial-Up Networking to wait until the remote system sends a particular prompt. For example, if the remote system prompts you to enter your username by displaying a `User Name:` prompt, you can use the `waitfor` command to tell the script to look for the `"User Name:"` string. Here's the syntax for the `waitfor` command:

```
waitfor string [, matchcase] [then label] [until seconds]
```

> `string`   The prompt you want the script to look for. You surround the prompt text with quotation marks (for example, `"User Name:"`).
>
> `matchcase`   If you include this optional parameter, Dial-Up Networking looks for a prompt that exactly matches the case of `string`. For example, if `string` is `"User Name:"` and the system prompts with `User name:`, the command fails.
>
> `then label`   If you include this optional parameter, when the `string` prompt is received, the script jumps to the line that begins with `label`.
>
> `until seconds`   This optional parameter specifies the number of `seconds` that the script waits to receive the `string` prompt. If you leave out this parameter, the script waits indefinitely.

If the prompt is received, the script sets a system variable called `$SUCCESS` to `TRUE`; otherwise, `$SUCCESS` is set to `FALSE`. (Scripting supports an `if...then...endif` command you can use to test the value of `$SUCCESS` and have the script proceed accordingly.)

Here's a piece of a script that uses the `waitfor` command:

```
waitfor "User Name:" until 30 then Continue
halt
Continue:
waitfor "Password:"
...
```

The first `waitfor` command looks for the `"User Name:"` prompt and, when it arrives, jumps to the `Continue` label (the third line); then another `waitfor` command is executed. If the prompt doesn't come within 30 seconds, however, the `halt` command runs instead to bail out of the script.

MULTIPLE WAITFOR STRINGS

You don't have to use the `waitfor` command to look for just a single string. Instead, you can repeat any combination of the `waitfor` parameters to look for multiple strings. This capability is handy for writing generic scripts that can be used for multiple dial-up servers. For example, suppose that you have two Internet service providers: one that prompts for your username with `User Name:`, and one that prompts with `Login:`. To handle both prompts with a single `waitfor`, you use the following command:

`waitfor "User Name" then DoThis, "Login:" then DoThat`

Here, if the `User Name:` prompt is received, the script jumps to the `DoThis` label; alternatively, if the `Login:` prompt is received, the script branches to the `DoThat` label.

The transmit Command

You use this command to send text to the remote system. Here's the syntax:

`transmit string [,raw]`

string	This is the text you want to send, enclosed in quotation marks. Two system variables, however, don't require quotation marks: `$USERID`, which sends the contents of the User name field from the Connect To dialog box, and `$PASSWORD`, which sends the contents of the Password field from the Connect To dialog box. You can also use several literal strings:

Literal	What It Sends
`^char`	Control characters (for example, `"^M"` sends Ctrl+M, the carriage return control character)
`<cr>`	Carriage return
`<lf>`	Line feed
`\"`	Quotation mark
`\^`	Caret
`\<`	Less-than sign
`\\`	Backslash
`raw`	If you include this optional parameter, the script sends carets and other control characters as literal values. So, for example, `"^M"` would be interpreted as `"^M"` and not as a carriage return.

A Sample Script

To make all this information more concrete, let's run through an example. In particular, let's see how you would handle the prompts shown in the terminal window in Figure 30.22. Here's a simple script that does the job:

```
proc main
    ; Delay for 3 seconds to allow the remote system
    ; enough time to send the initial characters.
    delay 3
    ; Now wait for the remote system to prompt for
    ; the user name. When it does, send the $USERID
    ; followed by a carriage return.
    waitfor "login:"
    transmit $USERID
    transmit "^M"
    ; Now wait for the remote system to prompt for
    ; the password. When it does, send the $PASSWORD
    ; followed by a carriage return.
    waitfor "Password:"
    transmit $PASSWORD
    transmit "^M"
    ; Next, wait for menu prompt.
    ; When it arrives, enter 3 for PPP
    ; followed by a carriage return.
    waitfor "choice:"
    transmit "3^M"
endproc
```

The procedure starts with a couple of lines that begin with semicolons (;). These are comments you can insert to make your script more readable. They're used for information purposes only; Dial-Up Networking ignores any lines that begin with a semicolon.

The first real command is delay 3, which delays the script for three seconds to give the remote system time to display its welcome messages.

Then the script uses a waitfor command to look for the login: prompt. (Notice that although the exact prompt in Figure 30.22 is hookup login:, you need to specify only the last part of the prompt.) When the prompt arrives, the script sends $USERID, followed by a carriage return.

Next, the script uses waitfor to look for the Password: prompt, and then it sends $PASSWORD and a carriage return.

Finally, one last waitfor command looks for the choice: menu prompt and enters "3" and a carriage return to select the PPP menu option.

MORE SCRIPTING INFORMATION

There are many other scripting commands that you can use. For a complete list, see the SCRIPT.DOC file that comes with the Dial-Up Scripting Tool. (You find this file in your main Windows 98 folder.) You also get several sample SCP files that you can customize to suit your needs.

Assigning a Script to a Connection

After you create the script you want to use, you need to assign it to the appropriate Dial-Up Networking connection. Before doing that, you do two things:

■ Open the connection and modify the modem configuration so that it no longer brings up the terminal window (the Dial-Up Scripting Tool has its own terminal window).

■ The script requires the correct username and password. The first time you use the script, you need to enter the correct values in the Connect To dialog box. If you told Dial-Up Networking not to display this dialog box, select Connection I Settings and activate the Prompt for information before dialing check box. After you run through a successful login, you can deactivate this check box, because Dial-Up Networking will remember the username and password in subsequent connections.

When those chores are done, open the properties sheet for the connectoid and then activate the Scripting tab. In the File name text box, enter the path and filename of the script (SCP) file you want to assign to the connectoid, as shown in Figure 30.23. You can also click the Browse button to choose the file from the Open dialog box.

FIGURE 30.23.

Use the Dial-Up Scripting Tool to assign a script to a Dial-Up Networking connection.

You also have the following options:

Step through script: If you activate this check box, Dial-Up Networking executes the script one line at a time. This feature is useful if your script isn't working properly. By stepping through the script, you can watch for error messages and see exactly where the script goes wrong.

Start terminal screen minimized: If you activate this check box, Dial-Up Networking displays the terminal screen minimized.

Click OK to close the properties sheet.

30

COMPUTING WITH
DIAL-UP
NETWORKING

Running the Connection with the Script

With the script assigned to the connection, everything operates more or less on autopilot from here. You just fire up the Dial-Up Networking connection, and the script takes care of everything for you. The script's terminal screen appears (unless you elected to run the script's terminal screen minimized), and you see the remote system's prompts and the script's responses. When the script has completed its labors, it shuts down the terminal screen, and your connection continues normally.

If you have problems, however, activate the Step through script option, as described in the preceding section. (You should also make sure that the Start terminal screen minimized check box is deactivated.) Then when you start the connection, you see not only the script's terminal screen, but also a window named Automated Script Test, shown in Figure 30.24. Each time you click the Step button, another line of the script is executed. By watching the terminal screen as each command runs, you can determine where the script is going wrong.

FIGURE 30.24.

Stepping through the script lets you watch for errors.

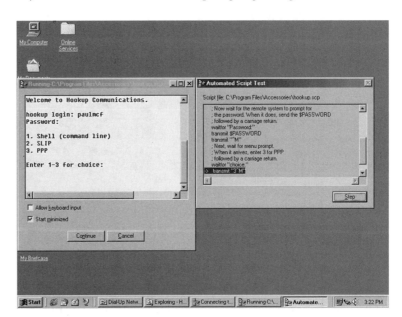

Using the Dial-Up Server

Although most people use Dial-Up Networking to connect to corporate networks, online services, and Internet service providers, your needs might not be so grandiose. You might just have a couple of Windows 98 machines—for example, one at home and one at the office—and you need to connect from one to the other occasionally. Fortunately, Windows 98 can act as a dial-up server. (In Windows 95, this was part of the Microsoft Plus! add-on.) This Dial-Up Server component turns your Windows 98 machine into a dial-up server that supports the following features:

- Remote machines running Windows 98 or Windows NT 3.5*x* can connect using the PPP dial-up protocol.

- Remote machines running Windows NT 3.1 or Windows for Workgroups 3.11 can connect using the RAS dial-up protocol.

- You can give remote callers access to the network via NetBEUI or IPX/SPX. Note that the Dial-Up Networking Server doesn't support TCP/IP connections, so you can't connect and get access to the Internet.

- You can set up security to allow only authorized users to call in.

- You can require an encrypted password for extra security.

The next section tells you how to configure the dial-up server.

Configuring the Dial-Up Server

To set up your Windows 98 machine for remote callers, you must set a few properties of the dial-up server. To view these properties, open the Dial-Up Networking folder and select Connections | Dial-Up Server. The dialog box that appears contains a tab for each installed modem, and the layout depends on whether your Windows 98 machine's access control is set to share-level or user-level.

Setting User-Level Caller Access

If you're set up for user-level access, you see the Dial-Up Server dialog box shown in Figure 30.25. In this case, you can specify the users who are allowed to dial in to the server. Here's how to do it:

1. If you have multiple modems, select the tab for the modem you want to use.
2. Activate the Allow caller access option.
3. Click the Add button. The Add Users dialog box, shown in Figure 30.26, appears.
3. For each user you want to allow access to the server, highlight the name in the Name list and click Add->.
4. When you're done, click OK to return to the Dial-Up Server dialog box.

The users you selected will appear in the User name list. To prevent a user from connecting, highlight his or her name and click the Remove button.

Setting Share-Level Caller Access

If your Windows 98 machine is set up for share-level access, you see the Dial-Up Server dialog box shown in Figure 30.27. In this case, you set up a single password that all callers must enter to access the server. Here are the steps to follow:

1. Activate the Allow caller access option.
2. Click the Change Password button to display the Dial-Up Networking Password dialog box.

30

COMPUTING WITH
DIAL-UP
NETWORKING

3. If this is the first time you've run this command, your "old password" will be blank, so you can bypass the Old password text box. Otherwise, use this text box to enter your existing password.

4. Enter the password you want to assign to the server in both the New password and the Confirm new password text boxes.

5. When you're done, click OK to return to the Dial-Up Server dialog box.

FIGURE 30.25.

You see this dialog box if your Windows 98 computer is set up for user-level access control.

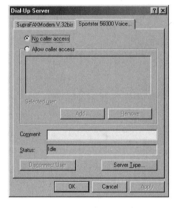

FIGURE 30.26.

Use this dialog box to select the users who are allowed access to the server.

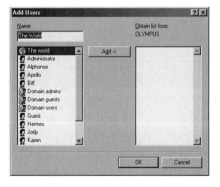

FIGURE 30.27.

You see this dialog box if your machine is set up to use share-level access control.

TROUBLESHOOTING: IF YOU FORGET YOUR PASSWORD

If you forget the password you've assigned to your dial-up server, you must boot Windows 98 in MS-DOS mode and then delete RNA.PWL from your main Windows 98 folder.

Other Configuration Options

To complete the configuration of the dial-up server, you need to set a few more properties. The Comment text box doesn't do all that much. It's just a field where you can enter descriptive information about the server, such as the access phone number.

If you click the Server Type button, you see the Server Types dialog box, shown in Figure 30.28. You have three options to work with:

Type of Dial-Up Server: Use this drop-down list to specify the type of server you want to run. If you select the Default option, the server first attempts to connect with the remote caller by using the PPP dial-up protocol. If that doesn't work, the server tries RAS (asynchronous NetBEUI). If, instead, you specify a server type, the server tries to connect with only the remote system using that protocol. If it can't negotiate the protocol, the server ends the connection.

Enable software compression: When this check box is activated, the server uses compression to send data to the remote system.

Require encrypted password: When this check box is activated, the server accepts only encrypted passwords during the logon. If the remote system sends a clear text (unencrypted) password, the server rejects the logon.

Click OK to return to the Dial-Up Server dialog box.

FIGURE 30.28.
Use this dialog box to configure your computer's server type.

Activating and Deactivating the Server

Your computer is now ready for duty as a dial-up server. To activate the server, click OK to close the Dial-Up Server dialog box. If you want to keep an eye on what's happening with the server, select Connections | Dial-Up Server again (or double-click the Dial-Up Server icon in the system tray). This time, you notice that the Status box says Monitoring to indicate that it's monitoring the serial port for incoming calls. When a remote call comes in, this box displays status messages to keep you apprised of the connection, as shown in Figure 30.29.

30

COMPUTING WITH DIAL-UP NETWORKING

FIGURE 30.29.

The Status box tells you the current state of the remote connection.

To shut down the server and prevent remote connections, activate the No caller access option and click OK.

DISCONNECTING A USER

If you suspect that someone has gained unauthorized access to the server, or if a forgetful user has neglected to disconnect, you can shut him or her down by clicking the Disconnect User button.

Summary

This chapter showed you how to connect to remote networks by using Windows 98's Dial-Up Networking. To give you a solid background in the fundamentals, I first told you how Dial-Up Networking works and gave you some info on the Dial-Up Networking client architecture, including the dial-up protocols and dial-up servers supported by the Dial-Up Networking client. From there, I took you step-by-step through the Dial-Up Networking configuration process: installing and configuring the Dial-Up Adapter, creating a new Dial-Up Networking connection, and configuring the connection. I then showed you how to connect to a dial-up server.

You also learned plenty of related features: how to use PPTP, how to configure Microsoft Mail for remote sessions, how to create and use scripts to automate remote logons, and how to set up a Windows 98 machine as a dial-up server.

Here's a list of chapters where you'll find related information:

- A modem is a must for Dial-Up Networking, and I show how to install and configure modems in Chapter 26, "Getting Started with Modem Communications."

- Dial-Up Networking is a networking client, so understanding how networks do their thing is essential. You can get all the info you need to know in Chapter 28, "Setting Up Windows 98 for Networking," and Chapter 29, "Working with Network Resources."

- If you want to use Dial-Up Networking to connect to your Internet service provider, you have to know how to configure the TCP/IP protocol. You can get the full scoop in Chapter 31, "Implementing TCP/IP for Internet and Intranet Connections."

- With your knowledge of Dial-Up Networking and TCP/IP in place, I put everything together and show you how to connect to the Internet from Windows 98 in Chapter 32, "Windows 98 and the Internet."

VII

PART

Unleashing Windows 98 for the Internet and Intranet

Implementing TCP/IP for Internet and Intranet Connections

> *There is, however, one Rosetta stone of the computer world that can link a wide variety of mainframe, minicomputer, and PC systems. That common denominator is called TCP/IP.*
>
> —*Frank J. Derfler, Jr.*

One of the problems facing network administrators these days is the need to support multiple protocols. If the network includes Windows NT servers and Windows machines, NetBEUI is often the protocol of choice. Throw in some NetWare nodes, and you also need IPX/SPX. If any UNIX boxes are on the network, or if the network has an Internet gateway, TCP/IP must also be supported. Diverse networks might also need to support AppleTalk, Banyan VINES, and who knows what else.

Increasingly, administrators are throwing up their hands and saying, "Enough already!" Instead of putting up with the headache of supporting umpteen protocols, they're simplifying both their networks and their lives by implementing a single protocol on *all* their network machines. That protocol is TCP/IP, thanks to its near-universal support by networking vendors, its large packet size and speed, its robustness, and its unmatched scalability.

But TCP/IP isn't just for network honchos. The explosion of interest in the Internet has thrust TCP/IP into the spotlight. That's because TCP/IP is the *lingua franca* of Internet communication, and you can't get online without it. So even if you're using a standalone machine with no network in sight, you need to know how to implement TCP/IP in Windows 98 to take advantage of all the Net has to offer.

This chapter will help you do just that. Whether you work with one machine or one thousand, you find everything you need to know to install and configure TCP/IP in the Windows 98 environment.

Understanding TCP/IP

If there's a downside to TCP/IP, it's that compared to other protocols, TCP/IP is much more complex to implement and manage. However, we're still not talking about brain surgery here. With just a smattering of background information, the mysteries of TCP/IP will become clear, and your configuration chores will become downright comprehensible. That's my goal in this section: to give you enough knowledge about TCP/IP plumbing to stand you in good stead when you get down to the brass tacks of actually setting up, using, and, if necessary, troubleshooting TCP/IP.

What Is TCP/IP?

Although people often speak of TCP/IP as being a protocol, it is in fact a suite of protocols (more than 100 in all!) housed under one roof. Here's a summary of the most important of these protocols:

> **Internet Protocol (IP):** This is a connectionless protocol that defines the Internet's basic packet structure and its addressing scheme, and that also handles routing of packets between hosts.

Transmission Control Protocol (TCP): This is a connection-oriented protocol that sets up a connection between two hosts and ensures that data is passed between them reliably. If packets are lost or damaged during transmission, TCP takes care of retransmitting the packets.

File Transfer Protocol (FTP): This protocol defines file transfers among computers on the Internet.

Simple Mail Transport Protocol (SMTP): This protocol describes the format of Internet email messages and how messages get delivered.

Hypertext Transfer Protocol (HTTP): This protocol defines the format of Uniform Resource Locator (URL) addresses and how World Wide Web data is transmitted between a server and a browser.

Network News Transport Protocol (NNTP): This protocol defines how Usenet newsgroups and postings are transmitted.

Of these, IP and TCP are the most important for our purposes, so the next two sections look at these protocols in greater detail.

THE TCP/IP STACK

You often see references to the *TCP/IP stack*. Networks are always implemented in a layered model that begins with the *application* and *presentation* layers at the top (these layers determine how programs interact with the operating system and user, respectively) and the *data-link* and *physical* layers at the bottom (these layers govern the network drivers and network adapters, respectively). Between those, you have a three-layer stack of protocols:

Session layer: These are protocols that enable applications to communicate across the network. Protocols such as FTP and SMTP reside here.

Transport layer: These are connection-oriented protocols that ensure that data is transmitted correctly. TCP resides here.

Network layer: These are connectionless protocols that handle the creation and routing of packets. IP resides here.

Understanding IP

As the name *Internet Protocol* implies, the Internet, in a very basic sense, *is* IP. That's because IP has a hand in everything that goes on in the Internet:

- The structure of all the data being transferred around the Internet is defined by IP.

- The structure of the address assigned to every host computer and router on the Internet is defined by IP.

- The process by which data gets from one address to another (this is called *routing*) is defined by IP.

Clearly, to understand the Internet (or, on a smaller scale, an intranet), you must understand IP. In turn, this understanding will make your life a lot easier when it comes time to implement TCP/IP in Windows 98.

The Structure of an IP Datagram

Network data is broken down into small chunks called *packets*. These packets include not only the data (such as part of a file), but also *header information* that specifies items such as the destination address and the address of the sender. On the Internet, data is transmitted in a packet format defined by IP. These IP packets are known as *datagrams*.

The datagram header can be from 160 to 512 bits in length, and it includes information such as the address of the host that sent the datagram and the address of the host that is supposed to receive the datagram. Although you don't need to know the exact format of a datagram header to implement TCP/IP, Table 31.1 spells it out in case you're interested.

Table 31.1. The structure of a datagram header.

Field	*Bits*	*Description*
Version	0 to 3	Specifies the format of the header.
Internet Header Length	4 to 7	The length of the header, in words (32 bits).
Type of Service	8 to 15	Specifies the quality of service desired (for example, this field can be used to set precedence levels for the datagram).
Total Length	16 to 31	The length of the datagram, including the header and data. Because this is a 16-bit value, datagrams can be as large as 65,536 bytes.
Identification	32 to 47	An identifying value that lets the destination reassemble a fragmented datagram. (Some systems can't handle packets larger than a particular size, so they'll fragment datagrams as needed. The header is copied to each fragment, and the next two fields are altered as necessary.)
Flags	48 to 50	One flag specifies whether a datagram can be fragmented. If it can't, and the host can't handle the datagram, it discards the datagram. If the datagram can be fragmented, another flag indicates whether this is the last fragment.

Field	Bits	Description
Fragment Offset	51 to 63	If the datagram is fragmented, this field specifies the position in the datagram of this fragment.
Time to Live	64 to 71	Specifies the maximum number of hosts through which the datagram can be routed. Each host decrements this value by 1, and if the value reaches 0 before arriving at its destination, the datagram is discarded. This prevents runaway datagrams from traversing the Internet endlessly.
Protocol	72 to 79	Represents the session layer protocol being used (such as FTP or SMTP).
Header Checksum	80 to 95	Used to check the integrity of the header (not the data).
Source Address	96 to 127	The IP address of the host that sent the datagram.
Destination Address	128 to 159	The IP address of the host that is supposed to receive the datagram.
Options	160 and over	This field can contain from 0 to 352 bits, and it specifies extra options such as security.

The rest of the datagram is taken up by the data that is to be transmitted to the destination host.

The Structure of an IP Address

You saw in the preceding section that the addresses of both the source and the destination hosts form an integral part of every IP datagram. This section looks at the structure of these so-called *IP addresses.* When setting up TCP/IP in Windows 98, you have to face the chore of entering the IP address of your computer (and, if you're an administrator, each computer on your network), as well as several other IP addresses. You therefore need to know how they work.

An IP address is a 32-bit value assigned to a computer by a network administrator or, if you've signed up for an Internet account, by your Internet service provider (ISP). As you'll see in a minute, these addresses are designed so that every host and router on the Internet or within a TCP/IP network has a unique address. That way, when an application needs to send data to a particular locale, it knows that the destination address it plops into the datagram header will make sure that everything ends up where it's supposed to.

Dotted-Decimal Notation

The problem with IP addresses is their "32-bitness." For example, here's the IP address of my Web server:

11001101110100000111000100000010

Not very inviting, is it? To make these numbers easier to work with, the TCP/IP powers-that-be came up with the *dotted-decimal notation* (also known in the trade as *dotted-quad notation*). This notation divides the 32 bits of an IP address into four groups of 8 bits each (each of these groups is called a *quad*), converts each group into its decimal equivalent, and then separates these numbers with dots.

Let's look at an example. Here's my Web server's IP address grouped into four 8-bit quads:

11001101 11010000 01110001 00000010

Now you convert each quad into its decimal equivalent. (Recall that you can do this easily by using the Calculator's Scientific view. Make sure that the Bin option is selected, enter the appropriate 1s and 0s, and activate the Dec option.) When you do, you end up with this:

```
11001101 11010000 01110001 00000010
   205      208      113       2
```

Now you shoehorn dots between each decimal number to get the dotted-decimal form of the address:

205.208.113.2

IP Address Classes

So how is it possible, with millions of hosts on the Internet the world over, to ensure that each computer has a unique IP address? The secret is that each network that wants on the Internet must register with the Internet Network Information Center (called the InterNIC, for short). In turn, the InterNIC assigns that network a block of IP addresses that the administrator can then dole out to each computer (or, in the case of an ISP, to each customer). These blocks come in three classes: A, B, and C.

In a *class A* network, the InterNIC assigns the first (that is, the leftmost) 8 bits of the address: The first bit is 0, and the remaining 7 bits are an assigned number. Two to the power of 7 is 128, so 128 class A networks are possible. The dotted-decimal versions of these IP addresses begin with the numbers 0 (that is, 00000000) through 127 (that is, 01111111). However, 0 isn't used and 127 is used for other purposes, so there are really only 126 possibilities.

NETWORK IDS AND HOST IDS

The numbers assigned by the InterNIC are called *network IDs*, and the numbers assigned by the network administrator are called *host IDs*. For example, consider the following address from a class A network: 115.123.234.1. The network ID is 115 (or it's sometimes written as 115.0.0.0), and the host ID is 123.234.1.

The number 126 might seem small, but consider that the remaining 24 address bits are available for the network to assign locally. In each quad, you have 254 possible numbers (0 and 255 aren't used), so you have $254 \times 254 \times 254$ possible addresses to assign, which comes out to a little more than 16 million. In other words, you need to have a large system to rate a class A network. (If you do have such a system, don't bother petitioning the InterNIC for a block of IP addresses, because all the class A networks were snapped up long ago by behemoths such as IBM.) Figure 31.1 shows the layout of the IP addresses used by class A networks.

FIGURE 31.1.

The IP address structure for class A networks.

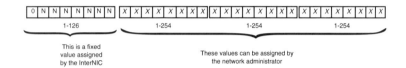

REGISTERED IP ADDRESSES ARE FOR INTERNET USE ONLY

Bear in mind that you need to register your network with the InterNIC only if you require Internet access. If you're just creating an internal TCP/IP network, you can create your own block of IP addresses and assign them at will.

In a *class B* network, the InterNIC assigns the first 16 bits of the address: The first two bits are 10, and the remaining 14 bits are an assigned number. This allows for a total of 16,384 (2 to the power of 14) class B networks, all of which have a first quad dotted-decimal value between 128 (that is, 10000000) and 191 (that is, 10111111). Note that, as with class A networks, all the possible class B numbers have been assigned.

Again, the network administrator can dole out the remaining 16 bits to the network hosts. Given 254 possible values in each of the two quads, that produces a total of 64,516 possible IP addresses. Figure 31.2 shows the layout of class B network IP addresses.

FIGURE 31.2.

The IP address structure for class B networks.

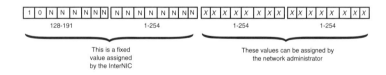

In a *class C* network, the InterNIC assigns the first 24 bits of the address: The first three bits are 110, and the remaining 21 bits are an assigned number. So the total number of class C networks available is 2,097,152 (2 to the power of 21), all of which have a first quad dotted-decimal value between 192 (that is, 11000000) and 223 (that is, 11011111).

This leaves only the remaining 8 bits in the fourth quad for network administrators to assign addresses to local computers. Again, 0 and 255 aren't used, so a class C network has a total of 254 possible IP addresses. The layout of class C network IP addresses is shown in Figure 31.3.

FIGURE 31.3.

The IP address structure for class C networks.

This is a fixed value assigned by the InterNIC

These values can be assigned by the network administrator

WHAT HAPPENED TO THE REST OF THE ADDRESSES?

Because the first quad of an IP address is 8 bits, the range of possible values should be between 0 and 255, but class A, B, and C networks usurp only 0 through 223. What happened to 224 through 255? Well, the values between 224 and 239 are used for special multicast protocols (these are class D addresses), and the values between 240 and 255 are used for experimental purposes (these are class E addresses).

CLASS C ADDRESS BLOCKS ARE GOING FAST!

I already mentioned that the address blocks for class A and class B networks are long gone, but with more than 2 million class C blocks available, there's plenty to go around, right? Wrong! These blocks are being gobbled up quickly, and it's predicted that the InterNIC will run out before too long. As you read this, the Internet Engineering Task Force and other industry mavens are busy hammering out an agreement for a 64-bit replacement to IP—usually known as IPng (next generation)—that will solve this crisis.

IP Routing

So far you've seen that IP datagrams include the source and destination IP addresses in their headers and that these addresses use the dotted-decimal notation. The next question is, how do the datagrams get from the source to the destination? The answer is that IP also defines how datagrams travel from host to host in a process called *routing.* (Each leap from one host to the next is called a *hop.*)

When IP is ready to send data, it compares the addresses in the datagram header to see whether the source and destination reside on the same network. If they do, IP just hands the packets over to the LAN for delivery, and the data is sent directly to the destination. If the addresses are on different networks, however, the packets must be routed outside the network.

Subnet Masks

At first blush, deciding whether the source and destination hosts are on the same network sounds easy: Just compare the network IDs of the two addresses. For example, consider the following two addresses:

Source	200.100.55.101
Destination	200.100.66.72

These are class C networks, so the source address has a network ID of 200.100.55, and the destination has a network ID of 200.100.66. Therefore, they're on different networks. Or are they? One of the consequences of having no more class A and class B address blocks is that many large corporations can handle their addressing needs only by obtaining multiple blocks of class C addresses. So it's entirely possible that the 200.100.55 and 200.100.66 network IDs belong to the same company and could therefore be part of the same network! If so, IP should look at only the first two quads (200.100) to determine whether the addresses are on the same network.

So how does IP know to compare the first one, two, or three quads? By using a *subnet mask*. A subnet is a subsection of a network that uses related IP addresses. On a class C network, for example, you could define the first 127 addresses to be on one subnet and the second 127 addresses to be on another subnet. On a larger scale, from the point of view of the Internet—which you can think of as being *the* network—each class A, B, and C network is a subnet.

The subnet mask is a 32-bit value that is usually expressed in the same dotted-decimal notation used by IP addresses. The purpose of the subnet mask is to let IP separate the network ID (or, as you saw in the preceding example, part of the network ID) from the full IP address and thus determine whether the source and destination are on the same network. Table 31.2 spells out the default subnet masks used for each type of network class.

Table 31.2. Normal subnet masks used for each network class.

Network	Subnet Mask	Bit Values
Class A	255.0.0.0	11111111 00000000 00000000 00000000
Class B	255.255.0.0	11111111 11111111 00000000 00000000
Class C	255.255.255.0	11111111 11111111 11111111 00000000

When IP applies the subnet mask to an IP address, the part of the mask that is all 0s strips off the corresponding section of the address. Consider the following example:

	IP Address	Mask	Result
Source	205.208.113.2	255.255.255.0	205.208.113.0
Destination	205.208.113.50	255.255.255.0	205.208.113.0

The mask produces the same result, so these two addresses are on the same network. Now consider the example I used earlier. In that case, you need to use a nonstandard mask of 255.255.0.0:

	IP Address	Mask	Result
Source	200.100.55.101	255.255.0.0	200.100.0.0
Destination	200.100.66.72	255.255.0.0	200.100.0.0

HOW THE SUBNET MASK WORKS

The operation of the subnet mask is a bit more complex than I've indicated. It's actually a two-step process. In the first step, the IP addresses are compared bit-by-bit with the subnet mask using a Boolean AND operation—if both bits are 1, a 1 is returned; otherwise, a 0 is returned:

Source:

205.208.113.2	11001101 11010000 01110001 00000010
255.255.255.0	11111111 11111111 11111111 00000000
Result of AND	11001101 11010000 01110001 00000000

Destination:

205.208.113.50	11001101 11010000 01110001 00110010
255.255.255.0	11111111 11111111 11111111 00000000
Result of AND	11001101 11010000 01110001 00000000

Now the two results are compared bit-by-bit using a Boolean Exclusive Or (XOR) operation—if both bits are 0 or both bits are 1, a 0 is returned; otherwise, a 1 is returned:

Source Result	11001101 11010000 01110001 00000000
Destination Result	11001101 11010000 01110001 00000000
Result of XOR	00000000 00000000 00000000 00000000

If the result of the XOR operation is all 0s, the source and destination are on the same network.

Routing and the Default Gateway

As I said, if IP determines that the source and destination exist on the same network, it hands the datagrams over to the LAN for immediate delivery. If the destination is outside the network, however, IP's routing capabilities come into play.

Routing is the process by which a datagram travels from the source host to a destination host on another network. The first part of the routing process involves defining a default gateway. This is the IP address of a computer or dedicated router on the same network as the source computer. When IP sees that the destination is on a different network, it sends the datagrams to the default gateway.

When the gateway gets the datagrams, it checks the IP header for the destination address and compares that address to its internal list of other gateways and network addresses on the Internet. In some cases, the gateway will be able to send the datagrams directly to the destination. More likely, though, the gateway will only be able to forward the packet to another system that's en route to the destination. This system repeats the procedure: It checks the destination and forwards the datagrams accordingly. Although many hops might be involved, the datagrams will eventually arrive at their destination.

THE TIME TO LIVE

Actually, if the datagram has to perform too many hops, it might never reach its destination. That's because each datagram is supplied with a Time to Live (TTL) value in its header (as described earlier). If the TTL value is 64, for example, and then if the datagram has made 64 hops before getting to its destination, it's discarded without a second thought. The TTL is useful for preventing datagrams from running amok and wandering the Internet's highways and byways endlessly.

USE TRACERT TO MONITOR HOPS

If you're curious about how many hops it takes to get from here to there (wherever "there" might be), TCP/IP provides a way to find out. You use a utility called TRACERT. I'll show you how it works later in this chapter (see "Wielding the TCP/IP Utilities").

Dynamic IP Addressing

If your network has just a few computers and if the organization of the network is static (the computers attached to the network remain attached at all times), it's easiest to assign an IP address to every computer from the block of addresses supplied by the InterNIC.

Managing IP addresses, however, can get quite cumbersome if the network has many computers or if the network configuration changes constantly, thanks to users logging on to the network remotely (using, for example, the Dial-Up Networking accessory you learned about in the preceding chapter) or computers being moved from one subnet to another. One way to solve this problem is to assign IP addresses to network computers dynamically. In other words, when a computer logs on to the network, it is assigned an IP address from a pool of available addresses. When the computer logs off, the address it was using is returned to the pool.

The system that manages this dynamic allocation of addresses is called *Dynamic Host Configuration Protocol* (DHCP), and the computers that implement DHCP are called *DHCP servers*. Windows 98 supports DHCP via either Windows NT DHCP servers on the network, or PPP dial-up routers.

Domain Name Resolution

Of course, when you're accessing a Web site or sending Internet email, you don't use IP addresses. Instead, you use "friendlier" names such as www.windows.com and president@whitehouse.gov. That's because TCP/IP, bless its heart, lets us mere humans use English-language equivalents of IP addresses. So, in the same way that IP addresses can be seen as network IDs and host IDs, these English-language alternatives are broken down into *domain names* and *host names.*

When you register with the InterNIC, what you're really doing is registering a domain name that is associated with your network. In my case, I'm registered under the domain name mcfedries.com, which points to my network ID of 205.208.113. The computers—or hosts— on my network have their own host names. For example, I have one machine with the host name hermes, so its full Internet name is hermes.mcfedries.com (this machine's IP address is 205.208.113.4); similarly, my Web server's host name is www, so its full Internet name is www.mcfedries.com (its IP address is 205.208.113.2).

COMPUTER NAMES AND HOST NAMES ARE NOT RELATED

You might recall from Chapter 28, "Setting Up Windows 98 for Networking," that I used the computer name Hermes as an example when I was going through the steps required for setting up a computer on a network. That is the same machine as hermes.mcfedries.com, but the computer name and host name are in no way related. I just happened to use the same name for both.

Even though domain names and host names look sort of like IP addresses (a bunch of characters separated by dots), there's no formula that translates one into the other. Instead, a process called *name resolution* is used to look up host names and domain names to find their underlying IP addresses (and vice versa). Three mechanisms are used to perform this task: the HOSTS file, the Domain Name System, and the Windows Internet Name System.

The HOSTS File

The simplest method of mapping a host name to an IP address is to use a HOSTS file. This is a simple text file that implements a two-column table with IP addresses in one column and their corresponding host names in the other, like so:

```
127.0.0.1 localhost
205.208.113.2 www.mcfedries.com
205.208.113.4 hermes.mcfedries.com
```

(The address 127.0.0.1 is a special IP address that refers to your computer. If you send a packet to 127.0.0.1, it comes back to your machine. For this reason, 127.0.0.1 is called a *loopback* address.) You just add an entry for every host on your network. In your main Windows 98 folder, you find a file named HOSTS.SAM that includes the loopback address. You can use this file as a start by copying it to a file named HOSTS (no extension). Note, however, that after you have the HOSTS file set up for your network, you must copy it to *every* machine on the network.

The Domain Name System

The HOSTS system is fine for resolving host names within a network, but with millions of hosts worldwide, it's obviously impractical for resolving the names of computers that reside outside of your subnet.

You might think that because the InterNIC handles all the registration duties for domains, your TCP/IP applications could just query some kind of central database at the InterNIC to resolve host names. There are two problems with this approach: The number of queries this database would have to handle would be astronomical (and thus extremely slow), and you'd have to contact the InterNIC every time you added a host to your network. Because it now takes a few weeks to get a domain registered, it's reasonable to assume that it would take at least as long to get your host onto the database, which is unacceptable.

Instead of one central database of host names and IP addresses, the Internet uses a distributed database system called the *Domain Name System* (DNS). The DNS databases use a hierarchical structure to organize domains. The top level of this hierarchy consists of seven categories, as described in Table 31.3.

Table 31.3. Top-level domains in the DNS.

Domain	*What It Represents*
com	Commercial businesses
edu	Educational institutions
gov	Governments
int	International organizations
mil	Military organizations
net	Networking organizations
org	Nonprofit organizations

Top-level domains also exist for various countries. Table 31.4 lists a few of these geographical domains.

Table 31.4. Some top-level geographical domains in the DNS.

Domain	*The Country It Represents*
at	Austria
au	Australia
ca	Canada
ch	Switzerland

continues

Table 31.4. continued

Domain	The Country It Represents
cn	China
de	Germany
dk	Denmark
es	Spain
fi	Finland
fr	France
hk	Hong Kong
ie	Ireland
il	Israel
jp	Japan
mx	Mexico
nl	Netherlands
no	Norway
nz	New Zealand
ru	Russia
se	Sweden
uk	United Kingdom
us	United States

NEW TOP-LEVEL DOMAINS PROPOSED

In February 1997, the International Ad Hoc Committee (IAHC) announced a plan to add seven new top-level domains to the DNS:

firm	Businesses or firms
store	Businesses offering goods to purchase
web	Organizations emphasizing activities related to the World Wide Web
arts	Organizations emphasizing cultural and entertainment activities
rec	Organizations emphasizing recreational activities
info	Organizations providing information services
nom	Individual or personal Internet sites (incomprehensibly, "nom" comes from the word *nomenclature*)

Below these top-level domains are the domain names, such as `whitehouse.gov` and `microsoft.com`. From there, you can have subdomains (subnetworks) and then host names at the bottom of the hierarchy. The database maintains a record of the corresponding IP address for each domain and host.

To handle name resolution, the DNS database is distributed around the Internet to various computers called *DNS servers*, or simply *name servers*. When you set up TCP/IP, you specify one of the DNS servers, and your TCP/IP software uses this server to resolve all host names into their appropriate IP addresses.

The Windows Internet Name Service

Earlier, I told you how DHCP can be used to assign IP addresses to hosts dynamically. On a Microsoft TCP/IP network, how are these addresses coordinated with host names? By using a name resolution feature called the *Windows Internet Name Service* (WINS). WINS maps NetBIOS names (the names you assign to computers in the Identification tab of the Network properties sheet) to the IP addresses assigned via DHCP.

Understanding TCP

IP is a connectionless protocol, so it doesn't care whether datagrams ever reach their eventual destinations. It just routes the datagrams according to the destination address and then forgets about them. This is why IP is also called an *unreliable* protocol.

We know from experience, however, that the Internet is reliable (most of the time!). So where does this reliability come from if not from IP? It comes from the rest of the TCP/IP equation: TCP. You can think of TCP as IP's better half, because through TCP, applications can make sure that their data gets where it's supposed to go and that it arrives there intact.

To help you visualize the difference between IP and TCP, imagine IP as analogous to sending a letter through the mail. You put the letter in an envelope, address the envelope, and drop it in a mailbox. You don't know when the letter gets picked up, how it gets to its destination, or even *whether* it gets there.

Suppose, however, that after mailing the letter you were to call up the recipient and tell him or her that a letter was on its way. You could give the recipient your phone number and have him or her call you when the letter is received. If the letter doesn't arrive after a preset length of time, the recipient could let you know so that you could resend it.

That phone link between you and the recipient is analogous to what TCP does for data transfers. TCP is a connection-oriented protocol that sets up a two-way communications channel between the source and the destination to monitor the IP routing.

TCP Sockets

In the TCP scheme of things, this communications channel is called a *socket*, and it has two components on each end:

IP address: You've already seen that each IP datagram header includes both the source and the destination IP address. For a TCP socket, these addresses are analogous to the sender and receiver having each other's phone number.

Port number: Having a phone number might not be enough to get in touch with someone. If the person works in an office, you might also have to specify his or her extension. Similarly, knowing the IP address of a host isn't enough information for TCP. It also must know which application sent the datagram. After all, in a multitasking environment such as Windows 98, you could be running a Web browser, an email client, and an FTP program all at the same time. To differentiate between programs, TCP uses a 16-bit number called a *port* that uniquely identifies each running process.

SOME PORT NUMBERS ARE FIXED

On the source host, the port number usually specifies an application. On the destination host, the port can also specify an application, but it's more likely that the port is a fixed number that is used by an Internet service. For example, FTP uses port 21, Telnet uses port 23, and HTTP uses port 80.

The Structure of a TCP Segment

When a TCP/IP application sends data, it divides the data into a number of *TCP segments*. These segments include part of the data along with a header that defines various parameters used in the TCP communication between the source and the destination. These TCP segments are then encapsulated within the data portion of an IP datagram and sent on their way.

Wait a minute. If TCP segments are sent inside IP datagrams, and I just said that IP is unreliable, how can TCP possibly be reliable? The trick is that, unlike straight IP, TCP expects a response from its TCP counterpart on the receiving end. Think of it this way: Imagine mailing a letter to someone and including a Post-it note on the letter that specifies your phone number and tells the recipient to call you when she receives the letter. If you don't hear from her, you know she didn't get the letter. To ensure reliable communications, TCP includes an electronic "Post-it Note" in its header that does two things:

- When the application requests that data be sent to a remote location, TCP constructs an initial segment that attempts to set up the socket interface between the two systems. No data is sent until TCP hears back from the receiving system that the sockets are in place and that it's ready to receive the data.

- When the sockets are ready to go, TCP starts sending the data within its segments and always asks the receiving TCP to acknowledge that these data segments have arrived. If no acknowledgment is received, the sending TCP retransmits the segment.

As with IP, you don't need to know the exact format of a TCP header. In case you're curious, however, I've laid it all out in Table 31.5.

Table 31.5. The structure of a TCP segment header.

Field	Bits	Description
Source Port	0 to 15	The source port number.
Destination Port	16 to 31	The destination port number.
Sequence Number	32 to 63	In the overall sequence of bytes being sent, this field specifies the position in this sequence of the segment's first data byte.
Acknowledgment Number	64 to 95	If the ACK Control Bit is set (see the Control Bits entry), this field contains the value of the next sequence number the sender of the segment is expecting the receiver to acknowledge.
Data Offset	96 to 99	The length of the TCP segment header, in 32-bit words. This tells the receiving socket where the data starts.
Reserved	100 to 105	This field is reserved for future use.
Control Bits	106 to 111	These codes specify various aspects of the communication. When set to 1, each bit controls a particular code, as listed here:
	106	URG: Urgent Pointer field significant.
	107	ACK: Acknowledgment Number field is to be used.
	108	PSH: Push function.
	109	RST: Reset the connection.
	110	SYN: Synchronize sequence numbers. This bit is set when the connection is opened.
	111	FIN: No more data from sender, so close the connection.

continues

Table 31.5. continued

Field	Bits	Description
Window	112 to 127	The number of data bytes that the sender can currently accept. This *sliding window* lets the sender and receiver vary the number of bytes sent and thus increase efficiency.
Checksum	128 to 143	This value lets the receiver determine the integrity of the data.
Urgent Pointer	144 to 159	If the URG Control Bit is set, this field indicates the location in the data where urgent data resides.
Options	160 and over	This variable-length field specifies extra TCP options, such as the maximum segment size.

TCP Features

To ensure that IP datagrams are transferred in an orderly, efficient, and reliable manner, TCP implements the following six features:

Connection opening: On the sending host, a process (such as a Web browser) issues a request to send data (such as a URL) to a destination host (such as a Web server). TCP creates an initial segment designed to open the connection between the sender and the receiver (the browser and server). In this initial contact, the two systems exchange IP addresses and port numbers (to create the socket interface) and set up the flow control and sequencing (discussed next).

Flow control: One of the parameters that the sending and receiving hosts exchange is the number of bytes each is willing to accept at one time. This way, one system doesn't end up sending more data than the other system can handle. This value can move up or down as circumstances change on each machine, so the systems exchange this information constantly to ensure efficient data transfers.

Sequencing: Every segment is assigned a sequence number (or, technically, the first data byte in every segment is assigned a sequence number). This technique enables the receiving host to reassemble any segments that arrive out of order.

Acknowledgment: When TCP transmits a segment, it holds the segment in a queue until the receiving TCP issues an acknowledgment that it has received the segment. If the sending TCP doesn't receive this acknowledgment, it retransmits the segment.

31

Error detection: A checksum value in the header enables the receiver to test the integrity of an incoming segment. If the segment is corrupted, the receiver fires back an error message to the sender, which then immediately retransmits the segment.

Connection closing: When the process on the sending host indicates that the connection should be terminated, the sending TCP sends a segment that tells the receiver that no more data will be sent and that the socket should be closed.

These features illustrate why Internet communications are generally reliable. They show that TCP acts as a sort of chaperone for the IP datagrams traveling from host to host.

Installing and Configuring TCP/IP

TCP/IP is a complex set of protocols (I've really only scratched the surface here), but the good news is that it's much easier to implement than it is to understand. With this chapter's background information in hand, after you've installed the protocol, configuring a computer to use TCP/IP becomes a simple matter of plugging in a few values. Here's what you need to know before getting started:

- Whether your network or ISP uses dynamic IP addressing.
- If dynamic addressing isn't used, the IP address that has been assigned to your computer and the appropriate subnet mask for your network.
- The IP address of your network's default gateway.
- The host name of your computer and the domain name of your network.
- Whether your network uses DNS. If it does, you need to know the IP address of one or more DNS servers.
- Whether your network uses WINS. If it does, you need to know the IP address of your WINS server.
- Which network clients and services use TCP/IP. For each of these clients and services, you need to bind the TCP/IP protocol.

After you have all this information in hand (which you can get from your network administrator or your ISP), you're ready to install TCP/IP on your computer.

Installing the TCP/IP Protocol

Unlike Windows 3.1, Windows 98 comes with its own TCP/IP stack. Before installing this TCP/IP stack, you need to make sure that you've installed the necessary network adapters. If you're running TCP/IP on a network, you need to install the driver for your network interface card, as described in Chapter 28. If you're connecting to the Internet, you need to install the

Dial-Up Adapter, as described in Chapter 30, "Remote Computing with Dial-Up Networking." After that's done, follow these steps to install the TCP/IP protocol:

1. Display the Network properties sheet, either by opening Control Panel's Network icon or by right-clicking the Network Neighborhood and selecting Properties from the context menu.

2. Click the Add button to display the Select Network Component Type dialog box.

3. Highlight Protocol and click Add. The Select Network Protocol dialog box appears, as shown in Figure 31.4.

FIGURE 31.4.

Use this dialog box to highlight the TCP/IP protocol.

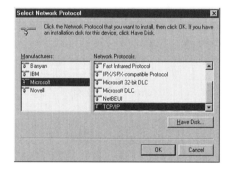

4. In the Manufacturers list, highlight Microsoft.

5. In the Network Protocols list, highlight TCP/IP.

6. Click OK and follow the prompts for inserting your Windows 98 source disc. Windows 98 then adds TCP/IP to the list of network components.

Windows 98 binds the TCP/IP protocol to the installed network adapters automatically. (To make sure, highlight the network adapter you'll be using with TCP/IP and click Properties. In the properties sheet that appears, select the Bindings tab and make sure that the check box beside the TCP/IP protocol is activated.)

MULTIPLE TCP/IP CONFIGURATIONS

Windows 98 is quite flexible when it comes to having multiple TCP/IP configurations. For example, you might need to use TCP/IP on your LAN with one configuration and through your ISP with a different configuration. In this case, you can run through one configuration using the LAN adapter and through another using the Dial-Up Adapter. What if you have multiple Internet accounts? No problem. Windows 98 lets you establish connection-specific TCP/IP configurations (as described later in this chapter in the "Connection-Specific TCP/IP Settings" section).

Configuring the TCP/IP Protocol

With TCP/IP safely ensconced on your system, you now need to configure it to your liking. To do this, highlight the TCP/IP protocol in the list of network components and then click Properties. (If TCP/IP is bound to multiple adapters, you have multiple entries for the TCP/IP protocol. In this case, highlight the appropriate binding and click Properties.) You see the TCP/IP Properties dialog box, which contains several tabs for configuring TCP/IP. The next few sections take you though each of these tabs.

IP Address Properties

You use the IP Address tab to tell Windows 98 about your computer's IP address. You have two options:

> **Obtain an IP address automatically:** Select this option if your network uses DHCP or if your ISP supplies you with an IP address on-the-fly whenever you log on.

> **Specify an IP address:** Select this option if your computer has been assigned a permanent IP address, which you then enter in dotted-decimal notation in the IP Address text box. Also, you need to enter the appropriate dotted-decimal subnet mask in the Subnet Mask text box, as shown in Figure 31.5.

FIGURE 31.5.

The IP Address tab with an IP address and a subnet mask filled in.

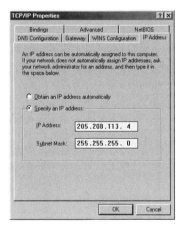

WINS Configuration Properties

If your network uses WINS for name resolution, select the WINS Configuration tab and activate the Enable WINS Resolution option, as shown in Figure 31.6. From here, you have two choices:

■ If your network has a DHCP server, activate the Use DHCP for WINS Resolution option. This option tells Windows 98 to use the DHCP server to get all the WINS information it needs.

■ If you aren't using DHCP, fill in the IP address of the Primary WINS Server and Secondary WINS Server, as well as the Scope ID. (Note that the last of these fields is usually left blank. If your network runs NetBIOS over TCP/IP, however, only computers with the same scope ID can talk to one another.)

FIGURE 31.6.

Use the WINS Configuration tab to enable WINS name resolution on your computer.

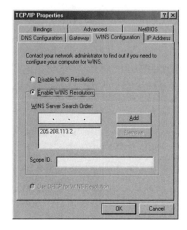

Gateway Properties

Your next chore is to tell Windows 98 the IP address of the machine to use as your gateway. This is the address either of a computer or router on your network, or of a computer on your ISP's system. In the Gateway tab, shown in Figure 31.7, enter the dotted-decimal IP address of the default gateway in the New gateway text box and then click Add to place it on the Installed gateways list. Repeat this procedure if your network uses multiple gateways. (Note that the gateway at the top of the list is the one that Windows 98 tries first.)

FIGURE 31.7.

You use the Gateway tab to enter your network's default gateway.

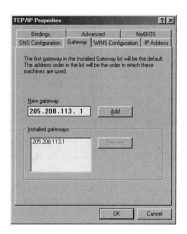

DNS Configuration Properties

The next item on the TCP/IP configuration agenda involves setting up DNS properties for the host. If your network uses DNS or if you're configuring the host for an Internet connection, select the DNS Configuration tab, shown in Figure 31.8, and then activate the Enable DNS option. Then fill in the following properties:

Host: This is the host name for your computer.

Domain: This is the domain name of your network or your ISP. DNS combines the host name and domain name to create the fully qualified domain name (FQDN) for the computer. In Figure 31.8, for example, the Host is `hermes` and the Domain is `mcfedries.com`, so this computer's FQDN is `hermes.mcfedries.com`. This is the name Windows 98 sends to the DNS for resolution into an IP address.

DNS Server Search Order: Use this group to enter the IP addresses for one or more (up to three) DNS servers, either on your network or on your ISP's network. For each server, enter the dotted-decimal IP address and then click Add. Windows 98 queries these servers in the order in which you enter them.

Domain Suffix Search Order: A host computer can belong to multiple domains. In my case, I have two domains—`mcfedries.com` and `logophilia.com`—so the `hermes` host has two FQDNs: `hermes.mcfedries.com` and `hermes.logophilia.com`. In case the DNS has trouble with the main FQDN, you can use the Domain Suffix Search Order group to specify all the domains Windows 98 can use when building an FQDN. Enter a domain name and click Add. You can specify as many domains as required.

FIGURE 31.8.

If you're using DNS, you need to fill in various properties in the DNS Configuration tab.

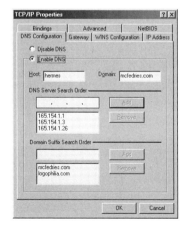

Bindings Properties

You next have to specify which clients and services should use the TCP/IP protocol. Select the Bindings tab, shown in Figure 31.9, and, for each network component that should use

TCP/IP, activate the appropriate check box. If your network uses a different protocol for these components (such as NetBEUI or IPX/SPX) or if you're using TCP/IP just to connect to an ISP, you can clear these check boxes.

FIGURE 31.9.

Use the Bindings tab to specify which network components will use TCP/IP.

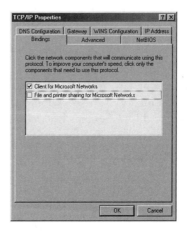

DON'T ENABLE SHARING FOR THE DIAL-UP ADAPTER

If you're configuring TCP/IP for the Dial-Up Adapter (for, say, an Internet connection), you create a huge security breach if you enable file and print sharing. I explain why in the next chapter (see the section titled "TCP/IP and Internet Security"), but for now, you should make sure that file and print sharing is disabled in the Bindings tab. This caution also applies if you use a network gateway to access the Internet. In this case, you want to make sure that TCP/IP over your network adapter is not bound to the file and print sharing service.

Advanced Properties

The Advanced properties tab, shown in Figure 31.10, is pretty stark compared to the other tabs. In this case, you have only one option: Set this protocol to be the default protocol. Again, you need to activate this option only if you're setting up this host on a local TCP/IP network. Leave this option deactivated if your network uses a different protocol or if you're using TCP/IP to connect to an ISP.

Finishing the Configuration

After you've filled in all the necessary options in the TCP/IP Properties dialog box, click OK to return to the Network properties sheet. Remember that if you want to use TCP/IP with multiple network adapters, you need to repeat the preceding configuration procedure for each adapter. When all that's done, click OK, and when Windows 98 asks whether you want to restart your computer, click Yes.

31

FIGURE 31.10.
You can use the Advanced tab to set TCP/IP as the default protocol.

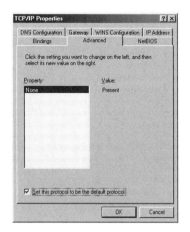

Connection-Specific TCP/IP Settings

You might be among the many people who have multiple Internet accounts. For example, you might have one account that you access for business and another that you access for personal use. You might also have to dial in to your company's TCP/IP network while you're on the road. What do you do if you often use the same computer for all these scenarios (such as a notebook computer that you lug between the office and home and to remote locations)? The prospect of modifying all those TCP/IP properties each time you need to access a particular account is unattractive, to say the least. Luckily, however, you don't have to. Windows 98 lets you set up a different TCP/IP configuration for each Dial-Up Networking connection you use. When you establish the connection, Dial-Up Networking uses the correct TCP/IP configuration automatically.

To set this up, follow these steps:

1. In the Dial-Up Networking folder, highlight the connection you want to work with.

2. Either select File | Properties or right-click the icon and click Properties.

3. In the properties sheet that appears, display the Server Types tab.

4. In the Allowed network protocols group, make sure that the TCP/IP check box is activated and then click TCP/IP Settings.

5. In the TCP/IP Settings dialog box, shown in Figure 31.11, configure the following options:

   Server assigned IP address: Activate this option if the dial-up server assigns an IP address automatically when you log on.

   Specify an IP address: Activate this option if you have a permanent IP address with this connection. Enter the dotted-decimal address in the IP address box.

   Server assigned name server addresses: Activate this option if the dial-up server assigns the addresses of DNS and WINS servers automatically.

Specify name server addresses: Activate this option if this connection uses specific IP addresses for DNS and WINS servers. Use the text boxes provided to enter up to two dotted-decimal IP addresses for DNS and WINS servers.

Use IP header compression: Activate this check box if the dial-up server supports IP header compression. If you have trouble using an Internet connection, one likely cause is that your ISP doesn't support IP compression, so you should deactivate this check box.

Use default gateway on remote network: When this check box is activated, the dial-up server's default gateway is used. If you deactivate this check box, the default gateway defined in your TCP/IP properties is used.

6. Click OK until you're back in the Dial-Up Networking folder.

FIGURE 31.11.

Use the TCP/IP Settings dialog box to configure TCP/IP properties specific to the current Dial-Up Networking connection.

Wielding the TCP/IP Utilities

Windows 98 TCP/IP comes with a few utilities you can use to review your TCP/IP settings and troubleshoot problems. Here's a list of the available utilities:

ARP: This DOS command displays (or modifies) the IP-to-Ethernet or IP-to-Token Ring address translation tables used by the Address Resolution Protocol (ARP) in TCP/IP. Enter the command `arp -?` for the syntax.

NBTSTAT: This DOS command displays the protocol statistics and the current TCP/IP connections using NBT (NetBIOS over TCP/IP). Enter `nbtstat -?` for the syntax.

NETSTAT: This DOS command displays the protocol statistics and current TCP/IP connections. The command `netstat -?` displays the syntax.

PING: This DOS command can check a network connection to a remote computer. This is one of the most commonly used TCP/IP diagnostic tools, so I describe it in more detail in the next section.

ROUTE: This DOS command can be used to manipulate a network routing table (HOSTS). Enter route -? for the syntax.

TRACERT: This DOS command can check the route taken to a remote host. I'll explain this valuable diagnostic command in more detail later.

WINIPCFG: This Windows 98 utility displays the current TCP/IP network configuration. Select Start|Run, enter winipcfg, and click OK to display the IP Configuration window. For each installed network adapter, this window tells you the adapter's physical address, IP address, subnet mask, and default gateway. Click More Info>> to expand the window, as shown in Figure 31.12.

FIGURE 31.12.

The WINIPCFG utility displays information about the TCP/IP configuration associated with each network adapter.

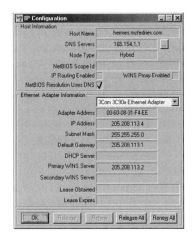

The PING Command

As you might know, a submarine can detect a nearby object by using sonar to send out a sound wave and then seeing whether the wave is reflected. This is called *pinging* an object.

TCP/IP has a PING command that performs a similar function. PING sends out a special type of IP packet—called an *Internet Control Message Protocol (ICMP) echo packet*—to a remote location. This packet requests that the remote location send back a response packet. PING then tells you whether the response was received. This way, you can check your TCP/IP configuration to see whether your host can connect with a remote host.

Here's the PING syntax:

```
ping [-t] [-a] [-n count] [-l length] [-f] [-i TTL] [-v TOS] [-r count]
    [-s count] [[-j route-list] ¦ [-k route-list]] [-w timeout] host
```

-t	Pings the specified *host* until you interrupt the command.
-a	Specifies not to resolve IP addresses to host names.

-n *count*	Sends the number of echo packets specified by *count*. The default is 4.
-l *length*	Sends echo packets containing the amount of data specified by *length*. The default is 32 bytes; the maximum is 8192.
-f	Sends a Do Not Fragment flag in the packet's header. The flag ensures that the packet won't be fragmented by gateways along the route.
-i *TTL*	Sets the Time To Live field to the value specified by *TTL* (the default is 32).
-v *TOS*	Sets the Type Of Service field to the value specified by *TOS*.
-r *count*	Records the route of the outgoing packet and the returning packet in the Record Route field. A minimum of 1 to a maximum of 9 hosts must be specified by *count*.
-s *count*	Specifies the time stamp for the number of hops specified by *count*.
-j *route-list*	Routes packets by means of the list of hosts specified by *host*. Consecutive hosts may be separated by intermediate gateways (loose source routed). The maximum number allowed by IP is 9.
-k *route-list*	Routes packets by means of the list of hosts specified by *host*. Consecutive hosts may not be separated by intermediate gateways (strict source routed). The maximum number allowed by IP is 9.
-w *timeout*	Specifies a time-out interval in milliseconds. The default is 1000 (1 second).
host	Specifies either the IP address or the host name (a fully qualified domain name) of the remote host you want to ping. (You can enter multiple hosts.)

Here's an example that uses PING on the Microsoft Web site (www.microsoft.com):

```
C:\>ping www.microsoft.com
Pinging www.microsoft.com [198.105.232.6] with 32 bytes of data:
Reply from 198.105.232.6: bytes=32 time=251ms TTL=19
Reply from 198.105.232.6: bytes=32 time=471ms TTL=19
Reply from 198.105.232.6: bytes=32 time=331ms TTL=19
Reply from 198.105.232.6: bytes=32 time=206ms TTL=19
C:\>
```

Here you see that each echo packet received a reply. If you can't connect to the remote host, PING returns a Request timed out message for each packet.

If you can't connect to a remote host, here are some notes on using PING to troubleshoot TCP/IP problems:

- First, check to see whether you can use PING successfully on the loopback address: ping 127.0.0.1. If you can't, make sure that you restarted Windows 98 after installing TCP/IP. If PING still doesn't work on the loopback address, you might need to remove TCP/IP and reinstall it.

- If your loopback test works properly, try using PING on your computer's IP address. (If you're using DHCP, run the IP Configuration utility to get your current IP address.) If you don't get a successful echo, it could be that you entered an invalid IP address or subnet mask.

- The next test you should run is on your default gateway. If you can't ping the gateway successfully, you won't be able to access remote Internet sites. In this case, check the IP address you entered for the gateway. Make sure that TCP/IP is bound to the network adapter you're using.

- If you get this far, now try using PING on the remote host you're trying to contact. If you're unsuccessful, check to make sure that you're using the correct IP address for the host and that the gateway (router) is set up to route IP packets.

- You can also try pinging the remote host by both its IP address and its host name. If you get a response with the IP address but not the host name, you likely have a name resolution problem.

The TRACERT Command

If you can't ping a remote host, it could be that your echo packets are getting held up along the way. To find out, you can use the TRACERT (trace route) command:

```
tracert [-d] [-h maximum_hops] [-j route-list] [-w timeout] host
```

-d	Specifies not to resolve IP addresses to host names.
-h *maximum_hops*	Specifies the maximum number of hops to search for the *host* (the default is 30).
-j *route-list*	Specifies loose source route along the *route-list*.
-w *timeout*	Waits the number of milliseconds specified by *timeout* for each reply.
host	Specifies the host name of the destination computer.

TRACERT operates by sending ICMP echo packets with varying TTL values. Recall that TTL places a limit on the number of hops a packet can take. Each host along the packet's route decrements the TTL value until, when the TTL value is 0, the packet is discarded (assuming that it hasn't reached its destination by then).

In TRACERT, the ICMP packets specify that whichever host decrements the echo packet to 0 should send back a response. So the first packet has a TTL value of 1, the second has a TTL value of 2, and so on. TRACERT keeps sending packets with incrementally higher TTL values until either a response is received from the remote host or a packet receives no response. Here's an example of a TRACERT command in action:

```
C:\>tracert www.mcp.com
Tracing route to www.mcp.com [206.246.150.10]over a maximum of 30 hops:
  1     5 ms     4 ms     4 ms  router.logophilia.com [205.208.113.1]
  2    39 ms    39 ms    41 ms  isdn-1.tor.hookup.net [165.154.125.54]
  3    88 ms    44 ms    44 ms  router.tor.hookup.net [165.154.1.10]
  4    64 ms    53 ms    52 ms  core-spc-tor-2-Serial5-7.Sprint-Canada.Net
[207.107.244.73]
  5    66 ms    48 ms    64 ms  core-spc-tor-1-fddi0/0.Sprint-Canada.Net
[204.50.251.31]
  6    79 ms    90 ms    90 ms  sl-pen-15-H11/0-T3.sprintlink.net [144.228.165.25]
  7    68 ms    62 ms    74 ms  sl-pen-17-F6/0/0.sprintlink.net [144.228.60.17]
  8   150 ms       *     294 ms  sl-chi-2-H1/0-T3.sprintlink.net [144.228.10.38]
  9   164 ms   317 ms   143 ms  sl-chi-19-F0/0.sprintlink.net [144.228.50.19]
 10       *     294 ms       *   sl-napnet-2-s-T3.sprintlink.net [144.228.159.18]
 11   140 ms   293 ms       *   iquest-fddi0.nap.net [206.54.225.250]
 12   134 ms   391 ms   156 ms  204.180.50.9
 13       *     107 ms   145 ms  www.mcp.com [206.246.150.10]

Trace complete.
C:\>
```

The first column is the hop number (that is, the TTL value set in the packet). Notice that, in my case, it took 13 hops to get to www.mcp.com. The next three columns contain round-trip times for an attempt to reach the destination with that TTL value. (Asterisks indicate that the attempt timed out.) The last column contains the host name (if it was resolved) and the IP address of the responding system.

TROUBLESHOOTING: TTL TOO LOW

One of the reasons your packets might not be getting to their destination is that the default TTL value used by Windows 98 might be set too low. The default is 32, as compared to 64 in most UNIX systems. To increase this value, start the Registry Editor and highlight the following key:

HKEY_LOCAL_MACHINE\System\CurrentControlSet\Services\VxD\MSTCP

Select Edit | New | String Value, enter DefaultTTL, and press Enter. Change the value of this new setting to 64.

Summary

This chapter showed you how to implement Microsoft's TCP/IP stack in Windows 98. I spent a good chunk of this chapter taking you through various TCP/IP concepts that are crucial if you hope to understand what you're doing when you set up TCP/IP on a computer. To that end, I showed you the basics behind the two main protocols: IP (including the structure of IP datagrams and addresses, IP routing, and name resolution) and TCP (including TCP sockets, segments, and features). From there, you dove right into TCP/IP installation and configuration. I showed you how to configure TCP/IP for an adapter and for a specific Dial-Up Networking connection. To finish, I showed you how to use various TCP/IP tools, especially the PING and TRACERT commands.

Here's a list of chapters where you'll find related information:

- For practical network knowledge—such as how to install adapters, clients, and services—check out Chapter 28, "Setting Up Windows 98 for Networking."

- To get the scoop on Dial-Up Networking, Chapter 30, "Remote Computing with Dial-Up Networking," is the place to be.

- You'll put all this TCP/IP know-how to good use when I show you how to use Windows 98 to connect to the Internet in Chapter 32, "Windows 98 and the Internet."

Windows 98 and the Internet

CHAPTER

32

A man may know the world without leaving his own home.

—*Lao-Tzu*

"Cachet to cliché" is a phrase I use to describe how concepts that were once hip and fashionable suddenly become yesterday's news and the victims of a none-too-subtle backlash. This hasn't happened to the Internet just yet (unless you count the righteous backlash leveled against the "Information Superhighway" metaphors that have been done to death). In fact, by just about any measure—popularity, technological innovation, number of industry millionaires—the Internet is still growing by leaps and bounds.

However, there's no shortage of neo-Luddites and other head-in-the-sand types willing to sound off on the nearest soapbox about what they perceive as the evils of all this technology. Even among industry pundits who should know better, it has become almost fashionable to predict an imminent Internet backlash. The rest of us who use the Internet in our daily lives and wonder how we ever got along without it just nod our heads at all this chin-wagging and get back to being productive.

If you're interested in getting on the Internet, this chapter shows you how to do it in Windows 98. I'll review the Internet-related concepts you've seen in previous chapters, and then I'll show you some alternative methods you can use to get connected. From there, you learn about Internet security and Windows 98's ftp and telnet utilities.

CHECK OUT MY WEB HOME

After you get yourself online and have a Web browser up and running, feel free to drop by my Web site and have a look around. Here's the address:

```
http://www.mcfedries.com/
```

Setting Up Windows 98 to Connect to the Internet

If you've been following along here in Parts VII and VIII, you already know everything you need to connect to the Internet in Windows 98. In fact, you're probably off investigating the Net's nooks and crannies right now. However, if you're just starting out at this chapter, this section will get your cyberjourney off the ground. You have three ways to proceed:

- Review the relevant material from the past few chapters, especially the information about Dial-Up Networking and TCP/IP.

■ Use the Internet Connection Wizard to take you step-by-step through the process of setting up a connection for your existing Internet account.

■ Use the Internet Connection Wizard to set up a new account with an Internet service provider.

The next three sections take you through each method.

What You've Learned So Far

Networking and the Internet are intimately related. After all, participating in the Internet is like logging on to a giant TCP/IP network, and networking a few computers is like creating your own mini-Internet. (TCP/IP-based private networks are known as *intranets*.)

Over the last few chapters, you've seen that many of the ideas we've looked at apply equally well to either setting up a network or setting up an Internet connection. These ideas are scattered among several chapters, however (mostly in Chapter 30, "Remote Computing with Dial-Up Networking," and Chapter 31, "Implementing TCP/IP for Internet and Intranet Connections"). So what I want to do now is review the relevant material and summarize everything in one nice, neat package. To that end, here's the general procedure you follow to set up an Internet connection in Windows 98 from scratch:

1. Make sure that your ISP has provided you with all the information required to create the connection (your IP address, subnet mask, default gateway, and so on). For a list of the TCP/IP settings you need, see the section "Installing and Configuring TCP/IP" in Chapter 31. You also need to find out the following information:

   ■ The phone number to dial, as well as your username and password.

   ■ Whether your connection is PPP or SLIP. (I explain the difference in the section "Dial-Up Networking Fundamentals" in Chapter 30.) For PPP, you need to know whether the connection supports software compression or encrypted passwords; for SLIP, whether it supports CSLIP.

   ■ For Internet email, you need to know the name of your account and your account password (these are usually the same as your logon name and password). You also need to know the type of email account you have (POP3 or IMAP) and the addresses of your service provider's incoming (POP3 or IMAP) email server and its outgoing (SMTP) email server.

   ■ For Internet newsgroups (Usenet), you need the name of your service provider's *news server* (also called an *NNTP server*) and whether you must log on to this server. If you do log on, you also need your logon name and password.

   ■ Whether your service provider provides an *Internet directory service* (often called *LDAP*—Lightweight Direct Access Protocol—service). If it does, you need the name of the *directory server* and whether you must log on to this server. If you do log on, you also need your logon name and password.

- If you're connecting over your company's network, whether that network uses a proxy server and, if so, the name of the proxy server.

- Whether the connection requires a specific modem setup (such as turning off compression).

2. Install your modem in Windows 98, and configure it to your liking. You'll find the relevant instructions in Chapter 26, "Getting Started with Modem Communications," in the section titled "Installing and Configuring a Modem."

3. Install Dial-Up Networking and configure the Dial-Up Adapter. (In Chapter 30, see the section "Setting Up Windows 98 for Dial-Up Networking.")

4. Install TCP/IP and make sure that TCP/IP is bound to the Dial-Up Adapter. (In Chapter 31, see "Installing the TCP/IP Protocol.")

5. Configure the Dial-Up Adapter's TCP/IP stack (the instructions are in the section "Configuring the TCP/IP Protocol" in Chapter 31). Alternatively, configure TCP/IP for the Dial-Up Networking connection you'll create for your ISP (in Chapter 31, see "Connection-Specific TCP/IP Settings").

6. Create and configure a Dial-Up Networking connection for your ISP. In particular, you probably need to configure the connection to display a terminal window after the connection is made. You use this window to enter your username, password, and possibly the connection type (PPP, SLIP, or dial-up). I showed you how to do all this in the section "Setting Up Windows 98 for Dial-Up Networking" in Chapter 30.

7. If you want to use the Dial-Up Scripting Tool, create the appropriate script for your logon and assign it to your Dial-Up Networking connection. (I explain how to do all this in Chapter 30, in the section "Using the Dial-Up Scripting Tool.")

8. Configure Outlook Express for your ISP email account. You'll find the details in Chapter 34, "Outlook Express and Internet Email."

That's it; you're ready for action on the Internet. From here, head to the section later in this chapter titled "Connecting to Your Service Provider" to run through the connection procedure.

A Note About WINSOCK.DLL

If you upgraded to Windows 98 over a Windows 3.*x* system that had an Internet connection installed, you might find that the connection no longer works in Windows 98. Similarly, you might install an Internet access program under Windows 98, set it up so that it works perfectly, and then find that it no longer works when you reboot Windows 98.

Both problems are related to the file that provides access to the TCP/IP protocol stack for Windows-based Internet applications. For 16-bit applications, this Windows socket (WinSock) support is provided by a file named WINSOCK.DLL. The problem is actually threefold:

■ When you install Dial-Up Networking, the TCP/IP protocol, or the IPX/SPX protocol, Windows 98 renames your existing WINSOCK.DLL file to WINSOCK.OLD and then copies its own version of WINSOCK.DLL.

■ If you install an Internet access program under Windows 98, the program will probably install its own version of WINSOCK.DLL. When you reboot, Windows 98 compares its DLL files with those in the Sysbckup subfolder (which you'll find in your main Windows 98 folder). If it finds a file that is different (such as WINSOCK.DLL), it "fixes the problem" by replacing the new file with the backup copy that exists in Sysbckup.

■ Some 16-bit WinSock applications aren't compatible with this new WINSOCK.DLL (and its supporting WinSock interface files).

Here's a list of programs known to experience problems with the new WINSOCK.DLL:

Chameleon

CompuServe Internet Dialer or CompuServe Net Launcher

FTP Software

Internet In a Box

Internet Office

Mosaic In a Box

NetCom Net Cruiser

Pipeline

Spry Air Series

Trumpet

To resolve this problem, you have two choices:

■ Connect to your ISP using Dial-Up Networking exclusively.

■ Copy the WINSOCK.OLD file into the folder that contains the program you're having problems with. Rename this WINSOCK.OLD to WINSOCK.DLL.

Starting the Internet Connection Wizard

If you don't feel like slogging through all the steps described earlier, the Internet Connection Wizard gives you an easier way to get your Windows 98 machine connected to the Internet. Note that you still need to know the various TCP/IP settings assigned by your ISP, as well as the other data mentioned earlier.

There are a couple of ways to launch the Internet Connection Wizard:

■ Open the icon named Connect to the Internet on your Windows 98 desktop. (This icon may not appear on the desktop, depending on the configuration of your system.)

- Open the icon named Internet Explorer on your Windows 98 desktop. (Note that this method works only once. After you've completed the Wizard, opening this icon runs Internet Explorer, Microsoft's World Wide Web browser.)
- Select Start | Programs | Internet Explorer | Connection Wizard.

The initial Wizard dialog box, shown in Figure 32.1, presents you with your first fork in the road. Here are the long-winded choices presented in this dialog box:

I want to sign up and configure my computer for a new Internet account: Activate this option if you don't have an existing Internet account.

I have an existing Internet account through my phone line or a local area network (LAN): Activate this option if you have an existing Internet account and you want to tell Windows 98 about it.

My computer is already set up for the Internet: Activate this option if you know you already have an Internet connection set up on your computer.

Make your choice and click Next >. The rest of this section assumes you selected the I Want to Sign Up and Configure My Computer for a New Internet Account option.

FIGURE 32.1.

Use this dialog box to tell the Wizard what route you want to take.

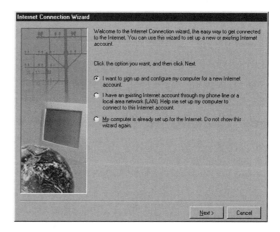

Setting Up a New Internet Account

At this point, you may trip over one of the following:

- If you see the Installing Files dialog box, it means Windows 98 needs to install the Dial-Up Adapter and a few other Internet-related files. In this case, click OK, follow the prompts that come your way, and then click OK when Windows 98 tells you it has to restart your machine.
- If you were negligent in your modem setup duties, Windows 98 will launch the Install New Modem Wizard so you can set up a modem. If this happens, refer to Chapter 26

to get the nitty-gritty on modem setup. Note that you may have to restart your computer when the dust clears.

■ If you have multiple modems set up on your computer, the Wizard will display the Choose Modem dialog box. Use the list box to pick out the modem you want to use for connecting to the Internet and then click OK.

■ If you already have TCP/IP installed and bound to the Dial-Up Adapter, and if you have the File and Print Sharing service bound to TCP/IP, the Wizard displays the warning shown in Figure 32.2. This setup is a major security risk, so Windows 98 will not let you set up an Internet connection under these circumstances. To find out more about this, see "TCP/IP and Internet Security" later in this chapter. For now, click OK to disable file and print sharing on the Dial-Up Adapter's TCP/IP protocol, and then click OK again when the Wizard tells you it will restart your computer.

FIGURE 32.2.
Windows 98 will not let you set up an Internet connection that uses file and print sharing.

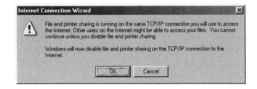

With all that out of the way, the Wizard dials your modem, connects to the Microsoft Internet Referral server, and downloads a list of the Internet service providers in your area. When that's done, the Wizard displays a window similar to the one shown in Figure 32.3. This window lists one or more providers and gives you some information about each one.

FIGURE 32.3.
You eventually see a list of service providers in your area.

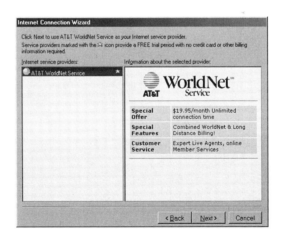

32

WINDOWS 98
AND THE INTERNET

When you decide which one you want, click Next >. The Wizard prompts you for your name, address, and phone number. The Wizard then connects you with the provider so you can complete the sign-up procedure. (This varies from provider to provider.)

Setting Up an Existing Internet Account

If you already have an Internet account, the Internet Connection Wizard makes it a breeze to set up a connection to the provider (or through your network gateway) in Windows 98. This section runs through the Wizard's dialog boxes.

After you select the I have an existing Internet account through my phone line or a local area network (LAN) option, the next dialog box tells you that you should use this Wizard only if you access the Internet through a service provider or a network. Click Next > to get to the dialog box shown in Figure 32.4, which presents you with a choice:

> **Connect using my phone line:** Activate this option if you'll be using your modem to connect to the Internet. Follow the instructions in the next section, "Connecting via a Modem."

> **Connect using my local area network (LAN):** Activate this option only if your computer is attached to a network and the network has an Internet connection. Head for the "Connecting via a Local Area Network" section, later in this chapter.

Make your selection and then click Next > to continue. As explained in the last section, the Wizard may now tell you it's going to install some files, or it may complain about your TCP/IP setup. Follow the instructions given earlier.

FIGURE 32.4.
Use this dialog box to let the Wizard know how you'll be connecting to the Internet.

Connecting via a Modem

If you'll be using a modem to connect to the Internet, the Wizard may ask you to choose one of your installed modems, or it may run the Install New Modem Wizard. Follow the onscreen prompts as described earlier.

If you've already created one or more Dial-Up Networking connectoids, the Wizard will also ask whether you want to use one of them for your Internet connection. This section assumes you need a new connectoid, so activate the Create a new dial-up connection option and click Next >.

The next wizard dialog box, shown in Figure 32.5, asks for the Area code, Telephone number, and Country name and code of the ISP's dial-in phone number. If the call isn't long distance, make sure you deactivate the Dial using the area code and country code check box. When you're done, click Next >.

FIGURE 32.5.

Use this dialog box to enter your provider's dial-in phone number.

The next item on the Wizard's to-do list is to ask for the User name and Password that you use to log on to your service provider (see Figure 32.6). Fill in the boxes and click Next >.

FIGURE 32.6.

Tell the Wizard the username and password that your service provider assigned to you.

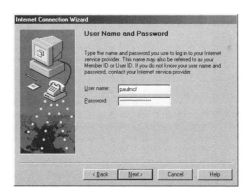

Now the Wizard wonders whether you want to work with the "advanced settings." Select Yes and click Next >. You then run through the following series of dialog boxes:

Connection Type: Whether your service provider uses a PPP or SLIP connection.

Logon Procedure: Whether you need to log on manually (that is, by typing your username and password at your service provider's logon screen). You can also assign a script to the connection.

IP Address: Whether your service provider assigns you an IP address automatically or whether you have a permanent IP address.

DNS Server Address: Whether the IP address of your service provider's DNS server is assigned automatically or whether they use a specific address.

You eventually end up at the Dial-Up Connection Name dialog box. Enter a name for your new connection and then click Next >.

Connecting via a Local Area Network

If you choose the Connect using my local area network option, the Wizard will take you through two more dialog boxes:

Proxy Server: Activate Yes if your network uses a proxy server or No if it doesn't.

Proxy Server Name: If you selected Yes in the Proxy Server dialog box, the Wizard will then prompt you for the name of the proxy server and the port.

Setting Up Your Internet Mail Account

The Wizard now asks whether you want to set up an Internet email account. Activate the Yes option if you do or the No option if you don't, and then click Next >.

If you told the Wizard you want to set up your email account, the following dialog boxes will come your way:

Your Name: This is the name that people see when you send them a message.

Internet E-mail Address: This is the email address that your service provider assigned to you.

E-mail Server Names: In this dialog box, you specify whether your provider's email server uses POP3 or IMAP. You also enter the names of the incoming mail server and the outgoing mail server (see Figure 32.7).

Internet Mail Logon: Enter the account name and password for your email account.

Friendly Name: Enter a name that you want to use to refer to this email account.

FIGURE 32.7.

This is one of the dialog boxes you have to deal with if you're setting up your Internet email account.

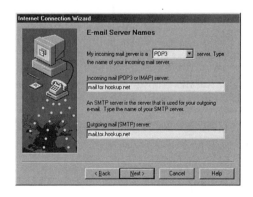

Setting Up Your Internet News Account

Next on the Wizard's agenda is whether you want to set up an Internet news account. Again, either activate Yes or No, and then click Next >.

If you told the Wizard you want to set up your news account, you'll be pestered with another series of dialog boxes:

Your Name: This is the name that people see when you send a message to a newsgroup.

Internet News E-mail Address: This is the email address that people on your newsgroups can use to send you a message. This will almost certainly be the same as the Internet email address you specified earlier.

AVOIDING SPAM

Unsolicited commercial email (otherwise known as *spam*) is a big problem on the Internet. Most folks receive dozens of these intrusive and annoying messages during the course of a week. Although there are many ways spam-spewers gather email addresses, one of the most popular is combing Usenet postings and extracting the sender's email address. Because of this, many savvy Usenetters use a fake email address for their news account.

Internet News Server Name: Enter the name of the news server that your provider uses (see Figure 32.8). If you have to log on to this server, activate the My news server requires me to log on check box.

Internet News Server Logon: If you have to log on to the news server, this dialog box enables you to enter the account name and password for your news account.

Friendly Name: Enter a name that you want to use to refer to this news account.

FIGURE 32.8.

This is one of the dialog boxes from the Internet news portion of the Wizard's show.

Setting Up Your Directory Service Account

Now the ever-curious Internet Connection Wizard asks you if you want to set up your Internet directory service. Again, select Yes or No, and then click Next >.

If you selected Yes in the previous wizard dialog box, it will come as absolutely no surprise that you have to trudge through another host of dialog boxes. Here's a summary:

Internet Directory Server Name: Enter the name of your service provider's Internet directory server. If you have to log on to this server, activate the My LDAP server requires me to log on check box.

Internet Directory Server Logon: If you have to log on to the directory server, use this dialog box to enter the account name and password for your directory server account.

Check E-mail Addresses: This dialog box wonders whether you want to check the email addresses you use in your outgoing messages with the email addresses in the Internet directory service. You probably want to select No here. However, if you're sure you want to perform this check, select Yes instead.

Friendly Name: Use this dialog box to type in the name that you want to use to refer to this Internet directory account.

Finishing Up

At long last, you're finally done! In the Complete Configuration dialog box, click Finish. If the Wizard prompts you to restart your computer, click Yes.

When you get back to Windows 98, you find a new connection in your Dial-Up Networking folder.

Changing the Connection Properties

If you need to adjust the connection settings down the road, you have two places to go:

■ For modem- and TCP/IP-related settings, open the Dial-Up Networking folder, highlight the connectoid, and then select File | Properties.

■ You can access all the connection settings by opening the Control Panel's Internet icon and then select the Connection tab in the properties sheet that appears (see Figure 32.9).

In the Connection group, click Connect to run the Internet Connection Wizard and create a new connection. You can also select the connection type: Connect to the Internet using a modem or Connect to the Internet using a local area network. If you select the former option, the Settings button becomes available. Clicking this button displays the Dial-Up Settings dialog box, shown in Figure 32.10. Here are the settings you get to work with:

FIGURE 32.9.

Use the Connection tab to change the settings for your Internet connection.

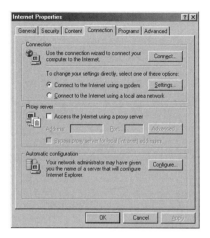

Use the following Dial-Up Networking connection: Use this list to select a different Dial-Up Networking connectoid. You can also click Add to create a new connectoid or click Properties to adjust the displayed connectoid.

Number of times to attempt connection: Sets the maximum number of dial attempts that Windows 98 will perform if it can't establish a connection.

Number of seconds to wait between attempts: Sets the number of seconds that Windows 98 delays before attempting the next connection.

Log on to this connection using the following information: These text boxes specify your logon data.

Disconnect if idle for *x* minutes: When this check box is activated, Windows 98 automatically disconnects you from the Internet after the connection has been idle for the number of minutes specified in the spinner. This is useful if you pay by the minute for your dial-up connection (or if your account is allowed only so many minutes before extra charges apply).

Connect automatically to update subscriptions: If you activate this check box, Windows 98 will connect to your service provider automatically in order to update any subscriptions you've defined with Internet Explorer. (I discuss subscriptions in the next chapter.)

Perform system security check before dialing: When this check box is activated, Windows 98 performs a security check before connecting. (This is the same TCP/IP-related security check that I mentioned earlier.) See "TCP/IP and Internet Security" later in this chapter for a detailed explanation of what Windows 98 checks and how you can safeguard your system.

When you're done, click OK to return to the Connection tab.

Figure 32.10.

Use this dialog box to adjust various parameters for your Internet modem connectoid.

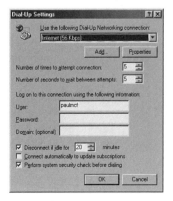

If you're connecting to the Internet through a LAN, you can configure a proxy server for extra security. A proxy server is a computer that processes Internet packets: All data heading out to the Internet and all data coming in from the Internet goes through the proxy server. This lets the proxy server filter this data selectively and thus prevent unauthorized access to the LAN.

If your LAN has a proxy server, activate the Access the Internet using a proxy server check box. Then enter the Address and Port number of the proxy server.

Clicking the Advanced button displays the Proxy Settings dialog box shown in Figure 32.11. This dialog box has two groups:

Servers: Use this group to specify multiple proxy server names and ports for different protocols.

Exceptions: If you want to access specific Internet or intranet resources (computers, domains, and IP addresses) without going through the proxy server, enter the appropriate values in this text box. Make sure you separate each value with a semicolon. Note, too, that you can use the asterisk (*) wildcard character. For example, `*.microsoft.com` gives you access to any host in the `microsoft.com` domain. Similarly, `200.100.50.*` gives you access to any host with an IP address that starts with 200.100.50.

Click OK to return to the Connection tab.

If you want to access intranet resources without going through the proxy server, be sure to activate the Bypass proxy server for local (Intranet) addresses check box.

Finally, the Automatic configuration group enables you to specify a server or file that contains configuration information for Internet Explorer. This configuration data includes browser settings, components that should be installed, proxy server settings, and more. Configuration information for Internet Explorer is created using the Internet Explorer Administration Kit, available from Microsoft's Web site:

`http://www.microsoft.com/ie/ieak/`

FIGURE 32.11.

Use the Proxy Settings dialog box to specify multiple proxy servers and proxy server exceptions.

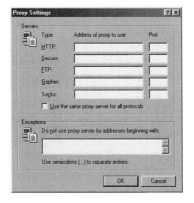

To set the name of the server or file that contains this data, click Configure, enter a URL in the Automatic Configuration dialog box (see Figure 32.12), and then click OK.

FIGURE 32.12.

Use this dialog box to enter the name of a server or file that provides configuration data for Internet Explorer.

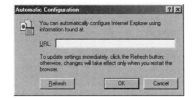

Connecting to Your Service Provider

With your Internet connection set up and ready for action, you can establish your Net session at any time. You have two ways to proceed:

- Open the appropriate Dial-Up Networking connection directly.
- Launch an Internet application and access a Net-based resource (such as a Web site or an FTP site). Windows 98 prompts you to initiate your Internet connection.

When you're connecting to your ISP, you may see the Post-Dial Terminal window, shown in Figure 32.13, where you can enter your logon options. Depending on the ISP (and whether you're using a script), you might have to enter some or all of the following information (if you just see a blank terminal window, try pressing Enter):

- Your username.
- Your password.
- The connection type. In some cases, you enter a command (such as ppp); in other cases, you select the connection type from a menu of choices.

When you've entered all your options, click the terminal window's Continue button or press F7. If you're establishing a SLIP connection, you need to fill in the dialog box shown in

Figure 32.14. Enter your dotted-decimal IP address (if the displayed address isn't correct for some reason) and then click OK.

FIGURE 32.13.

Connecting to a third-party ISP usually requires entering a few parameters in the terminal window.

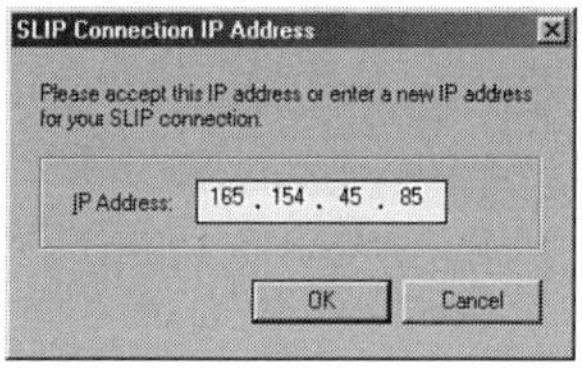

FIGURE 32.14.

You have to enter an IP address if you're establishing a SLIP connection.

TROUBLESHOOTING: GARBAGE CHARACTERS IN THE TERMINAL SCREEN

When you connect to your ISP, you might see garbage characters in the Post-Dial Terminal Screen. If you see these characters after you've logged on, you can ignore them. Simply click Continue, and your connection will be established normally. If, however, you see garbage characters as soon as the Post-Dial Terminal Screen appears, your ISP might not support your modem's compression. Open the properties sheet for the Dial-Up Networking connection you're using, click Configure, click Advanced in the Connection tab, and deactivate the Compress data check box.

TROUBLESHOOTING: YOU CAN'T ESTABLISH A CONNECTION

If you can't get a connection to your ISP, here are a few things to check:

■ If you have a PPP account, make sure that you're using the PPP server type.

■ If you have a SLIP account, check with your provider to see whether it's a SLIP or CSLIP connection. Also, be sure to enter the correct IP address in the SLIP Connection IP Address dialog box (refer to Figure 32.14).

■ Make sure that the Dial-Up Networking connection is using only the TCP/IP protocol. (In the properties sheet, display the Server Types tab and then deactivate the NetBEUI and IPX/SPX Compatible check boxes.)

■ While you're in the Server Types tab, try deactivating the Require encrypted password check box and the Require data encryption check box.

■ Use the PING utility that I described in the preceding chapter to check your TCP/IP settings.

■ Make sure that the modem's flow control matches what your ISP requires. For example, if the ISP requires hardware (RTS/CTS) flow control, make sure that your modem configuration doesn't specify software (XON/XOFF) flow control.

■ Some ISPs require that your modem's DTR signal be disabled. Use your modem manual to find the command that disables DTR (on many modems it's &D0). Open the properties sheet for the connection, click Configure, click Advanced in the Connection tab, and enter the command in the Extra settings text box.

■ If all else fails, sometimes a simple reboot will get Windows unstuck and enable you to make the connection.

32

WINDOWS 98
AND THE INTERNET

TCP/IP and Internet Security

Earlier in this chapter, I told you that Windows 98 performs a security check before connecting. Specifically, it checks to make sure that the TCP/IP protocol bound to the Dial-Up Adapter isn't also bound to the File and Print Sharing service.

Why is file and print sharing such a security risk? Because unless you're careful, folders and drives that you're sharing on your network can also be accessed by people on the Internet! In other words, if you bind file and print sharing to the Dial-Up Adapter's TCP/IP protocol, you extend your shared resources to the Internet as a whole. So it wouldn't be that hard for some total Net stranger to run amok in your files and folders.

Here's how people on the Net could access your shared resources:

■ They would need to be on a system running Microsoft Networking.

■ They would need to know the IP address and NetBIOS name of your computer.

■ They would need to add an entry in their LMHOSTS file that includes your IP address and NetBIOS name:

```
200.100.50.6 Biff
```

> ## LMHOSTS **IS SIMILAR TO** HOSTS
>
> LMHOSTS is similar to the HOSTS file I told you about in the preceding chapter. But whereas HOSTS mapped IP addresses to host names, LMHOSTS maps IP addresses to NetBIOS names. (This is the computer name you enter in the Identification tab in the Network properties sheet, as described in Chapter 28, "Setting Up Windows 98 for Networking.") You find a sample LMHOSTS file—named LMHOSTS.SAM—in your main Windows 98 folder.

Given these not-too-far-fetched conditions, the remote user could display a list of the resources being shared on your computer by entering the NET VIEW command at his or her DOS prompt:

```
NET VIEW \\NetBIOSName
```

Here, *NetBIOSName* is the NetBIOS name of your computer. This command displays a listing similar to this:

```
C:\>net view \\Biff
Shared resources at \\Biff

Sharename    Type          Comment
-------------------------------------------------------------
C            Disk          C'mon in and look around!
D            Disk          No password required!
H            Disk          CD-ROM (go ahead and start the program!)
The command was completed successfully.

C:\>
```

To map one of your resources to his computer, the person can use the NET USE command:

```
NET USE \\NetBIOSName\DriveLetter
```

Here, *DriveLetter* is the letter of the shared drive the person wants to map.

> ## MICROSOFT'S NET **COMMANDS**
>
> NET VIEW and NET USE are just two examples of the various NET commands available in Microsoft's network operating systems (including Windows 98). To see a complete list of these commands, enter net help at the DOS prompt.

To protect yourself, you should disable file and print sharing over the Dial-Up Adapter's TCP/IP protocol. If you use your LAN for Internet access, you need to disable file and print sharing for the network adapter's TCP/IP protocol. You can still use another protocol (such as NetBEUI) for sharing resources.

The only problem you might run into occurs if your network uses the TCP/IP protocol exclusively. In this case, it might be impractical to disable file and print sharing. Your alternative is to set up a reasonable level of security for the resources you share:

■ If you use share-level security, assign passwords to each shared resource. A remote user trying to access a shared resource has to enter the correct password.

■ If you use user-level security, your server will prevent access from any unauthorized interlopers. You should, however, make sure that you don't have The World or Guest with full access privileges to your shared folders.

A POOR MAN'S WAN

This apparent security breach I've just described can actually be a handy feature. By enabling TCP/IP over your Internet connection, you can set up a cheap wide area network (WAN) that gives remote users access to network resources. You just have to be sure to plan your security appropriately.

The Net Is Your Oyster

With your Internet connection up and running and the appropriate security measures in place, you're free to take full advantage of all the Net has to offer. To do that, you need the appropriate client applications, and the clients you use will depend on the Internet services you want to access. The various services—the World Wide Web, FTP, Telnet, Usenet, and so on—are separate pieces of the overall Internet puzzle, so they require separate applications. (Some applications, though—Web browsers, mostly—are making a bid for becoming the "Swiss army knife" of the Internet by offering access to several different services in one package.)

Many service providers supply their customers with collections of Internet programs. This is an easy way to get started, because you can usually download everything you need from the ISP's site with a single command, and most of the programs will be preconfigured with the appropriate options for your ISP.

Fortunately, Windows 98 ships with a wide array of Internet appliances. Here's a rundown:

Internet Explorer: This is the Windows 98 World Wide Web browser. See Chapter 33, "Exploring the Web with Internet Explorer."

Outlook Express: This program combines both Internet email and Usenet newsreading. See Chapter 34, "Outlook Express and Internet Email," and Chapter 35, "Outlook Express and Usenet News."

Microsoft NetMeeting: You can use this program to have voice and text conversations, send files, and collaborate on applications over the Internet. See Chapter 36, "Remote Collaboration with Microsoft NetMeeting."

FrontPage Express: You can use this program to create your own Web pages. See Chapter 37, "Web Page Publishing with Windows 98."

> **Web Page Publishing Wizard:** This Wizard enables you to upload your HTML pages, Web page graphics, and other files to your Web server. I also cover this program in Chapter 37.

> **ftp:** This is a command-line utility for transferring files via the FTP protocol. See the next section of this chapter, "Using FTP for Internet File Transfers."

> **Telnet:** This is a graphical terminal emulation client for connecting to remote Internet computers. See "Using Telnet for Remote Internet Sessions," later in this chapter.

> **Microsoft Chat:** This is a chat client that enables you to have text conversations using semi-animated characters via Internet-based chat servers. I don't cover this program in this book, but it's very simple to use. To try it out, select Start | Programs | Internet Explorer | Microsoft Chat.

If you want to use any other Windows Internet software (such as a graphical FTP client), the best place to start is the Consummate Winsock Applications Web site at the following address:

```
http://cws.internet.com/
```

Using FTP for Internet File Transfers

FTP sits just above TCP in the TCP/IP food chain. FTP's purpose in life is to coordinate file transfers to and from remote Internet sites. If you're just starting out on the Internet, for example, you can use FTP to download programs that enable you to access the services that interest you.

INTERNET EXPLORER AND FTP

If you just want to download files, you can use Internet Explorer. To do so, enter a URL that uses the following syntax:

```
ftp://domain/directory/filename
```

Here, *domain* is the domain name of the FTP server, *directory* is the full path of the directory you want to work with, and *filename* is the name of the file you want to download. If you leave off *filename*, Internet Explorer displays the contents of *directory*.

To initiate these transfers, you need an FTP client. This section shows you how to use the `ftp` command-line utility that ships with Windows 98. I won't explore this utility in any great depth because I'm assuming that you want to get a graphical FTP client at the earliest opportunity. The Internet has several free FTP clients designed for Windows, and the Consummate Winsock Applications site lists several at the following URL:

```
http://cws.internet.com/32ftp.html
```

The idea behind the ftp utility (and, indeed, any FTP client) is that you connect to a remote host that's running an FTP server and then use various commands to change directories, display files, and transfer files. It's a lot like working with files in a DOS session (which is why you likely want to get a graphical FTP client!).

Here's the syntax for Windows 98's ftp utility:

```
ftp [-v] [-n] [-i] [-d] [-g] [host] [-s: filename]
```

-v	Suppresses the display of the remote server's responses.
-n	Turns off autologon on initial connection.
-i	Turns off interactive prompting during multiple-file transfers.
-d	Enables debugging, displaying all FTP commands passed between the client and the server.
-g	Disables filename "globbing," which permits the use of wildcard characters in local file and pathnames.
host	Specifies the host name or IP address of the remote host to which you want to connect.
-s: *filename*	Specifies a text file containing FTP commands that will run automatically after the ftp utility starts. You can use this switch to automate your FTP sessions.

For example, the following command starts the ftp utility and initiates a connection to Microsoft's FTP site (ftp.microsoft.com):

```
ftp ftp.microsoft.com
```

Note that all the parameters in the ftp command are optional. If you like, you can just enter the ftp command by itself to start a local FTP session. This replaces the usual DOS prompt with the FTP prompt:

```
ftp>
```

From here, you can use the open command to start an FTP session with a remote server:

```
ftp> open ftp.microsoft.com
```

After you're connected to the remote computer, you are asked for a username and password. In most cases, you won't have an account on the remote machine, so you won't have a username or a password. This doesn't mean you're out of luck, however. Most FTP servers are *anonymous FTP sites*, which means they offer public access to their files. With anonymous FTP access, you don't need a username or password to access the remote computer. The remote machine accepts anonymous as your username and your email address as the password. After that, you can access files on the remote machine, although your wanderings are usually restricted to one or more public directories.

32

WINDOWS 98 AND THE INTERNET

A typical FTP session progresses in the following way:

1. Start FTP and connect to the host computer.
2. Change to the directory you want to work with.
3. Set some file transfer options.
4. Download (or upload) the file or files.
5. End the FTP session.

Table 32.1 summarizes the ftp commands you use most often during each step.

Table 32.1. A summary of frequently used ftp commands.

Command	Description
Working with Directories	
cd *remote_directory*	Changes the directory of the remote computer to *remote_directory*.
cd .. or cdup	Changes the directory of the remote computer to the parent of the current directory.
lcd *local_directory*	Changes the directory of the local computer to *local_directory*.
ls	Displays a short listing of the files in the current remote directory.
ls -l or dir	Displays a long listing of the files in the current remote directory.
mkdir *new_directory*	Creates the directory *new_directory* on the remote computer.
pwd	Prints (displays) the name of the current working directory on the remote computer.
rmdir *remote_directory*	Removes *remote_directory* from the remote computer.
Setting File Transfer Options	
ascii	Sets FTP to ASCII mode for transferring text files.
bell	Toggles the bell setting on and off. When it's on, ftp beeps your computer's speaker after each file is transferred.
binary	Sets FTP to binary mode for transferring binary files.
hash	Toggles display of # symbols for each data block transferred.
prompt	Toggles confirmation prompt for multiple-file transfers. The default setting is on.
status	Displays the current option settings.

Command	*Description*
	Working with Files
delete *rfile*	Deletes *rfile* from the remote computer.
get *rfile* [*lfile*]	Downloads *rfile* to your local computer and stores it as *lfile*.
mget *rfile1* [*rfile2*...]	Downloads the remote files *rfile1*, *rfile2*, and so on to your local computer.
mput *lfile1* [*lfile2*...]	Uploads the local files *lfile1*, *lfile2*, and so on from your local computer to the remote machine.
put *lfile rfile*	Uploads *lfile* from your computer to the remote machine and stores it as *rfile*.
rename *rfile new_name*	Renames *rfile* to *new_name* on the remote computer.
	Ending the FTP Session
bye or quit	Quits the ftp program and returns you to the DOS prompt.
close or disconnect	Ends the FTP session with the remote computer and returns you to the ftp> prompt.

32

WINDOWS 98
AND THE INTERNET

USE BINARY MODE FOR BINARY FILE TRANSFERS

Before downloading a binary file to your computer, be sure to run the binary command. Downloading a binary file while ftp is in ASCII mode will damage the file.

TURN OFF PROMPTS WITH MGET

If you're using the mget command to retrieve multiple files, be sure to use the prompt command first to turn off prompting. This will save you from having to answer the confirmation prompt for each file.

Using Telnet for Remote Internet Sessions

The command-line nature of the ftp utility will probably doom that program to the dustbin of unused Windows 98 accessories. After all, why wrestle with cryptic commands when excellent graphical clients are available that do everything ftp does, and more besides?

By contrast, Windows 98's other Internet utility—the Telnet program—will likely find a permanent place in most people's Internet tool chest. Not that the Telnet program is all that spectacular—some third-party clients have more features—but it's certainly more than adequate for those few times you need to use the telnet protocol.

What is the telnet protocol? It's another member of the TCP/IP suite. In this case, telnet is a terminal emulation protocol that lets you log on to remote systems and use their services as though you were sitting at a local terminal. For example, you can use telnet to log on to a library's server and access its card catalog database.

Starting the Telnet Client

To run the Windows 98 Telnet client, either open the `TELNET.EXE` file in your main Windows 98 folder, or select Start | Run, enter `telnet`, and click OK. You see the Telnet window, shown in Figure 32.15. The next few sections show you how to set preferences, connect to a remote host, and log your sessions.

FIGURE 32.15.

You can use Windows 98's Telnet client to connect to remote hosts.

Setting Telnet Preferences

Before connecting to a remote host, the Telnet client offers a few preferences you can use to customize your sessions. Select Terminal | Preferences to display the Terminal Preferences dialog box, shown in Figure 32.16.

FIGURE 32.16.

Use this dialog box to customize your Telnet sessions.

Here's a look at the various options you can work with:

Local Echo: The remote system might not "echo" the characters you enter, so you won't see anything onscreen as you type. In this case, you should activate the Local Echo check box so that you can see your typing. If you see double characters while you're typing, you should deactivate this check box.

Blinking Cursor: If you activate this check box, the cursor that tells you where your next typed character will appear blinks on and off.

Block Cursor: This check box toggles the cursor between a block and a line.

VT100 Arrows: This option determines how Telnet handles your keyboard's arrow keys. When the VT100 Arrows check box is activated, Telnet sends arrow keystrokes to the remote host; when it's deactivated, Telnet doesn't send the keystrokes but instead uses them to navigate locally.

Buffer Size: This text box specifies the number of lines of text from the remote host that Telnet stores in its buffer. You can use the window scrollbar to see the lines stored in this buffer.

USE A LARGER BUFFER SIZE

Some remote hosts will send you a large chunk of text (say, an introductory message) in one shot. In some cases, this text might contain more than 25 lines, so the first part of the text won't be preserved in the Telnet client's buffer. To prevent this situation, use a larger buffer size. I'd suggest starting with 50 lines and moving up as you need to (buffers of 100 lines are quite common).

Emulation: These options determine the type of terminal emulation Telnet uses with the remote host. The setting you use depends on the host, but you'll find that VT100/ ANSI should suffice for most hosts.

Fonts: Use this button to display the Font dialog box, from which you can choose the font you want the Telnet client to use when displaying text from the remote host.

Background Color: This button displays the Color dialog box, in which you can select the background color of the Telnet window. Note that if you select a darker color, you probably want to use the Fonts button to specify a lighter color for the text.

Click OK to put your new settings into effect.

Connecting to a Remote Host

When you're ready to initiate a telnet session, select Connect | Remote System. Telnet displays the Connect dialog box, shown in Figure 32.17. You need to specify three options for each connection:

Host Name: Use this combo box to specify the host to which you want to connect. You can enter a fully qualified domain name or an IP address. After you've connected to at least one host, your previous selections appear in the drop-down list.

Port: Use this combo box to choose the port to use for the connection. Most systems use the telnet port, but you can choose one of the other ports in the drop-down list or enter a specific port number.

TermType: If the remote host uses TermType subnegotiation, use this drop-down list to specify the terminal type string you want Telnet to send to the host.

FIGURE 32.17.

Use this dialog box to fill in your connection options.

After you enter your options, click Connect to initiate the telnet session.

COMMAND-LINE CONNECTIONS

If you have a telnet host that you use frequently, you can connect to the host directly by specifying the host name (and the port, if necessary) along with the TELNET command. Here's the syntax:

```
telnet host [port]
```

You might want to consider creating a shortcut for this remote host on the desktop or in one of the Start menus.

After Telnet makes the connection to the remote host, you'll likely have to log on. How you do this depends on the host. In Figure 32.18, for example, I logged on using www so that I could access a command-line World Wide Web browser (called Lynx) at the University of Kansas.

DELETING CHARACTERS

If you enter the wrong character while typing in the Telnet window, you might not be able to erase it with the Backspace key. In this case, try pressing Ctrl+H or Ctrl+Backspace to expunge the offending character.

FIGURE 32.18.

After the connection is established, you'll probably have to log on to the remote telnet server.

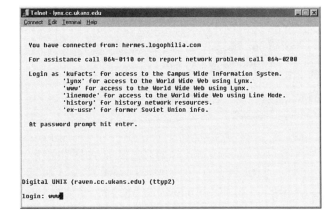

Logging a Telnet Session

To save the text that is displayed in a telnet session, the Telnet client gives you two choices:

■ For text that has already been displayed, drag the mouse over the text to highlight it and then select Edit | Copy. Alternatively, you can choose Edit | Select All to highlight all the text in the window and then copy it to the Clipboard.

■ For text that hasn't been displayed yet, select Terminal | Start Logging, specify a name and location for the log file in the Open log file dialog box, and click Open. All text that appears in the Telnet window will also be saved to the log file. When you're done, select Terminal | Stop Logging to close the file. Use Notepad or some other text editor to view the log file.

Disconnecting from the Remote Host

When your session is complete, select Connect | Disconnect.

Summary

This chapter showed how Windows 98 and the Internet get along. As you saw, they get along just fine, thank you. I began by summarizing what you've learned in previous chapters regarding modems, Dial-Up Networking, and TCP/IP, and then I distilled the information into a procedure for getting Internet access. I also showed you how to use the Internet Connection Wizard to set up both a new and existing Internet account. Other topics in this chapter include the relationship between TCP/IP and Internet security and how to use ftp and Telnet.

One more time, here's a list of chapters that contain all the information you need to get an Internet connection up and running in Windows 98:

■ For modem setup and configuration, connect to Chapter 26, "Getting Started with Modem Communications."

■ If you have a TCP/IP network with an Internet connection, getting your computer hooked up to the network and installing TCP/IP are all that's required to access the Net from your PC. For the networking part, see Chapter 28, "Setting Up Windows 98 for Networking."

■ For dial-up Internet connections, the key piece of Windows 98 technology is Dial-Up Networking. I gave you the full scoop in Chapter 30, "Remote Computing with Dial-Up Networking."

■ Whichever kind of connection you use, you can surf the Internet without running a TCP/IP stack on your computer. I explained TCP/IP in glorious detail in Chapter 31, "Implementing TCP/IP for Internet and Intranet Connections."

■ The next piece of the Windows 98 Internet puzzle is Internet Explorer, Microsoft's Web browser. You'll take it for a test drive in Chapter 33, "Exploring the Web with Internet Explorer."

■ See Chapter 34, "Outlook Express and Internet Email," and Chapter 35, "Outlook Express and Usenet News," to learn about Windows 98's email and Usenet client.

■ If you'd like to cobble together your own Web pages, Chapter 37, "Web Page Publishing with Windows 98," shows you how.

Exploring the Web with Internet Explorer

> *For my part, I travel not to go anywhere, but to go. I travel for travel's sake. The great affair is to move.*
>
> —*Robert Louis Stevenson*

You saw in Chapter 5, "Web Integration and the Active Desktop," that Windows 98's most famous (and, in some circles at least, most controversial) feature is the marriage between the Internet Explorer browser and the Windows interface. This "Web integration" enables you to navigate your local drives using more or less the same methods you use to navigate the World Wide Web.

However, an arm-in-arm relationship with Windows isn't the only trick that Internet Explorer has up its digital sleeve. The 4.*x* version of Microsoft's browser, released originally in August 1997, boasts many new features, including support for channels, the capability of setting up Web site subscriptions, support for dynamic HTML, enhanced security, improved history and search features, many new customization options, and numerous user interface improvements.

This chapter shows you how to use Internet Explorer to traverse the highways and byways of the World Wide Web. Besides extensive coverage of all the new features, I also show you how to navigate links, deal with files and multimedia, and set up Internet Explorer to your liking.

Starting Internet Explorer

As I've said, Internet Explorer is an integral part of the Windows 98 world, so after you've defined an Internet connection (as discussed in the previous chapter), you're ready to start your Web journeys. First, establish the connection to your Internet service provider. Then use any of the following methods to start Internet Explorer:

New to
98

- In the Quick Launch toolbar, click the Launch the Internet Explorer Browser icon.
- Launch the desktop's Internet Explorer icon.
- Select Start | Programs | Internet Explorer | Internet Explorer.

A Tour of the Internet Explorer Screen

When you crank up Internet Explorer, you see the Internet Start Web page, which will be similar to the one shown in Figure 33.1. (The content of this page changes from day to day.) This first page that appears is called the *home page.*

Here's a summary of the main features of this screen:

Title bar: The top line of the screen shows you the title of the current Web page.

Standard buttons: These toolbar buttons give you point-and-click access to some of Internet Explorer's main features.

FIGURE 33.1.
You see this Web page when you launch Internet Explorer.

Title bar   Links bar   Standard buttons

Address bar

Status bar

Current zone   Hypertext links   Content area

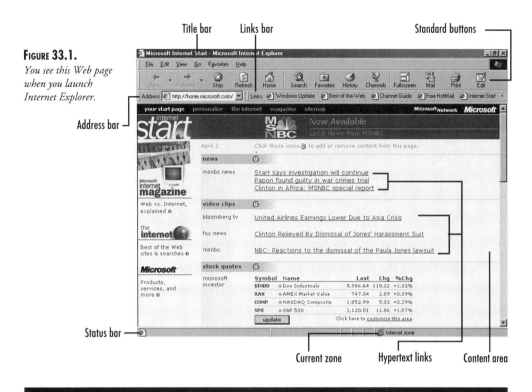

HIDING (AND SHOWING) INTERNET EXPLORER'S BARS

If you prefer to hide any of the Internet Explorer toolbars (because, for example, you want more screen real estate), you have two choices:

■ Select View | Toolbars.

■ Right-click a toolbar. (For the Address bar, right click Address; for the Links bar, right-click Links.)

In the menu that appears, the Standard Buttons, Address Bar, and Links commands toggle the toolbars on and off.

You can also eke out a bit more screen room by removing the text labels on the Standard buttons. To do so, right-click any toolbar and then deactivate the Text Labels command.

Note, too, that you can toggle the status bar on and off by selecting the View | Status Bar command.

Links bar: This toolbar contains buttons that represent five predefined Web sites that you can try out to get your Web feet wet. Here's a summary of each link:

■ **Best of the Web:** If you're not sure where to start your Web journey, this link can help. Clicking this button takes you to the Start Exploring page, which contains a large set of links arranged by category, as well as a few "showcase" links.

■ **Channel Guide:** This button takes you to the Channel Guide page, from which you can check out a large number of channels that work with Internet Explorer 4.*x*. See "Channel Surfing: Internet Explorer's Channels," later in this chapter.

■ **Customize Links:** This button takes you to a page that gives you brief instructions on how to give the Links bar a makeover. I talk about these techniques later in this chapter in the section titled "Customizing the Links Bar."

■ **Internet Explorer News:** Click this button to get the latest Internet Explorer news and updates.

■ **Internet Start:** This link returns you to the home page.

Address bar: This area shows you the URL (Uniform Resource Locator; see the next Note) of the current page. You also can enter URLs into the Address bar (as explained later).

Content area: This is the area below the Address bar that takes up the bulk of the Internet Explorer screen. It's where the body of each Web page is displayed. You can use the vertical scroll bar (and, occasionally, the horizontal scroll bar) to see more of the current document.

Status bar: This bar tells you Internet Explorer's current status, displays a description of the links you point to, and tells you the progress of the current Internet Explorer operation (such as downloading a file).

Hypertext links: Links to other documents (or to other places in the same document) are displayed underlined and in a different color. When you point to a link, Internet Explorer does two things: It changes the mouse pointer to a hand with a pointing finger, and in the Status bar it displays the address of the document the link will take you to. If you want to display that page, you just click the link text. Note, too, that although most Web page graphics are used just for show, some of them are used as links. In some cases, the image contains several different "hot spots." These types of graphics are called *image maps* and clicking different areas of the map takes you to different pages.

Current zone: This status bar text shows you the *security zone* of the current Web page. You can use these zones to define appropriate security levels for page content. See "Security Options," later in this chapter.

A FEW WORDS FROM THE WEB

Like all of the Internet's services, the Web has its own vernacular and acronyms. To make sure that we're reading from the same Web page, so to speak, here's a glossary of some common Web terms:

form   A Web document used for gathering information from the reader. Most forms have at least one text field where you can enter text data (such as your name or the keywords for a search). More sophisticated forms also include check boxes, option buttons, and command buttons.

HTML (Hypertext Markup Language)   The encoding scheme used to format a Web document. The various HTML tags define hypertext links, reference graphics files, and designate nontext items, such as buttons and check boxes.

HTTP (Hypertext Transfer Protocol)   The protocol used by the Web to transfer hypertext documents and other Net resources.

hyperlink Another name for a hypertext link.

URL (Uniform Resource Locator)   An Internet addressing scheme that spells out the exact location of a Net resource. Most URLs take the following form:

```
protocol://host.domain/directory/file.name
```

protocol	The TCP/IP protocol to use for retrieving the resource (such as http or ftp)
host.domain	The domain name of the host computer where the resource resides
directory	The host directory that contains the resource
file.name	The filename of the resource

Web server   A program that responds to requests from Web browsers to retrieve resources. This term is also used to describe the computer that runs the server program.

Navigating with Internet Explorer

Now that you're familiar with the lay of the Internet Explorer land, you can start using it to navigate sites. The next few sections take you through the various ways you can use Internet Explorer to wend your way through the Web.

Following the Links

As I've said, Internet Explorer displays hypertext links in an underlined font that's a different color from the rest of the text. To follow one of these links, you have three choices:

- Click it with the mouse. (Image maps work the same way: Position the mouse pointer over the portion of the map you want to see and then click.)

- Right-click the link and choose Open.
- Right-click the link and choose Open in New Window. This command spawns a new Internet Explorer window and opens the link URL in that window.

A NEW WINDOW ON INTERNET EXPLORER

You can open another Internet Explorer window at any time by selecting File | New | Window or by pressing Ctrl+N.

Here are a few notes about working with links in Internet Explorer:

- To find the address of the document that will open when you click a link, place the mouse pointer over the link, and the address will appear in the status bar. (If the status bar is hidden, you can also see the address of the link's URL by right-clicking the link and clicking Properties in the context menu.)

- To copy the link's URL (to reference the URL in an email message, for example), right-click the link and select Copy Shortcut from the context menu. This copies the URL to the Clipboard.

- If you select a link and then change your mind (or if a link is busy loading large graphics or animation files and you don't want to wait), you can stop the download by selecting View | Stop, by pressing Esc, or by clicking the Stop button on the toolbar.

- If you select a link and some of the objects don't load properly, you can reload the page by selecting View | Refresh, by pressing F5, or by clicking the toolbar's Refresh button.

- To email a link shortcut to someone, click the link to open the page and then select File | Send | Page By Email. A new email message window appears, and the message body contains a shortcut that points to the page's URL. (The messaging system used is the default for your system. You can specify the system in Internet Explorer's Options dialog box. See the section "Programs Options" later in this chapter.) Specify a recipient and then send the message. When the recipient gets the message, he or she can double-click the shortcut to load the Web page.

Entering a URL

If you want to head to a particular Web site, you can specify a URL by using any of the following methods:

- Click inside the Address bar, delete the current URL, type the one you want, and press Enter. One of the welcome interface enhancements found with Internet Explorer 4.*x* is called AutoComplete. This feature watches what you type in the Address bar and tries to match this with a URL you've visited previously. If it finds a match, Internet Explorer completes some or all of the URL. For example, if you type ho in the Address bar, Internet Explorer will complete the address as `home.microsoft.com`, as shown in Figure 33.2.

FIGURE 33.2.

As you type within the Address bar, Internet Explorer tries to automatically complete your address.

■ Select File | Open or press Ctrl+O. In the Open Internet Address dialog box that appears (see Figure 33.3), type your URL in the Open text box. Click OK when you're done.

FIGURE 33.3.

Use this dialog box to enter the URL you want to see.

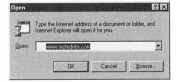

■ From Windows 98, select Start | Run. Enter the URL in the Run dialog box and click OK.

■ If you want to open an HTML file that resides on your hard disk or on your LAN, select File | Open, click the Browse button, highlight the file in the Open dialog box, and click Open.

SHORTER URLS

If the URL you want to see is a Web page, you can leave off the `http://` part. Internet Explorer assumes that an address that's missing the protocol is a Web page, so it appends `http://` automatically.

Retracing Your Steps

After you've started leaping through the Web's cyberspace, you'll often want to head back to a previous site, or even to your home page. (The Internet Start site is the default home page, but I'll show you later how to designate any URL as your home page.) Here's a rundown of the various techniques you can use to move to and fro in Internet Explorer:

■ To go back to the previous document, click the Back button on the toolbar, select Go | Back, or press Alt+left arrow.

■ After you've gone back to a previous document, you can move ahead to the next document by clicking the Forward button on the toolbar, selecting Go | Forward, or pressing Alt+right arrow.

■ Both the Back and Forward buttons do double duty as drop-down lists. When you click the drop-down arrow to the right of each button, Internet Explorer displays a list of the sites you've visited (see Figure 33.4). You can then click the site you want and Internet Explorer will take you straight there. Note that these lists are cleared when you return to the home page.

FIGURE 33.4.

The Back and Forward buttons contain lists of the sites you've visited.

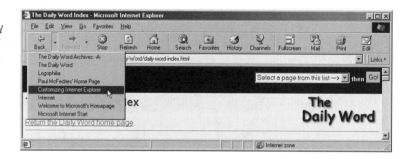

■ To return to the Internet Start page (or whatever page you've designated as your home page), either click the Home toolbar button or select Go | Home Page.

Creating a Shortcut to a URL

Another way to navigate Web sites via Internet Explorer is to create shortcuts that point to the appropriate URLs. To do this, use either of the following techniques:

■ Copy the URL to the Clipboard, create a new shortcut as described in Chapter 14, "File and Folder Tricks and Techniques," and then paste the URL into the Command line text box.

■ You can create a shortcut for the currently displayed page by using the page icon that appears in the Address bar (to the left of the address). Just drag this icon and drop it on the desktop (or whatever folder you want to use to store the shortcuts).

■ You can create a shortcut for any hypertext link by dragging the link text from the page.

After your shortcut is in place, you can open the Web site by launching the shortcut's icon.

SHORTCUTS ARE TEXT FILES

Internet shortcuts are simple text files that use the URL extension. They contain only the address of the Internet site, as in the following example:

```
[Internet Shortcut]
http://www.microsoft.com/
```

If you need to make changes to that address, it's possible to edit the shortcut by opening the URL file in Notepad.

The Handy History Bar

You saw in the last section how you can click the Back and Forward buttons to follow your own Web footsteps. However, Internet Explorer wipes those lists clean when you return to the home page or exit the program. What do you do when you want to revisit a site from a previous session? Happily, Internet Explorer keeps track of the addresses of all the pages you perused for the last 20 days.

New to **98**

The list of these pages is stored in a special screen area called the History bar, and you can view it using either of the following methods:

- Click the History button in the toolbar.
- Select the View | Explorer Bar | History command.

You then see the History bar on the left side of the window, as shown in Figure 33.5. To bring a site into view, follow these steps:

1. Click the day you want to work with. Internet Explorer displays a list of the domains you visited on that day.

2. Click the domain of the Web site that contains the page you want to see. Internet Explorer "opens" the domain to reveal all the pages you visited within that site.

3. Click the name of the page you want. Internet Explorer displays a cached version of the page in the right side of the content area.

Using the Search Bar

The navigation approaches you've tried so far have encompassed the two extremes of Web surfing: clicking on links randomly to see what happens, and entering addresses to display specific sites. However, what if you're looking for information on a particular topic, but you don't know any appropriate addresses and you don't want to waste time clicking aimlessly around the Web? In this case, you want to put the Web to work for you. That is, you want to rev up one of the Web's search engines to track down sites that contain the data you're looking for.

New to **98**

FIGURE 33.5.

The History bar keeps track of all the Web addresses you called on in the last 20 days.

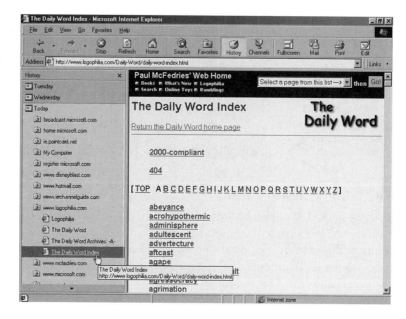

Conveniently, Internet Explorer contains a special Search bar that gives you easy access to a few of the Web's best search engines. Here's how you use this feature to perform a search:

1. Either click the toolbar's Search button or select the View | Explorer Bar | Search command. Internet Explorer adds a Search screen on the left side of the content area. (You may see a Security Warning dialog box asking whether you want to install the Internet Explorer Search Enhancements control. If so, click Yes.)

2. The Search bar usually displays a random search engine (this is called the Provider-of-the-day engine; see Figure 33.6). To use a different search engine, click Choose a Search Engine.

3. How you run the search depends on which search engine you have displayed. However, in all cases there is a text box that you use to enter a keyword (or two) that represents the type of site you want to find.

4. When you've entered your search text, click the Submit button. (This button may have a different name—such as Search, Find, Seek, or Go Get It—depending on the search engine.)

5. At this point, Internet Explorer may display a Security Alert dialog box. This is just a warning that when you submit data to a site, other people may be able to view the data. That's no problem here, so click Yes.

6. The search engine will rummage through its database of Web sites and then it will display a list of sites that contain the word or words you entered (if any). If so, click any of the offered links to check out the page. If no matches are found, repeat steps 4 and 5 using different search terms.

FIGURE 33.6.

Windows 98's Internet Explorer has a new Search bar that gives you access to some of the Web's top search engines.

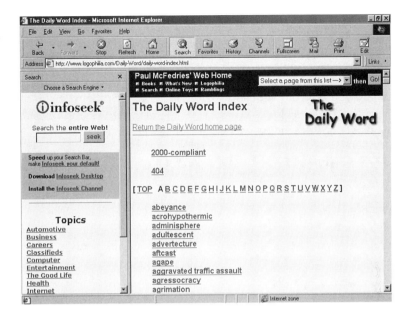

The Search bar is a quick and easy way to scour the Web's nooks and crannies for information. If you still can't find what you want, however, Internet Explorer can take you to a page that gives you more search options. To get there, select the Go | Search the Web command. (For best viewing, you should close the Search bar either by clicking the Search toolbar button or by selecting the View | Explorer Bar | None command.) The page that appears will be similar to the one shown in Figure 33.7.

FIGURE 33.7.

The Go | Search the Web command displays this page of searching solutions.

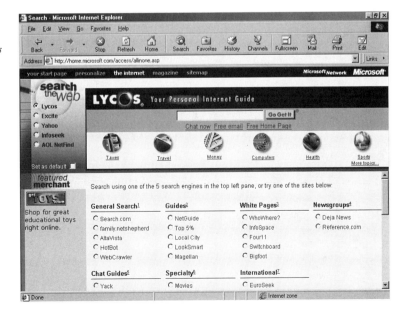

The frame on the left gives you access to the five search engines you worked with in the Search bar. When you select one of these engines, the top of the right frame gives you a slightly more advanced version of the search engine's features.

The bottom part of the right frame lists a few search categories. These are useful if you want to narrow your search. For example, if you're looking for something related to music, your best bet is to activate the Music option in the Specialty category. Whatever you pick, Internet Explorer displays the appropriate search form at the top of the page.

The Favorites Folder: Sites to Remember

The sad truth is that much of what you see on the Web will be utterly forgettable and not worth a second look. However, there are all kinds of gems out there waiting to be uncovered—sites you want to visit regularly. Instead of memorizing the appropriate URLs, jotting them down on sticky notes, or plastering your desktop with shortcuts, you can use Internet Explorer's handy Favorites feature to keep track of your choice sites.

The Favorites feature is really just a folder (you find it in your main Windows 98 folder) that you use to store Internet shortcuts. The advantage of using the Favorites folder as opposed to any other folder is that you can add, view, and link to the Favorites folder shortcuts directly from Internet Explorer.

Adding a Shortcut to the Favorites Folder

When you find a site that you'd like to declare as a favorite, follow these steps:

1. Select the Favorites | Add To Favorites command. The Add Favorite dialog box appears.

2. This dialog box asks whether you want to subscribe to the page. I'll hold off on this subscription business until later in this chapter (see "Setting Up Subscriptions"). For now, make sure the No, just add the page to my favorites option is activated.

3. The Name text box displays the title of the page. This is the text that appears later when you view the list of your favorites. Feel free to edit this text if you like.

4. Internet Explorer enables you to set up subfolders to hold related favorites. If you don't want to bother with this, skip to step 7. Otherwise, click the Create in button to expand the dialog box as shown in Figure 33.8.

5. To create a new folder, click New Folder, type the name of the folder in the dialog box that shows up, and then click OK. Windows 98 takes you back to the expanded Add Favorite dialog box.

6. Click the folder you want to use to store the favorite.

7. Click OK.

FIGURE 33.8.

Use this dialog box to add a shortcut to the Favorites folder.

Viewing the Favorites Folder

If you want to work with the Favorites folder directly, select Favorites | Organize Favorites. Figure 33.9 shows the Organize Favorites window that appears. From here, you can rename shortcuts, delete shortcuts, and create new subfolders to organize your shortcuts. Click Close when you're done.

FIGURE 33.9.

The Favorites folder stores your Internet shortcuts.

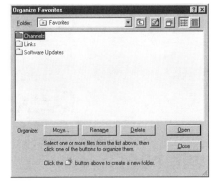

33

EXPLORING THE
WEB WITH IN-
TERNET EXPLORER

EXPLORING THE FAVORITES FOLDER

You can also work with the Favorites folder in Explorer or My Computer. Just open your main Windows 98 folder and highlight the Favorites subfolder.

Opening an Internet Shortcut from the Favorites Folder

The purpose of the Favorites folder, of course, is to give you quick access to the sites you visit regularly. To link to one of the shortcuts in your Favorites folder, you have three choices:

■ In Internet Explorer, the Favorites menu contains the complete list of your Favorites folder shortcuts. To link to a shortcut, pull down this menu and select the shortcut you want.

■ Click the Favorites toolbar button, or select View | Explorer Bar | Favorites, to display the Favorites bar, as shown in Figure 33.10. Click a link in the Favorites bar.

■ In the taskbar, select Start | Favorites and then click the favorite you want from the submenu that appears.

FIGURE 33.10.

The Favorites bar keeps your favorite links visible at all times.

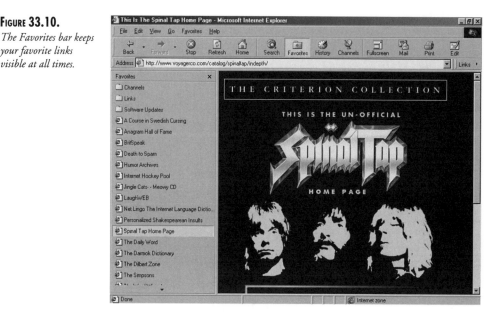

Dealing with Files

As you click your way around the Web, you find that some links don't take you to other pages but instead are tied directly to a file. In this case, you see the dialog box shown in Figure 33.11, which gives you two ways to proceed:

■ If you want to view the file (for example, if you want to open a text file in Notepad), select the Open this file from its current location option and click OK.

■ If you prefer to download the file to disk, activate the Save this file to disk option and click OK. In the Save As dialog box that appears, choose a location for the file and click Save.

FIGURE **33.11.**

*You see this dialog box
if a link is tied to a file.*

Setting Up Subscriptions

The Web is in a constant state of flux. Not only do new sites pop up all the time, but existing pages change regularly as Webmasters tweak their content. How are you supposed to keep up with the latest and greatest? The hard way is to set up a site as a favorite and then check out the site regularly. That route quickly loses its luster as your Favorites folder fattens up.

New to
98

Fortunately, Internet Explorer offers an easier way: *subscriptions.* The idea is that you subscribe to a particular page, and Internet Explorer regularly checks that page for changes. If there's something new for you to see, Internet Explorer can either download the page for "offline" viewing or send you an email to let you know.

To set up a subscription, follow these steps:

1. To begin, there are two paths you can take:

   ■ If the page is already part of your Favorites folder, select Favorites | Organize Favorites, right-click the page in the Organize Favorites dialog box, and then click Subscribe. You see the Subscribe Favorite dialog box, shown in Figure 33.12.

   ■ For any other site, first surf to the site you want to work with and then select the Favorites | Add to Favorites command to display the Add Favorite dialog box.

FIGURE **33.12.**

*Use this dialog box to
set up a subscription
for a Web page.*

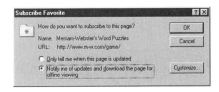

2. Either way, you are presented with two choices (the wording of each option varies slightly depending on the dialog box):

   Only tell me when this page is updated: If you activate this option, Internet Explorer sends you an email if it detects that the page has been updated.

Notify me of updates and download the page for offline viewing: If you choose this option, Internet Explorer not only sends you an email when it sees the page is changed, but it also downloads the new page so that you can view the update without having to connect to the Internet.

3. If you don't want to set up a custom schedule for the subscription, skip to step 8. Otherwise, click Customize to launch the Subscription Wizard, shown in Figure 33.13.

FIGURE 33.13.

Use the Subscription Wizard to set up a customized subscription.

4. In the first Wizard dialog box, select one of the following options and click Next >:

Download this page: Choose this option to have Internet Explorer download only the page specified by the subscription.

Download this page and pages linked to it: Select this option to download not only the subscribed page, but also any pages that are referred to in links on the subscribed page.

5. In the next Wizard dialog box, select whether you want Internet Explorer to send you an email message notifying you that the subscribed page has changed. If you select Yes, you can also click Change Address to specify the email address Internet Explorer should use. Click Next > when you're done.

6. Use the next Wizard dialog box, shown in Figure 33.14, to set up a schedule for the subscription update. You have two choices (click Next > when you're done):

Scheduled: If you activate this option, Internet Explorer will automatically check for changes. To set the frequency of those checks, click Edit and use the Custom Schedule dialog box to choose the frequency of the updates and what time of day they occur.

Manually: If you choose this option, Internet Explorer doesn't check for changes automatically. Instead, you have to run the Update All Subscriptions command, as described next.

7. The final Wizard dialog box asks whether the site requires a password. If it does, activate Yes and then enter the appropriate User name and Password. Click Finish to return to the Subscribe Favorite (or Add Favorite) dialog box.

FIGURE 33.14.
Use this Wizard dialog box to set up a schedule for the subscription update.

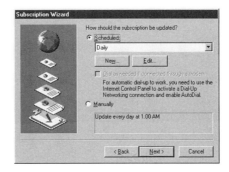

8. Click OK.

Now, each night (at whatever time you specified), Internet Explorer will connect to the Internet, check out your subscriptions, and then notify you about the updates. Note, too, that you can force Internet Explorer to update all your subscriptions at any time by selecting the Favorites | Update All Subscriptions command.

If you want to customize how Internet Explorer deals with your subscriptions, select the Favorites | Manage Subscriptions command. In the Subscriptions window that appears, highlight a subscription and then select File | Properties. The properties sheet that pops up (see Figure 33.15) contains three tabs:

Subscription: This tab gives you a summary of the subscription settings. If you no longer want to subscribe to the Web page, click the Unsubscribe button.

Receiving: Use this tab to specify a Subscription type (notification only or notification plus download). You can also use the Notification group to specify the email address used by Internet Explorer to notify you of updates.

Schedule: Use this tab to set up a schedule for the subscription update, as described earlier.

FIGURE 33.15.
Use this dialog box to adjust the properties of a subscription.

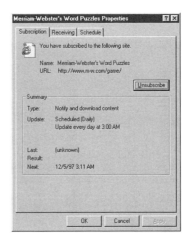

Channel Surfing: Internet Explorer's Active Channels

A typical Web surfing safari involves heading out onto the Web's waves and either paddling to sites you know about or cruising for new and interesting places. In other words, *you* do all the work. Happily, as you've seen, subscriptions relieve some of the burden by either sending you or notifying you about updated pages.

However, when it comes to surfing, Internet Explorer can go one better: *active channels*. An active channel is a special Web site that features content that changes regularly. It could be news, weather, sports scores, trivia, or even "live" broadcasts. The idea is that you subscribe to these channels, so the content is delivered to your desktop automatically. (In the vernacular, the information is "pushed" to your computer rather than "pulled" in by you.)

In Windows, you can get a rough measure of how important a particular feature is in the Microsoft scheme of things by counting the number of methods that exist to access that feature. Given that, it's safe to say that active channels play a big part in Microsoft's overall strategy because there are many different methods you can use to access them:

Use the Active Channel Guide: The Active Channel Guide is a Web site that acts as a sort of electronic equivalent of a TV guide. To get there, either select the Go | Channel Guide command, or click Channel Guide in the Links bar. As shown in Figure 33.16, the Web page that appears contains links to various categories. When you click a category, a new page displays icons for several channels, as well as number ranges for other channels, as shown in Figure 33.17. You can also run a search for channels that meet certain criteria.

Use the Favorites folder: The Favorites folder contains a Channels command that displays a submenu of channels and channel categories, as shown in Figure 33.18. Use this submenu to select the channel you want to view.

Use the Channels bar: The Channels bar is a separate window that lists the same channels and channel categories that you saw in the Channels submenu. The Channels bar is available on the Active Desktop or by clicking the Channels toolbar button in Internet Explorer.

At first, all the channels you check out will be just previews. In all cases, you see some kind of "subscription" button or link that you click to set up a subscription to the channel. Depending on the preview screen you're dealing with, this button may be named Subscribe, Add to Channels, or Add Active Channel.

Whatever the name, after you click the button, you run through the same subscription process that I told you about in the last section. In this case, though, you see a slightly different dialog box, which will look something like the one shown in Figure 33.19. You can either have the channel added to the Channels bar, or you can have Internet Explorer notify you of new content.

FIGURE 33.16.

Use the Channel Guide to get previews for the available channels.

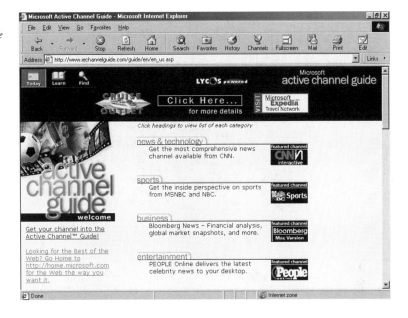

FIGURE 33.17.

Clicking a category in the Active Channel Guide produces a page with links to several active channels.

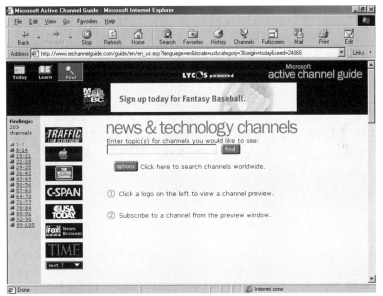

Note, too, that certain channels require extra information from you. For example, if you subscribe to PointCast, you have to fill in some personal details (such as your email address) and you have to pick which PointCast services you want delivered to your screen.

FIGURE 33.18.

In the Favorites folder's Channels menu, click the channel you want to watch.

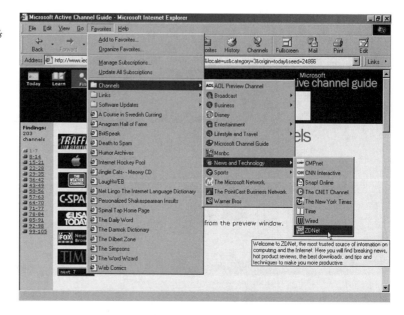

FIGURE 33.19.

This dialog box pops up when you subscribe to a channel.

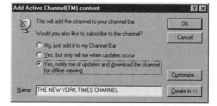

ACTIVE DESKTOP CHANNELS

You'll also notice that some preview pages have an Add to Desktop or Add to Active Desktop button. If you choose this option, the service adds a new Active Desktop item to your Windows 98 desktop.

Another thing about channels that may throw you for a loop at first is that Internet Explorer displays many of them in "Full Screen" mode, as shown in the preview of the Comics channel shown in Figure 33.20. Here are some notes about this new Internet Explorer mode:

■ In Full Screen mode, the channel consumes the entire screen with the exception of the toolbar strip across the top. You can toggle the Internet Explorer window between Full Screen and the regular screen by clicking the Full Screen toolbar button. (You can also toggle between screen modes by pressing F11.)

The Full Screen toolbar button

Figure 33.20.

Internet Explorer in Full Screen mode.

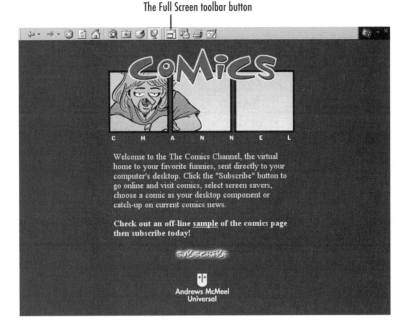

- To maximize the content area, right-click the toolbar and then activate the Auto Hide command. This removes the toolbar from view. To get the toolbar back, move your mouse pointer to the top of the screen.

- The other toolbars—the menu bar, the Address bar, and the Links bar—are all available in Full Screen mode. To view them, right-click the toolbar and then click the name of the bar that you want to display.

- You can bring the Channels bar into view by moving your mouse pointer to the left edge of the screen, as shown in Figure 33.21. When you move the mouse to the right, the Channels bar moves off the screen again.

- If you'd prefer to keep the Channels bar onscreen, click the pushpin icon.

Customizing Internet Explorer

Internet Explorer is chock-full of customization options that enable you to set up the program for the way you work and surf. For example, you saw earlier that you can use the commands on the View | Toolbars submenu to toggle the various toolbars on and off. The rest of this chapter examines the long list of other customization features.

Customizing the Links Bar

The Links bar gives you one-click access to Web pages, and so is more convenient than even the Favorites folder (unless you have the Favorites bar displayed). To take full advantage of this

33

EXPLORING THE WEB WITH INTERNET EXPLORER

convenience, you want to redesign the Links bar so that its links and setup are suitable for the way you work. Here's a list of a few techniques and options you can use to work with and customize the Links bar:

Click the pushpin icon to keep the Channels bar visible

FIGURE 33.21.

The Channels bar lurks on the left side of the screen when you're in Full Screen mode.

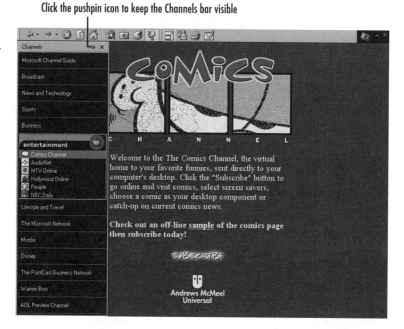

Moving the Links bar: By default, the Links bar appears to the right of the Address bar. This is fine if you're running Windows 98 on a large screen or with a high resolution, because the entire Links bar will be visible. If horizontal screen space is limited, however, you can still view the full Links bar by moving it so that it's flush with the left edge of the screen. To do this, move your mouse over the Links label and then drag the bar to the left side of the screen.

Sizing the Links bar: Rather than moving the Links bar, you may need only to change its size. To try this, position the mouse pointer over the vertical bar on the left side of the toolbar, then drag the bar left or right.

Scrolling the Links bar: If the Links bar is cut off on the right side of the screen, you can still get to the other buttons by clicking the arrow that appears on the right side of the Links bar. This will scroll the buttons to the left. To scroll back to the right, click the arrow that now appears on the left side of the Links bar.

Changing button positions: The positions of the Links bar buttons are not permanent. To move any button, use your mouse to drag the button left or right along the Links bar.

Link button properties: Each Links bar button is a shortcut object for a URL. As such, each button has various properties and methods you can access by right-clicking the button.

Changing the URL for a button: If you right-click a button and then click Properties, Internet Explorer displays the properties sheet for the shortcut. You can then use the Target URL text box to edit the URL for the button.

Adding a link button: To add a new Link bar button for the current page, drag the page icon from the Address bar into the Links bar. To add a new button for a hypertext link, drag the link into the Links bar.

Deleting a link: To remove a button from the Links bar, drag the button and then drop it in the Windows 98 Recycle Bin.

Setting Some Options

To get the most out of Internet Explorer, you should set up the program to suit your own personal style. This includes not only cosmetic options, such as the fonts and colors used by the program, but also more important concerns, such as your Usenet news server and the level of security that Internet Explorer uses.

To display these options, select View | Internet Options. (You can also get there by opening the Internet icon in the Control Panel folder.) You see the Internet Options dialog box, shown in Figure 33.22. The next few sections discuss the details of most of the tabs in this dialog box.

FIGURE 33.22.
Use the Internet Options dialog box to customize Internet Explorer to suit the way you work.

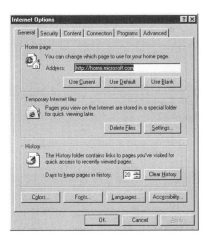

General Options

The General tab contains options that enable you to modify Internet Explorer's default home page, configure the disk cache, and configure the History folder.

To change the home page, click one of the following buttons:

Use Current: For this button, first navigate to the page you want to use. Then open the Internet Options dialog box and click the Use Current to change the home page to the current page.

Use Default: Click this button to revert to Internet Explorer's default home page.

Use Blank: Click this button if you'd prefer to launch Internet Explorer without loading a home page.

Internet Explorer sets up a folder named Temporary Internet Files within your main Windows 98 folder. This folder serves as a disk cache that Internet Explorer uses to store data from pages you visited recently. This lets Internet Explorer redisplay a page quickly (even one that's heavy on graphics) if you return to that page. In the Temporary Internet files group, you have two choices:

Delete Files: Click this button to remove all the files from the cache.

Settings: Click this button to display the Settings dialog box shown in Figure 33.23.

FIGURE 33.23.

The Settings dialog box enables you to configure Internet Explorer's disk cache.

Here's a quick review of the controls in the Settings dialog box:

Check for newer versions of stored pages: These options determine what Internet Explorer does when you visit a site that's already in the cache. If you select the Every visit to the page option, Internet Explorer updates each page as you visit it. To update all pages in the cache, activate the Every time you start Internet Explorer option. To bypass these checks, activate the Never option.

Amount of disk space to use: This slider determines the maximum size of the cache as a percentage of the total disk space on the hard disk where the cache folder resides. If you have a lot of free space available, specifying a larger cache size speeds up your browsing.

Move Folder: Click this button to specify the pathname of the folder where Internet Explorer keeps the cache files.

View Files: Click this button to view the cache files.

View Objects: Click this button to view a list of the Java applets, ActiveX controls, and other objects that have been installed on your system during your Web sessions.

The General tab has a History group that controls various options related to the History folder:

Days to keep pages in history: This spinner determines the maximum number of days that Internet Explorer will store a URL in its History list.

Clear History: Click this button to remove all URLs from the History folder.

The General tab also boasts four buttons at the bottom:

Colors: Click this button to display the Colors dialog box. From here, you can deactivate the Use Windows colors check box to set the default Text and Background colors used in the Internet Explorer window. (If you leave this check box activated, Internet Explorer uses the colors defined in the Display properties sheet; see Chapter 6, "Customizing the Taskbar, Start Menu, and Display.") You can also use the Visited and Unvisited buttons to set the default link colors. Finally, activate the Use hover color check box to have Internet Explorer change the color of a link when you position the mouse pointer over the link. (Use the Hover button to set the color.)

Fonts: Click this button to display the Fonts dialog box, which lets you determine how Web page fonts appear within Internet Explorer.

CHANGING FONT SIZES

To change the size of the fonts Internet Explorer uses, select View | Fonts and then choose a relative font size from the cascade menu (for example, Large or Small). Later on (see the "Advanced Options" section), I'll show you how to add a Fonts button to the toolbar, which enables you to cycle easily through the font sizes.

Languages: Click this button to display the Language Preferences dialog box, which enables you to add one or more languages to Internet Explorer. This enables Internet Explorer to handle foreign language pages. You can also use this dialog box to set up relative priorities for the designated languages.

Accessibility: Click this button to display the Accessibility dialog box. From here, you can tell Internet Explorer to ignore the colors, font styles, and font sizes specified on any Web page. You can also specify your own style sheet to use when formatting Web pages.

Security Options

A big push is on to turn the Web into a giant shopping mall where consumers can take conspicuous consumption (and their credit card balances) to new heights. This isn't surprising, because the Web's graphical nature makes it a natural venue for showing off products of all kinds and because it's easy to turn the Web's forms into full-fledged order forms.

The fly in this capitalistic ointment, however, is security. Those innocuous-looking order forms you fill out to buy your toys also contain sensitive data, such as your credit card number. You wouldn't leave credit card receipts lying in the street, but that's more or less what you're doing if you submit a normal Web form that has your Visa number on it.

Recognizing that most people are at least aware of the dangers involved in online commerce, would-be Web merchants realize that they won't break any sales records until the phrase "secure transaction" is no longer oxymoronic. So all kinds of programmers are working long hours to make the Web a safe place for consumers.

Internet Explorer supports many of the early security initiatives that have been developed. Moreover, the Internet Explorer window gives you visual cues that tell you whether a particular document is secure. For example, Figure 33.24 shows Internet Explorer displaying a secure Web page. Notice how a lock icon appears in the lower-right corner and that the URL of a secure page uses `https` rather than `http`. (HTTPS is a variation on regular HTTP that uses Netscape's Secure Sockets Layer to implement RSA encryption and other security features.) Both of these features tell you that the Web page has a security certificate that passed muster with Internet Explorer.

FIGURE 33.24.

An example of a secure Web document.

Lock icon —

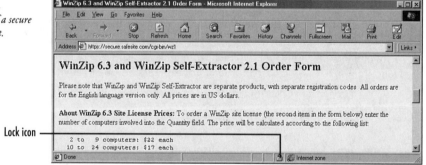

DISPLAYING SECURITY INFO

You can get some details about the current document's security level by selecting File | Properties. In the properties sheet that appears, click the Certificates button to see the properties of the site's security certificate.

Internet Explorer also implements security warnings. These are dialog boxes that warn you about concerns such as the following:

- Entering a secure Web site
- Secure Web sites that don't have a valid security certificate
- Leaving a secure Web site
- Being redirected to a page other than the one you specified
- Downloading and running objects, including files, ActiveX controls, Java applets, and scripts
- Submitting a form unsecurely, as shown in Figure 33.25.

Figure 33.25.

Internet Explorer warns you when you're about to send data from an unsecure form.

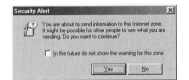

Note that these dialog boxes contain a check box that enables you to turn the warning off. You can also use the Security tab in the Options dialog box (see Figure 33.26) to toggle these warnings on and off and customize the level of security used by Internet Explorer.

Figure 33.26.

Use the Security tab to set a comfortable level of security.

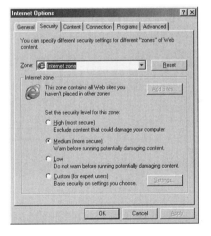

QUICK ACCESS TO THE SECURITY TAB

To get to the Security tab quickly, double-click the security zone information shown in the Internet Explorer status bar.

New to **98**

Internet Explorer 4.*x* implements security by using several different *zones* to classify Web pages. Each zone is a collection of Web pages that implements a common security level:

Local intranet zone: This zone covers Web pages on your local hard drives, your local area network (intranet), and any other pages that can be accessed without going through a proxy server. You can also add sites to this zone. Default security level: Medium.

Trusted sites zone: You use this zone to specify Web sites that you trust. That is, these are sites for which you're certain that any objects you download and run are safe. Default security level: Low.

Internet zone: This is a catchall zone that includes all Web pages that aren't in any of the other zones. Default security level: Medium.

Restricted sites zone: You use this zone to specify Web sites that you don't trust and so want to implement the tightest possible security. Default security level: High.

Adding Sites to a Zone

As mentioned in the previous section, you can add sites to three of Internet Explorer's security zones: Local intranet, Trusted sites, and Restricted sites. Here's how you do it:

1. In the Security tab, use the Zone drop-down list to choose the zone you want to work with.

2. Click the Add Sites button.

3. If you're working with the Local intranet zone, you see the dialog box shown in Figure 33.27. These check boxes determine the sites that are part of the default settings for this zone. If these settings are all you want to work with, make your selections and then click OK. To add specific sites to this zone, click Advanced.

FIGURE 33.27.

This dialog box appears if you're working with the Local intranet zone.

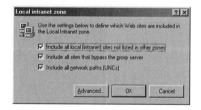

4. You use the dialog box shown in Figure 33.28 to add individual sites to a zone. (The exact layout of this dialog box varies from zone to zone.) To add a site, enter the address in the Add this Web site to the zone text box and then click Add.

5. To remove a site from the zone, highlight it in the Web sites list and then click Remove.

6. If you want Internet Explorer to make sure each site's Web server is using the HTTPS security protocol, activate the Require server verification (`https:`) for all sites in this zone check box.

7. Click OK.

FIGURE 33.28.

Use this dialog box to add and remove Web sites to the security zone.

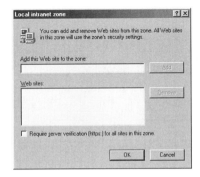

Customizing the Security Level for a Zone

Internet Explorer has three predefined security levels: High (most secure), Low (least secure), and Medium (between High and Low). You can assign any of these levels within the Security tab by first using the Zone list to choose the security zone and then activating the appropriate option button for the security level you want.

Internet Explorer also has a Custom level that you can use to set specific security settings. After you activate this option, click Settings to display the Security Settings dialog box shown in Figure 33.29. This dialog box lists various Web site objects and actions and offers several settings for each. In most cases, you have three choices:

> **Enable:** Internet Explorer accepts the content automatically.
>
> **Prompt:** Internet Explorer displays a Security Alert dialog box that enables you to accept or reject the content.
>
> **Disable:** Internet Explorer rejects the content automatically.

FIGURE 33.29.

Use the Security Settings dialog box to set specific permissions for Web content.

Here's a rundown of the various content categories and the default settings assigned to each security level:

Script ActiveX controls marked safe for scripting: Determines how Internet Explorer handles scripts that work with ActiveX controls. This setting applies only to ActiveX controls that have a signature that marks them as safe for scripting.

> Default High setting: Enable
> Default Medium setting: Enable
> Default Low setting: Enable

Run ActiveX controls and plugins: Determines whether Internet Explorer runs both ActiveX controls embedded in a Web page and plug-in programs required by Web page objects.

> Default High setting: Disable
> Default Medium setting: Enable
> Default Low setting: Enable

Download signed ActiveX controls: Determines whether Internet Explorer downloads ActiveX controls that come with a valid security signature.

> Default High setting: Disable
> Default Medium setting: Prompt
> Default Low setting: Enable

Download unsigned ActiveX controls: Determines whether Internet Explorer downloads ActiveX controls that don't come with a valid security signature.

> Default High setting: Disable
> Default Medium setting: Disable
> Default Low setting: Prompt

Initialize and script ActiveX controls not marked as safe: Determines how Internet Explorer handles scripts that work with ActiveX controls. This setting applies only to ActiveX controls that don't have a signature that marks them as safe for scripting.

> Default High setting: Disable
> Default Medium setting: Prompt
> Default Low setting: Prompt

Java permissions: Determines the level of permission assigned to Java applets that run on your computer. These permissions govern things such as access to local and network resources, whether the applet can run programs and print documents on your computer, whether the applet has access to system information and the Clipboard, and so on. There are three predefined levels: Low safety, Medium safety, and High safety. If you want to prevent Java programs from running altogether, activate the Disable Java option. To customize these permissions, activate the Custom option, click the Java Custom Settings button that appears and then use the controls in the dialog box (see Figure 33.30) to set the permissions.

> Default High setting: High safety
> Default Medium setting: High safety
> Default Low setting: Low safety

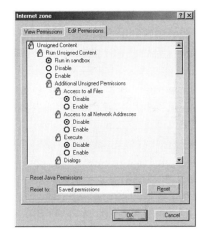

FIGURE 33.30.

Use this dialog box to set custom permissions for Java applets.

Active scripting: Determines how Internet Explorer handles scripts that manipulate ActiveX controls.

Default High setting:	Enable
Default Medium setting:	Enable
Default Low setting:	Enable

Scripting of Java applets: Determines how Internet Explorer handles scripts that manipulate Java applets controls.

Default High setting:	Disable
Default Medium setting:	Enable
Default Low setting:	Enable

File download: Determines how Internet Explorer handles file downloads.

Default High setting:	Disable
Default Medium setting:	Enable
Default Low setting:	Enable

Font download: Determines how Internet Explorer handles downloadable fonts.

Default High setting:	Prompt
Default Medium setting:	Enable
Default Low setting:	Enable

Logon: Determines how Internet Explorer logs on to sites that require a username and password.

Default High setting:	Prompt for username and password
Default Medium setting:	Automatic logon only in Intranet zone
Default Low setting:	Automatic logon with current username and password

33

EXPLORING THE WEB WITH IN-TERNET EXPLORER

Submit non-encrypted form data: Determines how Internet Explorer handles form submissions that send data without using encryption.

Default High setting: Prompt
Default Medium setting: Prompt
Default Low setting: Enable

Launching applications and files in an IFRAME: Determines whether Internet Explorer lets a Web page launch a program or display a file in an IFRAME window. (An IFRAME is a floating frame that displays content in a separate window.)

Default High setting: Disable
Default Medium setting: Prompt
Default Low setting: Enable

Installation of desktop items: Determines whether Internet Explorer lets a Web site install objects on your desktop.

Default High setting: Disable
Default Medium setting: Prompt
Default Low setting: Enable

Drag and drop or copy and paste files: Determines whether Internet Explorer enables you to drag files (such as images) from a Web page and drop them on a local resource.

Default High setting: Prompt
Default Medium setting: Enable
Default Low setting: Enable

Software channel permissions: Determines how Internet Explorer handles the downloading and installation of software distributed via active channels. The choices are Low safety (software is automatically downloaded and installed), Medium safety (software is downloaded automatically, but you are prompted to begin the installation), and High safety (you're prompted to begin both the download and the installation).

Default High setting: High safety
Default Medium setting: Medium safety
Default Low setting: Low safety

Content Options

The Content tab, shown in Figure 33.31, governs a mixed bag of settings related to Web site ratings, digital certificates, and your personal data.

Enable: Clicking this button displays the Create Supervisor Password dialog box, which you use to enter a password for the Content Advisor. When you've done that, the name of this button changes to Disable. You can turn off the ratings by clicking this button and entering your password.

FIGURE 33.31.

*The Content Advisor
group enables you to
control the type of
content that appears
in the browser.*

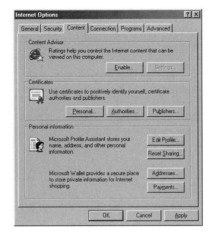

Settings: Clicking this button displays the Content Advisor (see Figure 33.32), which
you use to set site restrictions for people who don't know the password. You select a
category (such as Language or Nudity) and then move the Rating slider to set the
maximum level that nonpassword users can view. If a site is rated higher, users must
enter the supervisor password to download the site. There are two important settings
in the Content Advisor's General tab:

> **Users can see sites that have no rating:** Activate this check box if you
> want users to be able to view only rated sites.
>
> **Supervisor can type a password to allow users to view restricted
> content:** Deactivate this check box to prevent users from entering the
> supervisor password to see sites rated higher than their permissions allow.

FIGURE 33.32.

*Use the Content
Advisor to set up
restrictions for rated
Internet sites.*

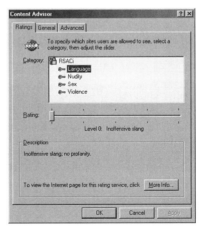

33

EXPLORING THE
WEB WITH IN-
TERNET EXPLORER

PROGRAMS THAT RESTRICT WEB CONTENT

The Internet has many tools that can help parents restrict the content their children can view online. These packages come with names such as CyberSitter, Net Nanny, and KinderGuard, so you get the idea. The Yahoo! Service has a list of these software packages at the following address:

```
http://www.yahoo.com/Business_and_Economy/Companies/Computers/Software/
➥System_Utilities/Security/
```

The Certificates group deals with site certificates that act as positive identifications on the Web. For example, when viewing a site that requires installing an ActiveX control, you see a dialog box like the one shown in Figure 33.33. This certificate tells you that the publisher of the control is legitimate. To install and run the control, click Yes. Also note that you can designate this publisher as "trustworthy" by activating the Always trust content from *x* check box in this dialog box.

FIGURE 33.33.

A certificate that tells you an ActiveX control is from a legitimate publisher.

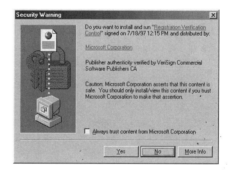

Internet Explorer stores this and other certificate data in the Certificates group:

> **Personal:** Your personal certificates (if any).
>
> **Authorities:** Certificates that have been issued by various Web sites.
>
> **Publishers:** Web publishers and credentials agencies that you've deemed trustworthy.

The Personal information group gives you a place to store some data about yourself. These controls are your interface for two new Internet Explorer features: Microsoft Profile Assistant and the Microsoft Wallet.

The Profile Assistant is a database of your personal demographic data, including your name, email address, home and business address and phone number, gender, and more. Web sites that support the World Wide Web Consortium's Platform for Privacy Preferences (P3) standard, can ask the Assistant for data from your profile. The Profile Assistant then alerts you that a Web site is requesting your data and supplies you with some background information (such as the URL of the requesting site, what data is being requested, whether the site uses a secure protocol, and so on). You use two buttons to interact with the Profile Assistant:

Edit Profile: Click this button to enter your profile data. Note that the dialog box that appears is the same as the dialog box for entering contact data in the Windows Address Book. (In fact, your profile is stored as an entry in the Address Book.)

Reset Sharing: After you've given a site permission to access your profile, that site will be able to get this data without prompting each time you visit the site. To prevent this access, click the Reset Sharing button and then click Yes to clear the list of sites that have access to your profile.

Note, too, that you can turn off the Profile Assistant any time you like. To learn how, see "Advanced Options," later in this chapter.

The second new Internet Explorer feature accessible from the Content tab is the Microsoft Wallet, which acts as a kind of electronic pocket book. The purpose of the Wallet is to make it easier and safer for you to conduct online shopping transactions. The idea is that you supply the Wallet with the basic data required by most online shopping sites, and the Wallet can then interact with those sites to provide the data and you don't have to type it in. To accomplish this, the Microsoft Wallet uses two components:

Address Manager: This component stores one or more shipping addresses. With this data in place, Wallet-enabled Web sites that would normally prompt you for your address can be told to just grab what they need from the Wallet's Address Manager. To access the Address Manager, click the Addresses button in the Content tab.

Payment Manager: This component stores payment information, which means one or more credit card numbers and expiration dates, as well as associated billing addresses and passwords. Again, Wallet-savvy sites can ask the Payment Manager for this data, which saves you from typing everything in by hand. The data is stored in encrypted form, and no one can use a credit card without entering the correct password. In the Content tab, use the Payments button to enter your credit card data.

Connection Options

The Connection tab controls how your Internet connection is established. I discussed the options in this tab in Chapter 32, "Windows 98 and the Internet."

Programs Options

The controls in the Programs tab, shown in Figure 33.34, determine the applications used to read mail, view Usenet newsgroups, and handle other types of Internet files:

Mail: This drop-down list determines the program you use to send Internet email. To launch the email program from within Internet Explorer, select Go|Mail. To start a new mail message from within Internet Explorer, select File|New|Message.

News: This drop-down list determines the Usenet newsreader to use while reading newsgroups from within Internet Explorer. To launch the newsreader from within Internet Explorer, select Go | News. To start a new Usenet message from within Internet Explorer, select File | New | Post.

Internet call: This drop-down list determines the program used to place voice calls over the Internet. To launch the program from within Internet Explorer, select Go | Internet Call. To initiate a voice call within Internet Explorer, select File | New | Internet Call.

Calendar: This list sets the program you use as a calendar.

Contact list: This list sets the program you use for your contacts database. To launch the program from within Internet Explorer, select Go | Address Book. To create a new contact within Internet Explorer, select File | New | Contact.

Internet Explorer should check to see whether it is the default browser: When you activate this option, Internet Explorer checks the Registry to see which browser is specified in the Open action for the Internet Document (HTML) file type. If the default isn't Internet Explorer (it won't be if, for example, you installed Netscape Navigator after installing Windows 98), you see a dialog box asking whether you want to set Internet Explorer as the default browser. Netscape Navigator does the same thing, so this seems to be a little game of one-upmanship on the part of Microsoft and Netscape. In the end, it's more annoying than anything else.

FIGURE 33.34.

Use the Programs tab to enable Internet Explorer's newsreader features.

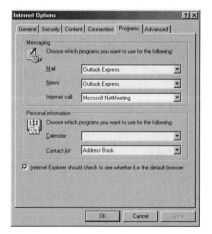

Advanced Options

The Advanced tab, shown in Figure 33.35, contains a long list of options that control everything from Internet Explorer's Accessibility settings to whether the program uses the HTTP 1.1 protocol.

FIGURE 33.35.

The Advanced tab contains dozens of settings for customizing Internet Explorer.

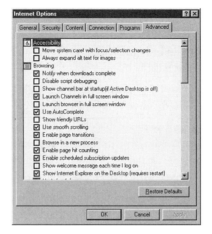

Let's begin with the Accessibility settings:

Move system caret with focus/selection changes: The system caret monitors where the current focus is on the screen. If you activate this check box, Internet Explorer moves the system caret whenever the focus or selected control changes. This is handy if you use a screen reader that uses the position of the system caret to determine which portion of the screen to magnify.

Always expand alt text for images: If you clear the Show pictures check box, as described below, Internet Explorer displays a text description of the picture, instead. This is known as the *alt text* (*alt* is short for *alternate*; this text is defined by the Webmaster). If you activate this dialog box, Internet Explorer expands the size of the image icon so that the entire alt text can be seen.

The Browsing branch has over a dozen settings that help you customize your browsing experience:

Notify when downloads complete: When Internet Explorer finishes downloading a file, it displays a dialog box telling you the download is complete. To avoid seeing this dialog box, deactivate this check box.

Disable script debugging: If you have a script debugger installed, activate this check box to disable the debugger.

Show channel bar at startup (if Active Desktop is off): If you've turned off the Active Desktop, activating this check box tells Windows 98 to display the Channel bar on the desktop at startup.

Launch Channels in full screen window: This check box determines whether active channel Web sites are displayed in full screen mode.

Launch browser in full screen window: This check box determines whether Internet Explorer is displayed in full screen mode at startup.

33

EXPLORING THE
WEB WITH IN-
TERNET EXPLORER

Use AutoComplete: This check box toggles the AutoComplete feature on and off.

Show friendly URLs: When this check box is turned on, the URLs displayed in the status bar contain only the filename of the Web page. Deactivate this check box if you prefer to see the full URL.

Use smooth scrolling: This check box toggles Internet Explorer's "smooth scrolling" feature on and off. When this feature is on, page scrolling occurs at a preset speed.

Enable page transitions: This check box toggles support for page transitions (such as the current page fading out and the next page fading in). These transitions are supported only by certain Web sites (particularly those that use Microsoft Internet Information Server with FrontPage extensions).

Browse in a new process: If you activate this check box, a new version of Internet Explorer is launched whenever you open an HTML file.

Enable page hit counting: When this check box is activated, Internet Explorer enables Web sites to track which pages you visit, even those pages that are downloaded and read offline. If you deactivate this check box, your page visits will not be logged.

Enable scheduled subscription updates: When this check box is activated, Internet Explorer updates your subscriptions at the specified times. If you don't want your subscriptions updated (if you're going on vacation, for example), deactivate this check box.

Show welcome message each time I log on: This check box toggles the Internet Explorer startup welcome message on and off.

Show Internet Explorer on the desktop (requires restart): If you deactivate this check box, Windows 98 no longer displays the Internet Explorer icon on the desktop. You need to restart Windows 98 to put this setting into effect.

Underline links: These options determine when Internet Explorer displays link text with an underline: Always, Never, or Hover (that is, when you position the mouse pointer over a link).

The Multimedia branch contains options that control how Internet Explorer gets along with various multimedia files:

Show pictures: When this check box is activated, Internet Explorer loads and displays whatever inline images are part of the Web page. If you're on a slow connection, you can speed up your Web work by turning off this option and thus preventing Web graphics from being displayed. Instead, you just see an icon that represents the image. If you then want to see a particular graphic, right-click the icon and select Show Picture from the context menu.

Play animations: This check box toggles the display of animated GIF images on and off. Again, when this option is off you can display an animated GIF image by right-clicking the icon and selecting Show Picture.

Play videos: Internet Explorer also supports inline AVI files. Turning off this check box prevents Internet Explorer from downloading and playing these AVI files.

Play sounds: When this check box is activated, Internet Explorer plays any sounds embedded in a Web page. Again, it can take quite a while to download sound files on a slow link, so you can turn off this option for faster loading (and to save your ears from the execrable MIDI files that most Webmasters seem to feature).

Smart image dithering: When this check box is activated, Internet Explorer "dithers" images in an attempt to smooth jagged edges.

The Security branch contains quite a few options for fine-tuning Internet Explorer security:

Enable Profile Assistant: This check box toggles the Profile Assistant on and off.

PCT 1.0: This check box toggles support for Microsoft's Private Communications Technology security protocol.

SSL 2.0: This check box toggles support for the Secure Sockets Layer Level 2 security protocol. This is the standard security protocol used on the Web.

SSL 3.0: This check box toggles support for the Secure Sockets Layer Level 3 security protocol. SSL 3.0 is more secure than SSL 2.0, but it doesn't yet have the broad support enjoyed by SSL 2.0.

Delete saved pages when browser closed: If you activate this check box, Internet Explorer clears out the Temporary Internet Files folder each time you shut down the program.

Do not save encrypted pages to disk: If you activate this check box, Internet Explorer will not cache any Web pages accessed via a secure server. This is a good idea if you share your computer and don't want other people to see these secure pages.

Warn if forms submit is being redirected: When this check box is activated, Internet Explorer warns you if the form data you submit is going to be sent to a server different than the one used to display the form page.

Warn if changing between secure and not secure mode: Activating this check box tells Internet Explorer to warn you when you switch between a secure document and an unsecure document.

Check for certificate revocation: If you activate this check box, Internet Explorer checks security certificates to see whether they have been revoked.

Warn about invalid site certificates: When this option is turned on, Internet Explorer displays a warning if a site provides a certificate that appears to be invalid.

Cookies: These options determine how Internet Explorer reacts when a Web page attempts to write a cookie to your computer. (A *cookie* is a small text file that Web sites store on your computer to save information about you, such as selections you've made in a Web "shopping cart.")

33

EXPLORING THE WEB WITH IN-TERNET EXPLORER

The Java VM branch controls various behaviors for Internet Explorer's Java Virtual Machine:

Java console enabled (requires restart): Toggles whether Internet Explorer uses a separate console window for Java applet output and error messages. When this option is activated (you need to restart Windows 98 to put the new setting into effect), select View | Java Console to open the console window.

Java JIT compiler enabled: Toggles whether Internet Explorer uses its internal "just-in-time" Java compiler to compile and run Java applets.

Java logging enabled: Toggles whether Internet Explorer keeps a log of all Java applet activity on your system.

The Printing branch contains a single option: Print background colors and images. If you activate this check box, Internet Explorer includes the page's background when you print the page. If the page has a busy background, you speed up your printing considerably if you turn off this setting.

The Searching branch controls what Internet Explorer does when you enter an incorrect URL:

Autoscan common root domains: When this check box is activated and a URL you entered cannot be found, Internet Explorer cycles through all the root domains (.com, .edu, .gov, .mil, .net, and .org) in an attempt to find the correct URL. For example, if Internet Explorer can't find www.whitehouse.org, it will try the other roots—www.whitehouse.com, www.whitehouse.edu, and so on—until it (hopefully) finds one that works (www.whitehouse.gov, in this case).

Search when URL fails: These options offer another searching alternative for those times when Internet Explorer can't find an address. In this case, the program can search for URLs that are similar to the one you entered.

The Toolbar branch has two check boxes that enable you to customize the Standard Buttons toolbar:

Show font button: This check box toggles the Fonts toolbar button on and off. Clicking the Fonts toolbar button produces a menu of font and language options.

Small icons: This check box toggles the toolbar between small icons and large icons. Note that the small icons are only marginally smaller, so you don't gain that much extra screen space by activating this setting.

Finally, the HTTP 1.1 settings branch has check boxes that control whether Internet Explorer uses the HTTP 1.1 protocol. (HTTP 1.1 replaces the original HTTP 1.0 protocol, and thanks to its support for persistent connections, improved security, and better caching control, is now the standard protocol on the Web.) You have two options:

Use HTTP 1.1: When this check box is activated, Internet Explorer uses HTTP 1.1 to communicate with Web servers. If you're having trouble establishing a connection to a Web site, the problem may be that the site uses HTTP 1.0, so deactivating this check box may help.

Use HTTP 1.1 through proxy connections: When this check box is activated, Internet Explorer uses HTTP 1.1 to communicate with Web servers only when connecting through a proxy server.

Summary

This chapter continued your look at Windows 98 and the Internet by showing you how to wield Windows 98's built-in Web browser: Internet Explorer. After showing you how to get Internet Explorer, I took you on a tour of the screen. From there, you learned some basic browsing techniques, including how to create Internet shortcuts, how to use the new Explorer bars (Search, Channels, Favorites, and History). You also learned how to customize Internet Explorer, and I ran through each of the settings available in the Internet Options dialog box.

Here are some pointers to related chapters:

- You can't explore the Web until you've set up Windows 98 to connect to the Internet. To find out how it's done, see Chapter 32, "Windows 98 and the Internet."

- See Chapter 34, "Outlook Express and Internet Email," and Chapter 35, "Outlook Express and Usenet News," to learn about the email and Usenet clients that are tied so closely with Internet Explorer.

- Internet Explorer also has ties to the NetMeeting collaboration software. I'll show you how to use it in Chapter 36, "Remote Collaboration with Microsoft NetMeeting."

- To learn how to build your own Web pages, see Chapter 37, "Web Page Publishing with Windows 98."

33

EXPLORING THE WEB WITH INTERNET EXPLORER

CHAPTER 34

Outlook Express and Internet Email

IN THIS CHAPTER

And none will hear the postman's knock
Without a quickening of the heart.
For who can bear to feel himself forgotten?

—W. H. Auden

With Windows 98, Microsoft has moved its messaging model away from the "universal inbox" concept that prevailed (however imperfectly) in Windows 95. For Internet email, the tool of choice in Windows 98 is Outlook Express—thanks to its built-in support for the SMTP and POP protocols, support for multiple email accounts and automatic signatures, its ability to handle HTML and other rich text formats, its support for secure messages, and much more. This chapter shows you how to use Outlook Express for exchanging notes with other Net denizens.

A Brief Email Primer

Although the Internet email system isn't complicated, there is a bit of background you should know if you're new to all this. Knowing how the email system works, what security issues are involved, the basics of email etiquette, and some fundamental jargon, acronyms, and symbols will stand you in good stead during your e-conversations. Rather than cluttering this chapter with all this background information, I've put together an online email primer that you can peruse at your leisure. You'll find the primer on my Web site at the following address:

`http://www.mcfedries.com/Ramblings/email-primer.html`

Getting Started with Outlook Express

It's worth mentioning at this point that I'm assuming you've set up both your Internet connection and your email account. If not, head back to Chapter 32, "Windows 98 and the Internet," to get the details.

ADDING NEW MAIL ACCOUNTS

Outlook Express supports multiple email accounts. To add a new account, select Tools | Accounts to display the Internet Accounts dialog box. Click the Add button and then click Mail to launch the Internet Connection Wizard. Run through the email account dialog boxes, as described in Chapter 32.

Note, too, that you can also use the Internet Accounts dialog box to adjust the properties of your mail accounts. I discuss this in detail later in this chapter (see "Setting Some Mail Account Options").

There are a number of methods you can use to get Outlook Express off the ground:

- Select Start | Programs | Internet Explorer | Outlook Express.
- Open the desktop's Outlook Express icon.
- Click the Launch Outlook Express icon in the taskbar's Quick Launch area.
- In Internet Explorer, select Go | Mail.

When you first launch Outlook Express, the program displays the Browse for Folder dialog box shown in Figure 34.1. This dialog box wants to know where you'd like your incoming email messages stored. The default folder is the `\Application Data\Microsoft\Outlook Express` subfolder of your main Windows 98 folder. If you'd prefer a different folder (for example, one on the same drive that you use to store your other data), use the folder tree to select the new location and then click OK.

FIGURE 34.1.

When you first start Outlook Express, you're prompted for a storage location.

Outlook Express then loads and you see the window shown in Figure 34.2. The Outlook Express window is a relatively simple affair, with two main components:

> **Folder List:** This is the list on the left side of the window. Outlook Express uses these folders to store messages, as follows:

>> **Inbox:** Stores incoming messages.

>> **Outbox:** Stores pending outgoing messages (that is, messages that won't be sent until you connect to the Internet).

>> **Sent Items:** Stores messages that have been sent.

>> **Deleted Items:** Stores messages that you delete. Like the Windows Recycle Bin, this is a temporary deletion area. (See "Working with Your Messages," later in this chapter for more information).

>> **Drafts:** Stores messages that you've saved but haven't sent.

> If you set up one or more Usenet news accounts, you see a folder for each one. As you'll learn later (see "Understanding the Message Folders"), you can create your own folders and subfolders to categorize the messages you receive.

34

OUTLOOK EXPRESS AND INTERNET EMAIL

Content area: This is the large box on the right. When you're working with any of the message folders, this area displays a list of the messages in the folder as well as a preview of the currently highlighted message. The default folder displayed at startup is the top-level Outlook Express folder, which gives you a few icons that point to common tasks. If you'd prefer that Outlook Express open the Inbox folder at startup, activate the When starting, go directly to my 'Inbox' folder check box.

QUICK INBOX ACCESS

Wherever you are in Outlook Express, you can jump to the Inbox folder quickly by pressing Ctrl+Shift+I.

FIGURE 34.2.

The Outlook Express window.

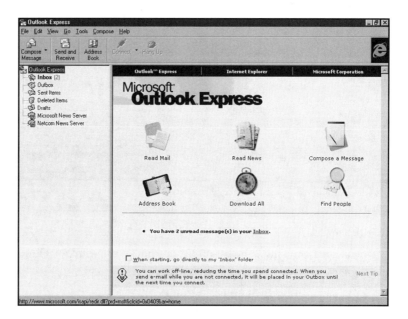

Understanding the Message Folders

You'll spend the bulk of your Outlook Express time working within one message folder or another, so you'll want to get comfortable with how these folders work. To that end, this section runs through a few folder techniques, including navigating the message lists, reading messages, customizing the layout, sorting and finding messages, and more.

Importing Messages and Addresses

If you had an email program installed on your machine when you installed Windows 98, when you select a message folder Outlook Express will offer to import the messages and address book from the old program (see the Figure 34.3). This is a good idea, so if you decide to go ahead, you need to follow these steps:

1. Make sure your old email program is highlighted in the Import from list.
2. Make sure both the Messages and Address Book check boxes are activated.
3. Click Next >.
4. If Outlook Express prompts you to choose a profile, make sure the appropriate profile is highlighted and then click OK.
5. Outlook Express then asks you to select the folders to import. You have two choices:

    All folders: Select this option to have Outlook Express import messages from every folder.

    Selected folders: Select this option to import only certain folders.

6. When you've made your choice, click Finish.

FIGURE 34.3.

Outlook Express may offer to import your old messages and address book.

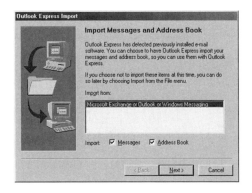

If Outlook Express didn't offer to import your old mail data, you can still fire up the import process by hand. Select the File | Import command to display a submenu with three choices:

Address Book: Select this command to display the Address Book Import Tool dialog box, shown in Figure 34.4. Highlight your address book type and then click Import. Depending on the address book type, you need to run through one or two more steps (such as selecting the address book file).

IMPORTING OTHER ADDRESS BOOKS

If your address book isn't listed in the Address Book Import Tool, all is not lost. Most address books enable you to export the data to a text file with comma-separated values (a CSV file). If your address book can do this, you can then import the data into Outlook Express by selecting the Text File (Comma Separated Values) option in the Address Book Import Tool.

Figure 34.4.

Use the Address Book Import Tool to import data from an existing address book or file.

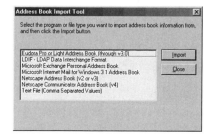

Messages: Select this command to start the Outlook Express Import Wizard; Figure 34.5 shows the initial dialog box. Select the mail client that contains the messages, click Next >, and follow the instructions the wizard provides.

Figure 34.5.

Use the Outlook Express Import Wizard to import messages from another email client.

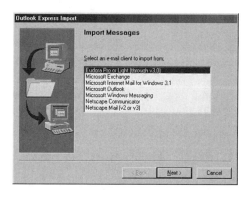

Mail Account Settings: Select this command to import the Internet email account settings from another client. For example, if your system has Windows Messaging (or Microsoft Exchange) with the Internet E-mail service installed, you could import the particulars of that account into an Outlook Express account.

A Look Around a Message Folder

When you finally get to a folder, you see a view something like the one shown in Figure 34.6. As you can see, the content area is divided into two sections: the messages list and the preview pane:

Messages: The top part of the window is a list of the messages that reside in the currently selected folder. In the default view, the messages list shows five columns:

Exclamation mark (!): This column tells you the priority of the message. A red exclamation mark indicates high priority, and a blue, downward-pointing arrow indicates low priority. If no priority was specified, no icon appears in this column.

Paper clip: When you see a paper clip icon beside a message in this column, it tells you that the message has a file attached to it.

From: This is the name of the person or company that sent the message.

Subject: This is the subject line of the message (which is usually a brief description of the message contents).

Received: This column shows the date and time the message was received.

Preview pane: The bottom part of the window displays a preview of the currently highlighted message.

FIGURE 34.6.

The Outlook Express window with a message folder selected.

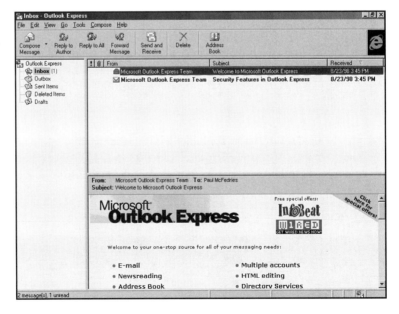

34

OUTLOOK EXPRESS
AND INTERNET
EMAIL

Creating New Folders

The four default folders that Outlook Express sets up are functional but not all that useful in the long term. At this early stage of your Outlook Express career, you might not have all that many messages in your Inbox folder, but it probably won't take long to fill up. Sure, you delete missives you don't want to bother with, but you'll still have plenty of messages to keep for posterity. So you still are faced with an unwieldy stack of messages before too long.

The problem here is that your messages aren't organized in any way. When you get paper memos and letters, you don't leave them cluttering your In basket, do you? No, you probably use file folders to store related correspondence. You can add the same level of organization to your email correspondence by creating new folders in which to store related messages. So, for example, you could create a folder for each Internet mailing list you subscribe to, one for correspondence between you and your boss, another for your current project, one each for all your wired friends, and so on.

To create a new folder, follow these steps:

1. Select the File | Folder | New Folder command to display the Create Folder dialog box, shown in Figure 34.7.

FIGURE 34.7.

Use this dialog box to select a home and enter a name for your new folder.

2. In the Folder List, select the folder within which you want the new folder to appear. For example, to create a first-level folder (that is, a folder on the same hierarchical level as Inbox, Outbox, and so on), you'd select the main Outlook Express folder.

3. Use the Folder name text box to enter the name of the new folder.

4. Click OK.

DELETING FOLDERS

To delete a folder you've created, select File | Folder | Delete and then choose the folder from the cascade menu that appears.

Other Folder Operations

Here's a quick look at a few other folder maintenance chores you may need from time to time:

Renaming a folder: The names of the five predefined Outlook Express folders are set in stone, but it's easy to rename any folder that you created yourself. To do so, use either of the following methods:

- Highlight the folder and then select File | Folder | Rename (or press F2). In the Rename Folder dialog box, enter the new name and then click OK.

- Click the folder once to highlight it, and then click the folder again to open a text box around the folder name. Edit the name, and then press Enter.

Compacting a folder: Within the storage location that you selected when you first launched Outlook Express, folder contents are stored in two files: an .mbx file that contains the contents of each message, and an .idx file that serves as an index for the .mbx file. When you move or delete messages, Outlook Express removes the corresponding data from the .mbx and .idx files, which results in "gaps" within these files. To remove these gaps and reduce the size of these files, you need to *compact* the folder. To do this, highlight the folder and then select File | Folder | Compact.

Compacting every folder: If you've been moving and deleting messages from a number of folders, you can get Outlook Express to compact all your folders in one pass by selecting the File | Folder | Compact All Folders command.

Moving a folder: If you want to move a folder to a different location, you have two ways to proceed:

- Highlight the folder and select File | Folder | Move To. In the Move dialog box, use the folder tree to highlight the new location for the folder and then click OK.

- In the Outlook Express Folder List, use your mouse to drag the folder and drop it on the new location.

Deleting a folder: To get rid of a folder you no longer need, highlight the folder and then select File | Folder | Delete. Outlook Express then warns you that the deletion can't be reversed and asks whether you want to proceed. Click Yes to delete the folder.

34

OUTLOOK EXPRESS AND INTERNET EMAIL

SAFER FOLDER DELETIONS

A safer deletion method is to move the folder to the Deleted Items folder. That way, if you change your mind down the road, you can easily restore the folder by moving it out of Deleted Items.

Working with the Windows Address Book

As you'll see a bit later, when you compose a new message or reply to a received message, Outlook Express provides fields in which you can specify the address of the recipient. If you have correspondents with whom you swap notes frequently, typing their email addresses each time can be a pain.

Instead of typing your recipients' addresses each time you compose a message, you can use the Windows Address Book to store these frequently used addresses for easy recall.

To display the Address Book, use any of the following techniques:

- Select Tools | Address Book or press Ctrl+Shift+B.
- Click the Address Book toolbar button.
- In Windows 98, select Start | Programs | Internet Explorer | Address Book.

Figure 34.8 shows the Address Book window with a few contacts already in place. As you can see, the bulk of the window is taken up by the list of contacts, which shows the name, email address, and home and business numbers of each contact.

FIGURE 34.8.

Use the Address Book to store your frequently used email addresses.

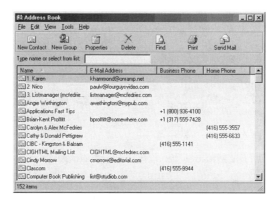

IMPORTING ADDRESSES

If you have names in your Exchange Address Book (or some other format), you can import them into the Windows Address Book by selecting the File | Import | Address Book command. In the Address Book Import Tool window that appears, highlight the address book type and then click Import. Follow the instructions that appear for selecting the appropriate address book file and whatever other steps are required. (The exact steps will depend on what type of address book you're importing.)

To find a specific name in the address list, use any of the following techniques:

■ Move into the list and scroll through it using the scrollbars or the navigation keys (up arrow, down arrow, Page Up, and Page Down).

SHOWING MORE NAMES

You can display more names in the Address Book window by pulling down the View menu and selecting either Large Icon, Small Icon, or List.

■ In the Type name or select from list text box, type the first few letters of the name you want.

■ Select View | Sort By and then choose a sort order in the cascade menu that appears.

Adding a New Address

To store a new address, follow these steps:

1. Select File | New Contact (or press Ctrl+N) or click the New Contact toolbar button. Outlook Express displays the Properties dialog box shown in Figure 34.9.

FIGURE 34.9.

Use this dialog box to define the specifics of the new address.

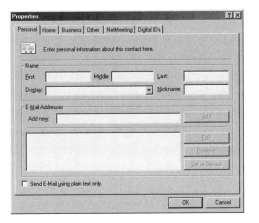

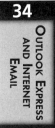

2. Fill in the fields in the Personal tab. Here are some notes:

■ The default value displayed in the contacts list is the person's first name, followed by the middle name, followed by the last name. If you'd rather display something else, enter that value in the Display text box.

PLACING COMMON ADDRESSES AT THE TOP

The Address Book is at its most convenient when the addresses you use most frequently appear at the top of the list. To make sure an address appears near the top, use the Display box to enter a number, followed by the person's name (for example, 1. Karen; see Figure 34.8 for some examples.)

- To specify an email address, enter the address in the Add new text box and then click Add. You can enter as many addresses as you like.
- If you enter multiple addresses for a contact, you can specify which address is the default by highlighting that address and then clicking Set as Default.
- I mentioned earlier that Outlook Express can read and send messages using rich text or HTML formatting. If you don't want formatting information sent to this person (if, say, you know or suspect it will mess up the person's email system), activate the Send E-Mail using plain text only check box.

3. Use the Home tab to enter the contact's home address and phone numbers, as well as the URL of his or her personal Web page (if there is one).

4. Use the Business tab to enter the contact's business address and phone numbers, job title, company Web address, and so on.

5. Use the Notes text box in the Other tab to jot down miscellaneous information about the contact (birthday, spouse and children's names, and so on).

6. The NetMeeting tab enables you to enter NetMeeting contact data, such as the conferencing email address and the names of one or more directory servers on which the person is listed.

7. Use the Digital IDs tab to import one or more digital IDs associated with the contact's email address.

8. When you're done, click OK.

Creating an Address Group

You'll see that the Address Book makes it a snap to include addresses in your correspondence. Even the Address Book method of choosing names can get tedious, however, if you regularly send messages to many people. For example, you might send a monthly bulletin to a few dozen recipients, or you might send notes to entire departments.

To make these kinds of mass mailings easier to manage, Outlook Express lets you group multiple email addresses under a single name. To send a message to every member of the group, you simply specify the group as the "recipient" of the message. Here are the steps to follow to create a group:

1. In the Address Book window, either select File | New Group (or press Ctrl+G) or click New Group in the toolbar. Outlook Express displays the Properties dialog box shown in Figure 34.10.

FIGURE 34.10.

Use this dialog box to define a new address group.

2. In the Group Name text box, enter the name you want to use for the group.
3. To include addresses (that is, *members*) in the group, click the Select Members button. Outlook Express displays the Select Group Members dialog box, shown in Figure 34.11.

FIGURE 34.11.

Use the Select Group Members dialog box to add email addresses to the group.

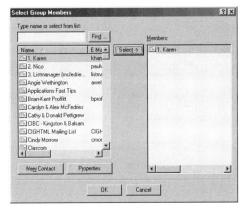

4. To add members, highlight the names and click Select->.
5. When you're done, click OK to return to the group properties sheet.
6. Click OK. Outlook Express adds the group to the Address Book.

In the Address Book window, address groups appear in bold blue text with a different icon. If you use groups frequently, the Address Book offers a convenient way to view the members of each group. If you activate the View | Groups List command, the window sprouts a list of all your defined groups. As you can see in Figure 34.12, highlighting a group displays the group's members on the right.

FIGURE 34.12.

Activate the View | Groups List command to display this list of your defined groups.

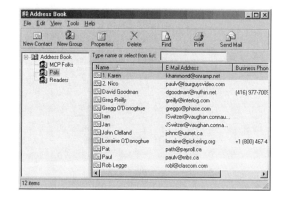

The Address Book and Electronic Business Cards (vCards)

The Windows Address Book offers built-in support for the new electronic business card format called vCard. A vCard is a cross-platform file format for personal data interchange. It can contain not only basic contact data (name, address, phone number, email, and so on), but also World Wide Web hyperlinks, graphics, audio files, and more. vCard has been proposed as an Internet standard, and already boasts wide industry support, including not only the Windows Address Book, but also Microsoft Outlook and Outlook Express, Netscape Communicator, Lotus Organizer 97, Sidekick 98, and the Four11 Internet directory service.

Later I show you how to use Outlook Express to create a vCard for yourself (see "Working with Stationery and Signatures"). For now, here are the Address Book techniques you can use to import and export vCards:

> **Importing a vCard:** To import a vCard file (.vcf extension) into the Address Book, select File | Import | Business Card (vCard). In the dialog box that appears, highlight the vCard file you want to Import and then click Open.

> **Exporting a vCard:** To export a contact to a vCard file, highlight the contact and then select File | Export | Business Card (vCard). In the dialog box, select a location for the file, adjust the filename if necessary, and then click Save.

Composing and Sending a New Message

It's time now to get down to the email nitty-gritty. For starters, I'll show you how to use Outlook Express to compose and send a message. You also learn how to embed objects in your messages, how to work with stationery and signatures, and more.

Outlook Express's Send Options

Before we get started, let's examine the various options that Outlook Express provides for sending email. Select Tools | Options, and in the Options dialog box that appears, display the Send tab. You see the controls shown in Figure 34.13.

FIGURE 34.13.

Outlook Express's options for sending email.

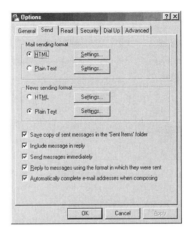

The Mail sending format group contains two options buttons that determine whether your messages contain formatting: HTML and Plain Text.

If you activate the HTML button, Outlook Express enables you to apply a number of formatting options to your messages. In effect, your message becomes a miniature Web page and can be formatted in much the same way that a Web page can (see Chapter 37, "Web Page Publishing with Windows 98"). Note, however, that this formatting will be visible only to recipients who have an HTML-enabled mail client. Clicking the Settings button beside the HTML option displays the HTML Settings dialog box, shown in Figure 34.14. Here's a synopsis of the available options:

> **Encode text using:** SMTP supports only 7-bit ASCII data, so binary messages or messages that include full 8-bit values (such as foreign characters), must be encoded. This list determines how (or whether) Outlook Express encodes message text:
>
> > **None:** Tells Outlook Express not to encode the text.
> >
> > **Quoted Printable:** Use this encoding if your messages have full 8-bit values. This encoding converts each of these characters into an equals sign (=) followed by the character's hexadecimal representation. This ensures SMTP compatibility. (Note that most 7-bit ASCII characters are not encoded.)

34

OUTLOOK EXPRESS
AND INTERNET
EMAIL

Base 64: Use this encoding if your message contains binary data. This encoding uses the Base 64 alphabet, which is a set of 64 character/value pairs: A through Z is 0 through 25; a through z is 26 through 51; 0 through 9 is 52 through 61; + is 62 and / is 63. All other characters are ignored.

Allow 8-bit characters in headers: When this check box is activated, characters that require 8 bits—including ASCII 128 or higher, foreign character sets, and double-byte character sets—will be allowed within the message header without being encoded. If you leave this check box deactivated, these characters are encoded.

Send pictures with messages: When this check box is activated, any pictures embedded in the message or used as the message background will be sent along with the message text.

Indent message on reply: When this check box is activated and you reply to a message, Outlook Express displays the original message indented below your message.

Automatically wrap text at *x* characters, when sending: This spinner determines the point at which Outlook Express wraps text onto a new line. Many Internet systems can't read lines longer than 80 characters, so you shouldn't select a value higher than that. A value somewhat less than 80 is best because it allows for extra greater-than signs (>), which are placed at the beginning of each line to indicate the original message in a reply. Note that the Quoted Printable and Base 64 encoding schemes require 76-character lines, so this option is available only if you select None in the Encode text using list.

FIGURE 34.14.

Use this dialog box to work with settings associated with the HTML sending format.

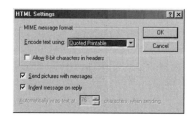

If you activate the Plain option, Outlook Express sends your message as regular text, without any formatting. Clicking the Settings button displays the Plain Text Settings dialog box, shown in Figure 34.15. This dialog box includes many of the same options as the HTML Settings dialog box shown earlier. Here's what's different:

MIME: MIME stands for Multipurpose Internet Mail Extensions and it's the standard encoding format for text-based messages. Each of the encoding options I discussed previously is MIME-based.

Uuencode: This is an older encoding format that is primarily used when sending binary files to Usenet newsgroups.

Indent the original text with > when replying or forwarding: It's standard on the Internet that original message text in a reply be indicated with a greater than sign (>) at the beginning of each line. (Colons are also sometimes used.) When this check box is activated, Outlook Express prefaces each line of the original message with whatever character you specify in the list.

FIGURE 34.15.

Use this dialog box to work with settings associated with the Plain Text sending format.

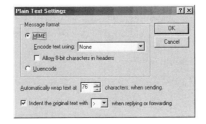

Here's a quick rundown of the rest of the options in the Send tab:

Save copy of sent messages in the 'Sent Items' folder: When this check box is activated, Outlook Express saves a copy of your message in the Sent Items folder. It's a good idea to leave this option checked because it gives you a record of the messages you send.

Include message in reply: If you activate this check box, Outlook Express includes the original message text as part of the new message when you reply to or forward a message.

Send messages immediately: When this check box is activated, Outlook Express passes your message to the SMPT server as soon as you click the Send button (more on this in the next section). If you deactivate this option, clicking the Send button when composing a message only stores that message in the Outbox folder. This is useful if you have a number of messages to compose and you use a dial-up connection to the Internet. That is, you can compose all your messages offline and store them in the Outbox folder. You can then connect to the Internet and send all your messages at once.

Reply to messages using the format in which they were sent: When this check box is activated, Outlook Express automatically selects either the HTML or Plain Text sending format depending on the format used in the original message. If you'd prefer to always use your default sending format, deactivate this check box.

Automatically complete e-mail addresses when composing: When this check box is activated, Outlook Express monitors the email addresses you enter when composing a message. If you've entered a similar address before, the program will complete the rest of the address automatically.

34

OUTLOOK EXPRESS
AND INTERNET
EMAIL

Composing a Message

Composing a message isn't all that different from composing a letter or memo in WordPad. You just need to add a few extra bits of information, such as the email address of your recipient and a description of your message.

To get started, use any of the following techniques:

- Select Compose | New Message (or press Ctrl+N).
- Click the Compose Message button on the toolbar.
- In Internet Explorer, select File | New | Message.

Whichever method you choose, the New Message window, shown in Figure 34.16, appears.

FIGURE 34.16.

Use the New Message window to enter the email addresses of your recipients, the Subject line, and the body of the message.

Check Names
Select Recipients
Insert file
Insert Signature
Digitally sign message
Encrypt message

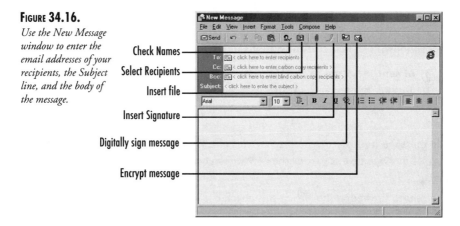

Here are the basic steps to follow to compose and send your message:

1. In the To field, enter the address of the recipient. If you want to send the message to multiple recipients, separate each address with a semicolon (;).

2. In the Cc (courtesy copy) field, enter the addresses of any recipients you want to receive copies of the message. Again, separate multiple addresses with semicolons.

3. In the Bcc (blind courtesy copy) field, enter the addresses of any recipients you want to receive blind copies of the message. (This means that recipients in the To and Cc fields will not see the names or addresses of the recipient's in the Bcc field.)

4. In the Subject field, enter a brief description of the message. This description will appear in the Subject column of the recipient's mail client, so make sure that it accurately describes your message.

5. Use the box below the Subject field to enter your message.

6. You can toggle the message sending format by pulling down the Format menu and selecting either Rich Text (HTML) or Plain Text. If you select the HTML sending format, feel free to use any of the formatting options found on the Format menu or the Formatting toolbar. Remember, however, that not all systems will transfer the rich text formatting.

7. To set the message priority, select Tools | Set Priority and then choose the importance level from the submenu that appears.

8. To send your message, you have two choices:

   ■ Select File | Send Message. This tells Outlook Express to send the message out to the Internet right away.

   ■ Select File | Send Later. This command tells Outlook Express to store the message in the Outbox folder. If you choose this route, Outlook Express displays a dialog box telling you that your message is stored in the Outbox folder. Click OK. When you're ready to send the message, select the Tools | Send command in the Outlook Express window.

SEND SHORTCUTS

The New Message window has two shortcut methods for sending a message: pressing Alt+S and clicking the Send button. However, it's important to note that these shortcuts apply to only one of the two Send commands: Send or Send Later. Which one they apply to depends on whether the Send tab's Send messages immediately check box is activated:

   ■ If this check box is activated, the shortcuts apply to the Send command.

   ■ If this check box is deactivated, the shortcuts apply to the Send Later command.

Using the Address Book to Specify Recipients

When you're composing a message, you can use the Address Book to add recipients without having to type their addresses. To display the Address Book from the New Message window, use any of the following techniques:

   ■ Click the 3×5 card icon that appears to the left of the To, Cc, and Bcc fields.

   ■ Choose the Tools | Select Recipients command.

   ■ Click the toolbar's Select Recipients button.

Figure 34.17 shows the slightly different version of the Address Book that appears.

FIGURE 34.17.

This dialog box appears when you invoke the Address Book from within the message composition window.

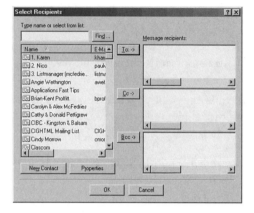

Highlight the recipient and then click either To-> (if you want the name to appear in the To field), Cc-> (if you want the name to appear in the Cc field), or Bcc-> (if you want the name to appear in the Bcc field). When you've added all the recipients for your message, click OK.

Inserting a File into a Message

Outlook Express's OLE support means that you can embed objects into your messages. These objects are sent to the recipient using the rich text format, so as long as the recipient's system supports this format (specifically, the remote gateway must be able to handle MIME or Uuencode attachments, and the recipient's email client must be MAPI-compliant), you can attach spreadsheets, word processing documents, graphics, files, and any other OLE object to your messages.

Depending on the type of object you want to work with, Outlook Express gives you two methods of inserting objects:

Inserting file text: If you have text in a separate file that you want to add to the message, select the Insert | Text from File command. In the Insert Text File dialog box that appears, highlight the file and then click Open. Outlook Express adds the file's contents to the message.

Inserting a file: To insert a file in the message, select Insert | File Attachment or click the toolbar's Insert File button. In the Insert Attachment dialog box that appears, highlight the file you want to send and then click Attach. Outlook Express embeds the file into the message as an icon.

PASTING DATA INTO A MESSAGE

Besides these file insertion techniques, you can also use the standard Windows techniques (Cut, Copy, and Paste; drag and drop; and so on) to insert text or other objects into your messages. See Chapter 19, "Sharing Data in Windows 98: The Clipboard and OLE."

Working with Stationery and Signatures

In the real world, stationery is paper that includes predefined text, colors, and images. Outlook Express lets you set up the electronic equivalent. That is, you can define email stationery that includes a background image and predefined text. This is essentially a Web page to which you can also add your own text.

You can also customize the default look of a message as follows:

- You can specify a message font.

- You can add a signature. (In Internet email circles, a *signature* is text that appears at the bottom of all your messages. Most people use a signature to provide their email and Web addresses, their company contact information, and perhaps a snappy quote or epigram that reflects their personality.)

- You can attach a vCard (electronic business card).

The next two sections show you how to work with these options.

Specifying a Font or Stationery

To set a default stationery or message font, first select Tools | Stationery to display the Stationery dialog box, shown in Figure 34.18.

FIGURE 34.18.

Use this dialog box to set up a default font and stationery.

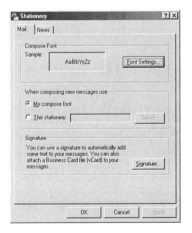

To set the message font, click Font Settings, use the standard Font dialog box to pick your font options, and then click OK. To use this font, head for the When composing new messages use group and make sure the My compose font option button is selected.

If you'd prefer to use stationery, move to the When composing new messages use group and activate the This stationery option. Then click Select to display the Select Stationery dialog box, shown in Figure 34.19. You have four choices here:

- To use one of the stationery samples that comes with Outlook Express, highlight it in the Stationery list and then click OK.

- To choose another Web page, click Browse and then use the Stationery dialog box to pick out the Web page you want to use.

- To make changes to an existing stationery, highlight it and then click Edit. This loads the stationery into FrontPage Express so that you can edit the page. (See Chapter 40.)

- You can download other stationery samples by clicking the Get More button, which takes you to the Microsoft Greetings Workshop on the Web.

Figure 34.19.

Use the Select Stationery dialog box to pick out the Web page pattern you want to use with your messages.

Rather than setting a default stationery, you may prefer to select a stationery to use only in a single message. Outlook Express gives you quite a few ways to do this.

To start a new message using a specific stationery, first try either of the following:

- Select Compose | New Message using.
- Click the downward-pointing arrow in the Compose Message toolbar button.

Either way, Outlook Express displays a menu of stationery options.

If you've already started a message, you can choose a stationery by selecting the Format | Apply Stationery command and then picking out the stationery you want from the submenu that appears.

Specifying a Signature or vCard

As I mentioned earlier, a signature is a few lines of text that provide contact information and other data. Outlook Express lets you define a signature and then have it appended to the bottom of every outgoing message (or you can insert it by hand in individual messages). Outlook Express also supports the vCard electronic business card format, and lets you create and add a vCard to your messages.

To do this, you must first follow these steps to define a signature or vCard:

1. In the main Outlook Express window, select Tools | Stationery.

2. Click the Signature button to display the Signature dialog box, shown in Figure 34.20.

FIGURE 34.20.

Use the Signature dialog box to define a signature and vCard.

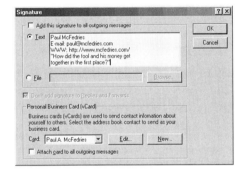

3. To define a text signature, activate the Text option and then enter your signature in the box provided.

4. If your signature text resides in a text file, activate the File option and then enter the full path to the file in the box provided. (Or click Browse to choose the file from a dialog box.)

5. If you want Outlook Express to add the signature to all your messages, activate the Add this signature to all outgoing messages check box.

6. If you'd rather use the signature only on original messages, leave the Don't add signature to Replies and Forwards check box activated.

7. If you have an Address Book entry for yourself, use the Card list to select that entry. Otherwise, click New to create a contact for yourself.

8. To send the vCard as an attachment with all your messages, activate the Attach card to all outgoing messages check box.

9. Click OK to put the signature options into effect.

If you choose not to have your signature and vCard added automatically, you can insert them manually by using either of the following techniques in the New Message window:

■ Select Insert | Signature or click the Insert Signature button on the toolbar.

■ Select Insert | Business Card.

34

OUTLOOK EXPRESS AND INTERNET EMAIL

Reading Incoming Mail

Of course, you won't be spending all your time firing off notes and missives to friends and colleagues. Those people will eventually start sending messages back to you, and you might start getting regular correspondence from mailing lists, administrators, and other members of the email community. This section shows you how to retrieve messages, read them, and then deal with them appropriately.

Retrieving Messages

Whether Outlook Express checks for new messages on your server automatically is controlled by a setting within the Options dialog box. To view this setting, select Tools | Options and make sure the General tab is displayed (see Figure 34.21). This tab actually has two settings related to retrieving messages:

> **Check for new messages every *x* minute(s):** Activate this check box to have Outlook Express automatically check for new messages using the interval specified in the spinner.

> **Play sound when new messages arrive:** Outlook Express plays a sound whenever a new message arrives. If you'd prefer the sounds of silence, deactivate this check box.

FIGURE 34.21.

The General tab has a couple of options related to retrieving messages.

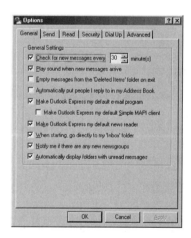

If you elected not to have Outlook Express check for new mail automatically, you can use any of the following techniques to check the server by hand:

- Select Tools | Send and Receive. (If you have multiple accounts, selecting this command displays a submenu that lists each account. From here, you can either select an individual account or select the All Accounts command.)
- Press Ctrl+M or F5.
- Click the Send and Receive toolbar button.

Each new message that arrives is stored in the Inbox folder's message list and appears in a bold font. To view the contents of any message, highlight it in the message list. Outlook Express then displays the message text in the preview pane.

If you find the preview pane too confining, you can open the highlighted message in its own window by selecting File | Open (or by pressing Ctrl+O).

ADDING CORRESPONDENTS TO THE ADDRESS BOOK

When you have a message displayed in its own window, you can easily add the sender's name and email address to the Address Book. There are two techniques you can use:

- Select Tools | Add To Address Book | Sender. (Note, too, that addresses listed in the Cc field also appear in this submenu.)
- Right-click the sender's name and then click Add To Address Book.

MESSAGES THAT YOU'VE READ ARE NO LONGER BOLD

After about five seconds, Outlook Express removes the bold from the message list item so that you know right away whether you've read the message. You can toggle boldfacing on and off by pulling down the Edit menu and selecting one of the following commands:

Mark as Read: Turns off boldfacing for the current message. Shortcut keys: Ctrl+Q or Ctrl+Enter. You can also right-click the message and then click Mark as Read.

Mark All as Read: Turns off boldfacing on all messages in the current folder.

Mark as Unread: Turns on boldfacing for the current message. Shortcut key: Ctrl+Shift+Enter. You can also right-click the message and then click Mark as Unread.

Note, too, that you can ask Outlook Express to display only unread messages by activating the View | Current View | Unread Messages command. (Select View | Current View | All Messages to return to the regular view.)

Outlook Express's Read Options

To help you work with your correspondence, you might want to check out Outlook Express's read-related properties. To view them, select Tools | Options and then display the Read tab in the Options dialog box, shown in Figure 34.22. Many of these settings are related to reading Usenet newsgroups, so I'll leave them until the next chapter. Here's a review of the mail-related controls:

> **Message is read after being previewed for *x* second(s):** Deactivate this check box to prevent Outlook Express from removing the bold while you're reading a message. Alternatively, you can use the spinner to adjust how long it takes Outlook Express to remove the bold.

Automatically show picture attachments in messages: When this check box is activated, Outlook Express displays attached picture files after the message text.

Show multiple pictures as a slide show: If you activate this check box, Outlook Express handles multiple picture attachments as a "slide show." That is, the first picture is displayed at the bottom of the message, and controls are added for viewing the other images, as shown in Figure 34.23. Click Next or Previous to cycle through the pictures one at a time. To have Outlook Express run through the pictures automatically, click Play. If you leave this check box deactivated, Outlook Express displays all the attached pictures at the bottom of the message.

Fonts: Click this button to display the Fonts dialog box, which displays a list of the character sets installed on your computer. For each character set, you can specify a proportional and fixed-width font, as well as a font size. You can also specify which character set to use as the default.

International Settings: Click this button to display the International Settings dialog box. You can have Outlook Express remap your default character set to a different character set for a given message. This dialog box lists all the remappings you've done. You can use the Remove button to stop remapping a character set. This dialog box also has a check box that lets you choose whether Outlook Express always uses English headers when replying to messages.

REMAPPING A CHARACTER SET

To remap a message character set, select View | Language and then select the character set you want to use from the submenu. Outlook Express will ask whether you want to use this new character set for all messages that have the same specified character set in the header as the current message. Click Yes or No, as appropriate.

FIGURE 34.22.

Use the Read tab to set various properties related to reading messages.

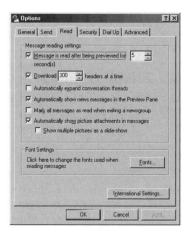

FIGURE 34.23.

Outlook Express can set up a slide show for multiple picture attachments.

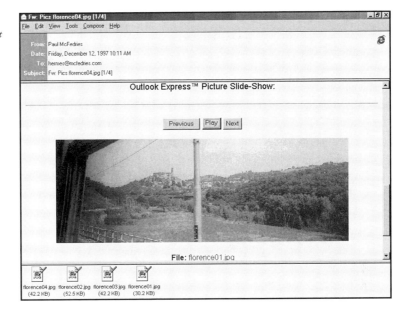

Working with Your Messages

When you have a message highlighted, you can do plenty of things with it (besides reading it, of course). You can print it, save it to a file, move it to another folder, delete it, and more. Most of these operations are straightforward, so I'll just summarize the basic techniques here:

Reading other messages: If you have several messages you want to read, you don't have to return to the message list to navigate your messages because the View | Next submenu gives you the following commands:

Next Message: Moves forward to the next message (the one below the current message in the message list). You can also press Ctrl+>.

Previous Message: Moves back to the preceding message (the one above the current message in the message list). You can also press Ctrl+<.

Next Unread Message: Moves forward to the next unread message. You can also press Ctrl+U.

Dealing with attachments: If a message has an attachment, it appears either as an icon or as an object embedded in the message. You can use the usual OLE methods of viewing the object (assuming that you have the correct server application; see Chapter 19 for more about OLE). You can also select File | Save Attachments to save the attached file to disk. (You can also drag an attachment from the message and drop it on a folder.)

Moving a message to a different folder: Later in this chapter, I'll show you how to create new folders you can use for storing related messages. To move a message to another folder, select Edit | Move To Folder (or File | Move To Folder in the message window) and then choose the destination folder from the Move dialog box that appears.

Copying a message: If you just want to make a copy of the message, use the Edit | Copy To Folder command (or File | Copy To Folder in the message window) command.

Saving a message: Instead of storing the message in a folder, you might prefer to save it to a file. To do this, select File | Save As. In the Save As dialog box, select a location, enter a filename, select a file type—Mail (.eml) or Text—and then click Save.

Saving a message as stationery: If you receive a formatted message and you like the layout, you can save it as stationery for your own use. To do so, select File | Save As Stationery. In the Save Message As Stationery dialog box, select a location, enter a filename, and then click Save.

Printing a message: To print a copy of the message, select File | Print to display the Print dialog box. Enter your print options (including whether you want to print any attachments) and then click OK.

Deleting a message: If you want to get rid of the message you're reading, select Edit | Delete (or File | Delete in the message window) or press Ctrl+D. You can also click the toolbar's Delete button. Note that Outlook Express doesn't really delete the message. Instead, it just moves it to the Deleted Items folder. If you change your mind and decide to keep the message, open the Deleted Items folder and move the message back. To remove a message permanently, open the Deleted Items folder and delete it from there.

Replying to a Message

If you receive a message from someone who is looking for some information from you, or if you think of a witty retort to a friend's or colleague's message, you want to send a reply. Instead of requiring you to create a new message from scratch, however, Outlook Express (like all email programs) has a Reply feature that saves you the following steps:

- Outlook Express starts a new message automatically.
- Outlook Express inserts the recipient automatically.
- Outlook Express inserts the original Subject line but adds RE: to the beginning of the text to identify this message as a reply.
- Outlook Express adds the header and the text of the original message in the body of the new message (unless, of course, you turned off this feature in the Send tab, as described earlier).

Outlook Express gives you two Reply options:

Reply to Author: This option sends the reply only to the person who shipped out the original message. Any names in the Cc line are ignored. To use this option, select Compose | Reply to Author or press Ctrl+R. You can also click the Reply to Author button on the toolbar.

Reply to All: This option sends the reply not only to the original author, but also to anyone else mentioned in the Cc line. To use this option, select Compose | Reply to All or press Ctrl+Shift+R. You can also click the Reply to All button on the toolbar.

Forwarding a Message

Instead of replying to a message, you might prefer to forward it to another person. For example, you might receive a message in error, or you might think that a friend or colleague might receive some benefit from reading a message you received. Whatever the reason, you can forward a message to another address by using either of the following commands:

Forward: Select Compose | Forward, press Ctrl+F, or click the Forward toolbar button.

Forward as Attachment: If you'd prefer to send the message as an attachment, select Compose | Forward as Attachment.

Outlook Express creates a new message, adds the original Subject line with Fw: (to identify this as a forwarded message), and inserts the original text as follows:

■ If you selected the Forward command, the full text of the original message is inserted in the body of the new message and a greater-than sign (>) is appended to the beginning of each line.

■ If you selected the Forward as Attachment command, Outlook Express packages the original message as an attachment, but it makes no changes to the message. The user who receives the forwarded message can then open this attachment and view the original message exactly as you received it.

If you like, you can add your own text as well.

Sorting the Messages

By default, Outlook Express sorts the messages in descending order according to the values in the Received column. But you're free to sort the messages based on any displayed column. Here are the techniques you can use:

■ Select View | Sort By and then use the submenu to select the name of a column by which you want to sort the messages. Descending is the default sort order, but you can change it to ascending by selecting View | Sort By and then activating the Ascending command.

34

OUTLOOK EXPRESS
AND INTERNET
EMAIL

■ Click the header for the column you want to use for the sort. An arrow appears beside the column name to tell you the direction of the sort (an up arrow for ascending and a down arrow for descending). Click the column header again to toggle the sort direction.

Exporting Messages to a Personal Folders File

If you want to view your messages within either Microsoft Outlook or Windows Messaging (formerly Microsoft Exchange), Outlook Express lets you export messages to your Personal Folders (.pst) file. Here are the steps to follow:

1. Select File | Export | Messages. Outlook Express tells you you're about to export messages.

2. Click OK. Outlook Express prompts you for your Windows Messaging profile.

3. Select a profile and then click OK. The Export Messages dialog box appears, shown in Figure 34.24.

FIGURE 34.24.

Use the Export Messages dialog box to choose which folders you want to export.

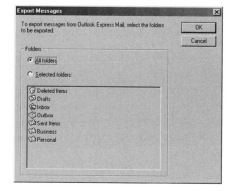

4. Select the All folders option to export all your messages. If you'd prefer to export individual folders, activate the Selected folders option and then use the folder tree to highlight the folders to export.

5. Click OK. Outlook Express exports the messages.

Using the Inbox Assistant to Filter Messages

As email becomes a ubiquitous feature on the business (and even home) landscape, you find that email chores take up more and more of your time. And I'm not just talking about the three Rs of email: reading, 'riting, and responding. Basic email maintenance—moving, deleting, and so on—also takes up large chunks of otherwise-productive time.

To help ease the email time crunch, Outlook lets you set up "rules" that allow Outlook Express to automatically move an incoming message to a specific folder if the message contains a particular keyword in the subject or body, or if it's from a particular person.

Outlook Express comes with an Inbox Assistant that makes it easy to set up and define these rules. To get started, select Tools | Inbox Assistant. In the Inbox Assistant dialog box that appears, click the Add button. You see the Properties dialog box shown in Figure 34.25.

FIGURE 34.25.

Use this dialog box to define a rule.

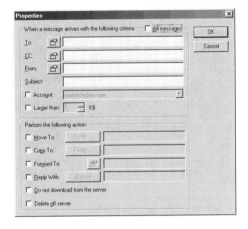

Your first step is to define the criteria that will cause Outlook Express to invoke this rule. That is, you specify what conditions an incoming message must meet for the rule to be applied to that message. That's the purpose of the controls in the When a message arrives with the following criteria group:

All messages: Activate this check box to invoke the rule on all incoming messages.

To: Use this text box to specify the addresses or names of the direct message recipients that will invoke the rule.

CC: Use this text box to specify the addresses or names of the Cc message recipients that will invoke the rule.

From: Use this text box to specify one or more email addresses or names. In this case, Outlook Express will invoke the rule for any message sent from one of these addresses.

Subject: Use this text box to enter a word or phrase that must appear in the Subject line to invoke the rule.

Account: Activate this check box and choose the mail account that will invoke the rule.

Larger than *x* KB: Activate this check box and set the message size that will invoke the rule.

After you've determined when the rule will be invoked, you need to specify the action Outlook Express should take with any message that satisfies these criteria:

Move To: Moves the message to the folder selected by clicking the Folder button.

Copy To: Copies the message to the folder selected by clicking the Folder button.

Forward To: Forwards the message to the recipient selected by clicking the Select Recipients button.

Reply With: Replies to the message using the file specified by clicking the Browse button. You can select a file that uses one of the following formats: Mail (.eml), News (.nws), HTML, or Text.

CREATING A MAIL FILE

Recall that earlier I showed you how to save a message as a file in the Mail format (see "Working with Your Messages"). To create a Mail file to use with the Reply With action, compose a message with the reply text and send it to yourself. When you receive the message, use File | Save As to save the message as a Mail file.

Do not download from that server: Activate this check box to leave the message on the server.

Delete off server: Activate this check box to delete the message from the server. In this case, you never see the message (although Outlook Express does tell you that the message was deleted from the server).

When you're done, click OK to add the new rule to the Inbox Assistant, shown in Figure 34.26.

FIGURE 34.26.

The rules you've defined appear in the Inbox Assistant dialog box.

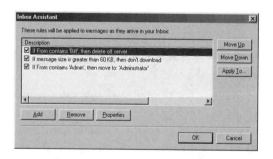

RULE MAINTENANCE

You can use the Inbox Assistant dialog box to maintain your rules:

- Each rule you've defined has a checkbox beside it that toggles the rule on and off.
- You can change a rule by highlighting it and clicking Properties.
- The Inbox Assistant processes the rules in the order they appear in the list. You can use the Move Up and Move Down buttons to change this order.
- The rules apply to the Inbox folder. If you'd like the rules to also apply to another folder, click Apply To and choose a folder in the Select Folder dialog box.
- To get rid of a rule, highlight it and click Remove.

Finding Text, Messages, and People

Outlook Express offers three search features that enable you to find text within a single message, a message within a folder, and a person with a directory service. This section shows you how to use all three search engines.

Finding Text in a Message

To find text within the current message, follow these steps:

1. Select Edit | Find Text. Outlook Express displays the Find dialog box, shown in Figure 34.27.

FIGURE 34.27.

Use the Find dialog box to find text within a message.

2. Use the Find what text box to enter your search text.

3. Select your Find options:

   Match whole word only: Outlook Express normally looks for partial word matches (entering pass will match *password* and *compass*, for example). If you prefer that Outlook Express match entire words, activate this check box.

   Match case: Activate this check box to perform a case-sensitive search.

   Direction: These options determine the direction Outlook Express searches from the current position.

4. Click Find Next to start the search. If Outlook Express finds a match it highlights the text. If this isn't the instance you want, keep clicking Find Next until you locate what you need (or until you hit the end of the message).

Finding Messages

Email is one of those things that just snowballs after you begin using it. You might get only a few messages a week at first, but then you start getting a few messages a day. Before you know it, a few dozen daily messages are streaming your way, and your folders are bursting at the seams. You'll probably find that you keep many of these messages because you never know when you'll need them again. But after you've accumulated many messages, finding the one you want down the road becomes a real challenge.

Fortunately, Outlook Express has a decent Find Message command that makes the task easy. This command isn't like the Find command you saw in Chapter 14, "File and Folder Tricks and Techniques," because it's geared toward searching through email messages. To take a look, first choose the folder in which you want to search and then select Edit | Find Message (or press Ctrl+Shift+F). Outlook Express displays the Find Message dialog box, shown in Figure 34.28.

Here's a summary of the various options you can use to define your search criteria:

From: Use this text box to specify a sender as part of the search criteria.

Sent to: Use this text box to specify a recipient as part of the search criteria.

Subject: Use this field to search for text in the Subject line of the messages.

Message body: Use this field to search for text within the body of the message.

Received After: Drop down this list to use the displayed calendar to pick the earliest received date for the message.

Received Before: Drop down this list to use the displayed calendar to pick the latest received date for the message.

Look in: If you didn't select the folder to search in beforehand, use this list to select it. You can also activate the Include subfolders check box to have Outlook Express look in the folder's subfolders, as well.

When you've specified your search criteria, click the Find Now button. If Outlook Express finds any matching messages, it displays them at the bottom of the Find Message dialog box.

FIGURE 34.28.

Outlook Express has a Find Message command that can scour parts of your email messages for text.

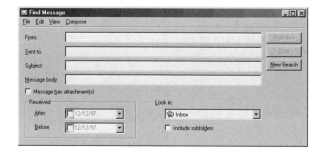

Finding People Using a Directory Service

A *directory service* is a database of names and email addresses that you can use to search for people you know (or would like to know). The protocol used to access and search these databases is known as the Lightweight Directory Access Protocol (LDAP). Outlook Express not only supports this protocol, but also offers predefined accounts for several of the most popular directory services, including Bigfoot, Four11, Verisign, and WhoWhere. (You can see a complete list of these accounts by selecting Tools | Accounts to display the Internet Accounts dialog box. Activate the Directory Service tab. Note, too, that you can also use this dialog box to add your own directory service accounts.)

To use one of directory services to find someone on the Internet, follow these steps:

1. Select Edit | Find People to display the Find People dialog box, shown in Figure 34.29.

FIGURE 34.29.

Use this dialog box to find a person on the Internet by using LDAP to access a directory service.

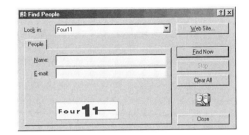

2. Use the Look in list to select the directory service you want to use. (You can also look for people in the Address Book.) If you want to find out more about a service before using it, click the Web Site button to load Internet Explorer and display the Web site for the highlighted directory service.

3. Use the Name text box to enter some or all of the name of the person you want to find.

4. Use the E-mail text box to enter the full email address of the person you want to find.

5. Click Find Now. Outlook Express connects to the directory service. If it finds any matches, it displays them at the bottom of the dialog box.

Customizing Outlook Express

Outlook Express comes with an extensive and welcome set of customization options that enable you to change the message folder columns, rearrange the basic interface, and much more. The rest of this chapter takes you through all these options.

Customizing the Message Columns

The default columns in Outlook Express tell you the basic information you need for any message. More information is available, however. For example, you might want to know the date and time the message was sent, the size of the message, and to whom the message was sent. All these items can be displayed as columns in the message list. Here are the steps to follow to customize the Outlook Express columns:

1. Select View | Columns. Outlook Express displays the Columns dialog box, shown in Figure 34.30.

FIGURE 34.30.

Use the Columns dialog box to customize the columns displayed in the message list.

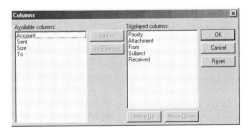

2. To add a column, highlight it in the Available columns list and click Add>>.

3. To remove a column, highlight it in the Displayed columns list and click <<Remove.

4. To change the order of the columns, highlight a column in the Displayed columns list and then use the Move Up and Move Down buttons to position the column where you want it. (Columns listed top to bottom are displayed left to right in the message list.)

5. When you're done, click OK.

Here are a few more column customization tricks:

■ To change the width of a displayed column, use your mouse to drag the right edge of the column's header to the left or right.

■ To change the width of a displayed column to fit its widest entry, double-click the right edge of the column's header.

■ To change the position of a column, use your mouse to drag the column's header left or right.

■ To change the size of the message list, use your mouse to drag the bar that separates the message list and the list of folders.

Modifying the Outlook Express Layout

Surprisingly, the layout of the Outlook Express interface isn't set. You can customize it by selecting the View | Layout command to display the Window Layout Properties dialog box, shown in Figure 34.31.

Figure 34.31.

Use this dialog box to customize the layout of the Outlook Express window.

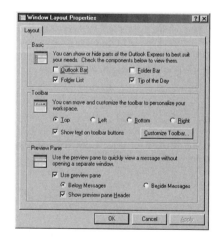

The Basic group contains four check boxes that toggle the following features on and off:

Outlook Bar: This is a strip that runs down the left side of the window (to the left of the Folder List). It contains icons for the various Outlook Express folders.

Folder Bar: This is a strip that runs across the window, just below the toolbar. It tells you the name of the current folder.

Folder List: This is the folder tree that appears to the left of the messages list.

Tip of the Day: This is a short tip that appears in the Outlook Express folder. When this feature is activated, a new tip appears each time you start Outlook Express.

NAVIGATING FOLDERS WITHOUT THE FOLDER LIST

If you elect to hide the Folder List, you can still navigate the folder tree by selecting the Go | Go To Folder command (or by pressing Ctrl+Y). In the Go to Folder dialog box that appears, use the folder tree to select the folder you want to work with and then click OK.

Note, too, that this dialog box also has a New Folder button that you can use to create folders.

The Toolbar group gives you four options—Top, Left, Bottom, and Right—that determine the position of the toolbar within the Outlook Express window. You can also use the Show text on toolbar buttons check box to toggle the toolbar text on and off. To customize the toolbar buttons, follow these steps:

1. Click the Customize Toolbar button to display the Customize Toolbar dialog box, shown in Figure 34.32.

FIGURE 34.32.

Use this dialog box to customize the Outlook Express toolbar.

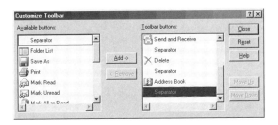

34

OUTLOOK EXPRESS
AND INTERNET
EMAIL

2. To add a button, highlight it in the Available buttons list and click Add->. (The Separator "button" adds a vertical separator bar.)

3. To remove a button, highlight it in the Toolbar buttons list and click <-Remove.

4. To change the order of the buttons, highlight a button in the Toolbar buttons list and then click Move Up and Move Down to position the button where you want it. (Buttons listed top to bottom are displayed left to right in the toolbar.)

5. When you're done, click Close.

The controls in the Preview Pane group set several options related to the preview pane:

Use preview pane: This check box toggles the preview pane on and off.

Below Messages or **Beside Messages:** These options determine where the preview pane sits in relation to the messages list.

Show preview pane header: This check box toggles the header at the top of the preview pane on and off.

Setting Some Mail Account Options

Outlook Express keeps track of a number of properties for each of your Internet email accounts. These properties include all the data you provided when setting up the account—email address, account name and password, server domains, and so on—as well as a few other useful options. To view these properties, select Tools | Accounts to display the Internet Accounts dialog box. In the Mail tab, highlight your account and then click Properties to open the properties sheet for the account.

The first three tabs—General, Servers, and Connection—contain the setup data for the account.

The Security tab contains options for implementing the S/MIME (Secure Multipurpose Internet Mail Extensions) security feature. This requires three steps:

1. Click Get Digital ID to launch Internet Explorer and open the Outlook Express Digital ID Web page. From here, you can connect to VeriSign (or some other provider of digital certificates) to get your digital ID.

2. Return to the Security tab and activate the Use digital ID when sending secure messages from check box.

3. Click the Digital ID button, highlight your digital ID in the dialog box that appears, and then click OK.

With that done, you can now send and receive messages that are digitally signed and/or encrypted.

The Advanced tab, shown in Figure 34.33, contains the following settings:

Server port numbers: These options determine the TCP/IP port used by the SMTP and POP3 protocols. You can also use the check boxes to tell Outlook Express whether each server requires a Secure Sockets Layer connection.

Server timeouts: This slider controls how long Outlook Express waits for a response from the servers. In general, the faster your Internet connection, the shorter you can set the timeout.

Leave a copy of messages on server: If you activate this check box, Outlook Express downloads your messages but doesn't delete them from the server. This is useful if you want to download the same messages into another email client.

Remove from server after *x* day(s): If you decide to leave a copy of your messages on the server, activate this check box to have Outlook Express clean out those messages after the specified number of days.

Remove from server when deleted from 'Deleted Items': If you decide to leave a copy of your messages on the server, activate this check box to have Outlook Express clean out those messages when you delete the downloaded copies from your Deleted Items folder.

Break apart messages larger than *x* KB: Some mail servers can't handle large messages (the usual limit in these cases is around 64KB). If you're working with such a server, activate this check box and specify a maximum message size in the spinner provided.

FIGURE 34.33.

The Advanced tab of the mail account properties sheet.

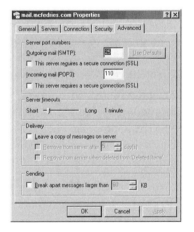

Setting Some Outlook Express Options

To complete this look at Outlook Express customization, I'll now examine the rest of the settings in the Options dialog box. (I talked about the Read and Send tabs earlier in this chapter.) Select Tools | Options to open this dialog box. Here's a review of the mail related settings in the General tab (refer to Figure 34.21):

Check for new messages every *x* minute(s): Activate this check box to have Outlook Express automatically check for new messages using the interval specified in the spinner.

Play sound when new messages arrive: Outlook Express plays a sound whenever a new message arrives. If you'd prefer the sounds of silence, deactivate this check box.

Empty messages from the 'Deleted Items' folder on exit: Activate this check box to force Outlook Express to clean out the Deleted Items folder each time you exit the program.

Automatically put people I reply to in my Address Book: If you activate this check box, Outlook Express adds to the Address Book the name and email address of the people you send replies to.

Make Outlook Express my default e-mail program: When this check box is activated, Outlook Express becomes the default email client. This means that Outlook Express is invoked if you click a "mailto" link in a Web page, select any mail-related commands in your Web browser, and select Send To | Mail Recipient in Windows 98.

Make Outlook Express my default Simple MAPI client: When this check box is activated, Outlook Express becomes the default Simple MAPI client. This means that Outlook Express is invoked when you select the File | Send command in an application that supports Simple MAPI operations.

When starting, go directly to my 'Inbox' folder: Activate this check box to force Outlook Express to open the Inbox folder at startup. When this option is deactivated, the top-level Outlook Express folder is displayed at startup.

Automatically display folders with unread messages: When this check box is activated, at startup Outlook Express looks for folders that have unread messages. If it finds any, it opens the appropriate branches in the Folder List tree so that you can see which folders have the unread messages. This is a useful option if you're using the Inbox Assistant to filter incoming messages to different folders.

The Dial Up tab, shown in Figure 34.34, contains a number of options that control how and when Outlook Express invokes your Internet dial-up connection. (The controls in this tab are active only if you've specified a dial-up connection in the Connection tab of the mail account's properties sheet.) Here's a quick look at each control:

When Outlook Express starts: These options determine whether Outlook Express connects to the Internet at startup. Select Do no dial a connection to work offline, or Dial this connection to connect using whatever Dial-Up Networking connection you select in the list. If you want to have a choice, activate Ask me if I would like to dial a connection.

Warn me before switching dial up connections: When this check box is activated, Outlook Express warns you if your connection is no longer working and offers to try another one (assuming you have multiple Dial-Up Networking connections defined).

Hang up when finished sending, receiving, or downloading: When this check box is activated, Outlook Express automatically severs your Internet connection as soon as it has finished with the server. This is a handy way to prevent your online time (and, possibly, your connection charges) from mounting unnecessarily.

Automatically dial when checking for new messages: When you turn on this option, Outlook Express connects to the Internet automatically whenever it checks for new messages. This is useful if you've set up the program to check for new messages at regular intervals. Note, however, that for true convenience you may need to create a Dial-Up Networking script that logs you on to your provider automatically. (See Chapter 30, "Remote Computing with Dial-Up Networking.")

FIGURE 34.34.

Use the Dial Up tab to configure the Outlook Express dial-up options.

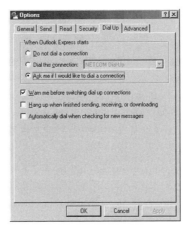

To finish with the Outlook Express options, let's turn to the Advanced tab, shown in Figure 34.35. The Local message files group applies only to Usenet newsgroup messages, so I'll deal with those options in the next chapter. For Internet mail, the only applicable settings are the two check boxes in the Logging Options group:

Mail Transport: Activate this option to create a log file of all commands sent to and received from your POP3 mail server. This file is named `Pop3.log`, and it's stored in the Mail subfolder of your Outlook Express application data folder:

`\Windows\Application Data\Microsoft\Outlook Express\Mail`

IMAP Transport: Activate this option to create a log file of all commands sent to and received from your IMAP mail server. This file is named `Imap.log`, and it's stored in the Mail subfolder of your Outlook Express application data folder.

34

OUTLOOK EXPRESS
AND INTERNET
EMAIL

FIGURE 34.35.

*Outlook Express's
Advanced options.*

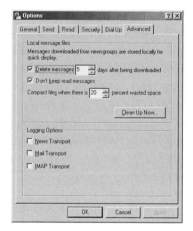

Summary

This chapter showed you how to use Microsoft's Outlook Express messaging client. I began by showing you around Outlook Express and showing you how to work with message folders. From there, I showed you how to work with the Address Book, how to compose new messages, and how to read incoming messages. You also learned some useful techniques for replying and forwarding, finding data and people, using rules to filter messages, and customizing the program.

Here's a list of chapters where you'll find related information:

- To get the goods on TCP/IP and other Net plumbing, turn to Chapter 31, "Implementing TCP/IP for Internet and Intranet Connections."

- To learn how to get an Internet connection established, see Chapter 32, "Windows 98 and the Internet."

- I showed you how to work with Internet Explorer in Chapter 33, "Exploring the Web with Internet Explorer."

- To learn how to wield the Usenet newsreader portion of Outlook Express, see Chapter 35, "Outlook Express and Usenet News."

Outlook Express and Usenet News

35

CHAPTER

"The time has come," the Walrus said,
"To talk of many things:
Of shoes—and ships—and sealing wax—
Of cabbages—and kings—
And why the sea is boiling hot—
And whether pigs have wings."

—Lewis Carroll

The vast majority of the attention, buzz, and hype about the Internet is centered on the World Wide Web. That's not surprising because it's the easiest Net service for novices to use, and it's where all the cutting-edge development is taking place. The rest of the Internet services fall into two categories: those that have fallen more or less into disuse (Gopher, for example) and those that just keep on keeping on.

A good example of the latter type of service is Usenet. Usenet is, in essence, a collection of topics available for discussion. These discussion groups (or *newsgroups*, as they're normally called) are open to all and sundry, and they won't cost you a dime (aside from the usual connection charges, of course).

Will you find anything interesting in these discussion groups? Well, let's put it this with way: with more than 25,000 (that's right, twenty-five *thousand*) groups to choose from, if you can't find anything that strikes your fancy, you'd better check your pulse. (Not all service providers offer the complete menu of Usenet groups, so the number available to you might be considerably less than 25,000.) On the other hand, most of Usenet has no central control, which means that many newsgroups have degenerated into a collection of rambling, off-topic posts and unsolicited commercial email. (One wag likened Usenet to a "verbal landfill.") Not all groups are this bad, but you need to be cautious when choosing which discussions you join.

In this chapter, I turn your attention to the Usenet service. I give you some background about Usenet and then show you how to wield the newsreader portion of the Outlook Express show.

USENET HISTORY

Usenet began its life back in 1979 at Duke University. A couple of resident computer whizzes (James Elliot and Tom Truscott) needed a way to easily share research, knowledge, and smart-aleck opinions among Duke students and faculty. So, in true hacker fashion, they built a program that would do just that. Eventually, other universities joined in, and the thing just mushroomed. Today, it's estimated that more than 20 million people participate in Usenet, sending a whopping 150,000 messages a day.

Some Usenet Basics

To get your Usenet education off on the right foot, this section looks at a few crucial concepts that will serve as the base from which you can explore the rest of Usenet:

article An individual message in a newsgroup discussion.

follow up To respond to an article. (Also: *follow-up*; the response itself.)

hierarchy Usenet divides its discussion groups into several classifications, or *hierarchies*. There are seven so-called *mainstream* hierarchies:

`comp`	Computer hardware and software
`misc`	Miscellaneous stuff that doesn't really fit anywhere else
`news`	Usenet-related topics
`rec`	Entertainment, hobbies, sports, and more
`sci`	Science and technology
`soc`	Sex, culture, religion, and politics
`talk`	Debates about controversial political and cultural topics

Most Usenet-equipped Internet service providers give you access to all the mainstream hierarchies. There's also a huge `alt` (alternative) hierarchy that covers just about anything that either doesn't belong in a mainstream hierarchy or is too wacky to be included with the mainstream groups. There are also many smaller hierarchies designed for specific geographic areas. For example, the `ba` hierarchy includes discussion groups for the San Francisco Bay area, the `can` hierarchy is devoted to Canadian topics, and so on.

newsgroup *Newsgroup* (or, often, simply *group*) is the official Usenet moniker for a discussion topic. Why are they called newsgroups? The original Duke University system was designed to share announcements, research findings, and commentary. In other words, people would use this system if they had some "news" to share with their colleagues. The name stuck, and now you often hear Usenet referred to as *Netnews* or simply as *the news*.

newsreader The software you use to read a newsgroup's articles and to post your own articles.

post To send an article to a newsgroup.

subscribe In a newsreader, to add a newsgroup to the list of groups you want to read. If you no longer want to read the group, you unsubscribe from the group.

thread A series of articles related to the same Subject line. A thread always begins with an original article and then progresses through one or more follow-ups.

35

OUTLOOK EXPRESS
AND USENET
NEWS

Figuring Out Newsgroup Names

Newsgroup names aren't too hard to understand, but you need to go through the drill to make sure that you're comfortable with them. In their basic guise, newsgroup names have three parts: the hierarchy to which they belong, followed by a dot, followed by the newsgroup's topic. For example, check out the following name:

```
rec.boats
```

Here, the hierarchy is `rec` (recreation), and the topic is `boats`. Sounds simple enough so far, but many newsgroups were too broad for some people, so they started breaking the newsgroups into subgroups. For example, the `rec.boats` people who were into canoeing got sick of speedboat discussions, so they created their own "paddle" newsgroup. Here's how its official name looks:

```
rec.boats.paddle
```

You'll see lots of these subgroups in your Usenet travels. (For example, there are also newsgroups named `rec.boats.building` and `rec.boats.racing`.) Occasionally, you see sub-subgroups, such as `soc.culture.african.american`, but these are still rare in most hierarchies (the exception is the `comp` hierarchy, in which you find all kinds of these sub-subgroups). One variation on this theme is to tack on extra subgroup names for emphasis. For example, consider the following newsgroup:

```
alt.tv.dinosaur.barney.die.die.die
```

This newsgroup, of course, is designed for people who don't exactly like TV's Barney the Dinosaur (to put it mildly).

Understanding Articles and Threads

Articles, as you can imagine, are the lifeblood of Usenet. As I mentioned earlier, every day tens of thousands of articles are posted to the different newsgroups. Some newsgroups might get only one or two articles a day, but many get a dozen or two, on average. (And some very popular groups—`rec.humor` is a good example—can get a hundred or more postings in a day.)

Happily, Usenet places no restrictions on article content. (However, a few newsgroups have *moderators* who decide whether an article is worth posting.) Unlike, say, the heavily censored America Online chat rooms, Usenet articles are the epitome of free speech. Articles can be as long or short as you like (although extremely long articles are frowned on because they take so long to retrieve), and they can contain whatever ideas, notions, and thoughts you feel like getting off your chest (within the confines of the newsgroup's subject matter). You're free to be inquiring, informative, interesting, infuriating, or even incompetent—it's entirely up to you.

USENET NETIQUETTE

If you want to get along with your fellow newshounds, you should follow the accepted Netiquette guidelines that apply to Usenet. To get some pointers on minding your Usenet Ps and Qs, please check out my online Usenet primer:

`http://www.mcfedries.com/Ramblings/usenet-primer.html`

Earlier I told you that newsgroups were "discussion topics," but that doesn't mean they work like a real-world discussion, where you have immediate conversational give and take. Instead, newsgroup discussions lurch ahead in discrete chunks (articles) and unfold over a relatively long period (sometimes even weeks or months).

To get the flavor of a newsgroup discussion, think of the "Letters to the Editor" section of a newspaper. Someone writes an article in the paper, and later someone else sends in a letter commenting on the content of the article. A few days after that, more letters might come in, such as a rebuttal from the original author, or someone else weighing in with his two cents worth. Eventually, the "discussion" dies out either because the topic has been exhausted or because everyone loses interest.

Newsgroups work in just the same way. Someone posts an article, and then the other people who read the group can, if they like, respond to the article by posting a *follow-up* article. Others can then respond to the response, and so on down the line. This entire discussion—from the original article to the last response—is called a *thread*.

Working with Newsgroups in Outlook Express

Now that you know a bit about Usenet, it's time to get down to more practical matters. Specifically, the rest of this chapter will show you how to use Outlook Express to subscribe to, read, and post to newsgroups. (I'm assuming here that you've set up an Outlook Express account for your news server, as described in Chapter 32, "Windows 98 and the Internet.")

In the Outlook Express window, head for the folder list and click on the folder that represents your news server account. The first time you do this, Outlook Express displays the dialog box shown in Figure 35.1, which asks whether you want to view a list of the available newsgroups.

With the configuration complete, Outlook Express connects to your news server and proceeds to download the list of newsgroups available on the server, as shown in Figure 35.1. Click Yes. If you use a dial-up connection for this server, Outlook Express will then prompt you to connect. Click Yes again.

35

OUTLOOK EXPRESS AND USENET NEWS

FIGURE 35.1.

After the configuration is complete, Outlook Express connects to your news server and downloads the list of available newsgroups.

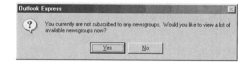

Outlook Express then connects to the news server and begins downloading a list of the available newsgroups. When that's done (it might take quite a while, depending on the speed of your connection), you see the Newsgroups dialog box, shown in Figure 35.2. (Note that the News servers list appears only if you've defined multiple servers.) To display this dialog box in the future, highlight the news server account in the Outlook Express window and then use any of the following techniques:

- Select Tools | Newsgroups.
- Press Ctrl+W.
- Click the News groups toolbar button.

ANOTHER WAY TO SELECT YOUR NEWS ACCOUNT

If you don't have the Outlook Express folders list displayed, you can still get to your news server account by selecting the Go | News command. If you have multiple news accounts, Outlook Express will go to the default account. To change the default, select Tools | Accounts and open the News tab in the Internet Accounts dialog box. Click the account and then click the Set as Default button.

FIGURE 35.2.

Use this dialog box to work with newsgroups in Outlook Express.

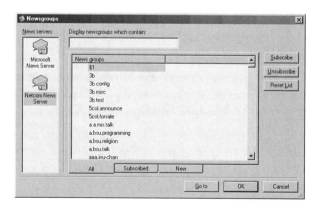

Newsgroups are at the heart of Usenet, so you need to become comfortable with basic newsgroup chores, such as subscribing and unsubscribing. This section takes you through the basics.

Subscribing to a Newsgroup

Before you can read or post articles, you have to add a newsgroup or two to your news server account. You have two ways of doing this: you can subscribe to a newsgroup or you can open a newsgroup without committing to a subscription.

Either way, you must first display the group you want in the News groups list. Begin by selecting the news server you want to use (if you have multiple servers defined). Then you can either scroll through the groups or type all or part of the newsgroup name in the Display newsgroups that contain a text box. Note that Outlook Express looks for group names that contain the text you type. If you type `startrek`, for example, Outlook Express will match `alt.startrek`, `rec.arts.startrek.fandom`, and so on. This example is shown in Figure 35.3.

FIGURE 35.3.

Outlook Express matches newsgroup names that contain the text you type.

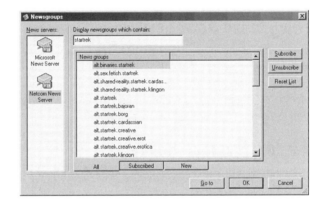

After you've highlighted a newsgroup, use either of the following techniques:

- If you just want to view the group without subscribing, click Go to. You are returned to the Outlook Express window with the newsgroup displayed. If you later want to subscribe to this group, select Tools | Subscribe to this newsgroup.

- If you want to subscribe to the group, click the Subscribe button. You can repeat this process for any other newsgroup subscriptions. In each case, Outlook Express adds the name of the group to the Subscribed tab. When you're done, click OK to return to the main Outlook Express window.

Unsubscribing from a Newsgroup

If you get tired of a newsgroup, you can unsubscribe at any time by using either of the following techniques:

- In the Newsgroups dialog box, select the Subscribed tab, highlight the newsgroup, and click Unsubscribe.

- In the Outlook Express window, use the Newsgroups list to select the group and then select Tools | Unsubscribe from this newsgroup.

Downloading Messages

With some newsgroups selected, you're now ready to start grabbing messages to read. With Outlook Express, you have two ways to proceed:

Online: Working online means you're connected to the news server. You can download message headers at any time, and highlighting a message downloads the message text immediately.

Offline: Working offline means that you connect briefly to get the available headers in a group. Then, while you're not connected, you examine the message Subject lines and mark those that you want to retrieve. You then connect once again and tell Outlook Express to download the marked messages.

Connecting to the News Server

In Outlook Express, you can connect to your news server at any time by selecting File | Connect | *Server* (where *Server* is the account name of the server). You can also click the Connect button. (Note that this applies only to dial-up users. If you connect to the Internet via your LAN, Outlook Express will establish the connection automatically. You can prevent this by activating the File | Work Offline command.)

Downloading Message Headers

After you're connected, Outlook Express offers the following methods for downloading a newsgroup's message headers:

■ Click the newsgroup in the folders list. Outlook Express will download the headers for you automatically. For busy groups, the default download limit of 300 might not grab every header. To get more headers, select Tools | Get Next 300 Headers. (As you'll see later, you can adjust this header limit to your liking.)

■ Click the newsgroup and then select the Tools | Download this Newsgroup command. In the Download Newsgroups dialog box, click OK. (I'll explain this dialog box in more detail a bit later.)

■ Highlight either your news server account or a subscribed group within that account. Then select Tools | Download *server*, where *server* is the name of your news server. This tells Outlook Express to grab the available headers for all the subscribed groups in the account.

Disconnecting from the News Server

If you're on a dial-up connection, you may want to disconnect at this point so that you can review the headers. To disconnect, select the File | Hang Up command or click the toolbar's Hang Up button.

Downloading Messages

To view the contents of any message (the message body) while you're online, just highlight it in the message list. Outlook Express then downloads the message body and displays the message text in the preview pane.

Working Offline: Marking Messages for Downloading

If you're working offline, you need to mark those messages that you want to download. Here are the techniques you can use:

> **To mark a single message for download:** Highlight the message and then select Tools | Mark for Retrieval | Mark Message. You can also right-click the message and then click Mark Message for Download.

> **To mark a thread for download:** Highlight any message in the thread and then select Tools | Mark for Retrieval | Mark Thread.

> **To mark all the messages for download:** Select Tools | Mark for Retrieval | Mark All Messages.

In each case, Outlook Express places a small, blue arrow to the left of the marked messages.

If you change your mind about downloading a message, highlight it and then select Tools | Mark for Retrieval | Unmark. (To start over again, first choose Edit | Select All to highlight every message, and then choose the Tools | Mark for Retrieval | Unmark command.)

Working Offline: Getting the Message Bodies

To get the message bodies, follow these steps:

1. Connect to the news server.
2. Select the Tools | Download this Newsgroup command to display the Download Newsgroup dialog box.
3. Activate the Get the following items check box, as shown in Figure 35.4.

FIGURE 35.4.

Use this dialog box to tell Outlook Express what you want to download.

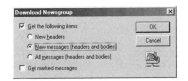

4. Select one of the following options:

   New headers: This option looks for new headers and downloads them.

   New messages (headers and bodies): This option looks for new messages and downloads both the headers and the bodies.

   All messages (headers and bodies): This option downloads every available header and body.

5. If you marked one or more messages for download, activate the Get marked messages check box.

6. Click OK. Outlook Express starts downloading the messages.

7. When the download is complete, disconnect from the news server.

Notes on Working with Newsgroup Messages

You can treat newsgroup messages in much the same way that you treat email messages. That is, you can view the message text in the preview pane, open the message in its own window, save the message, copy it to another folder, and so on. I discuss all these message techniques and quite a few others in Chapter 34, "Outlook Express and Internet Email." Here are a few notes on tasks that are specific to newsgroup messages:

Dealing with threads: If you see a plus sign (+) beside a message header, it means that replies have been posted. To see the other messages in the thread, click the plus sign, or highlight the message and press plus sign (+) on your numeric keypad.

Unscrambling ROT13 messages: Some messages are encoded using a scheme called ROT13. This scheme encodes the message by shifting the letters of the alphabet 13 positions to the right and wrapping around to the front of the alphabet when the end is reached. (*ROT* is short for *rotate*.) If you come across a message that has been encoded using ROT13, you can use Outlook Express's built-in decoder. To use it, select Edit|Unscramble (ROT13).

Canceling one of your messages: If you post a message and then have second thoughts, you can remove it from the newsgroup by highlighting it and selecting Compose|Cancel Message. (This command is available only for messages you've sent.)

Combining and decoding multiple attachments: Some multimedia groups post large binary files that are split into multiple posts. To extract the original binary file from these posts, first highlight all the posts. Then select Tools|Combine and Decode to display the Order for decoding dialog box (see Figure 35.5). Use the Move Up and Move Down buttons to order the posts (the Subject lines usually tell you the proper order) and then click OK.

FIGURE 35.5.

Use this dialog box to set the proper order for the posts that contain the various pieces of the file.

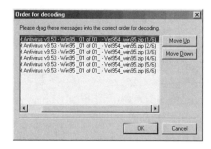

Writing a Rejoinder: Following Up a Message

Usenet is at its best when it's interactive: questions are asked and answered; the swords of conflicting opinions are crossed; debaters cut and parry to score points on contentious issues. The engine behind all this verbal jousting is, of course, the follow-up message. To post a follow-up with Outlook Express, follow these steps:

1. Highlight the original message in the message list.

2. Select Compose | Reply to Newsgroup. (You can also press Ctrl+G or click the Reply to Group toolbar button.) Outlook Express opens a message composition window and fills it with the text from the original article.

3. Cut out any unnecessary text from the original article.

4. Enter your own text in the article body.

5. Select File | Send Message. (Alternatives for faster service: Alt+S or click the Post button.) Outlook Express displays a dialog box telling you that your message has been sent to the news server and that it may not appear immediately.

6. Click OK.

REPLYING VIA EMAIL

Instead of posting a follow-up message, you might prefer to reply directly to the author via email. To do this, highlight the message and select Compose | Reply to Author. (Or else press Ctrl+R or click the Reply to Author button.)

If you want to send a message to both the group and the author, select Compose | Reply to Newsgroup and Author.

Posting a New Message

As I've said before, original messages are the lifeblood of Usenet because they get the discussions off the ground and give the rest of us something to read (as well as laugh at, sneer at, and hurl verbal abuse at). So if you're feeling creative, you can take advantage of this section, which shows you how to post a new message from Outlook Express.

To get started, select the newsgroup to which you want to post and then use any of the following techniques:

- Select Compose | New Message.
- Press Ctrl+N.
- Click the Compose Message button on the toolbar.

Whichever method you choose, the New Message window appears. This window is almost identical to the New Message window I discussed in the last chapter. The only difference is that the To field is replaced by a Newsgroups field.

The Newsgroups field should show the name of the current newsgroup. If you want to send the message to multiple newsgroups, separate each name with a comma (,). (Alternatively, run the Tools | Select Newsgroups command and then choose a newsgroup from the dialog box that appears.)

To post your message, select File | Send Message (or press Alt+S or click the Post button in the toolbar).

Filtering Newsgroup Messages

I mentioned at the top of this chapter that many newsgroups are riddled with spam (unsolicited commercial email) and off-topic rants and raves. Such groups are said to have a bad *signal-to-noise ratio*. To help improve this ratio, Outlook Express has a newsgroup filter feature that enables you to set up criteria for messages you don't want to see. Here are the steps to follow to set up a newsgroup filter:

1. Select Tools | Newsgroup Filters. Outlook Express displays the Newsgroup Filters dialog box.

2. Click the Add button. You see the Properties dialog box shown in Figure 35.6.

FIGURE 35.6.

Use this dialog box to define the criteria for those messages you don't want to see.

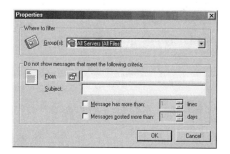

3. Use the Group(s) list to specify where you want your criteria applied. You can choose a specific (subscribed) newsgroup or server, or you can apply the filter to all your Usenet dealings (by selecting All Servers).

4. Use the following controls to define the criteria:

    From: Use this text box to specify one or more email addresses. In this case, Outlook Express won't display any messages that were sent from one of these addresses.

    Subject: Use this text box to filter out messages that contain a particular word or phrase in the Subject line.

> **Message has more than *x* lines:** Activate this check box to filter out messages that are longer than the number of lines specified in the spinner.

> **Message posted more than *x* days:** Activate this check box to filter out messages that are older than the number of days specified in the spinner.

5. Click OK to return to the Newsgroup Filters dialog box.

6. When you're finished, click OK to return to Outlook Express.

Setting News Options

You saw in the last chapter that Outlook Express has many options and settings that enable you to customize aspects of the Outlook Express email client. There are also quite a few options related to newsgroups, and this section runs through them all.

Options for Newsgroups and Messages

The options related to newsgroups and messages are in the Options dialog box, which you can get to by selecting the Tools | Options command.

The General Options

The General tab contains just two Usenet-related settings (see Chapter 34, "Outlook Express and Internet Email," for explanations of the other options in this tab):

> **Make Outlook Express my default news reader:** If you activate this check box, Outlook Express loads whenever you run your Web browser's "news" command. (In Internet Explorer, for example, select Go | News.)

> **Notify me if there are any new newsgroups:** When this check box is activated, Outlook Express polls the server for the names of newsgroups added since you last connected. If there are any, Outlook Express displays a dialog box to let you know. (A list of the new groups appears in the New tab of the Newsgroups dialog box.)

The Read Options

The Read tab, shown in Figure 35.7, boasts the following message-related settings (see Chapter 30 to learn about the other options in this tab):

> **Download *x* headers at a time:** If you deactivate this check box, Outlook Express does not download headers automatically when you select a newsgroup. If you leave this option activated, use the spinner to determine the maximum number of headers downloaded at a time.

> **Automatically expand conversation threads:** Activating this check box tells Outlook Express to expand all downloaded threads.

> **Automatically show news messages in the Preview Pane:** When this check box is activated and you're online, Outlook Express downloads and displays a message when

you highlight its header. If you'd prefer not to have messages downloaded automatically, deactivate this check box.

Mark all messages as read when exiting a newsgroup: If you activate this check box, Outlook Express marks every group message as read whenever you move to a different newsgroup.

Figure 35.7.

Use the Read tab to set various properties related to reading messages.

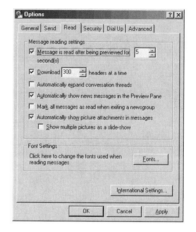

The Advanced Options

You find a few more message-related options in the Advanced tab, shown in Figure 35.8. Most of these options affect the local storage that Outlook Express uses for downloaded messages. Here's a summary:

Delete messages *x* days after being downloaded: When this check box is activated, Outlook Express deletes any downloaded message a specified number of days after the download.

Don't keep read messages: When this option is activated, Outlook Express removes read messages from local storage after you exit the program.

Compact files when there is *x* percent wasted space: This spinner determines the threshold point at which Outlook Express cleans up its local storage to reduce disk space usage. (Messages removed from local storage don't reduce the size of the cache, but just leave gaps. These gaps must be compacted to retrieve the disk space.)

Clean Up Now: Click this button to force Outlook Express to compact its local storage space immediately.

News Transport: Activate this check box to have Outlook Express maintain a log of commands sent to and from the news server. This log is stored in a file named inetnews.log, and it's saved in the server's subfolder of your Outlook Express application data folder:

\Windows\Application Data\Microsoft\Outlook Express\News\

FIGURE 35.8.

The Advanced tab contains various options related to the local storage of downloaded messages.

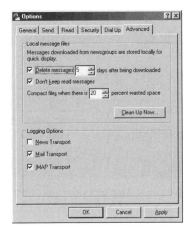

Options for Individual Newsgroups

Outlook Express also maintains a few properties related to individual newsgroups. To view these settings, highlight a newsgroup and then select File | Properties. The properties sheet that appears contains three tabs: General, Download, and Local Files. The General tab tells you the name of the newsgroup, the total number of available messages, and the number of those messages that are unread.

The Download tab, shown in Figure 35.9, enables you to set the default download setting for this newsgroup. These are the options that appear when you select the Tools | Download this Newsgroup command, discussed earlier in this chapter.

FIGURE 35.9.

Use the Download tab to set the default download option for this newsgroup.

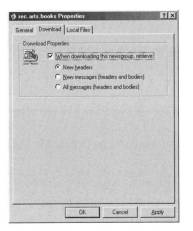

The Local Files tab, shown in Figure 35.10, contains settings that control the newsgroup's local message storage, which is a file in the server's subfolder of the main Outlook Express News folder:

`\Windows\Application Data\Microsoft\Outlook Express\News\`

The File Information group shows you the total size of the storage file, the size taken up by message headers, and the amount of wasted space in the file. You can adjust this storage by using the following buttons:

Compact: You saw earlier that Outlook Express deletes downloaded messages after a certain time, and it deletes read messages when you quit the program. These deletions create gaps in the local storage, which is the source of the wasted space value. To close these gaps and remove this wasted space, click the Compact button.

Remove Messages: Click this button to remove all the downloaded message bodies that are in the local storage file.

Delete: Click this button to clean out all the downloaded headers and message bodies from the local storage file.

Reset: Click this button to mark all read messages as unread. This enables you to download these headers again, and it prevents Outlook Express from deleting the marked messages when you quit the program.

Figure 35.10.

Use the Local Files tab to control the local storage for the newsgroup.

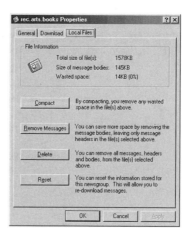

Summary

This chapter showed you how to use Outlook Express for reading Usenet news. I began by giving you quite a bit of Usenet background information. From there, you learned how to operate the Outlook Express program. I showed you how to work with newsgroups, how to download and read messages, how to post replies, and how to compose new messages. You also learned how to filter messages and how to work with the Usenet-related options.

Here's a list of chapters where you'll find related information:

■ To get the goods on TCP/IP and other Net plumbing, turn to Chapter 31, "Implementing TCP/IP for Internet and Intranet Connections."

■ To learn how to get an Internet connection established, see Chapter 32, "Windows 98 and the Internet."

■ Chapter 33, "Exploring the Web with Internet Explorer," shows you how to work with Internet Explorer.

■ To learn how to wield Outlook Express for Internet email, see Chapter 34, "Outlook Express and Internet Email."

Remote Collaboration with Microsoft NetMeeting

He sought to inject a few raisins of conversation into the tasteless dough of existence.

—O. Henry

As remote connection technologies improve, commuters find themselves morphing into telecommuters, and employees often end up with more freedom than ever to work where they want, when they want. In this new age of distance computing, the traditional definition of an office needs to be modified to include modern incarnations that are more "virtual" than physical.

Not only that, but the manner in which employees interact with each other also needs to be rethought. If members of, say, the editorial department are scattered all over the city, state, or even country, regular meetings just aren't possible. Sure, there is always email or company Web pages (or even that almost-forgotten device, the telephone) to keep distant workers informed, but these methods lack the interaction of a true meeting.

If you have users or colleagues who must collaborate regularly but who are too far flung to meet face-to-face, Microsoft NetMeeting might be the solution. NetMeeting is a communication and collaboration tool that allows users to establish "conferences" over an Internet, a network, or a modem connection. Within these conferences, remote users can interact in various ways:

■ They can have voice conversations using sound card/microphone combinations.

■ They can exchange files.

■ They can "chat" by sending text messages in real time.

■ They can use an electronic Whiteboard to collaborate on drawings.

■ They can share applications and even work together on the same document.

This chapter shows you how to set up NetMeeting and then takes you through all its collaboration features.

Configuring NetMeeting

I'm going to assume that you have an Internet/network connection set up and that you've installed NetMeeting. Given that, let's run through the steps necessary to configure the program. Begin by selecting Start|Programs|Internet Explorer|Microsoft NetMeeting. The first time you make this selection, Windows 98 launches the Microsoft NetMeeting Wizard. This dialog box just gives you an overview of NetMeeting's capabilities, so click Next > to proceed. You see the dialog box shown in Figure 36.1.

You can find other NetMeeting users (and they can find you) by logging in to a directory server (also known as an Internet Locator Server). NetMeeting will log you into one of these servers automatically at startup if you by leave the Log on to a directory server when NetMeeting starts check box activated. Use the drop-down list to select the domain name of a directory server. (You'll probably want to use the default ils.microsoft.com for now.) Click Next >.

FIGURE 36.1.

This dialog box sets up a couple of options for the User Location Service.

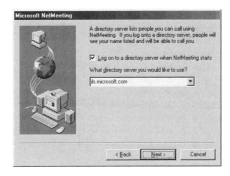

The next dialog box, shown in Figure 36.2, asks for a few particulars that help identify you in the NetMeeting user directory. At a minimum, you have to specify your first and last names and your email address to coax NetMeeting into continuing. (Don't worry—you can tell NetMeeting not to publish this information if you'd prefer to be incognito.) When you're done, click Next >.

FIGURE 36.2.

Use this dialog box to enter your personal data.

In the next wizard dialog box, shown in Figure 36.3, you're asked to categorize the data you entered in the previous step. Select For personal use, For business use, or For adults-only use, and then click Next >.

FIGURE 36.3.

Use this dialog box to categorize the data you entered.

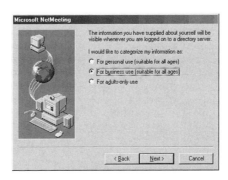

Now the wizard wonders what connection speed you'll be using for your NetMeeting collaborations. (Not surprisingly, the faster the connection, the better NetMeeting performs. However, for best results, you shouldn't select a connection speed that's faster than the one you'll be using.) Select the appropriate connection speed and then click Next >.

FIGURE 36.4.

Use this dialog box to select the speed of your NetMeeting connection.

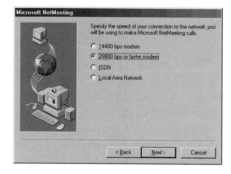

NetMeeting now launches the Audio Tuning Wizard, which checks your sound card to see whether it supports full-duplex (two-way) or half-duplex (one-way) sound. First, make sure that no other programs that use your sound card are running. This includes CD Player, Sound Recorder, Media Player, programs that use the sound card to broadcast messages ("You have mail!"), multimedia software, and so on. When that's done, click Next >.

The Audio Tuning Wizard first checks to see whether you have multiple audio devices in your computer. If you do, you see the dialog box shown in Figure 36.5. Select your Recording and Playback devices and then click Next >.

FIGURE 36.5.

The wizard may ask you to select recording and playback devices.

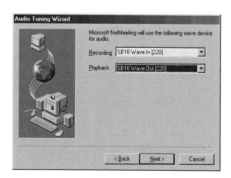

For the Audio Tuning Wizard's next chore, you see the dialog box shown in Figure 36.6. Click Test to play a sound and then adjust the Volume slider to taste. Click Next > when you're done.

Remote Collaboration with Microsoft NetMeeting

CHAPTER 36

977

36

COLLABORATION
WITH MICROSOFT
NETMEETING

FIGURE 36.6.

*Use this Audio Tuning
Wizard dialog box to
set the output audio
level.*

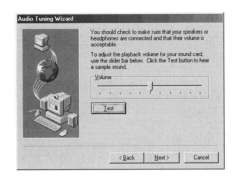

Now you use the dialog box shown in Figure 36.7 to adjust the input (microphone) volume.
Make sure that you have your sound card microphone plugged in and ready. Then speak into
the microphone using your normal voice (the Wizard displays some suggested text to read). As
you speak, the wizard adjusts the Record Volume slider automatically. Keep speaking until the
slider stabilizes. When the recording is complete, click Next > and then click Finish in the final
Wizard dialog box to continue loading NetMeeting.

FIGURE 36.7.

*Use this dialog box to
set the recording level
for your microphone.*

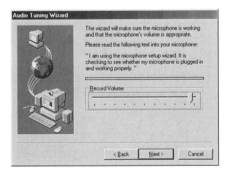

NETMEETING AND FIREWALLS

If your network has a firewall separating it from the Internet, the firewall must be configured
to allow Internet-based NetMeeting connections. Here are the ports NetMeeting uses for its
connections:

Port	Purpose	Protocol
389	ILS server	TCP
522	ULS server	TCP
1503	T.120	TCP
1720	H.323 call setup	TCP

continues

Port	Purpose	Protocol
continued		
1731	Audio call control	TCP
Dynamic	H.323 call control	TCP
Dynamic	H.323 stream	RTP over UDP

In other words, the firewall must be configured to allow TCP connections on ports 389, 522, 1503, 1720, and 1731, and secondary UDP connections on dynamically assigned ports.

A Tour of the NetMeeting Window

After the Wizard has completed its labors (and each subsequent time you select Start|Programs| Internet Explorer|Microsoft NetMeeting), the Microsoft NetMeeting window appears. Figure 36.8 shows how the window looks after you've logged on to a directory server. (If you didn't elect to log on to the directory at startup, you can log on at any time by selecting the Call|Log On to *server* command, where *server* is the domain name of your default directory server.)

FIGURE 36.8.

The NetMeeting window with an active conference.

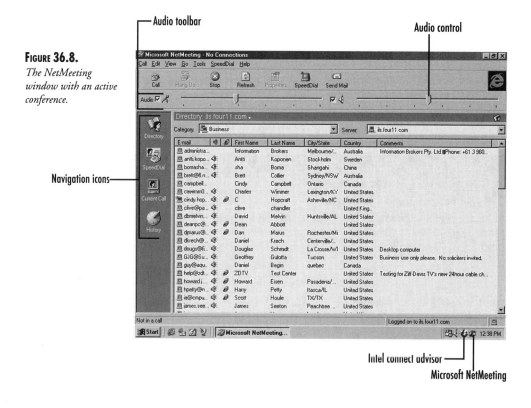

Here's a quick review of the NetMeeting window's features:

Toolbar: Provides point-and-click access to a few NetMeeting features. You can hide the toolbar by deactivating the View|Toolbar command.

Audio controls: The bottom half of the toolbar controls the NetMeeting volume. The slider on the left controls the volume of the microphone, and the slider on the right controls the volume of the speaker. You can mute either device by deactivating its check box.

Navigation icons: Clicking these icons takes you to the four main NetMeeting folders (you can also select the folder names from the View menu):

- Directory—This folder enables you to view the users logged on to a directory server.

- SpeedDial—You use this folder to create a list of frequently called users.

- Current Call—The folder opens when you connect with another user.

- History—This folder shows the results of your recent incoming and outgoing calls.

Note, too, that when NetMeeting is running it adds a couple of icons to the system tray:

Intel Connection Advisor: Double-clicking this icon opens the Intel Connection Advisor window. During a call, this window shows you the following audio and video properties: the transfer rate, the delay, and the percentage loss.

Microsoft NetMeeting: Click this icon for access to several NetMeeting features.

Placing NetMeeting Calls

After NetMeeting is configured and you have the Internet or network connection established, you can get right down to business. In this section, I'll show you how to make calls in NetMeeting, use the Directory to find folks to talk with, place advanced and SpeedDial calls, and more.

Placing Simple Calls

If you know who you want to call, NetMeeting is simple to use. Here are the steps to follow:

1. Select the Call|New Call command, or press Ctrl+N. (You can also click the Call button in the NetMeeting toolbar.) You see the New Call dialog box, shown in Figure 36.9.

FIGURE 36.9.

Use this dialog box to tell NetMeeting who you want to call.

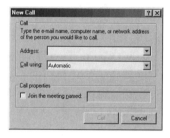

2. In the Address list, specify the person you want to call by entering one of the following:

   ■ If the person is logged on to the same directory server as you, type his or her email address.

   ■ If the person is logged on to a different directory server, type the server name, a slash (/), and then his or her email address (for example, `ils.microsoft.com/biff@newbie.net`).

   ■ If you're on a network, type the name that the person's computer uses on the network.

   ■ If the person is connected to the Internet, type the host name of his or her computer.

TRY IP ADDRESSES

If you can't connect to a user by entering his or her network computer name or Internet host name, try entering the user's IP address.

CALLING NETWARE USERS

If you want to call another user over a NetWare IPX network, the user's address must use the following format:

network:*node*

Here, *network* is the IPX network address, and *node* is the user's node address. Unfortunately, there is no built-in method for determining a user's network node address. However, Microsoft has created a tool that can sniff out network node addresses. The file is `IPXAddr.exe`, and you can download it from the following page on Microsoft's Web site:

`http://premium.microsoft.com/download/support/mslfiles/ipxaddr.exe`

3. In the Call using list, select either Network (TCP/IP) or Directory Server. (Alternatively, you can select Automatic and let NetMeeting figure it out.)

4. Click Call.

After NetMeeting finds the user and places the call, the other person hears a ring and sees a dialog box similar to the one shown in Figure 36.10. The remote user clicks Accept to "answer" the call or clicks Ignore to reject the call. (NetMeeting rejects an incoming call automatically if it isn't answered after five rings.)

FIGURE 36.10.

This dialog box appears when there is an incoming NetMeeting call.

If the call went through, your name and the remote user's name are added to the Current Call folder, and NetMeeting displays In a call in the status bar (see Figure 36.11).

FIGURE 36.11.

The Current Call folder with a call in progress.

User has audio capability

User has video capability

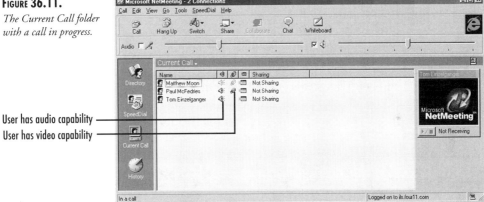

If the remote user is already involved in a conference, you see the dialog box shown in Figure 36.12. Click Yes to attempt to join the existing conference or click No if you prefer to try again later.

FIGURE 36.12.

This dialog box shows up if the remote user is already in a conference.

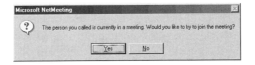

TROUBLESHOOTING: NO VOICE CONNECTION

If you can't seem to get a voice connection in NetMeeting (even when only two users are in the conference), make sure that you're connecting via the TCP/IP protocol. NetMeeting's voice features are enabled only on TCP/IP connections. To learn how to tell NetMeeting to use TCP/IP, see "Setting NetMeeting Properties" later in this chapter.

Here are some notes to bear in mind when you're connected:

- To talk to the other person, just speak into your microphone. If the sound cards used by you and the remote user can handle full-duplex audio, both of you can speak at the same time. If the cards support only half-duplex audio, only one of you can speak at a time.

- If the remote user complains that your voice isn't loud enough, you can increase your microphone volume or the remote user can increase his or her speaker volume.

- To find out the email address and other particulars about the remote user (depending on what that person entered into his or her NetMeeting configuration), right-click the user and select Properties from the context menu.

- As shown in Figure 36.11, users who have voice capability are shown with an icon in the audio column. Similarly, users with video capability have an icon in the video column.

- In a conference, only two people can communicate by voice or video at one time. If a third person joins the conference, that person can communicate only via Chat, Whiteboard, or some other NetMeeting feature. (For users who can't communicate by voice or video, NetMeeting grays out the icons in the audio and video columns.)

SWITCHING AUDIO AND VIDEO

Although NetMeeting allows audio and video contact for only two people, the other users in the conference aren't out of luck. NetMeeting enables you to switch the audio/video contact to another person by selecting the Tools | Switch Audio and Video command, and then selecting a user from the submenu that appears. This list of users also appears when you click the Switch toolbar button.

- Under ideal conditions, NetMeeting supports a maximum of 32 callers in a conference. In practice, the maximum number of participants might be less, depending on the available network bandwidth and the speed of the users' computers.

- If your system is capable of displaying video, the outgoing and incoming video streams are displayed in windows within the Current Call folder, as shown in Figure 36.13. (Even if you don't have a desktop camera or video capture device, NetMeeting will

Remote Collaboration with Microsoft NetMeeting

CHAPTER 36

983

36

COLLABORATION
WITH MICROSOFT
NETMEETING

still show incoming video.) You can toggle outgoing video on and off by selecting the Tools|Video|Send command. Similarly, you can toggle incoming video on and off by selecting the Tools|Video|Receive command. Note, too, that the Tools|Video submenu has two commands—Detach My Video and Detach Remote Video—that display the video streams in separate windows.

FIGURE 36.13.

The Current Call folder with outgoing and incoming video streams.

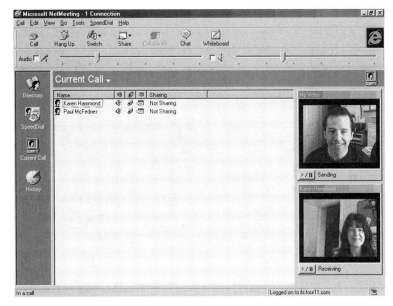

Hanging Up from a Call

When it's time to end a NetMeeting call, use any of the following techniques to hang up:

- Select Call|Hang Up.
- Click the Hang Up button on the toolbar.
- Select Call|Exit or close the NetMeeting window.

NetMeeting disconnects the call. If you began the conference and it includes three or more people, NetMeeting displays the warning dialog box shown in Figure 36.14. To disconnect everyone in the conference, click Yes.

FIGURE 36.14.

NetMeeting displays this dialog box when you attempt to hang up from a conference that contains three or more users.

Using the Directory to Make a Call

When you launch NetMeeting, the program automatically logs you on to a directory server (assuming you activated this option during configuration). This is a server that keeps track of the people who are currently running NetMeeting. If you're looking for someone to call, NetMeeting's Directory folder can provide you with a list of these users.

To open the Directory, either select the View|Directory command or click the Directory button on the toolbar. When you're in the folder, use the Server drop-down list to choose the directory server you want to work with. NetMeeting then connects to the server and downloads the list of users who are logged on. (Note that it might take a minute or two to complete the download of users, depending on the speed of your connection.) Figure 36.15 shows the Directory folder with the list of users.

FIGURE 36.15.

The Directory folder shows you a list of all the people who are logged on to the current server.

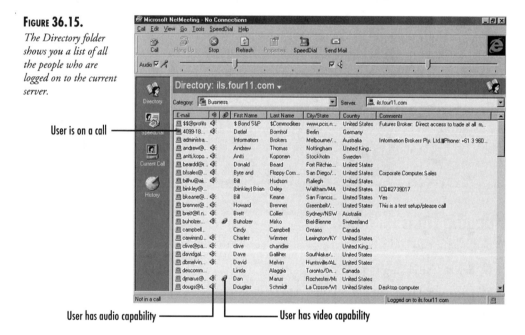

User is on a call

User has audio capability ——— ——— User has video capability

The Directory folder shows the email address, name, and location of each user, as well as the comments they entered in their configuration. Figure 36.15 points out the icons that tell you whether the user is on a call and whether the user has audio or video capability. Here are a few more notes about the Directory list:

■ The initial order of the users is by email address. To change the sort order, click the column headers. For example, click the Last Name header to sort the entries by last name in ascending order. Click the header again to switch to descending order.

■ You can use the Category drop-down list to filter the messages. For example, you can switch between Business users, Personal users, and All users. You can also select users who have video cameras and those who live in your country.

■ To see the latest user list for the current server, either select View|Refresh or press F5.

■ If you prefer to work with a different directory server, use the Server drop-down list and select the server you want.

When you've found someone you want to connect with, highlight that directory entry and then either select Call|New Call or click the Call button.

REMOVING YOUR NAME FROM THE SERVER

If you'd rather not have your name appear in your default directory server (which is sort of like having an unlisted NetMeeting number), NetMeeting gives you two methods for leaving your name off the list:

■ Log off the server by selecting Call | Log Off from *server* (where *server* is the domain of your default directory server). In the dialog box that appears, click OK. (Note that you still can use the service to find other people.)

■ Select Tools | Options, activate the Calling tab, and then activate the following check box: Do not list my name in the directory. People can call me if they know my email name.

Accessing the Web Directory

Microsoft also maintains a Web-based directory of NetMeeting users. To display the Web Directory, first use either of the following methods:

■ Select Go|Web Directory.

■ Enter the server URL into a Web browser. The URL of the main server is `http://ils.microsoft.com/`. Other server URLs take the form `http://ilsx.microsoft.com/`, where *x* is a number (1 through 5 at the time of this writing).

When you get to the server page, click the Directory link to display the form shown in Figure 36.16. Select the options you want to use to filter the user list and then click Submit. The directory then displays a list of the users that match your criteria.

The advantage of using the Web Directory is that after the page loads, you can use the browser's Find command to look for specific entries in the Directory. (If you're working in frames, you might need to click inside the list of users for the Find feature to operate properly.)

FIGURE 36.16.

Use this form to filter the user list.

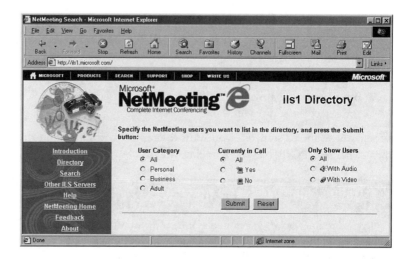

Use the links on the Web Directory page as a general guide for creating NetMeeting links on your own Web pages. Here's the general format to use:

```
<A HREF="callto:server/email">
```

Here, *server* is the domain name of your directory server, and *email* is the email address you used when configuring NetMeeting. Here's a sample link (see Chapter 37, "Web Page Publishing with Windows 98," for information on the <A> tag):

```
<A HREF="callto:ils1.microsoft.com/paul@mcfedries.com">
Click here to talk to me live!
</A>
```

Using the SpeedDial Feature

If you call certain people frequently, you can use NetMeeting's SpeedDial feature to connect to those users with only a couple of mouse clicks or keystrokes.

By default, NetMeeting adds SpeedDial entries automatically for users you call and users who call you. I'll show you later how to turn this feature off. If you do so, you can use either of the following methods to create a SpeedDial entry by hand:

- While you're connected to a user, right-click the user's name and click Add SpeedDial in the context menu.
- Select SpeedDial|Add SpeedDial to display the dialog box shown in Figure 36.17. Fill in the Address and Call using controls, make sure the Add to SpeedDial option is activated, and then click OK.

Remote Collaboration with Microsoft NetMeeting

CHAPTER 36

987

36

COLLABORATION
WITH MICROSOFT
NETMEETING

FIGURE 36.17.
Use this dialog box to add a new SpeedDial entry.

After you've added someone to the SpeedDial, you can call the person by pulling down the SpeedDial menu and selecting his or her name from the list that appears at the bottom of the menu. Alternatively, open the SpeedDial folder, right-click the user, and then click Call.

To remove someone from the SpeedDial menu, open the SpeedDial folder, right-click the user, and then click Delete SpeedDial (or you can press the Delete key).

CREATE A SPEEDDIAL FOR YOURSELF

If you want to give other people a SpeedDial shortcut that connects to you, select SpeedDial | Add SpeedDial. In the dialog box that appears, enter your NetMeeting address and calling method and then select one of the following options:

Send to mail recipient: Sends the SpeedDial shortcut via email.

Save on the desktop: Creates a SpeedDial shortcut on your desktop.

Hanging Out a "Do Not Disturb" Sign

If you have NetMeeting running but you don't want to accept any new calls for a while, you can hang an electronic "Do Not Disturb" sign by activating the Call|Do Not Disturb command (click OK in the dialog box that appears). While this command is active, others attempting to call you will receive a message telling them The other party did not accept your call.

ACCEPTING CALLS WITHOUT AUDIO

Instead of cutting off calls altogether, you might prefer to avoid only voice calls. To do that, start a NetMeeting conference beforehand by selecting Call | Host Meeting (click OK in the dialog box that appears). With the conference started, all incoming calls will be "No Voice" connections. To return to regular operations, hang up the call.

Exchanging Files in NetMeeting

Assuming that you've established a connection with one or more remote users, NetMeeting makes it easy to send files back and forth. To initiate a file transfer, use any of the following techniques:

- ■ Select Tools|File Transfer|Send File.
- ■ Press Ctrl+F.
- ■ If you have multiple users in your conference, you can send the file to an individual by right-clicking the person's name in the Current Call folder and then selecting Send File from the context menu.

NetMeeting then displays the Select a File to Send dialog box, as shown in Figure 36.18. Highlight the file you want to ship and then click Send. NetMeeting begins sending the file and displays the progress of the operation in the status bar. When the upload is complete, a dialog box lets you know.

FIGURE 36.18.

Use this dialog box to choose the file you want to send to the remote user.

On the remote end, the user sees a dialog box similar to the one shown in Figure 36.19. There are three ways to proceed:

- ■ To have NetMeeting store the file on your hard drive without further ado, click Accept. Alternatively, you can wait until the download is complete and then click Close.
- ■ To cancel the file transfer (or to remove the file after the transfer is finished), click Delete.
- ■ To work with the file after the transfer is done, click Open.

FILE TRANSFER OPTIONS

NetMeeting has a few options that enable you to prevent file downloads and specify the folder in which transferred files are stored (the default is \NetMeeting\Received Files). See "Setting NetMeeting Properties" later in this chapter for details.

Remote Collaboration with Microsoft NetMeeting

CHAPTER **36**

989

36

COLLABORATION
WITH MICROSOFT
NETMEETING

FIGURE 36.19.

This dialog box appears when a remote user attempts to send you a file.

Using the Chat Feature

If you have a "No Voice" connection in a conference, or if you don't have a microphone, NetMeeting's audio features won't do you much good. That doesn't mean you can't communicate with remote callers, however. For simple text communications in real time, NetMeeting's Chat feature is perfect.

To run Chat, use any of the following methods:

- Select Tools|Chat.
- Press Ctrl+T.
- Click the Chat toolbar button.

The Chat window that appears is shown in Figure 36.20.

FIGURE 36.20.

Use the Chat window to type messages to remote users in real time.

To use Chat, follow these steps:

1. Type your message in the Message text box.
2. Use the Send to list to select the recipient of the message.
3. Press Enter or click the Send button to the right of the Message text box.

These messages appear in the upper text box, along with the name of each person who sent them. Figure 36.21 shows a sample Chat session.

FIGURE 36.21.

A Chat session in progress.

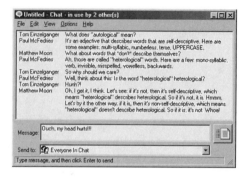

Chat also has a couple of customization features. For example, you can select Options|Font to choose the font that's displayed in the Chat window. Selecting Options|Chat Format displays the Chat Format dialog box shown in Figure 36.22. Here's a summary of the available options:

Information display: Use these check boxes to specify how much information Chat displays about each message. Besides the Person's name, you can also choose to display the Date and Time each message is sent.

Entire message is on one line: If you activate this option, each Chat message is displayed on a single line across the window.

Wrap (message appears next to information display): If you activate this option (this is the Chat default), the messages are wrapped within the Chat window, and they appear beside the person's name (or whatever is checked in the Information display group).

Wrap (message appears below information display): If you activate this option, the messages again are wrapped within the Chat window, but they appear below the displayed information.

FIGURE 36.22.

Use this dialog box to customize the Chat window.

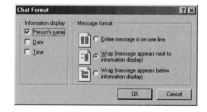

Using the Whiteboard

Whiteboards have become a standard feature in boardrooms and conference rooms across the land. Presenters, facilitators, and meeting leaders use them to record action points, highlight important information, and draw charts and diagrams.

If you're running a remote conference via NetMeeting, you can use its Whiteboard feature for the same purposes. The Whiteboard is basically a revamped version of the Paint window that allows you to enter text, highlight information, and draw lines and shapes. Everything you add to the Whiteboard is reflected on the other users' screens, so they see exactly what you're typing and drawing. You can create multiple Whiteboard "pages" and even save pages for later use.

To work with the Whiteboard, each user must display it by using any of the following techniques:

- Select Tools|Whiteboard.
- Press Ctrl+W.
- Click the Whiteboard toolbar button.

Figure 36.23 shows the Whiteboard window that appears.

FIGURE 36.23.

Use the Whiteboard to draw text and pictures that can be seen by the other users in the conference.

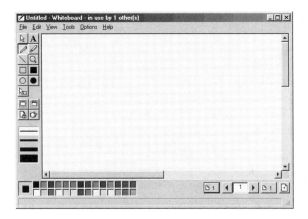

For basic operations, you use Whiteboard just as you use Paint. That is, you select a tool to work with, select a line width (if applicable for the tool), select a color, and then draw your shape or type your text.

However, Whiteboard has quite a few other techniques that aren't found in the Paint program. Here's a summary:

Locking the Whiteboard contents: To prevent other users from changing the Whiteboard screen while you work, either select Tools|Lock Contents or click the Lock Contents tool.

Using the remote pointer: Whiteboard has a remote pointer that, when activated, appears on each user's Whiteboard. To activate it, either select Tools| Remote Pointer or click the Remote Pointer On tool. After the pointer appears, use the mouse to drag it around the screen.

Displaying the contents of another window in the Whiteboard: Whiteboard has a Select Window feature that allows you to display the contents of another open window inside the Whiteboard. To activate this feature, either select Tools|Select Window or click the Select Window tool. Click OK in the Whiteboard Select Window dialog box that appears and then click the window you want to display.

 Displaying part of the screen in the Whiteboard: Rather than an entire window, you might prefer to display only part of the screen in the Whiteboard. To do this, either select Tools|Select Area or click the Select Area tool. Click OK in the Whiteboard Select Area dialog box that appears and then use the mouse to select the screen area you want to display.

Clearing the Whiteboard: If you want to start over, you can clear the contents of the Whiteboard either by selecting Edit|Clear Page or by pressing Ctrl+Delete.

 Adding another page to the Whiteboard: The Whiteboard is capable of displaying multiple pages. To add a new page, either select Edit|Insert Page After or click the Insert New Page button. You can insert a new page before an existing page by selecting Edit|New Page Before.

Navigating Whiteboard pages: When you have multiple pages in the Whiteboard, you can navigate among them by pressing Ctrl+Page Up (to move to the next page) or Ctrl+Page Down (to move to the previous page). Note that as you move from page to page, the remote users' Whiteboards also change pages. You can also use the following navigation buttons:

 Previous Page

 Next Page

Sorting Whiteboard pages: To change the order in which the Whiteboard pages appear, select Edit|Page Sorter. In the Page Sorter dialog box, use the mouse to drag the pages into the order you prefer.

Deleting a Whiteboard page: To remove the current page from the Whiteboard, select Edit|Delete page.

Preventing remote users from seeing your changes: If you want to make some changes to a page without the other users seeing them, deactivate the Tools|Synchronize command, move to the page and make your changes, and then activate Tools|Synchronize again. The remote users will remain on the original page while you make your edits.

Saving the Whiteboard: If you think you'll need to use your Whiteboard again, select File|Save and then choose a location and name for the new file (Whiteboard files use the .WHT extension). To reuse the Whiteboard, select File|Open and pick out the WHT file from the Open dialog box.

Sharing Programs

Chat and the Whiteboard are handy features, but their functionality is limited to text and simple drawings or screen shots. For truly collaborative computing, you need the ability to run a program on one computer and display what's happening on the remote machines. An even better scenario is one in which all the users can work with an application at the same time.

The good news is that NetMeeting can handle both situations, albeit with a few quirks and security concerns. The next two sections take you through NetMeeting's application-sharing features.

Sharing an Application in Work Alone Mode

NetMeeting's default method for application sharing is called Work Alone mode. In this mode, you select one of your running programs to share, and the program's window appears on the other users' screens. However, only you can access the program's features and edit the program's documents. This is perfect if you just want to demonstrate a feature or display a document.

To share an application in this way, first use either of the following techniques:

- ■ Select Tools|Share Application.
- ■ Click the Share button on the toolbar.

As you can see in Figure 36.24, a list of your running applications appears. Click the application you want to share, and in the NetMeeting dialog box that appears, click OK. A copy of the application's window is sent to each user, and any actions you perform within this window (including mouse movements) are mirrored on the remote screens. Note, too, that NetMeeting's Current Call folder displays Not Collaborating in the Sharing column of each user.

FIGURE 36.24.

The Share Application button and menu (shown here) contain a list of your running applications.

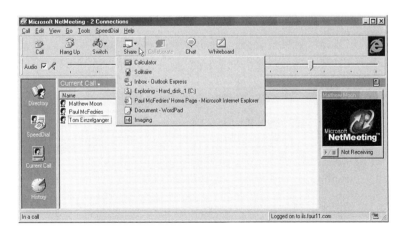

To end the sharing, either exit the program or select it again from the Share Application menu or button.

Sharing an Application in Collaborate Mode

Instead of merely demonstrating a program to the other users, you might prefer a more interactive approach that allows each user to work with the shared application. This is called Collaborate mode. After you've shared an application, you switch to this mode by using either of these methods:

- Activate the Tools|Start Collaborating command.
- Click the Collaborate toolbar button.

NetMeeting displays a dialog box warning you about possible security problems with Collaborate mode (which I discuss later). Click OK to continue. Note that each person who wants to collaborate on this application will also have to switch to Collaborate mode.

Figure 36.25 demonstrates a few features that come with Collaborate mode, as described here:

The sharing status: In the Current Call folder, the Sharing column reports the sharing status of each user: In Control for the user who currently controls the shared application, Collaborating for users who are collaborating on the application but don't have control, and Not Collaborating for users who aren't collaborating.

The shared application window: Above the upper-right corner of the window, NetMeeting displays the name of the user who is running the application. (This banner appears only in nonmaximized windows.)

Taking control of the shared application: Only one person can work in a shared application window at one time. To take control of the application, just click the mouse anywhere within the application's window.

To end the collaboration, either exit the application or use one of the following techniques:

- Activate the Tools|Stop Collaborating command.
- Click the Collaborate toolbar button.

Some Notes About Sharing Applications

NetMeeting's application-sharing features are a real boon to collaborative computing, but they come with a few "gotchas" and limitations. Here are a few notes to keep in mind when sharing applications:

Graphics-intensive applications and DOS programs: NetMeeting doesn't do the greatest job sharing graphics-intensive applications (especially those that use the DirectX APIs) and DOS programs. Try to avoid sharing these types of applications.

Remote Collaboration with Microsoft NetMeeting

CHAPTER **36**

995

36

COLLABORATION
WITH MICROSOFT
NETMEETING

The name of the user who is running the application

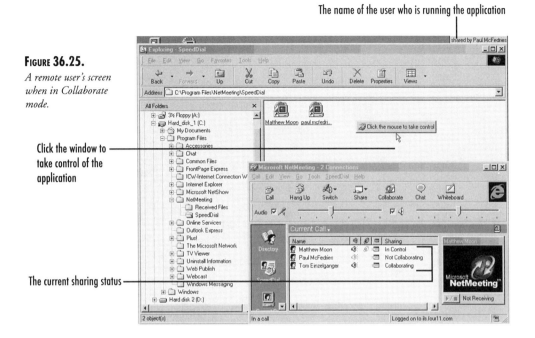

FIGURE 36.25.

A remote user's screen when in Collaborate mode.

Click the window to take control of the application

The current sharing status

Handling different screen resolutions: Application sharing works best when all users have their screens set to the same resolution. If a user running at high resolution (say 1,024×768) shares a maximized application with a user running at low resolution (say, 640×480), the user with the lower resolution sees only part of the shared application's window. However, that user can still see more of the window by moving the mouse pointer to the edge of the screen, which causes the window to scroll. (You have some control over this behavior; see the section "Setting NetMeeting Properties.")

Security concerns in Collaborate mode: When you share an application in Collaborate mode, remember that other people can assume control over that application and use it just as though they were sitting at your keyboard. Depending on the program, this might include the ability to open, save, and delete files, or even to launch programs.

Windows Explorer and Internet Explorer are shared simultaneously: Thanks to Windows 98's Web integration, if you share Windows Explorer and you have an Internet Explorer window open, Internet Explorer gets shared as well.

Hiding part of a shared window: If you have data in an application window that you want to hide from others, use another open window to cover that portion of the shared window. The remote users will see a pattern over the obscured section of the window.

Setting NetMeeting Properties

To finish our look at NetMeeting, this section shows you how to customize the program using its extensive list of properties. To work with these options, select Tools|Options to display the Options dialog box, shown in Figure 36.26. The next few sections run through the controls on each tab.

FIGURE 36.26.

Use the Options dialog box to customize NetMeeting.

The General Tab

The options in the General tab control a mixed bag of NetMeeting settings. Here's a review:

Show Microsoft NetMeeting icon on the taskbar: This check box toggles the NetMeeting icon on and off in the system tray.

Run when Windows starts and notify me of incoming calls: When this check box is activated, NetMeeting is launched automatically when you start Windows 98.

Automatically accept incoming calls: When this check box is activated, NetMeeting accepts all incoming calls.

Show the SpeedDial tab when NetMeeting starts: When this check box is activated, NetMeeting opens the SpeedDial folder each time you start the program.

Show Intel Connection Advisor icon on the taskbar: This check box toggles the Intel Connection Advisor icon on and off in the system tray.

Network bandwidth: Use this list to select your connection speed.

File transfer: This group shows you the folder that NetMeeting uses to store incoming files. Click View Files to open the folder; click Change Folder to select a different storage area.

The My Information Tab

The controls in the My Information tab display the personal NetMeeting data that you specified when configuring the program. Feel free to edit this information as needed.

The Calling Tab

The Calling tab, shown in Figure 36.27, controls various settings for your directory server and the SpeedDial feature:

Log on to the directory server when NetMeeting starts: If you deactivate this check box, NetMeeting will not log you on to the directory server. If you leave this check box activated, use the drop-down list to select the server on which you want your information published and onto which you log each time you start NetMeeting.

Do not list my name in the directory. People can call me if they know my e-mail name: Deactivate this check box if you prefer that your data not appear in the directory server.

Refresh directory listing when NetMeeting starts: When this check box is activated, NetMeeting connects to the default server and downloads an updated list of the users who are logged on.

Automatically add SpeedDials for people I call and people who call me: These options determine when NetMeeting creates SpeedDial entries automatically. Select either Never, Ask me after each call is accepted, or Always.

Refresh SpeedDial list when NetMeeting starts: When this check box is activated, NetMeeting runs through the SpeedDial entries and checks the server to see whether all users are logged on and whether they're participating in a call.

Automatically refresh SpeedDial list every *x* minutes: If you activate this setting, NetMeeting updates the data on each SpeedDial user at whatever interval you specify in the spinner.

Do not add more than *x* SpeedDials automatically: When this check box is activated, you can use the text box to set the maximum number of SpeedDial entries that NetMeeting can add automatically.

The Audio Tab

The Audio tab, shown in Figure 36.28, controls various settings related to the audio portion of the NetMeeting show. Here's a summary:

Enable full duplex audio so I can speak while receiving audio: This check box toggles full-duplex (two-way) audio on and off.

FIGURE 36.27.

*Use the Calling tab to
set a few options related
to the directory server
and the SpeedDial
feature.*

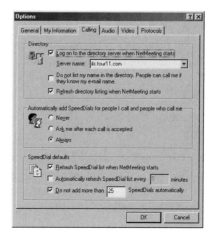

Enable auto-gain control: NetMeeting's automatic gain feature adjusts the microphone volume based on the volume of your voice. That is, if you speak quietly,
NetMeeting increases the microphone volume to compensate; if you speak loudly, the
value is decreased accordingly. If a noisy work environment causes the microphone
level to fluctuate unpredictably, deactivate this check box to shut off automatic gain.

Tuning Wizard: Click this button to run the Audio Tuning Wizard. This is a good
idea if you change your sound card or the speed of your connection. (You can also
launch the Audio Tuning Wizard by selecting Tools|Audio Tuning Wizard. Note
that this command is unavailable while you're in an audio conference.)

Advanced: Click this button if you'd like to configure your own audio codecs. In the
Advanced Compression Settings dialog box, activate the Manually configure compression settings check box. Then use the Up and Down buttons to determine the codec
order you want.

Microphone sensitivity: The sensitivity of your microphone is a measure of how it
handles background noises. A high sensitivity setting means the microphone will pick
up background noises. By default, NetMeeting adjusts this sensitivity automatically
(that is, the Adjust sensitivity automatically option button is activated). If you prefer
to make the adjustments yourself, activate the Let me adjust sensitivity myself option
and then use the slider to choose a setting (move the slider to the right for higher
sensitivity; move it to the left for lower sensitivity).

Use H.323 gateway: NetMeeting can use H.323 gateways to place calls to regular
telephones. To use this feature, activate this check box and then use the text box to
enter the name of the H.323 gateway.

Remote Collaboration with Microsoft NetMeeting

CHAPTER 36

999

36

COLLABORATION
WITH MICROSOFT
NETMEETING

FIGURE 36.28.

Use the Audio tab to customize NetMeeting's sound capabilities.

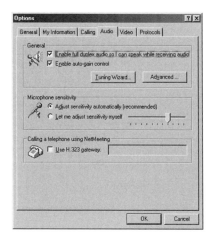

The Video Tab

If you have video capability on your system, use the controls in the Video tab, shown in Figure 36.29, to set up your video conferencing:

Automatically send video at the start of each call: When this check box is deactivated, you have to initiate the outgoing video stream by hand. Activating this check box tells NetMeeting to start sending the video immediately.

Automatically receive video at the start of each call: When this check box is activated, NetMeeting displays the incoming video stream when the call is connected. If you'd prefer not to see incoming video, deactivate this check box.

Send image size: These options determine the default size of the video image you send.

Video quality: As usual with video applications, in NetMeeting there is a trade-off between video speed and video quality. You can use this slider to set the level of quality you prefer. Move the slider to the left for a better frame rate; move the slider to the right for higher quality within each frame.

The video capture device I wish to use is: This list shows you the video device NetMeeting is using. If you have more than one device on your system, use this list to select the one you want to use. Click the Source button to display the Video Source dialog box, which enables you to adjust various settings related to the device.

FIGURE 36.29.

Use the Video tab to adjust NetMeeting's video settings.

The Protocols Tab

You use the Protocols tab, shown in Figure 36.30, to determine the networking protocols that are available to NetMeeting:

Network (TCP/IP): Activate this protocol to make TCP/IP-based connections over a network or the Internet.

Null Modem: Use this protocol for computers connected via a null-modem cable. You can set various properties for this protocol by highlighting it and clicking Properties.

FIGURE 36.30.

The Protocols tab determines the transport mechanisms available to NetMeeting.

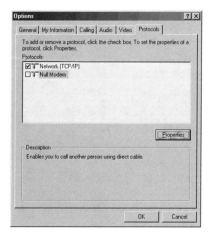

Summary

This chapter showed you how to work with Microsoft NetMeeting. After explaining how to configure the program, I gave you a tour of the NetMeeting window. From there, you learned various methods for placing calls within NetMeeting. I then showed you how to exchange files, how to use the Chat feature and the Whiteboard, and how to share applications. I finished by running through all NetMeeting's customization options.

Here's a list of chapters where you'll find related information:

- Windows video was the subject of Chapter 24, "DirectX and Windows 98 Video."
- To learn more about sound in Windows 98, see Chapter 25, "Windows 98 Audio Features."
- To set up a remote connection for use with NetMeeting, head for Chapter 32, "Windows 98 and the Internet."

36

COLLABORATION WITH MICROSOFT NETMEETING

Web Page Publishing with Windows 98

If you've seen some World Wide Web pages in your Internet travels, you might think you need a high-end word processor or page layout application to achieve all those fancy effects. Well, although you can use a sophisticated software package, the truth is that any basic text editor (such as Windows 98's Notepad accessory) is all you need to create attractive Web pages.

New to 98

On the other hand, forging pages manually isn't for everyone. If you'd prefer a more WYSIWYG (What You See Is What You Get) approach, Windows 98 can help there too, thanks to its FrontPage Express HTML (Hypertext Markup Language) editor.

This chapter takes you through both approaches. You get not only a primer on the basic elements that constitute HTML, but also the instructions for using FrontPage Express to create a page without having to deal with HTML. Why both? Well, even the most sophisticated HTML editor (and I'd rate FrontPage Express as a middle-of-the-pack editor) won't produce pages that look exactly the way you want. Inevitably, you need to tweak the underlying HTML code to get just the effect you want.

Understanding HTML Tags

Underneath all the bells and whistles, Web pages are relatively simple affairs. You just type in your text and then insert markers—called *tags*—that dictate how you want things to look. For example, if you'd like a word on your page to appear in bold text, you surround that word with the appropriate tags for boldness.

In general, tags use the following format:

```
<TAG>The text to be affected</TAG>
```

The *TAG* part is a code (usually just a few letters, but often an entire word) that specifies the type of effect you want. For example, the tag for bolding is <B>. So if you wanted the phrase "ACME Coyote Supplies" to appear in bold, you'd type the following into your document:

```
<B>ACME Coyote Supplies</B>
```

The first <B> tells the browser to display all the text that follows in a bold font. This continues until the </B> is reached. The slash (/) defines this as an *end tag*, which tells the browser to turn off the effect. As you'll see, there are tags for lots of other effects, including italics, paragraphs, headings, page titles, lists, and much more. HTML is just the sum total of all these tags.

HTML REFERENCES

This chapter presents only the briefest of introductions to HTML. Most of the tags I'll be talking about have a number of attributes that you can use to refine each tag's behavior. To learn more, you can find a number of HTML references on the Web. Yahoo! provides a list of these references at the following address:

```
http://www.yahoo.com/Computers_and_Internet/Information_and_Documentation/
➡Data_Formats/HTML/Reference/
```

Microsoft also maintains an excellent HTML reference (geared, of course, toward the capabilities of Internet Explorer) at the following address:

`http://www.microsoft.com/workshop/author/newhtml/default.htm`

The Basic Structure of Web Pages

Web pages range from dull to dynamic, inane to indispensable, but they all have the same underlying structure. This consistent structure—which, as you'll see, is nothing more than a small collection of HTML tags—is the reason why almost all browser programs running on almost all types of computers can successfully display almost all Web pages.

HTML files always start with the <HTML> tag. This tag doesn't do much except tell any Web browser that tries to read the file that it's dealing with a file that contains HTML codes. Similarly, the last line in your document will always be the </HTML> tag, which you can think of as the HTML equivalent of "The End."

The next items in the HTML tag catalog serve to divide the document into two sections: the *head* and the *body*.

The head section is like an introduction to the page. Web browsers use the head to glean various types of information about the page. Although a number of items can appear in the head section, the most common is the title of the page, which I'll talk about shortly. To define the head, you add a <HEAD> tag and a </HEAD> tag immediately below the <HTML> tag.

The body section is where you enter both the text that will actually appear on the Web page and the other tags that control the look of the page. To define the body, you place a <BODY> tag and a </BODY> tag after the head section (that is, below the </HEAD> tag).

These tags define the basic structure of every Web page:

```
<HTML>
<HEAD>
Header tags go here.
</HEAD>
<BODY>
The Web page text and tags go here.
</BODY>
</HTML>
```

Getting Started with FrontPage Express

This is as good a place as any to bring FrontPage Express into the discussion. To get the program started, select Start | Programs | Internet Explorer | FrontPage Express. Figure 37.1 shows the FrontPage Express window that appears.

37

WEB PAGE
PUBLISHING WITH
WINDOWS 98

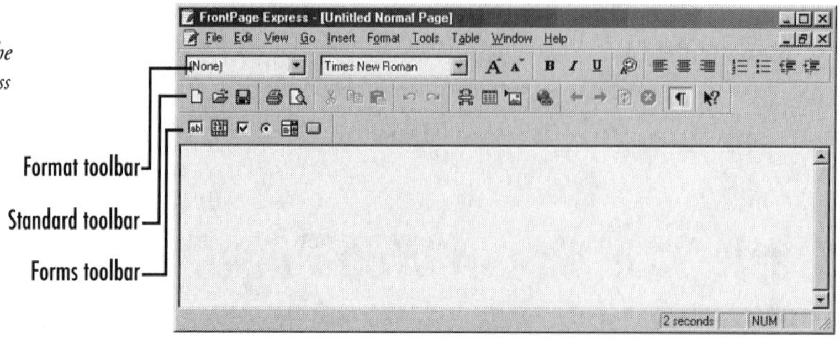

FIGURE 37.1.

The features of the FrontPage Express window.

Format toolbar⌐

Standard toolbar⌐

Forms toolbar⌐

PAGE DOWNLOAD TIME

If you look at the FrontPage Express status bar, you see that one of the boxes says 2 seconds. This is the estimated time that it would take to download the page using a 28.8Kbps connection. As you add text and graphics to your page, keep an eye on this download time to make sure it doesn't become too long.

Using FrontPage Express isn't all that much different than using WordPad or some other word processor. That is, you create your page by typing text, formatting that text appropriately, adding images and other objects, and so on. FrontPage Express also ships with a few wizards and templates that help you get your Web pages off the ground.

When you start the program, FrontPage Express creates a new Web page for you. This page is based on the Normal Page template, which is really just an empty page that includes only the basic HTML tags described in the last section.

To start a new page, follow these steps:

1. Select the File | New command, or press Ctrl+N. FrontPage Express displays the New Page dialog box, shown in Figure 37.2.

FIGURE 37.2.

Use this dialog box to specify the template or wizard to use when creating your new page.

2. Select one of the following templates and wizards:

    Normal Page: This option creates an empty Web page.

    Confirmation Form: This option creates a page suitable for displaying after the user has submitted a form.

    Form Page Wizard: This wizard helps you to build a form for gathering data.

    Personal Home Page Wizard: This wizard helps you put together a simple home page.

    Survey Form: This template also creates a form, but it takes the data submitted in the form and stores it in a file.

3. Click OK.

4. If you selected a wizard, fill in all the dialog boxes.

5. Many of the pages created using these templates and wizards contain "placeholders," which are fields where you need to fill in your own data. For example, in a Web page created using the Personal Home Page Wizard, you need to edit the data with your own email address, Web address, and telephone number.

VIEWING THE HTML TAGS

While you're working within FrontPage Express, you still have access to the page's underlying HTML tags. To see them, select the View | HTML command. In the View or Edit HTML window that appears, feel free to edit the tags as necessary and then click OK to return to the FrontPage Express window.

Adding a Title

The next item you need to add is the title of the Web page. The page's title is just about what you might think it is: the overall name of the page (not to be confused with the name of the file you're creating). If someone views the page in a graphical browser (such as Netscape or Internet Explorer), the title appears in the title bar of the browser's window.

To define a title, surround the text with the `<TITLE>` and `</TITLE>` tags. For example, if you want the title of your page to be My Home Sweet Home Page, you would enter it as follows:

```
<TITLE>My Home Sweet Home Page</TITLE>
```

Note that you always place the title inside the head section. Your basic HTML document will now look like this:

```
<HTML>
<HEAD>
<TITLE>My Home Sweet Home Page</TITLE>
</HEAD>
<BODY>
</BODY>
</HTML>
```

To define the page title in FrontPage Express, follow these steps:

1. Select File | Page Properties. FrontPage Express displays the Page Properties dialog box.

2. In the General tab, use the Title text box to enter the title of the page.

3. Click OK.

Entering Text and Paragraphs

With your page title firmly in place, you can now think about the text you want to appear in the body of the page. For the most part, you can simply type the text between the `<BODY>` and `</BODY>` tags. In FrontPage Express, you type your prose within the large text box that takes up the bulk of the screen.

When you're working with the HTML tags directly, things get a little tricky when you want to start a new paragraph. In most text editors and word processors (and in FrontPage Express), starting a new paragraph is a simple matter of pressing the Enter key to move to a new line. You can try doing that in your Web page, but the browsers that read your page will ignore this *whitespace*. Instead, you have to use the `<P>` tag to tell the browser that you want to move to a new paragraph:

```
<HTML>
<HEAD>
<TITLE>My Home Sweet Home Page</TITLE>
</HEAD>
<BODY>
This text appears in the body of the Web page.
<P>
This text appears in a new paragraph.
</BODY>
</HTML>
```

Adding Formatting and Headings

HTML has lots of tags that will spruce up your page text. You saw earlier how a word or phrase surrounded by the `<B>` and `</B>` tags will appear in bold in a browser. You can also display text in *italic* by bracketing it with the `<I>` and `</I>` tags, you can make your words appear in `monospace` by surrounding them with the `<TT>` and `</TT>` tags, and you can <u>underline</u> words by enclosing them with the `<U>` and `</U>` tags.

You can achieve other text effects by using the <FONT> tag:

```
<FONT SIZE=n FACE=name COLOR=color>
```

Here's a summary of the three attributes used in this tag:

SIZE=*n*: Specifies the text size, where *n* is a number between 1 and 6.

FACE=*name*: Specifies the typeface used to display the text, where *name* is the name of one or more fonts. Note, however, that the user will see this typeface only if they have the appropriate font installed on their computer.

COLOR=*color*: Specifies the text color. The *color* value is either a six-digit RGB code preceded by # (for example, #FF0000 for red), or a predefined color name. See the following page for a table of RGB values and color names:

```
http://www.mcfedries.com/books/cightml/x11colors.html
```

Like the chapters of a book, many Web pages have their contents divided into several sections. To help separate these sections and make life easier for the reader, you can use headings. Ideally, these headings act as mini-titles that convey some idea of what each section is all about. To make these titles stand out, HTML has a series of heading tags that display text in a larger, bold font. There are six heading tags in all, ranging from <H1>, which uses the largest font, down to <H6>, which uses the smallest font.

To create these effects in FrontPage Express, use the following techniques:

Text effects: Select Format | Font and use the Font dialog box to pick out the text options you want to work with. You can also use the Format toolbar to select your text effects (see Figure 37.3).

Headings: Select Format | Paragraph and then select a heading from the Paragraph Properties dialog box. You can also select a heading from the Change Style list in the Format toolbar.

To illustrate these text formatting and heading tags, let's use the following HTML code (FORMATS.HTM; see the following Note):

```
<HTML>
<HEAD>
<TITLE>My Home Sweet Home Page</TITLE>
</HEAD>
<BODY>
You can create various text formatting effects,
including <B>bold text</B>, <I>italic text</I>,
and <TT>monospaced text</TT>.
<H1>An H1 Heading</H1>
<H2>An H2 Heading</H2>
<H3>An H3 Heading</H3>
<H4>An H4 Heading</H4>
<H5>An H5 Heading</H5>
<H6>An H6 Heading</H6>
</BODY>
</HTML>
```

Figure 37.3 shows how this looks in FrontPage Express.

FIGURE 37.3.

Examples of text formatting and heading tags.

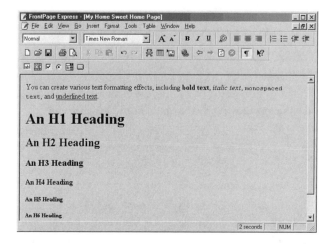

DOWNLOAD THE CODE

I've placed all the examples in this chapter on my Windows 98 Unleashed Web site:

`http://www.mcfedries.com/books/win98unleashed/`

So if you don't feel like typing in the examples, feel free to surf by and grab them with your browser. I'll provide you with the appropriate filenames when I introduce each chunk of code. For example, the filename for the code in this section is `FORMATS.HTM`, so you'd head for the following address:

`http://www.mcfedries.com/books/win98unleashed/formats.htm`

Setting Up Lists

HTML offers several different list styles, but I discuss only two of them in this section: numbered lists and bulleted lists.

If you want to include a numbered list of items—a Top Ten list, bowling league standings, or any kind of ranking—you don't need to add the numbers yourself. Instead, you can use HTML *ordered lists* to make the Web browser generate the numbers for you.

Ordered lists use two types of tags:

■ The entire list is surrounded by the `<OL>` and `</OL>` tags.

■ Each item in the list is preceded by the `<LI>` (list item) tag.

The general setup looks like this:

```
<OL>
<LI>First item.
<LI>Second item.
<LI>Third item.
<LI>You get the idea.
</OL>
```

Follow these steps to generate a numbered list within FrontPage Express:

1. Position the cursor where you want the list to appear.
2. Select the Format | Bullets and Numbering command to display the List Properties dialog box.
3. Activate the Numbered tab.
4. Click the numbering style you want to use.
5. Use the Start At spinner to set the starting number for the list.
6. Click OK.

If you want to list just a few points, a bulleted list might be more your style. They're called "bulleted" lists because a Web browser displays a small dot or square (depending on the browser) called a *bullet* to the left of each item.

The HTML tags for a bulleted list are pretty close to the ones you saw for a numbered list. As before, you precede each list item with the <LI> tag, but you enclose the entire list in the <UL> and </UL> tags. Why <UL>? Well, what the rest of the world calls a bulleted list, the HTML powers-that-be call an *unordered list*. Here's how they work:

```
<LI>First bullet point.
<LI>Second bullet point.
<LI>Third bullet point.
<LI>And so on
</UL>
```

To create a bulleted list in FrontPage Express, you follow the same steps outlined previously. In this case, however, you activate the Bulleted tab in the List Properties dialog box and you use this tab to select the bullet style you want to use.

Figure 37.4 shows how FrontPage Express displays these two list types (see LISTS.HTM).

Working with Hyperlinks

The *H* in HTML stands for *hypertext*, which is dynamic text that defines a link to another document. The user clicks the hypertext, and the browser takes him to the linked document.

The HTML tags that set up links are <A> and </A>. The <A> tag is a little different from the other tags you've seen. Specifically, you don't use it by itself; instead, you add the address of the document to which you want to link. Here's how it works:

```
<A HREF="address">
```

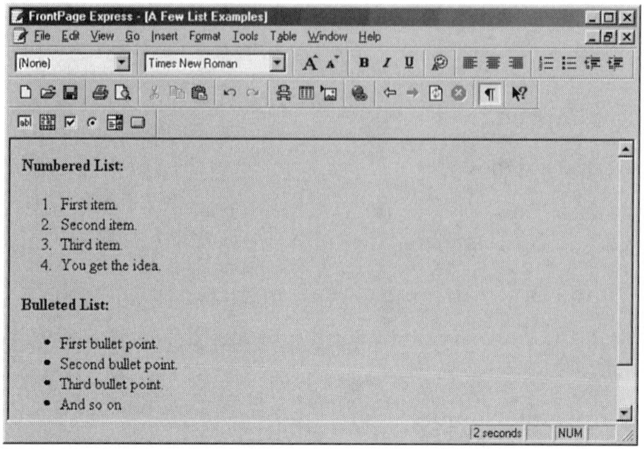

FIGURE 37.4.

A numbered list and a bulleted list in FrontPage Express.

Here, HREF stands for *hypertext reference*. Just replace `address` with the actual address of the Web page you want to use for the link (and, yes, you have to enclose the address in quotation marks). Here's an example:

```
<A HREF="http://www.mcp.com/sams/">
```

You're not done yet, though. Next, you have to give the reader some descriptive link text to click. All you do is insert the text between the `<A>` and `</A>` tags:

```
<A HREF="address">Link text goes here</A>
```

Here's an example:

```
Why not head to the <A HREF="http://www.mcp.com/sams">Sams home page</A>?
```

You can also use the `<A>` tag to create an email link. In this case, someone clicking the link will be presented with a screen (assuming his or her browser supports this kind of link, which most recent browsers do) that can be used to send a message to your email address.

This type of link is called a *mailto link* because you include the word `mailto` in the `<A>` tag. Here's the general form:

```
<A HREF="mailto:YourEmailAddress">The link text goes here</A>
```

Here, *YourEmailAddress* is your Internet email address. For example, suppose I want to include an email link in one of my Web pages. My email address is `paul@mcfedries.com`, so I'd set up the link as follows:

```
You can write to me at my
<A HREF="mailto:paul@mcfedries.com">e-mail address.</A>
```

If you want to try your hand at linking to other Net resources, here's a rundown of the type of URLs to use:

Resource	URL
FTP (directory)	`ftp://domain/directory/`
FTP (file)	`ftp://domain/directory/filename`
Gopher	`gopher://domain/`
Usenet	`news://newsgroup.name`
Telnet	`telnet://domain`

Forging hypertext links within FrontPage Express involves the following steps:

1. Type in the link text you want to use and then highlight it.
2. Select the Insert | Hyperlink command (or press Ctrl+K). FrontPage Express displays the Create Hyperlink dialog box.
3. Use the Hyperlink Type list to choose the type of link you want (such as `http:` for a Web page or `mailto:` for an email link).
4. Enter the link address in the URL text box.
5. If your site uses frames, you can use the Target Frame text box to enter the name of the frame in which you want the linked page to appear.
6. Click OK to insert the link.

Inserting Images, Sounds, and Video

If you feel like enhancing your page with a nice graphic or two, a background sound, or even a video, both HTML and FrontPage Express are up to the challenge. The next few sections show you how to add these multimedia elements to your page.

Adding an Image

If you're looking to make your Web site really stand out from the crowd, you need to go graphical with a few well-chosen images. How do you insert images if HTML files are text-only? As you'll see a bit later, all you are really doing (for each image you want to use) is adding a tag to the document that says, in effect, "Insert image here." This tag specifies the name of the graphics file, so the browser opens the file and displays the image.

Some computer wag once said that the nice thing about standards is that there are so many of them! Graphics files are no exception. It seems that every geek who ever gawked at graphics has invented his own format for storing them on disk. There are images in GIF, JPEG, BMP, PCX, TIFF, DIB, EPS, TGA and many more.

The good news is that the vast majority of browsers can handle only two formats: GIF and JPEG. (And some older browsers can't even handle JPEG.) Internet Explorer, however, can also work with Windows' native BMP and DIB formats.

As I mentioned a moment ago, there's an HTML code that tells a browser to display an image: the <IMG> tag. Here's how it works:

```
<IMG SRC="filename">
```

Here, SRC is short for *source*, and *filename* is the name and path of the graphics file you want to display. For example, suppose you have an image named logo.gif and it's located in the Graphics folder. To add it to your page, you'd use the following line:

```
<IMG SRC="/Graphics/logo.gif">
```

The <IMG> tag also supports the following attributes:

ALT=*text*: Specifies the *text* that will appear in place of the image for browsers that can't handle graphics (or that have had their graphics capabilities turned off by the user).

BORDER=*n*: Specifies the size of the border that is displayed around the image when the image is used as a hyperlink. (To use an image as a link, insert the <IMG> tag between the <A> and </A> tags.) Use BORDER=0 to turn off this border.

HEIGHT=*n*: Specifies the height of the image, where *n* is either a value in pixels or a percentage.

HSPACE=*n*: Specifies the amount of horizontal space between the image and the page text, where *n* is a pixel value.

VSPACE=*n*: Specifies the amount of vertical space between the image and the page text, where *n* is a pixel value.

WIDTH=*n*: Specifies the width of the image, where *n* is either a value in pixels or a percentage.

To insert an image in FrontPage Express, position the insertion point where you want the image to appear and then select the Insert | Image command. Use the Image dialog box to pick out the GIF or JPEG file you want to use, and then click OK.

STORE HTML AND OTHER FILES IN THE SAME FOLDER

Later, you'll be sending all your files—the HTML file, the image files, the sound files, and so on—to your Web server. When you do, it's likely that you'll store all the files in one place: your home directory on the server.

So whatever file you refer to in your page, things will be much simpler if you copy or move the file into the same folder that you're using to store your Web page. That way, when you specify the file in the Image dialog box (or wherever), you need only enter the name of the file and not the drive and folder. Otherwise, you'd have to strip out the extra drive and folder information before sending your files to the server.

When the image is in place, you can make a few adjustments by clicking the image and then selecting the Edit | Image Properties command. The Image Properties dialog box that pops up contains quite a few controls, but only a few are useful:

> **Setting alternative text:** Many Web users either have browsers that can't handle graphics, or else they surf with graphics turned off to speed things up. For these graphically challenged folks, you should provide a text alternative so that they know what your image represents. To do so, enter the text in the General tab's Text area.

> **Creating a link:** If you want to turn the image into a link, use the General tab's Location text box to enter the URL you want to use.

> **Setting alignment and spacing:** Use the Appearance tab's Alignment list to set the image alignment relative to the surrounding text. You can also use the Horizontal Spacing and Vertical Spacing controls to set the distance between the image and the nearby text, and so give the image a bit of breathing room.

> **Setting the border size:** For images used as links, you can set the width of the image border by using the Border Thickness spinner.

> **Specifying a size:** Web page text loads much quicker if the browser knows how much room each image on the page takes up. Therefore, you should always activate the Appearance tab's Specify Size check box. You can then use the Width and Height spinners to specify values either in Pixels or in Percent.

Adding a Background Sound

Next on the multimedia hit parade is specifying a background sound. This is a sound file that plays in the background automatically when the surfer loads your page. Before you decide to add a background sound, bear in mind that many (if not most) Web surfers find sounds that load automatically to be an annoying intrusion. On the other hand, most antiaudiophiles have also turned sounds off in their Web browsers, so this warning may be moot.

One way to do this is to use the <EMBED> tag, which is supported by both Netscape and Internet Explorer. At its simplest, you use the SRC attribute to specify the name of the sound file:

```
<EMBED SRC="playme.mid">
```

The browser displays a set of controls that enables the user to play and stop the sound file.

The `<EMBED>` tag also supports the following extras:

AUTOSTART=TRUE: If you add this attribute, the browser starts playing the sound file automatically as soon as the user surfs to your page.

LOOP=*value*: The LOOP attribute tells the browser how many times to play the sound. If you set *value* to 2, for example, the browser runs through the sound twice. If you really want to drive your visitors away, set *value* to TRUE to tell the browser to play the sound indefinitely.

HIDDEN=TRUE: If you add this attribute, the browser hides the controls.

With Internet Explorer, the `<EMBED>` tag isn't the only way to wire your site for sound. Specifically, Internet Explorer also supports the `<BGSOUND>` tag that enables you to specify a sound that will play automatically when someone surfs to your site (much like the `<EMBED>` tag's AUTOSTART=TRUE attribute). Here's the generic format:

```
<BGSOUND SRC="Filename" LOOP=Times>
```

The *Filename* part is the name of the sound file that you want to play (you can use AU, WAV, or MIDI files). The *Times* part tells the browser how many times to play the sound. You can either enter some positive number or else use LOOP=INFINITE to play the sound indefinitely. (Note that you can put this tag anywhere you like in the page.) Here's an example:

```
<BGSOUND SRC="MyTheme.mid" LOOP=1>
```

FrontPage Express only supports the `<BGSOUND>` method. To insert a background sound, select the Insert | Background Sound command, enter the name of the sound file in the Background Sound dialog box that appears, and then click OK.

INSERTING OTHER HTML TAGS

Although FrontPage Express doesn't support the `<EMBED>` tag, you can still use it by inserting the tag by hand. One way to do this would be to view the HTML (select View | HTML) and then type in the appropriate tags. Alternatively, select Insert | HTML Markup and then use the HTML Markup dialog box to enter the tags.

As with images, there are a few properties you can set for background sounds. To get these properties onto the screen, select File | Page Properties. In the Page Properties dialog box that shows up, the General tab has a Background Sound group. In this group, use the Loop spin box to set the number of times the sound should play. Alternatively, activate the Forever check box to have the sound play indefinitely.

Adding a Video

I don't recommend adding a video file to a Web page because they're normally huge files and take far too long to download. However, if you know your visitors will have a fast connection (if they're on your corporate intranet, for example), a slick video can add a nice touch.

To insert a video, use the following form of the `<IMG>` tag with Internet Explorer:

```
<IMG DYNSRC="Filename" CONTROLS LOOP=Times START=When>
```

`Filename` is a pointer to the video file you want to play. If you use the `CONTROLS` attribute, Internet Explorer displays a set of video controls (really just a Play button) underneath the video box. `Times` specifies how many times the video should play (use `LOOP=INFINITE` to play the video continuously). `When` tells the browser when to play the video: Use `START=FILEOPEN` to play the video as soon as the user loads the Web page; use `START=MOUSEOVER` to play the video whenever the user moves their mouse pointer over the video box.

To insert a video in FrontPage Express, first position the insertion point where you want the video to play. Then select Insert | Video, enter the filename in the dialog box that flies in for the occasion, and click OK.

To set video properties, click the video to select it and then run the Edit | Image Properties command. FrontPage Express loads the Image Properties dialog box and selects the Video tab for you. Here's a look at the cast of options featured in this tab:

Video Source: This text box holds the filename for your video.

Show Controls in Browser: If you activate this check box, FrontPage Express sets things up so that the video displays simple controls that enable the visitor to start and stop the video.

Repeat: These controls determine how many times the video plays. Use the Loop spin box to set the number of showings and use the Loop Delay spin box to set the amount of time between each showing. If you'd prefer that you video play *ad nauseum*, activate the Forever check box.

Start: When the On File Open check box is turned on, Internet Explorer starts playing the video as soon as anyone surfs to your page. If you activate the On Mouse Over check box, the video will start up again when users put their mouse pointers over the video.

Setting Up Tables

An HTML table is a rectangular grid of rows and columns in a Web page. You can enter all kinds of information into a table, including text, numbers, links, and even images. Your tables will always begin with the following basic container:

```
<TABLE>
</TABLE>
```

All the other table tags fit between these two tags. There are two things you need to know about the <TABLE> tag:

- If you want your table to show a border, use the <TABLE BORDER=*n*> tag (where *n* is the size of the border).
- If you don't want a border, just use <TABLE>.

When that's done, most of your remaining table chores will involve the following four-step process:

1. Add a row.
2. Divide the row into the number of columns you want.
3. Insert data into each cell.
4. Repeat steps 1 through 3 until done.

To add a row, you toss a <TR> (table row) tag and a </TR> tag (its corresponding end tag) between <TABLE> and </TABLE>:

```
<TABLE BORDER>
<TR>
</TR>
</TABLE>
```

Now you divide that row into columns by placing the <TD> (table data) and </TD> tags between <TR> and </TR>. Each <TD>/</TD> combination represents one column (or, more specifically, an individual cell in the row). Therefore, if you want a three-column table, you'd do this:

```
<TABLE BORDER>
<TR>
<TD></TD>
<TD></TD>
<TD></TD>
</TR>
</TABLE>
```

Now you enter the row's cell data by typing text between each <TD> tag and its </TD> end tag:

```
<TABLE BORDER>
<TR>
<TD>Row 1, Column1</TD>
<TD>Row 1, Column2</TD>
<TD>Row 1, Column3</TD>
</TR>
</TABLE>
```

Remember that you can put any of the following within the <TD> and </TD> tags:

- Text
- HTML text-formatting tags (such as <B> and <I>)
- Links
- Lists
- Images

TABLE HEADINGS

If you want to include headings at the top of each column, use (table heading) tags in the first row. Most browsers display text within a /</TH> combination in bold type. (Note, too, that you can just as easily use tags in the first column to create headers for each row.)

After you have your first row firmly in place, you simply repeat the procedure for the other rows in the table. For our sample table, here's the HTML that includes the data for all the rows (see TABLE.HTM):

```
<TABLE BORDER>
<TR>
<TD>Row 1,  Column1</TD>
<TD>Row 1, Column2</TD>
<TD>Row 1, Column3</TD>
</TR>
<TR>
<TD>Row 2,  Column1</TD>
<TD>Row 2, Column2</TD>
<TD>Row 2, Column3</TD>
</TR>
<TR>
<TD>Row 3,  Column1</TD>
<TD>Row 3, Column2</TD>
<TD>Row 3, Column3</TD>
</TR>
</TABLE>
```

Figure 37.5 shows a table displayed in FrontPage Express.

FIGURE 37.5.

An HTML table in FrontPage Express.

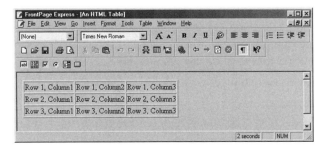

In FrontPage Express, the easiest way to get a table started is to click the Insert Table button in the Standard toolbar (see Figure 37.6). FrontPage Express displays a grid. You then drag your mouse into this grid to select the number of rows and columns you want, as shown in the next figure. When you release the mouse, FrontPage Express cranks out the new table.

FIGURE 37.6.

Tables are easy to build if you use the Insert Table button.

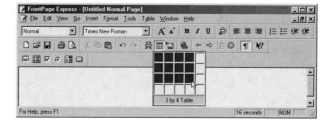

You can get a bit more control over the finished table product if you follow these steps instead:

1. Move the insertion point to where you want the new table to appear.
2. Select the Table | Insert Table command. FrontPage Express displays the Insert Table dialog box, shown in Figure 37.7.

FIGURE 37.7.

The Insert Table dialog box lets you specify a few extra table tidbits.

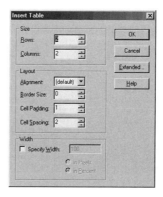

3. In the Size group, use the Rows and Columns spin boxes to set the number of rows and columns you want in the table. (If you're not sure about this, don't sweat it too much because you can always add and delete rows and columns later on.)
4. The Layout group offers the following goodies:

   Alignment: Use this list to specify the table's horizontal alignment within the page.

   Border Size: This spin box determines the size of the border that surrounds the table.

   Cell Padding: This spin box sets the amount of white space that surrounds the data within each cell.

   Cell Spacing: This spin box sets the amount of space between each table cell.

5. To set the width of the table, activate the Specify Width check box and then use the text box to enter the width you want. (Note that you can enter a value either in Pixels or in Percent.)
6. Click OK to insert the table.

When your table is in place, the FrontPage Express Table menu boasts an impressive array of commands for table touch-ups. Here's a quick summary (make sure the insertion point is inside the table):

Insert Rows or Columns: Use this command to add more rows and/or columns to the table.

Insert Cell: This command adds a new cell to the table.

Insert Caption: When you select this command, FrontPage Express moves the insertion point just above the table. You can type in a caption that describes or names the table.

Merge Cells: If you selected two or more cells in advance, you can use this command to merge those cells into a single cell.

Split Cells: Use this command to split a single cell into two or more rows or columns.

Select Cell: This command selects the current cell.

Select Row: This command selects the current row.

Select Column: This command selects the current column.

Select Table: This command selects the entire table.

Caption Properties: Use this command to display the caption either at the top of the table or at the bottom. (Note that you need to put the insertion point into the caption before you can select this command).

Cell Properties: Selecting this command displays the Cell Properties dialog box. Use the controls in this dialog box to set the cell alignment and width, specify a background image or color, set the border colors, and more.

Table Properties: When you select this command, the Table Properties dialog box appears. This dialog box contains many of the same options you saw in the Cell Properties dialog box. (The difference is that the Table Properties options apply to the entire table.)

DON'T REINVENT THE TABLE WHEEL

Complex tables require quite a bit of work to get them right, particularly if you're trying to recreate a table that you build in Microsoft Word, a range from Microsoft Excel, or some records from an Access database. For these cases, note that the Office 97 versions of these programs have a Save As HTML command that will convert these tabular objects into HTML tables. You can find the details in my book *Paul McFedries' Office 97 Unleashed, Professional Reference Edition.*

37

WEB PAGE
PUBLISHING WITH
WINDOWS 98

A Few More FrontPage Express Techniques

To round out our look at the FrontPage Express Web page creation techniques, this section runs through a few more techniques for inserting objects and formatting the page.

A Few More Things to Insert

This section shows you how to insert a few more bits and pieces, including horizontal rules, special symbols, and more. All these items are available using the following Insert menu commands:

Break: This command inserts a *line break*. A line break forces the browser to start a new line, but it doesn't create a new paragraph. This is equivalent to the <BR> tag in HTML.

Horizontal Line: This command inserts a horizontal line across the page. This is equivalent to the <HR> tag in HTML.

Symbol: This commands displays the Symbol dialog box, which contains a list of special characters you can insert into the page. Highlight the character you want and then click Insert.

Comment: Use this to add *comments* to your Web page. A comment is text that appears within the file, but isn't displayed by the browser. This is handy for things such as writing explanatory notes about the page contents. To enter comments in HTML, precede the text with <!-- and close the text with -->.

File: You can use this command to insert the contents of another file into your Web page. You use this most often to insert other HTML files, but you can also insert text files, WordPad files, and more.

WebBot Component: This command enables you to add a WebBot to your page. A WebBot is a special Web page object that implements nonstandard functionality. For example, the Timestamp WebBot displays the date and time the Web page was last modified. For these WebBots to function, the page must be displayed using a Web server that understands WebBots, such as Internet Information Server or Personal Web Server.

Other Components: This command displays a submenu of components you can insert, including ActiveX controls and Java applets.

Form Field: This command displays a list of form controls that you can insert. In most cases, you're better off using one of the form-related wizards to set up a Web page form.

Marquee: This command enables you to add a scrolling text object to your page. Note that only Internet Explorer supports the Marquee object. This is equivalent to the `<MARQUEE>` tag in HTML.

Script: Use this command to insert either a VBScript or JavaScript program. In HTML, you'd use either `<SCRIPT LANGUAGE="VBscript">` or `<SCRIPT LANGUAGE= "JavaScript">`.

A Few More Things to Format

Now let's take a quick run through a few more of the FrontPage Express formatting options:

Setting the page background: To specify the page background, select the Format|Background command to display the Background tab of the Page Properties dialog box (shown in Figure 37.8). To set a background image, activate the Background Image check box and then enter the image filename (or click Browse). Alternatively, use the Background list to choose a background color.

FIGURE **37.8.**

Use the dialog box to set the page background. You also use it to set the default colors for text and links.

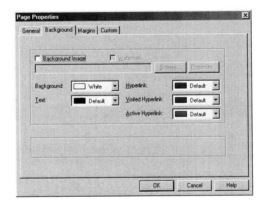

Setting the default colors for text and links: While you're in the Background tab, you can also use the Text list to set the default color for the page text. You can use the other color lists to set the default colors for each Hyperlink, Visited Hyperlink, and Active Hyperlink. (The latter is a link that has been clicked and the user is waiting for the page to load.)

Aligning paragraphs: FrontPage Express gives you three different paragraph alignment options: Left, Center, and Right. To set the alignment, select Format|Paragraph and then use the Paragraph Alignment list in the Paragraph Properties dialog box. You can also click the appropriate alignment button in the Format toolbar.

Setting page margins: Internet Explorer supports margins at the top and left side of the page. To set these margins, select File | Page Properties and then display the Margins tab in the Page Properties dialog box. Activate the Specify Top Margin check box and then use the spinner to set the height of the margin. Similarly, activate the Specify Left Margin check box and use the spinner to set the width of the margin.

Publishing Pages Using the Web Publishing Wizard

When your pages are suitable for public consumption, it's time to put them on the Web. Assuming you have access to a Web server, this process involves uploading the Web pages, graphics, and other files to your home directory on the server. Depending on the server, you use one of the following methods:

- For an intranet, you copy the files to the appropriate network directory.
- For most Web hosting providers, you use FTP to upload the files to your home directory on the Web server.
- Use the Web Publishing Wizard to take a step-by-step approach to uploading the files. The Web Publishing Wizard comes with Windows 98.

Here are the steps to follow to upload files using the Web Publishing Wizard:

1. Select Start | Programs | Internet Explorer | Web Publishing Wizard.

2. The first wizard dialog box just gives you an overview, so click Next >. The Select a File or Folder dialog box appears, as shown in Figure 37.9.

FIGURE 37.9.

Use this wizard dialog box to pick out the folders or files you want to publish on the Web.

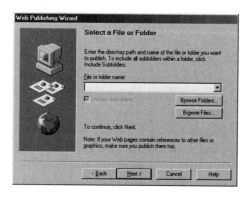

3. Type the name of the folder or file you want to publish (you need to include the drive and folder name). Alternatively, click either Browse Folders or Browse Files to pick out your Web files from a dialog box. If you choose a folder, you can tell the wizard to publish all the subfolders, as well, by activating the Include subfolders check box. Click Next > when you're ready to move on.

4. In the Name the Web Server dialog box that materializes, enter a descriptive name for your provider's Web server.

5. To specify how the wizard should send the files, click Advanced and use the Service provider to choose one of the following:

   Automatically Select a Service Provider: Choose this option if you're not sure where to send your files. In this case, the Wizard will ask you for the Internet address you use to access your files on the Web and the Internet address of your Web home. Given this, the wizard will attempt to figure out the appropriate place to send your files.

   FrontPage Extended Web: Select this item if your Web server has FrontPage (the big brother of FrontPage Express) enabled. You need to provide the Internet address you use to access your files on the Web and the Internet address of your Web home.

   FTP: This item publishes the files using the Internet's FTP service. This is by far the most common choice.

   HTTP Post: Only select this command if your service provider accepts files submitted using the HTTP Post method. You need to know the proper posting command.

   Microsoft Content Replication System: Choose this item if your Web server runs the Content Replication System (CRS). You need to enter the name of the CRS server and supply the name of the CRS project.

6. Click Next >. Note that the rest of these steps assume you chose the FTP option.

7. The wizard now displays the Specify the URL and Directory dialog box. Click Next > after filling in the following text boxes:

   URL or Internet address: Enter the main URL for your Web site. This address usually takes the form `http://provider.domain/~user`, where `provider.domain` is the domain name of your Web provider and *user* is your username.

   Local directory: Enter the name of the folder on your computer that corresponds to the main directory on your Web server.

8. Now the wizard conjures up the Specify the FTP Server and Subfolder dialog box. Click Next > after supplying the wizard with the following information:

   FTP server name: Enter the domain name of your provider's FTP server.

   Subfolder containing your Web pages: Enter the full name of the directory assigned to you for file storage on the FTP site.

9. In the Publish Your Files dialog box that appears, click Finish. The wizard will now likely display the Enter Network Password dialog box.

10. Enter your User name and Password and then click OK. The wizard then connects to the provider, posts the files, and displays a dialog box to tell you all went well.

11. Click OK.

The next time you run the wizard, you follow the first three steps as just outlined. The wizard will then display the Select a Web Server dialog box so that you can choose the Web server name you entered in step 4. (If you want to define a new Web server, click New.) After you've done that, you can skip to step 9 and publish your files without further ado.

Summary

This chapter introduced you to both HTML and the FrontPage Express HTML editor. You learned the basic structure of a page, as well as how to add a title, enter text and paragraphs, format text and headings, add lists, images, and hyperlinks, insert multimedia and tables, and much more. In all cases, I showed you both the HTML tags and the FrontPage Express equivalents.

Here are some pointers to related chapters:

- You can't explore the Web until you've set up Windows 98 to connect to the Internet. To find out how it's done, see Chapter 32, "Windows 98 and the Internet."

- To learn more about Internet Explorer, see Chapter 33, "Exploring the Web with Internet Explorer."

I

INDEX